Basics of
Social Research

Basics of
Social Research

Qualitative and Quantitative Approaches

SECOND EDITION

W. Lawrence Neuman

University of Wisconsin–Whitewater

PEARSON

Boston   New York   San Francisco
Mexico City   Montreal   Toronto   London   Madrid   Munich   Paris
Hong Kong   Singapore   Tokyo   Cape Town   Sydney

Senior Series Editor: *Jeff Lasser*
Editorial Assistant: *Erikka Adams*
Senior Marketing Manager: *Kelly May*
Production Editor: *Roberta Sherman*
Composition Buyer: *Linda Cox*
Manufacturing Buyer: *JoAnne Sweeney*
Editorial Production Services and Electronic Composition: *Publishers' Design and Production Services, Inc.*
Cover Administrator: *Kristina Mose-Libon*

For related titles and support materials, visit our online catalog at www.ablongman.com.

Between the time Website information is gathered and then published, it is not unusual for some sites to have closed. Also, the transcription of URLs can result in typographical errors. The publisher would appreciate notification where these errors occur so that they may be corrected in subsequent editions.

Cataloging-in-Publication data unavailable at press time.

0-205-48437-9

Printed in the United States of America

10 9 8 7 6 5 4   RRD-VA 10 09 08

BRIEF CONTENTS

CONTENTS

Many students approach a first course on social research with anxiety and trepidation. Sometimes this is because they associate the course with mathematics and statistics with which they had an unpleasant past experience, sometimes they struggled in natural science courses that used experiments, and sometimes they do not know what to expect but believe it is beyond them and only for advanced, very smart scholars.

Basics of Social Research introduces you to social research and presents "what researchers do and why" in a nonthreatening manner that captures both the excitement and importance of doing "real" research. The "nuts and bolts" of methods for doing research requires disciplined thinking and has rigor, but it is easily within reach of almost all undergraduate students. Once you overcome any anxiety and recognize what research is actually about, you will probably find it fascinating. A course in social research methodology differs from most other social sciences courses. Most courses examine content topics, such as inequality, crime, racial divisions, gender relations, urban society, and so forth. A methodology course is relevant, both in preparing you to think more systematically about the content and in revealing how content findings are created.

This book aims to be easy to understand and very accessible, but accessible does not mean it is "Mickey Mouse" or "fluff." Indeed, proper research is a serious activity and often how well a study was conducted can have real consequences. Also, researchers deal with significant ethical issues, their findings shape policy decisions and service delivery concerns, and ultimately research produces new knowledge, or what we really know about issues of importance. Just as the actual daily work of a nurse, social worker, police officer, teacher, physician, or counselor often involves serious issues that have real implications for people's lives, so does social research.

Basics of Social Research has three goals. First, it seeks to show you that social research is simultaneously a very important enterprise and one that is not beyond you—you *can* understand it. Second, it uses many examples from "real research" in published studies to show you the origins of the findings and information found in textbooks or in the media. Last, it gives you a foundation for further learning about doing research and shows you that this activity requires dedication, creativity, and mature judgment.

Social research is not a matter of simply following a cookbook recipe, looking up the correct formula, or blindly following fixed procedures or routines without thinking. It is a creative process that requires personal integrity, moral choices, and a deep commitment to the free and open inquiry into questions about the social world.

This book is a shortened version of a larger, in-depth textbook on social research that I first wrote 15 years ago and that has been updated many times since then. It was written to provide an uncomplicated introduction to social research for students with less background. It reflects what my students taught me over the 25 years that I have been helping undergraduates understand and appreciate social research methods.

Like most written works, this book reflects its author. From the beginning I have been firmly committed to the value of both quantitative and qualitative approaches to research. I believe each approach offers a distinct and complementary perspective to understanding the social world, and that both are equally important and necessary. Revisions in this second edition include updated examples from the recent literature, rewording for greater clarity, two new charts for emphasis, and a reorganization of material to make the presentation smoother.

Doing Social Research

INTRODUCTION

Social research is all around us. Educators, government officials, business managers, human service providers, and health care professionals regularly use social research methods and findings. People use social research to raise children, reduce crime, improve public health, sell products, or just understand one's life. Reports of research appear on broadcast news programs, in popular magazines, in newspapers, and on the Internet.

Research findings can affect people's daily lives and public policies. For example, I recently heard a debate regarding a U.S. federal government program to offer teenagers sexual abstinence counseling. A high-level government official argued for such counseling and strongly opposed offering teens birth control information. An independent health administrator noted that there is no scientific evidence showing that abstinence-only counseling works. He said that 80 percent of teens are already sexually active by the age of 18, therefore it is essential to provide birth control information. He pointed to many research studies showing that birth control instruction for teens reduces pregnancy rates and the spread of sexually transmitted diseases. The government abstinence-only advocate relied on moral persuasion because he had no research evidence. Ideology, faith, and politics shape many government programs rather than solid research evidence, but good social research can help all of us make informed decisions. The evidence also explains why many programs fail to accomplish much or may do more harm than good.

This book is about social research. In simple terms, research is a way of going about finding answers to questions. Professors, professional researchers, practitioners, and students in many fields conduct research to seek answers to questions about the social world. You probably already have some notion of what social research entails. First, let me end some possible misconceptions. When I asked students in my classes what they think social research entails, they gave the following answers:

- It is based on facts alone; there is no theory or personal judgment.
- Only experts with a Ph.D. degree or college professors read it or do it.
- It means going to the library and finding a lot of magazine articles or books on a topic.
- It is when someone hangs around a group and observes.
- It means conducting a controlled experiment.
- Social research is drawing a sample of people and giving them questionnaires to complete.
- It is looking up lots of statistical tables and information from official government reports.
- To do it, one must use computers to create statistics, charts, and graphs.

The first two answers are wrong, and the others describe only part of what constitutes social research. It is unwise to confuse one part with the whole.

People conduct social research to learn something new about the social world; or to carefully document guesses, hunches, or beliefs about it; or to refine their understanding of how the social world works. A researcher combines theories or ideas with facts in a careful, systematic way and uses creativity. He or she learns to organize and plan carefully and to select the appropriate technique to address a specific kind of question. A researcher also must treat the people in a study in ethical and moral ways. In addition, a researcher must fully and clearly communicate the results of a study to others.

Social research is a process in which people combine a set of principles, outlooks, and ideas (i.e., methodology) with a collection of specific practices, techniques, and strategies (i.e., a method of inquiry) to produce knowledge. It is an exciting process of discovery, but it requires persistence, personal integrity, tolerance for ambiguity, interaction with others, and pride in doing quality work.

Reading this book cannot transform you into an expert researcher, but it can teach you to be a better consumer of research results, help you to understand how the research enterprise works, and prepare you to conduct small research projects. After studying this book, you will be aware of what research can and cannot do, and why properly conducted research is important.

ALTERNATIVES TO SOCIAL RESEARCH

Unless you are unusual, most of what you know about the social world is not based on doing social research. You probably learned most of what you know using an alternative to social research. It is based on what your parents and other people (e.g., friends, teachers) have told you. You also have knowledge based on your personal experiences, the books and magazines you have read, and the movies and television you have watched. You may also use plain old "common sense."

More than a collection of techniques, social research is a process for producing knowledge. It is a more structured, organized, and systematic process than the alternatives that most of us use in daily life. Knowledge from the alternatives is often correct, but knowledge based on research is more likely to be true and have fewer errors. Although research does not always produce perfect knowledge, compared to the alternatives it is much less likely to be flawed. Let us review the alternatives before examining social research.

Authority

You have acquired knowledge from parents, teachers, and experts as well as from books, television, and other media. When you accept something as being true because someone in a position of authority says it is true or because it is in an authoritative publication, you are relying on authority as a basis for knowledge. Relying on the wisdom of authorities is a quick, simple, and cheap way to learn something. Authorities often spend time and effort to learn something, and you can benefit from their experience and work.

There are also limitations to relying on authority. First, it is easy to overestimate the expertise of other people. You may assume that they are right when they are not. History is full of past experts whom we now see as being misinformed. For example, some "experts" of the past measured intelligence by counting bumps on the skull; other "experts" used bloodletting to try to cure diseases. Their errors seem obvious now, but can you be certain that today's experts will not become tomorrow's fools? Second, authorities may not agree, and all authorities may not be equally dependable. Whom should we believe if authorities disagree? Third, authorities may speak on fields they know little about or be plain wrong. An expert who is very informed about one area may use his or her authority in an unrelated area. Also, using the halo effect (discussed later), expertise in one area may spill over illegitimately to be authority in a totally different area. Have you ever seen television commercials where a movie star uses his or her fame as authority to convince you to buy a car? We need to ask: Who is or is not an authority?

An additional issue is the misuse of authority. Sometimes organizations or individuals give an appearance of authority so they can convince others to agree to something that they might not otherwise agree to. A related situation occurs when a person with little training and expertise is named as a "senior fellow" or "adjunct scholar" in a private "think tank" with an impressive name, such as the Center for the Study of X or the Institute on Y Research. Some think tanks are legitimate research centers, but many are mere fronts created by wealthy special-interest groups to engage in advocacy politics. Think tanks can make anyone a "scholar" to facilitate the mass media accepting the person as an authority on an issue. In reality, the person may not have any real expertise.[1] Also, too much reliance on authorities can be dangerous to a democratic society. Experts may promote ideas that strengthen their own power and position. When we accept the authority of experts, but do not know how they arrived at their knowledge, we lose the ability to evaluate what the experts say and lose control of our destiny.

Tradition

People sometimes rely on tradition for knowledge. Tradition is a special case of authority—the authority of the past. Tradition means you accept something as being true because "it's the way things have always been." For example, my father-in-law says that drinking a shot of whiskey cures a cold. When I asked about his statement, he said that he had learned it from his father when he was a child, and it had come down from past generations. Tradition was the basis of the knowledge for the cure. Here is an example from the social world: Many people believe that children who are raised at home by their mothers grow up to be better adjusted and have fewer personal problems than those raised in other settings. People "know" this, but how did they learn it? Most accept it because they believe (rightly or wrongly) that it was true in the past or is the way things have always been done. Some traditional social knowledge begins as simple prejudice. You might rely on tradition without being fully aware of it with a belief such as "People from that side of the tracks will never amount to anything" or "You never can trust that type of person" or "That's the way men (or women) are." Even if traditional knowledge was once true, it can become distorted as it is passed on, and soon it is no longer true. People may cling to traditional knowledge without real understanding; they assume that because something may have worked or been true in the past, it will continue to be true.

Common Sense

You know a lot about the social world from your everyday reasoning or common sense. You rely on what everyone knows and what "just makes sense." For example, it "just makes sense" that murder rates are higher in nations that do not have a death penalty, because people are less likely to kill if they face execution for doing so. This and other widely held commonsense beliefs, such as that poor youth are more likely to commit deviant acts than those from the middle class or that most Catholics do not use birth control, are false.

Common sense is valuable in daily living, but it allows logical fallacies to slip into thinking. For example, the so-called gambler's fallacy says: "If I have a long string of losses playing a lottery, the next time I play, my chances of winning will be better." In terms of probability and the facts, this is false. Also, common sense contains contradictory ideas that often go unnoticed because people use the ideas at different times, such as "opposites attract" and "birds of a feather flock together." Common sense can originate in tradition. It is useful and sometimes correct, but it also contains errors, misinformation, contradiction, and prejudice.

Media Myths

Television shows, movies, and newspaper and magazine articles are important sources of information. For example, most people have no contact with criminals but learn about crime by watching television shows and movies and by reading newspapers. However, the television portrayals of crime, and of many other things, do not accurately reflect social reality. The writers who create or "adapt" images from life for television shows and movie scripts distort reality either out of ignorance or because they rely on authority, tradition, and common sense. Their primary goal is to entertain, not to represent reality accurately. Although many journalists try to present a realistic picture of the world, they must write stories in short time periods with limited information and within editorial guidelines.

Unfortunately, the media tend to perpetuate the myths of a culture. For example, the media show that most people who receive welfare are Black (actually, most are White), that most people who are mentally ill are violent and dangerous (only a small percentage actually are), and that most people who are elderly are senile and in nursing homes (a tiny minority are). Also, mass media "hype" can create a feeling that a major problem exists when it may not (see Box 1.1). People are misled by visual images more easily than other forms of "lying"; this means that stories or stereotypes that appear on film and television can have a powerful effect on people. For example, television repeatedly shows low-income, inner-city, African American youth using illegal drugs. Eventually, most people "know" that urban Blacks use illegal drugs at a higher rate than other groups in the United States, even though this notion is false.

Competing interests use the media to win public support.[2] Public relations campaigns try to alter what the public thinks about scientific findings, making it difficult for the public to judge research findings. For example, a large majority of scientific research supports the global warming thesis (i.e., pollutants from industrialization and massive deforestation are raising the earth's temperature and will cause dramatic climate change and bring about environmental disasters). The scientific evidence is growing and gets stronger each year. The media give equal attention to a few dissenters who question global warming, creating the impression in the public mind that "no one really knows" or that scientists are undecided about the issue of global warming. The media sources fail to mention that the dissenters represent less than 2 percent of all scientists, or that most dissenting studies are paid for by heavily polluting industries. The industries also spend millions of dollars to publicize the findings because their goal is to deflect growing criticism and delay en-

vironmental regulations, not to advance knowledge.

Newspapers offer horoscopes, and television programs or movies report on supernatural powers, ESP (extrasensory perception), UFOs (unidentified flying objects), and angels or ghosts. Although no scientific evidence exists for such, between 25 and 50 percent of the U.S. public accepts them as true, and the percentage with

---

| Box 1.1 | Is Road Rage a Media Myth? |

Americans hear a lot about *road rage. Newsweek* magazine, *Time* magazine, and newspapers in most major cities have carried headlines about it. Leading national political officials have held public hearings on it, and the federal government gives millions of dollars in grants to law enforcement and transportation departments to reduce it. Today, even psychologists specialize in this disorder.

The term *road rage* first appeared in 1988, and by 1997, the print media were carrying over 4,000 articles per year on it. Despite media attention about "aggressive driving" and "anger behind the wheel," there is no scientific evidence for road rage. The term is not precisely defined and can refer to anything from gunshots from cars, use of hand gestures, running bicyclists off the road, tailgating, and even anger over auto repair bills! All the data on crashes and accidents show declines during the period when road rage reached an epidemic.

Perhaps media reports fueled perceptions of road rage. After hearing or reading about road rage and having a label for the behavior, people began to notice rude driving behavior and engaged in *selective observation.* We will not know for sure until it is properly studied, but the amount of such behavior may be unchanged. It may turn out that the national epidemic of road rage is a widely held myth stimulated by reports in the mass media. (For more information, see Michael Fumento, "Road Rage versus Reality," *Atlantic Monthly* [August 1998].)

such beliefs has been growing over time as the entertainment media give the phenomenon more prominence.[3]

Personal Experience

If something happens to you, if you personally see it or experience it, you accept it as true. Personal experience, or "seeing is believing," has a strong impact and is a powerful source of knowledge. Unfortunately, personal experience can lead you astray. Something similar to an optical illusion or mirage can occur. What appears true may actually be due to a slight error or distortion in judgment. The power of immediacy and direct personal contact is very strong. Even knowing that, people fall for illusions. Many people believe what they see or personally experience rather than what very carefully designed research has discovered.

The four errors of personal experience reinforce each other and can occur in other areas, as well. They are a basis for misleading people through propaganda, cons or fraud, magic, stereotyping, and some advertising. The most frequent problem is _overgeneralization_; it occurs when some evidence supports your belief, but you falsely assume that it applies to many other situations, too. Limited generalization may be appropriate; under certain conditions, a small amount of evidence can explain a larger situation. The problem is that many people generalize far beyond limited evidence. For example, over the years, I have known five blind people. All of them were very friendly. Can I conclude that all blind people are friendly? Do the five people with whom I happened to have personal experience with represent all blind people?

The second error, _selective observation_, occurs when you take special notice of some people or events and tend to seek out evidence that confirms what you already believe and ignore contradictory information. People often focus on or observe particular cases or situations, especially when they fit preconceived ideas. We are sensitive to features that confirm what we think, but ignore features that contradict it. For example, I believe tall people are excellent singers. This may be because of stereotypes, what my mother told me, or whatever. I observe tall people and, without awareness, pay particular attention to their singing. I look at a chorus or top vocalist and notice those who are tall. Without realizing it, I notice and remember people and situations that reinforce my preconceived ideas. Psychologists found that people tend to "seek out" and distort their memories to make them more consistent with what they already think.[4]

A third error is _premature closure_. It often operates with and reinforces the first two errors. Premature closure occurs when you feel you have the answer and do not need to listen, seek information, or raise questions any longer. Unfortunately, most of us are a little lazy or get a little sloppy. We take a few pieces of evidence or look at events for a short while and then think we have it figured out. We look for evidence to confirm or reject an idea and stop when a small amount of evidence is present. In a word, we jump to conclusions. For example, I want to learn whether people in my town support Mary Smith or Jon Van Horn for mayor. I ask 20 people; 16 say they favor Mary, 2 are undecided, and only 2 favor Jon, so I stop there and believe Mary will win.

Another common error is the _halo effect_; it is when we overgeneralize from what we accept as being highly positive or prestigious and let its strong reputation or prestige "rub off" onto other areas. Thus, I pick up a report by a person from a prestigious university, say Harvard or Cambridge University. I assume that the author is smart and talented and that the report will be excellent. I do not make this assumption about a report by someone from Unknown University. I form an opinion and prejudge the report and may not approach it by considering its own merits alone. How the various alternatives to social research might address the issue of laundry is shown in Table 1.1.

TABLE 1.1   Alternatives to Social Research

Alternative Explanation to Social Research	Example Issue: In the division of household tasks by gender, why do women tend to do the laundry?
Authority	Experts say that as children, females are taught to make, select, mend, and clean clothing as part of a female focus on physical appearance and on caring for children or others in a family. Women do the laundry based on their childhood preparation.
Tradition	Women have done the laundry for centuries, so it is a continuation of what has happened for a long time.
Common Sense	Men just are not as concerned about clothing as much as women, so it only makes sense that women do the laundry more often.
Media Myth	Television commercials show women often doing laundry and enjoying it, so they do laundry because they think it's fun.
Personal Experience	My mother and the mothers of all my friends did the laundry. My female friends did it for their boyfriends, but never the other way around. It just feels natural for the woman to do it.

HOW SCIENCE WORKS

Although it builds on some aspects of the alternative ways of developing knowledge, science is what separates social research. Social research involves thinking scientifically about questions about the social world and following scientific processes. This suggests that we examine the meaning of science and how its works.

Science

The term *science* suggests an image of test tubes, computers, rocket ships, and people in white lab coats. These outward trappings are a part of science, especially natural science (i.e., astronomy, biology, chemistry, geology, and physics,), that deals with the physical and material world (e.g., plants, chemicals, rocks, stars, and electricity). The social sciences, such as anthropology, psychology, political science, and sociology, involve the study of people—their beliefs, behavior, interaction, institutions, and so forth. Fewer people associate these disciplines with the word *science*. Science is a social institution and a way to produce knowledge. Not everyone is well informed about science. For example, a 2001 survey found that about only one-third of U.S. adults could correctly explain the basics of science.[5]

Scientists gather data using specialized techniques and use the data to support or reject theories. *Data* are the empirical evidence or information that one gathers carefully according to rules or procedures. The data can be *quantitative* (i.e., expressed as numbers) or *qualitative* (i.e., expressed as words, visual images, sounds, or objects). *Empirical evidence* refers to observations that people experience through the senses—touch, sight, hearing, smell, and taste. This confuses people, because researchers cannot use their senses to directly observe many aspects of the social world about which they seek answers (e.g., intelligence, attitudes, opinions, feelings, emotions, power, authority, etc.). Researchers have many specialized techniques to observe and indirectly measure such aspects of the social world.

The Scientific Community

Science comes to life through the operation of the scientific community, which sustains the assumptions, attitudes, and techniques of science. The *scientific community* is a collection of people who practice science and a set of norms, behaviors, and attitudes that bind them together. It is a professional community—a group of interacting people who share ethical principles, beliefs and values, techniques and training, and career paths. For the most part, the scientific community includes both the natural and social sciences.[6]

Many people outside the core scientific community use scientific research techniques. A range of practitioners and technicians apply research techniques that scientists developed and refined. Many use the research techniques (e.g., a survey) without possessing a deep knowledge of scientific research. Yet, anyone who uses the techniques or results of science can do so better if they also understand the principles and processes of the scientific community.

The boundaries of the scientific community and its membership are defined loosely. There is no membership card or master roster. Many people treat a Ph.D. degree in a scientific field as an informal "entry ticket" to membership in the scientific community. The Ph.D., which stands for doctorate of philosophy, is an advanced graduate degree beyond the master's that prepares one to conduct independent research. Some researchers do not have Ph.D.s and not all those who receive Ph.D.s enter occupations in which they conduct research. They enter many occupations and may have other responsibilities (e.g., teaching, administration, consulting, clinical practice, advising, etc.). In fact, about one-half of the people who receive scientific Ph.D.s do not follow careers as active researchers.

At the core of the scientific community are researchers who conduct studies on a full-time or part-time basis, usually with the help of assistants. Many research assistants are graduate students, and some are undergraduates. Working as a research assistant is the way that most scientists gain a real grasp on the details of doing research. Colleges and universities employ most members of the scientific community's core. Some scientists work for the government or private industry in organizations such as the National Opinion Research Center and the Rand Corporation. Most, however, work at the approximately 200 research universities and institutes located in a dozen advanced industrialized countries. Thus, the scientific community is scattered geographically, but its members tend to work together in small clusters.

How big is the scientific community? This is not an easy question to answer. Using the broadest definition (including all scientists and those in science-related professions, such as engineers), it includes about 15 percent of the labor force in advanced industrialized countries. A better way to look at the scientific community is to examine the basic unit of the larger community: the discipline (e.g., sociology, biology, psychology, etc.). Scientists are most familiar with a particular discipline because knowledge is specialized. Compared to other fields with advanced training, the numbers are very small. For example, each year, about 500 people receive Ph.D.s in sociology, 16,000 receive medical degrees, and 38,000 receive law degrees.

A discipline such as sociology may have about 8,000 active researchers worldwide. Most researchers complete only two or three studies in their careers, whereas a small number of highly active researchers conduct many dozens of studies. In a specialty or topic area (e.g., study of the death penalty, social movements, divorce), only about 100 researchers are very active and conduct most research studies. Although research results represent what humanity knows and it has a major impact on the lives of many millions of people, only a small number of people are actually producing most new scientific knowledge.

The Scientific Method and Attitude

You have probably heard of the scientific method, and you may be wondering how it fits into all this. The *scientific method* is not one single thing; it refers to the ideas, rules, techniques, and approaches that the scientific community uses. The method arises from a loose consensus within the community of scientists. It includes a way of looking at the world that places a high value on professionalism, craftsmanship, ethical integrity, creativity, rigorous standards, and diligence. It also includes strong professional norms such as honesty and uprightness in doing research, great candor and openness about how one conducted a study, and a focus on the merits of the research itself and not on any characteristics of individuals who conducted the study.

Journal Articles in Science

Consider what happens once a researcher finishes a study. First, he or she writes a detailed description of the study and the results as a research report or a paper using a special format. Often, he or she also gives an oral presentation of the paper before other researchers at a conference or a meeting of a professional association and seeks comments and suggestions. Next, the researcher sends several copies to the editor of a scholarly journal. Each editor, a respected researcher chosen by other scientists to oversee the journal, removes the title page, which is the only place the author's name appears, and sends the article to several reviewers. The reviewers are respected scientists who have conducted studies in the same specialty area or topic. The reviewers do not know who did the study, and the author of the paper does not know who the reviewers are. This reinforces the scientific principle of judging a study on its merits alone. Reviewers evaluate the research based on its clarity, originality, standards of good research methods, and advancing knowledge. They return their evaluations to the editor, who decides to reject the paper, ask the author to revise and resubmit it, or accept it for publication. It is a very careful, cautious method to ensure quality control.

The scholarly journals that are highly respected and regularly read by most researchers in a field receive far more papers than they can publish. They accept only 10 to 15 percent of submitted manuscripts. Even lower-ranked journals regularly reject half of the submissions. Thus, several experienced researchers screen a journal article based on its merits alone, and publication represents the study's tentative acceptance by the scientific community as a valid contribution to knowledge. Unlike the authors of articles for the popular magazines found at newsstands, scientists are not paid for publishing in scholarly journals. In fact, they may have to pay a small fee to help defray costs just to have their papers considered. Researchers are happy to make their research available to their peers (i.e., other scientists and researchers) through scholarly journals. The article communicates the results of a study that a researcher might have devoted years of his or her life to, and it is the way researchers gain respect and visibility among their professional peers. Likewise, the reviewers are not paid for reviewing papers, but consider it an honor to be asked to conduct the reviews and to carry out one of the responsibilities of being in the scientific community. The scientific community imparts great respect to researchers who publish many articles in the foremost scholarly journals because these researchers are directly advancing the scientific community's primary goal—the accumulation of carefully developed knowledge. A researcher gains prestige and honor and a reputation as an accomplished researcher through such publications.

You may never publish an article in a scholarly journal, but you will probably read many such articles. It is important to see how they are a vital component in the system of scientific research. Researchers actively read what appears in the journals to learn about new research findings and the methods used to conduct a study. Eventually, the new knowledge is disseminated in textbooks, new reports, or public talks.

STEPS IN THE RESEARCH PROCESS

Social research proceeds in a sequence of steps, although various approaches to research suggest slightly different steps. Most studies follow the seven steps discussed here. To begin the process, you select a *topic*—a general area of study or issue, such as domestic abuse, homelessness, or powerful corporate elites. A topic is too broad for conducting a study. This makes the next step crucial. You must then narrow down the topic, or *focus* the topic into a specific research question for a study (e.g., "Are people who marry younger more likely to engage in physical abuse of a spouse under conditions of high stress than those who marry older?"). As you learn about a topic and narrow the focus, you should review past research, or the *literature,* on a topic or question. You also want to develop a possible answer, or hypothesis, and theory can be important at this stage.

After specifying a research question, you have to develop a highly detailed plan on how you will carry out the study. This third step requires that you decide on the many practical details of doing the research (e.g., whether to use a survey or qualitative observing in the field, how many subjects to use, etc.). It is only after completing the design stage that you are ready to *gather the data* or evidence (e.g., ask people the questions, record answers, etc.). Once you have very carefully collected the data, your next step is to manipulate or *analyze the data.* This will help you see any patterns in it and help you to give meaning to or *interpret* the data (e.g., "People who marry young and grew up in families with abuse have higher rates of physical domestic abuse than those with different family histories"). Finally, you must *inform others* by writing a report that describes the study's background, how you conducted it, and what you discovered.

The seven-step process shown in Figure 1.1 is oversimplified. In practice, you will rarely complete one step totally then leave it behind to move to the next step. Rather, the process is interactive in which the steps blend into each other. What you do in a later step may stimulate you to reconsider and slightly adjust your thinking in a previous one. The process is not strictly linear and may flow back and forth before reach-

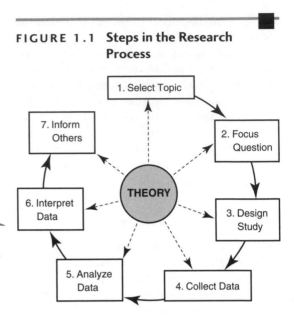

FIGURE 1.1   Steps in the Research Process

ing an end. The seven steps are for one research project; it is one cycle of going through the steps in a single study on a specific topic.

Science is an ongoing enterprise that builds on prior research and builds a larger, collectively created body of knowledge. Any one study is a small part of the much larger whole of science. A single researcher may be working on multiple research projects at once, or several researchers may collaborate on one project. Likewise, one project may result in one scholarly article or several, and sometimes several smaller projects are reported in a single article.

DIMENSIONS OF RESEARCH

Three years after they graduated from college. Tim and Sharon met for lunch. Tim asked Sharon, "So, how is your new job as a researcher for Social Data, Inc.? What are you doing?" Sharon answered, "Right now I'm working on an applied research project on day care quality in which we're doing a cross-sectional survey to get descriptive data for an evaluation study." Sharon touched on four dimensions of social research as she described her research on day care.

Social research comes in several shapes and sizes. Before you begin a study, you will need to make several decisions about the specific type of research you are going to conduct. Researchers need to understand the advantages and disadvantages of each type, although most end up specializing in doing one type. We can think of the types as fitting into one of the categories in each of four dimensions of research.

The first dimension is a distinction in how research is used, or between applied and basic research. The next is the purpose of doing research, or its goal, to explore, describe, or explain. The next two dimensions are more specific: how time is incorporated into the study design, and the specific data collection technique used.

The dimensions overlap, in that certain dimensions are often found together (e.g., the goal of a study and a data collection technique). Once you learn the dimensions, you will begin to see how the particular research questions you might want to investigate tend to be more compatible with certain ways of designing a study and collecting data. In addition, being aware of the dimensions of research will make it easier to understand the research reports by others.

Use of Research

For over a century, science has had two wings. Some researchers adopt a detached, purely scientific, and academic orientation; others are more activist, pragmatic, and interventionist oriented. This is not a rigid separation. Researchers in the two wings cooperate and maintain friendly relations. Some individuals move from one wing to another at different stages in their careers. In simple terms, some researchers concentrate on advancing general knowledge over the long term, whereas others conduct studies to solve specific, immediate problems. Those who concentrate on examining the fundamental nature of social reality are engaged in basic research.

Basic Research. Basic social research advances fundamental knowledge about the social world. Basic researchers focus on refuting or supporting theories that explain how the social world operates, what makes things happen, why social relations are a certain way, and why society changes. Basic research is the source of most new scientific ideas and ways of thinking about the world. Many nonscientists criticize basic research and ask, "What good is it?" and consider it to be a waste of time and money. Although basic research often lacks a practical application in the short term, it provides a foundation for knowledge that advances understanding in many policy areas, problems, or areas of study. Basic research is the source of most of the tools, methods, theories, and ideas about underlying causes of how people act or think used by applied researchers. It provides the major breakthroughs that significant advances in knowledge; it is the painstaking study of broad questions that has the potential of shifting how we think about a wide range of issues. It may have an impact for the next 50 years or century. Often, the applications of basic research appear many years or decades later. Practical applications may be apparent only after many accumulated advances in basic knowledge build over a long time period. For example, in 1984, Alec Jeffreys, a geneticist at the University of Leicester in England, was engaged in basic research studying the evolution of genes. As an indirect accidental side effect of a new technique he developed, he discovered a way to produce what is now call human DNA "fingerprints" or unique markings of the DNA of individuals. This was not his intent. He even said he would have never thought of the technique if DNA fingerprints had been his goal. Within 10 years applied uses of the technique were developed. Today, DNA analysis is a widely used technique in criminal investigations.

Applied Research. Applied social research is designed to address a specific concern or to offer solutions to a problem identified by an employer, club, agency, social movement, or organization. Applied social researchers are rarely concerned with building, testing, or connecting to a larger theory, developing a long-term general understanding, or carrying out a large-scale investigation that might span years. Instead, they usually conduct a quick, small-scale study that provides practical results for use in the short term (i.e., next month or next year). For example, the student government of University X wants to know whether the number of University X students who are arrested for driving while intoxicated or involved in auto accidents will decline if it sponsors alcohol-free parties next year. Applied research would be most applicable for this situation.

People employed in businesses, government offices, health care facilities, social service agencies, political organizations, and educational institutions often conduct applied research and use the results in decision making. Applied research affects decisions such as the following: Should an agency start a new program to reduce the wait time before a client receives benefits? Should a police force adopt a new type of response to reduce spousal abuse? Should a political candidate emphasize his or her stand on the environment instead of the economy? Should a company market a skin care product to mature adults instead of teenagers?

The scientific community is the primary consumer of basic research. The consumers of applied research findings are practitioners such as teachers, counselors, and social workers, or decision makers such as managers, agency administrators, and public officials. Often, someone other than the researcher who conducted the study uses the results.

Applied research results are less likely to enter the public domain in publications and may be available only to few decision makers or practitioners. This means that applied research findings often are not widely disseminated and that well-qualified researchers rarely get to judge the quality of applied studies.

The decision makers who use the results of an applied study may or may not use them wisely. Sometimes despite serious problems with a study's methodology and cautions from the researchers, politicians use results to justify cutting programs they dislike or to advance programs they favor. Because applied research often has immediate implications or involves controversial issues, it often generates conflict. One famous researcher, William Whyte (1984), encountered conflict over findings in his applied research on a factory in Oklahoma and on restaurants in Chicago. In the first case, the management was more interested in defeating a union than in learning about employment relations; in the other, restaurant owners really sought to make the industry look good and did not want findings on the nitty-gritty of its operations made public.

Applied and basic researchers adopt different orientations toward research methodology (see Table 1.2). Basic researchers emphasize high methodological standards and try to conduct near-perfect research. Applied researchers must make more tradeoffs. They may compromise scientific rigor to get quick, usable results, but compromise is never an excuse for sloppy research. Applied researchers try to squeeze research into the constraints of an applied setting and balance rigor against practical needs. Such balancing requires an in-depth knowledge of research and an awareness of the consequences of compromising standards.

Types of Applied Research. There are many specific types of applied research. Here, you will learn about three major types: evaluation, action, and social impact assessment.

Evaluation Research Study. Evaluation research study is applied research designed to find out whether a program, a new way of doing something, a marketing campaign, a policy, and so forth, is effective—in other words, "Does it work?" The most widely used type of applied research is evaluation research.[7] This type of research is widely used in large bureaucratic organizations (e.g., businesses, schools, hospi-

TABLE 1.2   Basic and Applied Social Research Compared

Basic	Applied
1. Research is intrinsically satisfying and judgments are by other sociologists.	1. Research is part of a job and is judged by sponsors who are outside the discipline of sociology.
2. Research problems and subjects are selected with a great deal of freedom.	2. Research problems are "narrowly constrained" to the demands of employers or sponsors.
3. Research is judged by absolute norms of scientific rigor, and the highest standards of scholarship are sought.	3. The rigor and standards of scholarship depend on the uses of results. Research can be "quick and dirty" or may match high scientific standards.
4. The primary concern is with the internal logic and rigor of research design.	4. The primary concern is with the ability to generalize findings to areas of interest to sponsors.
5. The driving goal is to contribute to basic, theoretical knowledge.	5. The driving goal is to have practical payoffs or uses for results.
6. Success comes when results appear in a scholarly journal and have an impact on others in the scientific community.	6. Success comes when results are used by sponsors in decision making.

Source: Adapted from Freeman and Rossi (1984:572–573).

tals, government, large nonprofit agencies) to demonstrate the effectiveness of what they are doing. An evaluation researcher does not use techniques different from those of other social researchers. The difference lies in the fact that decision makers, who may not be researchers themselves, define the scope and purpose of the research. Also, their objective is to use results in a practical situation.[8]

Evaluation research questions might include: Does a Socratic teaching technique improve learning over lecturing? Does a law-enforcement program of mandatory arrest reduce spouse abuse? Does a flextime program increase employee productivity? Evaluation researchers measure the effectiveness of a program, policy, or way of doing something and often use several research techniques (e.g., survey and field). If it can be used, the experimental technique is usually preferred. Practitioners involved with a pol-

icy or program may conduct evaluation research for their own information or at the request of outside decision makers. The decision makers may place limits on the research by fixing boundaries on what can be studied and by determining the outcome of interest. This often creates ethical dilemmas for a researcher.

Ethical and political conflicts often arise in evaluation research because people can have opposing interests in the findings. The findings of research can affect who gets or keeps a job, it can build political popularity, or it may help promote an alternative program. People who are personally displeased with the findings may attack the researcher or his or her methods.

Evaluation research has several limitations: The reports of research rarely go through a peer review process, raw data are rarely publicly available, and the focus is narrowed to select inputs and outputs more than the full process by which a program affects people's lives. In addition, decision makers may selectively use or ignore evaluation findings.

Action Research Study.   *Action research* is applied research that treats knowledge as a form of power and abolishes the division between creating knowledge and using knowledge to engage in political action. There are several types of action research, but most share five characteristics: (1) the people being studied actively participate in the research process; (2) the research incorporates ordinary or popular knowledge; (3) the research focuses on issues of power; (4) the research seeks to raise consciousness or increase awareness of issues; and (5) the research is tied directly to a plan or program of political action. Action research tends to be associated with a social movement, political cause, or advocacy for an issue. It can be conducted to advance a range of political positions. Some action research has an insurgent orientation with goals of empowering the powerless, fighting oppression and injustice, and reducing inequality. Wealthy and powerful groups or organizations also sponsor and conduct action research to defend their status, position, and privileges in society.

Most action researchers are explicitly political, not value neutral. Because the primary goal is to affect sociopolitical conditions, publishing results in formal reports, articles, or books is secondary. Most action researchers also believe that knowledge develops from direct experience, particularly the experience of engaging in sociopolitical action.

For example, most feminist research is action research. It has a dual mission: to create social change by transforming gender relations and to contribute to the advancement of knowledge. A feminist researcher who studies sexual harassment might recommend policy changes to reduce it as well as to inform potential victims so they can protect themselves and defend their rights. At times, researchers will explain study results in a public hearing to try to modify new policies or laws. The authors of a study on domestic violence that will be discussed shortly as an explanatory study example (Cherlin et al., 2004) testified in the United States Senate. The study findings and the testimony helped to alter marriage promotion provisions in a 2005 welfare reform law.[9]

Social Impact Assessment Research Study.   A researcher who conducts *social impact assessment* (SIA) estimates the likely consequences of a planned intervention or intentional change to occur in the future. It may be part of a larger environmental impact statement required by government agencies and used for planning and making choices among alternative policies. He or she forecasts how aspects of the social environment may change and suggests ways to mitigate changes likely to be adverse from the point of view of an affected population. *Impacts* are the difference between a forecast of the future with the project or policy and without the project or policy. For example, the SIA might estimate the ability of a local hospital to respond to an earthquake, determine how housing availability for the elderly will change if a major new highway is built, or assess the impact on college admissions if students receive interest-free loans. Researchers who conduct SIAs often examine a range of social outcomes and work in an interdisciplinary research team to estimate the social outcomes. The outcomes include measuring "quality of life" issues, such as access to health care, illegal drug and alcohol use, employment opportunities, schooling quality, teen pregnancy rates, commuting time and traffic congestion, availability of parks and recreation facilities, shopping choices, viable cultural institutions, crime rates, interracial tensions, or social isolation. There is an international professional association for SIA research that advances SIA techniques and promotes SIA by governments, corporations, and other organizations.

Social impact assessments are rarely required, but a few governments mandate them. For example, in New South Wales, Australia, a registered club or hotel cannot increase the number of poker machines unless the Liquor Administration Board in the Department Gaming and Racing approves an SIA for the club or hotel. The SIA enables the board to assess the likely local community impact from increasing the number of poker machines. The format includes a matrix that allows the board to identify the social and economic impacts, positive and negative, financial or nonfinancial, quantified or qualitative. In New Zealand, the Gambling Act of 2003 requires an SIA before expanding gambling. In one 2004 study in New Zealand for the Auckland City Council, it noted that 90 percent of New Zealand's adults gamble, 10 percent gamble regularly (once a week or more often), and about 1 percent are problem gamblers, although this varies by age, income, and ethnicity. The SIA recommended limiting the locations of new gambling venues, monitoring their usage, and tracing the amount of gambling revenues that are returned to the community in various ways (e.g., clubs, trusts, etc.). It contained a matrix with social (e.g, arrests, divorce, domestic violence), economic (e.g., unemployment, bankruptcy, tourism expansion), and cultural impacts (e.g., time away from other leisure activity) listed by their effect on all gamblers, problem gamblers, the local community, and the region.[10]

Purpose of a Study

If you ask someone why he or she is conducting a study, you might get a range of responses: "My boss told me to"; "It was a class assignment"; "I was curious"; "My roommate thought it would be a good idea." There are almost as many reasons to do research as there are researchers. Yet, the purposes of social research may be organized into three groups based on what the researcher is trying to accomplish—explore a new topic, describe a social phenomenon, or explain why something occurs. Studies may have multiple purposes (e.g., both to explore and to describe), but one of three major purposes is usually dominant (see Box 1.2).

<table>
<tr><td>Box
1.2</td><td colspan="3">**Purpose of Research**</td></tr>
</table>

Exploratory	**Descriptive**	**Explanatory**
■ Become familiar with the basic facts, setting, and concerns.	■ Provide a detailed, highly accurate picture.	■ Test a theory's predictions or principle.
■ Create a general mental picture of conditions.	■ Locate new data that contradict past data.	■ Elaborate and enrich a theory's explanation.
■ Formulate and focus questions for future research.	■ Create a set of categories or classify types.	■ Extend a theory to new issues or topics.
■ Generate new ideas, conjectures, or hypotheses.	■ Clarify a sequence of steps or stages.	■ Support or refute an explanation or prediction.
■ Determine the feasibility of conducting research.	■ Document a causal process or mechanism.	■ Link issues or topics with a general principle.
■ Develop techniques for measuring and locating future data.	■ Report on the background or context of a situation.	■ Determine which of several explanations is best.

Exploration. Perhaps you have explored a new topic or issue in order to learn about it. If the issue was new or no researchers had written about it, you began at the beginning. In *exploratory research,* a researcher examines a new area to formulate precise questions that he or she can address in future research. Exploratory research may be the first stage in a sequence of studies. A researcher may need to conduct an exploratory study in order to know enough to design and execute a second, more systematic and extensive study. It addresses the "what?" question: "What is this social activity really about?"

Many higher-education officials are concerned about college students' low retention rates, especially students from minority-disadvantaged social backgrounds. For example, of Latinos who enroll in college, 80 percent leave without receiving a degree. Officials seek ways to reduce dropouts and increase the chances that students who begin college will stay until they earn a degree. Garza and Landeck (2004) conducted an exploratory study of over 500 Latino students at a college along the Texas–Mexico border who had dropped out. They wanted to learn the influencing factors and rationales in student decision making. The authors discovered that the primary factors and rationales were unrelated to teaching quality or university services. Instead, the students who dropped out had been overwhelmed by personal problems or had serious difficulties with family or job responsibilities. Such factors were a major reason given by over 80 percent of the students who dropped out.

Exploratory researchers tend to use qualitative data and not be wedded to a specific theory or research question. Exploratory research rarely yields definitive answers. If you conduct an exploratory study, you may get frustrated and feel it is difficult because there are few guidelines to follow. Everything is potentially important, the steps are not well defined, and the direction of inquiry changes frequently. You need to be creative, open-minded, and flexible; adopt an investigative stance; and explore all sources of information.

Description. Perhaps you have a more highly developed idea about a social phenomenon and want to describe it. *Descriptive research* presents a picture of the specific details of a situation, social setting, or relationship; it focuses on "how?" and "who?" questions: "How did it happen?" "Who is involved?" A great deal of social research is descriptive. Descriptive researchers use most data-gathering techniques—surveys, field research, content analysis, and historical-comparative research. Only experimental research is less often used. Much of the social research found in scholarly journals or used for making policy decisions is descriptive.

Descriptive and exploratory research often blur together in practice. In descriptive research, a researcher begins with a well-defined subject and conducts a study to describe it accurately and the outcome is a detailed picture of the subject. The results may indicate the percentage of people who hold a particular view or engage in specific behaviors—for example, that 8 percent of parents physically or sexually abuse their children. A descriptive study presents a picture of types of people or of social activities.

Stack, Wasserman, and Kern (2004) conducted a descriptive study on pornography use on the Internet by people in the United States. They found that the greatest users were those with weak social bonds. More specifically, the types of people who were adult users of pornography tended to be males with unhappy marriages and weak ties to organized religion. Pornography users were also more likely to have engaged in nonconventional sexual behavior (i.e., had an extramarital affair or engaged in paid sex) but not other forms of deviance, such as illegal drug use.

Explanation. When you encounter an issue that is well recognized and have a description of it, you might begin to wonder why things are the way they are. *Explanatory research* identifies the sources of social behaviors, beliefs, conditions, and events; it documents causes, tests theories, and provides reasons. It builds on exploratory and descriptive research. For example, an exploratory study discovers a new type of abuse by parents; a descriptive researcher documents that 10 percent of parents abuse their children in this new way and describes the kinds of parents and conditions for which it is most frequent; the explanatory researcher focuses on why certain parents are abusing their children in this manner. Cherlin, Burton, Hurt, and Purvin (2004) explained instability in marriage or cohabitation using a woman's past experience with sexual or physical abuse. They tested the hypothesis that women with a history of abuse would be less likely marry than those without such histories. The authors reasoned that those who were abused have fewer social supports and resources to resist or avoid abusive partners, and they are more likely to harbor feelings of self-blame, guilt, and low self-esteem that inhibit the formation of healthy romantic relationships. An abusive experience also creates greater emotional distance and a hesitancy to make long-term commitments. Using quantitative and qualitative data gathered in low-income neighborhoods in three cities—Boston, Chicago, and San Antonio—they found that adult women who had experienced past abuse were less likely to be married, and those with multiple forms of abuse were most likely to remain single. It appears that women without a past history of abuse who found themselves in an abusive relationship as an adult were likely to withdraw from it, but women who had been abused as children were less likely to leave and tended to enter into a series of unstable, transitory relations.

Time Dimension in Research

An awareness of how a study uses the time dimension will help you read or conduct research. This is because different research questions or issues incorporate time differently. Some studies give a snapshot of a single, fixed time point and allow you to analyze it in detail (cross-sectional). Other studies provide a moving picture that lets you follow events, people, or social relations over several time points (longitudinal). Quantitative studies generally look at many cases, people, or units, and measure limited features about them in the form of numbers. By contrast, a qualitative study usually involves qualitative data and examines many diverse features of a small number of cases across either a short or long time period (see Figure 1.2).

Cross-Sectional Research. Most social research studies are *cross-sectional*; they examine a single point in time or take a one-time snapshot approach. Cross-sectional research is usually the simplest and least costly alternative. Its disadvantage is that it cannot capture social processes or change. Cross-sectional research can be exploratory, descriptive, or explanatory, but it is most consistent with a descriptive approach to research. The descriptive study by Stack, Wasserman, and Kern (2004) on pornography use was cross-sectional, based on a national U.S. survey conducted in 2000.

Longitudinal Research. Researchers using *longitudinal research* examine features of people or other units at more than one time. It is usually more complex and costly than cross-sectional research, but it is also more powerful and informative. Descriptive and explanatory researchers use longitudinal approaches. Let us now look at the three main types of longitudinal research: time series, panel, and cohort.

Time-Series Study. A *time-series study* is longitudinal research in which a researcher gathers the same type of information across two or more time periods. Researchers can observe stability or change in the features of the units or can track conditions over time. The specific individuals may change but the overall pattern is clear. For example, there has been a nationwide survey of a large sample of incoming freshman students since 1966. Since it began, over 11 million students at more than 1,800 colleges participated. The fall 2003 survey of 276,449 students found many facts and trends, such as only 34 percent of

FIGURE 1.2   The Time Dimension in Social Research

CROSS-SECTIONAL: Observe a collection of people at one time.

February 2007

TIME SERIES: Observe different people at multiple times.

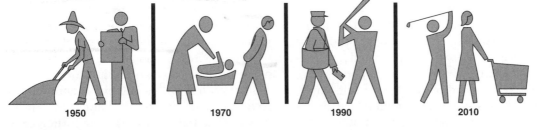

1950   1970   1990   2010

PANEL: Observe the exact same people at two or more times.

1986   1996   2006

COHORT: Observe people who shared an experience at two or more times.

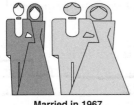

Married in 1967   1987   2007

CASE STUDY: Observe a small set intensely across time.

2005 → 2007

entering freshmen studied six or more hours per week. This was the lowest level since the question was asked in 1987 (when it was 47 percent). Yet, alcohol consumption was down. In 2003, 44.8 percent reported drinking beer, which represented a steady decline from 73.7 percent in 1982. In 2003, freshmen were more interested in keeping up with politics. The 33.9 percent who said it was very important to stay politically informed was up from a low of 28.1 percent in 2000, and 22.5 percent said they discussed politics regularly, up from 19.4 percent in 2002 (which had been the highest since a low point in 1993). These figures are still far lower than the 60.3 percent who expressed an interest in politics in 1966, or the one-third who discussed politics regularly in 1968. The importance of family has steadily increased over the years, with 74.8 percent of students calling it essential or very important. This is up from the low point of 58.8 percent in 1977 when the question was first asked. However, religious involvement declined. The percentage of students who attended religious services regularly was at its lowest level in 35 years. In addition, the percent claiming "none" as a religious preference reached a record high of 17.6 percent, compared to a record low of 6.6 percent in 1966. Another trend over the past two decades has been a steady growth in opposition to the death penalty. Nearly one in three incoming students advocated ending capital punishment. This is the highest score since 1980 (when it was 33.2 percent), although the percent withholding an opinion was far higher earlier in time; it exceeded 60 percent in the 1970.[11]

Panel Study. The *panel study* is a powerful type of longitudinal research in which the researcher observes exactly the same people, group, or organization across multiple time points. It is more difficult to conduct than time-series research. Panel research is formidable to conduct and very costly. Tracking people over time is often difficult because some people die or cannot be located. Nevertheless, the results of a well-designed panel study are very valuable. Even short-term panel studies can clearly show the impact of a particular life event. For example, Oesterle, Johnson, and Mortimer (2004) examined panel data from a longitudinal study that began in 1988 with 1,000 ninth-grade students enrolled in the St. Paul, Minnesota, public school district and looked at volunteering activities during late adolescence and young adulthood, covering nine years from age 18–19 (1992) to age 26–27 (2000). They found that volunteering at an earlier stage strongly affected whether one volunteered at a later stage. Also, people who devoted full time to working or parenting at an earlier stage (18–19 years old) were less likely to volunteer at a later stage (26–27 years old) than those whose major activity was attending school.

Cohort Study. A *cohort study* is similar to a panel study, but rather than observing the exact same people, the study focuses on a category of people who share a similar life experience in a specified time period. Researchers examine the category as a whole for important features and focus on the cohort, or category, not on specific individuals. Commonly used cohorts include all people born in the same year (called *birth cohorts*), all people hired at the same time, and all people who graduate in a given year. Unlike panel studies, researchers do not have to find the exact same people for cohort studies; rather, they need only to identify those who experienced a common life event. In a study of Generation X in the United States, Andolina and Mayer (2003) focused on the cohort of people born between 1967 and 1974. They compared 10 birth cohorts at different time periods over several decades, tracing questions across 24 years. The authors found that White Xers are distinct in their support for school racial integration and for government action to enforce such efforts, compared to other birth cohorts, but not in their attitudes toward employment opportunities or affirmative action. Despite greater general support than other cohorts for equality through integration, it does not extend to issues beyond the schoolyard.

Case Studies.   In cross-sectional and longitudinal research, a researcher examines features on many people or units, either at one time period or across time periods, and measures several common features on them, often using numbers. In *case-study research,* a researcher examines, in depth, many features of a few cases over a duration of time with very detailed, varied, and extensive data, often in a qualitative form. The researcher carefully selects a few key cases to illustrate an issue and study it (or them) in detail and considers the specific context of each case. This contrasts with other longitudinal studies in which the researcher gathers data on many units or cases, then looks for general patterns in the mass of numbers.

For example, Snow and Anderson (1992) conducted a case study on homeless people in Austin, Texas. It provided a wealth of details about the lives and conditions of homeless people, identified several types of homeless people, outlined the paths by which they became homeless, and discussed several processes that kept them homeless. This case study used many types of detailed qualitative and quantitative data, with exploratory, descriptive, and explanatory phases to reveal a great amount of unexpected and new information.[12]

Data Collection Techniques

Social researchers collect data using one or more specific techniques. This section gives you a brief overview of the major techniques. In later chapters, you will read about these techniques in detail and learn how to use them. Some techniques are more effective when addressing specific kinds of questions or topics. It takes skill, practice, and creativity to match a research question to an appropriate data collection technique. The techniques fall into two categories based on whether the data being gathered are quantitative or qualitative.

Quantitative Data Collection Techniques.
Techniques for quantitative data collection include experiments, surveys, content analyses, and existing statistics.

Experiments.   Experimental research closely follows the logic and principles found in natural science research; researchers create situations and examine their effects on participants. A researcher conducts experiments in laboratories or in real life with a relatively small number of people and a well-focused research question. Experiments are most effective for explanatory research. In the typical experiment, the researcher divides the people being studied into two or more groups. He or she then treats both groups identically, except that one group but not the other is given a condition he or she is interested in: the "treatment." The researcher measures the reactions of both groups precisely. By controlling the setting for both groups and giving only one group the treatment, the researcher can conclude that any differences in the reactions of the groups are due to the treatment alone.

Surveys.   A survey researcher asks people questions in a written questionnaire (mailed or handed to people) or during an interview and then records answers. The researcher manipulates no situation or condition; he or she simply asks many people numerous questions in a short time period. Typically, he or she then summarizes answers to questions in percentages, tables, or graphs. Researchers use survey techniques in descriptive or explanatory research. Surveys give the researcher a picture of what many people think or report doing. Survey researchers often use a sample or a smaller group of selected people (e.g., 150 students), but generalize results to a larger group (e.g., 5,000 students) from which the smaller group was selected. Survey research is very widely used in many fields.

Content Analyses.   A content analysis is a technique for examining information, or content, in written or symbolic material (e.g., pictures, movies, song lyrics, etc.). In content analysis, a researcher first identifies a body of material to analyze (e.g., books, newspapers, films, etc.) and then creates a system for recording specific aspects of it. The system might include counting how often certain words or themes occur. Finally, the researcher records what was found in the material. He or she often measures information in the content as numbers and presents it as tables or graphs. This technique lets a researcher discover features in the content of large amounts of material that might otherwise go unnoticed. Researchers can use content analysis for exploratory and explanatory research, but primarily it is used for descriptive research.

Existing Statistics. In *existing statistics research,* a researcher locates previously collected information, often in the form of government reports or previously conducted surveys, then reorganizes or combines the information in new ways to address a research question. Locating sources can be time consuming, so the researcher needs to consider carefully the meaning of what he or she finds. Frequently, a researcher does not know whether the information of interest is available when he or she begins a study. Sometimes, the existing quantitative information consists of stored surveys or other data that a researcher reexamines using various statistical procedures. Existing statistics research can be used for exploratory, descriptive, or explanatory purposes, but it is most frequently used for descriptive research.

Qualitative Data Collection Techniques. Techniques for qualitative data collection include field research and historical-comparative research.

Field Research. Most field researchers conduct case studies looking at a small group of people over a length of time (e.g., weeks, months, years). A *field researcher* begins with a loosely formulated idea or topic, selects a social group or natural setting for study, gains access and adopts a social role in the setting, and observes

in detail. The researcher gets to know personally the people being studied, may conduct open-ended and informal interviews, and takes detailed notes on a daily basis. After leaving the field site, the researcher carefully rereads the notes and prepares written reports. Field research is used most often for exploratory and descriptive studies; it is rarely used for explanatory research.

Historical-Comparative Research. *Historical-comparative researchers* examine aspects of social life in a past historical era or across different cultures. Researchers who use this technique may focus on one historical period or several, compare one or more cultures, or mix historical periods and cultures. Like field research, a researcher combines theory building/testing with data collection and begins with a loosely formulated question that is refined during the research process. Researchers often gather a wide array of evidence, including existing statistics and documents (e.g., novels, official reports, books, newspapers, diaries, photographs, and maps) for study. In addition, they may make direct observations and conduct interviews. Historical-comparative research can be exploratory, descriptive, or explanatory and can blend types.

CONCLUSION

This chapter gave you an overview of social research. You saw how social research differs from the ordinary ways of learning-knowing about the social world, how doing research is based on science and the scientific community, and about several types of social research based on its dimensions (e.g., its purpose, the technique used to gather data, etc.). The dimensions of research loosely overlap with each other. The dimensions of social research are a kind of "road map" to help you make your way through the terrain of social research. In the next chapter, we turn to social theory. You read about it a little in this chapter. In the next chapter, you will learn how theory and research methods work together and about several types of theory.

Key Terms

action research study
applied social research
basic social research
case study
cohort study
cross-sectional research
data
descriptive research
empirical evidence
evaluation research study
existing statistics research
experimental research
explanatory research
exploratory research
field research
halo effect
historical comparative research
longitudinal research
overgeneralization
panel study
premature closure
qualitative data
quantitative data
scientific community
scientific method
selective observation

social impact assessment study
social research
survey research
time-series study

Endnotes

1. See Rampton and Stauber (2001:247–277 and 305–306).
2. See Best (2001:15) on advocates and media.
3. See National Science Board (2002:735–739).
4. Schacter (2001) provides a summary of memory issues.
5. National Science Board (2002:739).
6. Discussions of the scientific community can be found in Cole and Gordon (1995), Crane (1972), Hagstrom (1965), Merton (1973), Mulkay (1991), and Ziman (1999).
7. See Patton (2001) and Weiss (1997) for a more detailed discussion of recent advances in evaluation research.
8. Beck (1995) provides a useful overview.
9. See Herring and Ebner (2005) on the use of domestic violence study findings.
10. See Adams (2004) for more information on the Auckland City study.
11. See the website at www.gseis.ucla.edu/heri/heri.html.
12. Also see Snow and Anderson (1991) for a discussion of the case-study method in their study of homeless people. Also see George and Bennett (2005) on the case-study method generally.

Theory and Social Research

INTRODUCTION

Suppose you want to make sense of the hostility between people of different races. Trying to understand it, you ask a teacher, who responds:

Most racially prejudiced people learn negative stereotypes about another racial group from their families, friends, and others in their immediate surroundings. If they lack sufficient intimate social contact with members of the group or intense information that contradicts those stereotypes, they remain prejudiced.

This makes sense to you because it is consistent with what you know about how the social world works. This is an example of a small-scale social theory, a type that researchers use when conducting a study.

What do you think of when you hear the word *theory*? Theory is one of the least well understood terms for students learning social science. My students' eyelids droop if I begin a class by saying, "Today we are going to examine the theory of . . ." The mental picture many students have of theory is something that floats high among the clouds. My students have called it "a tangled maze of jargon" and "abstractions that are irrelevant to the real world."

Contrary to these views, theory has an important role in research and is an essential ally for the researcher. Researchers use theory differently in various types of research, but some type of theory is present in most social research. It is less evident in applied or descriptive than in basic or explanatory research. In simple terms, researchers interweave a story about the operation of the social world (the theory) with what they observe when they examine it systematically (the data).

People who seek absolute, fixed answers for a specific individual or a particular one-time event may be frustrated with science and social theories. To avoid frustration, it is wise to keep in mind three things about how social scientific theories work. First, social theories explain recurring patterns, not unique or one-time events. For example, they are not good for explaining why terrorists decided to attack New York's World Trade Center on September 11, 2001, but they can explain patterns, such as the conditions that generally lead to increased levels of fear and feelings of patriotism in a people. Second, social theories are explanations for aggregates, not particular individuals. *Aggregates* are collections of many individuals, cases, or other units (e.g., businesses, schools, families, clubs, cities, nations, etc.). A social theory rarely can explain why Josephine decided to major in nursing rather than engineering, but it can explain why females more than males in general choose nursing over engineering as a major. Third, social theories state a probability, chance, or tendency for events to occur, rather than state that one event must absolutely follow another. For example, instead of stating that when someone is abused as a child, that person will always later abuse his or her own children, a theory might state that when someone experiences abuse during his or her childhood, that person will *tend to* or is *more likely to* become an abusive parent when an adult. Likewise, it might state that people who did not experience childhood abuse might become abusive parents, but they are *less likely to* than someone who has experienced abuse as a child.

WHAT IS THEORY?

In Chapter 1, *social theory* was defined as a system of interconnected abstractions or ideas that condenses and organizes knowledge about the social world. It is a compact way to think of the social world. People are constantly developing new theories about how the world works.

Some people confuse the history of social thought, or what great thinkers said, with social theory. The classical social theorists (e.g., Durkheim, Weber, Marx, and Tonnies) played an important role in generating innovative ideas. They developed original theories that laid the foundation for subsequent generations of social thinkers. People study the classical theorists because they provided many creative and interrelated ideas at once. They radically changed the way people understood and saw the social world. We study them because geniuses who generate many original, insightful ideas and fundamentally shift how people saw the social world are rare.

At times people confuse theory with a hunch or speculative guessing. They may say, "It's only a theory" or ask, "What's your theory about it?" This lax use of the term *theory* causes confusion. Such guessing differs from a serious social theory that has been carefully built and debated over many years by dozens of researchers who found support for the theory's key parts in repeated empirical tests. A related confusion is when what people consider to be a "fact" (i.e., light a match in a gasoline-filled room and it will explode) is what scientists call a theory (i.e., a theory of how combining certain quantities of particular chemicals with oxygen and a level of heat is likely to produce the outcome of explosive force). People use simple theories without making them explicit or labeling them as such. For example, newspaper articles or television reports on social issues usually have unstated social theories embedded within them. A news report on the difficulty of implementing a school desegregation plan will contain an implicit theory about race relations. Likewise, political leaders frequently express social theories when they discuss public issues. Politicians who claim that inadequate education causes poverty or that a decline in traditional moral values causes higher crime rates are expressing theories. Compared to the theories of social scientists, such laypersons' theories are less systematic, less well formulated, and harder to test with empirical evidence.

Almost all research involves some theory, so the question is less *whether* you should use theory than *how* you should use it. Being explicit about the theory makes it easier to read someone else's research or to conduct your own. An awareness of how theory fits into the research process produces better designed, easier to understand, and better conducted studies. Most researchers disparage atheoretical or "crude empiricist" research.

Blame Analysis

Blame analysis is a type of counterfeit argument presented as if it were a theoretical explanation. It substitutes attributing blame for a causal explanation that is backed by supporting empirical evidence. Blame belongs to the realm of making moral, legal, or ideological claims. It implies an intention, negligence, or responsibility for an event or situation (usually an unfavorable one). It shifts the focus from Why did it occur? to Who is responsible? Blame analysis assumes there is a party or source to which a fixed amount of responsibility can be attached. The goal of inquiry is to identify a responsible party. Often, some sources are exempted or shielded. This may be the injured party, members of a sympathetic audience, or a sacred value or principle.

Blame analysis clouds discussion because it confuses blame with cause; it gives an account (or story) instead of a logical explanation with intervening causal mechanisms; and it fails to explore empirical evidence for and against several alternative causes. Blame analysis first presents an unfavorable event or situation. It could be a bank is robbed, a group is systematically paid less in the labor force, or traffic congestion is terrible in an urban area. It next identifies one or more responsible parties, then it provides selective evidence that shields certain parties or sources (e.g., employment conditions, the choices available to the underpaid group, transportation policy, and land cost).[1]

THE PARTS OF THEORY

Concepts

All theories contain concepts, and concepts are the building blocks of theory.[2] A *concept* is an idea expressed as a symbol or in words. Natural science concepts are often expressed in symbolic forms, such as Greek letters (e.g., δ) or formulas (e.g., $s = d/t$; s = speed, d = distance, t = time). Most social science concepts are expressed as words. The exotic symbols of natural science concepts make many people nervous, as the use of everyday words in specialized social science concepts can create confusion.

I do not want to exaggerate the distinction between concepts expressed as words and concepts expressed as symbols. Words, after all, are symbols, too; they are symbols we learn with language. Height is a concept with which you are already familiar. For example, I can say the word *height* or write it down; the spoken sounds and written words are part of the English language. The combination of letters in the sound symbolizes, or stands for, the idea of a *height*. Chinese or Arabic characters, the French word *hauteur,* the German word *höhe*, the Spanish word *altura*— all symbolize the same idea. In a sense, a language is merely an agreement to represent ideas by sounds or written characters that people learned at some point in their lives. Learning concepts and theory is like learning a language.[3]

Concepts are everywhere, and you use them all the time. Height is a simple concept from everyday experience. What does it mean? It is easy to use the concept of *height,* but describing the concept itself is difficult. It represents an abstract idea about physical relations. How would you describe it to a very young child or a creature from a distant planet who was totally unfamiliar with it? A new concept from a social theory may seem just as alien when you encounter it for the first time. Height is a characteristic of a physical object, the distance from top to bottom. All people, buildings, trees, mountains, books, and so forth have a height. We can

measure height or compare it. A height of zero is possible, and height can increase or decrease over time. As with many words, we use the word in several ways. Height is used in the expressions *the height of the battle, the height of the summer,* and *the height of fashion.*

The word *height* refers to an abstract idea. We associate its sound and its written form with that idea. There is nothing inherent in the sounds that make up the word and the idea it represents. The connection is arbitrary, but it is still useful. People can express the abstract idea to one another using the symbol alone.

Concepts have two parts: a *symbol* (word or term) and a *definition.* We learn definitions in many ways. I learned the word *height* and its definition from my parents. I learned it as I learned to speak and was socialized to the culture. My parents never gave me a dictionary definition. I learned it through a diffuse, nonverbal, informal process. My parents showed me many examples; I observed and listened to others use the word; I used the word incorrectly and was corrected; and I used it correctly and was understood. Eventually, I mastered the concept.

This example shows how people learn concepts in everyday language and how we share concepts. Suppose my parents had isolated me from television and other people, then taught me that the word for the idea *height* was *zdged.* I would have had difficulty communicating with others. People must share the terms for concepts and their definitions if they are to be of value.

Everyday life is filled with concepts, but many have vague and unclear definitions. Likewise, the values, misconceptions, and experiences of people in a culture may limit everyday concepts. Social scientists borrow concepts from everyday culture, but they refine these concepts and add new ones. Many concepts such as *sexism, life-style, peer group, urban sprawl,* and *social class* began as precise, technical concepts in social theory but have diffused into the larger culture and become less precise.

We create concepts from personal experience, creative thought, or observation. The classical theorists originated many concepts. Example concepts include *family system, gender role, socialization, self-worth, frustration,* and *displaced aggression.*

Some concepts, especially simple, concrete concepts such as *book* or *height,* can be defined through a simple nonverbal process. Most social science concepts are more complex and abstract. They are defined by formal, dictionary-type definitions that build on other concepts. It may seem odd to use concepts to define other concepts, but we do this all the time. For example, I defined *height* as a distance between top and bottom. *Top, bottom,* and *distance* are all concepts. We often combine simple, concrete concepts from ordinary experience to create more abstract concepts. *Height* is more abstract than *top* or *bottom.* Abstract concepts refer to aspects of the world we do not directly experience. They organize thinking and extend understanding of reality.

Researchers define scientific concepts more precisely than those we use in daily discourse. Social theory requires well-defined concepts. The definition helps to link theory with research. A valuable goal of exploratory research, and of most good research, is to clarify and refine concepts. Weak, contradictory, or unclear definitions of concepts restrict the advance of knowledge.

Concept Clusters. Concepts are rarely used in isolation. Rather, they form interconnected groups, or *concept clusters.* This is true for concepts in everyday language as well as for those in social theory. Theories contain collections of associated concepts that are consistent and mutually reinforcing. Together, they form a web of meaning. For example, if I want to discuss a concept such as *urban decay,* I will need a set of associated concepts (e.g., *urban expansion, economic growth, urbanization, suburbs, center city, revitalization, mass transit,* and *racial minorities*).

Some concepts take on a range of values, quantities, or amounts. Examples of this kind of concept are *amount of income, temperature, density of population, years of schooling,* and *degree of violence.* These are called *variables,* and you will read about them in a later chapter. Other concepts express types of nonvariable phenomena (e.g., *bureaucracy, family, revolution, homeless,* and *cold*). Theories use both kinds of concepts.

Classification Concepts. Some concepts are simple; they have one dimension and vary along a single continuum. Others are complex; they have multiple dimensions or many subparts. You can break complex concepts into a set of simple, or single-dimension, concepts. For example, Rueschemeyer and associates (1992:43–44) stated that democracy has three dimensions: (1) regular, free elections with universal suffrage; (2) an elected legislative body that controls government; and (3) freedom of expression and association. The authors recognized that each dimension varies by degree. They combined the dimensions to create a set of types of regimes. Regimes very low on all three dimensions are totalitarian, those high on all three are democracies, and ones with other mixes are either authoritarian or liberal oligarchies.

Classifications are partway between a single, simple concept and a theory.[4] They help to organize abstract, complex concepts. To create a new classification, a researcher logically specifies and combines the characteristics of simpler concepts. You can best grasp this idea by looking at some examples.

The *ideal type* is a well-known classification. Ideal types are pure, abstract models that define the essence of the phenomenon in question. They are mental pictures that define the central aspects of a concept. Ideal types are not explanations because they do not tell why or how something occurs. They are smaller than theories, and researchers use them to build a theory. They are broader, more abstract concepts that bring together several narrower, more concrete concepts. Qualitative researchers often use ideal types to see how well observable phenomena match up to the ideal model. For example, Max

Weber developed an ideal type of the concept *bureaucracy*. Many people use Weber's ideal type (see Box 2.1). It distinguishes a bureaucracy from other organizational forms (e.g., social movements, kingdoms, etc.). It also clarifies critical features of a kind of organization that people once found nebulous and hard to think about. No real-life organization perfectly matches the ideal type, but the model helps us think about and study bureaucracy.

Scope.   Concepts vary by scope. Some are highly abstract, some are at a middle level of abstraction, and some are at a concrete level (i.e., they are easy to directly experience with the senses such as sight or touch). More abstract concepts have wider scope; that is, they can be used for a much broader range of specific time points and situations. More concrete concepts are easy to recognize but apply to fewer situations. The concepts *skin pigmentation, casting a ballot in an election,* and *age based on the date on a birth certificate* are less abstract and more concrete than the concepts *racial group, democracy,* and *maturity.* Theories that use many abstract concepts can apply to a wider range of social phenomena than those with concrete concepts. An example of a theoretical relationship is: Increased size creates centralization, which in turn creates greater formalization. *Size, centralization,* and *formalization* are very abstract concepts. They can refer to features of a group, organization, or society. We can translate this to say that as an organization or group gets bigger, authority and power relations within it become centralized and concentrated in a small elite. The elite will tend to rely more on written policies, rules, or laws to control and organize others in the group or organization. When you think explicitly about the scope of concepts, you make a theory stronger and will be able to communicate it more clearly to others.

Assumptions

Concepts contain built-in *assumptions,* statements about the nature of things that are not observable or testable. We accept them as a necessary starting point. Concepts and theories build on assumptions about the nature of human beings, social reality, or a particular phenomenon. Assumptions often remain hidden or unstated. One way for a researcher to deepen his or her understanding of a concept is to identify the assumptions on which it is based.

For example, the concept *book* assumes a system of writing, people who can read, and the existence of paper. Without such assumptions, the idea of a *book* makes little sense. A social science concept, such as *racial prejudice,* rests on several assumptions. These include people who make distinctions among individuals based on their racial heritage, attach specific motivations

---

Box 2.1

Max Weber's Ideal Type of Bureaucracy

- It is a continuous organization governed by a system of rules.
- Conduct is governed by detached, impersonal rules.
- There is division of labor, in which different offices are assigned different spheres of competence.
- Hierarchical authority relations prevail; that is, lower offices are under control of higher ones.
- Administrative actions, rules, and so on are in writing and maintained in files.
- Individuals do not own and cannot buy or sell their offices.
- Officials receive salaries rather than receiving direct payment from clients in order to ensure loyalty to the organization.
- Property of the organization is separate from personal property of officeholders.

Source: Adapted from Chafetz (1978:72).

and characteristics to membership in a racial group, and make judgments about the goodness of specific motivations and characteristics. If race became irrelevant, people would cease to distinguish among individuals on the basis of race, to attach specific characteristics to a racial group, and to make judgments about characteristics. If that occurred, the concept of *racial prejudice* would cease to be useful for research. All concepts contain assumptions about social relations or how people behave.

Relationships

Theories contain concepts, their definitions, and assumptions. More significantly, theories specify how concepts relate to one another. Theories tell us whether concepts are related or not. If they are related, the theory states how they relate to each other. In addition, theories give reasons for why the relationship does or does not exist. It is a relationship, such as: Economic distress among the White population caused an increase in mob violence against African Americans. When a researcher empirically tests or evaluates such a relationship, it is called a *hypothesis*. After many careful tests of a hypothesis with data confirm the hypothesis, it is treated as a *proposition*. A proposition is a relationship in a theory in which the scientific community starts to gain greater confidence and feels it is likely to be truthful.

THE ASPECTS OF THEORY

Theory can be baffling because it comes in so many forms. To simplify, we can categorize a theory by (1) the direction of its reasoning, (2) the level of social reality that it explains, (3) the forms of explanation it employs, and (4) the overall framework of assumptions and concepts in which it is embedded. Fortunately, all logically possible combinations of direction, level, explanation, and framework are not equally viable. There are only about half a dozen serious contenders.

Direction of Theorizing

Researchers approach the building and testing of theory from two directions. Some begin with abstract thinking. They logically connect the ideas in theory to concrete evidence, then test the ideas against the evidence. Others begin with specific observations of empirical evidence. On the basis of the evidence, they generalize and build toward increasingly abstract ideas. In practice, most researchers are flexible and use both approaches at various points in a study (see Figure 2.1).

Deductive. In a *deductive approach,* you begin with an abstract, logical relationship among concepts, then move toward concrete empirical evidence. You may have ideas about how the world operates and want to test these ideas against "hard data."

Weitzer and Tuch (2004, 2005) used a deductive approach in a study of perceptions of police misconduct. They began with Group Position theory (a middle-range theory discussed later) within the conflict theory framework (see Range of Theory later in this chapter). Group position theory states that dominant and subordinate racial–ethnic groups are in competition for resources and status in a multiethnic society that has a racial hierarchy, and such competition affects racial beliefs and attitudes. Dominant groups believe they are entitled to privileges and a position of superiority, and they fear losing their privileges. Subordinate groups believe their position can be enhanced if they challenge the existing order. The authors deduced that group competition extends beyond attitudes to perceptions of social institutions, especially institutions of social control such as policing. They argued that subordinate group members (i.e., Blacks and Latino/Hispanics) would preceive police misconduct (measured as unjustified stops of citizens, verbal abuse by police, an excessive use of force, and police corruption) differently than members of the dominant group (Whites). The authors thought that perceptions operated via three mechanisms:

FIGURE 2.1 Deductive and Inductive Theorizing

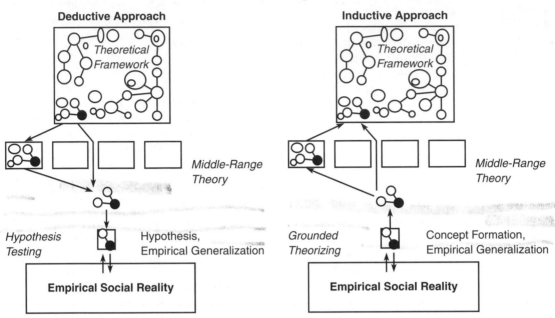

personal encounters with the police; reports of police encounters by friends, family, or neighbors; and noticing and interpreting news reports about police activity. In these three areas, they predicted that non-Whites would interpret negative events or reports as strong evidence of serious and systematic police misconduct. By contrast, Whites would tend to ignore or dismiss such events or reports or see them as isolated incidents. Data from a national survey of U.S. metropolitan areas (over 100,000 population) supported predictions of the theory.

Inductive. If you use an *inductive approach*, you begin with detailed observations of the world and move toward more abstract generalizations and ideas. When you begin, you may have only a topic and a few vague concepts. As you observe, you refine the concepts, develop empirical generalizations, and identify preliminary relationships. You build the theory from the ground up.

Duneier (1999) used an inductive approach in his study of life on the sidewalk. He noted that in much of social science, both quantitative secondary analysis research and qualitative field research, a researcher develops a theoretical understanding only after data have been collected. He stated, "I began to get ideas from the things I was seeing and hearing on the street" (p. 341). Many researchers who adopt an inductive approach use grounded theory. *Grounded theory* is part of an inductive approach in which a researcher builds ideas and theoretical generalizations based on closely examining and creatively thinking about the data (see Box 2.2). A researcher creates grounded theory out of a process of trying to explain, interpret, and render meaning from data. It arises from trying to account for, understand, or "make sense of" the evidence. Duneier (1999:342) has suggested that the process is similar to seeing many symptoms and later arriving at a diagnosis (i.e., a story that explains the source of the symptoms).

Box **2.2**	**What Is Grounded Theory?**

Grounded theory is a widely used approach in qualitative research. It is not the only approach and it is not used by all qualitative researchers. *Grounded theory* is "a qualitative research method that uses a systematic set of procedures to develop an inductively derived theory about a phenomenon" (Strauss and Corbin, 1990:24). The purpose of grounded theory is to build a theory that is faithful to the evidence. It is a method for discovering new theory. In it, the researcher compares unlike phenomena with a view toward learning similarities. He or she sees micro-level events as the foundation for a more macro-level explanation. Grounded theory shares several goals with more positivist-oriented theory. It seeks theory that is comparable with the evidence that is precise and rigorous, capable of replication, and generalizable. A grounded theory approach pursues generalizations by making comparisons across social situations.

Qualitative researchers use alternatives to grounded theory. Some qualitative researchers offer an in-depth depiction that is true to an informant's worldview. They excavate a single social situation to elucidate the micro processes that sustain stable social interaction. The goal of other researchers is to provide a very exacting depiction of events or a setting. They analyze specific events or settings in order to gain insight into the larger dynamics of a society. Still other researchers apply an existing theory to analyze specific settings that they have placed in a macro-level historical context. They show connections among micro-level events and between micro-level situations and larger social forces for the purpose of reconstructing the theory and informing social action.

Range of Theory

Social theories operate with varying ranges. One source of the confusion about theories involves the range at which a theory operates. At one end are highly specific theories with concrete concepts of limited scope. At the opposite end are whole systems with many theories that are extremely abstract. As part of the task of theory building, verifying, and testing, a researcher connects theoretical statements of different ranges together, like a series of different-sized boxes that fit into one another or a set of Russian dolls.

Empirical Generalization. An empirical generalization is the least abstract theoretical statement and has a very narrow range. It is a simple statement about a pattern or generalization among two or more concrete concepts that are very close to empirical reality. For example, "More men than women choose engineering as a college major." This summarizes a pattern between gender and choice of college major. It is

easy to test or observe. It is called a generalization because the pattern operates across many time periods and social contexts. The finding in the study on Internet pornography discussed in Chapter 1 that unhappily married men are more likely than happily married men to use Internet porn is an empirical generalization.

Middle-Range Theory. Middle-range theories are slightly more abstract than empirical generalizations or a specific hypothesis. A middle-range theory focuses on a specific substantive topic area (e.g., domestic violence, military coups, student volunteering), includes a multiple empirical generalization, and builds a theoretical explanation (see Forms of Explanation later in this chapter). As Merton (1967:39) stated, "Middle-range theory is principally used in sociology to guide empirical inquiry." A middle-range theory used in a study discussed in Chapter 1 said that girls who suffer physical or sexual abuse experience self-blame and guilt feelings that inhibits them from developing a healthy social network or forming stable romantic relationships, and that these factors lead to them staying single or experiencing greater marital instability when they become adults.

Theoretical Frameworks. A theoretical framework (also called a paradigm or theoretical system) is more abstract than a middle-range theory. Figure 2.1 shows the levels and how they are used in inductive and deductive approaches to theorizing. Few researchers make precise distinctions among the ranges of theorizing. They rarely use a theoretical framework directly in empirical research. A researcher may test parts of a theory on a topic and occasionally contrast parts of the theories from different frameworks. Box 2.3 illustrates the various degrees of abstrac-

---

Box 2.3

Kalmijn's Levels of Theory in "Shifting Boundaries" and Weitzer and Tuch's "Race and Perceptions of Police Misconduct"

Theoretical Framework

Kalmijn.   Structural functionalism holds that the processes of industrialization and urbanization change human society from a traditional to a modern form. In this process of modernization, social institutions and practices evolve. This evolution includes those that fill the social system's basic needs, socialize people to cultural values, and regulate social behavior. Institutions that filled needs and maintained the social system in a traditional society (such as religion) are superseded by modern ones (such as formal schooling).

Weitzer and Tuch.   Conflict theory holds that established social, political, and legal institutions protect the dominant or privileged groups of a society. Major institutions operate in ways that contain or suppress the activities of nondominant groups in society, especially if they challenge or threaten the established social–economic hierarchy. Thus, conflict between the dominant and subordinate social groups is reflected in how major institutions operate, especially institutions that are charged with maintaining order and engaged in formal social control, such as law enforcement.

Middle-Range Substantive Theory

Kalmijn.   A theory of intermarriage patterns notes that young adults in modern society spend less time in small, local settings, where family, religion, and community all have a strong influence. Instead, young adults spend increasing amounts of time in school settings. In these settings, especially in col-

lege, they have opportunities to meet other unmarried people. In modern society, education has become a major socialization agent. It affects future earnings, moral beliefs and values, and leisure interests. Thus, young adults select marriage partners less on the basis of shared religious or local ties and more on the basis of common educational levels.

Weitzer and Tuch.   Group-position theory uses group competition over material rewards, power, and status to explain intergroup attitudes and behaviors. Each group perceives and experiences real or imagined threats to its social position differently. Members of a dominant group tend to view police or government actions taken to defend its interests as being fair or favorable, whereas members of subodorinate groups tend to see the same actions negatively.

Empirical Generalization

Kalmijn.   Americans once married others with similar religious beliefs and affiliation. This practice is being replaced by marriage to others with similar levels of education.

Weitzer and Tuch.   Non-Whites experience more negative interpersonal encounters with police and tend to interpret media reports about police misconduct as evidence of serious and systematic problems with the police. By contrast, Whites have different police encounters or interpret their encounters and media reports about police actions more favorably.

tion with Kalmijn's study of changing marriage partner selection (see also page 40).

Sociology and other social sciences have several major theoretical frameworks.[5] The frameworks are orientations or sweeping ways of looking at the social world. They provide collections of assumptions, concepts, and forms of explanation. Frameworks include theories for many substantive areas (e.g., theories of crime, theories of the family, etc.). Thus, there can be a structural functional theory, an exchange theory, and a conflict theory of the family. Theories within the same framework share assumptions and major concepts. Some frameworks are oriented more to the micro level; others focus more on macro-level phenomena (see Levels of Theory next). Box 2.4 shows four major frameworks

in sociology and briefly describes the key concepts and assumptions of each.

Levels of Theory

Social theories can be divided into three broad groupings by the level of social reality with which they deal. Most of us devote the majority of our time to thinking about the micro level of reality, the individuals we see and interact with on a day-by-day basis. Micro-level theory deals with small slices of time, space, or numbers of people. The concepts are usually not very abstract.

Brase and Richmond (2004) used a micro-level theory about doctor–patient interactions and perceptions. The theory stated that physican attire affects doctor–patient interactions. It sug-

---

 Box 2.4 **Major Theoretical Frameworks in Sociology**

Structural Functionalism

Major Concepts.   System, equilibrium, dysfunction, division of labor

Key Assumptions.   Society is a system of interdependent parts that is in equilibrium or balance. Over time, society has evolved from a simple to a complex type, which has highly specialized parts. The parts of society fulfill different needs or functions of the social system. A basic consensus on values or a value system holds society together.

Exchange Theory (also Rational Choice)

Major Concepts.   Opportunities, rewards, approval, balance, credit

Key Assumptions.   Human interactions are similar to economic transactions. People give and receive resources (symbolic, social approval, or material) and try to maximize their rewards while avoiding pain, expense, and embarrassment. Exchange relations tend to be balanced. If they are unbalanced, persons with credit can dominate others.

Symbolic Interactionism

Major Concepts.   Self, reference group, role-playing, perception

Key Assumptions.   People transmit and receive symbolic communication when they socially interact. People create perceptions of each other and social settings. People largely act on their perceptions. How people think about themselves and others is based on their interactions.

Conflict Theory

Major Concepts.   Power, exploitation, struggle, inequality, alienation

Key Assumptions.   Society is made up of groups that have opposing interests. Coercion and attempts to gain power are ever-present aspects of human relations. Those in power attempt to hold on to their power by spreading myths or by using violence if necessary.

gested that a patient makes judgments about a physician's abilities based on attire and that a patient's trust-openness toward a physican is also affected. It said that perceptions of physician authority increased with traditional professional formal attire over informal attire, but that trust-openness was influenced in the opposite direction as authority. Thirty-eight male and 40 female research participants rated their perceptions of same- and opposite-gender models who were identified as being medical doctors, but who were wearing different attire. Findings showed that a white coat and formal attire are clearly superior to casual attire in establishing physician authority, but it did not reduce trust-openness as expected.

Meso-level theory links macro and micro levels and operates at an intermediate level. Theories of organizations, social movements, and communities are often at this level.

Roscigno and Danaher (2001) used meso-level theory in a study on the 1930s labor movement among southern textile workers. The researchers used a theory of movement subculture and political opportunity to explain growing labor movement strength and increased strike activity among workers in one industry in a region of the United States across several years. They expected strike activity to grow as the result of a strong movement subculture that carried a message of injustice and a "political opportunity" or the expectation among people that collective action at a particular time would produce positive results. Their study showed that a technological innovation (i.e., the spread of new radio stations with songs and discussions of working conditions and unfair treatment) contributed to the growth of a subculture of movement solidarity among the textile workers and fostered self-identity as a worker who had common interests with the other textile workers. The technological innovation and events in the political environment (i.e., union organizers and speeches by the President of the United States) also created a political opportunity for the workers. The workers believed that collection action (i.e., strike) was necessary to achieve justice and

would produce gains because other workers and government authorities would support their actions.

Macro-level theory concerns the operation of larger aggregates such as social institutions, entire cultural systems, and whole societies. It uses more concepts that are abstract.

Marx's study (1998) on race in the United States, South Africa, and Brazil used a macro-level theory. He wanted to explain the conditions that led Black people to engage in protest to gain full citizenship rights and he examined patterns of national racial politics in three counties across two centuries. His theory said that protest resulted in an interaction between (1) race-based political mobilization and (2) national government policies of racial domination (i.e., apartheid in South Africa, Jim Crow laws in southern United States, and no legalized race-based domination in Brazil). Policies of racial domination developed from practices of slavery, exploitation, and discrimination that justified White superiority. The policies reinforced specific racial ideologies that shaped national development during the twentieth century. A critical causal factor was how national political elites used the legalized domination of Blacks to reduce divisions among Whites. In nations that had large regional or class divisions among Whites, national elites tried to increase White backing for the national government by creating legalized forms of racial domination. Over time, such legalized domination froze racial divisions, which promoted a sense of racial identity and consciousness among Blacks. The strong sense of racial identity became a key resource when Blacks mobilized politically to demand full citizenship rights. Legalized racial domination also intensified the Blacks' protest and directed it against the national government as the societal institution that reinforced their experience of racial inequality.

Forms of Explanation

Prediction and Explanation. A theory's primary purpose is to explain. Many people confuse prediction with explanation. There are two meanings or uses of the term *explanation.* Researchers focus on *theoretical explanation,* a logical argument that tells why something occurs. It refers to a general rule or principle. These are a researcher's theoretical argument or connections among concepts. The second type of explanation, *ordinary explanation,* makes something clear or describes something in a way that illustrates it and makes it intelligible. For example, a good teacher "explains" in the ordinary sense. The two types of explanation can blend together. This occurs when a researcher explains (i.e., makes intelligible) his or her explanation (i.e., a logical argument involving theory).

Prediction is a statement that something will occur. It is easier to predict than to explain, and an explanation has more logical power than prediction because good explanations also predict. An explanation rarely predicts more than one outcome, but the same outcome may be predicted by opposing explanations. Although it is less powerful than explanation, many people are entranced by the dramatic visibility of a prediction.

A gambling example illustrates the difference between explanation and prediction. If I enter a casino and consistently and accurately predict the next card to appear or the next number on a roulette wheel, it will be sensational. I may win a lot of money, at least until the casino officials realize I am always winning and expel me. Yet, my method of making the predictions is more interesting than the fact that I can do so. Telling you what I do to predict the next card is more fascinating than being able to predict.

Here is another example. You know that the sun "rises" each morning. You can predict that at some time, every morning, whether or not clouds obscure it, the sun will rise. But why is this so? One explanation is that the Great Turtle carries the sun across the sky on its back. Another explanation is that a god sets his arrow ablaze, which appears to us as the sun, and shoots it across the sky. Few people today believe these ancient explanations. The explanation you

probably accept involves a theory about the rotation of the earth and the position of the sun, the star of our solar system. In this explanation, the sun only appears to rise. The sun does not move; its apparent movement depends on the earth's rotation. We are on a planet that both spins on its axis and orbits around a star millions of miles away in space. All three explanations make the same prediction: The sun rises each morning. As you can see, a weak explanation can produce an accurate prediction. A good explanation depends on a well-developed theory and is confirmed in research by empirical observations.

Causal Explanation. *Causal explanation,* the most common type of explanation, is used when the relationship is one of cause and effect. We use it all the time in everyday language, which tends to be sloppy and ambiguous. What do we mean when we say *cause?* For example, you may say that poverty causes crime or that looseness in morals causes an increase in divorce. This does not tell how or why the causal process works. Researchers try to be more precise and exact when discussing causal relations.

Philosophers have long debated the idea of cause. Some people argue that causality occurs in the empirical world, but it cannot be proved. Causality is "out there" in objective reality, and researchers can only try to find evidence for it. Others argue that causality is only an idea that exists in the human mind, a mental construction, not something "real" in the world. This second position holds that causality is only a convenient way of thinking about the world. Without entering into the lengthy philosophical debate, many researchers pursue causal relationships.

You need three things to establish causality: temporal order, association, and the elimination of plausible alternatives. An implicit fourth condition is an assumption that a causal relationship makes sense or fits with broader assumptions or a theoretical framework. Let us examine the three basic conditions.

The *temporal order* condition means that a cause must come before an effect. This commonsense assumption establishes the direction of causality: from the cause toward the effect. You may ask, How can the cause come after what it is to affect? It cannot, but temporal order is only one of the conditions needed for causality. Temporal order is necessary but not sufficient to infer causality. Sometimes people make the mistake of talking about "cause" on the basis of temporal order alone. For example, a professional baseball player pitches no-hit games when he kisses his wife just before a game. The kissing occurred before the no-hit games. Does that mean the kissing is the cause of the pitching performance? It is very unlikely. As another example, race riots occurred in four separate cities in 1968, one day after an intense wave of sunspots. The temporal ordering does not establish a causal link between sunspots and race riots. After all, all prior human history occurred before some specific event. The temporal order condition simply eliminates from consideration potential causes that occurred later in time.

It is not always easy to establish temporal order. With cross-sectional research, temporal order is tricky. For example, a researcher finds that people who have a lot of education are also less prejudiced than others. Does more education cause a reduction in prejudice? Or do highly prejudiced people avoid education or lack the motivation, self-discipline, and intelligence needed to succeed in school? Here is another example. The students who get high grades in my class say I am an excellent teacher. Does getting high grades make them happy, so they return the favor by saying that I am an excellent teacher (i.e., high grades cause a positive evaluation)? Or am I doing a great job, so students study hard and learn a lot, which the grades reflect (i.e., their learning causes them to get high grades)? It is a chicken-or-egg problem. To resolve it, a researcher needs to bring in other information or design research to test for the temporal order.

Simple causal relations are unidirectional, operating in a single direction from the cause to the effect. Most studies examine unidirectional relations. More complex theories specify reciprocal-effect causal relations—that is, a mutual causal relationship or simultaneous causality. For example, studying a lot causes a student to get good grades, but getting good grades also motivates the student to continue to study. Theories often have reciprocal or feedback relationships, but these are difficult to test. Some researchers call unidirectional relations nonrecursive and reciprocal-effect relations recursive.

A researcher also needs an *association* for causality. Two phenomena are associated if they occur together in a patterned way or appear to act together. People sometimes confuse correlation with association. *Correlation* has a specific technical meaning, whereas *association* is a more general idea. A correlation coefficient is a statistical measure that indicates the amount of association, but there are many ways to measure association. Figure 2.2 shows 38 people from a lower-income neighborhood and 35 people from an upper-income neighborhood. Can you see an association between race and income level?

More people mistake association for causality than confuse it with temporal order. For example, when I was in college, I got high grades on the exams I took on Fridays but low grades on those I took on Mondays. There was an association between the day of the week and the exam grade, but it did not mean that the day of the week caused the exam grade. Instead, the reason was that I worked 20 hours each weekend and was very tired on Mondays. As another example, the number of children born in India increased until the late 1960s, then slowed in the 1970s. The number of U.S.-made cars driven in the United States increased until the late 1960s, then slowed in the 1970s. The number of Indian children born and the number of U.S. cars driven are associated: They vary together or increase and decrease at the same time. Yet there is no causal connection. By coincidence, the Indian government instituted a birth control program that slowed the number of births at the same time that Americans were buying more imported cars.

FIGURE 2.2   Association of Income and Race

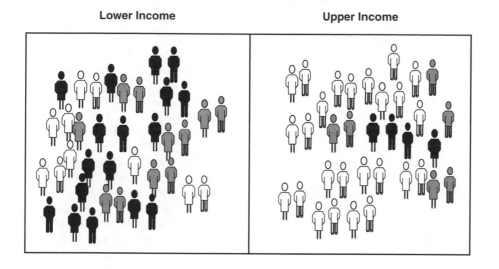

If a researcher cannot find an association, a causal relationship is unlikely. This is why researchers attempt to find correlations and other measures of association. Yet, a researcher can often find an association without causality. The association eliminates potential causes that are not associated, but it cannot definitely identify a cause. It is a necessary but not a sufficient condition. In other words, you need it for causality, but it is not enough alone.

An association does not have to be perfect (i.e., every time one variable is present, the other also is) to show causality. In the example involving exam grades and days of the week, there is an association if on 10 Fridays I got 7 As, 2 Bs, and 1 C, whereas my exam grades on 10 Mondays were 6 Ds, 2 Cs, and 2 Bs. An association exists, but the days of the week and the exam grades are not perfectly associated. The race and income-level association shown in Figure 2.2 is also an imperfect association.

Eliminating alternatives means that a researcher interested in causality needs to show that the effect is due to the causal variable and not to something else. It is also called *no spuriousness* because an apparent causal relationship that is actually due to an alternative but unrec-

ognized cause is called a spurious relationship, which is discussed in Chapter 4 (see Box 2.5).

Researchers can observe temporal order and associations. They cannot observe the elimination of alternatives. They can only demonstrate it indirectly. Eliminating alternatives is an ideal because eliminating all possible alternatives is impossible. A researcher tries to eliminate major alternative explanations in two ways: through built-in design controls and by measuring potential hidden causes. Experimental researchers build controls into the study design itself to eliminate alternative causes. They isolate an experimental situation from the influence of all variables except the main causal variable.

Researchers also try to eliminate alternatives by measuring possible alternative causes. This is common in survey research and is called *controlling for* another variable. Researchers use statistical techniques to learn whether the causal variable or something else operates on the effect variable.

Causal explanations are usually in a linear form or state cause and effect in a straight line: *A* causes *B*, *B* causes *C*, *C* causes *D*.

The study by Brasc and Richmond (2004) on doctor–patient interactions discussed earlier

Box
2.5   **Learning to See Causal Relations**

As I was driving home from the university one day, I heard a radio news report about gender and racial bias in standardized tests. A person who claimed that bias was a major problem said that the tests should be changed. Since I work in the field of education and disdain racial or gender bias, the report caught my attention. Yet, as a social scientist, I critically evaluated the news story. The evidence for a bias charge was the consistent pattern of higher scores in mathematics for male high school seniors versus female high school seniors, and for European-background students versus African American students. Was the cause of the pattern of different test scores a bias built into the tests?

When questioned by someone who had designed the tests, the person charging bias lacked a crucial piece of evidence to support a claim of test bias: the educational experience of students. It turns out that girls and boys take different numbers and types of mathematics courses in high school. Girls tend to take fewer math courses. Among the girls who complete the same mathematics curriculum as boys, the gender difference dissolves. Likewise, a large percentage of African Americans attend racially segregated, poor-quality schools in inner cities or in impoverished rural areas. For African Americans who attend high-quality suburban schools and complete the same courses, racial differences in test scores disappear. This evidence suggests that inequality in education causes test score differences. Although the tests may have problems, identifying the real cause implies that changing the tests without first improving or equalizing education could be a mistake.

used a causal explanation; it said physican attire causes certain types of patient perceptions. The study by Weitzer and Tuch (2004, 2005) on police misconduct cited earlier used a causal explanation. The cause was a person's group position and competitive pressure with other groups. These are causally linked to police encounters, either directly or indirectly, and interpretions of news reports, which differ by group position. The police encounters and the interpretations of news reports cause very different perceptions of police misconduct. We can restate the logic in a deductive causal form: If the proposition is true, then we observe certain things in the empirical evidence. Good causal explanations identify a causal relationship and specify a causal mechanism. A simple causal explanation is: X causes Y or Y occurs because of X, where X and Y are concepts (e.g., early marriage and divorce). Some researchers state causality in a predictive form: If X occurs, then Y follows. Causality can be stated in many ways:

X leads to Y, X produces Y, X influences Y, X is related to Y, the greater X the higher Y.

Here is a simple causal theory: A rise in unemployment causes an increase in child abuse. The subject to be explained is an increase in the occurrence of child abuse. What explains it is a rise in unemployment. We "explain" the increase in child abuse by identifying its cause. A complete explanation also requires elaborating the causal mechanism. My theory says that when people lose their jobs, they feel a loss of self-worth. Once they lose self-worth, they become easily frustrated, upset, and angry. Frustrated people often express their anger by directing violence toward those with whom they have close personal contact (e.g., friends, spouse, children, etc.). This is especially true if they do not understand the source of the anger or cannot direct it toward its true cause (e.g., an employer, government policy, or "economic forces").

The unemployment and child abuse example illustrates a chain of causes and a causal mechanism. Researchers can test different parts of the chain. They might test whether unemployment rates and child abuse occur together, or whether frustrated people become violent toward the people close to them. A typical research strategy is to divide a larger theory into parts and test various relationships against the data.

Relationships between variables can be positive or negative. Researchers imply a positive relationship if they say nothing. A *positive relationship* means that a higher value on the causal variable goes with a higher value on the effect variable. For example, the more education a person has, the longer his or her life expectancy is. A *negative relationship* means that a higher value on the causal variable goes with a lower value on the effect variable. For example, the more frequently a couple attends religious services, the lower the chances of their divorcing each other. In diagrams, a plus sign (+) signifies a positive relationship and a negative sign (−) signifies a negative relationship.

Structural Explanation.   A *structural explanation* is used with three types of theories: network, sequential, and functional theories. Unlike a causal effect chain, which is similar to a string of balls lined up that hit one another causing each to bounce in turn, it is more similar to a wheel with spokes from a central idea or a spider web in which each strand forms part of the whole. A researcher making a structural explanation uses a set of interconnected assumptions, concepts, and relationships. Instead of causal statements, he or she uses metaphors or analogies so that relationships "make sense." The concepts and relations within a theory form a mutually reinforcing system. In structural explanations, a researcher specifies a sequence of phases or identifies essential parts that form an interlocked whole.

Structural explanations are used in network theory. Sanders, Nee, and Sernau (2002) explained Asian immigrant job seeking with network theory. They used interview data on immigrants from the Philippines, Korea, Taiwan, and China in Los Angeles and found that social networks matched and sorted immigrants with jobs. New immigrants with limited language and job skills sought employment either with a co-ethnic employer or through informal social ties (i.e., they consulted experienced friends, relatives, and acquaintances and asked them to be intermediaries). Network users expanded job opportunities beyond employers in their own ethnic group. Thus, ethnic network ties were "bridge ties" (i.e., they helped immigrants get jobs beyond their ethnic community by using co-ethnics who already made the transition to mainstream employment). Over time, as language and job skills improved, these immigrants moved on to mainstream jobs. Immigrants lacking social ties, in limited networks, or who worked for co-ethnics found it difficult to get a mainstream job. Thus, a person's network location, access to a large and diverse network, and use of network ties is what facilitated obtaining a mainstream job.

Structural explanations are also used in sequence theory. The panel study on volunteerism by Oesterle, Johnson, and Mortimer (2004) discussed in Chapter 1 employs sequence theory. The authors used a "life course" perspective in which the impact of an event happening at one phase of a person's life differs what it would have been if the same happened at other phases, and early events generally shape events in later phases. The authors noted that the transition to adulthood is a critical stage when a person learns new social roles and adult expectations. They found that the amounts and types of volunteer activity in the last stage they observed (age 26–27) was strongly influenced by such activities at prior stages of a person's life (age 18–19). People who volunteered at an early stage tended to volunteer at later stages. Those who did not volunteer at an early stage or who devoted full time to working or parenting at other prior stages (18–19 years old) were less likely to volunteer at a later stage (26–27 years old). Thus, later events flowed from an interconnected process in which earlier stages set a course or direction that pointed to specific events in a later stage.

Additionally, structural explanations are used in *functional theory*.[6] Functional theorists explain an event by locating it within a larger, ongoing, balanced social system. They often use biological metaphors. These researchers explain something by identifying its function within a larger system or the need it fulfills for the system. Functional explanations are in this form: "*L* occurs because it serves needs in the system *M*." Theorists assume that a system will operate to stay in equilibrium and to continue over time. A functional theory of social change says that, over time, a social system, or society, moves through developmental stages, becoming increasingly differentiated and more complex. It evolves a specialized division of labor and develops greater individualism. These developments create greater efficiency for the system as a whole. Specialization and individualism create temporary disruptions. The traditional ways of doing things weaken, but new social relations emerge. The system generates new ways to fulfill functions or satisfy its needs.

Kalmijn (1991) used a functional explanation to explain a shift in how people in the United States select marriage partners. He relied on secularization theory, which holds that ongoing historical processes of industrialization and urbanization shape the development of society. During these modernization processes, people rely less on traditional ways of doing things. Religious beliefs and local community ties weaken, as does the family's control over young adults. People no longer live their entire lives in small, homogeneous communities. Young adults become more independent from their parents and from the religious organizations that formerly played a critical role in selecting marriage partners.

Society has a basic need to organize the way people select marriage partners and find partners with whom they share fundamental values.

In modern society, people spend time away from small local settings in school settings. In these school settings, especially in college, they meet other unmarried people. Education is a major socialization agent in modern society. Increasingly, it affects a person's future earnings, moral beliefs and values, and ways of spending leisure time. This explains why there has been a trend in the United States for people to marry less within the same religion and increasingly to marry persons with a similar level of education. In traditional societies, the family and religious organization served the function of socializing people to moral values and linking them to potential marriage partners who held similar values. In modern society, educational institutions largely fulfill this function for the social system.

Interpretive Explanation.   The purpose of an *interpretive explanation* is to foster understanding. The interpretive theorist attempts to discover the meaning of an event or practice by placing it within a specific social context. He or she tries to comprehend or mentally grasp the operation of the social world, as well as get a feel for something or to see the world as another person does. Because each person's subjective worldview shapes how he or she acts, the researcher attempts to discern others' reasoning and view of things. The process is similar to decoding a text or work of literature. Meaning comes from the context of a cultural symbol system.

Duneier's (1999) study of sidewalk life in New York City discussed earlier in this chapter used an interpretive explanation. An interpretive explanation is also illustrated by Edelman, Fuller, and Mara-Drita's (2001) study of how companies adopted policies related to diversity issues in the early 1990s—that is, affirmative action and equal opportunity. The authors examined what managers said, or their rhetoric, about diversity concerns. Rhetoric included various statements about diversity made by professional managers, business school professors, and consultants in professional workshops, meetings, specialized magazines, and electronic forums.

Edelman and colleagues (2001) found that managers took legal ideas, terms, and concepts and converted them into ones that fit into their organizational setting. Professional managers converted vague legal mandates and terms that were based on ideas about racial discrimination and ending injustice. They interjected their own views, values, training, and interests and produced slightly different ideas and procedures. Management rhetoric changed legal ideas from taking specific actions to end racial–ethnic or gender discrimination and changed them into a "new idea" for effective corporate management. The "new idea" was that corporations benefit from a culturally diverse workforce. Simply put, diversity is good for company profits. They consolidated various studies and discussions on how to improve corporate operations around the new idea—a socially heterogeneous workforce is more creative, productive, and profitable.

The authors created a theory of "managerialization of law" from their data. This theory states that professional managers operate in a corporate environment. They will not simply take ideas and mandates created in a government-legal environment and impose them directly onto a corporation's internal operations. In fact, on the issue of affirmative action, many corporate officials saw the legal ideas and requirements as hostile or alien. So the managers converted, or translated, the legal ideas into an acceptable form—one acceptable from a managerial point of view. They used new forms to move their corporations in a direction that would comply with the legal requirements. This is an interpretive explanation because the authors explained a social event (i.e., corporations embracing programs and rhetoric to favor cultural diversity) by examining how the managers subjectively constructed new ways of looking at, thinking about, and talking about the diversity issue (i.e., they constructed a new interpretation).

THE THREE MAJOR APPROACHES TO SOCIAL SCIENCE

We began this chapter by looking at small-scale parts of a theory (i.e., ideas or concepts). We moved toward larger aspects of social theory, and arrived at major theoretical frameworks in the last section. Now, we move to an even a broader, more abstract level of the linkage between theory and research—fundamental approaches to social science. It involves issues sometimes called *meta-methodological* (i.e., beyond or supersized methodological concerns) and blurs into areas of philosophy that studies what science means. We only briefly touch on the issues here, but we cannot ignore them because they affect how people do social research studies.

About 45 years ago, a now famous philosopher of science, Thomas Kuhn, argued that the way science develops in a specific field across time is based on researchers sharing a general approach, or paradigm. A *paradigm* is an integrated set of assumptions, beliefs, models of doing good research, and techniques for gathering and analyzing data. It organizes core ideas, theoretical frameworks, and research methods. Kuhn observed that scientific fields tend to be held together around a paradigm for a long period of time. Very few researchers question the paradigm, and most focus on operating within its general boundaries to accumulate new knowledge. On rare occasions in history, intellectual difficulties increase, unexpected issues grow, and troubling concerns over proper methods multiply. Slowly, the members of a scientific field shift in how they see things and switch to a new paradigm. Once the new paradigm becomes fully established and widely adopted, the process of accumulating knowledge begins anew.

Kuhn's explanation covered how most sciences operate most of the time, but some fields operate with multiple or competing paradigms. This is the case in several of the social sciences. This greatly bothers some social scientists, and they believe having multiple paradigms hinders the growth of knowledge. They see multiple paradigms as a sign of the immaturity or underdevelopment of the "science" in the social sciences. Some believe all social science researchers should embrace a single paradigm and stop using alternatives to it.

Other social scientists accept the coexistence of multiple paradigms. They recognize that this can be confusing and often makes communicating difficult among those who use a different approach. Despite this, they argue that each social science paradigm provides important kinds of knowledge and insights, so to drop one would limit what we can learn about the social world. These social scientists note that no one definitely can say which approach is "best" or even whether it is necessary or highly desirable to have only one paradigm. So instead of closing off an approach that offers innovative ways to study social life and gain insight into human behavior, they argue for keeping a diversity of approaches.

In this section, we will look at three fundamental paradigms or approaches used in social science. Each approach has been around for over 150 years and is used by many highly respected professional researchers. These approaches are unequal in terms of the number of followers, quantity of new studies, and types of issues addressed. Often, people who strongly adhere to one approach disagree with researchers who use another, or see the other approaches as being less valuable or less "scientific" than their approach. Although adherents to each approach may use various research techniques, theories, and theoretical frameworks, researchers who adopt one approach tend to favor certain research techniques, theories, or theoretical frameworks over others. The three approaches are positivism, interpretive, and critical; each has internal divisions, offshoots, and extensions, but these are the core ideas of the three major approaches.

Positivist Approach

Positivism is the most widely practiced social science approach, especially in North America.

Positivism sees social science research as fundamentally the same as natural science research; it assumes that social reality is made up of objective facts that value-free researchers can precisely measure and use statistics to test causal theories. Large-scale bureaucratic agencies, companies, and many people in the general public favor a positivist approach because it emphasizes getting objective measures of "hard facts" in the form of numbers.

Positivists put a great value on the principle of replication, even if only a few studies are replicated. *Replication* occurs when researchers or others repeat the basics of a study and get identical or very similar findings. Positivists emphasize replication and the ultimate test of knowledge. This is because they believe that different observers looking at the same facts will get the same results if they carefully specify their ideas, precisely measure the facts, and follow the standards of objective research. When many studies by independent researchers yield similar findings, confidence grows that we accurately captured the workings of social reality and therefore scientific knowledge increases.

If a researcher repeats a study and does not get similar findings, one or more of five possibilities may be occurring: (1) the initial study was an unusual fluke or based on a misguided understanding of the social world; (2) important conditions were present in the initial study, but no one was aware of their significance so they were not specified; (3) the initial study, or the repeat of it, was sloppy—it did not include very careful, precise measures; (4) the initial study, or the repeat of it, was improperly conducted—researchers failed to closely follow the highest standards for procedures and techniques, or failed to be completely objective; or (5) the repeated study was an unusual fluke.

The positivist approach is *nomothetic;* it means explanations use law or law-like principles. Positivists may use inductive and deductive inquiry, but the ideal is to develop a general causal law or principle then use logical deduction to specify how it operates in concrete situations. Next, the researcher empirically tests outcomes predicted by the principle in concrete settings using very precise measures. In this way, a general law or principle covers many specific situations. For example, a general principle says that when two social groups are unequal and compete for scarce resources, in-group feelings and hostility toward the other groups intensify, and the competing groups are likely to engage in conflict. The principle applies to sports teams, countries, ethnic groups, families, and other social groupings. A researcher might deduce that in cities with high levels of interracial inequality, when jobs become more scarce and thereby increase economic competition, each group will express greater hostility about the other racial groups, and intergroup conflict (e.g., riots, demonstrations, violent attacks) will increase.

The vast majority of positivist studies are quantitative, and positivists generally see the experiment as the ideal way to do research. Positivist researchers also use other quantitative research techniques, such as surveys or existing statistics, but tend to see them as approximations of the experiment for situations where an experiment is impossible. Positivist researchers advocate value-free science, seek precise quantitative measures, test causal theories with statistics, and believe in the importance of replicating studies.

Interpretive Approach

The interpretive approach is also scientific, but its sees the idea of "scientific" differently from positivism. Unlike the positivist approach, interpretive researchers say that human social life is qualitatively different from other things studied by science. This means that social scientists cannot just borrow the principles of science from the natural sciences. Instead, they believe it is necessary to create a special type of science, one based on the uniqueness of humans and one that can really capture human social life.

Most researchers who use an interpretive approach adopt a version of the constructionist

view of social reality. This view holds that human social life is based less on objective, hard, factual reality than on the ideas, beliefs, and perceptions that people hold about reality. In other words, people socially interact and respond based as much, if not more, on what they believe to be real than what is objectively real. This means that social scientists will be able to understand social life only if they study how people go about constructing social reality. As people grow up, interact, and live their daily lives, they continuously create ideas, relationships, symbols, and roles that they consider to be meaningful or important. These include things such as intimate emotional attachments, religious or moral ideals, beliefs in patriotic values, racial–ethnic or gender differences, and artistic expressions. Rarely do people relate to the objective facts of reality directly; instead, they do so through the filter of these socially constructed beliefs and perceptions. What positivists and many people view to be objective facts (e.g., a person's height), interpretive researchers say are only at the trivial surface level of social life. Or, the "facts" are images/categories that humans created (i.e., I am two meters tall) and we "forget" that people originated the images/categories but now treat them as being separate from people and objectively real.

Interpretive researchers are skeptical of the positivist attempts to produce precise quantitative measures of objective facts. This is because they view social reality as very fluid. For most humans, social reality is largely the shifting perceptions that they are constantly constructing, testing, reinforcing, or changing and that have become embedded in social traditions or institutions. For this reason, interpretive researchers tend to trust and favor qualitative data. They believe that qualitative data can more accurately capture the fluid processes of social reality. In addition, they favor interpretive over causal forms of theory (see discussion earlier in this chapter).

Interpretive researchers are not likely to adopt a nomothetic approach, but instead favor an idiographic form of explanation and use inductive reasoning. *Idiographic* literally means specific description and refers to explaining an aspect of the social world by offering a highly detailed picture or description of a specific social setting, process, or type of relationship. For example, qualitative researchers do not see replication as the ultimate test of knowledge. Instead, they emphasize *verstehen* or empathetic understanding. *Verstehen* is the desire of a researcher to get inside the worldview of those he or she is studying and accurately represent how the people being studied see the world, feel about it, and act. In other words, the best test of good social knowledge is not replication but whether the researcher can demonstrate that he or she really captured the inner world and personal perspective of the people studied.

Critical Approach

The critical approach shares many features with an interpretive approach, but it blends an objective/materialist with a constructionist view of social reality. The key feature of the critical approach is a desire to put knowledge into action and a belief that research is not value free. Research is the creation of knowledge, and people regularly use knowledge to advance political-moral ends. This gives doing social research a strong connection to political-moral issues. The researcher can decide to ignore and help those with power and authority in society, or advance social justice and empower the powerless.

Critical approach emphasizes the multilayered nature of social reality. On the surface level, there is often illusion, myth, and distorted thinking. The critical approach notes that people are often misled, are subject to manipulated messages, or hold false ideas. Yet, beneath the surface level at a deeper, often hidden level lies "real" objective reality. Part of the task of social research is to strip away the surface layer of illusion or falsehood. Although a researcher wants to see beyond this layer, he or she does not entirely ignore it. Such an outer layer is important

because it profoundly shapes much of human action.

The critical approach has an activist orientation and favors action research. *Praxis* is the ultimate test of how good an explanation is in the critical approach. It is a blending of theory and concrete action; theory informs one about the specific real-world actions one should take to advance social change, and one uses the experiences of engaging in action for social change to reformulate the theory. All the approaches see a mutual relationship between abstract theory and concrete empirical evidence, but the critical approach goes further and tries to dissolve the gap between abstract theory and the empirical experiences of using the theory to make changes in the world.

THE DYNAMIC DUO

You have seen that theory and research are interrelated. Only the naive, new researcher mistakenly believes that theory is irrelevant to research or that a researcher just collects the data. Researchers who attempt to proceed without theory may waste time collecting useless data. They easily fall into the trap of hazy and vague thinking, faulty logic, and imprecise concepts. They find it difficult to converge onto a crisp research issue or to generate a lucid account of their study's purpose. They also find themselves adrift as they attempt to design or conduct empirical research.

The reason is simple. Theory frames how we look at and think about a topic. It gives us concepts, provides basic assumptions, directs us to the important questions, and suggests ways for us to make sense of data. Theory enables us to connect a single study to the immense base of knowledge to which other researchers contribute. To use an analogy, theory helps a researcher see the forest instead of just a single tree. Theory increases a researcher's awareness of interconnections and of the broader significance of data (see Table 2.1).

TABLE 2.1   Major Aspects and Types of Social Theory

Aspect	Types of Social Theory
Direction	Inductive or deductive
Level	Micro, meso, or macro
Explanation	Causal, interpretive, or structural
Abstraction	Empirical generalization, middle range, framework, or paradigm

Theory has a place in virtually all research, but its prominence varies. It is generally less central in applied-descriptive research than in basic-explanatory research. Its role in applied and descriptive research may be indirect. The concepts are often more concrete, and the goal is not to create general knowledge. Nevertheless, researchers use theory in descriptive research to refine concepts, evaluate assumptions of a theory, and indirectly test hypotheses.

Theory does not remain fixed over time; it is provisional and open to revision. Theories grow into more accurate and comprehensive explanations about the make-up and operation of the social world in two ways. They advance as theorists toil to think clearly and logically, but this effort has limits. The way a theory makes significant progress is by interacting with research findings.

The scientific community expands and alters theories based on empirical results. Researchers who adopt a more deductive approach use theory to guide the design of a study and the interpretation of results. They refute, extend, or modify the theory on the basis of results. As researchers continue to conduct empirical research in testing a theory, they develop confidence that some parts of it are true. Researchers may modify some propositions of a theory or reject them if several well-conducted studies have negative findings. A theory's core propositions and central tenets are more difficult to test and are refuted less often. In a slow process, researchers may decide to abandon or change a theory as the evidence against it mounts over time and cannot be logically reconciled.

Researchers adopting an inductive approach follow a slightly different process. Inductive theorizing begins with a few assumptions and broad orienting concepts. Theory develops from the ground up as the researchers gather and analyze the data. Theory emerges slowly, concept by concept and proposition by proposition in a specific area. The process is similar to a long pregnancy. Over time, the concepts and empirical generalizations emerge and mature. Soon, relationships become visible, and researchers weave together knowledge from different studies into more abstract theory.

CONCLUSION

In this chapter, you learned about social theory—its parts, purposes, and types. The dichotomy between theory and research is an artificial one. The value of theory and its necessity for conducting good research should be clear. Researchers who proceed without theory rarely conduct top-quality research and frequently find themselves in a quandary. Likewise, theorists who proceed without linking theory to research or anchoring it to empirical reality are in jeopardy of floating off into incomprehensible speculation and conjecture. You are now familiar with the scientific community, the dimensions of research, and social theory.

Key Terms

association
assumption
blame analysis
causal explanation
classification concept
concept cluster

deductive approach
empirical generalization
functional theory
grounded theory
ideal type
idiographic
inductive approach
macro-level theory
meso-level theory
micro-level theory
negative relationship
nomothetic
paradigm
positive relationship
praxis
prediction
proposition
replication
verstehen

Endnotes

1. See Felson (1991), Felson and Felson (1993), and Logan (1991) for a discussion of blame analysis.
2. For more detailed discussions of concepts, see Chafetz (1978:45–61), Hage (1972:9–85), Kaplan (1964:34–80), Mullins (1971:7–18), Reynolds (1971), and Stinchcombe (1968, 1973).
3. Turner (1980) discussed how sociological explanation and theorizing can be conceptualized as translation.
4. Classifications are discussed in Chafetz (1978: 63–73) and Hage (1972).
5. Introductions to alternative theoretical frameworks and social theories are provided in Craib (1984), Phillips (1985:44–59), and Skidmore (1979).
6. An introduction to functional explanation can be found in Chafetz (1978:22–25).

Ethics in Social Research

INTRODUCTION

Ethics include the concerns, dilemmas, and conflicts that arise over the proper way to conduct research. Ethics help to define what is or is not legitimate to do, or what "moral" research procedure involves. This is not as simple as it may appear, because there are few ethical absolutes and only agreed-upon broad principles. These principles require judgment to apply and some may conflict with others in practice. Many ethical issues ask you to balance two values: the pursuit of knowledge and the rights of research participants or of others in society. Social researchers balance potential benefits—such as advancing the understanding of social life, improving decision making, or helping research participants—against potential costs—such as loss of dignity, self-esteem, privacy, or democratic freedoms.

Social researchers confront many ethical dilemmas and must decide how to act. They have a moral and professional obligation to be ethical, even if research participants are unaware of or unconcerned about ethics.

Many areas of professional practice have ethical standards (e.g., journalists, police departments, business corporations, etc.), but the ethical standards for doing social research are often stricter. To do professional social research, you must both know the proper research techniques (e.g., sampling) and be sensitive to ethical concerns. This is not always easy. For centuries, moral, legal, and political philosophers debated the issues researchers regularly face.

It is difficult to appreciate fully the ethical dilemmas experienced by researchers until you actually begin to do research, but waiting until the middle of a study is too late. You need to prepare yourself ahead of time and consider ethical concerns as you design a study so that you can build sound ethical practices into a study's design. In addition, by developing sensitivity to ethical issues, you will be alert to potential ethical concerns that can arise as you make decisions while conducting a study. Also, an ethical awareness will help you better understand the overall research process.

Ethics begin and end with you, the individual social researcher. A strong personal moral code by the researcher is the best defense against unethical behavior. Before, during, and after conducting a study, a researcher has opportunities to, and *should,* reflect on the ethics of research actions and consult his or her conscience. Ultimately, ethical research depends on the integrity of an individual researcher.

WHY BE ETHICAL?

Given that most people who conduct social research are genuinely concerned about others, you might ask, Why would any researcher ever act in an ethically irresponsible manner? Most unethical behavior is due to a lack of awareness and pressures on researchers to take ethical shortcuts. Researchers face pressures to build a career, publish new findings, advance knowledge, gain prestige, impress family and friends, hold on to a job, and so forth. Ethical research will take longer to complete, cost more money, be more complicated, and be less likely to produce unambiguous results. Plus, there are many opportunities in research to act unethically, the odds of getting caught are small, and written ethical standards are in the form of vague, loose principles.

The ethical researcher gets few rewards and wins no praise. The unethical researcher, if caught, faces public humiliation, a ruined career, and possible legal action. The best preparation for ethical behavior is to internalize a sensitivity to ethical concerns, to adopt a serious professional role, and to interact regularly with other researchers. Moreover, the scientific community demands ethical behavior without exceptions.

Scientific Misconduct

The research community and agencies that fund research oppose a type of unethical behavior called scientific misconduct; it includes research fraud and plagiarism. *Scientific misconduct* occurs when a researcher falsifies or distorts the data or the methods of data collection, or plagiarizes the work of others. It also includes significant, unjustified departures from the generally accepted scientific practices for doing and reporting on research. *Research fraud* occurs when a researcher fakes or invents data that he or she did not really collect, or fails to honestly and fully report how he or she conducted a study. Although rare, it is considered a very serious violation. The most famous case of research fraud was that of Sir Cyril Burt, the father of British educational psychology. Burt died in 1971 as an esteemed researcher who was famous for his studies with twins that showed a genetic basis of intelligence. In 1976, it was discovered that he had falsified data and the names of coauthors. Unfortunately, the scientific community had been misled for nearly 30 years. More recently, a social psychologist was discovered to have fabricated data for several experiments on sex bias conducted at Harvard University in the 1990s. *Plagiarism* occurs when a researcher "steals" the ideas or writings of another or uses them without citing the source. Plagiarism also includes stealing the work of another researcher, an assistant, or a student, and misrepresenting it as one's own. These are serious breaches of ethical standards.[1]

Unethical but Legal

Behavior may be unethical but legal (i.e., not break any law). A plagiarism case illustrates the distinction between legal and ethical behavior. The American Sociological Association documented that a 1988 book without any footnotes by a dean from Eastern New Mexico University contained large sections of a 1978 dissertation that a sociology professor at Tufts University wrote. Copying the dissertation was not *illegal*; it did not violate copyright law because the sociologist's dissertation did not have a copyright filed with the U.S. government. Nevertheless, it was

FIGURE 3.1   Typology of Legal and Moral Actions in Social Research

LEGAL	ETHICAL	
	Yes	No
Yes	Moral and Legal	Legal but Immoral
No	Illegal but Moral	Immoral and Illegal

clearly *unethical* according to standards of professional behavior.[2] (See Figure 3.1 for relations between legal and moral actions.)

POWER RELATIONS

A professional researcher and the research participants or employee-assistants are in a relationship of unequal power and trust. An experimenter, survey director, or research investigator has power over participants and assistants, and in turn, they trust his or her judgment and authority. The researcher's credentials, training, professional role, and the place of science in modern society legitimate the power and make it into a form of expert authority. Some ethical issues involve an abuse of power and trust. A researcher's authority to conduct social research and to earn the trust of others is accompanied always by an unyielding ethical responsibility to guide, protect, and oversee the interests of the people being studied.

When looking for ethical guidance, researchers are not alone. They can turn to a number of resources: professional colleagues, ethical advisory committees, institutional review boards or human subjects committees at a college or institution (discussed later), codes of ethics by professional associations (discussed later in this chapter), and writings on ethics in research. The larger research community firmly supports and upholds ethical behavior, even if an individual researcher is ultimately responsible to do what is ethical in specific situations.

ETHICAL ISSUES INVOLVING RESEARCH PARTICIPANTS

Have you ever been a participant in a research study? If so, how were you treated? More attention is focused on the possible negative effects of research on those being studied than any other ethical issue, beginning with concerns about biomedical research. Acting ethically requires that a researcher balance the value of advancing knowledge against the value of noninterference in the lives of others. Either extreme causes problems. Giving research participants absolute rights of noninterference could make empirical research impossible, but giving researchers absolute rights of inquiry could nullify participants' basic human rights. The moral question becomes: When, if ever, are researchers justified in risking physical harm or injury to those being studied, causing them great embarrassment or inconvenience, violating their privacy, or frightening them?

The law and codes of ethics recognize some clear prohibitions: Never cause unnecessary or irreversible harm to subjects; secure prior voluntary consent when possible; and never unnecessarily humiliate, degrade, or release harmful information about specific individuals that was collected for research purposes. In other words, you should always show respect for the research participant. These are minimal standards and are subject to interpretation (e.g., What does *unnecessary* mean in a specific situation?).

Origins of Research Participant Protection

Concern over the treatment of research participants arose after the revelation of gross violations of basic human rights in the name of science. The most notorious violations were "medical experiments" conducted on Jews and others in Nazi Germany, and similar "medical experiments" to test biological weapons by Japan in the 1940s. In these experiments, terrible tortures were committed. For example, people were placed in freezing water to see how long it took them to die, people were purposely starved to death, people were intentionally infected with horrible diseases, and limbs were severed from children and transplanted onto others.[3]

Such human rights violations did not occur only long ago. In a famous case of unethical research, the Tuskegee Syphilis Study, also known as *Bad Blood,* the President of the United States admitted wrongdoing and formally apologized in 1997 to the participant-victims. Until the 1970s, when a newspaper report caused a scandal to erupt, the U.S. Public Health Service sponsored a study in which poor, uneducated African American men in Alabama suffered and died of untreated syphilis, while researchers studied the severe physical disabilities that appear in advanced stages of the disease. The unethical study began in 1929, before penicillin was available to treat the disease, but it continued long after treatment was available. Despite their unethical treatment of the people, the researchers were able to publish their results for 40 years. The study ended in 1972, but a formal apology took another 25 years.[4]

Unfortunately, the Bad Blood scandal is not unique. During the Cold War era, the U.S. government periodically compromised ethical research principles for military and political goals. In 1995, reports revealed that the government authorized injecting unknowing people with radioactive material in the late 1940s. In the 1950s, the government warned Eastman Kodak and other film manufacturers about nuclear fallout from atomic tests to prevent fogged film, but it did not warn nearby citizens of health hazards. In the 1960s, the U.S. army gave unsuspecting soldiers LSD (a hallucinogenic drug), causing serious trauma. Today, researchers widely recognize these to be violations of two fundamental ethical principles: Avoid physical harm and obtain informed consent.[5]

Physical Harm, Psychological Abuse, and Legal Jeopardy

Social research can harm a research participant in several ways: physical, psychological, and legal harm, as well as harm to a person's career, reputation, or income. Different types of harm are more likely in other types of research (e.g., in experiments versus field research). It is a researcher's responsibility to be aware of all types of potential harm and to take specific actions to minimize the risk to participants at all times.

Physical Harm.   Physical harm is rare. Even in biomedical research, where the intervention into a person's life is much greater, 3 to 5 percent of studies involved any person who suffered any harm.[6] A straightforward ethical principle is that researchers should never cause physical harm. An ethical researcher anticipates risks before beginning a study, including basic safety concerns (e.g., safe buildings, furniture, and equipment). This means that he or she screens out high-risk subjects (those with heart conditions, mental breakdown, seizures, etc.) if great stress is involved and anticipates possible sources of injury or physical attacks on research participants or assistants. The researcher accepts moral and legal responsibility for injury due to participation in research and terminates a project immediately if he or she can no longer fully guarantee the physical safety of the people involved (see the Zimbardo study in Box 3.1).

Psychological Abuse, Stress, or Loss of Self-Esteem.   The risk of physical harm is rare, but social researchers can place people in highly stressful, embarrassing, anxiety-producing, or unpleasant situations. Researchers want to learn about people's responses in real-life, high-anxiety–producing situations, so they might place people in realistic situations of psychological discomfort or stress. Is it unethical to cause discomfort? The ethics of the famous Milgram obedience study are still debated (see Box 3.1). Some say that the precautions taken and the knowledge gained outweighed the stress and potential psychological harm that research participants experienced. Others believe that the extreme stress and the risk of permanent harm were too great. Such an experiment could not be conducted today because of heightened sensitivity to the ethical issues involved.

Social researchers have created high levels of anxiety or discomfort. They have exposed participants to gruesome photos; falsely told male students that they have strong feminine personality traits; falsely told students that they have failed; created a situation of high fear (e.g., smoke entering a room in which the door is locked); asked participants to harm others; placed people in situations where they face social pressure to deny their convictions; and had participants lie, cheat, or steal.[7] Researchers who study helping behavior often place participants in emergency situations to see whether they will lend assistance. For example, Piliavin and associates (1969) studied helping behavior in subways by faking someone's collapse onto the floor. In the field experiment, the riders in the subway car were unaware of the experiment and did not volunteer to participate in it.

The only researchers who might even consider conducting a study that purposely induces great stress or anxiety in research participants are very experienced and take all necessary precautions before inducing anxiety or discomfort. The researchers should consult with others who have conducted similar studies and mental health professionals as they plan the study. They should screen out high-risk populations (e.g., those with emotional problems or weak hearts), and arrange for emergency interventions or termination of the research if dangerous situations arise. They must always obtain written informed consent (to be discussed) before the research and debrief the people immediately afterward (i.e., explain any deception and what actually happened in the study). Researchers should never create *unnecessary* stress (i.e., beyond the minimal amount needed to create the desired effect) or stress that lacks a very clear, legitimate research purpose. Knowing what "minimal

Box 3.1   Three Cases of Ethical Controversy

Stanley Milgram's *obedience study* (Milgram, 1963, 1965, 1974) attempted to discover how the horrors of the Holocaust under the Nazis could have occurred by examining the strength of social pressure to obey authority. After signing "informed consent forms," subjects were assigned, in rigged random selection, to be a "teacher" while a confederate was the "pupil." The teacher was to test the pupil's memory of word lists and increase the electric shock level if the pupil made mistakes. The pupil was located in a nearby room, so the teacher could hear but not see the pupil. The shock apparatus was clearly labeled with increasing voltage. As the pupil made mistakes and the teacher turned switches, she or he also made noises as if in severe pain. The researcher was present and made comments such as "You must go on" to the teacher. Milgram reported, "Subjects were observed to sweat, tremble, stutter, bite their lips, groan and dig their fingernails into their flesh. These were characteristic rather than exceptional responses to the experiment" (Milgram, 1963:375). The percentage of subjects who would shock to dangerous levels was dramatically higher than expected. Ethical concerns arose over the use of deception and the extreme emotional stress experienced by subjects.

In Laud Humphreys's (Humphreys, 1975) *tearoom trade study* (a study of male homosexual encounters in public restrooms), about 100 men were observed engaging in sexual acts as Humphreys pretended to be a "watchqueen" (a voyeur and lookout). Subjects were followed to their cars, and their license numbers were secretly recorded. Names and addresses were obtained from police registers when Humphreys posed as a market researcher. One year

later, in disguise, Humphreys used a deceptive story about a health survey to interview the subjects in their homes. Humphreys was careful to keep names in safety deposit boxes, and identifiers with subject names were burned. He significantly advanced knowledge of homosexuals who frequent "tearooms" and overturned previous false beliefs about them. There has been controversy over the study: The subjects never consented; deception was used; and the names could have been used to blackmail subjects, to end marriages, or to initiate criminal prosecution.

In the *Zimbardo prison experiment* (Zimbardo, 1972, 1973; Zimbardo et al., 1973, 1974), male students were divided into two role-playing groups: guards and prisoners. Before the experiment, volunteer students were given personality tests, and only those in the "normal" range were chosen. Volunteers signed up for two weeks, and prisoners were told that they would be under surveillance and would have some civil rights suspended, but that no physical abuse was allowed. In a simulated prison in the basement of a Stanford University building, prisoners were deindividualized (dressed in standard uniforms and called only by their numbers) and guards were militarized (with uniforms, nightsticks, and reflective sunglasses). Guards were told to maintain a reasonable degree of order and served 8-hour shifts, while prisoners were locked up 24 hours per day. Unexpectedly, the volunteers became too caught up in their roles. Prisoners became passive and disorganized, while guards became aggressive, arbitrary, and dehumanizing. By the sixth day, Zimbardo called off the experiment for ethical reasons. The risk of permanent psychological harm, and even physical harm, was too great.

amount" means comes with experience. It is best to begin with too little stress, risking a finding of no effect, than to create too much. It is always wise to work in collaboration with other researchers when the risk to participants is high, because the involvement of several ethically sensitive researchers reduces the chances of making an ethical misjudgment.

Research that induces great stress and anxiety in participants also carries the danger that experimenters will develop a callous or manipulative attitude toward others. Researchers have reported feeling guilt and regret after conducting experiments that caused psychological harm to people. Experiments that place subjects in anxiety-producing situations may produce significant personal discomfort for the ethical researcher.

Legal Harm.   A researcher is responsible for protecting research participants from increased risk of arrest. If participation in research increases the risk of arrest, few individuals will trust researchers or be willing to participate in future research. Potential legal harm is one criticism of Humphreys's 1975 tearoom trade study (see Box 3.1).

A related ethical issue arises when a researcher learns of illegal activity when collecting data. A researcher must weigh the value of protecting the researcher-subject relationship and the benefits to future researchers against potential serious harm to innocent people. The researcher bears the cost of his or her judgment. For example, in his field research on police, Van Maanen (1982:114–115) reported seeing police beat people and witnessing illegal acts and irregular procedures, but said, "On and following these troublesome incidents I followed police custom: I kept my mouth shut."

Field researchers in particular can face difficult ethical decisions. For example, when studying a mental institution, Taylor (1987) discovered the mistreatment and abuse of inmates by the staff. He had two choices: Abandon the study and call for an immediate investigation, or keep quiet and continue with the study for several months, publicize the findings afterwards, and then become an advocate to end the abuse. After weighing the situation, he followed the latter course and is now an activist for the rights of mental institution inmates.

In some studies, observing illegal behavior may be central to the research project. If a researcher covertly observes and records illegal behavior, then supplies the information to law-enforcement authorities, he or she is violating ethical standards regarding research participants and is

undermining future social research. At the same time, a researcher who fails to report illegal behavior is indirectly permitting criminal behavior. He or she could be charged as an accessory to a crime. Cooperation with law-enforcement officials raises the question, Is the researcher a professional scientist who protects research participants in the process of seeking knowledge, or a free-lance undercover informant who is really working for the police trying to "catch" criminals?

Other Harm to Participants

Research participants may face other types of harm. For example, a survey interview may create anxiety and discomfort if it asks people to recall unpleasant or traumatic events. An ethical researcher must be sensitive to any harm to participants, consider precautions, and weigh potential harm against potential benefits.

Another type of harm is a negative impact on the careers, reputations, or incomes of research participants. For example, a researcher conducts a survey of employees and concludes that the supervisor's performance is poor. As a consequence, the supervisor loses her job. Or, a researcher studies homeless people living on the street. The findings show that many engage in petty illegal acts to get food. As a consequence, a city government "cracks down" on the petty illegal acts and the homeless people can no longer eat. What is the researcher's responsibility? The ethical researcher considers the consequences of research for those being studied. The general goal is not to cause any harm simply because someone was a research participant. However, there is no set answer to such questions. A researcher must evaluate each case, weigh potential harm against potential benefits, and bear the responsibility for the decision.

Deception

Has anyone ever told you a half-truth or lie to get you to do something? How did you feel about it? Social researchers follow the ethical *principle of voluntary consent*: Never force anyone to participate in research, and do not lie to anyone unless it is necessary and the only way to accomplish a legitimate research purpose. The people who participate in social research should explicitly agree to participate. A person's right not to participate can be a critical issue whenever the researcher uses deception, disguises the research, or uses covert research methods.

Social researchers sometimes deceive or lie to participants in field and experimental research. A researcher might misrepresent his or her actions or true intentions for legitimate methodological reasons. For example, if participants knew the true purpose, they would modify their behavior, making it impossible to learn of their real behavior. Another situation occurs when access to a research site would be impossible if the researcher told the truth. Deception is never preferable if the researcher can accomplish the same thing without using deception.

Experimental researchers often deceive subjects to prevent them from learning the hypothesis being tested and to reduce "reactive effects" (see Chapter 8). Deception is acceptable only if a researcher can show that it has a clear, specific methodological purpose, and even then, the researcher should use it only to the minimal degree necessary. Researchers who use deception should always obtain informed consent, never misrepresent risks, and always explain the actual conditions to participants afterwards. You might ask, How can a researcher obtain prior informed consent and still use deception? He or she can describe the basic procedures involved and conceal only specific information about hypotheses being tested.

Sometimes field researchers use covert observation to gain entry to field research settings. In studies of cults, small extremist political sects, illegal or deviant behavior, or behavior in a large public area, it may be impossible to conduct research if a researcher announces and discloses her or his true purpose. If a covert stance is not essential, a researcher should not use it. If he or she does not know whether covert access is necessary, then a strategy of gradual disclosure may

be best. When in doubt, it is best to err in the direction of disclosing one's true identity and purpose. Covert research remains controversial, and many researchers feel that all covert research is unethical. Even those who accept covert research as ethical in certain situations say that it should be used only when overt observation is impossible. Whenever possible, the researcher should inform participants of the observation immediately afterwards and give them an opportunity to express concerns.

Deception and covert research may increase mistrust and cynicism as well as diminish public respect for social research. Misrepresentation in field research is analogous to being an undercover agent or government informer in nondemocratic societies. The use of deception has a long-term negative effect. It increases distrust among people who are frequently studied and makes doing social research more difficult in the long term.

Informed Consent

A fundamental ethical principle of social research is: Never coerce anyone into participating; participation *must* be voluntary at all times. Permission alone is not enough; people need to know what they are being asked to participate in so that they can make an informed decision. Participants can become aware of their rights and what they are getting involved in when they read and sign a statement giving *informed consent*—an agreement by participants stating they are willing to be in a study and they know something about what the research procedure will involve.

Governments vary in the requirement for informed consent. The U.S. federal government does not require informed consent in all research involving human subjects. Nevertheless, researchers should get written informed consent unless there are good reasons for not obtaining it (e.g., covert field research, use of secondary data, etc.) as judged by an institutional review board (IRB) (see the later discussion of IRBs).

Informed consent statements provide specific information (see Box 3.2). A general statement about the kinds of procedures or questions involved and the uses of the data are sufficient for informed consent. Studies suggest that participants who receive a full informed consent statement do not respond differently from those who do not. If anything, people who refused to sign such a statement were more likely to guess or answer "no response" to questions.

It is unethical to coerce people to participate, including offering them special benefits that they cannot otherwise attain. For example, it is unethical for a commanding officer to order a soldier to participate in a study, for a professor to require a student to be a research subject in order to pass a course, or for an employer to expect an employee to complete a survey as a con-

dition of continued employment. It is unethical even if someone other than the researcher (e.g., an employer) coerces people (e.g., employees) to participate in research.

Full disclosure with the researcher's identification helps to protect research participants against fraudulent research and to protect legitimate researchers. Informed consent lessens the chance that a con artist in the guise of a researcher will defraud or abuse people. It also reduces the chance that someone will use a bogus researcher identity to market products or obtain personal information on people for unethical purposes.

Legally, a signed informed consent statement is optional for most survey, field, and secondary data research, but it is often mandatory for experimental research. Informed consent is impossible to obtain in existing statistics and documentary research. The general rule is: The greater the risk of potential harm to research participants, the greater the need to obtain a written informed consent statement from them. In sum, there are many sound reasons to get informed consent and few reasons not to get it.

Special Populations and New Inequalities

Some populations or groups of research participants are not capable of giving true voluntary informed consent. *Special populations* are people who lack the necessary cognitive competency to give valid informed consent or people in a weak position who might cast aside their freedom to refuse to participate in a study. Students, prison inmates, employees, military personnel, the homeless, welfare recipients, children, and the developmentally disabled may not be fully capable of making a decision, or they may agree to participate only because they see their participation as a way to obtain a desired good—such as higher grades, early parole, promotions, or additional services. It is unethical to involve "incompetent" people (e.g., children, mentally disabled, etc.) in research unless a researcher meets two

Box	
3.2	**Informed Consent**

Informed consent statements contain the following:

1. A brief description of the purpose and procedure of the research, including the expected duration of the study

2. A statement of any risks or discomfort associated with participation

3. A guarantee of anonymity and the confidentiality of records

4. The identification of the researcher and of where to receive information about subjects' rights or questions about the study

5. A statement that participation is completely voluntary and can be terminated at any time without penalty

6. A statement of alternative procedures that may be used

7. A statement of any benefits or compensation provided to subjects and the number of subjects involved

8. An offer to provide a summary of findings

minimal conditions: (1) a legal guardian grants written permission and (2) the researcher follows all standard ethical principles to protect participants from harm. For example, a researcher wants to conduct a survey of high school students to learn about their sexual behavior and drug/alcohol use. If the survey is conducted on school property, school officials must give official permission. For any research participant who is a legal minor (usually under 18 years old), written parental permission is needed. It is best to ask permission from each student, as well.

The use of coercion to participate can be a tricky issue, and it depends on the specifics of a situation. For example, a convicted criminal faces the alternative of imprisonment or participation in an experimental rehabilitation program. The convicted criminal may not believe in the benefits of the program, but the researcher may believe that it will help the criminal. This is a case of coercion. A researcher must honestly judge whether the benefits to the criminal and to society greatly outweigh the ethical prohibition on coercion. This is risky. History shows many cases in which a researcher believed he or she was doing something "for the good of" someone in a powerless position (e.g., prisoners, students, homosexuals), but it turned out that the "good" actually was for the researcher or a powerful organization in society, and it did more harm than good to the research participant.

You may have been in a social science class in which a teacher required you to participate as a subject in a research project. This is a special case of coercion and is usually ethical. Teachers have made three arguments in favor of requiring student participation: (1) it would be difficult and prohibitively expensive to get participants otherwise, (2) the knowledge created from research with students serving as subjects benefits future students and society, and (3) students will learn more about research by experiencing it directly in a realistic research setting. Of the three arguments, only the third justifies limited coercion. This limited coercion is acceptable only as long as it meets three conditions: it is attached to a clear educational objective, the students have a choice of research experience or an alternative activity, and all other ethical principles of research are followed.

Avoid Creating New Inequalities. Another type of harm occurs when one group of people is denied a service or benefit as a result of participating in a research project. For example, a researcher might have a new treatment for people with a terrible disease, such as acquired immune deficiency syndrome (AIDS). To determine the effects of the new treatment, half the group is randomly chosen to receive the treatment, while others receive nothing. The design may clearly show whether the treatment is effective, but participants in the group who receive no treatment may die. Of course, those receiving the treatment may also die, until more is known about whether it is effective. Is it ethical to deny people who have been randomly assigned to a study group the potentially life-saving treatment? What if a clear, definitive test of whether a treatment is effective requires that one study group receive no treatment?

A researcher can reduce creating a new inequality among research participants when the outcome has a major impact on their survival or quality of life in three ways. First, the people who do not receive the "new, improved" treatment continue to receive the best previously acceptable treatment. In other words, instead of denying all assistance, they get the best treatment available prior to the new one being tested. This ensures that people will not suffer in absolute terms, even if they temporarily fall behind in relative terms. Second, researchers can use a *crossover design,* which is when a study group that gets no treatment in the first phase of the experiment becomes the group with the treatment in the second phase, and vice versa. Finally, the researcher continuously monitors results. If it appears early in the study that the new treatment is highly effective, the researcher should offer it to those in the control group. Also, in high-risk experiments with medical treatments or possible physical harm, researchers may use animal or other surrogates for humans.

Privacy, Anonymity, and Confidentiality

How would you feel if private details about your personal life were shared with the public without your knowledge? Because social researchers sometimes transgress the privacy of people in order to study social behavior, they must take several precautions to protect research participants' privacy.

Privacy.   Survey researchers invade a person's privacy when they probe into beliefs, backgrounds, and behaviors in a way that reveals intimate private details. Experimental researchers sometimes use two-way mirrors or hidden microphones to "spy" on subjects. Even if people know they are being studied, they are unaware of what the experimenter is looking for. Field researchers may observe private aspects of behavior or eavesdrop on conversations.

In field research, privacy may be violated without advance warning. When Humphreys (1975) served as a "watchqueen" in a public restroom where homosexual contacts took place, he observed very private behavior without informing subjects. When Piliavin and colleagues (1969) had people collapse on subways to study helping behavior, those in the subway car had the privacy of their ride violated. People have been studied in public places (e.g., in waiting rooms, walking down the street, in classrooms, etc.), but some "public" places are more private than others (consider, for example, the use of periscopes to observe people who thought they were alone in a public toilet stall).

Eavesdropping on conversations and observing people in quasi-private areas raises ethical concerns. To be ethical, a researcher violates privacy only to the minimum degree necessary and only for legitimate research purposes. In addition, he or she takes steps to protect the information on participants from public disclosure.

Anonymity.   Researchers protect privacy by not disclosing a participant's identity after information is gathered. This takes two forms, both of which require separating an individual's identity from his or her responses: anonymity and confidentiality. *Anonymity* means that people remain anonymous or nameless. For example, a field researcher provides a social picture of a particular individual, but gives a fictitious name and location, and alters some characteristics. The subject's identity is protected, and the individual remains unknown or anonymous. Survey and experimental researchers discard the names or addresses of subjects as soon as possible and refer to participants by a code number only to protect anonymity. If a researcher uses a mail survey and includes a code on the questionnaire to determine which respondents failed to respond, he or she is not keeping respondents anonymous during that phase of the study. In panel studies, researchers track the same individuals over time, so they do not uphold participant anonymity within the study. Likewise, historical researchers use specific names in historical or documentary research. They may do so if the original information was from public sources; if the sources were not publicly available, a researcher must obtain written permission from the owner of the documents to use specific names.

It is difficult to protect research participant anonymity. In one study about a fictitious town, "Springdale," in *Small Town in Mass Society* (Vidich and Bensman, 1968), it was easy to identify the town and specific individuals in it. Town residents became upset about how the researchers portrayed them and staged a parade mocking the researchers. People often recognize the towns studied in community research. Yet, if a researcher protects the identities of individuals with fictitious information, the gap between what was studied and what is reported to others raises questions about what was found and what was made up. A researcher may breach a promise of anonymity unknowingly in small samples. For example, let us say you conduct a survey of 100 college students and ask many questions on a questionnaire, including age, sex, religion, and hometown. The sample contains one 22-year-old Jewish male born in Stratford, Ontario. With this information, you could find out who the specific individual is and how he answered very personal questions, even though his name was not directly recorded on the questionnaire.

Confidentiality.   Even if a researcher cannot protect anonymity, he or she always should protect participant confidentiality. Anonymity means protecting the identity of specific individuals from being known. Confidentiality can include information with participant names attached, but the researcher holds it in confidence or keeps it secret from public disclosure. The researcher releases data in a way that does not permit linking specific individuals to responses and presents it publicly only in an aggregate form (e.g., as percentages, statistical means, etc.).

A researcher can provide anonymity without confidentiality, or vice versa, although they usually go together. Anonymity without confidentiality occurs if all the details about a specific individual are made public, but the individual's name is withheld. Confidentiality without anonymity occurs if detailed information is not made public, but a researcher privately links individual names to specific responses.

Attempts to protect the identity of subjects from public disclosure has resulted in elaborate procedures: eliciting anonymous responses, using a third-party custodian who holds the key to coded lists, or using the random-response technique. Past abuses suggest that such measures may be necessary. For example, Diener and Crandall (1978:70) reported that during the 1950s, the U.S. State Department and the FBI requested research records on individuals who had been involved in the famous Kinsey sex study. The Kinsey Sex Institute refused to comply with the government. The institute threatened to destroy all records rather than release any. Eventually, the government agencies backed down. The moral duty and ethical code of the researchers obligated them to destroy the records rather than give them to government officials.

Confidentiality can sometimes protect research participants from legal or physical harm. In a study of illegal drug users in rural Ohio, Draus and associates (2005) took great care to protect the research participants. They conducted interviews in large multiuse buildings, avoided references to illegal drugs in written documents, did not mention of names of drug dealers and locations, and did not affiliate with drug rehabilitation services, which had ties to law enforcement. They noted, "We intentionally avoided contact with local police, prosecutors, or parole officers" and "surveillance of the project by local law enforcement was a source of concern" (p. 169). In other situations, other principles may take precedence over protecting research participant confidentiality. For example, when studying patients in a mental hospital, a researcher discovers that a patient is preparing to kill an attendant. The researcher must weigh the benefit of confidentiality against the potential harm to the attendant.

Social researchers can pay high personal costs for being ethical. Although he was never accused or convicted of breaking any law and he closely followed the ethical principles of the American Sociological Association, Professor Rik Scarce spent 16 weeks in a Spokane jail for contempt of court because he refused to testify before a grand jury and break the confidentiality of social research data. Scarce had been studying radical animal liberation groups and had already published one book on the subject. He had interviewed a research participant who was suspected of leading a group that broke into animal facilities and caused $150,000 damage. Two judges refused to acknowledge the confidentiality of social research data.[8]

A special concern with anonymity and confidentiality arises when a researcher studies "captive" populations (e.g., students, prisoners, employees, patients, and soldiers). Gatekeepers, or those in positions of authority, may restrict access unless they receive information on subjects.[9] For example, a researcher studies drug use and sexual activity among high school students. School authorities agree to cooperate under two conditions: (1) students need parental permission to participate and (2) school officials get the names of all drug users and sexually active students in order to assist the students with counseling and to inform the students' parents. An ethical researcher will refuse to continue rather than meet the second condition. Even though the officials claim to have the participants' best interests in mind, the privacy of participants will be violated and they could be in legal harm as a result of disclosure. If the school officials really want to assist the students and not use researchers as spies, they could develop an outreach program of their own.

Mandated Protections of Research Participants

Many governments have regulations and laws to protect research participants and their rights. In the United States, legal restraint is found in rules and regulations issued by the U.S. Department of Health and Human Services Office for the Protection from Research Risks. Although this is only one federal agency, most researchers and other government agencies look to it for guidance. The National Research Act (1974) established the National Commission for the Protection of Human Subjects in Biomedical and Behavioral Research, which significantly expanded regulations and required informed consent in most social research. The responsibility for safeguarding ethical standards was assigned to research institutes and universities. The Department of Health and Human Services issued regulations in 1981, which are still in force. Federal regulations follow a biomedical model and protect subjects from physical harm. Other rules require institutional review boards (IRBs) at all research institutes, colleges, and universities to review all use of human subjects. An *IRB* is a committee of researchers and community members that oversees, monitors, and reviews the im-

pact of research procedures on human participants and applies ethical guidelines by reviewing research procedures at a preliminary stage when first proposed. Some forms of research, educational tests, normal educational practice, most nonsensitive surveys, most observation of public behavior, and studies of existing data in which individuals cannot be identified are exempt from institutional review boards.

ETHICS AND THE SCIENTIFIC COMMUNITY

Physicians, attorneys, family counselors, social workers, and other professionals have a *code of ethics* and peer review boards or licensing regulations. The codes formalize professional standards and provide guidance when questions arise in practice. Social researchers do not provide a service for a fee, they receive limited ethical training, and rarely are they licensed. They incorporate ethical concerns into research because it is morally and socially responsible, and to protect social research from charges of insensitivity or abusing people. Professional social science associations have codes of ethics that identify proper and improper behavior. They represent a consensus of professionals on ethics. All researchers may not agree on all ethical issues, and ethical rules are subject to interpretation, but researchers are expected to uphold ethical standards as part of their membership in a professional community.

Codes of research ethics can be traced to the Nuremberg code adopted during the Nuremberg Military Tribunal on Nazi war crimes held by the Allied Powers immediately after World War II. The code, developed as a response to the cruelty of concentration camp experiments, outlines ethical principles and rights of human subjects. These include the following:

- The principle of voluntary consent
- Avoidance of unnecessary physical and mental suffering

- Avoidance of any experiment where death or disabling injury is likely
- Termination of research if its continuation is likely to cause injury, disability, or death
- The principle that experiments should be conducted by highly qualified people using the highest levels of skill and care
- The principle that the results should be for the good of society and unattainable by any other method

The principles in the Nuremberg code dealt with the treatment of human subjects and focused on medical experimentation, but they became the basis for the ethical codes in social research. Similar codes of human rights, such as the 1948 Universal Declaration of Human Rights by the United Nations and the 1964 Declaration of Helsinki, also have implications for social researchers. Box 3.3 lists some of the basic principles of ethical social research.

Professional social science associations have committees that review codes of ethics and hear about possible violations, but there is no formal policing of the codes. The penalty for a minor violation rarely goes beyond a letter of complaint. If laws have not been violated, the most extreme penalty is the negative publicity surrounding a well-documented and serious ethical violation. The publicity may result in the loss of employment, a refusal to publish the researcher's findings in scholarly journals, and a prohibition from receiving funding for research—in other words, banishment from the community of professional researchers.

Codes of ethics do more than codify thinking and provide individual researchers with guidance; they also help universities and other institutions defend ethical research against abuses. For example, after interviewing 24 staff members and conducting observations, a researcher in 1994 documented that the staff at the Milwaukee Public Defenders Office were seriously overworked and could not effectively provide legal defense for poor people. Learning of the findings, top officials at the office contacted

---

Box 3.3 Basic Principles of Ethical Social Research

- Ethical responsibility rests with the individual researcher.
- Do not exploit subjects or students for personal gain.
- Some form of informed consent is highly recommended or required.
- Honor all guarantees of privacy, confidentiality, and anonymity.
- Do not coerce or humiliate subjects.
- Use deception only if needed, and always accompany it with debriefing.
- Use the research method that is appropriate to a topic.
- Detect and remove undesirable consequences to research subjects.
- Anticipate repercussions of the research or publication of results.
- Identify the sponsor who funded the research.
- Cooperate with host nations when doing comparative research.
- Release the details of the study design with the results.
- Make interpretations of results consistent with the data.
- Use high methodological standards and strive for accuracy.
- Do not conduct secret research.

---

the university and demanded to know who on their staff had talked to the researcher, with implications that there might be reprisals. The university administration defended the researcher and refused to release the information, citing widely accepted codes that protect human research participants.[10]

ETHICS AND THE SPONSORS OF RESEARCH

Whistle-Blowing

You might find a job where you do research for a sponsor—an employer, a government agency, or a private firm that contracts with a researcher to conduct research. Special ethical problems arise when a sponsor pays for research, especially applied research. Researchers may be asked to compromise ethical or professional research standards as a condition for receiving a contract or for continued employment. Researchers need to set ethical boundaries beyond which they will refuse the sponsor's demands. When confronted with an illegitimate demand from a sponsor, a researcher has three basic choices: loyalty to an organization or larger group, exiting from the situation, or voicing opposition.[11] These present themselves as caving in to the sponsor, quitting, or becoming a whistle-blower. The researcher must choose his or her own course of action, but it is best to consider ethical issues early in a relationship with a sponsor and to express concerns up front. Whistle-blowing involves the researcher who sees an ethical wrongdoing, and who cannot stop it after informing superiors and exhausting internal avenues to resolve the issue. He or she then turns to outsiders and informs an external audience, agency, or the media. The whistle-blowing researcher must be convinced that the breach of ethics is serious and approved of in the organization. It is risky. The outsiders may or may not be interested in the problem or able to help. Outsiders often have their own priorities (making an organization look bad, sensationalizing the problem, etc.) that differ from the researcher's primary concern (ending the unethical behavior). Supervisors or managers may try to discredit or punish anyone who exposes problems and acts disloyal. Under the best of conditions, the issue may take a long time to resolve and create great emotional strain. By doing what is moral, a whistle-blower needs to be prepared to make sacrifices—loss of a job or no promotions, lowered pay, an undesirable transfer, abandonment by friends at work, or incurring legal costs. There is no guarantee that doing the ethical-moral thing will stop the unethical behavior or protect the honest researcher from retaliation.

Applied social researchers in sponsored research settings need to think seriously about their professional roles. They may want to maintain some independence from an employer and affirm their membership in a community of dedicated professionals. Many find a defense against sponsor pressures by participating in professional organizations (e.g., the Evaluation Research Society), maintaining regular contacts with researchers outside the sponsoring organization, and staying current with the best research practices. The researcher least likely to uphold ethical standards in a sponsored setting is someone who is isolated and professionally insecure. Whatever the situation, unethical behavior is never justified by the argument that "If I didn't do it, someone else would have."

Arriving at Particular Findings

What should you do if a sponsor tells you, directly or indirectly, what results you should come up with before you do a study? An ethical researcher will refuse to participate if he or she is told to arrive at specific results as a precondition for doing research. Legitimate research is conducted without restrictions on the possible findings that a study might yield.

An example of pressure to arrive at particular findings is in the area of educational testing. Standardized tests to measure achievement by U.S. school children have come under criticism. For example, children in about 90 percent of school districts in the United States score "above average" on such tests. This was called the *Lake Wobegon effect* after the mythical town of Lake Wobegon, where, according to radio show host Garrison Keillor, "all the children are above average." The main reason for this finding was that the researchers compared scores of current students with those of students many years ago. Many teachers, school principals, superintendents, and school boards pressured for a type of result that would allow them to report to parents and voters that their school district was "above average."[12]

Limits on How to Conduct Studies.   Is it ethically acceptable for a sponsor to limit research by defining what a researcher can study or by limiting the techniques used? Sponsors can legitimately set some conditions on research techniques used (e.g., survey versus experiment) and limit costs for research. However, the researcher must follow generally accepted research methods. Researchers must give a realistic appraisal of what can be accomplished for a given level of funding. The issue of limits is common in contract research, when a firm or government agency asks for work on a particular research project. There is often a tradeoff between quality and cost. Plus, once the research begins, a researcher may need to redesign the project, or costs may be higher. The contract procedure makes midstream changes difficult. A researcher may find that he or she is forced by the contract to use research procedures or methods that are less than ideal. The researcher then confronts a dilemma: complete the contract and do low-quality research, or fail to fulfill the contract and lose money and future jobs.

A researcher should refuse to continue a study if he or she cannot uphold generally accepted standards of research. If a sponsor demands a biased sample or leading survey questions, the ethical researcher should refuse to cooperate. If a legitimate study shows a sponsor's pet idea or project to be disaster, a researcher may anticipate the end of employment or pressure to violate professional research standards. In the long run, the sponsor, the researcher, the scientific community, and society in general are harmed by the violation of sound research practice. The researcher has to decide whether he or she is a "hired hand" who always gives the sponsors whatever they want, even if it is ethically wrong, or a professional who is obligated to teach, guide, or even oppose sponsors in the service of higher moral principles.

A researcher should ask: Why would sponsors want the social research conducted if they are not interested in using the findings or in the truth? The answer is that some sponsors are not interested in the truth and have no respect for the scientific process. They see social research only as "a cover" to legitimate a decision or practice that they plan to carry out, but use research to justify their action or deflect criticism. They abuse the researcher's professional status and undermine integrity of science to advance their own narrow goals. They are being deceitful by trying to "cash in" on social research's reputation for honesty. When such a situation occurs, an ethical researcher has a moral responsibility to expose and stop the abuse.

Suppressing Findings

What happens if you conduct a study and the findings make the sponsor look bad, then the sponsor does not want to release the results? This is a common situation for many applied researchers. For example, a sociologist conducted a study for a state government lottery commission on the effects of state government-sponsored gambling. After she completed the report, but before releasing it to the public, the commission asked her to remove sections that outlined the many negative social effects of gambling and to eliminate her recommendations to create social services to help the anticipated increase of compulsive gamblers. The researcher found herself in a difficult position and faced two conflicting values: do what the sponsor requested and paid for, or reveal the truth to the public but then suffer the consequences?[13]

Government agencies may suppress scientific information that contradicts official policy or embarrasses high officials. Retaliation against social researchers employed by government agencies who make the information public also occurs. In 2004, leading scientists, Nobel laureates, leading medical experts, former federal agency directors, and university chairs and presidents signed a statement voicing concern over the misuse of science by the George W. Bush administration. Major accusations included suppressing research findings and stacking scientific advisory committees with ideologically committed advocates rather than impartial scientists. Other complaints included limiting the public release studies on auto-saftey data, negative data about pharmaceuticals, and studies on pollution. These involved industries that were major political campaign supporters of the administration. Additional criticisms appeared over removing a government fact sheet citing studies that showed no relationship between abortions and breast cancer, removing study results about positive effects of condom use in pregnancy prevention, holding back information on positive aspects of stem cell research, and requiring researchers to revise their study findings on dangers of arctic oil drilling and endangered species so they would conform to the administration's political agenda. An independent 2005 survey of 460 biologists who worked for Fisheries Service found that about one-third said they were directed to suppress findings for nonscientific reasons or to inappropriately exclude or alter technical information from an official scientific document. In June 2005, it was discovered that a political appointee without scientific training who had previously been an oil industry lobbyist was charged with editing official government reports to play down the research findings that documented linkages between such emissions and global warming.[14]

In sponsored research, a researcher can negotiate conditions for releasing findings *prior to beginning* the study and sign a contract to that effect. It may be unwise to conduct the study without such a guarantee, although competing researchers who have fewer ethical scruples may do so. Alternatively, a researcher can accept the sponsor's criticism and hostility and release the findings over the sponsor's objections. Most researchers prefer the first choice, since the second one may scare away future sponsors.

Social researchers sometimes self-censor or delay the release of findings. They do this to protect the identity of informants, to maintain access to a research site, to hold on to their jobs, or to protect the personal safety of themselves or family members.[15] This is a less disturbing type of censorship because it is not imposed by an outside power. It is done by someone who is close to the research and who is knowledgeable about possible consequences. Researchers shoulder the ultimate responsibility for their research. Often, they can draw on many different resources but they face many competing pressures, as well.

Concealing the True Sponsor

Is it ethical to keep the identity of a sponsor secret? For example, an abortion clinic funds a study on members of religious groups who oppose abortion, but it tells the researcher not to reveal to participants who is funding the study. The researcher must balance the ethical rule that it is usually best to reveal a sponsor's identity to participants against both the sponsor's desire for confidentiality and reduced cooperation by participants in the study. In general, an ethical researcher will tell subjects who is sponsoring a study unless there is a strong methodological reason for not doing so. When reporting or publishing results, the ethical mandate is very clear: A researcher must always reveal the sponsor who provides funds for a study.

POLITICS OF RESEARCH

Ethics largely address moral concerns and standards of professional conduct in research that are under the researcher's control. Political concerns also affect social research, but many are beyond the control of researchers. The politics of research usually involve actions by organized advocacy groups, powerful interests in society, governments, or politicians trying to restrict or control the direction of social research. Historically, the political influence over social research has included preventing researchers from conducting a study, cutting off or redirecting funds for research, harassing individual researchers, censoring the release of research findings, and using social research as a cover or guise for covert government intelligence/military actions. For example, U.S. Congress members targeted and eliminated funding for research projects that independent panels of scientists recommended because Congress did not like the topics that would be studied, and politically appointed officials shifted research funds to support more studies on topics consistent with their political views while ending support for studies on topics that might contradict their views. A large company threatened an individual researcher with a lawsuit for delivering expert testimony in public about research findings that revealed its past bad conduct. Until about a decade ago, social researchers who appeared to be independent were actually conducting covert U.S. government intelligence activities.[16]

Most uses of political or financial influence to control social research share a desire to limit knowledge creation or restrict the autonomous scientific investigation of controversial topics. Attempts at control seem motivated by a fear that researchers might discover something damaging if they have freedom of inquiry. This shows that free scientific inquiry is connected to fundamental political ideals of open public debate, democracy, and freedom of expression.

The attempts to block and steer social research have three main reasons. First, some people defend or advance positions and knowledge that originate in deeply held ideological, political, or religious beliefs, and fear that social researchers might produce knowledge that contradicts them. Second, powerful interests want to protect or advance their political-financial position, and fear social researchers might yield findings showing that their actions are harmful to the public or some sectors of society. And third, some people in society do not respect the ideals of science to pursue truth/knowledge and instead view scientific research only as cover for advancing private interests (see Box 3.4).

VALUE-FREE AND OBJECTIVE RESEARCH

You have undoubtedly heard about "value-free" research and the importance of being "objective" in research. This is not as simple at it might first appear for several reasons. First, there are different meanings of the terms *value free* and *objective*. Second, different approaches to social science (positivism, interpretative, critical) hold different views on the issue. And last, even researchers who agree that social research should be value free and objective do not believe that it needs to be totally devoid of all values.

There are two basic ways the term *value free* is used: research that is free from any prior assumptions, theoretical stand, or value position, and research that is conducted free of influence from an individual researcher's personal prejudices/beliefs. Likewise, *objective* can mean focusing only on what is external or visible, or it can mean following clear and publicly accepted research procedures and not haphazard, personal ones.

The three approaches to social science that you read about in Chapter 2 hold different positions on the importance of value-free, objective research. Positivism puts a high value on such research. An interpretive approach seriously questions whether it is possible, since human values/beliefs pervade all aspects of human activities, including research. Instead of eliminating values and subjective dimension, it suggests a relativist stance—no single value position is bet-

**Box
3.4   What Is Public Sociology?**

Michael Burawoy (2004, 2005) distinguished among four ideal types of social research: policy, professional, critical, and public. The aim of public sociology (or social science, more generally) is to enrich public debate over moral and political issues by infusing such debate with social theory and research. Public sociology frequently overlaps with action-oriented research. Burawoy argued that the place of social research in society centers on how one answers two questions: Knowledge for whom? and Knowledge for what? The first question focuses on the sources of research questions and how results are used. The second question looks at the source of research goals. Are they handed down by some external sponsor or agency or are they concerned with debates over larger societal political-moral issues? Public social science tries to generate a conversation or debate between researchers and public. By constrast, policy social science focuses on finding solutions to specific problems as defined by sponsors or

clients. Both rely on professional social science for theories, bodies of knowledge, and techniques for gathering and analyzing data. Critical social science, as was discussed in Chapter 2, emphasizes demystifying and raising questioning about basic conditions.

The primary audience for professional and critical social science are members of the scientific community, whereas the main audience for public and policy research are nonexperts and practitioners. Both critical and public social science seek to infuse a moral, value dimension into social research and they try to generate debates over moral-political values. Professional and policy social science are less concerned about debates over moral or value issues and may avoid them. Instead, their focus is more on being effective in providing advances to basic knowledge or specific solutions to practical problems. Both public and policy social science are applied research and have a relevance beyond the community of scientific researchers.

---

ter than any other. A critical approach also questions value-free research, but sees it often as a sham.

Value free means free of everyone's values except those of science, and *objective* means following established rules or procedures that some people created, without considering who they represent and how they created the rules. In other words, a critical approach sees all research as containing some values, so those who claim to be value free are just hiding theirs. Those who follow an interpretive and critical approach and reject value-free research do not embrace sloppy and haphazard research, research procedures that follow a particular researcher's whims, or a study that has a foregone conclusion and automatically supports a specific value position. They believe that a researcher should make his

or her own value position explicit, reflect carefully on reasons for doing a study and the procedures used, and communicate in a candid, clear manner exactly how the study was conducted. In this way, other researchers see the role of a researcher's values and judge for themselves whether the values unfairly influenced a study's findings.

Even highly positivist researchers who advocate value-free and objective studies admit a limited place for some personal, moral values. Many hold that a researcher's personal, moral position can enter when it comes to deciding what topic to study and how to disseminate findings. Being value free and objective only refers to actually conducting the study. This means that you can study the issues you believe to be important and after completing a study you can share the results with specific interest groups in addition to making them available to the scientific community.

CONCLUSION

In Chapter 1, we discussed the distinctive contribution of science to society and how social research is a source of knowledge about the social world. The perspectives and techniques of social research can be powerful tools for understanding the world. Nevertheless, with that power to discover comes responsibility—a responsibility to yourself, a responsibility to your sponsors, a responsibility to the community of scientific researchers, and a responsibility to the larger society. These responsibilities can conflict with each other. Ultimately, you personally must decide to conduct research in an ethical manner, to uphold and defend the principles of the social science approach you adopt, and to demand ethical conduct by others. The truthfulness of knowledge produced by social research and its use or misuse depends on individual researchers like you, reflecting on their actions and on the serious role of social research in society. In the next chapter, we examine basic design approaches and issues that appear in both qualitative and quantitative research.

Key Terms

anonymity
confidentiality
crossover design
informed consent
institutional review board (IRB)
plagiarism
principle of voluntary consent
public sociology
research fraud
scientific misconduct
special populations
whistle-blower

Endnotes

1. For a discussion of research fraud, see Broad and Wade (1982), Diener and Crandall (1978), and Weinstein (1979). Hearnshaw (1979) and Wade (1976) discuss the Cyril Burt case, and see Holden (2000) on the social psychologist case. Kusserow (1989) discusses the concept of scientific misconduct.

2. See Blum (1989) and D'Antonio (1989) for details on this case. Also see Goldner (1998) on legal versus scientific views of misconduct. Gibelman (2001) discusses several cases and the changing definition of misconduct.

3. See Lifton (1986) on Nazi experiments, and Williams and Wallace (1989) discuss Japanese experiments. Harris (2002) argues that the Japanese experiments were more horrific, but the United States did not prosecute the Japanese scientists as the Germans were because the U.S. military wanted the results to develop its own biological warfare program.

4. See Jones (1981) and Mitchell (1997) on "Bad Blood."

5. Diener and Crandall (1978:128) discuss examples.

6. A discussion of physical harm to research participants can be found in Kelman (1982), Reynolds (1979, 1982), and Warwick (1982).

7. For a discussion, see Diener and Crandall (1978:21–22) and Kidder and Judd (1986:481–484).

8. See Monaghan (1993a, 1993b, 1993c).

9. Broadhead and Rist (1976) discuss gatekeepers.

10. See "UW Protects Dissertation Sources," *Capital Times* (Madison, Wisconsin), December 19, 1994, p. 4.

11. See Hirschman (1970) on loyalty, exit, or voice.

12. See Edward Fiske, "The Misleading Concept of 'Average' on Reading Test Changes, More Students Fall Below It," *New York Times* (July 12, 1989). Also see Koretz (1988) and Weiss and Gruber (1987).

13. See "State Sought, Got Author's Changes of Lottery Report," *Capital Times* (Madison, Wisconsin), July 28, 1989, p. 21.

14. Andrew Revkin, "Bush Aide Edited Climate Reports," *New York Times* (June 8, 2005). "White House Calls Editing Climate Files Part of Usual Review," *New York Times* (June 9, 2005). Union of Concerned Scientists, "Politics Trumps Science at

U.S. Fish and Wildlife Service" (February 9, 2005)." Specific Examples of the Abuse of Science www.ucsusa.org/global_environment/rsi/page.cf m?pageID=1398, downloaded August 3, 2005. "Summary of National Oceanic & Atmospheric Administration Fisheries Service Scientist Survey" by Union of Concerned Scientists (June 2005). E. Shogren, "Researchers Accuse Bush of Manipulating Science," *Los Angeles Times* (July 9, 2004). Jeffrey McCracker, "Government Bans Release of Auto-Safety Data," *Detroit Free Press* (August 19, 2004). Garddiner Harris, "Lawmaker Says FDA Held Back Drug Data," *New York Times* (September 10, 2004). James Glanz, "Scientists Say Administration Distorts Facts," *New York Times* (February 19, 2004). Dylan O. Krider, "The Politicization of Science in the Bush Administration," *Skeptic* Vol. 11, Number 2 (2004) at www. Skeptic.com. C. Orstein, "Politics Trumps Science in Condom Fact Sheet," *New York Times* (December 27, 2002). "Scientist Says Officials Ignored Advice on Water Levels," *Washington Post* (October 29, 2002).

15. See Adler and Adler (1993).

16. See Neuman (2003, Chapter 16) for a discussion of political issues in social research.

CHAPTER 4

Reviewing the Scholarly Literature and Planning a Study

INTRODUCTION

In the past three chapters, you have learned about the main principles and types of social research, discovered how researchers use theory in a study, and examined the place of ethics in social research. You are now ready to get into the specifics of how to go about designing a study. Recall from Chapter 1 that a researcher usually begins with a general topic, then narrows the topic down into a specific research question, and then makes decisions about the specifics of designing a study that will address the research question.

Where do topics for study come from? They come from many sources: previous studies, television or film, personal experiences, discussions with friends and family, or something you read about in a book, magazine, or newspaper. A topic often begins as something that arouses your curiosity, about which you hold deep commitments or strong feelings, or that you believe is really wrong and want to change. To apply social research, a topic must be about social patterns that operate in aggregates and be empirically measurable or observable. This rules out topics about one unique situation (e.g., why your boy/girlfriend dumped you yesterday, why your friend's little sister hates her school teacher), or one individual case (e.g., your own family), or something one can never observe, even indirectly (e.g., unicorns, ghosts with supernatural powers, etc.). This may rule out some interesting topics, but many tens of thousands remain to be investigated.

How you proceed differs slightly depending on whether you adopt an inductive or a deductive approach. Compared to an inductive researcher, those who choose a deductive approach and gather quantitative data will devote much more time to specifying the research question very precisely and planning many details of a study in advance. It will take you a while to develop the judgment skills for deciding whether it might be better to conduct a more deductive-quantitative or an inductive-qualitative study to address a topic and research question. Three things can help you learn what is the most effective type of study to pursue for a question:

1. Reading studies that others have conducted on a topic
2. Grasping issues that operate in qualitative and quantitative approaches to research
3. Understanding how to use various research techniques as well as their strengths and limitations

This chapter introduces you to the first two of these, whereas many of the remaining chapters of the book discuss the third item in the list.

LITERATURE REVIEW

Reading the "literature," or the collection of studies already published on a topic, serves several very important functions. First, it helps you narrow down a broad topic by showing you how others conducted their studies. The studies by others give you a model of how narrowly focused a research question should be, what kinds of study designs others have used, and how to measure variables or analyze data. Second, it informs you about the "state of knowledge" on a topic. From the studies by others, you can learn the key ideas, terms, and issues that surround a topic. You should consider replicating, testing, or extending what others already found. Third, the literature often stimulates your creativity and curiosity. Last, even if you never get to conduct or publish your own research study, a published study offers you an example of what the final report on a study looks like, its major parts, its form, and its style of writing. Another reason is more practical. Just as attentively reading a lot of top-quality writing can help you improve your own writing skills, reading many reports of good-quality social research enables you to grasp better the elements that go into conducting a research study.

It is best to be organized and not haphazard as you locate and read the scholarly or academic literature on a topic and associated research questions. Also, it is wise to plan to prepare a written literature review. There are many specialized types of reviews, but in general a literature review is a carefully crafted summary of the recent studies conducted on a topic that includes key findings and methods researchers used while making sure to document the sources. For most purposes, you must first locate the relevant studies; next, read thoroughly to discover the major findings, central issues, and methods of the studies, and take conscientious notes on what you read. While the reading is still fresh in your mind and with the notes in front of you, you need to organize what you have learned and write clearly about the studies in a way that builds a context around a specific research question that is of interest to you.

A literature review is based on the assumption that knowledge accumulates and that people learn from and build on what others have done. Scientific research is a collective effort of many researchers who share their results with one another and who pursue knowledge as a community. Although some studies may be especially important and individual researchers may become famous, a specific research project is just a tiny part of the overall process of creating knowledge. Today's studies build on those of yesterday. Researchers read studies to compare, replicate, or criticize them for weaknesses.

Reviews vary in scope and depth. Different kinds of reviews are stronger at fulfilling one or another of four goals (see Box 4.1). It may take a researcher over a year to complete an extensive professional summary review of all the literature on a broad question. The same researcher might complete a highly focused review in a very specialized area in a few weeks. When beginning a review, a researcher decides on a topic, how much depth to go into, and the kind of review to conduct.

Where to Find Research Literature

Researchers present reports of their research projects in several written forms: periodicals,

---

> **Box 4.1 Goals of a Literature Review**
>
> 1. *To demonstrate a familiarity with a body of knowledge and establish credibility.* A review tells a reader that the researcher knows the research in an area and knows the major issues. A good review increases a reader's confidence in the researcher's professional competence, ability, and background.
>
> 2. *To show the path of prior research and how a current project is linked to it.* A review outlines the direction of research on a question and shows the development of knowledge. A good review places a research project in a context and demonstrates its relevance by making connections to a body of knowledge.
>
> 3. *To integrate and summarize what is known in an area.* A review pulls together and synthesizes different results. A good review points out areas where prior studies agree, where they disagree, and where major questions remain. It collects what is known up to a point in time and indicates the direction for future research.
>
> 4. *To learn from others and stimulate new ideas.* A review tells what others have found so that a researcher can benefit from the efforts of others. A good review identifies blind alleys and suggests hypotheses for replication. It divulges procedures, techniques, and research designs worth copying so that a researcher can better focus hypotheses and gain new insights.

---

books, dissertations, government documents, or policy reports. They also present them as papers at the meetings of professional societies, but for the most part, you can find them only in a college or university library. This section briefly discusses each type and gives you a simple road map on how to access them.

Periodicals.   You can find the results of social research in newspapers, in popular magazines, on television or radio broadcasts, and in Internet news summaries, but these are not the full, complete reports of research required to prepare a literature review. They are selected, condensed summaries prepared by journalists for a general audience, and they lack many essential details needed for a serious evaluation of the study. Textbooks and encyclopedias also present condensed summaries as introductions to readers who are new to a topic, but, again, these are inadequate for preparing a literature review because many essential details about the study are absent.

It is easy for someone preparing a first literature review to be confused about the many types of periodicals. With skill, you will be able to distinguish among (1) mass market newspapers and magazines written for the general public, (2) popularized social science magazines, (3) opinion magazines in which intellectuals debate and express their views, and (4) scholarly academic journals in which researchers present the findings of studies or provide other communication to the scientific community. Peer-reviewed empirical research findings appear in a complete form only in the last type of publication, although articles in the other types occasionally talk about findings published elsewhere.

Mass market publications (e.g., *McCleans, Time, Newsweek, Economist, The Nation, American Spectator,* and *Atlantic Monthly*) are sold at newsstands and designed to provide the general public with news, opinion, and entertainment. A researcher might occasionally use them as a source on current events, but they do not provide full reports of research studies in the form needed to prepare a literature review.

Popularized social science magazines and professional publications (e.g., *Society* and *Psychology Today*) are sometimes peer reviewed. Their purpose is to provide the interested, educated lay public a simplified version of findings or a commentary, but not to be an outlet for original research findings. At best, popularized social science magazines can supplement to other sources in a literature review.

It is harder to recognize serious opinion magazines (e.g., *American Prospect, Commentary, Dissent,* and *Public Interest*). Larger bookstores in major cities sell them. Leading scholars often write articles for opinion magazines about topics on which they may also conduct empirical research (e.g., welfare reform, prison expansion, voter turnout). They differ in purpose, look, and scope from scholarly journals of social science research findings. The publications are an arena where intellectuals debate current issues, not where researchers present findings of their studies to the broader scientific community.

Scholarly Journals.   The primary type of periodical to use for a literature review is the scholarly journal filled with peer-reviewed reports of research (e.g., *American Sociological Review, Social Problems, American Journal of Sociology, Criminology,* and *Social Science Quarterly*). One rarely finds them outside of college and university libraries. Recall from Chapter 1 that researchers disseminate findings of new studies in scholarly journals.

Some scholarly journals are specialized. Instead of reports of research studies, they have only book reviews that provide commentary and evaluations on a book (e.g., *Contemporary Sociology*), or they contain only literature review essays (e.g., *Annual Review of Sociology, Annual Review of Psychology,* and *Annual Review of Anthropology*) in which researchers give a "state of the field" essay for others. Publications that specialize in literature reviews can be helpful if an article was recently published on a specific topic of interest. Many other scholarly journals have a mix of articles that are literature reviews, books reviews, reports on research studies, and theoretical essays.

No simple solution or "seal of approval" distinguishes scholarly journals, the kind of publications on which to build a serious literature review from other periodicals, or instantly distinguishes the report on a research study from other types of articles. One needs to develop judgment or ask experienced researchers or professional librarians. Nonetheless, distinguishing among types of publications is essential to build on a body of research. One of the best ways to learn to distinguish among types of publications is to read many articles in scholarly journals.

The number of journals varies by field. Psychology has over 400 journals, whereas sociology has about 250 scholarly journals, political science and communication have slightly fewer than sociology, anthropology-archaeology and social work have about 100, urban studies and women studies have about 50, and there are about a dozen journals in criminology. Each publishes from a few dozen to over 100 articles a year.

Many, but not all, scholarly journals may be viewed via the Internet. Usually, this is limited to selected years and to libraries that paid special subscription fees. A few Internet services provide full, exact copies of scholarly journal articles over the Internet. For example, JSTOR provides exact copies, but only for a small number of scholarly journals and only for past years. Other Internet services, such as EBSCO HOST, offer a full-text version of recent articles for a limited number of scholarly journals, but they are not in the same format as a print version of an article. This can make it impossible to find a specific page number or see an exact copy of a chart. It is best to visit the library and see what a full-print version of the scholarly article looks like. An added benefit is that it makes it easy for you to browse the Table of Contents of the journals. Browsing can be very useful for generating new ideas for research topics, seeing an established topic in creative ways, or learning how to expand an idea into new areas. Only a tiny handful of new Internet-only scholarly journals, called *e-journals,* present peer-reviewed research studies (e.g., *Sociological Research Online, Current Research in Social Psychology,* and *Journal of World Systems Research*). Eventually, the Internet format may replace print versions. But for now, 99 percent of scholarly journals are available in print form and about one-third of these are also available in a full-text version over the Internet

and only then if a library pays for a special on-line subscription service.

Once you locate a scholarly journal that reports on social science research studies, you need to make sure that a particular article presents the results of a study, since the journal may have other types of articles. It is easier to identify quantitative studies because they usually have a methods or data section and charts, statistical formulas, and tables of numbers. Qualitative research articles are more difficult to identify, and many students confuse them with theoretical essays, literature review articles, idea-discussion essays, policy recommendations, book reviews, and legal case analyses. To distinguish among these types requires a good grasp of the varieties of research as well as experience in reading many articles.

Your college library has a section for scholarly journals and magazines, or, in some cases, they may be mixed with books. Look at a map of library facilities or ask a librarian to find this section. The most recent issues, which look like thin paperbacks or thick magazines, are often physically separate in a "current periodicals" section. This is done to store them temporarily and make them available until the library receives all the issues of a volume. Most often, libraries bind all issues of a volume together as a book before adding them to their permanent collections.

Scholarly journals from many different fields are placed together with popular magazines. All are periodicals, or *serials* in the jargon of librarians. Thus, you will find popular magazines (e.g., *Time, Road and Track, Cosmopolitan,* and *Atlantic Monthly*) next to journals for astronomy, chemistry, mathematics, literature, and philosophy as well as sociology, psychology, social work, and education. Some fields have more scholarly journals than others. The "pure" academic fields usually have more than the "applied" or practical fields such as marketing or social work. The journals are listed by title in a card catalog or a computerized catalog system. Libraries can provide you with a list of the periodicals to which they subscribe.

Scholarly journals are published as rarely as once a year or as frequently as weekly. Most appear four to six times a year. For example, *Sociological Quarterly* appears four times a year. To assist in locating articles, librarians and scholars have developed a system for tracking scholarly journals and the articles in them. Each issue is assigned a date, volume number, and issue number. This information makes it easier to locate an article. Such information—along with details such as author, title, and page number—is called an article's *citation* and is used in bibliographies. When a journal is first published, it begins with volume 1, number 1, and continues increasing the numbers thereafter. Although most journals follow a similar system, there are enough exceptions that you have to pay close attention to citation information. For most journals, each volume is one year. If you see a journal issue with volume 52, for example, it probably means that the journal has been in existence for 52 years. Most, but not all, journals begin their publishing cycle in January.

Most journals number pages by volume, not by issue. The first issue of a volume usually begins with page 1, and page numbering continues throughout the entire volume. For example, the first page of volume 52, issue 4, may be page 547. Most journals have an index for each volume and a table of contents for each issue that lists the title, the author's or authors' names, and the page on which the article begins. Issues contain as few as 1 or 2 articles or as many as 50. Most have 8 to 18 articles, which may be 5 to 50 pages long. The articles often have *abstracts*, short summaries on the first page of the article or grouped together at the beginning of the issue.

Many libraries do not retain physical, paper copies of older journals. To save space and costs, they retain only microfilm versions. There are hundreds of scholarly journals in most academic fields, with each costing $50 to $2,500 per year. Only the large research libraries subscribe to all of them. You may have to borrow a journal or photocopy of an article from a distant library through an *interlibrary loan service,* a system by which libraries lend books or materials to other libraries. Few libraries allow people to check out recent issues of scholarly journals. You should plan to use these in the library. Some, not all, scholarly journals are available via the Internet.

Once you find the periodicals section, wander down the aisles and skim what is on the shelves. You will see volumes containing many research reports. Each title of a scholarly journal has a call number like that of a regular library book. Libraries often arrange them alphabetically by title. Because journals change titles, it may create confusion if the journal is shelved under its original title.

Citation Formats.   An article's citation is the key to locating it. Suppose you want to read the study by Weitzer and Tuch (2005) on perceptions of police misconduct discussed in Chapter 2. Its citation is as follows:

> Weitzer, Ronald, and Steven Tuch. 2005. "Racially Biased Policing: Determinants of Citizen Perceptions." *Social Forces* 83:1009–1030.

This tells you that you can find the article in an issue of *Social Forces* published in 2005. The citation does not provide the issue or month, but it gives the volume number, 83, and the page numbers, 1009 to 1030.

There are many ways to cite the literature. Formats for citing literature in the text itself vary, with the internal citation format of using an author's last name and date of publication in parentheses being very popular. The full citation appears in a separate bibliography or reference section. There are many styles for full citations of journal articles, with books and other types of works each having a separate style. When citing articles, it is best to check with an instructor, journal, or other outlet for the desired format. Almost all include the names of authors, article title, journal name, and volume and page numbers. Beyond these basic elements, there is great variety. Some include the authors' first names, others use initials only. Some include all authors, others give only the first one. Some include information on the issue or month of publication, others do not (see Figure 4.1).

Citation formats can get complex. Two major reference tools on the topic in social science are *Chicago Manual of Style,* which has nearly 80 pages on bibliographies and reference formats, and *American Psychological Association Publication Manual,* which devotes about 60 pages to the topic. In sociology, the *American Sociological Review* style, with 2 pages of style instructions, is widely followed.

Books.   Books communicate many types of information, provoke thought, and entertain. There are many types of books: picture books, textbooks, short story books, novels, popular fiction or nonfiction, religious books, children's books, and others. Our concern here is with those books containing reports of original research or collections of research articles. Libraries shelve these books and assign call numbers to them, as they do with other types of books. You can find citation information on them (e.g., title, author, publisher) in the library's catalog system.

It is not easy to distinguish a book that reports on research from other books. You are more likely to find such books in a college or university library. Some publishers, such as university presses, specialize in publishing them. Nevertheless, there is no guaranteed method for identifying one without reading it.

Some types of social research are more likely to appear in book form than others. For example, studies by anthropologists and historians are more likely to appear in book-length reports than are those of economists or psychologists. Yet, some anthropological and historical studies are articles, and some economic and psychological studies appear as books. In education, social work, sociology, and political science, the results of long, complex studies may appear both in two or three articles and in book form. Studies that involve detailed clinical or ethnographic descriptions and complex theoretical or philosophical discussions usually appear as books. Finally, an author who wants to communicate to scholarly peers and to the educated public may write a book that bridges the scholarly, academic style and a popular nonfiction style.

Locating original research articles in books can be difficult because there is no single source listing them. Three types of books contain collections of articles or research reports. The first is designed for teaching purposes. Such books, called *readers,* may include original research reports. Usually, articles on a topic from scholarly journals are gathered and edited to be easier for nonspecialists to read and understand.

The second type of collection is designed for scholars and may gather journal articles or may contain original research or theoretical essays on a specific topic. Some collections contain articles from journals that are difficult to locate. They may include original research reports organized around a specialized topic. The table of contents lists the titles and authors. Libraries shelve these collections with other books, and some library catalog systems include them.

Citations or references to books are shorter than article citations. They include the author's name, book title, year and place of publication, and publisher's name.

Dissertations.   All graduate students who receive the Ph.D. degree are required to complete a work of original research, which they write up as a dissertation thesis. The dissertation is bound and shelved in the library of the university that granted the Ph.D. About half of all dissertations are eventually published as books or articles. Because dissertations report on original research, they can be valuable sources of information. Some students who receive the master's degree conduct original research and write a master's thesis, but fewer master's theses involve serious research, and they are much more difficult to locate than unpublished dissertations.

Specialized indexes list dissertations completed by students at accredited universities. For

FIGURE 4.1 Different Reference Citations for a Journal Article

The oldest journal of sociology in the United States, *American Journal of Sociology,* reports on a study of virginity pledges by Peter Bearman and Hannah Bückner. It appeared on pages 859 to 913 of the January 2001 issue (number 4) of the journal, which begins counting issues in March. It was in volume 106, or the journal's 106th year. Here are ways to cite the article. Two very popular styles are those of *American Sociological Review (ASR)* and *American Psychological Association (APA).*

ASR Style

Bearman, Peter and Hannah Bückner. 2001. "Promising the Future: Virginity Pledges and First Intercourse."
   American Journal of Sociology 106:859–912.

APA Style

Bearman, P., and Bückner, H. (2001). Promising the future: Virginity pledges and first intercourse. *American
   Journal of Sociology 106,* 859–912.

Other Styles

Bearman, P., and H. Bückner. "Promising the Future: Virginity Pledges and First Intercourse," *American Journal
   of Sociology* 106 (2001), 859–912.
Bearman, Peter and Hannah Bückner, 2001.
   "Promising the future: Virginity pledges and first Intercourse." *Am. J. of Sociol.* 106:859– 912.
Bearman, P. and Bückner, H. (2001). "Promising the Future: Virginity Pledges and First Intercourse." *American Journal of Sociology* 106 (January): 859–912.
Bearman, Peter and Hannah Bückner. 2001.
   "Promising the future: Virginity pledges and first Intercourse." *American Journal of Sociology* 106
   (4):859–912.
Bearman, P. and H. Bückner. (2001). "Promising the future: Virginity pledges and first intercourse." *American
   Journal of Sociology* 106, 859–912.
Peter Bearman and Hannah Bückner, "Promising the Future: Virginity Pledges and First Intercourse," *American
   Journal of Sociology* 106, no. 4 (2001): 859–912.

example, *Dissertation Abstracts International* lists dissertations with their authors, titles, and universities. This index is organized by topic and contains an abstract of each dissertation. You can borrow most dissertations via interlibrary loan from the degree-granting university if the university permits this.

Government Documents.   The federal government of the United States, the governments of other nations, state- or provincial-level governments, the United Nations, and other international agencies such as the World Bank, all sponsor studies and publish reports of the re-

search. Many college and university libraries have these documents in their holdings, usually in a special "government documents" section. These reports are rarely found in the catalog system. You must use specialized lists of publications and indexes, usually with the help of a librarian, to locate these reports. Most college and university libraries hold only the most frequently requested documents and reports.

Policy Reports and Presented Papers.   A researcher conducting a thorough review of the literature will examine these two sources, which are difficult for all but the trained specialist to obtain. Research institutes and policy centers (e.g., Brookings Institute, Institute for Research on Poverty, Rand Corporation, etc.) publish papers and reports. Some major research libraries purchase these and shelve them with books. The only way to be sure of what has been published is to write directly to the institute or center and request a list of reports.

Each year, the professional associations in academic fields (e.g., sociology, political science, psychology) hold annual meetings. Thousands of researchers assemble to give, listen to, or discuss oral reports of recent research. Most of these oral reports are available as written papers to those attending the meeting. People who do not attend the meetings but who are members of the association receive a program of the meeting, listing each paper to be presented with its title, author, and author's place of employment. They can write directly to the author and request a copy of the paper. Many, but not all, of the papers are later published as articles. The papers may be listed in indexes or abstract services (to be discussed).

How to Conduct a Systematic Literature Review

Define and Refine a Topic.   Just as a researcher must plan and clearly define a topic and research question when beginning a research project, you need to begin a literature review with a clearly defined, well-focused research question and a plan. A good review topic should be as focused as a research question. For example, "divorce" or "crime" is much too broad. A more appropriate review topic might be "the stability of families with stepchildren" or "economic inequality and crime rates across nations." If you conduct a context review for a research project, it should be slightly broader than the specific research question being tested. Often, a researcher will not finalize a specific research question for a study until he or she has reviewed the literature. The review helps bring greater focus to the research question.

Design a Search.   After choosing a focused research question for the review, the next step is to plan a search strategy. The reviewer needs to decide on the type of review, its extensiveness, and the types of materials to include. The key is to be careful, systematic, and organized. Set parameters on your search: how much time you will devote to it, how far back in time you will look, the minimum number of research reports you will examine, how many libraries you will visit, and so forth.

Also, decide how to record the bibliographic citation for each reference you find and how to take notes (e.g., in a notebook, on 3 × 5 cards, in a computer file). Develop a schedule, because several visits are usually necessary. You should begin a file folder or computer file in which you can place possible sources and ideas for new sources. As the review proceeds, it should become more focused.

Locate Research Reports.   Locating research reports depends on the type of report or "outlet" of research being searched. As a general rule, use multiple search strategies in order to counteract the limitations of a single search method.

Articles in Scholarly Journals.   As discussed earlier, most social research is published in scholarly journals. There are dozens of journals, many going back decades, each containing many articles. The task of searching for articles can be formidable. Luckily, specialized publications make the task easier.

You may have used an index for general publications, such as *Reader's Guide to Periodical Literature.* Many academic fields have "abstracts" or "indexes" for the scholarly literature (e.g., *Psychological Abstracts, Social Sciences Index, Sociological Abstracts,* and *Gerontological Abstracts*). For education-related topics, the Educational Resources Information Center (ERIC) system is especially valuable. There are over 100 such publications. You can usually find them in the reference section of a library. Many abstracts or index services as well as ERIC are available via computer access, which speeds the search process.

Abstracts or indexes are published on a regular basis (monthly, six times a year, etc.) and allow a reader to look up articles by author name or subject. The journals covered by the abstract or index are listed in it, often in the front. An index, such as the *Social Sciences Index,* lists only the citation, whereas an abstract, such as *Sociological Abstracts,* lists the citation and has a copy of the article's abstract. Abstracts do not give you all the findings and details of a research project. Researchers use abstracts to screen articles for relevance, then locate the more relevant articles. Abstracts may also include papers presented at professional meetings.

It may sound as if all you have to do is to go find the index in the reference section of the library or on the Internet and look up a topic. Unfortunately, things are more complicated than that. In order to cover the studies across many years, you may have to look through many issues of the abstracts or indexes. Also, the subjects or topics listed are broad. The specific research question that interests you may fit into several subject areas. You should check each one. For example, for the topic of illegal drugs in high schools, you might look up these subjects: drug addiction, drug abuse, substance abuse, drug laws, illegal drugs, high schools, and secondary schools. Many of the articles under a subject area will not be relevant for your literature review. Also, there is a 3- to 12-month time lag between the publication of an article and its appearance in the abstracts or indexes. Unless you are at a major research library, the most useful article may not be available in your library. You can obtain it only by using an interlibrary loan service, or it may be in a foreign language that you do not read.

The computerized literature search works on the same principle as an abstract or an index. Researchers organize computerized searches in several ways—by author, by article title, by subject, or by keyword. A *keyword* is an important term for a topic that is likely to be found in a title. You will want to use six to eight keywords in most computer-based searches and consider several synonyms. The computer's searching method can vary and most only look for a keyword in a title or abstract. If you choose too few words or very narrow terms, you will miss a lot of relevant articles. If you choose too many words or very broad terms, you will get a huge number of irrelevant articles. The best way to learn the appropriate breadth and number of keywords is by trial and error.

In a study I conducted on how college students define *sexual harassment* (Neuman, 1992), I used the following keywords: *sexual harassment, sexual assault, harassment, gender equity, gender fairness,* and *sex discrimination.* I later discovered a few important studies that lacked any of these keywords in their titles. I also tried the keywords *college student* and *rape,* but got huge numbers of unrelated articles that I could not even skim.

There are numerous computer-assisted search databases or systems. A person with a computer and an Internet hook-up can search some article index collections, the catalogs of libraries, and other information sources around the globe if they are available on the Internet.

All computerized searching methods share a similar logic, but each has its own method of operation to learn. In my study, I looked for sources in the previous seven years and used five computerized databases of scholarly literature: *Social Science Index, CARL (Colorado Area Research Library), Sociofile, Social Science Citation Index,* and *PsychLit.*

Often, the same articles will appear in multiple scholarly literature databases, but each database may identify a few new articles not found in the others. For example, I discovered several excellent sources not listed in any of the computerized databases that had been published in earlier years by studying the bibliographies of the relevant articles.

The process in my study was fairly typical. Based on my keyword search, I quickly skimmed or scanned the titles or abstracts of over 200 sources. From these, I selected about 80 articles, reports, and books to read. I found about 49 of the 80 sources valuable, and they appear in the bibliography of the published article.

Scholarly Books.   Finding scholarly books on a subject can be difficult. The subject topics of library catalog systems are usually incomplete and too broad to be useful. Moreover, they list only books that are in a particular library system, although you may be able to search other libraries for interlibrary loan books. Libraries organize books by call numbers based on subject matter. Again, the subject matter classifications may not reflect the subjects of interest to you or all the subjects discussed in a book. Once you learn the system for your library, you will find that most books on a topic will share the main parts of the call number. In addition, librarians can help you locate books from other libraries. For example, the *Library of Congress National Union Catalog* lists all books in the U.S. Library of Congress. Librarians have access to sources that list books at other libraries, or you can use the Internet. There is no sure-fire way to locate relevant books. Use multiple search methods, including a look at journals that have book reviews and the bibliographies of articles.

Taking Notes

As you gather the relevant research literature, it is easy to feel overwhelmed by the quantity of information, so you need a system for taking notes. The old-fashioned approach is to write notes onto index cards. You then shift and sort the note cards, place them in piles, and so forth as you look for connections among them or develop an outline for a report or paper. This method still works. Today, however, most people use word-processing software and gather photocopies or printed versions of many articles.

As you discover sources, it is a good idea to create two kinds of files for your note cards or computer documents: a *Source File* and a *Content File*. Record *all* the bibliographic information for each source in the Source File, even

though you may not use some and later erase them. Do not forget anything in a complete bibliographic citation, such as a page number or the name of the second author; you will regret it later. It is far easier to erase a source you do not use than to try to locate bibliographic information later for a source you discover that you need or from which you forgot one detail.

I recommend creating two kinds of Source Files, or divide a master file into two parts: *Have File* and *Potential File.* The Have File is for sources that you have found and for which you have already taken content notes. The Potential File is for leads and possible new sources that you have yet to track down or read. You can add to the Potential File anytime you come across a new source or in the bibliography of something you read. Toward the end of writing a report, the Potential File will disappear while the Have File will become your bibliography.

Your note cards or computer documents go into the Content File. This file contains substantive information of interest from a source, usually its major findings, details of methodology, definitions of concepts, or interesting quotes. If you directly quote from a source or want to take some specific information from a source, you need to record the specific page number(s) on which the quote appears. Link the files by putting key source information, such as author and date, on each content file.

What to Record.   You will find it much easier to take all notes on the same type and size of paper or card, rather than having some notes on sheets of papers, others on cards, and so on. Researchers have to decide what to record about an article, book, or other source. It is better to err in the direction of recording too much rather than too little. In general, record the hypotheses tested, how major concepts were measured, the main findings, the basic design of the research, the group or sample used, and ideas for future study (see Box 4.2). It is wise to examine the report's bibliography and note sources that you can add to your search.

| Box 4.2 | How to Read Journal Articles |

1. Read with a clear purpose or goal in mind. Are you reading for basic knowledge or to apply it to a specific question?

2. Skim the article before reading it all. What can you learn from the title, abstract, summary and conclusions, and headings? What are the topic, major findings, method, and main conclusion?

3. Consider your own orientation. What is your bias toward the topic, the method, the publication source, and so on, that may color your reading?

4. Marshal external knowledge. What do you already know about the topic and the methods used? How credible is the publication source?

5. Evaluate as you read the article. What errors are present? Do findings follow the data? Is the article consistent with assumptions of the approach it takes?

6. Summarize information as an abstract with the topic, the methods used, and the findings. Assess the factual accuracy of findings and cite questions about the article.

Source: Adapted from Katzer, Cook, and Crouch (1991: 199–207).

Photocopying all relevant articles or reports will save you time recording notes and will ensure that you will have an entire report. Also, you can make notes on the photocopy. There are several warnings about this practice. First, photocopying can be expensive for a large literature search. Second, be aware of and obey copyright laws. U.S. copyright laws permit photocopying for personal research use. Third, remember to record or photocopy the entire article, including all citation information. Fourth, organizing entire articles can be cumbersome, especially if several different parts of a single article are being used. Finally, unless you highlight carefully or take good notes, you may have to reread the entire article later.

Organize Notes.   After gathering a large number of references and notes, you need an organizing scheme. One approach is to group studies or specific findings by skimming notes and creating a mental map of how they fit together. Try several organizing schemes before settling on a final one. Organizing is a skill that improves with practice. For example, place notes into piles representing common themes, or draw charts comparing what different reports state about the same question, noting agreements and disagreements.

In the process of organizing notes, you will find that some references and notes do not fit and should be discarded as irrelevant. Also, you may discover gaps or areas and topics that are relevant but that you did not examine. This necessitates return visits to the library.

There are many organizing schemes. The best one depends on the purpose of the review. Usually, it is best to organize reports around a specific research question or around core common findings of a field and the main hypotheses tested.

Writing the Review

A literature review requires planning and good, clear writing, which requires a lot of rewriting. This step is often merged with organizing notes. All the rules of good writing (e.g., clear organizational structure, an introduction and conclusion, transitions between sections, etc.) apply to writing a literature review. Keep your purposes in mind when you write, and communicate clearly and effectively.

To prepare a good review, read articles and other literature critically. Recall that skepticism is a norm of science. It means that you should not accept what is written simply on the basis of the authority of its having been published. Question what you read, and evaluate it. The first hurdle to overcome is thinking something must be perfect just because it has been published.

Critically reading research reports requires skills that take time and practice to develop. Despite a peer-review procedure and high rejection rates, errors and sloppy logic slip in. Read carefully to see whether the introduction and title really fit with the rest of the article. Sometimes, titles, abstracts, or the introduction are misleading. They may not fully explain the research project's method and results. An article should be logically tight, and all the parts should fit together. Strong logical links should exist between parts of the argument. Weak articles make leaps in logic or omit transitional steps. Likewise, articles do not always make their theory or approach to research explicit. Be prepared to read the article more than once. (See Figure 4.2 on taking notes on an article.)

What a Good Review Looks Like

An author should communicate a review's purpose to the reader by its organization. The *wrong* way to write a review is to list a series of research reports with a summary of the findings of each. This fails to communicate a sense of purpose. It reads as a set of notes strung together. Perhaps the reviewer got sloppy and skipped over the important organizing step in writing the review. The *right* way to write a review is to organize common findings or arguments together. A well-accepted approach is to address the most important ideas first, to logically link statements or findings, and to note discrepancies or weaknesses in the research (see Box 4.3 for an example).

USING THE INTERNET FOR SOCIAL RESEARCH

The Internet (see Box 4.4) has revolutionized how social researchers work. A mere decade ago, it was rarely used; today, most social researchers use the Internet regularly to help them review the literature, to communicate with other researchers, and to search for other information

sources. The Internet continues to expand and change at an explosive rate.

The Internet has been a mixed blessing for social research, but it has not proved to be the panacea that some people first thought it might be. It provides new and important ways to find information, but it remains one tool among others. It can quickly make some specific pieces of information accessible. For example, from my home computer, I was able to go to the U.S. Federal Bureau of Prisons and in less than three minutes locate a table showing me that in 1980, 139 people per 100,000 were incarcerated in the United States, whereas in 2004 (the most recent data available), it was 486 per 100,000. The Internet is best thought of as a supplement rather than as a replacement for traditional library research. There are "up" and "down" sides to using the Internet for social research:

The Up Side

1. The Internet is easy, fast, and cheap. It is widely accessible and can be used from many locations. This near-free resource allows people to find source material from almost anywhere—local public libraries, homes, labs or classrooms, or anywhere a computer is connected to the Internet system. Also, the Internet does not close; it operates 24 hours a day, seven days a week. With minimal training, most people can quickly perform searches and get information on their computer screens that would have required them to take a major trip to large research libraries a few years ago. Searching a vast quantity of information electronically has always been easier and faster than a manual search, and the Internet greatly expands the amount and variety of source material. More and more information (e.g., *Statistical Abstract of the United States*) is available on the Internet. In addition, once the information is located, a researcher can often store it electronically or print it at a local site.

2. The Internet has "links" that provide additional ways to find and connect to many other

FIGURE 4.2   Example of Notes on an Article

FULL CITATION ON BIBLIOGRAPHY (SOURCE FILE)

Bearman, Peter, and Hannah Bückner. 2001. "Promising the Future: Virginity Pledges and First Intercourse." *American Journal of Sociology* 106:859–912. (January, issue no. 4).

NOTE CARD (CONTENT FILE)

Bearman and Bückner 2001   **Topics:**   Teen pregnancy & sexuality, pledges/promises, virginity, first sexual intercourse, S. Baptists, identity movement

Since 1993, the Southern Baptist Church sponsored a movement among teens whereby the teens make a public pledge to remain virgins until marriage. Over 2.5 million teens have made the pledge. This study examines whether the pledge affected the timing of sexual intercourse and whether pledging teens differ from nonpledging teens. Critics of the movement are uncomfortable with it because pledge supporters often reject sex education, hold an overly romanticized view of marriage, and adhere to traditional gender roles.

Hypothesis

Adolescents will engage in behavior that adults enjoy but that is forbidden to them based on the amount of social controls that constrain opportunities to engage in forbidden behavior. Teens in nontraditional families with greater freedom and less supervision are more likely to engage in forbidden behavior (sex). Teens in traditional families and who are closer to their parents will delay sexual activity. Teens closely tied to "identity movements" outside the family will modify behavior based on norms the movements teach.

Method

Data are from a national health survey of U.S. teens in grades 7–12 who were in public or private schools in 1994–1995. A total of 90,000 students in 141 schools completed questionnaires. A second questionnaire was completed by 20,000 of the 90,000 students. The questionnaire asked about a pledge, importance of religion, and sexual activity.

Findings

The study found a substantial delay in the timing of first intercourse among pledgers. Yet, the effect of pledging varies by the age of the teen. In addition, pledging only works in some social contexts (i.e., where it is at least partially a social norm). Pledgers tend to be more religious, less developed physically, and from more traditional social and family backgrounds.

Box 4.3   Examples of Bad and Good Reviews

Example of Bad Review

Sexual harassment has many consequences. Adams, Kottke, and Padgitt (1983) found that some women students said they avoided taking a class or working with certain professors because of the risk of harassment. They also found that men and women students reacted differently. Their research was a survey of 1,000 men and women graduate and undergraduate students. Benson and Thomson's study in *Social Problems* (1982) lists many problems created by sexual harassment. In their excellent book, *The Lecherous Professor,* Dziech and Weiner (1990) give a long list of difficulties that victims have suffered.

Researchers study the topic in different ways. Hunter and McClelland (1991) conducted a study of undergraduates at a small liberal arts college. They had a sample of 300 students and students were given multiple vignettes that varied by the reaction of the victim and the situation. Jaschik and Fretz (1991) showed 90 women students at a mideastern university a videotape with a classic example of sexual harassment by a teaching assistant. Before it was labeled as *sexual harassment,* few women called it that. When asked whether it was sexual harassment, 98 percent agreed. Weber-Burdin and Rossi (1982) replicated a previous study on sexual harassment, only they used students at the University of Massachusetts. They had 59 students rate 40 hypothetical situations. Reilley, Carpenter, Dull, and Bartlett (1982) conducted a study of 250 female and 150 male undergraduates at the University of California at Santa Barbara. They also had a sample of 52 faculty. Both samples completed a questionnaire in which respondents were presented vignettes of sexual-harassing situations that they were to rate. Popovich and Colleagues (1986) created a nine-item scale of sexual harassment. They studied 209 undergraduates at a medium-sized university in groups of 15 to 25. They found disagreement and confusion among students.

Example of Better Review

The victims of sexual harassment suffer a range of consequences, from lowered self-esteem and loss of self-confidence to withdrawal from social interaction, changed career goals, and depression (Adams, Kottke, and Padgitt, 1983; Benson and Thomson, 1982; Dziech and Weiner, 1990). For example, Adams, Kottke, and Padgitt (1983) noted that 13 percent of women students said they avoided taking a class or working with certain professors because of the risk of harassment.

Research into campus sexual harassment has taken several approaches. In addition to survey research, many have experimented with vignettes or presented hypothetical scenarios (Hunter and McClelland, 1991; Jaschik and Fretz, 1991; Popovich et al., 1987; Reilley, Carpenter, Dull, and Barlett, 1982; Rossi and Anderson, 1982; Valentine-French and Radtke, 1989; Weber-Burdin and Rossi, 1982). Victim verbal responses and situational factors appear to affect whether observers label a behavior as harassment. There is confusion over the application of a sexual harassment label for inappropriate behavior. For example, Jaschik and Fretz (1991) found that only 3 percent of the women students shown a videotape with a classic example of sexual harassment by a teaching assistant initially labeled it as *sexual harassment.* Instead, they called it "sexist," "rude," "unprofessional," or "demeaning." When asked whether it was sexual harassment, 98 percent agreed. Roscoe and colleagues (1987) reported similar labeling difficulties.

---

sources of information. Many websites, home pages, and other Internet resource pages have "hot links" that can call up information from related sites or sources simply by clicking on the link indicator (usually a button or a highlighted word or phrase). This connects people to more information and provides "instant" access to cross-referenced material. Links make embed-

The Internet

The Internet is not a single thing in one place. Rather, the Internet is a system or interconnected web of computers around the world. It is changing very rapidly. I cannot describe everything on the Internet; many large books attempt to do that. Plus, even if I tried, it would be out of date in six months. The Internet is changing, in a powerful way, how many people communicate and share information.

The Internet provides low-cost (often free), worldwide, fast communication among people with computers or between people with computers and information in the computers of organizations (e.g., universities, government agencies, businesses). There are special hardware and software requirements, but the Internet potentially can transmit electronic versions of text material, up to entire books, as well as photos, music, video, and other information.

To get onto the Internet, a person needs an account in a computer that is connected to the Internet. Most college mainframe computers are connected, many business or government computers are connected, and individuals with modems can purchase a connection from an Internet service provider that provides access over telephone lines, special DSL lines, or cable television lines. In addition to a microcomputer, the person needs only a little knowledge about using computers.

ding one source within a network of related sources easy.

3. The Internet speeds the flow of information around the globe and has a "democratizing" effect. It provides rapid transmission of information (e.g., text, news, data, and photos) across long distances and international borders. Instead of waiting a week for a report or having to send off for a foreign publication and wait for a month, the information is often available in seconds at no cost. There are virtually no restrictions on who can put material on the Internet or what appears on it, so many people who had dif-

ficulty publishing or disseminating their materials can now do so with ease.

4. The Internet is the provider of a very wide range of information sources, some in formats that are more dynamic and interesting. It can send and be a resource for more than straight black and white text, as in traditional academic journals and sources. It transmits information in the form of bright colors, graphics, "action" images, audio (e.g., music, voices, sounds), photos, and video clips. Authors and other creators of information can be creative in their presentations.

The Down Side

1. There is no quality control over what gets on the Internet. Unlike standard academic publications, there is no peer-review process or any review. Anyone can put almost anything on a website. It may be poor quality, undocumented, highly biased, totally made up, or plain fraudulent. There is a lot of real "trash" out there! Once a person finds material, the real work is to distinguish the "trash" from valid information. One needs to treat a webpage with the same caution that one applies to a paper flyer someone hands out on the street; it could contain the drivel of a "nut" or be really valuable information. A less serious problem is that the "glitz" of bright colors, music, or moving images found in sites can distract unsophisticated users. The "glitz" may attract them more than serious content, and they may confuse glitz for high-caliber information. The Internet is better designed for a quick look and short attention spans rather than the slow, deliberative, careful reading and study of content.

2. Many excellent sources and some of the most important resource materials (research studies and data) for social research are *not* available on the Internet (e.g., *Sociofile*, GSS datafiles, and recent journal articles). Much information is available only through special subscription services that can be expensive.

Contrary to popular belief, the Internet has *not* made all information free and accessible to everyone. Often, what is free is limited, and fuller information is available only to those who pay. In fact, because some libraries redirected funds to buy computers for the Internet and cut the purchases for books and paper copies of documents, the Internet's overall impact may have actually reduced what is available for some users.

3. Finding sources on the Internet can be very difficult and time consuming. It is not easy to locate specific source materials. Also, different "search engines" can produce very different results. It is wise to use multiple search engines (e.g., Yahoo, Excite, and Google), since they work differently. Most search engines simply look for specific words in a short description of the webpage. This description may not reveal the full content of the source, just as a title does not fully tell what a book or article is about. In addition, search engines often come up with tens of thousands of sources, far too many for anyone to examine. The ones at the "top" may be there because they were recently added to the Internet or because their short description had several versions of the search word. The "best" or most relevant source might be buried as the 150th item found in a search. Also, one must often wade through a lot of commercials and advertisements to locate "real" information.

4. Internet sources can be "unstable" and difficult to document. After one conducts a search on the Internet and locates webpages with information, it is important to note the specific "address" (usually it starts http://) where it resides. This address refers to an electronic file sitting in a computer somewhere. If the computer file is moved, it may not be at the same address two months later. Unlike a journal article that will be stored on a shelf or on microfiche in hundreds of libraries for many decades to come and available for anyone to read, webpages can quickly vanish. This means it may not be possible to check someone's web references easily, verify a quote in a document, or go back to orig-

inal materials and read them for ideas or to build on them. Also, it is easy to copy, modify, or distort, then reproduce copies of a source. For example, a person could alter a text passage or a photo image then create a new webpage to disseminate the false information. This raises issues about copyright protection and the authenticity of source material.

There are few rules for locating the best sites on the Internet—ones that have useful and truthful information. Sources that originate at universities, research institutes, or government agencies usually are more trustworthy for research purposes than ones that are individual home pages of unspecified origin or location, or that a commercial organization or a political/social issue advocacy group sponsors. In addition to moving or disappearing, many webpages or sources fail to provide complete information to make citation easy. Better sources provide fuller or more complete information about the author, date, location, and so on.

As you prepare a review of the scholarly literature and more narrowly focus a topic, you should be thinking about how to design a study. The specifics of design can vary somewhat depending on whether your study will primarily employ a quantitative-deductive-positivist approach or a qualitative-inductive-interpretive/critical approach. The two approaches have a great deal in common and mutually complement one another, but there several places where "branches in the path" of designing a study diverge depending on the approach you adopt.

QUALITATIVE AND QUANTITATIVE ORIENTATIONS TOWARD RESEARCH

Qualitative and quantitative research differ in many ways, but they complement each other, as well. All social researchers systematically collect and analyze empirical data and carefully examine the patterns in them to understand and explain social life. One of the differences between the two styles comes from the nature of the data. *Soft data*, in the form of impressions, words, sentences, photos, symbols, and so forth, dictate different research strategies and data collection techniques than *hard data*, in the form of numbers. Another difference is that qualitative and quantitative researchers often hold different assumptions about social life and have different objectives. These differences can make tools used by the other style inappropriate or irrelevant. People who judge qualitative research by standards of quantitative research are often disappointed, and vice versa. It is best to appreciate the strengths each style offers.

To appreciate the strengths of each style, it is important to understand the distinct orientations of researchers. Qualitative researchers often rely on interpretive or critical social science, follow a nonlinear research path, and speak a language of "cases and contexts." They emphasize conducting detailed examinations of cases that arise in the natural flow of social life. They usually try to present authentic interpretations that are sensitive to specific social-historical contexts.

Almost all quantitative researchers rely on a positivist approach to social science. They follow a linear research path, speak a language of "variables and hypotheses," and emphasize precisely measuring variables and testing hypotheses that are linked to general causal explanations.

Researchers who use one style alone do not always communicate well with those using the other, but the languages and orientations of the styles are mutually intelligible. It takes time and effort to understand both styles and to see how they can be complementary.

Linear and Nonlinear Paths

Researchers follow a path when conducting research. The path is a metaphor for the sequence of things to do: what is finished first or where a researcher has been, and what comes next or where he or she is going. The path may be well worn and marked with signposts where many

other researchers have trod. Alternatively, it may be a new path into unknown territory where few others have gone, and without signs marking the direction forward.

In general, quantitative researchers follow a more linear path than do qualitative researchers. A *linear research path* follows a fixed sequence of steps; it is like a staircase leading in one clear direction. It is a way of thinking and a way of looking at issues—the direct, narrow, straight path that is most common in western European and North American culture.

Qualitative research is more nonlinear and cyclical. Rather than moving in a straight line, a *nonlinear research path* makes successive passes through steps, sometimes moving backward and sideways before moving on. It is more of a spiral, moving slowly upward but not directly. With each cycle or repetition, a researcher collects new data and gains new insights.

People who are used to the direct, linear approach may be impatient with a less direct cyclical path. From a strict linear perspective, a cyclical path looks inefficient and sloppy. But the diffuse cyclical approach is not merely disorganized, undefined chaos. It can be highly effective for creating a feeling for the whole, for grasping subtle shades of meaning, for pulling together divergent information, and for switching perspectives. It is not an excuse for doing poor-quality research, and it has its own discipline and rigor. It borrows devices from the humanities (e.g., metaphor, analogy, theme, motif, and irony) and is oriented toward constructing meaning. A cyclical path is suited for tasks such as translating languages, where delicate shades of meaning, subtle connotations, or contextual distinctions can be important.

Preplanned and Emergent Research Questions

Your first step when beginning a research project is to select a topic. There is no formula for this task. Whether you are an experienced researcher or just beginning, the best guide is to conduct research on something that interests you.

All research begins with a topic but a topic is only a starting point that researchers must narrow into a focused research question. Qualitative and quantitative researchers tend to adopt different approaches to turn a topic to a focused research question for a specific study. Qualitative researchers often begin with vague or unclear research questions. The topic emerges slowly during the study. The researchers often combine focusing on a specific question with the process of deciding the details of study design that occurs while they are gathering data. By contrast, quantitative researchers narrow a topic into a focused question as a discrete planning step before they finalize study design. They use it as a step in the process of developing a testable hypothesis (to be discussed later) and to guide the study design before they collect any data.

The qualitative research style is flexible and encourages slowly focusing the topic throughout a study. In contrast to quantitative research, only a small amount of topic narrowing occurs in an early research planning stage, and most of the narrowing occurs after a researcher has begun to collect data.

The qualitative researcher begins data gathering with a general topic and notions of what will be relevant. Focusing and refining continues after he or she has gathered some of the data and started preliminary analysis. Qualitative researchers use early data collection to guide how they adjust and sharpen the research question(s) because they rarely know the most important issues or questions until after they become fully immersed in the data. Developing a focused research question is a part of the data collection process, during which the researcher actively reflects on and develops preliminary interpretations. The qualitative researcher is open to unanticipated data and constantly reevaluates the focus early in a study. He or she is prepared to change the direction of research and follow new lines of evidence.

Typical research questions for qualitative researchers include: How did a certain condition or social situation originate? How is the condition/situation maintained over time? What are the processes by which a condition/situation changes, develops, or operates? A different type of question tries to confirm existing beliefs or assumptions. A last type of question tries to discover new ideas.

Research projects are designed around research problems or questions. Before designing a project, quantitative researchers focus on a specific research problem within a broad topic. For example, your personal experience might suggest labor unions as a topic. "Labor unions" is a topic, not a research question or a problem. In any large library, you will find hundreds of books and thousands of articles written by sociologists, historians, economists, management officials, political scientists, and others on unions. The books and articles focus on different aspects of the topic and adopt many perspectives on it. Before proceeding to design a research project, you must narrow and focus the topic. An example research question is, "How much did U.S. labor unions contribute to racial inequality by creating barriers to skilled jobs for African Americans in the post–World War II period?"

When starting research on a topic, ask yourself: What is it about the topic that is of greatest interest? For a topic about which you know little, first get background knowledge by reading about it. Research questions refer to the relationships among a small number of variables. Identify a limited number of variables and specify the relationships among them.

A research question has one or a small number of causal relationships. Box 4.5 lists some ways to focus a topic into a research question. For example, the question, "What causes divorce?" is not a good research question. A better research question is, "Is age at marriage associated with divorce?" The second question suggests two variables: age of marriage and divorce.

Box 4.5	Techniques for Narrowing a Topic into a Research Question

1. *Examine the literature.* Published articles are an excellent source of ideas for research questions. They are usually at an appropriate level of specificity and suggest research questions that focus on the following:

    a. Replicate a previous research project exactly or with slight variations.

    b. Explore unexpected findings discovered in previous research.

    c. Follow suggestions an author gives for future research at the end of an article.

    d. Extend an existing explanation or theory to a new topic or setting.

    e. Challenge findings or attempt to refute a relationship.

    f. Specify the intervening process and consider linking relations.

2. *Talk over ideas with others.*

    a. Ask people who are knowledgeable about the topic for questions about it that they have thought of.

    b. Seek out those who hold opinions that differ from yours on the topic and discuss possible research questions with them.

3. *Apply to a specific context.*

    a. Focus the topic onto a specific historical period or time period.

    b. Narrow the topic to a specific society or geographic unit.

    c. Consider which subgroups or categories of people/units are involved and whether there are differences among them.

4. *Define the aim or desired outcome of the study.*

    a. Will the research question be for an exploratory, explanatory, or descriptive study?

    b. Will the study involve applied or basic research?

Another technique for focusing a research question is to specify the *universe* to which the answer to the question can be generalized. All research questions, hypotheses, and studies apply to some group or category of people, organizations, or other units. The *universe* is the set of all units that the research covers, or to which it can be generalized. For example, your research question is about the effects of a new attendance policy on learning by high school students. The universe, in this case, is all high school students.

When refining a topic into a research question and designing a research project, you also need to consider practical limitations. Designing a perfect research project is an interesting academic exercise, but if you expect to carry out a research project, practical limitations will have an impact on its design.

Major limitations include time, costs, access to resources, approval by authorities, ethical concerns, and expertise. If you have 10 hours a week for five weeks to conduct a research project, but the answer to a research question will take five years, reformulate the research question more narrowly. Estimating the amount of time required to answer a research question is difficult. The research question specified, the research technique used, and the type of data collected all play significant roles. Experienced researchers are the best source of good estimates.

Cost is another limitation. As with time, there are inventive ways to answer a question within limitations, but it may be impossible to answer some questions because of the expense involved. For example, a research question about the attitudes of all sports fans toward their team mascot can be answered only with a great investment of time and money. Narrowing the research question to how students at two different colleges feel about their mascots might make it more manageable.

Access to resources is a common limitation. Resources can include the expertise of others, special equipment, or information. For example, a research question about burglary rates and family income in many different nations is almost impossible to answer because information on burglary and income is not collected or available for most countries. Some questions require the approval of authorities (e.g., to see medical records) or involve violating basic ethical principles (e.g., causing serious physical harm to a person to see the person's reaction). The expertise or background of the researcher is also a limitation. Answering some research questions involves the use of data collection techniques, statistical methods, knowledge of a foreign language, or skills that the researcher may not have. Unless the researcher can acquire the necessary training or can pay for another person's services, the research question may not be practical.

In summary, styles of qualitative and quantitative researchers have much in common, but the researchers often differ on design issues, such as taking a linear or nonlinear research path and developing a research question (see Table 4.1). In addition, researchers tend to adopt a different language and approach to study design, which we will consider next.

QUALITATIVE DESIGN ISSUES

The Language of Cases and Contexts

Qualitative researchers use a language of cases and contexts, examine social processes and cases in their social context, and look at interpretations or the creation of meaning in specific settings. They try look at social life from multiple points of view and explain how people construct identities. Only rarely do they use variables or test hypotheses, or try to convert social life into numbers.

Qualitative researchers see most areas and activities of social life as being intrinsically qualitative. To them, qualitative data are not imprecise or deficient; they are highly meaningful.

TABLE 4.1   Quantitative Reasearch versus Qualitative Research

Quantitative Research	Qualitative Research
Test hypothesis that the researcher begins with.	Capture and discover meaning once the researcher becomes immersed in the data.
Concepts are in the form of distinct variables.	Concepts are in the form of themes, motifs, generalizations, and taxonomies.
Measures are systematically created before data collection and are standardized.	Measures are created in an ad hoc manner and are often specific to the individual setting or researcher.
Data are in the form of numbers from precise measurement.	Data are in the form of words and images from documents, observations, and transcripts.
Theory is largely causal and is deductive.	Theory can be causal or noncausal and is often inductive.
Procedures are standard, and replication is assumed.	Research procedures are particular, and replication is very rare.
Analysis proceeds by using statistics, tables, or charts and discussing how what they show relates to hypotheses.	Analysis proceeds by extracting themes or generalizations from evidence and organizing data to present a coherent, consistent picture.

Instead of trying to convert social life into variables or numbers, qualitative researchers borrow ideas from the people they study and place them within the context of a natural setting. They examine motifs, themes, distinctions, and ideas instead of variables, and they adopt the inductive approach of *grounded theory.*

Some people believe that qualitative data are "soft," intangible, and immaterial. Such data are so fuzzy and elusive that researchers cannot really capture them. This is not necessarily the case. Qualitative data are empirical. They involve documenting real events, recording what people say (with words, gestures, and tone), observing specific behaviors, studying written documents, or examining visual images. These are all concrete aspects of the world. For example, some qualitative researchers take and closely scrutinize photos or videotapes of people or social events. This evidence is just as "hard" and physical as that used by quantitative researchers to measure attitudes, social pressure, intelligence, and the like.

Grounded Theory

A qualitative researcher develops theory during the data collection process. This more inductive method means that theory is built from data or grounded in the data. Moreover, conceptualization and operationalization occur simultaneously with data collection and preliminary data analysis. It makes qualitative research flexible and lets data and theory interact. Qualitative researchers remain open to the unexpected, are willing to change the direction or focus of a research project, and may abandon their original research question in the middle of a project.

A qualitative researcher builds theory by making comparisons. For example, when a researcher observes an event (e.g., a police officer confronting a speeding motorist), he or she immediately ponders questions and looks for similarities and differences. When watching a police officer stop a speeder, a qualitative researcher asks: Does the police officer always radio in the car's license number before proceeding? After radioing the car's location, does the officer ask the motorist to get out of the car sometimes, but in others casually walk up to the car and talk to the seated driver? When data collection and theorizing are interspersed, theoretical questions arise that suggest future observations, so new data are tailored to answer theoretical questions that came from thinking about previous data.

The Context Is Critical

Qualitative researchers emphasize the social context for understanding the social world. They hold that the meaning of a social action or statement depends, in an important way, on the context in which it appears. When a researcher removes an event, social action, answer to a question, or conversation from the social context in which it appears, or ignores the context, social meaning and significance are distorted.

Attention to social context means that a qualitative researcher notes what came before or what surrounds the focus of study. It also implies that the same events or behaviors can have different meanings in different cultures or historical eras. For example, instead of ignoring the context and counting votes across time or cultures, a qualitative researcher asks: What does voting mean in the context? He or she may treat the same behavior (e.g., voting for a presidential candidate) differently depending on the social context in which it occurs. Qualitative researchers place parts of social life into a larger whole. Otherwise, the meaning of the part may be lost. For example, it is hard to understand what a baseball glove is without knowing something about the game of baseball. The whole of the game—innings, bats, curve balls, hits—gives meaning to each part, and each part without the whole has little meaning.

The Case and Process

In quantitative research, cases are usually the same as a unit of analysis, or the unit on which variables are measured (discussed later). Quantitative researchers typically measure variables of their hypotheses across many cases. For example, if a researcher conducts a survey of 450 individuals, each individual is a case or unit on which he or she measures variables. Qualitative researchers tend to use a "case-oriented approach [that] places cases, not variables, center stage" (Ragin, 1992:5). They examine a wide variety of aspects of one or a few cases. Their analyses emphasize contingencies in "messy" natural settings (i.e., the co-occurrence of many specific factors and events in one place and time). Explanations or interpretations are complex and may be in the form of an unfolding plot or a narrative story about particular people or specific events. Rich detail and astute insight into the cases replace the sophisticated statistical analysis of precise measures across a huge number of units or cases found in quantitative research.

The passage of time is integral to qualitative research. Qualitative researchers look at the sequence of events and pay attention to what happens first, second, third, and so on. Because qualitative researchers examine the same case or set of cases over time, they can see an issue evolve, a conflict emerge, or a social relationship develop. The researcher can detect process and causal relations.

In historical research, the passage of time may involve years or decades. In field research, the passage of time is shorter. Nevertheless, in both, a researcher notes what is occurring at different points in time and recognizes that *when* something occurs is often important.

Interpretation

Interpretation means to assign significance or a coherent meaning to something. Quantitative and qualitative researchers both interpret data, but they do so in different ways. A quantitative researcher gives meaning by rearranging, examining, and discussing the numbers by using charts and statistics to explain how patterns in the data relate to the research question. A qualitative researcher gives meaning by rearranging, examining, and discussing textual or visual data in a way that conveys an authentic voice, or that remains true to the original understandings of the people and situations that he or she studied.

Instead of relying on charts, statistics, and displays of numbers, qualitative researchers put a greater emphasis on interpreting the data. Their data are often "richer" or more complex and full of meaning. The qualitative researcher interprets to "translate" or make the originally gathered data understandable to other people. The process of qualitative interpretation moves through three stages or levels.

A researcher begins with the point of view of the people he or she is studying, and the researcher wants to grasp fully how they see the world, how they define situations, or what things mean to them. A *first-order interpretation* contains the inner motives, personal reasons, and point of view of the people who are being studied in the original context. As the researcher discovers and documents this first-order interpretation, he or she remains one step removed from it. The researcher offers a *second-order interpretation,* which is an acknowledgment that however much a researcher tries to get very close and "under the skin" of those he or she is studying, a researcher is still "on the outside looking in." In the second-order interpretation, the researcher tries to elicit an underlying coherence or sense of overall meaning in the data. To reach an understanding of what he or she sees or hears, a researcher often places the data into a context of the larger flow of events and behaviors. A qualitative researcher will often move to the third step and link the understanding that he or she achieved to larger concepts, generalizations, or theories. The researcher can share this broader interpretation with other people who are unfamiliar with the original data, the people and events studied, or the social situations observed by the researcher. This level of meaning translates the researcher's own understanding in a way that facilitates communication with people who are more distant from the original source, and it represents a *third-order interpretation.*

QUANTITATIVE DESIGN ISSUES

The Language of Variables and Hypotheses

Variation and Variables. The *variable* is a central idea in quantitative research. Simply defined, a variable is a concept that varies. Quantitative research uses a language of variables and relationships among variables.

In Chapter 2, you learned about two types of concepts: those that refer to a fixed phenomenon (e.g., the ideal type of bureaucracy) and those that vary in quantity, intensity, or amount (e.g., amount of education). The second type of concept and measures of the concepts are variables. Variables take on two or more values. Once you begin to look for them, you will see variables everywhere. For example, gender is a variable; it can take on two values: male or female. Marital status is a variable; it can take on the values of never married single, married, divorced, or widowed. Type of crime committed is a variable; it can take on values of robbery, burglary, theft, murder, and so forth. Family income is a variable; it can take on values from zero to billions of dollars. A person's attitude toward abortion is a variable; it can range from strongly favoring legal abortion to strongly believing in antiabortion.

The values or the categories of a variable are its *attributes.* It is easy to confuse variables with attributes. Variables and attributes are related, but they have distinct purposes. The confusion arises because the attribute of one variable can itself become a separate variable with a slight change in definition. The distinction is between concepts themselves that vary and conditions within concepts that vary. For example, "male" is not a variable; it describes a category of gender and is an attribute of the variable "gender." Yet, a related idea, "degree of masculinity," is a vari-

able. It describes the intensity or strength of attachment to attitudes, beliefs, and behaviors associated with the concept of *masculine* within a culture. "Married" is not a variable; it is an attribute of the variable "marital status." Related ideas such as "number of years married" or "depth of commitment to a marriage" are variables. Likewise, "robbery" is not a variable; it is an attribute of the variable "type of crime." "Number of robberies," "robbery rate," "amount taken during a robbery," and "type of robbery" are all variables because they vary or take on a range of values.

Quantitative researchers redefine concepts of interest into the language of variables. As the examples of variables and attributes illustrate, slight changes in definition change a nonvariable into a variable concept. As you saw in Chapter 2, concepts are the building blocks of theory; they organize thinking about the social world. Clear concepts with careful definitions are essential in theory.

Types of Variables. Researchers who focus on causal relations usually begin with an effect, then search for its causes. Variables are classified into three basic types, depending on their location in a causal relationship. The cause variable, or the one that identifies forces or conditions that act on something else, is the *independent variable.* The variable that is the effect or is the result or outcome of another variable is the *dependent variable.* The independent variable is "independent of" prior causes that act on it, whereas the dependent variable "depends on" the cause.

It is not always easy to determine whether a variable is independent or dependent. Two questions help you identify the independent variable. First, does it come before other variables in time? Independent variables come before any other type. Second, if the variables occur at the same time, does the author suggest that one variable has an impact on another variable? Independent variables affect or have an impact on other variables. Research topics are often phrased in terms of the dependent variables because dependent variables are the phenomenon to be explained. For example, suppose a researcher examines the reasons for an increase in the crime rate in Dallas, Texas; the dependent variable is the crime rate.

A basic causal relationship requires only an independent and a dependent variable. A third type of variable, the *intervening variable*, appears in more complex causal relations. It comes between the independent and dependent variables and shows the link or mechanism between them. Advances in knowledge depend not only on documenting cause-and-effect relationships but also on specifying the mechanisms that account for the causal relation. In a sense, the intervening variable acts as a dependent variable with respect to the independent variable and acts as an independent variable toward the dependent variable.

For example, French sociologist Emile Durkheim developed a theory of suicide that specified a causal relationship between marital status and suicide rates. Durkheim found evidence that married people are less likely to commit suicide than single people. He believed that married people have greater social integration (i.e., feelings of belonging to a group or family). He thought that a major cause of one type of suicide was that people lacked a sense of belonging to a group. Thus, his theory can be restated as a three-variable relationship: marital status (independent variable) causes the degree of social integration (intervening variable), which affects suicide (dependent variable). Specifying the chain of causality makes the linkages in a theory clearer and helps a researcher test complex explanations.[1]

Simple theories have one dependent and one independent variable, whereas complex theories can contain dozens of variables with multiple independent, intervening, and dependent variables. For example, a theory of criminal behavior (dependent variable) identifies four independent variables: an individual's economic hardship, opportunities to commit crime easily, membership in a deviant subgroup of society that does not disapprove of crime, and lack of punishment for criminal acts. A multicause explanation usually specifies the independent variable that has the greatest causal effect.

A complex theoretical explanation contains a string of multiple intervening variables that are linked together. For example, family disruption causes lower self-esteem among children, which causes depression, which causes poor grades in school, which causes reduced prospects for a good job, which causes a lower adult income. The chain of variables is: family disruption (independent), childhood self-esteem (intervening), depression (intervening), grades in school (intervening), job prospects (intervening), adult income (dependent).

Two theories on the same topic may have different independent variables or predict different independent variables to be important. In addition, theories may agree about the independent and dependent variables but differ on the intervening variable or causal mechanism. For example, two theories say that family disruption causes lower adult income, but for different reasons. One theory holds that disruption encourages children to join deviant peer groups that are not socialized to norms of work and thrift. Another emphasizes the impact of the disruption on childhood depression and poor academic performance, which directly affect job performance.

A single research project usually tests only a small part of a causal chain. For example, a research project examining six variables may take the six from a large, complex theory with two dozen variables. Explicit links to a larger theory strengthen and clarify a research project. This applies especially for explanatory, basic research, which is the model for most quantitative research.

Causal Theory and Hypotheses

The Hypothesis and Causality.   A *hypothesis* is a proposition to be tested or a tentative statement of a relationship between two variables. Hypotheses are guesses about how the social

> **Box 4.6** **Five Characteristics of Causal Hypotheses**
>
> 1. It has at least two variables.
> 2. It expresses a causal or cause-effect relationship between the variables.
> 3. It can be expressed as a prediction or an expected future outcome.
> 4. It is logically linked to a research question and a theory.
> 5. It is falsifiable; that is, it is capable of being tested against empirical evidence and shown to be true or false.

world works; they are stated in a value-neutral form.

A causal hypothesis has five characteristics (see Box 4.6). The first two characteristics define the minimum elements of a hypothesis. The third restates the hypothesis. For example, the hypothesis that attending religious services reduces the probability of divorce can be restated as a prediction: Couples who attend religious services frequently have a lower divorce rate than do couples who rarely attend religious services. The prediction can be tested against empirical evidence. The fourth characteristic states that the hypothesis should be logically tied to a research question and to a theory. Researchers test hypotheses to answer the research question or to find empirical support for a theory. The last characteristic requires that a researcher use empirical data to test the hypothesis. Statements that are necessarily true as a result of logic, or questions that are impossible to answer through empirical observation (e.g., What is the "good life"? Is there a God?) cannot be scientific hypotheses.

Testing and Refining Hypothesis. Knowledge rarely advances on the basis of one test of a single hypothesis. In fact, it is easy to get a distorted picture of the research process by focusing on a single research project that tests one hypothesis. Knowledge develops over time as researchers throughout the scientific community test many hypotheses. It grows from shifting and winnowing through many hypotheses. Each hypothesis represents an explanation of a dependent variable. If the evidence fails to support some hypotheses, they are gradually eliminated from consideration. Those that receive support remain in contention. Theorists and researchers constantly create new hypotheses to challenge those that have received support. Figure 4.3 represents an example of the process of shifting through hypotheses over time.

Scientists are a skeptical group. Support for a hypothesis in one research project is not sufficient for them to accept it. The principle of replication says that a hypothesis needs several tests with consistent and repeated support to gain broad acceptance. Another way to strengthen confidence in a hypothesis is to test related causal linkages in the theory from which it comes.

Types of Hypotheses. Hypotheses are links in a theoretical causal chain and can take several forms. Researchers use them to test the direction and strength of a relationship between variables. When a hypothesis defeats its competitors, or offers alternative explanations for a causal relation, it indirectly lends support to the researcher's explanation. A curious aspect of hypothesis testing is that researchers treat evidence that supports a hypothesis differently from evidence that opposes it. They give negative evidence more importance. The idea that negative evidence is critical when evaluating a hypothesis comes from the *logic of disconfirming hypotheses.*[2] It is associated with Karl Popper's idea of falsification and with the use of null hypotheses (see later in this section).

A hypothesis is never proved, but it can be disproved. A researcher with supporting evidence can say only that the hypothesis remains a possibility or that it is still in the running. Nega-

FIGURE 4.3   How the Process of Hypotheses Testing Operates over Time

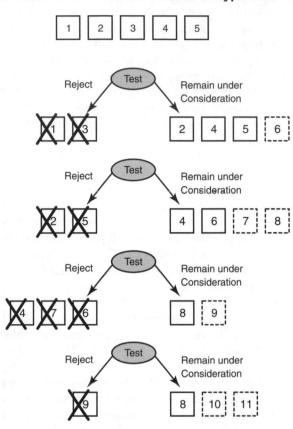

1966

There are five possible hypotheses.

1976

Two of the original five hypotheses
are rejected.
A new one is developed.

1986

Two hypotheses are rejected.
Two new ones are developed.

1996

Three hypotheses are rejected.
A new one is developed.

2006

One hypothesis is rejected.
Two new ones are developed.

In 2006, 3 hypotheses are in contention, but from 1966 to 2006, 11 hypotheses were considered, and over time, 8 of them were rejected in one or more tests.

tive evidence is more significant because the hypothesis becomes "tarnished" or "soiled" if the evidence fails to support it. This is because a hypothesis makes predictions. Negative and disconfirming evidence shows that the predictions are wrong. Positive or confirming evidence for a hypothesis is less critical because alternative hypotheses may make the same prediction. A researcher who finds confirming evidence for a prediction may not elevate one explanation over its alternatives.

For example, a man stands on a street corner with an umbrella and claims that his umbrella protects him from falling elephants. His hypothesis that the umbrella provides protection has supporting evidence. He has not had a single elephant fall on him in all the time he has had his umbrella open. Yet, such supportive evidence is weak; it also is consistent with an alternative hypothesis—that elephants do not fall from the sky. Both predict that the man will be safe from falling elephants. Negative evidence for the hypothesis—the one elephant that falls on him and his umbrella, crushing both—would destroy the hypothesis for good.

Researchers test hypotheses in two ways: a straightforward way and a null hypothesis way. Many quantitative researchers, especially experimenters, frame hypotheses in terms of a *null hypothesis* based on the logic of the disconfirming hypotheses. They test hypotheses by looking for evidence that will allow them to accept or reject the null hypothesis. Most people talk about a hypothesis as a way to predict a relationship. The null hypothesis does the opposite. It predicts no relationship. For example, Sarah believes that students who live on campus in dormitories get higher grades than students who live off campus and commute to college. Her null hypothesis is that there is no relationship between residence and grades. Researchers use the null hypothesis with a corresponding *alternative hypothesis* or experimental hypothesis. The alternative hypothesis says that a relationship exists. Sarah's alternative hypothesis is that students' on-campus residence has a positive effect on grades.

For most people, the null hypothesis approach is a backward way of hypothesis testing. Null hypothesis thinking rests on the assumption that researchers try to discover a relationship, so hypothesis testing should be designed to make finding a relationship more demanding. A researcher who uses the null hypothesis approach only directly tests the null hypothesis. If evidence supports or leads the researcher to accept the null hypothesis, he or she concludes that the tested relationship does not exist. This implies that the alternative hypothesis is false. On the other hand, if the researcher can find evidence to reject the null hypothesis, then the alternative hypotheses remain a possibility. The researcher cannot prove the alternative; rather, by testing the null hypotheses, he or she keeps the alternative hypotheses in contention. When null hypothesis testing is added to confirming evidence, the argument for an alternative hypothesis can grow stronger over time.

Many people find the null hypothesis to be confusing. Another way to think of it is that the scientific community is extremely cautious. It prefers to consider a causal relationship to be false until mountains of evidence show it to be true. This is similar to the Anglo-American legal idea of innocent until proved guilty. A researcher assumes, or acts as if, the null hypothesis is correct until *reasonable doubt* suggests otherwise. Researchers who use null hypotheses generally use it with specific statistical tests (e.g., t-test or F-test). Thus, a researcher may say there is reasonable doubt in a null hypothesis if a statistical test suggests that the odds of it being false are 99 in 100. This is what a researcher means when he or she says that statistical tests allow him or her to "reject the null hypothesis at the .01 level of significance."

Aspects of Explanation

Clarity about Units and Levels of Analysis. It is easy to become confused at first about the ideas of units and levels of analysis. Nevertheless, they are important for clearly thinking through and planning a research project. All studies have both units and levels of analysis, but few researchers explicitly identify them as such. The levels and units of analysis are restricted by the topic and the research question.

A *level of analysis* is the level of social reality to which theoretical explanations refer. The level of social reality varies on a continuum from micro level (e.g., small groups or individual processes) to macro level (e.g., civilizations or structural aspects of society). The level includes a mix of the number of people, the amount of space, the scope of the activity, and the length of time. For example, an extreme micro-level analysis can involve a few seconds of interaction between two people in the same small room. An extreme macro-level analysis can involve billions of people on several continents across centuries. Most social research uses a level of analysis that lies between these extremes.

The level of analysis delimits the kinds of assumptions, concepts, and theories that a researcher uses. For example, I want to study the topic of dating among college students. I use a micro-level analysis and develop an explanation that uses concepts such as interpersonal contact, mutual friendships, and common interests. I think that students are likely to date someone with whom they have had personal contact in a class, share friends in common, and share common interests. The topic and focus fit with a micro-level explanation because they are targeted at the level of face-to-face interaction among individuals. Another example topic is how inequality affects the forms of violent behavior in a society. Here, I have chosen a more macro-level explanation because of the topic and the level of social reality at which it operates. I am interested in the degree of inequality (e.g., the distribution of wealth, property, income, and other resources) throughout a society and in patterns of societal violence (e.g., aggression against other societies, sexual assault, feuds between families). The topic and research question suggest macro-level concepts and theories.

The *unit of analysis* refers to the type of unit a researcher uses when measuring. Common units in sociology are the individual, the group (e.g., family, friendship group), the organization (e.g., corporation, university), the social category (e.g., social class, gender, race), the social institution (e.g., religion, education, the family), and the society (e.g., a nation, a tribe). Although the individual is the most commonly used unit of analysis, it is by no means the only one. Different theories emphasize one or another unit of analysis, and different research techniques are associated with specific units of analysis. For example, the individual is usually the unit of analysis in survey and experimental research.

As an example, the individual is the unit of analysis in a survey in which 150 students are asked to rate their favorite football player. The individual is the unit because each individual student's response is recorded. On the other

hand, a study that compares the amounts different colleges spend on their football programs would use the organization (the college) as the unit of analysis because the spending by colleges is being compared and each college's spending is recorded.

Researchers use units of analysis other than individuals, groups, organizations, social categories, institutions, and societies. For example, a researcher wants to determine whether the speeches of two candidates for president of the United States contain specific themes. The researcher uses content analysis and measures the themes in each speech of the candidates. Here, the speech is the unit of analysis. Geographic units of analysis are also used. A researcher interested in determining whether cities that have a high number of teenagers also have a high rate of vandalism would use the city as the unit of analysis. This is because the researcher measures the percentage of teenagers in each city and the amount of vandalism for each city.

The units of analysis determine how a researcher measures variables or themes. They also correspond loosely to the level of analysis in an explanation. Thus, social-psychological or micro levels of analysis fit with the individual as a unit of analysis, whereas macro levels of analysis fit with the social category or institution as a unit. Theories and explanations at the micro level generally refer to features of individuals or interactions among individuals. Those at the macro level refer to social forces operating across a society or relations among major parts of a society as a whole.

Researchers use levels and units of analysis to design research projects, and being aware of them helps researchers avoid logical errors. For example, a study that examines whether colleges in the North spend more on their football programs than do colleges in the South implies that a researcher gathers information on spending by college and the location of each college. The unit of analysis—the organization or, specifically, the college—flows from the research problem and tells the researcher to collect data from each college.

Researchers choose among different units or levels of analysis for similar topics or research questions. For example, a researcher could conduct a project on the topic of patriarchy and violence with society as the unit of analysis for the research question, "Are patriarchal societies more violent?" He or she would collect data on societies and classify each society by its degree of patriarchy and its level of violence. On the other hand, if the research question was "Is the degree of patriarchy within a family associated with violence against a spouse?" the unit of analysis could be the group or the family, and a more micro level of analysis would be appropriate. The researcher could collect data on families by measuring the degree of patriarchy within different families and the level of violence between spouses in these families. The same topic can be addressed with different levels and units of analysis because patriarchy can be a variable that describes an entire society, or it can describe social relations within one family. Likewise, violence can be defined as general behavior across a society, or as the interpersonal actions of one spouse toward the other.

Ecological Fallacy. The *ecological fallacy* arises from a mismatch of units of analysis. It refers to a poor fit between the units for which a researcher has empirical evidence and the units for which he or she wants to make statements. It is due to imprecise reasoning and generalizing beyond what the evidence warrants. Ecological fallacy occurs when a researcher gathers data at a *higher* or an *aggregated* unit of analysis but wants to make a statement about a *lower* or *disaggregated* unit. It is a fallacy because what happens in one unit of analysis does not always hold for a different unit of analysis. Thus, if a researcher gathers data for large aggregates (e.g., organizations, entire countries, etc.) and then draws conclusions about the behavior of individuals from those data, he or she is committing the ecological fallacy. You can avoid this error by ensuring that the unit of analysis you use in an explanation is the same as or very close

to the unit on which you collect data (see Box 4.7).

Example. Tomsville and Joansville each have about 45,000 people living in them. Tomsville has a high percentage of upper-income people. Over half of the households in the town have family incomes of over $200,000. The town also has more motorcycles registered in it than any other town of its size. The town of Joansville has many poor people. Half its households live be-

Box 4.7 The Ecological Fallacy

Researchers have criticized the famous study *Suicide* ([1897] 1951) by Emile Durkheim for the ecological fallacy of treating group data as though they were individual-level data. In the study, Durkheim compared the suicide rates of Protestant and Catholic districts in nineteenth-century western Europe and explained observed differences as due to differences between people's beliefs and practices in the two religions. He said that Protestants had a higher suicide rate than Catholics because they were more individualistic and had lower social integration. Durkheim and early researchers only had data by district. Since people tended to reside with others of the same religion, Durkheim used group-level data (i.e., region) for individuals.

Later researchers (van Poppel and Day, 1996) reexamined nineteenth-century suicide rates only with individual-level data that they discovered for some areas. They compared the death records and looked at the official reason of death and religion, but their results differed from Durkheim's. Apparently, local officials at that time recorded deaths differently for people of different religions. They recorded "unspecified" as a reason for death far more often for Catholics because of a strong moral prohibition against suicide among Catholics. Durkheim's larger theory may be correct, yet the evidence he had to test it was weak because he used data aggregated at the group level while trying to explain the actions of individuals.

low the poverty line. It also has fewer motorcycles registered in it than any other town its size. But it is a *fallacy* to say, on the basis of this information alone, that rich people are more likely to own motorcycles or that the evidence shows a relationship between family income and motorcycle ownership. The reason is that we do not know which families in Tomsville or Joansville own motorcycles. We only know about the two variables—average income and number of motorcycles—for the towns as a whole. The unit of analysis for observing variables is the town as a whole. Perhaps all of the low- and middle-income families in Tomsville belong to a motorcycle club, and not a single upper-income family belongs. Or perhaps one rich family and five poor ones in Joansville each own motorcycles. In order to make a statement about the relationship between family ownership of motorcycles and family income, we have to collect information on families, not on towns as a whole.

Reductionism. Another problem involving mismatched units of analysis and imprecise reasoning about evidence is *reductionism,* also called the *fallacy of nonequivalence* (see Box 4.8). This error occurs when a researcher explains macro-level events but has evidence only about specific individuals. It occurs when a researcher observes a *lower* or *disaggregated* unit of analysis but makes statements about the operations of *higher* or *aggregated* units. It is a mirror image of the mismatch error in the ecological fallacy. A researcher who has data on how individuals behave but makes statements about the dynamics of macro-level units is committing the error of reductionism. It occurs because it is often easier to get data on concrete individuals. Also, the operation of macro-level units is more abstract and nebulous. As with the ecological fallacy, you can avoid this error by ensuring that the unit of analysis in your explanation is very close to the one for which you have evidence.

Researchers who fail to think precisely about the units of analysis and those who do not couple data with the theory are likely to commit

the ecological fallacy or reductionism. They make a mistake about the data appropriate for a research question, or they may seriously overgeneralize from the data.

You can make assumptions about units of analysis other than the ones you study empirically. Thus, research on individuals rests on assumptions that individuals act within a set of social institutions. Research on social institutions is based on assumptions about individual behavior. We know that many micro-level units form macro-level units. The danger is that it is easy to slide into using the causes or behavior of micro units, such as individuals, to explain the actions of macro units, such as social institutions. What happens among units at one level does not necessarily hold for different units of analysis. Sociology is a discipline that rests on the fundamental belief that a distinct level of social reality exists beyond the individual. Explanations of this level require data and theory that go beyond the individual alone. The causes, forces, structures, or processes that exist among macro units cannot be reduced to individual behavior.

Example. Why did World War I occur? You may have heard that it was because a Serbian shot an archduke in the AustroHungarian Empire in 1914. This is reductionism. Yes, the assassination was a factor, but the macro-political event between nations—war—cannot be reduced to a specific act of one individual. If it could, we could also say that the war occurred because the assassin's alarm clock worked and woke him up that morning. If it had not worked, there would have been no assassination, so the alarm clock caused the war! The event, World War I, was much more complex and was due to many social, political, and economic forces that came together at a point in history. The actions of specific individuals had a role, but only a minor one compared to these macro forces. Individuals affect events, which eventually, in combination with larger-scale social forces and organizations, affect others and move nations,

Box 4.8	Error of Reductionism

Suppose you pick up a book and read the following:

American race relations changed dramatically during the Civil Rights Era of the 1960s. Attitudes among the majority, white population shifted to greater tolerance as laws and court rulings changed across the nation. Opportunities that had been legally and officially closed to all but the white population—in the areas of housing, jobs, schooling, voting rights, and so on—were opened to people of all races. From the Brown vs. Board of Education *decision in 1955, to the Civil Rights Act of 1964, to the War on Poverty from 1966 to 1968, a new, dramatic outlook swept the country. This was the result of the vision, dedication, and actions of America's foremost civil rights leader, Dr. Martin Luther King Jr.*

This says: *dependent variable* = major change in U.S. race relations over a 10- to 13-year period; *independent variable* = King's vision and actions.

If you know much about the civil rights era, you see a problem. The entire civil rights movement and its successes are attributed to a single individual. Yes, one individual does make a difference and helps build and guide a movement, but the *movement* is missing. The idea of a social-political movement as a causal force is reduced to its major leader. The distinct social phenomenon—a movement—is obscured. Lost are the actions of hundreds of thousands of people (marches, court cases, speeches, prayer meetings, sit-ins, rioting, petitions, beatings, etc.) involved in advancing a shared goal and the responses to them.

The movement's ideology, popular mobilization, politics, organization, and strategy are absent. Related macro-level historical events and trends that may have influenced the movement (e.g., Vietnam War protest, mood shift with the killing of John F. Kennedy, African American separatist politics, African American migration to urban North) are also ignored.

This error is not unique to historical explanations. Many people think only in terms of individual actions and have an individualist bias, sometimes called *methodological individualism*. This is especially true in the extremely individualistic U.S. culture. The error is that it disregards units of analysis or forces beyond the individual. The *error of reductionism* shifts explanation to a much lower unit of analysis. One could continue to reduce from an individual's behavior to biological processes in a person, to micro-level neurochemical activities, to the subatomic level.

Most people live in "social worlds" focused on local, immediate settings and their interactions with a small set of others, so their everyday sense of reality encourages seeing social trends or events as individual actions or psychological processes. Often, they become blind to more abstract, macro-level entities—social forces, processes, organizations, institutions, movements, or structures. The idea that all social actions cannot be reduced to individuals alone is the core of sociology. In his classic work *Suicide,* Emile Durkheim fought methodological individualism and demonstrated that larger, unrecognized social forces explain even highly individual, private actions.

---

but individual actions alone are not the cause. Thus, it is likely that a war would have broken out at about that time even if the assassination had not occurred.

Spuriousness. To call a relationship between variables *spurious* means that it is false, a mirage. Researchers get excited if they think they have found a spurious relationship because they can show that what appears on the surface is false

and a more complex relation exists. Any association between two variables might be spurious, so researchers are cautious when they discover that two variables are associated; upon further investigation, it may not be the basis for a real causal relationship. It may be an illusion, just like the mirage that resembles a pool of water on a road during a hot day.

Spuriousness occurs when two variables appear to be associated but are not causally related

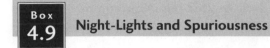

Box 4.9   Night-Lights and Spuriousness

For many years, researchers observed a strong positive association between the use of a night-light and children who were nearsighted. Many thought that the night-light was somehow causing the children to develop vision problems (illustrated as **a** below). Other researchers could think of no reason for a causal link between night-light use and developing nearsightedness. A 1999 study provided the answer. It found that nearsighted parents are more likely to use night-lights; they also genetically pass on their vision deficiency to their children. The study found no link between night-light use and nearsightedness once parental vision was added to the explanation (see **b** below). Thus the initial causal link was misleading or spurious (from *New York Times,* May 22, 2001).

a. Initial relationship

POSITIVE ASSOCIATION

b. Addition of the missing true causal factor

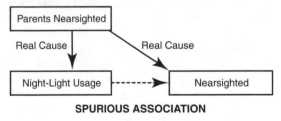

SPURIOUS ASSOCIATION

because an unseen third factor is the real cause (see Box 4.9). The unseen third or other variable is the cause of both the independent and the dependent variable in the apparent but illusionary relationship and accounts for the observed association. In terms of conditions for causality, the unseen factor is a more powerful alternative explanation.

You now understand that you should be wary of correlations or associations, but how can

you tell whether a relationship is spurious, and how do you find out what the mysterious third factor is? You will need to use statistical techniques (discussed later in this book) to test whether an association is spurious. To use them, you need a theory or at least a guess about possible third factors. Actually, spuriousness is based on commonsense logic that you already use. For example, you already know that there is an association between the use of air conditioners and ice cream cone consumption. If you measured the number of air conditioners in use and the number of ice cream cones sold for each day, you would find a strong correlation, with more cones sold on the days when more air conditioners are in use. But you know that eating ice cream cones does not cause people to turn on air conditioners. Instead, both variables are caused by a third factor: hot days. You could verify the same thing through statistics by measuring the daily temperature as well as ice cream consumption and air conditioner use. In social research, opposing theories help people figure out which third factors are relevant for many topics (e.g., the causes of crime or the reasons for war or child abuse).

Example 1. Some people say that taking illegal drugs causes suicide, school dropouts, and violent acts. Advocates of "drugs are the problem" position point to the positive correlations between taking drugs and being suicidal, dropping out of school, and engaging in violence. They argue that ending drug use will greatly reduce suicide, dropouts, and violence. Others argue that many people turn to drugs because of their emotional problems or high levels of disorder of their communities (e.g., high unemployment, unstable families, high crime, few community services, lack of civility). The people with emotional problems or who live in disordered communities are also more likely to commit suicide, drop out, and engage in violence. This means that reducing emotional problems and community disorder will cause illegal drug use, dropping out, suicide, and violence all to decline greatly. Reducing drug taking alone will have only a limited effect because it ignores the root causes. The "drugs are the problem" argument is spurious because the initial relationship between taking illegal drugs and the problems is misleading. The emotional problems and community disorder are the true and often unseen causal variables.

Example 2.   In the United States and Canada, we observe an empirical association between students classified as being in a non-White racial category and scoring lower academic tests (compared to students classifed as in a White category). The relationship between racial classification and test scores is illusionary, because a powerful and little-recognized variable is the true cause of both the racial classification and the test scores (see Figure 4.4). In this case, the true cause operates directly on the independent variable (racial classification) but indirectly through an intervening process on the dependent variable (test scores). A belief system that is based on classifying people as belonging to racial groups and assigning great significance to superficial physical appearance, such as skin color, is the basis of what people call "race." Such a belief system also is the basis for prejudice and discriminatory behavior. In such a situation, people are seen as belonging to different races and

treated differently because of it, such as having different job opportunities and housing choices. Discriminated-against people who are in some racial categories find limits in their housing choices. This means they get separated or grouped together in undesirable areas. Poor housing gets combined with unequal schooling, such that the lowest-quality schools are located in areas with the least desirable housing. Since the relationship between school quality and test scores is very strong, students from families living in less desirable housing areas with low-quality schools get lower test scores.

We can now turn from the errors in causal explanation to avoid and more to other issues involving hypotheses. Table 4.2 provides a review of the major errors.

From the Research Question to Hypotheses

It is difficult to move from a broad topic to hypotheses, but the leap from a well-formulated research question to hypotheses is a short one. Hints about hypotheses are embedded within a good research question. In addition, hypotheses are tentative answers to research questions (see Box 4.10).

FIGURE 4.4   Example of a Spurious Relationship between Belonging to a Non-White "Race" and Getting Low Academic Test Scores

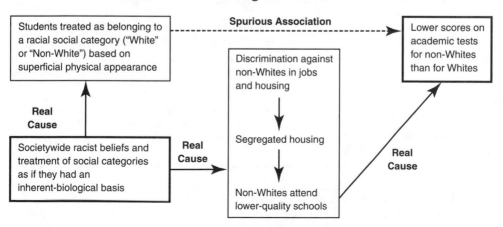

TABLE 4.2   Summary of Errors in Explanation

Type of Error	Short Definition	Example
Ecological Fallacy	The empirical observations are at too high a level for the causal relationship that is stated.	New York has a high crime rate. Joan lives in New York. Therefore, she probably stole my watch.
Reductionism	The empirical observations are at too low a level for the causal relationship that is stated.	Because Steven lost his job and did not buy a new car, the country entered a long economic recession.
Spuriousness	An unseen third variable is the actual cause of both the independent and dependent variable.	Hair length is associated with TV programs. People with short hair prefer watching football; people with long hair prefer romance stories. (*Unseen:* Gender)

Box 4.10   Examples of Bad and Good Research Questions

Bad Research Questions

Not Empirically Testable, Nonscientific Questions
- Should abortion be legal?
- Is it right to have capital punishment?

General Topics, Not Research Questions
- Treatment of alcohol and drug abuse
- Sexuality and aging

Set of Variables, Not Questions
- Capital punishment and racial discrimination
- Urban decay and gangs

Too Vague, Ambiguous
- Do police affect delinquency?
- What can be done to prevent child abuse?

Need to Be Still More Specific
- Has the incidence of child abuse risen?
- How does poverty affect children?
- What problems do children who grow up in poverty experience that others do not?

Good Research Questions

Exploratory Questions
- Has the actual incidence of child abuse changed in Wisconsin in the past 10 years?

Descriptive Questions
- Is child abuse, violent or sexual, more common in families that have experienced a divorce than in intact, never-divorced families?
- Are the children raised in poverty households more likely to have medical, learning, and social-emotional adjustment difficulties than nonpoverty children?

Explanatory Questions
- Does the emotional instability created by experiencing a divorce increase the chances that divorced parents will physically abuse their children?
- Is a lack of sufficent funds for preventive treatment a major cause of more serious medical problems among children raised in families in poverty?

Consider an example research question: "Is age at marriage associated with divorce?" The question contains two variables: "age at marriage" and "divorce." To develop a hypothesis, a researcher asks, "Which is the independent variable?" The independent variable is "age at marriage" because marriage must logically precede divorce. The researcher also asks, "What is the direction of the relationship?" The hypothesis could be: "The lower the age at time of marriage, the greater the chances that the marriage will end in divorce." This hypothesis answers the research question and makes a prediction. Notice that the research question can be reformulated and better focused now: "Are couples who marry younger more likely to divorce?"

Several hypotheses can be developed for one research question. Another hypothesis from the same research question is: "The smaller the difference between the ages of the marriage partners at the time of marriage, the less likely that the marriage will end in divorce." In this case, the variable "age at marriage" is specified differently.

Hypotheses can specify that a relationship holds under some conditions but not others. For example, a hypothesis states: "The lower the age of the partners at time of marriage, the greater the chances that the marriage will end in divorce, unless it is a marriage between members of a tight-knit traditional religious community in which early marriage is the norm."

Formulating a research question and a hypothesis do not have to proceed in fixed stages. A researcher can formulate a tentative research question, then develop possible hypotheses; the hypotheses then help the researcher state the research question more precisely. The process is interactive and involves creativity.

You may be wondering: Where does theory fit into the process of moving from a topic to a hypothesis I can test? Recall from Chapter 2 that theory takes many forms. Researchers use general theoretical issues as a source of topics. Theories provide concepts that researchers turn into variables as well as the reasoning or mechanism that helps researchers connect variables into a research question. A hypothesis can both answer a research question and be an untested proposition from a theory. Researchers can express a hypothesis at an abstract, conceptual level or restate it in a more concrete, measurable form.

Examples of specific studies may help to illustrate the parts of the research process. For examples of three quantitative studies, see Table 4.3; for two qualitative studies, see Table 4.4.

TABLE 4.3 Examples of Quantitative Studies

Study Citation (using ASA format style)	Goar, Carla and Jane Sell. 2005. "Using Task Definition to Modify Racial Inequality Within Task Groups" *Sociological Quarterly* 46:525–543.	Musick, Mark, John Wilson, and William Bynum. 2000. "Race and Formal Volunteering: The Differential Effects of Class and Religion" *Social Forces* 78: 1539–70.	Lauzen, Martha M. and David M. Dozier. 2005. "Maintaining the Double Standard: Portrayals of Age and Gender in Popular Films." *Sex Roles* 52: 437–446.
Methodological Technique	Experiment	Survey	Content Analysis

(continued)

TABLE 4.3 *(Continued)*

Topic	Mixed race group working on a task. A test of "expectation states theory"	Rates of volunteering by White and Black adults	Age and Gender Stereotypes in U.S. Mass Media
Research Question	If a group is presented with a task that is complex and requires many diverse skills, does this result in greater equality in participation across racial groups because people believe different racial groups possess different skills?	Do different kinds of resources available to Blacks and Whites explain why Blacks are less likely to volunteer?	Do contemporary films show a double standard, in which males acquire greater status and leadership as they age, while females are not permittted to gain status and leadership with increased age?
Main Hypothesis Tested	Groups exposed to instructions that suggest complex and diverse skills are required to complete a task will show less racial inequality in their operations to complete a task than groups without such instructions.	For Whites and Blacks, social class and religion affect whether a person volunteers in different ways.	As with past popular U.S. films and in other popular mass media, a double standard still exists.
Main Independent Variable(s)	Whether groups were told they were to a complete a complex task that requires diverse skills or not.	Social class, religious attendance, race.	The age and gender of major film characters.
Main Dependent Variable(s)	The amount of time/involvement by people of different races to resolve a group task.	Whether a person said he or she volunteered for any of five organizations (religious, education, political or labor, senior citizen, or local).	Whether a character has a leadership role, high occupational status, and goals.
Unit of Analysis	Mixed race task group	Individual adult	The movie

TABLE 4.3 *(Continued)*

Specific Units in the Study	90 undergraduate females in 3-person groups comprised of one Black and two White students.	Random sample of 2,867 U.S. adults interviewed twice (panel) in 1986 and 1989.	100 top-grossing domestic U.S. films in 2002.
Universe	All task groups that have a diverse set of members.	All adult Whites and Blacks in the United States.	All films.

TABLE 4.4   Examples of Qualitative Studies

Study Citation (using ASA format style)	Lu, Shun and Gary Fine. 1995. "The Presentation of Ethnic Authenticity: Chinese Food as a Social Accomplishment" *Sociological Quarterly* 36:535–53.	Molotch, Harvey, William Freudenburg, and Krista Paulsen. 2000. "History Repeats Itself, but How? City Character, Urban Tradition, and the Accomplishment of Place." *American Sociological Review* 65:791–823.
Methodological Technique	Field Research	Historical-Comparative Research
Topic	The ways ethnic cultures are displayed within the boundaries of being acceptable in the United States and how they deploy cultural resources.	The ways cities develop a distinct urban "character."
Research Question	How do Chinese restaurants present food to balance, giving a feeling of cultural authenticity and yet satisfying non-Chinese U.S. customers?	Why did the California cities of Santa Barbara and Ventura, which appear very similar on the surface, develop very different characters?

(continued)

TABLE 4.4 *(Continued)*

Grounded Theory	Ethnic restaurants Americanize their food to fit local tastes but also construct an impression of authenticity. It is a negotiated process of meeting the customer's expectations/taste conventions and the desire for an exotic and authentic eating experience.	The authors used two concepts—"lash up" (interaction of many factors) and structure (past events create constraints on subsequent ones)—to elaborate on character and tradition. Economic, political, cultural, and social factors combine to create distinct cultural-economic places. Similar forces can have opposite results depending on context.
Social Process	Restaurants make modifications to fit available ingredients, their market niche, and the cultural and food tastes of local customers.	Conditions in the two cities contributed to two different economic development responses to the oil industry and highway development. The city of Ventura formed an industrial-employment base around the oil industry and encouraged new highways. The city of Santa Barbara limited both the oil industry and highway growth. It instead focused on creating a strong tourism industry.
Social Context or Field Site	Chinese restaurants, especially four in Athens, Georgia.	The middle part of California's Pacific coast over the past 100 years.

CONCLUSION

In this chapter, you encountered the groundwork to begin a study. You saw how differences in the qualitative and quantitative styles or approaches to social research direct a researcher to prepare for a study differently. All social researchers narrow their topic into a more specific, focused research question. The styles of research suggest a different form and sequence of decisions, and different answers to when and how to focus the research. The style that a researcher uses will depend on the topic he or she selects, the researcher's purpose and intended use of study results, the orientation toward social science that he or she adopts, and the individual researcher's own assumptions and beliefs.

Quantitative researchers take a linear path and emphasize objectivity. They tend to use explicit, standardized procedures and a causal explanation. Their language of variables and hypotheses is found across many other areas of science. The process is often deductive with a sequence of discrete steps that precede data collection: Narrow the topic to a more focused question, transform nebulous theoretical concepts into more exact variables, and develop one or more hypotheses to test. In actual practice, researchers move back and forth, but the general process flows in a single, linear direction. In addition, quantitative researchers take special care to avoid logical errors in hypothesis development and causal explanation.

Qualitative researchers follow a nonlinear path and emphasize becoming intimate with the details of a natural setting or a particular cultural-historical context. They use fewer standardized procedures or explicit steps, and often devise on-the-spot techniques for one situation or study. Their language of cases and contexts directs them to conduct detailed investigations of particular cases or processes in their search for authenticity. They rarely separate planning and design decisions into a distinct pre–data collection stage, but continue to develop the study design throughout early data collection. The inductive qualitative style encourages a slow, flexible evolution toward a specific focus based on a researcher's ongoing learning from the data. Grounded theory emerges from the researcher's continuous reflections on the data.

Too often, the qualitative and quantitative distinction is overdrawn and presented as a rigid dichotomy. Adherents of one style of social research frequently judge the other style on the basis of the assumptions and standards of their own style. The quantitative researcher demands to know the variables used and the hypothesis tested. The qualitative researcher balks at turning humanity into cold numbers. The challenge for the well-versed, prudent social researcher is to understand and appreciate each style or approach on its own terms, and to recognize the strengths and limitations of each. The ultimate goal is to develop a better understanding and explanation of events in the social world. This comes from an appreciation of the value that each style has to offer.

Key Terms

abstract
alternative hypothesis
attributes
citation
dependent variable
ecological fallacy
first-order interpretation
hypothesis
independent variable
intervening variable
level of analysis
linear research path
literature review
nonlinear research path
null hypothesis
reductionism
second-order interpretation
spuriousness
third-order interpretation
unit of analysis
universe
variable

Endnotes

1. For a discussion of the "logic of the disconfirming hypothesis," see Singleton and associates (1988:456–460).
2. See Bailey (1987:43) for a discussion.

CHAPTER 5

Qualitative and Quantitative Measurement

INTRODUCTION

You may have heard of the Stanford Binet IQ test to measure intelligence, the Index of Dissimilarity to measure racial segregation, the Poverty Line to measure whether one is poor, or Uniform Crime Reports to measure the amount of crime. When social researchers test a hypothesis, evaluate an explanation, provide empirical support for a theory, or systematically study an applied issue or some area of the social world, they measure concepts and variables. How social researchers measure the numerous aspects of the social world—such as intelligence, segregation, poverty, crime, self-esteem, political power, alienation, or racial prejudice—is the focus of this chapter.

Quantitative researchers are far more concerned about measurement issues than are qualitative researchers. They treat measurement as a distinct step in the research process that occurs prior to data collection, and have developed special terminology and techniques for it. Using a deductive approach, they begin with a concept then create empirical measures that precisely and accurately capture it in a form that can be expressed in numbers.

Qualitative researchers approach measurement very differently. They develop ways to capture and express variable and nonvariable concepts using various alternatives to numbers. They often take an inductive approach, so they measure features of social life as part of a process that integrates creating new concepts or theories with measurement.

How people conceptualize and operationalize variables can significantly affect social issues beyond concerns of research methodology. For example, psychologists debate the meaning and measurement of intelligence. Most intelligence tests that people use in schools, on job applications, and in making statements about racial or other inherited superiority measure only analytic reasoning (i.e., one's capacity to think abstractly and to infer logically). Yet, many argue that there are other types of intelligence in addition to analytic. Some say there is practical and creative intelligence. Others suggest more types, such as social-interpersonal, emotional, body-kinesthetic, musical, or spatial. If there are many forms of intelligence but people narrowly limit measurement to one type, it seriously restricts how schools identify and nurture learning; how larger society evaluates, promotes, and recognizes the contributions of people; and how a society values diverse human abilities.

Likewise, different policymakers and researchers conceptualize and operationalize poverty differently. How people measure poverty will determine whether people get assistance from numerous social programs (e.g., subsidized housing, food aid, health care, child care, etc.). For example, some say that people are poor only if they cannot afford the food required to prevent malnutrition. Others say that people are poor if they have an annual income that is less than one-half of the average (median) income. Still others say that people are poor if they earn below a "living wage" based on a judgment about the income needed to meet minimal community standards of health, safety, and decency in hygiene, housing, clothing, diet, transportation, and so forth. Decisions about how to conceptualize and measure a variable—poverty—can greatly influence the daily living conditions of millions of people.

WHY MEASURE?

We use many measures in our daily lives. For example, this morning I woke up and hopped onto a bathroom scale to see how well my diet is working. I glanced at a thermometer to find out whether to wear a coat. Next, I got into my car and checked the gas gauge to be sure I could make it to campus. As I drove, I watched the speedometer so I would not get a speeding ticket. By 8:00 A.M., I had measured weight, temperature, gasoline volume, and speed—all measures about the physical world. Such precise, well-developed measures, which we use in daily life, are fundamental in the natural sciences.

We also measure the nonphysical world in everyday life, but usually in less exact terms. We are measuring when we say that a restaurant is excellent, that Pablo is really smart, that Karen has a negative attitude toward life, that Johnson is really prejudiced, or that the movie last night had a lot of violence in it. However, such everyday judgments as "really prejudiced" or "a lot of violence" are imprecise, vague measures.

Measurement also extends our senses. The astronomer or biologist uses the telescope or the microscope to extend natural vision. In contrast to our senses, scientific measurement is more sensitive, varies less with the specific observer, and yields more exact information. You recognize that a thermometer gives more specific, precise information about temperature than touch can. Likewise, a good bathroom scale gives you more specific, constant, and precise information about the weight of a 5-year-old girl than you get by lifting her and calling her "heavy" or "light." Social measures provide precise information about social reality.

In addition, measurement helps us observe what is otherwise invisible. Measurement extends human senses. It lets us observe things that were once unseen and unknown but were predicted by theory.

Before you can measure, you need a clear idea about what you are interested in. For example, you cannot see or feel magnetism with your natural senses. Magnetism comes from a theory about the physical world. You observe its effects indirectly; for instance, metal flecks move near a magnet. The magnet allows you to "see" or measure the magnetic fields. Natural scientists have invented thousands of measures to "see" very tiny things (molecules or insect organs) or very large things (huge geological land masses or planets) that are not observable through ordinary senses. In addition, researchers are constantly creating new measures.

Some of the things a social researcher is interested in measuring are easy to see (e.g., age, sex, skin color, etc.), but most cannot be directly observed (e.g., attitudes, ideology, divorce rates, deviance, sex roles, etc.). Like the natural scientist who invents indirect measures of the "invisible" objects and forces of the physical world, the social researcher devises measures for difficult-to-observe aspects of the social world.

QUANTITATIVE AND QUALITATIVE MEASUREMENT

Both qualitative and quantitative researchers use careful, systematic methods to gather high-quality data. Yet, differences in the styles of research and the types of data mean they approach the measurement process differently. The two approaches to measurement have three distinctions.

One difference between the two styles involves timing. Quantitative researchers think about variables and convert them into specific actions during a planning stage that occurs before and separate from gathering or analyzing data. Measurement for qualitative researchers occurs during the data collection process.

A second difference involves the data itself. Quantitative researchers develop techniques that can produce quantitative data (i.e., data in the form of numbers). Thus, the researcher moves from abstract ideas to specific data collection techniques to precise numerical information produced by the techniques. The numerical information is an empirical representation of the abstract ideas. Data for qualitative researchers sometimes is in the form of numbers; more often, it includes written or spoken words, actions, sounds, symbols, physical objects, or visual images (e.g., maps, photographs, videos, etc.). The qualitative researcher does not convert all observation into a single medium such as numbers. Instead, he or she develops many flexible, ongoing processes to measure that leaves the data in various shapes, sizes, and forms.

All researchers combine ideas and data to analyze the social world. In both research styles, data are empirical representations of concepts, and measurement links data to concepts. A third difference is how the two styles make such linkages. Quantitative researchers contemplate and reflect on concepts before they gather any data. They construct measurement techniques that bridge concepts and data.

Qualitative researchers also reflect on ideas before data collection, but they develop many, if not most, of their concepts during data collection. The qualitative researcher reexamines and evaluates the data and concepts simultaneously and interactively. Researchers start gathering data and creating ways to measure based what they encounter. As they gather data, they reflect on the process and develop new ideas.

PARTS OF THE MEASUREMENT PROCESS

When a researcher measures, he or she links a concept, idea, or construct[1] to a measure (i.e., a technique, a process, a procedure, etc.) by which he or she can observe the idea empirically. Quantitative researchers primarily follow a deductive route. They begin with the abstract idea, follow with a measurement procedure, and end with empirical data that represent the ideas. Qualitative researchers primarily follow an inductive route. They begin with empirical data, follow with abstract ideas, relate ideas and data, and end with a mixture of ideas and data. Actually, the process is more interactive in both styles of research. As a quantitative researcher develops measures, the constructs become refined and clearer, and as the researcher applies the measures to gather data, he or she often adjusts the measurement technique. As a qualitative researcher gathers data, he or she uses some preexisting ideas to assist in data collection, and will then mix old with new ideas that are developed from the data.

Both qualitative and quantitative researchers use two processes: conceptualization and operationalization in measurement. Conceptualization is the process of taking a construct and refining it by giving it a conceptual or theoretical

definition. A conceptual definition is a definition in abstract, theoretical terms. It refers to other ideas or constructs. There is no magical way to turn a construct into a precise conceptual definition. It involves thinking carefully, observing directly, consulting with others, reading what others have said, and trying possible definitions.

How might I develop a conceptual definition of the construct *prejudice*? When beginning to develop a conceptual definition, researchers often rely on multiple sources—personal experience and deep thinking, discussions with other people, and the existing scholarly literature. I might reflect on what I know about prejudice, ask others what they think about it, and go the library and look up its many definitions. As I gather definitions, the core idea should get clearer, but I have many definitions and need to sort them out. Most definitions state that prejudice is an attitude about another group and involves a prejudgment, or judging prior to getting specific information.

As I think about the construct, I notice that all the definitions refer to prejudice as an attitude, and usually it is an attitude about the members of another group. There are many forms of prejudice, but most are negative views about persons of a different racial-ethnic group. Prejudice could be about other kinds of groups (e.g., people of a religion, of a physical stature, or from a certain region), but it is always about a collectivity to which one does not belong. Many constructs have multiple dimensions or types, so I should consider whether there can be different types of prejudice—racial prejudice, religious prejudice, age prejudice, gender prejudice, nation prejudice, and so forth.

I also need to consider the units of analysis that best fit my definition of the construct. Prejudice is an attitude. Individuals hold and express attitudes, but so might groups (e.g., families, clubs, churches, companies, media outlets). I need to decide, Do I want my definition of prejudice to include only the attitudes of individuals or should it include attitudes held by groups, organizations, and institutions as well? Can I say,

The school or newspaper was prejudiced? I also must distinguish my construct from closely related ones. For example, I must ask, How is prejudice similar to or different from ideas such as discrimination, stereotype, or racism?

Conceptualization is the process of carefully thinking through the meaning of a construct. At this stage, I believe that *prejudice* means an inflexible negative attitude that an individual holds and is directed toward a race or ethnic group that is an out-group. It can, but does not always, lead to behavior, such as treating people unequally (i.e., discrimination), and it generally relies on a person's stereotypes of out-group members. Thus, my initial thought, "Prejudice is a negative feeling," has become a precisely defined construct. Even with all my conceptualization, I need to be even more specific. For example, if prejudice is a negative attitude about a race or an ethnic group of which one is not a member, I need to consider the meaning of *race* or *ethnic group*. I should not assume everyone sees racial-ethnic categories the same. Likewise, it is possible to have a positive prejudgment, and if so is that a kind of prejudice? The main point is that conceptualization requires that I become very clear and state what I mean very explicitly for others to see.

Operationalization links a conceptual definition to a specific set of measurement techniques or procedures, the construct's *operational definition* (i.e., a definition in terms of the specific operations of actions a researcher carries out). An operational definition could be a survey questionnaire, a method of observing events in a field setting, a way to measure symbolic content in the mass media, or any process carried out by the researcher that reflects, documents, or represents the abstract construct as it is expressed in the conceptual definition.

There are usually multiple ways to measure a construct. Some are better or worse and more or less practical than others. The key is to fit your measure to your specific conceptual definition, to the practical constraints within which you must operate (e.g., time, money, available subjects,

Box 5.1 **Five Suggestions for Coming Up with a Measure**

1. *Remember the conceptual definition.* The underlying principle for any measure is to match it to the specific conceptual definition of the construct that will be used in the study.
2. *Keep an open mind.* Do not get locked into a single measure or type of measure. Be creative and constantly look for better measures.
3. *Borrow from others.* Do not be afraid to borrow from other researchers, as long as credit is given. Good ideas for measures can be found in other studies or modified from other measures.
4. *Anticipate difficulties.* Logical and practical problems often arise when trying to measure variables of interest. Sometimes a problem can be anticipated and avoided with careful forethought and planning.
5. *Do not forget your units of analysis.* Your measure should fit with the units of analysis of the study and permit you to generalize to the universe of interest.

etc.), and to the research techniques you know or can learn. You can develop a new measure from scratch, or it can be a measure that is already being used by other researchers (see Box 5.1).

Operationalization links the language of theory with the language of empirical measures. Theory is full of abstract concepts, assumptions, relationships, definitions, and causality. Empirical measures describe how people concretely measure specific variables. They refer to specific operations or things people use to indicate the presence of a construct that exists in observable reality.

Quantitative Conceptualization and Operationalization

The measurement process for quantitative research flows in a straightforward sequence: first conceptualization, followed by operationalization, followed by applying the operational definition or measuring to collect the data. Quantitative researchers developed several ways to rigorously link abstract ideas to measurement procedures that will produce precise quantitative information about empirical reality.

Figure 5.1 illustrates the measurement process for two variables that are linked together in a theory and a hypothesis. There are three levels to consider: conceptual, operational, and empirical. At the most abstract level, the researcher is interested in the causal relationship between two constructs, or a *conceptual hypothesis*. At the level of operational definitions, the researcher is interested in testing an *empirical hypothesis* to determine the degree of association between indicators. This is the level at which correlations, statistics, questionnaires, and the like are used. The third level is the concrete empirical world. If the operational indicators of variables (e.g., questionnaires) are logically linked to a construct (e.g., racial discrimination), they will capture what happens in the empirical social world and relate it to the conceptual level.

The measurement process links together the three levels, moving deductively from the abstract to the concrete. A researcher first conceptualizes a variable, giving it a clear conceptual definition. Next, he or she operationalizes it by developing an operational definition or set of indicators for it. Last, he or she applies the indicators in the empirical world. The links from abstract constructs to empirical reality allow the researcher to test empirical hypotheses. Those tests are logically linked back to a conceptual hypothesis and causal relations in the world of theory.

A hypothesis has at least two variables, and the processes of conceptualization and operationalization are necessary for each variable. In the preceding example, prejudice is not a hypothesis. It is one variable. It could be a dependent variable caused by something else, or it could be an independent variable causing something else. It depends on my theoretical explanation.

We can return to the quantitative study by Weitzer and Tuch on perceptions of police bias and misconduct discussed in Chapter 2 for an

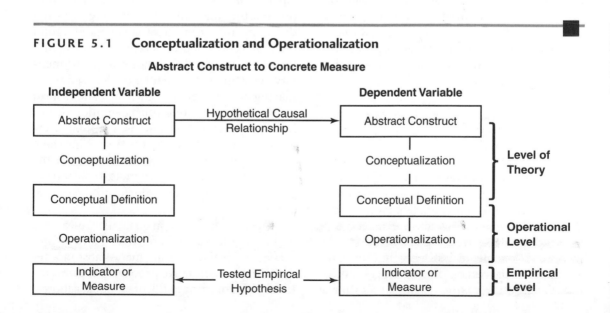

FIGURE 5.1   Conceptualization and Operationalization

Abstract Construct to Concrete Measure

example of how researchers conceptualize and operationalize variables. It is an explanatory study with two main variables in a causal hypothesis. The researchers began with the *conceptual hypothesis*: Members of a nondominant racial group are more likely than a dominant racial group to believe that policing is racially biased, and their experience with policing and exposure to media reports on police racial bias increase the perception of racial bias. They *conceptualized* the independent variable, dominant racial group, as White and the nondominant group as non-White subdivided into Black and Hispanic. The researchers *conceptualized* the dependent variable, racially biased policing, as unequal treatment by the police of Whites and non-Whites and racial prejudice by police officers. The researchers *operationalized* the independent variable by self-identification to a survey question about race. They *operationalized* the dependent variable by using four sets of survey questions: (1) questions about whether police treat Blacks better, the same, or worse than Whites, and the same question with Hispanics substituted for Blacks; (2) questions about whether police treat Black neighbhorhoods better, the same, or worse than Whites ones, with the same question asked for Hispanic neighborhoods; (3) a question about whether there is racial-ethnic prejudice among police officers in the city; and (4) a question about whether police are more likely to stop some drivers because they are Black or Hispanic.

Qualitative Conceptualization and Operationalization

Conceptualization. The conceptualization process in qualitative research also differs from that in quantitative research. Instead of refining abstract ideas into theoretical definitions early in the research process, qualitative researchers refine rudimentary "working ideas" during the data collection and analysis process. Conceptualization is a process of forming coherent theoretical definitions as one struggles to "make

sense" or organize the data and one's preliminary ideas.

As the researcher gathers and analyzes qualitative data, he or she develops new concepts, formulates definitions for the concepts, and considers relationships among the concepts. Eventually, he or she links concepts to one another to create theoretical relationships that may or may not be causal. Qualitative researchers form the concepts as they examine their qualitative data (i.e., field notes, photos and maps, historical documents, etc.). Often, this involves a researcher asking theoretical questions about the data (e.g., Is this a case of class conflict? What is the sequence of events and could it be different? Why did this happen here and not somewhere else?).

A qualitative researcher conceptualizes by developing clear, explicit definitions of constructs. The definitions are somewhat abstract and linked to other ideas, but usually they are also closely tied to specific data. They can be expressed in the words and concrete actions of the people being studied. In qualitative research, conceptualization is largely determined by the data.

Operationalization. The operationalization process for qualitative research significantly differs from that in quantitative research and often precedes conceptualization. A researcher forms conceptual definitions out of rudimentary "working ideas" that he or she used while making observations or gathering data. Instead of turning refined conceptual definitions into a set of measurement operations, a qualitative researcher operationalizes by describing how specific observations and thoughts about the data contributed to working ideas that are the basis of conceptual definitions and theoretical concepts.

Operationalization in qualitative research is an after-the-fact description more than a before-the-fact preplanned technique. Almost in a reverse of the quantitative process, data gathering occurs with or prior to full operationalization.

Just as quantitative operationalization deviates from a rigid deductive process, the process followed by qualitative researchers is one of mutual interaction. The researcher draws on ideas from beyond the data of a specific research setting. Qualitative operationalization describes how the researcher collects data, but it includes the researcher's use of preexisting techniques and concepts that were blended with those that emerged during the data collection process. In qualitative research, ideas and evidence are mutually interdependent.

We can see an example of qualitative operationalization in the study on managerialization of law by Edelman and associates (2001) discussed in Chapter 2. It is a descriptive study that developed one main construct. The researchers began with an interest in how major U.S. corporations came to accept legal mandates from the late 1970s to early 1990s. The mandates stated that firms must institute policies to equalize and improve the hiring and promotion of racial minorities and women, something the firms initially opposed. The researcher's *empirical data* consisted of articles in magazines written for and by corporate managers, or "managerial rhetoric" (i.e., debates and discussion within the community of leading professional managers on important issues). After gathering numerous articles, the researchers *operationalized* the data by developing working ideas and concepts from an inductive examination of the data. The researchers discovered that as managers discussed and deliberated, they had created a set of new nonlegal terms, ideas, and justifications. The operationalization moved inductively from looking at articles to creating working ideas based on what researchers found in the rhetoric. The researchers *conceptualized* their working ideas into the abstract construct "managerialization of law." The researchers saw that that corporate managers had altered and reformulated the original legal terms and mandates, and created new ones that were more consistent with the values and views of major corporations. The researchers documented a historical process that moved from re-

sistance to reformulation to acceptance, and with acceptance came new corporate policy. The researchers also drew on past studies to argue that the "managerialization of law" illustrates one role of top corporate managers—they innovate and alter internal operations by creating new terms, justifications, and maneuvers that help firms adjust to potential "disruptions" and requirements originating in the corporation's external political-legal environment.

RELIABILITY AND VALIDITY

Reliability and validity are central issues in all measurement. Both concern how concrete measures are connected to constructs. Reliability and validity are salient because constructs in social theory are often ambiguous, diffuse, and not directly observable. Perfect reliability and validity are virtually impossible to achieve. Rather, they are ideals for which researchers strive.

All social researchers want their measures to be reliable and valid. Both ideas are important in establishing the truthfulness, credibility, or believability of findings. Both terms also have multiple meanings. Here, they refer to related, desirable aspects of measurement.

Reliability means dependability or consistency. It suggests that the same thing is repeated or recurs under the identical or very similar conditions. The opposite of reliability is a measurement that yields erratic, unstable, or inconsistent results.

Validity suggests truthfulness and refers to the match between a construct, or the way a researcher conceptualizes the idea in a conceptual definition, and a measure. It refers to how well an idea about reality "fits" with actual reality. The absence of validity occurs if there is poor fit between the constructs a researcher uses to describe, theorize, or analyze the social world and what actually occurs in the social world. In simple terms, validity addresses the question of how well the social reality being measured through research matches with the constructs researchers use to understand it.

Qualitative and quantitative researchers want reliable and valid measurement, but beyond an agreement on the basic ideas at a general level, each style sees the specifics of reliability and validity in the research process differently.

Reliability and Validity in Quantitative Research

Reliability. As just stated, reliability means dependability. It means that the numerical results produced by an indicator do not vary because of characteristics of the measurement process or measurement instrument itself. For example, I get on my bathroom scale and read my weight. I get off and get on again and again. I have a reliable scale if it gives me the same weight each time—assuming, of course, that I am not eating, drinking, changing clothing, and so forth. An unreliable scale will register different weights each time, even though my "true" weight does not change. Another example is my car speedometer. If I am driving at a constant slow speed on a level surface, but the speedometer needle jumps from one end to the other, my speedometer is not a reliable indicator of how fast I am traveling.

How to Improve Reliability. It is rare to have perfect reliability. There are four ways to increase the reliability of measures: (1) clearly conceptualize constructs, (2) use a precise level of measurement, (3) use multiple indicators, and (4) use pilot-tests.

Clearly Conceptualize All Constructs. Reliability increases when a single construct or subdimension of a construct is measured. This means developing unambiguous, clear theoretical definitions. Constructs should be specified to eliminate "noise" (i.e., distracting or interfering information) from other constructs. Each measure should indicate one and only one concept.

Otherwise, it is impossible to determine which concept is being "indicated." For example, the indicator of a pure chemical compound is more reliable than one in which the chemical is mixed with other material or dirt. In the latter case, it is difficult to separate the "noise" of other material from the pure chemical.

Increase the Level of Measurement. Levels of measurement are discussed later. Indicators at higher or more precise levels of measurement are more likely to be reliable than less precise measures because the latter pick up less detailed information. If more specific information is measured, then it is less likely that anything other than the construct will be captured. The general principle is: Try to measure at the most precise level possible. However, it is more difficult to measure at higher levels of measurement. For example, if I have a choice of measuring prejudice as either high or low, or in 10 categories from extremely low to extremely high, it would be better to measure it in 10 refined categories.

Use Multiple Indicators of a Variable. A third way to increase reliability is to use multiple indicators, because two (or more) indicators of the same construct are better than one. Figure 5.2 illustrates the use of multiple indicators in hypothesis testing. Three indicators of the one independent variable construct are combined into an overall measure, *A,* and two indicators of a dependent variable are combined into a single measure, *B.*

For example, I create three indicators of the variable, racial-ethnic prejudice. My first indicator is an attitude question on a survey. I ask research participants their beliefs and feelings about many different racial and ethnic groups. For a second indicator, I observe research participants from various races and ethnic groups interacting together over the course of three days. I look for those who regularly either (1) avoid eye contact, appear to be tense, and sound cool and distant; or (2) make eye contact, appear

FIGURE 5.2   Measurement Using Multiple Indicators

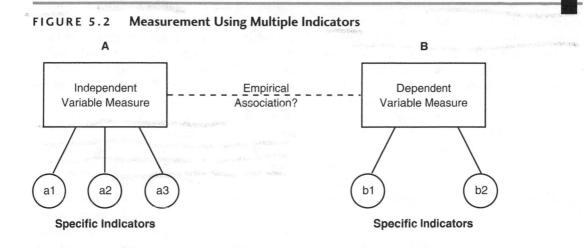

relaxed, and sound warm and friendly as they interact with people of their same or with people of a different racial-ethnic group. Last, I create an experiment. I ask research participants to read the grade transcripts, resumes, and interview reports on 30 applicants for five jobs— youth volunteer coordinator, office manager, janitor, clothing store clerk, and advertising account executive. The applicants have many qualifications, but I secretly manipulate their racial or ethnic group to see whether a research participant decides on the best applicant for the jobs based on an applicant's race and ethnicity.

Multiple indicators let a researcher take measurements from a wider range of the content of a conceptual definition. Different aspects of the construct can be measured, each with its own indicator. Also, one indicator (e.g., one question on a questionnaire) may be imperfect, but several measures are less likely to have the same (systematic) error. Multiple indicator measures tend to be more stable than measures with one item.

Use Pretests, Pilot Studies, and Replication. Reliability can be improved by using a pretest or pilot version of a measure first. Develop one or more draft or preliminary versions of a measure and try them before applying the final version in

a hypothesis-testing situation. This takes more time and effort.

The principle of using pilot-tests extends to replicating the measures other researchers have used. For example, I search the literature and find measures of prejudice from past research. I may want to build on and use a previous measure if it is a good one, citing the source, of course. In addition, I may want to add new indicators and compare them to the previous measure.

Validity.   *Validity* is an overused term. Sometimes, it is used to mean "true" or "correct." There are several general types of validity. Here, we are concerned with *measurement validity.* There are also several types of measurement validity. Nonmeasurement types of validity are discussed later.

When a researcher says that an indicator is valid, it is valid for a particular purpose and definition. The same indicator can be valid for one purpose (i.e., a research question with units of analysis and universe) but less valid or invalid for others. For example, the measure of prejudice discussed here might be valid for measuring prejudice among teachers but invalid for measuring the prejudice of police officers.

At its core, measurement validity refers to how well the conceptual and operational definitions mesh with each other. The better the fit, the greater the measurement validity. Validity is more difficult to achieve than reliability. We cannot have absolute confidence about validity, but some measures are *more valid* than others. The reason we can never achieve absolute validity is that constructs are abstract ideas, whereas indicators refer to concrete observation. This is the gap between our mental pictures about the world and the specific things we do at particular times and places. Validity is part of a dynamic process that grows by accumulating evidence over time. Without it, all measurement becomes meaningless.

Three Types of Measurement Validity

Face Validity.   The easiest to achieve and the most basic kind of validity is *face validity*. It is a judgment by the scientific community that the indicator really measures the construct. It addresses the question, On the face of it, do people believe that the definition and method of measurement fit? It is a consensus method. For example, few people would accept a measure of college student math ability using a question that asked students: $2 + 2 = ?$ This is not a valid measure of college-level math ability on the face of it. Recall that in the scientific community, aspects of research are scrutinized by others. See Table 5.1 for a summary of types of measurement validity.

TABLE 5.1   Summary of Measurement Validity Types

Validity (True Measure)

Face—in the judgment of others

Content—captures the entire meaning

Criterion—agrees with an external source

• Concurrent—agrees with a preexisting measure

• Predictive—agrees with future behavior

Content Validity.   Content validity is a special type of face validity. It addresses the question, Is the full content of a definition represented in a measure? A conceptual definition holds ideas; it is a "space" containing ideas and concepts. Measures should represent all ideas or areas in the conceptual space. Content validity involves three steps. First, specify fully the entire content in a construct's definition. Next, sample from all areas of the definition. Finally, develop an indicator that taps all of the parts of the definition.

An example of content validity is my definition of *feminism* as a person's commitment to a set of beliefs creating full equality between men and women in areas of the arts, intellectual pursuits, family, work, politics, and authority relations. I create a measure of feminism in which I ask two survey questions: (1) Should men and women get equal pay for equal work and (2) Should men and women share household tasks? My measure has low content validity because the two questions ask only about pay and household tasks. They ignore the other areas (intellectual pursuits, politics, authority relations, and other aspects of work and family). For a content-valid measure, I must either expand the measure or narrow the definition.

Criterion Validity.   Criterion validity uses some standard or criterion to indicate a construct accurately. The validity of an indicator is verified by comparing it with another measure of the same construct that is widely accepted. There are two subtypes of this kind of validity.

Concurrent Validity.   To have concurrent validity, an indicator must be associated with a preexisting indicator that is judged to be valid (i.e., it has face validity). For example, you create a new test to measure intelligence. For it to be concurrently valid, it should be highly associated with existing IQ tests (assuming the same definition of intelligence is used). This means that most people who score high on the old measure should also score high on the new one, and vice versa. The two measures may not be perfectly associated, but if they measure the same or a similar construct, it is logical for them to yield similar results.

Predictive Validity. Criterion validity whereby an indicator predicts future events that are logically related to a construct is called *predictive validity*. It cannot be used for all measures. The measure and the action predicted must be distinct from but indicate the same construct. Predictive measurement validity should not be confused with prediction in hypothesis testing, where one variable predicts a different variable in the future. For example, the Scholastic Assessment Test (SAT) that many U.S. high school students take measures scholastic aptitude—the ability of a student to perform in college. If the SAT has high predictive validity, then students who get high SAT scores will subsequently do well in college. If students with high scores perform the same as students with average or low scores, then the SAT has low predictive validity.

Another way to test predictive validity is to select a group of people who have specific characteristics and predict how they will score (very high or very low) vis-à-vis the construct. For example, I have a measure of political conservatism. I predict that members of conservative groups (e.g., John Birch Society, Conservative Caucus, Daughters of the American Revolution, Moral Majority) will score high on it, whereas members of liberal groups (e.g., Democratic Socialists, People for the American Way, Americans for Democratic Action) will score low. I "validate" the measure with the groups—that is, I pilot-test it by using it on members of the groups. It can then be used as a measure of political conservatism for the general public.

Reliability and Validity in Qualitative Research

Most qualitative researchers accept the principles of reliability and validity, but use the terms infrequently because of their close association with quantitative measurement. In addition, qualitative researchers apply the principles differently in practice.

Reliability. Reliability means dependability or consistency. Qualitative researchers use a variety of techniques (e.g., interviews, participation, photographs, document studies, etc.) to record their observations consistently. Qualitative researchers want to be consistent (i.e., not vacillating and erratic) in how, over time, they make observations, similar to the idea of stability reliability. One difficulty is that they often study processes that are not stable over time. Moreover, they emphasize the value of a changing or developing interaction between the researcher and what he or she studies.

Qualitative researchers believe that the subject matter and a researcher's relationship to it should be a growing, evolving process. The metaphor for the relationship between a researcher and the data is one of an evolving relationship or living organism (e.g., a plant) that naturally matures. Most qualitative researchers resist the quantitative approach to reliability, which they see as a cold, fixed mechanical instrument that one repeatedly injects into or applies to some static, lifeless material.

Qualitative researchers consider a range of data sources and employ multiple measurement methods. They accept that different researchers or that researchers using alternative measures will get distinctive results. This is because qualitative researchers see data collection as an interactive process in which particular researchers operate in an evolving setting and the setting's context dictates using a unique mix of measures that cannot be repeated. The diverse measures and interactions with different researchers are beneficial because they can illuminate different facets or dimensions of a subject matter. Many qualitative researchers question the quantitative researcher's quest for standard, fixed measures. They fear that such measures ignore the benefits of having a variety of researchers with many approaches and may neglect key aspects of diversity that exist in the social world.

Validity. ~~Validity~~ means truthful. It refers to the bridge between a construct and the data. Qualitative researchers are more interested in authenticity than validity. *Authenticity* means giving a fair, honest, and balanced account of social life from the viewpoint of someone who lives it everyday. Qualitative researchers are less concerned with trying to match an abstract concept to empirical data and more concerned with giving a candid portrayal of social life that is true to the experiences of people being studied. Most qualitative researchers concentrate on ways to capture an inside view and provide a detailed account of how those being studied feel about and understand events.

Qualitative researchers have developed several methods that serve as substitutes for the quantitative approach to validity. These emphasize conveying the insider's view to others. Historical researchers use internal and external criticisms to determine whether the evidence they have is real or they believe it to be. Qualitative researchers adhere to the core principle of validity, to be truthful (i.e., avoid false or distorted accounts). They try to create a tight fit between their understanding, ideas, and statements about the social world and what is actually occurring in it.

Relationship between Reliability and Validity

Reliability is necessary for validity and is easier to achieve than validity. Although reliability is necessary in order to have a valid measure of a concept, it does not guarantee that a measure will be valid. It is not a sufficient condition for validity. A measure can produce the same result over and over (i.e., it has reliability), but what it measures may not match the definition of the construct (i.e., validity).

A measure can be reliable but invalid. For example, I get on a scale and get weighed. The weight registered by the scale is the same each time I get on and off. But then I go to another scale—an "official" one that measures true weight—and it says that my weight is twice as great. The first scale yielded reliable (i.e., dependable and consistent) results, but it did not give a valid measure of my weight.

A diagram might help you see the relationship between reliability and validity. Figure 5.3 illustrates the relationship between the concepts by using the analogy of a target. The bull's-eye represents a fit between a measure and the definition of the construct.

Validity and *reliability* are usually complementary concepts, but in some situations they

FIGURE 5.3   Illustration of Relationship between Reliability and Validity

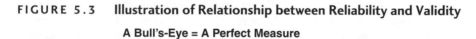

A Bull's-Eye = A Perfect Measure

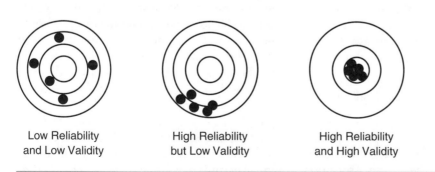

| Low Reliability and Low Validity | High Reliability but Low Validity | High Reliability and High Validity |

Source: Adapted from Babbie (2004:145).

conflict with each other. Sometimes, as validity increases, reliability is more difficult to attain, and vice versa. This occurs when the construct has a highly abstract and not easily observable definition. Reliability is easiest to achieve when the measure is precise and observable. Thus, there is a strain between the true essence of the highly abstract construct and measuring it in a concrete manner. For example, "alienation" is a very abstract, highly subjective construct, often defined as a deep inner sense of loss of one's humanity that diffuses across many aspects of one's life (e.g., social relations, sense of self, orientation toward nature). Highly precise questions in a questionnaire give reliable measures, but there is a danger of losing the subjective essence of the concept.

Other Uses of the Terms *Reliable* and *Valid*

Many words have multiple definitions, including *reliability* and *validity*. This creates confusion unless we distinguish among alternative uses of the same word.

Reliability.   We use *reliability* in everyday language. A reliable person is one who is dependable, stable, and responsible; a reliable car is dependable and trustworthy. This means the person responds in similar, predictable ways in different times and conditions; the same can be said for the car. In addition to measurement reliability, researchers sometimes say a study or its results are reliable. By this, they mean that the method of conducting a study or the results from it can be reproduced or replicated by other researchers.

Internal Validity. *Internal validity* means there are no errors internal to the design of the research project. It is used primarily in experimental research to talk about possible errors or alternative explanations of results that arise despite attempts to institute controls. High internal validity means there are few such errors. Low internal validity means that such errors are likely.

External Validity.   *External validity* is used primarily in experimental research. It is the ability to generalize findings from a specific setting and small group to a broad range of settings and people. It addresses the question, If something happens in a laboratory or among a particular group of subjects (e.g., college students), can the findings be generalized to the "real" (nonlaboratory) world or to the general public (nonstudents)? High external validity means that the results can be generalized to many situations and many groups of people. Low external validity means that the results apply only to a very specific setting.

Statistical Validity.   *Statistical validity* means that the correct statistical procedure is chosen and its assumptions are fully met. Different statistical tests or procedures are appropriate for different conditions, which are discussed in textbooks that describe the statistical procedures.

All statistics are based on assumptions about the mathematical properties of the numbers being used. A statistic will be invalid and its results nonsense if the major assumptions are violated. For example, to compute an average (actually the mean, which is discussed in a later chapter), one cannot use information at the nominal level of measurement (to be discussed). For example, suppose I measure the race of a class of students. I give each race a number: White = 1, African American = 2, Asian = 3, others = 4. It makes no sense to say that the "mean" race of a class of students is 1.9 (almost African American?). This is a misuse of the statistical procedure, and the results are invalid even if the computation is correct. The degree to which statistical assumptions can be violated or bent (the technical term is *robustness*) is a topic in which professional statisticians take great interest.

A GUIDE TO QUANTITATIVE MEASUREMENT

Thus far, you have learned about the principles of measurement, including the principles of reliability and validity. Quantitative researchers have developed ideas and specialized measures to help them in the process of creating operational definitions that will be reliable and valid measures and yield numerical data for their variable constructs. This section of the chapter is a brief guide to these ideas and a few of the measures.

Levels of Measurement

Levels of measurement is an abstract but important and widely used idea. Basically, it says that some ways a researcher measures a construct are at a higher or more refined level, and others are crude or less precisely specified. The level of measurement depends on the way in which a construct is conceptualized—that is, assumptions about whether it has particular characteristics. The level of measurement affects the kinds of indicators chosen and is tied to basic assumptions in a construct's definition. The way in which a researcher conceptualizes a variable limits the levels of measurement that he or she can use and has implications for how measurement and statistical analysis can proceed.

Continuous and Discrete Variables. Variables can be thought of as being either continuous or discrete. *Continuous variables* have an infinite number of values or attributes that flow along a continuum. The values can be divided into many smaller increments; in mathematical theory, there is an infinite number of increments. Examples of continuous variables include temperature, age, income, crime rate, and amount of schooling. *Discrete variables* have a relatively fixed set of separate values or variable attributes. Instead of a smooth continuum of values, discrete variables contain distinct categories. Examples of discrete variables include gender (male or female), religion (Protestant, Catholic, Jew, Muslim, atheist), and marital status (never married single, married, divorced or separated, widowed). Whether a variable is continuous or discrete affects its level of measurement.

Four Levels of Measurement

Precision and Levels.   The idea of levels of measurement expands on the difference between continuous and discrete variables and organizes types of variables for their use in statistics. The four *levels of measurement* categorize the degree of precision of measurement.

Deciding on the appropriate level of measurement for a construct often creates confusion. The appropriate level of measurement for a variable depends on two things: (1) how a construct is conceptualized and (2) the type of indicator or measurement that a researcher uses.

The way a researcher conceptualizes a construct can limit how precisely it can be measured. For example, some of the variables listed earlier as continuous can be reconceptualized as discrete. Temperature can be a continuous variable (e.g., degrees, fractions of degrees) or it can be crudely measured with discrete categories (e.g., hot or cold). Likewise, age can be continuous (how old a person is in years, months, days, hours, and minutes) or treated as discrete categories (infancy, childhood, adolescence, young adulthood, middle age, old age). Yet, most discrete variables cannot be conceptualized as continuous variables. For example, sex, religion, and marital status cannot be conceptualized as continuous; however, related constructs *can* be conceptualized as continuous (e.g., femininity, degree of religiousness, commitment to a marital relationship, etc.).

The level of measurement limits the statistical measures that can be used. A wide range of powerful statistical procedures are available for the higher levels of measurement, but the types of statistics that can be used with the lowest levels are very limited.

There is a practical reason to conceptualize and measure variables at higher levels of measurement. You can collapse higher levels of measurement to lower levels, but the reverse is not true. In other words, it is possible to measure a construct very precisely, gather very specific information, and then ignore some of the precision. But it is not possible to measure a construct with less precision or with less specific information and then make it more precise later.

Distinguishing among the Four Levels.   The four levels from lowest to greatest or highest precision are nominal, ordinal, interval, and ratio. Each level gives a different type of information (see Table 5.2). *Nominal* measures indicate only that there is a difference among categories (e.g., religion: Protestant, Catholic, Jew, Muslim; racial heritage: African, Asian, Caucasian, Hispanic, other). *Ordinal* measures indicate a difference, *plus* the categories can be ordered or ranked (e.g., letter grades: A, B, C, D, F; opinion measures: Strongly Agree, Agree, Disagree, Strongly Disagree). *Interval* measures everything the first two do, *plus* it can specify the amount of distance between categories (e.g., Fahrenheit or Celsius temperature: 5°, 45°, 90°; IQ scores: 95, 110, 125). Arbitrary zeroes may be used in interval measures; they are just there to help keep score. *Ratio* measures do everything all the other levels do, *plus* there is a true zero, which makes it possible to state relations in terms of proportion or ratios (e.g., money income: $10, $100, $500; years of formal schooling: 1 year, 10 years, 13 years).

In most practical situations, the distinction between interval and ratio levels makes little difference. The arbitrary zeroes of some interval measures can be confusing. For example, a rise in temperature from 30 to 60 degrees is not really a doubling of the temperature, although the numbers double, because zero degrees is not the absence of all heat.

Discrete variables are nominal and ordinal, whereas continuous variables can be measured at the interval or ratio level. A ratio-level measure can be turned into an interval, ordinal, or nominal level. The interval level can always be turned into an ordinal or nominal level, but the process does not work in the opposite way!

In general, use at least five ordinal categories and obtain many observations. This is because the distortion created by collapsing a continuous construct into a smaller number of ordered categories is minimized as the number of categories and the number of observations increase.

The ratio level of measurement is rarely used in the social sciences. For most purposes, it is indistinguishable from interval measurement. The only difference is that ratio measurement has a "true zero." This can be confusing because some measures, like temperature, have zeroes that are not true zeroes. The temperature can be zero, or below zero, but zero is an arbitrary number when it is assigned to temperature. This can be illustrated by comparing zero degrees Celsius with zero degrees Fahrenheit—they are different temperatures. In addition, doubling the degrees in one system does not double the degrees in the other. Likewise, it does not make sense to say that it is "twice as warm," as is possible with ratio measurement, if the temperature rises from 2 to 4 degrees, from 15 to 30 degrees, or from 40 to 80 degrees. Another common ex-

TABLE 5.2   Characteristics of the Four Levels of Measurement

Level	Different Categories	Ranked	Distance between Categories Measured	True Zero
Nominal	Yes			
Ordinal	Yes	Yes		
Interval	Yes	Yes	Yes	
Ratio	Yes	Yes	Yes	Yes

ample of arbitrary—not true—zeroes occurs when measuring attitudes where numbers are assigned to statements (e.g., -1 = disagree, 0 = no opinion, $+1$ = agree). True zeroes exist for variables such as income, age, or years of education. Examples of the four levels of measurement are shown in Table 5.3.

Specialized Measures: Scales and Indexes

Researchers have created thousands of different scales and indexes to measure social variables. For example, scales and indexes have been developed to measure the degree of formalization in bureaucratic organizations, the prestige of occupations, the adjustment of people to a marriage, the intensity of group interaction, the level of social activity in a community, the degree to which a state's sexual assault laws reflect feminist values, and the level of socioeconomic development of a nation. I cannot discuss the thousands of scales and indexes. Instead, I will focus on principles of scale and index construction and explore some major types.

Keep two things in mind. First, virtually every social phenomenon can be measured. Some constructs can be measured directly and produce precise numerical values (e.g., family income). Other constructs require the use of surrogates or proxies that indirectly measure a variable and may not be as precise (e.g., predisposition to commit a crime). Second, a lot can be learned from measures used by other researchers. You are fortunate to have the work of thousands of researchers to draw on. It is not always necessary to start from scratch. You can use a past scale or index, or you can modify it for your own purposes.

Indexes and Scales. You might find the terms *index* and *scale* confusing because they are often used interchangeably. One researcher's scale is another's index. Both produce ordinal- or interval-level measures of a variable. To add to the confusion, scale and index techniques can be combined in one measure. Scales and indexes give a researcher more information about variables and make it possible to assess the quality of measurement. Scales and indexes increase relia-

TABLE 5.3 Example of Levels of Measurement

Variable (Level of Measurement)	How Variable Measured
Religion (nominal)	Different religious denominations (Jewish, Catholic, Lutheran, Baptist) are not ranked, just different (unless one belief is conceptualized as closer to heaven).
Attendance (ordinal)	"How often do you attend religious services? (0) Never, (1) less than once a year, (3) several times a year, (4) about once a month, (5) two or three times a week, or (8) several times a week?" This might have been measured at a ratio level if the exact number of times a person attended was asked instead.
IQ Score (interval)	Most intelligence tests are organized with 100 as average, middle, or normal. Scores higher or lower indicate distance from the average. Someone with a score of 115 has somewhat above average measured intelligence for people who took the test, while 90 is slightly below. Scores of below 65 or above 140 are rare.
Age (ratio)	Age is measured by years of age. There is a true zero (birth). Note that a 40-year-old has lived twice as long as a 20-year-old.

Box 5.2 Scales and Indexes: Are They Different?

For most purposes, you can treat scales and indexes as interchangeable. Social researchers do not use a consistent nomenclature to distinguish between them.

A *scale* is a measure in which a researcher captures the intensity, direction, level, or potency of a variable construct. It arranges responses or observations on a continuum. A scale can use a single indicator or multiple indicators. Most are at the ordinal level of measurement.

An *index* is a measure in which a researcher adds or combines several distinct indicators of a construct into a single score. This composite score is often a simple sum of the multiple indicators. It is used for content and convergent validity. Indexes are often measured at the interval or ratio level.

Researchers sometimes combine the features of scales and indexes in a single measure. This is common when a researcher has several indicators that are scales (i.e., that measure intensity or direction). He or she then adds these indicators together to yield a single score, thereby creating an index.

---

bility and validity, and they aid in data reduction; that is, they condense and simplify the information that is collected (see Box 5.2).

Mutually Exclusive and Exhaustive Attributes. Before discussing scales and indexes, it is important to review features of good measurement. The attributes of all measures, including nominal-level measures, should be mutually exclusive and exhaustive.

Mutually exclusive attributes means that an individual or case fits into one and only one attribute of a variable. For example, a variable measuring type of religion—with the attributes Christian, non-Christian, and Jewish—is not mutually exclusive. Judaism is both a non-Christian religion and a Jewish religion, so a Jewish person fits into both the non-Christian and

the Jewish category. Likewise, a variable measuring type of city, with the attributes river port city, state capital, and interstate highway exit, lacks mutually exclusive attributes. One city could be all three (a river port state capital with an interstate exit), any one of the three, or none of the three.

Exhaustive attributes means that all cases fit into one of the attributes of a variable. When measuring religion, a measure with the attributes Catholic, Protestant, and Jewish is not exclusive. The individual who is a Buddhist, a Moslem, or an agnostic does not fit anywhere. The attributes should be developed so that every possible situation is covered. For example, Catholic, Protestant, Jewish, or other is an exclusive and mutually exclusive set of attributes.

Unidimensionality. In addition to being mutually exclusive and exhaustive, scales and indexes should also be unidimensional, or one dimensional. *Unidimensionality* means that all the items in a scale or index fit together, or measure a single construct. Unidimensionality was suggested in discussions of content and concurrent validity. Unidimensionality says: If you combine several specific pieces of information into a single score or measure, have all the pieces work together and measure the same thing. Researchers use a statistical measure called Cronbach's alpha to assess unidimenionality. Alpha ranges from a maximum of 1.0 for a perfect score to zero. To be considered a good measure, the alpha should be .70 or higher.

There is an apparent contradiction between using a scale or index to combine parts or subparts of a construct into one measure and the criteria of unidimensionality. It is only an apparent contradiction, however, because constructs are theoretically defined at different levels of abstraction. General, higher-level or more abstract constructs can be defined as containing several subparts. Each subdimension is a part of the construct's overall content.

For example, I define the construct "feminist ideology" as a general ideology about gender. Feminist ideology is a highly abstract and general construct. It includes specific beliefs and attitudes toward social, economic, political, family, and sexual relations. The ideology's five belief areas are parts of the single general construct. The parts are mutually reinforcing and together form a system of beliefs about the dignity, strength, and power of women.

If feminist ideology is unidimensional, then there is a unified belief system that varies from very antifeminist to very profeminist. We can test the validity of the measure that includes multiple indicators that tap the construct's subparts. If one belief area (e.g., sexual relations) is consistently distinct from the other areas in empirical tests, then we question its unidimensionality.

It is easy to become confused: A specific measure can be an indicator of a unidimensional construct in one situation and indicate a part of a different construct in another situation. This is possible because constructs can be used at different levels of abstraction.

For example, a person's attitude toward gender equality with regard to pay is more specific and less abstract than feminist ideology (i.e., beliefs about gender relations throughout society). An attitude toward equal pay can be both a unidimensional construct in its own right and a subpart of the more general and abstract unidimensional construct, *ideology toward gender relations.*

INDEX CONSTRUCTION

The Purpose

You hear about indexes all the time. For example, U.S. newspapers report the Federal Bureau of Investigation (FBI) crime index and the consumer price index (CPI). The FBI index is the sum of police reports on seven so-called index crimes (criminal homicide, aggravated assault, forcible rape, robbery, burglary, larceny of $50 or more, and auto theft). It began with the Uniform Crime Report in 1930. The CPI, which is a measure of

inflation, is created by totaling the cost of buying a list of goods and services (e.g., food, rent, and utilities) and comparing the total to the cost of buying the same list in the previous year. The consumer price index has been used by the U.S. Bureau of Labor Statistics since 1919; wage increases, union contracts, and social security payments are based on it. An *index* is a combination of items into a single numerical score. Various components or subparts of a construct are each measured, then combined into one measure.

There are many types of indexes. For example, if you take an exam with 25 questions, the total number of questions correct is a kind of index. It is a composite measure in which each question measures a small piece of knowledge, and all the questions scored correct or incorrect are totaled to produce a single measure.

Indexes measure the most desirable place to live (based on unemployment, commuting time, crime rate, recreation opportunities, weather, and so on), the degree of crime (based on combining the occurrence of different specific crimes), the mental health of a person (based on the person's adjustment in various areas of life), and the like.

One way to demonstrate that indexes are not very complicated is to use one. Answer yes or no to the seven questions that follow on the characteristics of an occupation. Base your answers on your thoughts regarding the following four occupations: long-distance truck driver, medical doctor, accountant, telephone operator. Score each answer 1 for yes and 0 for no.

1. Does it pay a good salary?
2. Is the job secure from layoffs or unemployment?
3. Is the work interesting and challenging?
4. Are its working conditions (e.g., hours, safety, time on the road) good?
5. Are there opportunities for career advancement and promotion?
6. Is it prestigious or looked up to by others?
7. Does it permit self-direction and the freedom to make decisions?

Total the seven answers for each of the four occupations. Which had the highest and which had the lowest score? The seven questions are my operational definition of the construct *good occupation.* Each question represents a subpart of my theoretical definition. A different theoretical definition would result in different questions, perhaps more than seven.

Creating indexes is so easy that it is important to be careful that every item in the index has face validity. Items without face validity should be excluded. Each part of the construct should be measured with at least one indicator. Of course, it is better to measure the parts of a construct with multiple indicators.

Weighting

An important issue in index construction is whether to weight items. Unless it is otherwise stated, assume that an index is unweighted. Likewise, unless you have a good theoretical reason for assigning different weights, use equal weights. An *unweighted index* gives each item equal weight. It involves adding up the items without modification, as if each were multiplied by 1 (or −1 for items that are negative).

In a weighted index, a researcher values or weights some items more than others. The size of weights can come from theoretical assumptions, the theoretical definition, or a statistical technique such as factor analysis. Weighting changes the theoretical definition of the construct.

Weighting can produce different index scores, but in most cases, weighted and unweighted indexes yield similar results. Researchers are concerned with the relationship between variables, and weighted and unweighted indexes usually give similar results for the relationships between variables.

Missing Data

Missing data can be a serious problem when constructing an index. Validity and reliability are threatened whenever data for some cases are missing. There are four ways to attempt to resolve the problem, but none fully solve it.

For example, I construct an index of the degree of societal development in 1975 for 50 nations. The index contains four items: life expectancy, percentage of homes with indoor plumbing, percentage of population that is literate, and number of telephones per 100 people. I locate a source of United Nations statistics for my information. The values for Belgium are 68 + 87 + 97 + 28; for Turkey, the scores are 55 + 36 + 49 + 3; for Finland, however, I discover that literacy data are unavailable. I check other sources of information, but none has the data because they were not collected.

Rates and Standardization

You have heard of crime rates, rates of population growth, and the unemployment rate. Some indexes and single-indicator measures are expressed as rates. Rates involve standardizing the value of an item to make comparisons possible. The items in an index frequently need to be standardized before they can be combined.

Standardization involves selecting a base and dividing a raw measure by the base. For example, City A had 10 murders and City B had 30 murders in the same year. In order to compare murders in the two cities, the raw number of murders needs to be standardized by the city population. If the cities are the same size, City B is more dangerous. But City B may be safer if it is much larger. For example, if City A has 100,000 people and City B has 600,000, then the murder rate per 100,000 is 10 for City A and 5 for City B.

Standardization makes it possible to compare different units on a common base. The process of standardization, also called *norming,* removes the effect of relevant but different characteristics in order to make the important differences visible. For example, there are two classes of students. An art class has 12 smokers and a biology class has 22 smokers. A researcher can compare the rate or incidence of smokers by standardizing the number of smokers by the size of the classes. The art class has 32 students and the biology class has 143 students. One method of standardization that you already know is the use of percentages, whereby measures are standardized to a common base of 100. In terms of percentages, it is easy to see that the art class has more than twice the rate of smokers (37.5 percent) than the biology class (15.4 percent).

A critical question in standardization is deciding what base to use. In the examples given, how did I know to use city size or class size as the base? The choice is not always obvious; it depends on the theoretical definition of a construct.

Different bases can produce different rates. For example, the unemployment rate can be defined as the number of people in the work force who are out of work. The overall unemployment rate is:

$$\text{Unemployment rate} = \frac{\text{Number of unemployed people}}{\text{Total number of people working}}$$

We can divide the total population into subgroups to get rates for subgroups in the population such as White males, African American females, African American males between the ages of 18 and 28, or people with college degrees. Rates for these subgroups may be more relevant to the theoretical definition or research problem. For example, a researcher believes that unemployment is an experience that affects an entire household or family and that the base should be households, not individuals. The rate will look like this:

$$\text{New Unemployment rate} = \frac{\text{Number of households with at least one unemployed person}}{\text{Total number of households}}$$

Different conceptualizations suggest different bases and different ways to standardize.

When combining several items into an index, it is best to standardize items on a common base (see Box 5.3).

SCALES

The Purpose

Scaling, like index construction, creates an ordinal, interval, or ratio measure of a variable expressed as a numerical score. Scales are common in situations where a researcher wants to measure how an individual feels or thinks about something. Some call this the hardness or potency of feelings.

Scales are used for two related purposes. First, scales help in the conceptualization and operationalization processes. Scales show the fit between a set of indicators and a single construct. For example, a researcher believes that there is a single ideological dimension that underlies people's judgments about specific policies (e.g., housing, education, foreign affairs, etc.). Scaling can help determine whether a single construct— for instance, "conservative/ liberal ideology"—underlies the positions people take on specific policies.

Second, scaling produces quantitative measures and can be used with other variables to test hypotheses. This second purpose of scaling is our primary focus because it involves scales as a technique for measuring a variable.

Logic of Scaling

As stated before, scaling is based on the idea of measuring the intensity, hardness, or potency of a variable. Graphic rating scales are an elementary form of scaling. People indicate a rating by checking a point on a line that runs from one extreme to another. This type of scale is easy to construct and use. It conveys the idea of a continuum, and assigning numbers helps people think about quantities. A built-in assumption of scales is that people with the same subjective feeling mark the graphic scale at the same place.

Box
5.3

Standardization and the Real Winners at the Olympics

Sports fans in the United States were jubilant about "winning" at the 2000 Olympics by carrying off the most gold medals. However, because they failed to *standardize*, the "win" is an illusion. Of course, the world's richest nation with the third largest population does well in one-on-one competition among all nations. To see what really happened, one must standardize on a base of the population or wealth. Standardization yields a more accurate picture by adjusting the results as if the nations had equal pop-

ulations and wealth. The results show that the Bahamas, with less than 300,000 citizens (smaller than a medium-sized U.S. city), proportionately won the most gold. Adjusted for its population size or wealth, the United States is not even near the top; it appears to be the leader only because of its great size and wealth. Sports fans in the United States can perpetuate the illusion of being at the top only if they ignore the comparative advantage of the United States.

TOP TEN GOLD MEDAL WINNING COUNTRIES AT THE 2000 OLYMPICS IN SYDNEY

Unstandardized Rank			Standardized Rank[*]			
Rank	*Country*	*Total*	*Country*	*Total*	*Population*	*GDP*
1	USA	39	Bahamas	1	33.3	20.0
2	Russia	32	Slovenia	2	10	10.0
3	China	28	Cuba	11	9.9	50.0
4	Australia	16	Norway	4	9.1	2.6
5	Germany	14	Australia	16	8.6	4.1
6	France	13	Hungry	8	7.9	16.7
7	Italy	13	Netherlands	12	7.6	3.0
8	Netherlands	12	Estonia	1	7.1	20.0
9	Cuba	11	Bulgaria	5	6.0	41.7
10	Britain	11	Lithuania	2	5.4	18.2
	EU15[**]	80	EU15	80	2.1	0.9
			USA	39	1.4	0.4

Note: [*]Population is gold medals per 10 million people and GDP is gold medals per $10 billion;
[**]EU15 is the 15 nations of the European Union treated as a single unit.
Source: Adapted from *The Economist,* October 7, 2000, p. 52.

Figure 5.4 is an example of a "feeling thermometer" scale that is used to find out how people feel about various groups in society (e.g., the National Organization of Women, the Ku Klux Klan, labor unions, physicians, etc.). This type of measure has been used by political scientists in the National Election Study since 1964 to measure attitudes toward candidates, social groups, and issues.

Commonly Used Scales

Likert Scale. You have probably used *Likert scales;* they are widely used and very common in

FIGURE 5.4 "Feeling Thermometer" Graphic Rating Scale

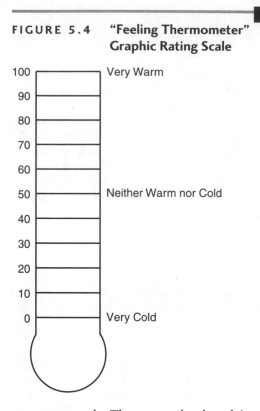

100	Very Warm
90	
80	
70	
60	
50	Neither Warm nor Cold
40	
30	
20	
10	
0	Very Cold

survey research. They were developed in the 1930s by Rensis Likert to provide an ordinal-level measure of a person's attitude. Likert scales usually ask people to indicate whether they agree or disagree with a statement. Other modifications are possible; people might be asked whether they approve or disapprove, or whether they believe something is "almost always true." Box 5.4 presents several examples of Likert scales.

Likert scales need a minimum of two categories, such as "agree" and "disagree." Using only two choices creates a crude measure and forces distinctions into only two categories. It is usually better to use four to eight categories. A researcher can combine or collapse categories after the data are collected, but data collected with crude categories cannot be made more precise later.

You can increase the number of categories at the end of a scale by adding "strongly agree," "somewhat agree," "very strongly agree," and so

forth. Keep the number of choices to eight or nine at most. More distinctions than that are probably not meaningful, and people will become confused. The choices should be evenly balanced (e.g., "strongly agree," "agree" with "strongly disagree," "disagree").

Researchers have debated about whether to offer a neutral category (e.g., "don't know," "undecided," "no opinion") in addition to the directional categories (e.g., "disagree," "agree"). A neutral category implies an odd number of categories.

A researcher can combine several Likert scale questions into a composite index if they all measure a single construct. Consider the Social Dominance Index that van Laar and colleagues (2005) used in their study of racial-ethnic attitudes among college roommates (see Box 5.5). As part of a larger survey, they asked four questions about group inequality. The answer to each question was a seven-point Likert scale with choices from Strongly Disagree to Strongly Agree. They created the index by adding the answers for each student to create scores that ranged from 4 to 28. Notice that they worded question number four in a reverse direction from the other questions. The reason for switching directions in this way is to avoid the problem of the *response set*. The response set, also called *response style* and *response bias*, is the tendency of some people to answer a large number of items in the same way (usually agreeing) out of laziness or a psychological predisposition. For example, if items are worded so that saying "strongly agree" always indicates self-esteem, we would not know whether a person who always strongly agreed had high self-esteem or simply had a tendency to agree with questions. The person might be answering "strongly agree" out of habit or a tendency to agree. Researchers word statements in alternative directions, so that anyone who agrees all the time appears to answer inconsistently or to have a contradictory opinion.

Researchers often combine many Likert-scaled attitude indicators into an index. The scale and indexes have properties that are associ-

Box 5.4   Examples of Types of Likert Scales

The Rosenberg Self-Esteem Scale

All in all, I am inclined to feel that I am a failure:
1. Almost always true
2. Often true
3. Sometimes true
4. Seldom true
5. Never true

A Student Evaluation of Instruction Scale

Overall, I rate the quality of instruction in this course as:

    Excellent   Good   Average   Fair   Poor

A Market Research Mouthwash Rating Scale

Brand	Dislike Completely	Dislike Somewhat	Dislike a Little	Like a Little	Like Somewhat	Like Completely
X	____	____	____	____	____	____
Y	____	____	____	____	____	____

Work Group Supervisor Scale

My supervisor:

	Never	Seldom	Sometimes	Often	Always
Lets members know what is expected of them	1	2	3	4	5
Is friendly and approachable	1	2	3	4	5
Treats all unit members as equals	1	2	3	4	5

ated with improving reliability and validity. An index uses multiple indicators, which improves reliability. The use of multiple indicators that measure several aspects of a construct or opinion improves content validity. Finally, the index scores give a more precise quantitative measure of a person's opinion. For example, each person's opinion can be measured with a number from 10 to 40, instead of in four categories: "strongly agree," "agree," "disagree," and "strongly disagree."

Instead of scoring Likert items, as in the previous example, the scores -2, -1, $+1$, $+2$ could be used. This scoring has an advantage in that a zero implies neutrality or complete ambiguity, whereas a high negative number means an attitude that opposes the opinion represented by a high positive number.

The numbers assigned to the response categories are arbitrary. Remember that the use of a zero does not give the scale or index a ratio level of measurement. Likert scale measures are at the

Box 5.5   Examples of Creating Indexes

Example 1

In a study of college roommates and racial–ethnic groups, van Laar and colleagues (2005) measured Social Dominance (i.e., a feeling that groups are fundamentally unequal) with the following four-item index that used a Likert scale, from 1 (Strongly Disagree) to 7 (Strongly Agree).

1. It is probably a good thing that certain groups are at the top and other groups are at the bottom.
2. Inferior groups should stay in their place.
3. We should do all we can to equalize the conditions of different groups.
4. We should increase social equality.*

*NOTE: This item was reverse scored.

The scores for the Likert responses (1 to 7) for items 1 to 4 were added to yield an index that ranged from 4 to 28 for each respondent. They report a Cronbach's alpha for this index as .74.

Example 2

In a study of perceptions of police misconduct, Weitzer and Tuch (2004) measured a respondent's experiences with police by asking seven questions

that had yes or no answers to create two composite indexes. The index for vicarious experiences was the sum of items 2, 4, and 6, with "yes" scored as 1 and "no" scored as zero. An index of personal experience was the sum of answers to items 1, 3, 5, and 7, with "yes" scored as 1 and "no" scored as zero.

1. Have you ever been stopped by police on the street without a good reason?
2. Has anyone else in your household been stopped by police on the street without a good reason?
3. Have the police ever used insulting language toward you?
4. Have the police ever used insulting language toward anyone else in your household?
5. Have the police ever used excessive force against you?
6. Have the police ever used excessive force against anyone else in your household?
7. Have you ever seen a police officer engage in any corrupt activities (such as taking bribes or involvement in drug trade)?

Weitzer and Tuch (2004) report a Cronbach's alpha for the personal experiences index as .78 and for vicarious experience index as .86.

---

ordinal level of measurement because responses indicate a ranking only. Instead of 1 to 4 or −2 to +2, the numbers 100, 70, 50, and 5 would have worked. Also, do not be fooled into thinking that the distances between the ordinal categories are intervals just because numbers are assigned. Although the number system has nice mathematical properties, the numbers are used for convenience only. The fundamental measurement is only ordinal.

The simplicity and ease of use of the Likert scale is its real strength. When several items are combined, more comprehensive multiple indi-

cator measurement is possible. The scale has two limitations: Different combinations of several scale items can result in the same overall score or result, and the response set is a potential danger.

Bogardus Social Distance Scale. The Bogardus social distance scale measures the social distance separating ethnic or other groups from each other. It is used with one group to determine how much distance it feels toward a target or "out-group."

The scale has a simple logic. People respond to a series of ordered statements; those that are most threatening or most socially distant are at one end, and those that might be least threatening or socially intimate are at the other end. The logic of the scale assumes that a person who refuses contact or is uncomfortable with the so-

cially distant items will refuse the socially closer items (see Box 5.6).

Researchers use the scale in several ways. For example, people are given a series of statements: People from Group X are entering your country,

---

| Box 5.6 | Replication of the Original Bogardus Social Distance Scale Study |

In 1993, Kleg and Yamamoto (1998) replicated the original 1925 study by Emory Bogardus that first used the social distance scale. The original study had 110 subjects from the Pacific Coast. Participants included 107 White Americans of non-Jewish European ancestry, 1 Jewish White, 1 Chinese, and 1 Japanese (about 70 percent were female). In their 1993 replication, Kleg and Yamamoto selected 135 middle school teachers from an affluent school district in a Colorado metropolitan area. There were 119 non-Jewish Whites, 7 Jewish Whites, 6 African Americans, 1 American Indian, 1 Asian, and 1 unknown (65 percent were female). There were three minor deviations from the 1925 study. First, the original Bogardus respondents were given a list of 39 groups. Those in the replication had a list of 36 groups. The two lists shared 24 groups in common. Three target groups were renamed: Negroes in 1925 versus African Americans in 1993; Syrians versus Arabs; and German-Jews and Russian-Jews vs. Jews. Second, both studies contained seven cate-

gories, but they were worded slightly differently (see below). Third, both studies had seven categories (called anchor points) printed left to right at the top. In the Bogardus original it said: "According to my first feeling reactions I would willingly admit members of each race (as a class, and not the best I have known, nor the worst members) to one or more of the classifications under which I have placed a cross (x)." In the 1993 replication it said: "Social distance means the degree that individuals desire to associate with others. This scale relates to a special form of social distance known as person to group distance. You are given a list of groups. Across from each group there are boxes identified by the labels at the top. Place an "x" in the boxes that indicate the degree of association you would desire to have with each group. Give your first reaction." The main finding was that although the average social distance declined a great deal over over 68 years, the ranking of the 25 groups changed very little (see below).

Instructions

Original 1925 Study	1993 Replication
I would willingly admit members of each race:	*The degree of association I would desire to have with members of each group is:*
1. To close kinship by marriage	To marry into group
2. To my club as personal chums	To have as best friend
3. To my street as neighbors	To have as next-door neighbors
4. To employment in my occupation in my country	To work in the same office
5. To citizenship in my country	To have as speaking acquaintances only
6. As visitors only to my country	To have as visitors to my country
7. Would exclude from my country	To keep out of my country

**BOX
5.6**   *Continued*

Results

Group	1925 Original		1993 Replication	
	Mean Score	*Rank*	*Mean Score*	*Rank*
English	1.27	1	1.17	2
Scottish	1.69	2	1.22	6
Irish	1.93	3	1.14	1
French	2.04	4	1.20	4
Dutch	2.12	5	1.25	9
Swedish	2.44	6	1.21	5
Danish	2.48	7	1.23	7
Norwegian	2.67	8	1.25	8
German	2.89	9	1.27	10
Spanish	3.28	10	1.29	11
Italian	3.98	11	1.19	3
Hindu	4.35	12	1.95	23
Polish	4.57	13	1.30	12
Russian	4.57	14	1.33	13
Native American	4.65	15	1.44	16
Jewish	4.83*	16	1.42	15
Greek	4.89	17	1.38	14
Arab	5.00*	18	2.21	24
Mexican	5.02	19	1.56	18
Black American	5.10*	20	1.55	17
Chinese	5.28	21	1.68	20
Japanese	5.30	22	1.62	19
Korean	5.55	23	1.72	21
Turk	5.80	24	1.77	22
Grand Mean	3.82		1.43	

*Slight change in name of group.

are in your town, work at your place of employment, live in your neighborhood, become your personal friends, and marry your brother or sister. People are asked whether they feel comfortable with the statement or if the contact is acceptable. It is also possible to ask whether they feel uncomfortable with the relationship. People may be asked to respond to all statements, or they may keep reading statements until they are not comfortable with a relationship. There is no set number of statements required; the number usually ranges from five to nine. The measure of social distance can be used as either an independent or a dependent variable.

A researcher can use the Bogardus scale to see how distant people feel from one out-group versus another. In addition to studying racial–ethnic groups, it has been used to examine doctor–patient distance. For example, Gordon and associates (2004) found that college students reported different social distance toward people with different disabilities. Over 95 percent would be willing to be a friend with someone with arthritis, cancer, diabetes, or a heart condition. Fewer than 70 percent would ever consider being a friend to someone with mental retardation. The social distance scale is a convenient way to determine how close a respondent feels toward a social group. It has two potential limitations. First, a researcher needs to tailor the categories to a specific out-group and social setting. Second, it is not easy for a researcher to compare how a respondent feels toward several different groups unless the respondent completes a similar social distance scale for all out-groups at the same time. Of course, how a respondent completes the scale and the respondent's actual behavior in specific social situations may differ.

Semantic Differential. Semantic Differential provides an indirect measure of how a person feels about a concept, object, or other person. The technique measures subjective feelings toward something by using adjectives. This is because people communicate evaluations through adjectives in spoken and written language. Because most adjectives have polar opposites (e.g., *light/dark, hard/soft, slow/fast*), it uses polar opposite adjectives to create a rating measure or scale. The Semantic Differential captures the connotations associated with whatever is being evaluated and provides an indirect measure of it.

The Semantic Differential has been used for many purposes. In marketing research, it tells how consumers feel about a product; political advisers use it to discover what voters think about a candidate or issue; and therapists use it to determine how a client perceives himself or herself (see Box 5.7).

To use the Semantic Differential, a researcher presents subjects with a list of paired opposite adjectives with a continuum of 7 to 11 points between them. The subjects mark the spot on the continuum between the adjectives that expresses their feelings. The adjectives can be very diverse and should be well mixed (e.g., positive items should not be located mostly on either the right or the left side). Studies of a wide variety of adjectives in English found that they fall into three major classes of meaning: evaluation (*good–bad*), potency (*strong–weak*), and activity (*active–passive*). Of the three classes of meaning, evaluation is usually the most significant. The analysis of results is difficult, and a researcher needs to use statistical procedures to analyze a subject's feelings toward the concept.

Results from a Semantic Differential tell a researcher how one person perceives different concepts or how different people view the same concept. For example, political analysts might discover that young voters perceive their candidate as traditional, weak, and slow, and as halfway between good and bad. Elderly voters perceive the candidate as leaning toward strong, fast, and good, and as halfway between traditional and modern.

Guttman Scaling. Guttman scaling, or cumulative scaling, differs from the previous scales or indexes in that researchers use it to evaluate data after they are collected. This means that researchers must design a study with the Guttman scaling technique in mind.

Guttman scaling begins with measuring a set of indicators or items. These can be questionnaire items, votes, or observed characteristics. Guttman scaling measures many different phenomena (e.g., patterns of crime or drug use, characteristics of societies or organizations, voting or political participation, psychological disorders). The indicators are usually measured in a simple yes/no or present/absent fashion. From 3 to 20 indicators can be used. The researcher se-

Box
5.7 **Example of Using the Semantic Differential**

As part of her undergraduate thesis, Daina Hawkes studied attitudes toward women with tattoos using the semantic differential (Hawkes, Senn, and Thorn, 2004). The researchers had 268 students at a medium-sized Canadian university complete a semantic differential form in response to several scenarios about a 22-year-old woman college student with a tattoo. They had five scenarios in which they varied the size of the tattoo (small versus large) and whether or not it was visible, and one with no details about the tattoo. The authors also varied features of the senario: weight problem or not; part-time job at restaurant, clothing store, or grocery store; boyfriend or not; average grades or failing grades. They used a semantic differential with 22 adjective pairs. They also had participants complete two scales: Feminist and Women's Movement scale and Neosexism scale. The semantic differential terms were selected to indicate three factors: evaluative, activity, and potency (strong/weak). Based on statistical analysis three adjectives were dropped. The 19 items used are listed below. Among other findings, the authors found that there were more negative feelings toward a woman with a visible tattoo.

Good	___	___	___	___	___	___	Bad[*]
Beautiful	___	___	___	___	___	___	Ugly
Clean	___	___	___	___	___	___	Dirty
Kind	___	___	___	___	___	___	Cruel[*]
Rich	___	___	___	___	___	___	Poor[*]
Honest	___	___	___	___	___	___	Dishonest[*]
Pleasant	___	___	___	___	___	___	Unpleasant[*]
Successful	___	___	___	___	___	___	Unsuccessful
Reputable	___	___	___	___	___	___	Disreputable
Safe	___	___	___	___	___	___	Dangerous
Gentle	___	___	___	___	___	___	Violent[*]
Feminine	___	___	___	___	___	___	Masculine
Weak	___	___	___	___	___	___	Powerful[*]
Passive	___	___	___	___	___	___	Active[*]
Cautious	___	___	___	___	___	___	Rash[*]
Soft	___	___	___	___	___	___	Hard
Weak	___	___	___	___	___	___	Strong
Mild	___	___	___	___	___	___	Intense
Delicate	___	___	___	___	___	___	Rugged[*]

[*]These items were presented in reverse order.

lects items on the belief that there is a logical relationship among them. He or she then places the results into a Guttman scale and determines whether the items form a pattern that corresponds to the relationship. (See Box 5.8 for an example of a study using Guttman scaling.)

Once a set of items is measured, the researcher considers all possible combinations of responses for the items. For example, three items are measured: whether a child knows her age, her telephone number, and three local elected political officials. The little girl may know her

Box 5.8 Guttman Scale Example

Crozat (1998) examined public responses to various forms of political protest. He looked at survey data on the public's acceptance of forms of protest in Great Britain, Germany, Italy, Netherlands, and the United States in 1974 and 1990. He found that the pattern of the public's acceptance formed a Guttman scale. Those who accepted more intense forms of protest (e.g., strikes and sit-ins) almost always accepted more modest forms (e.g., petitions or demon-

strations), but not all who accepted modest forms accepted the more intense forms. In addition to showing the usefulness of the Guttman scale, Crozat also found that people in different nations saw protest similarily and the degree of Guttman scalability increased over time. Thus, the pattern of acceptance of protest activities was Guttman "scalable" in both time periods, but it more closely followed the Guttman pattern in 1990 than 1974.

FORM OF PROTEST

	Petitions	Demonstrations	Boycotts	Strike	Sit-In
Guttman Patterns					
	N	N	N	N	N
	Y	N	N	N	N
	Y	Y	N	N	N
	Y	Y	Y	N	N
	Y	Y	Y	Y	N
	Y	Y	Y	Y	Y
Other Patterns (examples only)					
	N	Y	N	Y	N
	Y	N	Y	Y	N
	Y	N	Y	N	N
	N	Y	Y	N	N
	Y	N	N	Y	Y

age but no other answer, or all three, or only her age and telephone number. In fact, for three items there are eight possible combinations of answers or patterns of responses, from not knowing any through knowing all three. There is a mathematical way to compute the number of combinations (e.g., 2^3), but you can write down all the combinations of yes or no for three questions and see the eight possibilities.

The logical relationship among items in Guttman scaling is hierarchical. Most people or cases have or agree to lower-order items. The smaller number of cases that have the higher-order items also have the lower-order ones, but not vice versa. In other words, the higher-order items build on the lower ones. The lower-order items are necessary for the appearance of the higher-order items.

An application of Guttman scaling, known as *scalogram analysis*, lets a researcher test whether a hierarchical relationship exists among the items. For example, it is easier for a child to know her age than her telephone number, and to know her telephone number than the names of political leaders. The items are called *scalable*, or capable of forming a Guttman scale, if a hierarchical pattern exists.

The patterns of responses can be divided into two groups: scaled and errors (or nonscalable). The scaled patterns for the child's knowledge example would be as follows: not knowing any item, knowing only age, knowing only age plus phone number, knowing all three. Other combinations of answers (e.g., knowing the political leaders but not her age) are possible but are nonscalable. If a hierarchical relationship exists among the items, then most answers fit into the scalable patterns.

The strength or degree to which items can be scaled is measured with statistics that measure whether the responses can be reproduced based on a hierarchical pattern. Most range from zero to 100 percent. A score of zero indicates a random pattern, or no hierarchical pattern. A score of 100 percent indicates that all responses to the answer fit the hierarchical or scaled pattern. Alternative statistics to measure scalability have also been suggested.

CONCLUSION

In this chapter, you learned about the principles and processes of measurement in quantitative and qualitative research. All researchers conceptualize—or refine and clarify their ideas into conceptual definitions. All researchers operationalize—or develop a set of techniques or processes that will link their conceptual definitions to empirical reality. Qualitative and quantitative researchers differ in how they approach these processes, however. The quantitative researcher takes a more deductive path, whereas the qualitative researcher takes a more inductive path. The goal remains the same: to establish unambiguous links between a reseacher's abstract ideas and empirical data.

You also learned about the principles of reliability and validity. Reliability refers to the dependability or consistency of a measure; validity refers to its truthfulness, or how well a construct and data for it fit together. Quantitative and qualitative styles of research significantly diverge in how they understand these principles. Nonetheless, both quantitative and qualitative researchers try to measure in a consistent way, and both seek a tight fit between the abstract ideas they use to understand social world and what occurs in the actual, empirical social world. In addition, you saw how quantitative researchers apply the principles of measurement when they create indexes and scales, and you read about some major scales they use.

Beyond the core ideas of reliability and validity, good measurement requires that you create clear definitions for concepts, use multiple indicators, and, as appropriate, weigh and standardize the data. These principles hold across all fields of study (e.g., family, criminology, inequality, race relations, etc.) and across the many research techniques (e.g., experiments, surveys, etc.).

As you are probably beginning to realize, research involves doing a good job in each phase of a study. Serious mistakes or sloppiness in any one phase can do irreparable damage to the results, even if the other phases of the research project were conducted in a flawless manner.

Key Terms

Bogardus Social Distance Scale
conceptual definition
conceptual hypothesis
conceptualization
concurrent validity
content validity
continuous variables
criterion validity
discrete variables
empirical hypothesis
exhaustive attributes
external validity
face validity
Guttman scaling
index
internal validity
interval-level measurement
levels of measurement
Likert scale
measurement validity

multiple indicators
mutually exclusive attributes
nominal-level measurement
operational definition
operationalization
ordinal-level measurement
predictive validity
ratio-level measurement
reliability
scale
Semantic Differential
standardization
unidimensionality
validity

Endnote

1. The terms *concept, construct,* and *idea* are used more or less interchangeably, but there are differences in meaning between them. An *idea* is any mental image, belief plan, or impression. It refers to any vague impression, opinion, or thought. A *concept* is a thought, a general notion, or a generalized idea about a class of objects. A *construct* is a thought that is systematically put together, an orderly arrangement of ideas, facts, and impressions. The term *construct* is used here because its emphasis is on taking vague concepts and turning them into systematically organized ideas.

CHAPTER 6

Qualitative and Quantitative Sampling

INTRODUCTION

Qualitative and quantitative researchers approach sampling differently. Most discussions of sampling come from researchers who use the quantitative style. Their primary goal is to get a representative sample, or a small collection of units or cases from a much larger collection or population, such that the researcher can study the smaller group and produce accurate generalizations about the larger group. They tend to use sampling based on theories of probability from mathematics (called probability sampling).

Researchers have two motivations for using probability or random sampling. The first motivation is saving time and cost. If properly conducted, results from a sample may yield results at 1/1,000 the cost and time. For example, instead of gathering data from 20 million people, a researcher may draw a sample of 2,000; the data from those 2,000 are equal for most purposes to the data from all 20 million. The second purpose of probability sampling is accuracy. The results of a well-designed, carefully executed probability sample will produce results that are equally if not more accurate than trying to reach every single person in the whole population. A census is usually an attempt to count everyone. In 2000, the U.S. Census Bureau tried to count everyone in the nation, but it would have been more accurate if it used very specialized statistical sampling.

Qualitative researchers focus less on a sample's representativeness or on detailed techniques for drawing a probability sample. Instead, they focus on how the sample or small collection of cases, units, or activities illuminates key features of social life. The purpose of sampling is to collect cases, events, or actions that clarify and deepen understanding. Qualitative researchers' concern is to find cases that will enhance what the researchers learn about the processes of social life in a specific context. For this reason, qualitative researchers tend to collect a second type of sampling: nonprobability sampling.

NONPROBABILITY SAMPLING

Qualitative researchers rarely draw a representative sample from a huge number of cases to intensely study the sampled cases—the goal in quantitative research. Instead, they use nonprobability or nonrandom samples. This means they rarely determine the sample size in advance and have limited knowledge about the larger group or population from which the sample is taken. Unlike the quantitative researcher who uses a preplanned approach based on mathematical theory, the qualitative researcher selects cases gradually, with the specific content of a case determining whether it is chosen. Table 6.1

TABLE 6.1   Types of Nonprobability Samples

Type of Sample	Principle
Haphazard	Get any cases in any manner that is convenient.
Quota	Get a preset number of cases in each of several predetermined categories that will reflect the diversity of the population, using haphazard methods.
Purposive	Get all possible cases that fit particular criteria, using various methods.
Snowball	Get cases using referrals from one or a few cases, and then referrals from those cases, and so forth.
Deviant Case	Get cases that substantially differ from the dominant pattern (a special type of purposive sample).
Sequential	Get cases until there is no additional information or new characteristics (often used with other sampling methods).

shows a variety of nonprobability sampling techniques.

Haphazard, Accidental, or Convenience Sampling

Haphazard sampling can produce ineffective, highly unrepresentative samples and is not recommended. When a researcher haphazardly selects cases that are convenient, he or she can easily get a sample that seriously misrepresents the population. Such samples are cheap and quick; however, the systematic errors that easily occur make them worse than no sample at all. The person-on-the-street interview conducted by television programs is an example of a haphazard sample. Television interviewers go out on the street with camera and microphone to talk to a few people who are convenient to interview. The people walking past a television studio in the middle of the day do not represent everyone (e.g., homemakers, people in rural areas, etc.). Likewise, television interviewers often select people who look "normal" to them and avoid people who are unattractive, poor, very old, or inarticulate.

Another example of a haphazard sample is that of a newspaper that asks readers to clip a questionnaire from the paper and mail it in. Not everyone reads the newspaper, has an interest in the topic, or will take the time to cut out the questionnaire and mail it. Some people will, and the number who do so may seem large (e.g., 5,000), but the sample cannot be used to generalize accurately to the population. Such haphazard samples may have entertainment value, but they can give a distorted view and seriously misrepresent the population.

Quota Sampling

Quota sampling is an improvement over haphazard sampling. In quota sampling, a researcher first identifies relevant categories of people (e.g., male and female; or under age 30, ages 30 to 60, over age 60, etc.), then decides how many to get

in each category. Thus, the number of people in various categories of the sample is fixed. For example, a researcher decides to select 5 males and 5 females under age 30, 10 males and 10 females aged 30 to 60, and 5 males and 5 females over age 60 for a 40-person sample. It is difficult to represent all population characteristics accurately (see Figure 6.1).

Quota sampling is an improvement because the researcher can ensure that some differences are in the sample. In haphazard sampling, all those interviewed might be of the same age, sex, or race. But once the quota sampler fixes the categories and number of cases in each category, he or she uses haphazard sampling. For example, the researcher interviews the first five males under age 30 he or she encounters, even if all five just walked out of the campaign headquarters of a political candidate. Not only is misrepresentation possible because haphazard sampling is used within the categories, but nothing prevents the researcher from selecting people who "act friendly" or who want to be interviewed.

A case from the history of sampling illustrates the limitations of quota sampling. George Gallup's American Institute of Public Opinion, using quota sampling, successfully predicted the outcomes of the 1936, 1940, and 1944 U.S. presidential elections. But in 1948, Gallup predicted the wrong candidate. The incorrect prediction had several causes (e.g., many voters were undecided, interviewing stopped early), but a major reason was that the quota categories did not accurately represent all geographical areas and all people who actually cast a vote.

Purposive or Judgmental Sampling

Purposive sampling is used in situations in which an expert uses judgment in selecting cases with a specific purpose in mind. It is inappropriate if it is used to pick the "average housewife" or the "typical school." With purposive sampling, the researcher never knows whether the cases selected represent the population. It is often used in exploratory research or in field research.

FIGURE 6.1   Quota Sampling

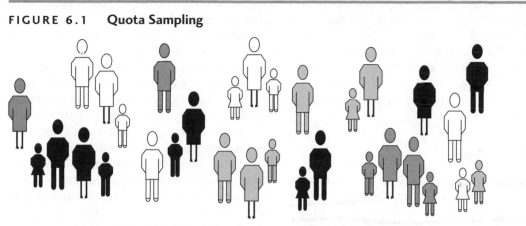

Of 32 adults and children in the street scene, select 10 for the sample:

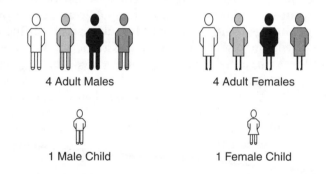

4 Adult Males   4 Adult Females

1 Male Child   1 Female Child

Purposive sampling is appropriate in three situations. First, a researcher uses it to select unique cases that are especially informative. For example, a researcher wants to use content analysis to study magazines to find cultural themes. He or she selects a specific popular women's magazine to study because it is trend setting.

Second, a researcher may use purposive sampling to select members of a difficult-to-reach, specialized population (see Hidden Populations later in this chapter). For example, the researcher wants to study prostitutes. It is impossible to list all prostitutes and sample randomly from the list. Instead, he or she uses subjective information (e.g., locations where prostitutes solicit, social groups with whom prostitutes associate, etc.) and experts (e.g., police who work on vice units, other prostitutes,

etc.) to identify a "sample" of prostitutes for inclusion in the research project. The researcher uses many different methods to identify the cases, because his or her goal is to locate as many cases as possible.

Another situation for purposive sampling occurs when a researcher wants to identify particular types of cases for in-depth investigation. The purpose is less to generalize to a larger population than it is to gain a deeper understanding of types. For example, Gamson (1992) used purposive sampling in a focus group study of what working-class people think about politics. (Chapter 11 discusses focus groups.) Gamson wanted a total of 188 working-class people to participate in one of 37 focus groups. He sought respondents who had not completed college but who were diverse in terms of age, ethnicity, religion, interest in politics, and type of occupation. He recruited people from 35 neighborhoods in the Boston area by going to festivals, picnics, fairs, and flea markets and posting notices on many public bulletin boards. In addition to explaining the study, he paid the respondents well so as to attract people who would not traditionally participate in a study.

Snowball Sampling

Snowball sampling (also called *network, chain referral,* or *reputational sampling*) is a method for identifying and sampling (or selecting) the cases in a network. It is based on an analogy to a snowball, which begins small but becomes larger as it is rolled on wet snow and picks up additional snow. Snowball sampling is a multistage technique. It begins with one or a few people or cases and spreads out on the basis of links to the initial cases.

One use of snowball sampling is to sample a network. Social researchers are often interested in an interconnected network of people or organizations. The network could be scientists around the world investigating the same problem, the elites of a medium-sized city, the members of an organized crime family, persons who sit on the boards of directors of major banks and corporations, or people on a college campus who have had sexual relations with each other. The crucial feature is that each person or unit is connected with another through a direct or indirect linkage. This does not mean that each person directly knows, interacts with, or is influenced by every other person in the network. Rather, it means that, taken as a whole, with direct and indirect links, they are within an interconnected web of linkages.

Researchers represent such a network by drawing a *sociogram*—a diagram of circles connected with lines. For example, Sally and Tim do not know each other directly, but each has a good friend, Susan, so they have an indirect connection. All three are part of the same friendship network. The circles represent each person or

case, and the lines represent friendship or other linkages (see Figure 6.2).

Researchers also use snowball sampling in combination with purposive sampling as in the case of Kissane (2003) in a descriptive field research study of low-income women in Philadelphia. The U.S. policy to provide aid and services to low-income people changed in 1996 to increase assistance (e.g., food pantries, domestic violence shelters, drug rehabilitation services, clothing distribution centers) delivered by nonpublic as opposed to government/public agencies. As frequently occurs, the policy change was made without a study of its consequences in advance. No one knew whether the affected low-income people would use the assistance provided by nonpublic agencies as much as that provided by public agencies. One year after the new policy, Kissane studied whether low-income women were equally likely to use nonpublic aid. She focused on the Kensington area of Philadelphia. It had a high (over 30 percent)

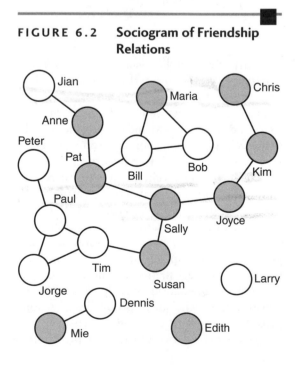

FIGURE 6.2   Sociogram of Friendship Relations

poverty rate and was a predominately White (85 percent) section of the city. First, she identified nonpublic service providers by using telephone books, the Internet, referral literature, and walking down every street of the area until she identified 50 nonpublic social service providers. She observed that a previous study found low-income women in the area distrusted outsiders and intellectuals. Her snowball sample began asking service providers for the names of a few low-income women in the area. She then asked those women to refer her to others in a similar situation, and asked those respondents to refer her to still others. She identified 20 low-income women aged 21 to 50, most who had received public assistance. She conducted in-depth, open-ended interviews about their awareness and experience with nonpublic agencies. She learned that the women were less likely to get nonpublic than public assistance. Compared to public agencies, the women were less aware of nonpublic agencies. Nonpublic agencies created more social stigma, generated greater administrative hassles, were in worse locations, and involved more scheduling difficulties because of limited hours.

Deviant Case Sampling

A researcher uses *deviant case sampling* (also called *extreme case sampling*) when he or she seeks cases that differ from the dominant pattern or that differ from the predominant characteristics of other cases. Similar to purposive sampling, a researcher uses a variety of techniques to locate cases with specific characteristics. Deviant case sampling differs from purposive sampling in that the goal is to locate a collection of unusual, different, or peculiar cases that are not representative of the whole. The deviant cases are selected because they are unusual, and a researcher hopes to learn more about the social life by considering cases that fall outside the general pattern or including what is beyond the main flow of events.

For example, a researcher is interested in studying high school dropouts. Let us say that previous research suggested that a majority of dropouts come from families that have low income, are single parent or unstable, have been geographically mobile, and are racial minorities. The family environment is one in which parents and/or siblings have low education or are themselves dropouts. In addition, dropouts are often engaged in illegal behavior and have a criminal record prior to dropping out. A researcher using deviant case sampling would seek majority-group dropouts who have no record of illegal activities and who are from stable two-parent, upper-middle–income families who are geographically stable and well educated.

Sequential Sampling

Sequential sampling is similar to purposive sampling with one difference. In purposive sampling, the researcher tries to find as many relevant cases as possible, until time, financial resources, or his or her energy is exhausted. The goal is to get every possible case. In sequential sampling, a researcher continues to gather cases until the amount of new information or diversity of cases is filled. In economic terms, information is gathered until the marginal utility, or incremental benefit for additional cases, levels off or drops significantly. It requires that a researcher continuously evaluate all the collected cases. For example, a researcher locates and plans in-depth interviews with 60 widows over 70 years old who have been living without a spouse for 10 or more years. Depending on the researcher's purposes, getting an additional 20 widows whose life experiences, social backgrounds, and worldviews differ little from the first 60 may be unnecessary.

PROBABILITY SAMPLING

A specialized vocabulary or jargon has developed around terms used in probability sampling. Before examining probability sampling, it is important to review its language.

Populations, Elements, and Sampling Frames

A researcher draws a sample from a larger pool of cases, or *elements*. A *sampling element* is the unit of analysis or case in a population. It can be a person, a group, an organization, a written document or symbolic message, or even a social action (e.g., an arrest, a divorce, or a kiss) that is being measured. The large pool is the *population*, which has an important role in sampling. Sometimes, the term *universe* is used interchangeably with *population*. To define the population, a researcher specifies the unit being sampled, the geographical location, and the temporal boundaries of populations. Consider the examples of populations in Box 6.1. All the examples include the elements to be sampled (e.g., people, businesses, hospital admissions,

---

Box 6.1   Examples of Populations

1. All persons aged 16 or older living in Singapore on December 2, 1999, who were not incarcerated in prison, asylums, and similar institutions

2. All business establishments employing more than 100 persons in Ontario Province, Canada, that operated in the month of July 2005

3. All admissions to public or private hospitals in the state of New Jersey between August 1, 1988, and July 31, 1993

4. All television commercials aired between 7:00 A.M. and 11:00 P.M. Eastern Standard Time on three major U.S. networks between November 1 and November 25, 2006

5. All currently practicing physicians in Australia who received medical degrees between January 1, 1960, and the present

6. All African American male heroin addicts in the Vancouver, British Columbia, or Seattle, Washington, metropolitan areas during 2003

---

commercials, etc.) and geographical and time boundaries.

A researcher begins with an idea of the population (e.g., all people in a city) but defines it more precisely. The term *target population* refers to the specific pool of cases that he or she wants to study. The ratio of the size of the sample to the size of the target population is the *sampling ratio*. For example, the population has 50,000 people, and a researcher draws a sample of 150 from it. Thus, the sampling ratio is 150/50,000 = 0.003, or 0.3 percent. If the population is 500 and the researcher samples 100, then the sampling ratio is 100/500 = 0.20, or 20 percent.

A population is an abstract concept. How can population be an abstract concept, when there are a given number of people at a certain time? Except for specific small populations, one can never truly freeze a population to measure it. For example, in a city at any given moment, some people are dying, some are boarding or getting off airplanes, and some are in cars driving across city boundaries. The researcher must decide exactly who to count. Should he or she count a city resident who happens to be on vacation when the time is fixed? What about the tourist staying at a hotel in the city when the time is fixed? Should he or she count adults, children, people in jails, those in hospitals? A population, even the population of all people over the age of 18 in the city limits of Milwaukee, Wisconsin, at 12:01 A.M. on March 1, 2006, is an abstract concept. It exists in the mind but is impossible to pinpoint concretely.

Because a population is an abstract concept, except for small specialized populations (e.g., all the students in a classroom), a researcher needs to estimate the population. As an abstract concept, the population needs an operational definition. This process is similar to developing operational definitions for constructs that are measured.

A researcher operationalizes a population by developing a specific list that closely approximates all the elements in the population. This list is a *sampling frame*. He or she can choose from many types of sampling frames: telephone directories, tax records, driver's license records, and so on. Listing the elements in a population sounds simple. It is often difficult because there may be no good list of elements in a population.

A good sampling frame is crucial to good sampling. A mismatch between the sampling frame and the conceptually defined population can be a major source of error. Just as a mismatch between the theoretical and operational definitions of a variable creates invalid measurement, so a mismatch between the sampling frame and the population causes invalid sampling. Researchers try to minimize mismatches. For example, you would like to sample all people in a region of the United States, so you decide to get a list of everyone with a driver's license. But some people do not have driver's licenses, and the lists of those with licenses, even if updated regularly, quickly go out of date. Next, you try income tax records. But not everyone pays taxes; some people cheat and do not pay, others have no income and do not have to file, some have died or have not begun to pay taxes, and still others have entered or left the area since the last time taxes were due. You try telephone directories, but they are not much better; some people are not listed in a telephone directory, some people have unlisted numbers, and others have recently moved. With a few exceptions (e.g., a list of all students enrolled at a university), sampling frames are almost always inaccurate. A sampling

frame can include some of those outside the target population (e.g., a telephone directory that lists people who have moved away) or might omit some of those inside it (e.g., those without telephones).

Any characteristic of a population (e.g., the percentage of city residents who smoke cigarettes, the average height of all women over the age of 21, the percent of people who believe in UFOs) is a population *parameter.* It is the true characteristic of the population. Parameters are determined when all elements in a population are measured. The parameter is never known with absolute accuracy for large populations (e.g., an entire nation), so researchers must estimate it on the basis of samples. They use information from the sample, called a *statistic,* to estimate population parameters (see Figure 6.3).

A famous case in the history of sampling illustrates the limitations of the technique. The *Literary Digest,* a major U.S. magazine, sent postcards to people before the 1920, 1924, 1928, and 1932 U.S. presidential elections. The magazine took the names for the sample from automobile registrations and telephone directories—the sampling frame. People returned the postcards indicating whom they would vote for. The magazine correctly predicted all four election outcomes. The magazine's success with predictions was well known, and in 1936, it increased the sample to 10 million. The magazine predicted a huge victory for Alf Landon over

FIGURE 6.3   A Model of the Logic of Sampling

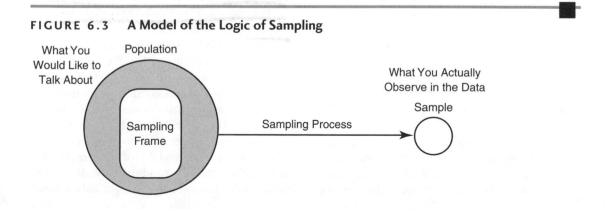

Franklin D. Roosevelt. But the *Literary Digest* was wrong; Franklin D. Roosevelt won by a landslide.

The prediction was wrong for several reasons, but the most important were mistakes in sampling. Although the magazine sampled a large number of people, its sampling frame did not accurately represent the target population (i.e., all voters). It excluded people without telephones or automobiles, a sizable percentage of the population in 1936, during the worst of the Great Depression of the 1930s. The frame excluded as much as 65 percent of the population and a segment of the voting population (lower income) that tended to favor Roosevelt. The magazine had been accurate in earlier elections because people with higher and lower incomes did not differ in how they voted. Also, during earlier elections, before the Depression, more lower-income people could afford to have telephones and automobiles.

You can learn two important lessons from the *Literary Digest* mistake. First, the sampling frame is crucial. Second, the size of a sample is less important than whether or not it accurately represents the population. A representative sample of 2,500 can give more accurate predications about the U.S. population than a nonrepresentative sample of 1 million or 10 million.

Why Random?

The area of applied mathematics called probability theory relies on random processes. The word *random* has a special meaning in mathematics. It refers to a process that generates a mathematically random result; that is, the selection process operates in a truly random method (i.e., no pattern), and a researcher can calculate the probability of outcomes. In a true random process, each element has an equal probability of being selected.

Probability samples that rely on random processes require more work than nonrandom ones. A researcher must identify specific sampling elements (e.g., person) to include in the

sample. For example, if conducting a telephone survey, the researcher needs to try to reach the specific sampled person, by calling back four or five times, to get an accurate random sample.

Random samples are most likely to yield a sample that truly represents the population. In addition, random sampling lets a researcher statistically calculate the relationship between the sample and the population—that is, the size of the *sampling error*. A nonstatistical definition of the sampling error is the deviation between sample results and a population parameter due to random processes.

Random sampling is based on a great deal of sophisticated mathematics. This chapter focuses on the fundamentals of how sampling works, the difference between good and bad samples, how to draw a sample, and basic principles of sampling in social research. This does not mean that random sampling is unimportant. It is essential to first master the fundamentals. If you plan to pursue a career using quantitative research, you should get more statistical background than space permits here.

Types of Probability Samples

Simple Random. The *simple random sample* is both the easiest random sample to understand and the one on which other types are modeled. In simple random sampling, a researcher develops an accurate sampling frame, selects elements from the sampling frame according to a mathematically random procedure, then locates the exact element that was selected for inclusion in the sample.

After numbering all elements in a sampling frame, a researcher uses a list of random numbers to decide which elements to select. He or she needs as many random numbers as there are elements to be sampled; for example, for a sample of 100, 100 random numbers are needed. The researcher can get random numbers from a *random-number table,* a table of numbers chosen in a mathematically random way. Random-number tables are available in most statistics and research methods books. The numbers are generated by a pure random process so that any number has an equal probability of appearing in any position. Computer programs can also produce lists of random numbers.

You may ask, Once I select an element from the sampling frame, do I then return it to the sampling frame or do I keep it separate? The common answer is that it is not returned. Unrestricted random sampling is random sampling with replacement—that is, replacing an element after sampling it so it can be selected again. In simple random sampling without replacement, the researcher ignores elements already selected into the sample.

The logic of simple random sampling can be illustrated with an elementary example—sampling marbles from a jar. I have a large jar full of 5,000 marbles, some red and some white. The 5,000 marbles are my population, and the parameter I want to estimate is the percentage of red marbles in it. I randomly select 100 marbles (I close my eyes, shake the jar, pick one marble, and repeat the procedure 99 times). I now have a random sample of marbles. I count the number of red marbles in my sample to estimate the percentage of red versus white marbles in the population. This is a lot easier than counting all 5,000 marbles. My sample has 52 white and 48 red marbles.

Does this mean that the population parameter is 48 percent red marbles? Maybe not. Because of random chance, my specific sample might be off. I can check my results by dumping the 100 marbles back in the jar, mixing the marbles, and drawing a second random sample of 100 marbles. On the second try, my sample has 49 white marbles and 51 red ones. Now I have a problem. Which is correct? How good is this random sampling business if different samples from the same population can yield different results? I repeat the procedure over and over until I have drawn 130 different samples of 100 marbles each (see Box 6.2 for results). Most people might empty the jar and count all 5,000, but I want to see what is going on. The results of my

130 different samples reveal a clear pattern. The most common mix of red and white marbles is 50/50. Samples that are close to that split are more frequent than those with more uneven splits. The population parameter appears to be 50 percent white and 50 percent red marbles.

Mathematical proofs and empirical tests demonstrate that the pattern found in Box 6.2 always appears. The set of many random samples is my *sampling distribution*. It is a distribution of different samples that shows the frequency of different sample outcomes from many separate random samples. The pattern will appear if the sample size is 1,000 instead of 100; if there are 10 colors of marbles instead of 2; if the population has 100 marbles or 10 million marbles instead of 5,000; and if the population is people, automobiles, or colleges instead of marbles. In fact, the pattern will become clearer as more and more independent random samples are drawn from the population.

The pattern in the sampling distribution suggests that over many separate samples, the true population parameter (i.e., the 50/50 split in the preceding example) is more common than any other result. Some samples deviate from the population parameter, but they are less common. When many different random samples are plotted as in the graph in Box 6.2, then the sampling distribution looks like a normal or bell-shaped curve. Such a curve is theoretically important and is used throughout statistics.

The *central limit theorem* from mathematics tells us that as the number of different random samples in a sampling distribution increases toward infinity, the pattern of samples and the population parameter become more predictable. With a huge number of random samples, the sampling distribution forms a normal curve, and the midpoint of the curve approaches the population parameter as the number of samples increases.

Perhaps you want only one sample because you do not have the time or energy to draw many different samples. You are not alone. A researcher rarely draws many samples. He or she

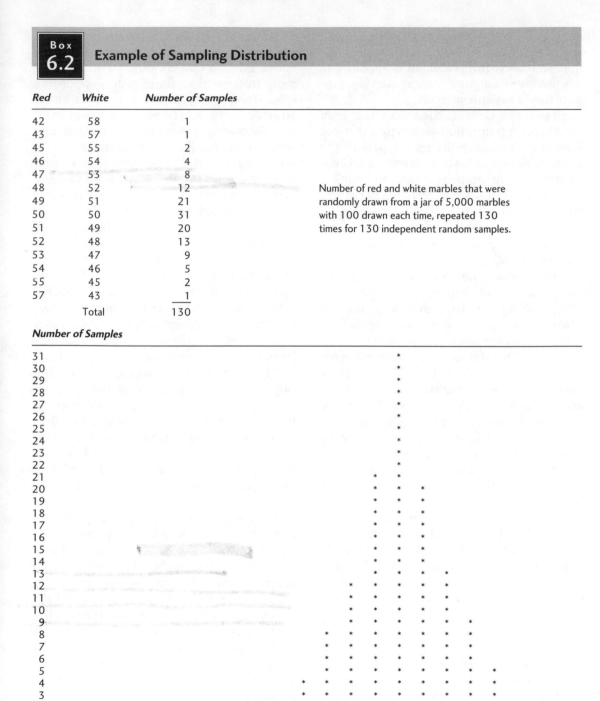

Box 6.2   Example of Sampling Distribution

Red	White	Number of Samples
42	58	1
43	57	1
45	55	2
46	54	4
47	53	8
48	52	12
49	51	21
50	50	31
51	49	20
52	48	13
53	47	9
54	46	5
55	45	2
57	43	1
	Total	130

Number of red and white marbles that were randomly drawn from a jar of 5,000 marbles with 100 drawn each time, repeated 130 times for 130 independent random samples.

Number of Samples

Number of Red Marbles in a Sample

usually draws only one random sample, but the central limit theorem lets him or her generalize from one sample to the population. The theorem is about many samples, but lets the researcher calculate the probability of a particular sample being off from the population parameter.

Random sampling does not guarantee that every random sample perfectly represents the population. Instead, it means that most random samples will be close to the population most of the time, and that one can calculate the probability of a particular sample being inaccurate. A researcher estimates the chance that a particular sample is off or unrepresentative (i.e., the size of the sampling error) by using information from the sample to estimate the sampling distribution. He or she combines this information with knowledge of the central limit theorem to construct *confidence intervals.*

The confidence interval is a relatively simple but powerful idea. When television or newspaper polls are reported, you may hear about something called the margin of error being plus or minus 2 percentage points. This is a version of confidence intervals. A confidence interval is a range around a specific point used to estimate a population parameter. A range is used because the statistics of random processes do not let a researcher predict an exact point, but they let the researcher say with a high level of confidence (e.g., 95 percent) that the true population parameter lies within a certain range.

The calculations for sampling errors or confidence intervals are beyond the level of this discussion, but they are based on the idea of the sampling distribution that lets a researcher calculate the sampling error and confidence interval. For example, I cannot say, "There are precisely 2,500 red marbles in the jar based on a random sample." However, I can say, "I am 95 percent certain that the population parameter lies between 2,450 and 2,550." I can combine characteristics of the sample (e.g., its size, the variation in it) with the central limit theorem to predict specific ranges around the parameter with a great deal of confidence.

Systematic Sampling. Systematic sampling is simple random sampling with a shortcut for random selection. Again, the first step is to number each element in the sampling frame. Instead of using a list of random numbers, a researcher calculates a *sampling interval,* and the interval becomes his or her quasi-random selection method. The sampling interval (i.e., 1 in k, where k is some number) tells the researcher how to select elements from a sampling frame by skipping elements in the frame before selecting one for the sample.

For instance, I want to sample 300 names from 900. After a random starting point, I select every third name of the 900 to get a sample of 300. My sampling interval is 3. Sampling intervals are easy to compute. I need the sample size and the population size (or sampling frame size as a best estimate). You can think of the sampling interval as the inverse of the sampling ratio. The sampling ratio for 300 names out of 900 is 300/900 = .333 = 33.3 percent. The sampling interval is 900/300 = 3.

In most cases, a simple random sample and a systematic sample yield virtually equivalent results. One important situation in which systematic sampling cannot be substituted for simple random sampling occurs when the elements in a sample are organized in some kind of cycle or pattern. For example, a researcher's sampling frame is organized by married couples with the male first and the female second (see Table 6.2). Such a pattern gives the researcher an unrepresentative sample if systematic sampling is used. His or her systematic sample can be nonrepresentative and include only wives because of how the cases are organized. When his or her sample frame is organized as couples, even-numbered sampling intervals result in samples with all husbands or all wives.

Table 6.3 illustrates simple random sampling and systematic sampling. Notice that different names were drawn in each sample. For example, H. Adams appears in both samples, but C. Droullard is only in the simple random sample. This is because it is rare for any two random samples to be identical.

TABLE 6.2   Problems with Systematic Sampling of Cyclical Data

Case	
1	Husband
2[a]	Wife
3	Husband
4	Wife
5	Husband
6[a]	Wife
7	Husband
8	Wife
9	Husband
10[a]	Wife
11	Husband
12	Wife

Random start = 2; Sampling interval = 4.
[a]Selected into sample.

The sampling frame contains 20 males and 20 females (gender is in parenthesis after each name). The simple random sample yielded 3 males and 7 females, and the systematic sample yielded 5 males and 5 females. Does this mean that systematic sampling is more accurate? No. To check this, draw a new sample using different random numbers; try taking the first two digits and beginning at the end (e.g., 11 from 11921, then 43 from 43232). Also draw a new systematic sample with a different random start. The last time the random start was 18. Try a random start of 11. What did you find? How many of each sex?

Stratified Sampling.   In *stratified sampling*, a researcher first divides the population into subpopulations (strata) on the basis of supplementary information. After dividing the population into strata, the researcher draws a random sample from each subpopulation. He or she can sample randomly within strata using simple ran-

TABLE 6.3   How to Draw Simple Random and Systematic Samples

1. Number each case in the sampling frame in sequence. The list of 40 names is in alphabetical order, numbered from 1 to 40.

2. Decide on a sample size. We will draw two 25 percent (10-name) samples.

3. For a *simple random sample,* locate a random-number table (see excerpt). Before using random-number table, count the largest number of digits needed for the sample (e.g., with 40 names, two digits are needed; for 100 to 999, three digits; for 1,000 to 9,999, four digits). Begin anywhere on the random number table (we will begin in the upper left) and take a set of digits (we will take the last two). Mark the number on the sampling frame that corresponds to the chosen random number to indicate that the case is in the sample. If the number is too large (over 40), ignore it. If the number appears more than once (10 and 21 occurred twice in

the example), ignore the second occurrence. Continue until the number of cases in the sample (10 in our example) is reached.

4. For a *systematic sample,* begin with a random start. The easiest way to do this is to point blindly at the random number table, then take the closest number that appears on the sampling frame. In the example, 18 was chosen. Start with the random number, then count the sampling interval, or 4 in our example, to come to the first number. Mark it, and then count the sampling interval for the next number. Continue to the end of the list. Continue counting the sampling interval as if the beginning of the list was attached to the end of the list (like a circle). Keep counting until ending close to the start, or on the start if the sampling interval divides evenly into the total of the sampling frame.

TABLE 6.3 *Continued*

No.	Name (Gender)	Simple Random	Systematic	No.	Name (Gender)	Simple Random	Systematic
01	Abrams, J. (M)			21	Hjelmhaug, N. (M)	Yes*	
02	Adams, H. (F)	Yes	Yes (6)	22	Huang, J. (F)	Yes	Yes (1)
03	Anderson, H. (M)			23	Ivono, V. (F)		
04	Arminond, L. (M)			24	Jaquees, J. (M)		
05	Boorstein, A. (M)			25	Johnson, A. (F)		
06	Breitsprecher, P. (M)	Yes	Yes (7)	26	Kennedy, M. (F)		Yes (2)
07	Brown, D. (F)			27	Koschoreck, L. (F)		
08	Cattelino, J. (F)			28	Koykkar, J. (M)		
09	Cidoni, S. (M)			29	Kozlowski, C. (F)	Yes	
10	Davis, L. (F)	Yes*	Yes (8)	30	Laurent, J. (M)		Yes (3)
11	Droullard, C. (M)	Yes		31	Lee, R. (F)		
12	Durette, R. (F)			32	Ling, C. (M)		
13	Elsnau, K. (F)	Yes		33	McKinnon, K. (F)		
14	Falconer, T. (M)		Yes (9)	34	Min, H. (F)	Yes	Yes (4)
15	Fuerstenberg, J. (M)			35	Moini, A. (F)		
16	Fulton, P. (F)			36	Navarre, H. (M)		
17	Gnewuch, S. (F)			37	O'Sullivan, C. (M)		
18	Green, C. (M)		START, Yes (10)	38	Oh, J. (M)		Yes (5)
19	Goodwanda, T. (F)	Yes		39	Olson, J. (M)		
20	Harris, B. (M)			40	Ortiz y Garcia, L. (F)		

Excerpt from a Random-Number Table (for Simple Random Sample)

15010	18590	00102	42210	94174	22099
90122	38221	21529	00013	04734	60457
67256	13887	94119	11077	01061	27779
13761	23390	12947	21280	44506	36457
81994	66611	16597	44457	07621	51949
79180	25992	46178	23992	62108	43232
07984	47169	88094	82752	15318	11921

*Numbers that appeared twice in random numbers selected.

dom or systematic sampling. In stratified sampling, the researcher controls the relative size of each stratum, rather than letting random processes control it. This guarantees representativeness or fixes the proportion of different strata within a sample. Of course, the necessary supplemental information about strata is not always available.

In general, stratified sampling produces samples that are more representative of the population than simple random sampling if the stratum information is accurate. A simple example illustrates why this is so. Imagine a population that is 51 percent female and 49 percent male; the population parameter is a sex ratio of 51 to 49. With stratified sampling, a researcher draws random samples among females and among males so that the sample contains a 51 to 49 percent sex ratio. If the researcher had used simple random sampling, it would be possible for a random sample to be off from the true sex ratio in the population. Thus, he or she makes fewer errors representing the population and has a smaller sampling error with stratified sampling.

Researchers use stratified sampling when a stratum of interest is a small percentage of a population and random processes could miss the stratum by chance. For example, a researcher draws a sample of 200 from 20,000 college students. He or she gets information from the college registrar indicating that 2 percent of the 20,000 students, or 400, are divorced women with children under the age of 5. This group is important to include in the sample. There would be 4 such students (2 percent of 200) in a representative sample, but the researcher could miss them by chance in one simple random sample. With stratified sampling, he or she obtains a list of the 400 such students from the registrar and randomly selects 4 from it. This guarantees that the sample represents the population with regard to the important strata (see Box 6.3).

In special situations, a researcher may want the proportion of a stratum in a sample to differ from its true proportion in the population. For example, the population contains 0.5 percent Aleuts, but the researcher wants to examine Aleuts in particular. He or she oversamples so that Aleuts make up 10 percent of the sample. With this type of disproportionate stratified sample, the researcher cannot generalize directly from the sample to the population without special adjustments.

In some situations, a researcher wants the proportion of a stratum or subgroup to differ from its true proportion in the population. For example, Davis and Smith (1992) reported that the 1987 General Social Survey (explained in a later chapter) oversampled African Americans. A random sample of the U.S. population yielded 191 Blacks. Davis and Smith conducted a separate sample of African Americans to increase the total number of Blacks to 544. The 191 Black respondents are about 13 percent of the random sample, roughly equal to the percentage of Blacks in the U.S. population. The 544 Blacks are 30 percent of the disproportionate sample. The researcher who wants to use the entire sample must adjust it to reduce the number of sampled African Americans before generalizing to the U.S. population. Disproportionate sampling helps the researcher who wants to focus on issues most relevant to a subpopulation. In this case, he or she can more accurately generalize to African Americans using the 544 respondents than using a sample of only 191. The larger sample is more likely to reflect the full diversity of the African American subpopulation.

Cluster Sampling. *Cluster sampling* addresses two problems: Researchers lack a good sampling frame for a dispersed population and the cost to reach a sampled element is very high. For example, there is no single list of all automobile mechanics in North America. Even if a researcher got an accurate sampling frame, it would cost too much to reach the sampled mechanics who are geographically spread out. Instead of using a single sampling frame, researchers use a sampling design that involves multiple stages and clusters.

A *cluster* is a unit that contains final sampling elements but can be treated temporarily as a sampling element itself. A researcher first samples clusters, each of which contains elements, then draws a second sample from within the clusters selected in the first stage of sampling. In other words, the researcher randomly samples clusters, then randomly samples elements from within the selected clusters. This has a big practical advantage. He or she can create a good sampling frame of clusters, even if it is impossible to create one for sampling elements. Once the researcher gets a sample of clusters, creating a

**Box
6.3   Illustration of Stratified Sampling**

SAMPLE OF 100 STAFF OF GENERAL HOSPITAL, STRATIFIED BY POSITION

Position	Population		Simple Random Sample	Stratified Sample	Errors Compared to the Population
	N	Percent	n	n	
Administrators	15	2.88	1	3	−2
Staff physicians	25	4.81	2	5	−3
Intern physicians	25	4.81	6	5	+1
Registered nurses	100	19.23	22	19	+3
Nurse assistants	100	19.23	21	19	+2
Medical technicians	75	14.42	9	14	+5
Orderlies	50	9.62	8	10	−2
Clerks	75	14.42	5	14	+1
Maintenance staff	30	5.77	3	6	−3
Cleaning staff	25	4.81	3	5	−2
Total	520	100.00	100	100	

Randomly select 3 of 15 administrators, 5 of 25 staff physicians, and so on.
Note: Traditionally, *N* symbolizes the number in the population and *n* represents the number in the sample.
The simple random sample overrepresents nurses, nursing assistants, and medical technicians, but underrepresents
administrators, staff physicians, maintenance staff, and cleaning staff. The stratified sample gives an accurate representation
of each type of position.

sampling frame for elements within each cluster becomes more manageable. A second advantage for geographically dispersed populations is that elements within each cluster are physically closer to one another. This may produce a savings in locating or reaching each element.

A researcher draws several samples in stages in cluster sampling. In a three-stage sample, stage 1 is random sampling of big clusters; stage 2 is random sampling of small clusters within each selected big cluster; and the last stage is sampling of elements from within the sampled small clusters. For example, a researcher wants a sample of

individuals from Mapleville. First, he or she randomly samples city blocks, then households within blocks, then individuals within households (see Box 6.4). Although there is no accurate list of all residents of Mapleville, there is an accurate list of blocks in the city. After selecting a random sample of blocks, the researcher counts all households on the selected blocks to create a sample frame for each block. He or she then uses the list of households to draw a random sample at the stage of sampling households. Finally, the researcher chooses a specific individual within each sampled household.

Illustration of Cluster Sampling

Goal: Draw a random sample of 240 people in Mapleville.

Step 1:   Mapleville has 55 districts. Randomly select 6 districts.

1 2 3* 4 5 6 7 8 9 10 11 12 13 14 15* 16 17 18 19 20 21 22 23 24 25 26
27* 28 29 30 31* 32 33 34 35 36 37 38 39 40* 41 42 43 44 45 46 47 48
49 50 51 52 53 54* 55

* = Randomly selected.

Step 2:   Divide the selected districts into blocks. Each district contains 20 blocks. Randomly select 4 blocks from the district.
Example of District 3 (selected in step 1):

1 2 3 4* 5 6 7 8 9 10* 11 12 13* 14 15 16 17* 18 19 20

* = Randomly selected.

Step 3:   Divide blocks into households. Randomly select households.
Example of Block 4 of District 3 (selected in step 2):

Block 4 contains a mix of single-family homes, duplexes, and four-unit apartment buildings. It is bounded by Oak Street, River Road, South Avenue, and Greenview Drive. There are 45 households on the block. Randomly select 10 households from the 45.

1	#1 Oak Street	16	"	31*	"	
2	#3 Oak Street	17*	#154 River Road	32*	"	
3*	#5 Oak Street	18	#156 River Road	33	"	
4	"	19*	#158 River Road	34	#156 Greenview Drive	
5	"	20*	"	35*	"	
6	"	21	#13 South Avenue	36	"	
7	#7 Oak Street	22	"	37	"	
8	"	23	#11 South Avenue	38	"	
9*	#150 River Road	24	#9 South Avenue	39	#158 Greenview Drive	
10*	"	25	#7 South Avenue	40	"	
11	"	26	#5 South Avenue	41	"	
12	"	27	#3 South Avenue	42	"	
13	#152 River Road	28	#1 South Avenue	43	#160 Greenview Drive	
14	"	29*	"	44	"	
15	"	30	#152 Greenview Drive	45	"	

* = Randomly selected.

Step 4:   Select a respondent within each household.
Summary of cluster sampling:

1 person randomly selected per household
10 households randomly selected per block
4 blocks randomly selected per district
6 districts randomly selected in the city
1 × 10 × 4 6 = 240 people in sample

Cluster sampling is usually less expensive than simple random sampling, but it is less accurate. Each stage in cluster sampling introduces sampling errors. This means a multistage cluster sample has more sampling errors than a one-stage random sample.

A researcher who uses cluster sampling must decide the number of clusters and the number of elements within each cluster. For example, in a two-stage cluster sample of 240 people from Mapleville, the researcher could randomly select 120 clusters and select 2 elements from each, or randomly select 2 clusters and select 120 elements in each. Which is best? The general answer is that a design with more clusters is better. This is because elements within clusters (e.g., people living on the same block) tend to be similar to each other (e.g., people on the same block tend to be more alike than those on different blocks). If few clusters are chosen, many similar elements could be selected, which would be less representative of the total population. For example, the researcher could select two blocks with relatively wealthy people and draw 120 people from each. This would be less representative than a sample with 120 different city blocks and 2 individuals chosen from each.

When a researcher samples from a large geographical area and must travel to each element, cluster sampling significantly reduces travel costs. As usual, there is a tradeoff between accuracy and cost.

For example, Alan, Ricardo, and Barbara each plan to visit and personally interview a sample of 1,500 students who represent the population of all college students in North America. Alan obtains an accurate sampling frame of all students and uses simple random sampling. He travels to 1,000 different locations to interview one or two students at each. Ricardo draws a random sample of three colleges from a list of all 3,000 colleges, then visits the three and selects 500 students from each. Barbara draws a random sample of 300 colleges. She visits the 300 and selects 5 students at each. If travel costs average $250 per location, Alan's travel bill is

$250,000, Ricardo's is $750, and Barbara's is $75,000. Alan's sample is highly accurate, but Barbara's is only slightly less accurate for one-third the cost. Ricardo's sample is the cheapest, but it is not representative at all.

Probability Proportionate to Size (PPS).   There are two methods of cluster sampling. The method just described is proportionate or unweighted cluster sampling. It is proportionate because the size of each cluster (or number of elements at each stage) is the same. The more common situation is for the cluster groups to be of different sizes. When this is the case, the researcher must adjust the probability or sampling ratio at various stages in sampling (see Box 6.5).

The foregoing cluster sampling example with Alan, Barbara, and Ricardo illustrates the problem with unweighted cluster sampling. Barbara drew a simple random sample of 300 colleges from a list of all 3,000 colleges, but she made a mistake—unless every college has an identical number of students. Her method gave each college an equal chance of being selected—a 300/3,000 or 10 percent chance. But colleges have different numbers of students, so each student does not have an equal chance to end up in her sample.

Barbara listed every college and sampled from the list. A large university with 40,000 students and a small college with 400 students had an equal chance of being selected. But if she chose the large university, the chance of a given student at that college being selected was 5 in 40,000 ($5/40,000 = 0.0125$ percent), whereas a student at the small college had a 5 in 400 ($5/400 = 1.25$ percent) chance of being selected. The small-college student was 100 times more likely to be in her sample. The total probability of being selected for a student from the large university was 0.125 percent (10×0.0125), while it was 12.5 percent (10×1.25) for the small-college student. Barbara violated a principle of random sampling—that each element has an equal chance to be selected into the sample.

Example Sample

Sampling has many terms for the different parts of samples or types of samples. A complex sample illustrates how researchers use them. Look at the 1980 sample for the best-known national U.S. survey in sociology, the General Social Survey.

The *population* is defined as all resident adults (18 years or older) in the U.S. for the *universe* of all Americans. The *target population* consists of all English-speaking adults who live in households, excluding those living in institutional settings such as college dormitories, nursing homes, or military quarters. The researchers estimated that 97.3 percent of all resident adults lived in households and that 97 percent of the household population spoke sufficient English to be interviewed.

The researchers used a complex multistage probability sample that is both a *cluster sample* and a *stratified sample*. First, they created a national *sampling frame* of all U.S. counties, independent cities, and Standard Metropolitan Statistical Areas (SMSAs), a Census Bureau designation for larger cities and surrounding areas. Each *sampling element* at this first level had about 4,000 households. They divided these elements into strata. The strata were the four major geographic regions as defined by the Census Bureau, divided into metropolitan and nonmetropolitan areas. They then sampled from each strata using *probability proportionate to size (PPS)* random selection, based on the number of housing units in each

county or SMSA. This gave them a sample of 84 counties or SMSAs.

For the second stage, the researchers identified city blocks, census tracts, or the rural equivalent in each county or SMSA. Each *sampling element* (e.g., city block) had a minimum of 50 housing units. In order to get an accurate count of the number of housing units for some counties, a researcher counted addresses in the field. The researchers selected 6 or more blocks within each county or SMSA using PPS to yield 562 blocks.

In the third stage, the researchers used the household as a *sampling element*. They randomly selected households from the addresses in the block. After selecting an address, an interviewer contacted the household and chose an eligible respondent from it. The interviewer looked at a selection table for possible respondents and interviewed a type of respondent (e.g., second oldest) based on the table. In total, 1,934 people were contacted for interviews and 75.9 percent of interviews were completed. This gave a final sample size of 1,468. We can calculate the *sampling ratio* by dividing 1,468 by the total number of adults living in households, which was about 150 million, which is 0.01 percent. To check the representativeness of their sample, the researchers also compared characteristics of the sample to census results (see Davis and Smith, 1992: 31–44).

If Barbara uses *probability proportionate to size (PPS)* and samples correctly, then each final sampling element or student will have an equal probability of being selected. She does this by adjusting the chances of selecting a college in the first stage of sampling. She must give large colleges with more students a greater chance of being selected and small colleges a smaller chance. She adjusts the probability of selecting a college on the basis of the proportion of all students in the population who attend it. Thus, a college

with 40,000 students will be 100 times more likely to be selected than one with 400 students. (See Box 6.6 for another example.)

Random-Digit Dialing. Random-digit dialing (RDD) is a special sampling technique used in research projects in which the general public is interviewed by telephone. It differs from the traditional method of sampling for telephone interviews because a published telephone directory is not the sampling frame.

Box 6.6   Cluster Sample Example

Vaquera and Kao (2005) studied displays of affection among adolescent couples in which the couple were either from the same or different racial groups. Their data were from a national longitudinal study of adolescent health given to students in grades 7 through 12 in 80 randomly selected U.S. high schools. There were over 90,000 students in these schools. After the schools were sampled, approximately 200 students were sampled for interviews from within those schools. Thus, the first cluster was the school, and students were sampled from within the school. Because the schools were not of the same size, ranging from 100 to 3,000 students, the authors adjusted using probabilities proportionate to size (PPS). They found that 53 percent of respondents had a relationship with someone of the opposite sex in the previous 18 months. Whites and Blacks were more likely to have same-race relationships (90 percent) compared to Asians and Hispanics (70 percent). The authors found that same- and mixed-race couples differed little in showing intimate affection, but the interracial couples were less likely to do so in public than the same-race couples.

Three kinds of people are missed when the sampling frame is a telephone directory: people without telephones, people who have recently moved, and people with unlisted numbers. Those without phones (e.g., the poor, the uneducated, and transients) are missed in any telephone interview study, but the proportion of the general public with a telephone is nearly 95 percent in advanced industrialized nations. As the percentage of the public with telephones has increased, the percentage with unlisted numbers has also grown. Several kinds of people have unlisted numbers: people who want to avoid collection agencies; the very wealthy; and those who want privacy and want to avoid obscene calls, salespeople, and prank calls. In some urban areas, the percentage of unlisted numbers is as

high as 50 percent. In addition, people change their residences, so directories that are published annually or less often have numbers for people who have left and do not list those who have recently moved into an area. Plus, directories do not list cell phone numbers. A researcher using RDD randomly selects telephone numbers, thereby avoiding the problems of telephone directories. The population is telephone numbers, not people with telephones. Random-digit dialing is not difficult, but it takes time and can frustrate the person doing the calling.

Here is how RDD works in the United States. Telephone numbers have three parts: a three-digit area code, a three-digit exchange number or central office code, and a four-digit number. For example, the area code for Madison, Wisconsin, is 608, and there are many exchanges within the area code (e.g., 221, 993, 767, 455); but not all of the 999 possible three-digit exchanges (from 001 to 999) are active. Likewise, not all of the 9,999 possible four-digit numbers in an exchange (from 0000 to 9999) are being used. Some numbers are reserved for future expansion, are disconnected, or are temporarily withdrawn after someone moves. Thus, a possible U.S. telephone number consists of an active area code, an active exchange number, and a four-digit number in an exchange.

In RDD, a researcher identifies active area codes and exchanges, then randomly selects four-digit numbers. A problem is that the researcher can select any number in an exchange. This means that some selected numbers are out of service, disconnected, pay phones, or numbers for businesses; only some numbers are what the researcher wants—working residential phone numbers. Until the researcher calls, it is not possible to know whether the number is a working residential number. This means spending a lot of time getting numbers that are disconnected, for businesses, and so forth.

Remember that the sampling element in RDD is the phone number, not the person or the household. Several families or individuals can share the same phone number, and in other situations each person may have a separate phone number or more than one phone number. This means that after a working residential phone is reached, a second stage of sampling is necessary, within household sampling, to select the person to be interviewed.

Box 6.5 presents an example of how the many sampling terms and ideas can be used together in a specific real-life situation.

Hidden Populations

In contrast to sampling the general population or visible and accessible people, sampling *hidden populations* (i.e., people who engage in concealed activities) is a recurrent issue in the studies of deviant or stigmatized behavior. It illustrates the creative application of sampling principles, mixing qualitative and quantitative styles of research and often using nonprobability techniques. Examples of hidden populations include illegal drug users, prostitutes, homosexuals, people with HIV/AIDS, homeless people, and others.

Tyldum and Brunovskis (2005) described ways to measure the hidden population of women and children victims of sex trafficking in Norway. They suggested using multiple sampling approaches and thinking of in terms of several overlapping populations in which victims are a subset. One population is all working prostitutes. By telephoning all identifiable escort and massage services, then calculating response rates and the number of women per phone, the authors estimated that 600 female prostitutes worked in the Oslo metro area in October 2003. Based on number of months most women work in prostitution and their turnover rate each year, they estimated that 1,100 different women work as prostitutes in Oslo in a year. Of these, about 80 percent of them are of non-Norwegian origin. Victims of sex trafficking are a subset among the roughly 800 non-Norwegians who work as prostitutes who are being exploited by others and working involuntary. A second population is the women law-enforcement officials or non-

government service agencies identified as victims. Law-enforcement estimates depend on the specific level of enforcement efforts and are most likely to identify a small percent of the most visible and serious cases. Similar difficulties exist with nongovernment service agencies that provide aid to victims. Thus, during the first 10 months of 2004, Norwegian police detected 42 sex trafficking victims. This is subset of all possible trafficking victims. For this population Tyldum and Brunovskis suggested using a capture-recapture method borrowed from biology. In capture-recapture, a percentage of the same cases will reappear across multiple attempts to "capture" cases (with a release after past capture). This percentage recaptured allows researchers to estimate the size of the total population. A third population is that of migrants who have returned to their country of origin. By surveying returnees and estimating the proportion of them who are former trafficking victims, researchers have another way to estimate the size of the hidden population.

Draus and associates (2005) described their sampling a hidden population in a field research study of illicit drug users in four rural Ohio counties. They used respondent-driven sampling (RDS), which is a version of snowball sampling and appropriate when members of a hidden population are likely to maintain contact with one another. This type of sampling begins by identifying an eligible case or participant. This person, called a "seed," is given referral coupons to distribute among other eligible people who engage in the same activity. For each successful referral, the "seed" receives some money. This process is repeated with several waves of new recuits until the a point of saturation (see Sequential Sampling earlier in this chapter). In the study by Draus and associates, each interviewed drug-using participant was paid $50 for an initial two-hour interview and $35 for an hour-long follow-up interview. The participants received three referral coupons at the end of the initial interview and got $10 for each eligible participant they referred who completed an initial interview. No participant received more than three referral coupons. Sometimes this yielded no new participants, but at other times more than the three people with referral coupons were recruited. In one case, a young man heard about the study at a local tatoo parlor and called the study office in July 2003. He (participant 157) had been a powder cocaine user and in his interview said he knew many other drug users. He referred two new participants (participants 161 and 146) who came in about one month later. Participant 161 did not refer anyone new, but participant 146 referred four new people, and two of the four (154 and 148) referred still others. Participant 154 referred four new people and 146 referred one new person, and that one person, (participant 158) referred four others. This sampling process that took place in different geographic locations produced 249 users of cocaine or methanmphetamine between June 2002 and February 2004.

You are now familiar with several major types of probability samples (see Table 6.4) and supplementary techniques used with them (e.g., PPS, within-household, RDD, and RDS) that may be appropriate. In addition, you have seen how researchers combine nonprobability and probability sampling for special situations, such as hidden populations. Next, we turn to determining a sample size for probability samples.

How Large Should a Sample Be?

Students and new researchers often ask, "How large does my sample have to be?" The best answer is, "It depends." It depends on the kind of data analysis the researcher plans, on how accurate the sample has to be for the researcher's purposes, and on population characteristics. As you have seen, a large sample size alone does not guarantee a representative sample. A large sample without random sampling or with a poor sampling frame is less representative than a smaller one with random sampling and an excellent sampling frame. Good samples for qualitative purposes can be very small.

TABLE 6.4   Types of Probability Samples

Type of Sample	Technique
Simple Random	Create a sampling frame for all cases, then select cases using a purely random process (e.g., random-number table or computer program).
Stratified	Create a sampling frame for each of several categories of cases, draw a random sample from each category, then combine the several samples.
Systematic	Create a sampling frame, calculate the sampling interval 1/k, choose a random starting place, then take every 1/k case.
Cluster	Create a sampling frame for larger cluster units, draw a random sample of the cluster units, create a sampling frame for cases within each selected cluster unit, then draw a random sample of cases, and so forth.

The question of sample size can be addressed in two ways. One is to make assumptions about the population and use statistical equations about random sampling processes. The calculation of sample size by this method requires a statistical discussion that is beyond the level of this text. The researcher must make assumptions about the degree of confidence (or number of errors) that is acceptable and the degree of variation in the population.

A second and more frequently used method is a rule of thumb—a conventional or commonly accepted amount. Researchers use it because they rarely have the information required by the statistical method and because it gives sample sizes close to those of the statistical method. Rules of thumb are not arbitrary but are based on past experience with samples that have met the requirements of the statistical method.

One principle of sample sizes is, the smaller the population, the bigger the sampling ratio has to be for an accurate sample (i.e., one with a high probability of yielding the same results as the entire population). Larger populations permit smaller sampling ratios for equally good samples. This is because as the population size grows, the returns in accuracy for sample size shrink.

For small populations (under 1,000), a researcher needs a large sampling ratio (about 30 percent). For example, a sample size of about 300 is required for a high degree of accuracy. For moderately large populations (10,000), a smaller sampling ratio (about 10 percent) is needed to be equally accurate, or a sample size of around 1,000. For large populations (over 150,000), smaller sampling ratios (1 percent) are possible, and samples of about 1,500 can be very accurate. To sample from very large populations (over 10 million), one can achieve accuracy using tiny sampling ratios (0.025 percent) or samples of about 2,500. The size of the population ceases to be relevant once the sampling ratio is very small, and samples of about 2,500 are as accurate for populations of 200 million as for 10 million. These are approximate sizes, and practical limitations (e.g., cost) also play a role in a researcher's decision.

A related principle is that for small samples, small increases in sample size produce big gains in accuracy. Equal increases in sample size produce more of an increase in accuracy for small than for large samples.

A researcher's decision about the best sample size depends on three things: (1) the degree of accuracy required, (2) the degree of variability or diversity in the population, and (3) the number of different variables examined simultaneously in data analysis. Everything else being equal, larger samples are needed if one wants high accuracy, if the population has a great deal of variability or heterogeneity, or if one wants to examine many variables in the data analysis simultaneously. Smaller samples are sufficient when less accuracy is acceptable, when the population is homogeneous, or when only a few variables are examined at a time.

The analysis of data on subgroups also affects a researcher's decision about sample size. If the researcher wants to analyze subgroups in the population, he or she needs a larger sample. For example, I want to analyze four variables for males between the ages of 30 and 40 years old. If this sample is of the general public, then only a small proportion (e.g., 10 percent) of sample cases will be males in that age group. A rule of thumb is to have about 50 cases for each subgroup to be analyzed. Thus, if I want to analyze a group that is only 10 percent of the population, then I should have 10 × 50 or 500 cases in the sample to be sure I get enough for the subgroup analysis.

Drawing Inferences

A researcher samples so he or she can draw inferences from the sample to the population. In fact, a subfield of statistical data analysis that concerns drawing accurate inferences is called *inferential statistics*. The researcher directly observes variables using units in the sample. The sample stands for or represents the population. Researchers are not interested in samples in themselves; they want to infer to the population. Thus, a gap exists between what the researcher concretely has (a sample) and what is of real interest (a population) (see Figure 6.4).

In the last chapter, you saw how the logic of measurement could be stated in terms of a gap between abstract constructs and concrete indicators. Measures of concrete, observable data are approximations for abstract constructs. Researchers use the approximations to estimate what is of real interest (i.e., constructs and causal laws). Conceptualization and operationalization

FIGURE 6.4   Model of the Logic of Sampling and of Measurement

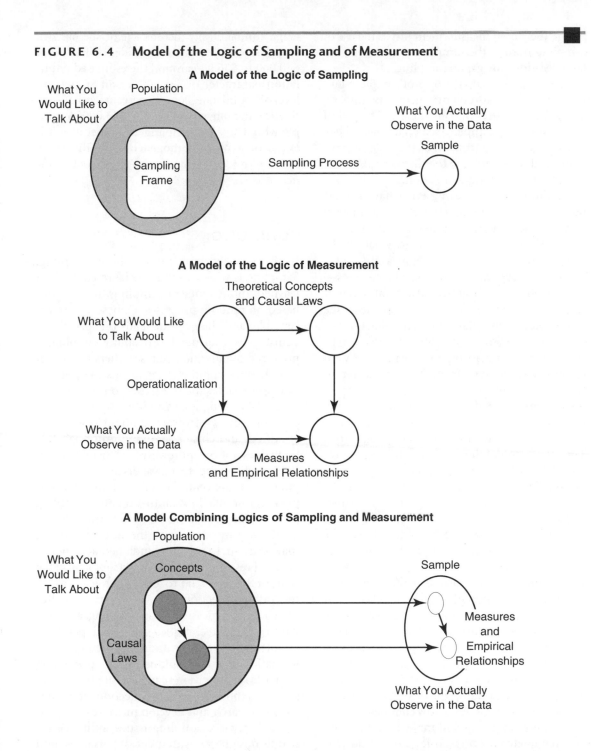

bridge the gap in measurement just as the use of sampling frames, the sampling process, and inference bridge the gap in sampling.

Researchers put the logic of sampling and the logic of measurement together by directly observing measures of constructs and empirical relationships in samples (see Figure 6.4). They infer or generalize from what they can observe empirically in samples to the abstract causal laws and constructs in the population.

Validity and sampling error have similar functions, as can be illustrated by the analogy between the logic of sampling and the logic of measurement—that is, between what is observed and what is discussed. In measurement, a researcher wants valid indicators of constructs—that is, concrete indicators that accurately represent abstract constructs. In sampling, he or she wants samples that have little sampling error—concrete collections of cases that accurately represent unseen and abstract populations. A valid measure deviates little from the construct it represents. A sample with little sampling error permits estimates that deviate little from population parameters.

Researchers try to reduce sampling errors. The calculation of the sampling error is not presented here, but it is based on two factors: the sample size and the amount of diversity in the sample. Everything else being equal, the larger the sample size, the smaller the sampling error. Likewise, the greater the homogeneity (or the less the diversity) in a sample, the smaller its sampling error.

Sampling error is also related to confidence intervals. If two samples are identical except that one is larger, the one with more cases will have a smaller sampling error and narrower confidence intervals. Likewise, if two samples are identical except that the cases in one are more similar to each other, the one with greater homogeneity will have a smaller sampling error and narrower confidence intervals. A narrow confidence interval means more precise estimates of the population parameter for a given level of confidence. For example, a researcher wants to estimate av-

erage annual family income. He or she has two samples. Sample 1 gives a confidence interval of $30,000 to $36,000 around the estimated population parameter of $33,000 for an 80 percent level of confidence. For a 95 percent level of confidence, the range is $23,000 to $43,000. A sample with a smaller sampling error (because it is larger or is more homogeneous) might give a $30,000 to $36,000 range for a 95 percent confidence level.

CONCLUSION

In this chapter, you learned about sampling. Sampling is widely used in social research. You learned about types of sampling that are not based on random processes. Only some are acceptable, and their use depends on special circumstances. In general, probability sampling is preferred by quantitative researchers because it produces a sample that represents the population and enables the researcher to use powerful statistical techniques. In addition to simple random sampling, you learned about systematic, stratified, and cluster sampling. Although this book does not cover the statistical theory used in random sampling, from the discussion of sampling error, the central limit theorem, and sample size, it should be clear that random sampling produces more accurate and precise sampling.

Before moving on to the next chapter, it may be useful to restate a fundamental principle of social research: Do not compartmentalize the steps of the research process; rather, learn to see the interconnections between the steps. Research design, measurement, sampling, and specific research techniques are interdependent. Unfortunately, the constraints of presenting information in a textbook necessitate presenting the parts separately, in sequence. In practice, researchers think about data collection when they design research and develop measures for variables. Likewise, sampling issues influence research design, measurement of variables, and data collection strategies. As you will see in future chapters, good social research depends on simultaneously controlling quality at several different steps—research design, conceptualization, measurement, sampling, and data collection and handling. The researcher who makes major errors at any one stage may make an entire research project worthless.

Key Terms

central limit theorem
cluster sampling
confidence intervals
deviant case sampling
haphazard sampling
hidden populations
inferential statistics
nonrandom sample
parameter
population

probability proportionate to size (PPS)
purposive sampling
quota sampling
random-digit dialing (RDD)
random-number table
random sample
sample
sampling distribution
sampling element
sampling error
sampling frame
sampling interval
sampling ratio
sequential sampling
simple random sampling
snowball sampling
sociogram
statistic
stratified sampling
systematic sampling
target population

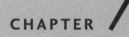

Survey Research

INTRODUCTION

Someone hands you a sheet of paper full of questions. The first reads: "I would like to learn your opinion of the Neuman research methods textbook. Would you say it is (a) well organized, (b) adequately organized, or (c) poorly organized?" You probably would not be shocked by this. It is a kind of survey, and most of us are accustomed to surveys by the time we reach adulthood.

The survey is the most widely used data-gathering technique in sociology, and it is used in many other fields, as well. In fact, surveys are almost too popular. People sometimes say, "Do a survey" to get information about the social world, when they should be asking, "What is the most appropriate research design?" Despite the popularity of surveys, it is easy to conduct a survey that yields misleading or worthless results. Good surveys require thought and effort.

All surveys are based on the professional social research survey. In this chapter, you will learn the main ingredients of good survey research, as well as the limitations of the survey method.

Research Questions Appropriate for a Survey

Survey research developed within the positivist approach to social science. The survey asks many people (called *respondents*) about their beliefs, opinions, characteristics, and past or present behavior.

Surveys are appropriate for research questions about self-reported beliefs or behaviors. They are strongest when the answers people give to questions measure variables. Researchers usually ask about many things at one time in surveys, measure many variables (often with multiple indicators), and test several hypotheses in a single survey.

Although the categories overlap, the following can be asked in a survey:

1. *Behavior.* How frequently do you brush your teeth? Did you vote in the last city election? When did you last visit a close relative?
2. *Attitudes/beliefs/opinions.* What kind of job do you think the mayor is doing? Do you think other people say many negative things about you when you are not there? What is the biggest problem facing the nation these days?
3. *Characteristics.* Are you married, never married, single, divorced, separated, or widowed? Do you belong to a union? What is your age?
4. *Expectations.* Do you plan to buy a new car in the next 12 months? How much schooling do you think your child will get? Do you think the population in this town will grow, shrink, or stay the same?
5. *Self-classification.* Do you consider yourself to be liberal, moderate, or conservative? Into which social class would you put your family? Would you say you are highly religious or not religious?
6. *Knowledge.* Who was elected mayor in the last election? About what percentage of the people in this city are non-White? Is it legal to own a personal copy of Karl Marx's *Communist Manifesto* in this country?

Researchers warn against using surveys to ask "why?" questions (e.g., Why do you think crime occurs?). "Why?" questions are appropriate, however, if a researcher wants to discover a respondent's subjective understanding or informal theory (i.e., the respondent's own view of "why" he or she acts a certain way). Because few respondents are fully aware of the causal factors that shape their beliefs or behavior, such questions are not a substitute for the researcher developing a consistent causal theory of his or her own that builds on the existing scientific literature.

An important limitation of survey research is that it provides data only of what a person or organization says, and this may differ from what he or she actually does. This is illustrated by Pager and Quillian (2005), who compared telephone survey responses from Milwaukee-area employers about their willingness to hire ex-offenders of different races with an "audit." In the audit, a trained pair of young males with specific characteristics applied for 350 job openings in December 2001. Employers agreed to hire 34 percent of White and 14 percent of Black applicants. The applicants had identical job experience and credentials and no criminal records. The same employers agreed to hire 17 percent of Whites and 5 percent of Blacks with identical job experience and credentials but also with a criminal record for illegal drug use. The employers were telephoned a few months later. Pager and Quillian found in the telephone survey far more employers expressed a willingness to hire an ex-offender (67 percent) and there were no differences in the offender's race. Also, certain employers said they were more willing to hire an ex-offender, but in the audit all employers acted the same. The authors said, "Survey responses have very little connection to the actual behaviors exhibited by these employers" (2005:367).

THE LOGIC OF SURVEY RESEARCH

What Is a Survey?

Survey researchers sample many respondents who answer the same questions. They measure many variables, test multiple hypotheses, and infer temporal order from questions about past behavior, experiences, or characteristics. For example, years of schooling or a respondent's race are prior to current attitudes. An association among variables is measured with statistical techniques. Survey researchers think of alternative explanations when planning a survey, measure variables that represent alternative explanations (i.e., control variables), then statistically examine their effects to rule out alternative explanations.

Survey research is often called *correlational*. Survey researchers use questions as control variables to approximate the rigorous test for causality that experimenters achieve with their physical control over temporal order and alternative explanations.

Steps in Conducting a Survey

The survey researcher follows a deductive approach. He or she begins with a theoretical or applied research problem and ends with empirical measurement and data analysis. Once a researcher decides that the survey is an appropriate method, basic steps in a research project can be divided into the substeps outlined in Figure 7.1.

In the first phase, the researcher develops an instrument—a survey questionnaire or interview schedule—that he or she uses to measure variables. Respondents read the questions themselves and mark answers on a *questionnaire*. An *interview schedule* is a set of questions read to the respondent by an interviewer, who also records responses. To simplify the discussion, I will use only the term *questionnaires*.

A survey researcher conceptualizes and operationalizes variables as questions. He or she writes and rewrites questions for clarity and completeness, and organizes questions on the questionnaire based on the research question, the respondents, and the type of survey. (The types of surveys are discussed later.)

When preparing a questionnaire, the researcher thinks ahead to how he or she will record and organize data for analysis. He or she pilot-tests the questionnaire with a small set of respondents similar to those in the final survey. If interviewers are used, the researcher trains them with the questionnaire. He or she asks respondents in the pilot-test whether the questions were clear and explores their interpretations to see if his or her intended meaning was clear. The researcher also draws the sample during this phase.

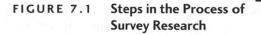

FIGURE 7.1   Steps in the Process of Survey Research

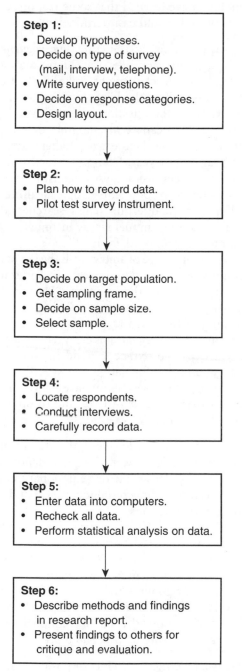

Step 1:
- Develop hypotheses.
- Decide on type of survey (mail, interview, telephone).
- Write survey questions.
- Decide on response categories.
- Design layout.

Step 2:
- Plan how to record data.
- Pilot test survey instrument.

Step 3:
- Decide on target population.
- Get sampling frame.
- Decide on sample size.
- Select sample.

Step 4:
- Locate respondents.
- Conduct interviews.
- Carefully record data.

Step 5:
- Enter data into computers.
- Recheck all data.
- Perform statistical analysis on data.

Step 6:
- Describe methods and findings in research report.
- Present findings to others for critique and evaluation.

After the planning phase, the researcher is ready to collect data. This phase is usually shorter than the planning phase. He or she locates sampled respondents in person, by telephone, or by mail. Respondents are given information and instructions on completing the questionnaire or interview. The questions follow, and there is a simple stimulus/response or question/answer pattern. The researcher accurately records answers or responses immediately after they are given. After all respondents complete the questionnaire and are thanked, he or she organizes the data and prepares them for statistical analysis.

Survey research can be complex and expensive and it can involve coordinating many people and steps. The administration of survey research requires organization and accurate record keeping. The researcher keeps track of each respondent, questionnaire, and interviewer. For example, he or she gives each sampled respondent an identification number, which also appears on the questionnaire. He or she then checks completed questionnaires against a list of sampled respondents. Next, the researcher reviews responses on individual questionnaires, stores original questionnaires, and transfers information from questionnaires to a format for statistical analysis. Meticulous bookkeeping and labeling are essential. Otherwise, the researcher may find that valuable data and effort are lost through sloppiness.

CONSTRUCTING THE QUESTIONNAIRE

Principles of Good Question Writing

A good questionnaire forms an integrated whole. The researcher weaves questions together so they flow smoothly. He or she includes introductory remarks and instructions for clarification and measures each variable with one or more survey questions.

Three principles for effective survey questions are: Keep it clear, keep it simple, and keep the respondent's perspective in mind. Good survey questions give the researcher valid and reliable measures. They also help respondents feel that they understand the question and that their answers are meaningful. Questions that do not mesh with a respondent's viewpoint or that respondents find confusing are not good measures. A survey researcher must exercise extra care if the respondents are heterogeneous or come from different life situations than his or her own.

Researchers face a dilemma. They want each respondent to hear exactly the same questions, but will the questions be equally clear, relevant, and meaningful to all respondents? If respondents have diverse backgrounds and frames of reference, the exact same wording may not have the same meaning. Yet, tailoring question wording to each respondent makes comparisons almost impossible. A researcher would not know whether the wording of the question or the differences in respondents accounted for different answers.

Question writing is more of an art than a science. It takes skill, practice, patience, and creativity. The principles of question writing are illustrated in the following 12 things to avoid when writing survey questions. The list does not include every possible error, only the more frequent problems.

1. *Avoid jargon, slang, and abbreviations.* Jargon and technical terms come in many forms. Plumbers talk about *snakes,* lawyers about a contract of *uberrima fides,* psychologists about the *Oedipus complex.* Slang is a kind of jargon within a subculture—for example, the homeless talk about a *snowbird* and skiers about a *hotdog.* Also avoid abbreviations. *NATO* usually means North Atlantic Treaty Organization, but for a respondent, it might mean something else (National Auto Tourist Organization, Native Alaskan Trade Orbit, or North African Tea Office). Avoid slang and jargon unless a specialized population is being surveyed. Target the vocabulary and grammar to the respondents sampled.

For the general public, this is the language used on television or in the newspaper (about an eighth-grade reading vocabulary). Survey researchers have learned that some respondents may not understand basic terminology.

2. *Avoid ambiguity, confusion, and vagueness.* Ambiguity and vagueness plague most question writers. A researcher might make implicit assumptions without thinking of the respondents. For example, the question, "What is your income?" could mean weekly, monthly, or annual; family or personal; before taxes or after taxes; for this year or last year; from salary or from all sources. The confusion causes inconsistencies in how different respondents assign meaning to and answer the question. The researcher who wants before-tax annual family income for last year must explicitly ask for it.[1]

Another source of ambiguity is the use of indefinite words or response categories. For example, an answer to the question, "Do you jog regularly? Yes _____ No _____," hinges on the meaning of the word *regularly.* Some respondents may define *regularly* as every day, others as once a week. To reduce respondent confusion and get more information, be specific—ask whether a person jogs "about once a day," "a few times a week," "once a week," and so on. (See Box 7.1 on improving questions.)

3. *Avoid emotional language.* Words have implicit connotative as well as explicit denotative meanings. Words with strong emotional connotations can color how respondents hear and answer survey questions.

Use neutral language. Avoid words with emotional "baggage," because respondents may react to the emotionally laden words rather than to the issue. For example, the question, "What do you think about a policy to pay murderous terrorists who threaten to steal the freedoms of peace-loving people?" is full of emotional words (*murderous, freedoms, steal,* and *peace*).

4. *Avoid prestige bias.* Titles or positions in society (e.g., president, expert, etc.) carry prestige

Box 7.1 Improving Unclear Questions

Here are three survey questions written by experienced professional researchers. They revised the original wording after a pilot test revealed that 15 percent of respondents asked for clarification or gave inadequate answers (e.g., don't know). As you can see, question wording is an art that may improve with practice, patience, and pilot testing.

Original Question	Problem	Revised Question
Do you exercise or play sports regularly?	What counts as exercise?	Do you do any sports or hobbies, physical activities, or exercise, including walking, on a regular basis?
What is the average number of days each week you have butter?	Does margarine count as butter?	The next question is just about butter—not including margarine. How many days a week do you have butter?
[Following question on eggs] What is the number of servings in a typical day?	How many eggs is a serving? What is a typical day?	On days when you eat eggs, how many eggs do you usually have?

	Responses to Question		Percentage Asking for Clarification	
	Original	*Revision*	*Original*	*Revision*
Exercise question (% saying "yes")	48%	60%	5%	0%
Butter question (% saying "none")	33%	55%	18%	13%
Egg question (% saying "one")	80%	33%	33%	0%

Source: Adapted from Fowler (1992).

or status. Issues linked to people with high social status can color how respondents hear and answer survey questions. Avoid associating a statement with a prestigious person or group. Respondents may answer on the basis of their feelings toward the person or group rather than addressing the issue. For example, saying, "Most doctors say that cigarette smoke causes lung disease for those near a smoker. Do you agree?" affects people who want to agree with doctors. Likewise, a question such as, "Do you support the president's policy regarding Kosovo?" will be answered by respondents who have never heard of Kosovo on the basis of their view of the president.

5. *Avoid double-barreled questions.* Make each question about one and only one topic. A *double-barreled question* consists of two or more questions joined together. It makes a respon-

dent's answer ambiguous. For example, if asked, "Does this company have pension and health insurance benefits?" a respondent at a company with health insurance benefits only might answer either yes or no. The response has an ambiguous meaning, and the researcher cannot be certain of the respondent's intention. A researcher who wants to ask about the joint occurrence of two things—for example, a company with both health insurance and pension benefits—should ask two separate questions.

6. *Do not confuse beliefs with reality.* Do not confuse what a respondent believes with what you, the researcher, measures. A respondent may think that a relationship exists between two variables but this is not an empirical measurement of variables in a relationship. For example, a researcher wants to find out if students rate teachers higher who tell many jokes in class. The two variables are "teacher tells jokes" and "rating the teacher." The *wrong* way to approach the issue is to ask students, "Do you rate a teacher higher if the teacher tells many jokes?" This measures whether or not students *believe* that they rate teachers based on joke telling; it does not measure the empirical relationship. The *correct* way is to ask two separate empirically based questions: "How do you rate this teacher?" and "How many jokes does the teacher tell in class?" Then the researcher can examine answers to the two questions to determine if there is an association between them. People's beliefs about a relationship among variables are distinct from an actual empirical relationship.

7. *Avoid leading questions.* Make respondents feel that all responses are legitimate. Do not let them become aware of an answer that the researcher wants. A *leading* (or *loaded*) *question* is one that leads the respondent to choose one response over another by its wording. There are many kinds of leading questions. For example, the question, "You don't smoke, do you?" leads respondents to state that they do not smoke.

Loaded questions can be stated to get either positive or negative answers. For example,

"Should the mayor spend even more tax money trying to keep the streets in top shape?" leads respondents to disagree, whereas "Should the mayor fix the pot-holed and dangerous streets in our city?" is loaded for agreement.

8. *Avoid asking questions that are beyond respondents' capabilities.* Asking something that few respondents know frustrates respondents and produces poor-quality responses. Respondents cannot always recall past details and may not know specific factual information. For example, asking an adult, "How did you feel about your brother when you were 6 years old?" is probably worthless. Asking respondents to make a choice about something they know nothing about (e.g., a technical issue in foreign affairs or an internal policy of an organization) may result in an answer, but one that is unreliable and meaningless. When many respondents are unlikely to know about an issue, use a full-filter question form (to be discussed).

Phrase questions in the terms in which respondents think. For example, few respondents will be able to answer, "How many gallons of gasoline did you buy last year for your car?" Yet, respondents may be able to answer a question about gasoline purchases for a typical week, which the researcher can multiply by 52 to estimate annual purchases.[2]

9. *Avoid false premises.* Do not begin a question with a premise with which respondents may not agree, then ask about choices regarding it. Respondents who disagree with the premise will be frustrated and not know how to answer. For example, the question, "The post office is open too many hours. Do you want it to open four hours later or close four hours earlier each day?" leaves those who either oppose the premise or oppose both alternatives without a meaningful choice.

A better question explicitly asks the respondent to assume a premise is true, then asks for a preference. For example, "Assuming the post office has to cut back its operating hours, which would you find more convenient, opening four hours later or closing four hours earlier each day?" Answers to a hypothetical situation are not very reliable, but being explicit will reduce frustration.

10. *Avoid asking about intentions in the distant future.* Avoid asking people about what they might do under hypothetical circumstances far in the future. Responses are poor predictors of behavior removed far from their current situation or far in the future. Questions such as, "Suppose a new grocery store opened down the road in three years. Would you shop at it?" are usually a waste of time. It is better to ask about current or recent attitudes and behavior. In general, respondents answer specific, concrete questions that relate to their experiences more reliably than they do those about abstractions that are beyond their immediate experiences.

11. *Avoid double negatives.* Double negatives in ordinary language are grammatically incorrect and confusing. For example, "I ain't got no job" logically means that the respondent does have a job, but the second negative is used in this way for emphasis. Such blatant errors are rare, but more subtle forms of the double negative are also confusing. They arise when respondents are asked to agree or disagree with a statement. For example, respondents who *dis*agree with the statement, "Students should not be required to take a comprehensive exam to graduate" are logically stating a double negative because they *disagree* with *not* doing something.

12. *Avoid overlapping or unbalanced response categories.* Make response categories or choices mutually exclusive, exhaustive, and balanced. *Mutually exclusive* means that response categories do not overlap. Overlapping categories that are numerical ranges (e.g., 5–10, 10–20, 20–30) can be easily corrected (e.g., 5–9, 10–19, 20–29). The ambiguous verbal choice is another type of overlapping response category—for example, "Are you satisfied with your job or are there things you don't like about it?" *Exhaustive* means that every respondent has a choice—a

place to go. For example, asking respondents, "Are you working or unemployed?" leaves out respondents who are not working but do not consider themselves unemployed (e.g., full-time homemakers, people on vacation, students, people with disabilities, retired people, etc.). A researcher first thinks about what he or she wants to measure and then considers the circumstances of respondents. For example, when asking about a respondent's employment, does the researcher want information on the primary job or on all jobs? On full-time work only or both full- and part-time work? On jobs for pay only or on unpaid or volunteer jobs as well?

Keep response categories *balanced.* A case of unbalanced choices is the question, "What kind of job is the mayor doing: outstanding, excellent, very good, or satisfactory?" Another type of unbalanced question omits information—for example, "Which of the five candidates running for mayor do you favor: Eugene Oswego or one of the others?" Researchers can balance responses by offering bipolar opposites. It is easy to see that the terms *honesty* and *dishonesty* have different meanings and connotations. Asking respondents to rate whether a mayor is highly, somewhat, or not very *honest* is not the same as asking them to rate the mayor's level of *dishonesty.* Unless there is a specific purpose for doing otherwise, it is better to offer respondents equal polar opposites at each end of a continuum.[3] For example, "Do you think the mayor is: very honest, somewhat honest, neither honest nor dishonest, somewhat dishonest, or very dishonest?" (see Table 7.1).

Aiding Respondent Recall

Recalling events accurately takes more time and effort than the five seconds that respondents have to answer survey questions. Also, one's ability to recall accurately declines over time. Studies in hospitalization and crime victimization show that although most respondents can recall significant events that occurred in the past several weeks, half are inaccurate a year later.

TABLE 7.1   Summary of Survey Question Writing Pitfalls

Things to Avoid	Not Good	A Possible Improvement
1. Jargon, slang, abbreviations	Did you drown in brew until you were totally blasted last night?	Last night, about how much beer did you drink?
2. Vagueness	Do you eat out often?	In a typical week, about how many meals do you eat away from home, at a restaurant, cafeteria, or other eating establishment?

3. Emotional language
4. Prestige bias
	"The respected Grace Commission documents that a staggering $350 BILLION of our tax dollars are being completely wasted through poor procurement practices, bad management, sloppy bookkeeping, 'defective' contract management, personnel abuses and other wasteful practices. Is cutting pork barrel spending and eliminating government waste a top priority for you?"*	How important is it to you that Congress adopt measures to reduce government waste?
		  Very Important
		  Somewhat Important
		  Neither Important or Unimportant
		  Somewhat Unimportant
		  Not Important At All

5. Double-barreled questions	Do you support or oppose raising social security benefits and increased spending for the military?	Do you support or oppose raising social security benefits? Do you support or oppose increasing spending on the military?
6. Beliefs as real	Do you think more educated people smoke less?	What is your education level? Do you smoke cigarettes?
7. Leading questions	Did you do your patriotic duty and vote in the last election for mayor?	Did you vote in last month's mayoral election?
8. Issues beyond respondent capabilities	Two years ago, how many hours did you watch TV every month?	In the past two weeks, about how many hours do you think you watched TV on a typical day?
9. False premises	When did you stop beating your girl/boyfriend?	Have you ever slapped, punched, or hit your girl/boyfriend?
10. Distant future intentions	After you graduate from college, get a job, and are settled, will you invest a lot of money in the stock market?	Do you have definite plans to put some money into the stock market within the coming two months?
11. Double negatives	Do you disagree with those who do not want to build a new city swimming pool?	There is a proposal to build a new city swimming pool. Do you agree or disagree with the proposal?
12. Unbalanced responses	Did you find the service at our hotel to be, Outstanding, Excellent, Superior, or Good?	Please rate the service at our hotel: Outstanding, Very Good, Adequate, or Poor.

*Actual question taken from a mail questionnaire that was sent to me in May 1998 by the National Republican Congressional Committee. It is also a double-barreled question.

Survey researchers recognize that memory is less trustworthy than was once assumed. It is affected by many factors—the topic, events occurring simultaneously and subsequently, the significance of an event for a person, situational conditions (question wording and interview style), and the respondent's need to have internal consistency.

The complexity of respondent recall does not mean that survey researchers cannot ask about past events; rather, they need to customize questions and interpret results cautiously. Researchers should provide respondents with special instructions and extra thinking time. They should also provide aids to respondent recall, such as a fixed time frame or location references. Rather than ask, "How often did you attend a sporting event last winter?" they should say, "I want to know how many sporting events you attended last winter. Let's go month by month. Think back to December. Did you attend any sporting events for which you paid admission in December? Now, think back to January. Did you attend any sporting events in January?"

Types of Questions and Response Categories

Threatening Questions. Survey researchers sometimes ask about sensitive issues or issues that respondents may believe threaten their presentation of self, such as questions about sexual behavior, drug or alcohol use, mental health problems, or deviant behavior. Respondents may be reluctant to answer the questions or to answer completely and truthfully. Survey researchers who wish to ask such questions must do so with great care and must be extra cautious about the results[4] (see Table 7.2).

Threatening questions are part of a larger issue of self-presentation and ego protection. Respondents often try to present a positive image of themselves to others. They may be ashamed, embarrassed, or afraid to give truthful answers, or find it emotionally painful to confront their own actions honestly, let alone admit them to

TABLE 7.2   Threatening Questions and Sensitive Issues

Topic	Percentage Very Uneasy
Masturbation	56
Sexual intercourse	42
Use of marijuana or hashish	42
Use of stimulants and depressants	31
Getting drunk	29
Petting and kissing	20
Income	12
Gambling with friends	10
Drinking beer, wine, or liquor	10
Happiness and well-being	4
Education	3
Occupation	3
Social activities	2
General leisure	2
Sports activity	1

Source: Adapted from Bradburn and Sudman (1980:68).

other people. They may underreport or self-censor reports of behavior or attitudes they wish to hide or believe to be in violation of social norms. Alternatively, they may overreport positive behaviors or generally accepted beliefs (social desirability bias is discussed later).

People are likely to underreport having an illness or disability (e.g., cancer, mental illness, venereal disease), engaging in illegal or deviant behavior (e.g., evading taxes, taking drugs, consuming alcohol, engaging in uncommon sexual practices), or revealing their financial status (e.g., income, savings, debts) (see Table 7.3).

Survey researchers have created several techniques to increase truthful answers to threatening questions. Some techniques involve the context and wording of the question itself. Researchers should ask threatening questions only after a warm-up, when an interviewer has developed rapport and trust with the respondents, and they should tell respondents that they

TABLE 7.3   Over- and Underreporting Behavior on Surveys

	Percentage Distorted or Erroneous Answers		
	Face to Face	*Phone*	*Self-Administered*
Low Threat/Normative			
Registered to vote	+15	+17	+12
Voted in primary	+39	+31	+36
Have own library card	+19	+21	+18
High Threat			
Bankruptcy	−32	−29	−32
Drunk driving	−47	−46	−54

Source: Adapted from Bradburn and Sudman (1980:8).

want honest answers. They can phrase the question in an "enhanced way" to provide a context that makes it easier for respondents to give honest answers. For example, the following enhanced question was asked of heterosexual males: "In past surveys, many men have reported that at some point in their lives they have had some type of sexual experience with another male. This could have happened before adolescence, during adolescence, or as an adult. Have you ever had sex with a male at some point in your life?" In contrast, a standard form of the question would have asked, "Have you ever had sex with another male?"

Also, by embedding a threatening response within more serious activities, it may be made to seem less deviant. For example, respondents might hesitate to admit shoplifting if it is asked first, but after being asked about armed robbery or burglary, they may admit to shoplifting because it appears less serious.

Socially Desirable Questions.   *Social desirability bias* occurs when respondents distort answers to make their reports conform to social norms. People tend to overreport being cultured (i.e., reading, attending high-culture events), giving

money to charity, having a good marriage, loving their children, and so forth. For example, one study found that one-third of people who reported in a survey that they gave money to a local charity really did not. Because a norm says that one should vote in elections, many report voting when they did not. In the United States, those under the greatest pressure to vote (i.e., highly educated, politically partisan, highly religious people who had been contacted by an organization that urged them to vote) are the people most likely to overreport voting.

Questionnaire writers try to reduce social desirability bias by phrasing questions in ways that make norm violation appear less objectionable and that presents a wider range of behavior as acceptable. They can also offer multiple response categories that give respondents "face-saving" alternatives.

Knowledge Questions.   Studies suggest that a large majority of the public cannot correctly answer elementary geography questions or identify important political documents (e.g., the Declaration of Independence). Researchers sometimes want to find out whether respondents know about an issue or topics, but knowledge questions can be threatening because respondents do not want to appear ignorant. Surveys may measure opinions better if they first ask about factual information, because many people have inaccurate factual knowledge.

Some simple knowledge questions, such as the number of people living in a household, are not always answered accurately in surveys. In some households, a marginal person—the boyfriend who left for a week, the adult daughter who left after an argument about her pregnancy, or the uncle who walked out after a dispute over money—may be reported as not living in a household, but he or she may not have another permanent residence and consider himself or herself to live there.[5]

Others have found that many Americans oppose foreign aid spending. Their opposition is based on extremely high overestimates of the cost of the programs. When asked what they would prefer to spend on foreign aid, most give an amount much higher than what now is being spent.

A researcher pilot-tests questions so that questions are at an appropriate level of difficulty. Little is gained if 99 percent of respondents cannot answer the question. Knowledge questions can be worded so that respondents feel comfortable saying they do not know the answer—for example, "How much, if anything, have you heard about . . . ."

Skip or Contingency Questions. Researchers avoid asking questions that are irrelevant for a respondent. Yet, some questions apply only to specific respondents. A *contingency question* is a two- (or more) part question. The answer to the first part of the question determines which of two different questions a respondent next receives. Contingency questions select respondents for whom a second question is relevant. Sometimes they are called *screen* or *skip questions*. On the basis of the answer to the first question, the respondent or an interviewer is instructed to go to another or to skip certain questions.

The following example is a contingency question, adapted from deVaus (1986:79).

1. Were you born in Australia?
   [ ] Yes (GO TO QUESTION 2)
   [ ] No _____
      (a) What country were you born in? _____
      (b) How many years have you lived in Australia? _____
      (c) Are you an Australian citizen?
         [ ] Yes [ ] No
   NOW GO TO QUESTION 2

Open versus Closed Questions

There has long been a debate about open versus closed questions in survey research. An *open-ended* (unstructured, free response) *question* asks a question (e.g., "What is your favorite television program?") to which respondents can give any answer. A *closed-ended* (structured, fixed response) *question* both asks a question and gives the respondent fixed responses from which to choose (e.g., "Is the president doing a very good, good, fair, or poor job, in your opinion?").

Each form has advantages and disadvantages (see Box 7.2). The crucial issue is not which form is best. Rather, it is under what conditions a form is most appropriate. A researcher's choice to use an open- or closed-ended question depends on the purpose and the practical limitations of a research project. The demands of using open-ended questions, with interviewers writing verbatim answers followed by time-consuming coding, may make them impractical for a specific project.

Large-scale surveys have closed-ended questions because they are quicker and easier for both respondents and researchers. Yet something important may be lost when an individual's beliefs and feelings are forced into a few fixed categories that a researcher created. To learn how a respondent thinks, to discover what is really important to him or her, or to get an answer to a question with many possible answers

Box 7.2   Closed versus Open Questions

Advantages of Closed

- It is easier and quicker for respondents to answer.
- The answers of different respondents are easier to compare.
- Answers are easier to code and statistically analyze.
- The response choices can clarify question meaning for respondents.
- Respondents are more likely to answer about sensitive topics.
- There are fewer irrelevant or confused answers to questions.
- Less articulate or less literate respondents are not at a disadvantage.
- Replication is easier.

Disadvantages of Closed

- They can suggest ideas that the respondent would not otherwise have.
- Respondents with no opinion or no knowledge can answer anyway.
- Respondents can be frustrated because their desired answer is not a choice.
- It is confusing if many (e.g., 20) response choices are offered.
- Misinterpretation of a question can go unnoticed.
- Distinctions between respondent answers may be blurred.
- Clerical mistakes or marking the wrong response is possible.
- They force respondents to give simplistic responses to complex issues.
- They force people to make choices they would not make in the real world.

Advantages of Open

- They permit an unlimited number of possible answers.
- Respondents can answer in detail and can qualify and clarify responses.
- Unanticipated findings can be discovered.
- They permit adequate answers to complex issues.
- They permit creativity, self-expression, and richness of detail.
- They reveal a respondent's logic, thinking process, and frame of reference.

Disadvantages of Open

- Different respondents give different degrees of detail in answers.
- Responses may be irrelevant or buried in useless detail.
- Comparisons and statistical analysis become very difficult.
- Coding responses is difficult.
- Articulate and highly literate respondents have an advantage.
- Questions may be too general for respondents who lose direction.
- Responses are written verbatim, which is difficult for interviewers.
- A greater amount of respondent time, thought, and effort is necessary.
- Respondents can be intimidated by questions.
- Answers take up a lot of space in the questionnaire.

(e.g., age), open questions may be best. In addition, sensitive topics (e.g., sexual behavior, liquor consumption) may be more accurately measured with closed questions.

The disadvantages of a question form can be reduced by mixing open-ended and closed-ended questions in a questionnaire. Mixing them also offers a change of pace and helps interviewers establish rapport. Periodic probes (i.e., follow-up questions by interviewers) with closed-ended questions can reveal a respondent's reasoning.

Having interviewers periodically use probes to ask about a respondent's thinking is a way to check whether respondents are understanding the questions as the researcher intended. However, probes are not substitutes for writing clear questions or creating a framework of understanding for the respondent. Unless carefully stated, probes might shape the respondent's answers or force answers when a respondent does not have an opinion or information. Yet, flexible or conversational interviewing in which interviewers use many probes can improve accuracy on questions about complex issues on which respondents do not clearly understand basic terms or about which they have difficulty expressing their thoughts. For example, to the question, "Did you do any work for money last week?" a respondent might hesitate then reply, "Yes." An interviewer probes, "Could you tell me exactly what work you did?" The respondent may reply, "On Tuesday and Wednesday, I spent a couple hours helping my buddy John move into his new apartment. For that he gave me $40, but I didn't have any other job or get paid for doing anything else." If the researcher's intention was only to get reports of regular employment, the probe revealed a misunderstanding. Researchers also use *partially open questions* (i.e., a set of fixed choices with a final open choice of "other"), which allows respondents to offer an answer that the researcher did not include.

Open-ended questions are especially valuable in early or exploratory stages of research. For large-scale surveys, researchers use open questions in pilot-tests, then develop closed-question responses from the answers given to the open questions.

Researchers writing closed questions have to make many decisions. How many response choices should be given? Should they offer a middle or neutral choice? What should be the order of responses? What types of response choices? How will the direction of a response be measured?

Answers to these questions are not easy. For example, two response choices are too few, but more than five response choices are rarely effective. Researchers want to measure meaningful distinctions and not collapse them. More specific responses yield more information, but too many specifics create confusion. For example, rephrasing the question, "Are you satisfied with your dentist?" (which has a yes/no answer) to "How satisfied are you with your dentist: very satisfied, somewhat satisfied, somewhat dissatisfied, or not satisfied at all?" gives the researcher more information and a respondent more choices.

Nonattitudes and the Middle Positions. Survey researchers debate whether to include choices for neutral, middle, and nonattitudes (e.g., "not sure," "don't know," or "no opinion").[6] Two types of errors can be made: accepting a middle choice or "no attitude" response when respondents hold a nonneutral opinion, or forcing respondents to choose a position on an issue when they have no opinion about it.

Many fear that respondents will choose nonattitude choices to evade making a choice. Yet, it is usually best to offer a nonattitude choice, because people will express opinions on fictitious issues, objects, and events. By offering a nonattitude (middle or no opinion) choice, researchers identify those holding middle positions or those without opinions.

The issue of nonattitudes can be approached by distinguishing among three kinds of attitude questions: standard-format, quasi-filter, and full-filter questions (see Box 7.3). The *standard-format question* does not offer a "don't know"

Box	
7.3	**Standard-Format, Quasi-Filter, and Full-Filter Questions**

Standard Format

Here is a question about an other country. Do you agree or disagree with this statement? "The Russian leaders are basically trying to get along with America."

Quasi-Filter

Here is a statement about an other country: "The Russian leaders are basically trying to get along with America." Do you agree, disagree, or have no opinion on that?

Full Filter

Here is a statement about an other country. Not everyone has an opinion on this. If you do not have an opinion, just say so. Here's the statement: "The Russian leaders are basically trying to get along with America." Do you have an opinion on that? If yes, do you agree or disagree?

Example of Results from Different Question Forms

	Standard Form (%)	Quasi-Filter (%)	Full Filter (%)
Agree	48.2	27.7	22.9
Disagree	38.2	29.5	20.9
No opinion	13.6*	42.8	56.3

*Volunteered

Source: Adapted from Schuman and Presser (1981:116–125). Standard format is from Fall 1978; quasi- and full-filter are from February 1977.

choice; a respondent must volunteer it. A *quasi-filter question* offers respondents a "don't know" alternative. A *full-filter question* is a special type of contingency question. It first asks if respondents have an opinion, then asks for the opinion of those who state that they do have an opinion.

Many respondents will answer a question if a "no opinion" choice is missing, but they will choose "don't know" when it is offered, or say that they do not have an opinion if asked. Such respondents are called *floaters* because they "float" from giving a response to not knowing. Their responses are affected by minor wording changes, so researchers screen them out using quasi-filter or full-filter questions. Filtered questions do not eliminate all answers to nonexistent issues, but they reduce the problem.

Agree/Disagree, Rankings or Ratings? Survey researchers who measure values and attitudes have debated two issues about the responses offered.[7] Should questionnaire items make a statement and ask respondents whether they agree or disagree with it, or should it offer respondents specific alternatives? Should the questionnaire include a set of items and ask respondents to rate them (e.g., approve, disapprove), or should it give them a list of items and force them to rank-order items (e.g., from most favored to least favored)?

It is best to offer respondents explicit alternatives. For example, instead of asking, "Do you agree or disagree with the statement, 'Men are better suited to. . . .' " instead ask, "Do you think men are better suited, women are better suited, or both are equally suited?" Less well educated respondents are more likely to agree with a statement, whereas forced-choice alternatives encourage thought and avoid the *response set* bias—a tendency of some respondents to agree and not really decide.

Researchers create bias if question wording gives respondents a reason for choosing one alternative. For example, respondents were asked whether they supported or opposed a law on energy conservation. The results changed when respondents heard, "Do you support the law or do you oppose it because the law would be difficult to enforce?" instead of simply, "Do you support or oppose the law?"

It is better to ask respondents to choose among alternatives by ranking instead of rating items along an imaginary continuum. Respondents can rate several items equally high, but will place them in a hierarchy if asked to rank them.[8]

Wording Issues

Survey researchers face two wording issues. The first, discussed earlier, is to use simple vocabulary and grammar to minimize confusion. The second issue involves effects of specific words or phrases. This is trickier because it is not possible to know in advance whether a word or phrase affects responses.

The well-documented difference between *forbid* and *not allow* illustrates the problem of wording differences. Both terms have the same meaning, but many more people are willing to "not allow" something than to "forbid" it. In general, less well educated respondents are most influenced by minor wording differences.

Certain words seem to trigger an emotional reaction, and researchers are just begin-

ning to learn of them. For example, Smith (1987) found large differences (e.g., twice as much support) in U.S. survey responses depending on whether a question asked about spending "to help the poor" or "for welfare." He suggested that the word *welfare* has such strong negative connotations for Americans (lazy people, wasteful and expensive programs, etc.) that it is best to avoid it.

Many respondents are confused by words or their connotations. For example, respondents were asked whether they thought television news was impartial. Researchers later learned that large numbers of respondents had ignored the word *impartial*—a term the middle-class, educated researchers assumed everyone would know. Less than half the respondents had interpreted the word as intended with its proper meaning. Over one-fourth ignored it or had no idea of its meaning. Others gave it unusual meanings, and one-tenth thought it was directly opposite to its true meaning. Researchers need to be cautious, because some wording effects (e.g., the difference between *forbid* and *not allow*) remain the same for decades, while other effects may appear.[9]

Questionnaire Design Issues

Length of Survey or Questionnaire. How long should a questionnaire be or an interview last? Researchers prefer long questionnaires or interviews because they are more cost effective. The cost for extra questions—once a respondent has been sampled, has been contacted, and has completed other questions—is small. There is no absolute proper length. The length depends on the survey format (to be discussed) and on the respondent's characteristics. A 5-minute telephone interview is rarely a problem and may be extended to 20 minutes. A few researchers stretched this to beyond 30 minutes. Mail questionnaires are more variable. A short (3- or 4-page) questionnaire is appropriate for the general population. Some researchers have had success with questionnaires as long as 10 pages (about 100 items) with the general public, but responses drop significantly for longer questionnaires. For highly educated respondents and a salient topic, using questionnaires of 15 pages may be possible. Face-to-face interviews lasting an hour are not uncommon. In special situations, face-to-face interviews as long as three to five hours have been conducted.

Question Order or Sequence.   A survey researcher faces three question sequence issues: organization of the overall questionnaire, question order effects, and context effects.

Organization of Questionnaire.   In general, you should sequence questions to minimize the discomfort and confusion of respondents. A questionnaire has opening, middle, and ending questions. After an introduction explaining the survey, it is best to make opening questions pleasant, interesting, and easy to answer to help a respondent feel comfortable about the questionnaire. Avoid asking many boring background questions or threatening questions first. Organize questions into common topics. Mixing questions on different topics causes confusion. Orient respondents by placing questions on the same topic together and introduce the section with a short introductory statement (e.g., "Now I would like to ask you questions about housing"). Make question topics flow smoothly and logically, and organize them to assist respondents' memory or comfort levels. Do not end with highly threatening questions, and always end with a "thank you."

Order Effects.   Researchers are concerned that the order in which they present questions may influence respondent answers. Such "order effects" appear to be strongest for people who lack strong views, for less educated respondents, and for older respondents or those with memory loss.[10] For example, support for an unmarried woman having an abortion rises if the question is preceded by a question about abortion being acceptable when a fetus has serious defects, but not when the question is by itself or before a question about fetus defects. A classic example of order effects is presented in Box 7.4.

Respondents may not perceive each issue of a survey as isolated and separate. They respond to survey questions based on the set of issues and their order of presentation in a questionnaire. Previous questions can influence later ones in two ways: through their content (i.e., the issue) and through the respondent's response. For example, a student respondent is asked, "Do you support or favor an educational contribution for students?" Answers vary depending on the topic of the preceding question. If it comes after, "How much tuition does the average U.S. student pay?" respondents interpret "contribution" to mean support for what students will pay. If it comes after "How much does the Swedish government pay to students?" respondents interpret it to mean a contribution that the government will pay. Responses can be also influenced by previous answers, because a respondent having already answered one part will assume no overlap. For example, a respondent is asked, "How is your wife?" The next question is, "How is your family?" Most respondents will assume that the second question means family members other than the wife because they already gave an answer about the wife.[11]

Context Effects.   Researchers found powerful context effects in surveys. As a practical matter, two things can be done regarding context effects. Use a *funnel sequence* of questions—that is, ask more general questions before specific ones (e.g., ask about health in general before asking about specific diseases). Or, divide the number of respondents in half and give half of the questions in one order and the other half in the alternative order, then examine the results to see whether question order mattered. If question order effects are found, which order tells you what the respondents really think? The answer is that you cannot know for sure.

For example, a few years ago, a class of my students conducted a telephone survey on two

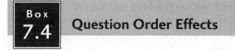

Question Order Effects

Question 1

"Do you think that the United States should let Communist newspaper reporters from other countries come in here and send back to their papers the news as they see it?"

Question 2

"Do you think a Communist country like Russia should let American newspaper reporters come in and send back to America the news as they see it?"

	Percentage Saying Yes	
	Yes to #1	*Yes to #2*
Heard First	*(Communist Reporter)*	*(American Reporter)*
#1	54%	75%
#2	64%	82%

The context created by answering the first question affects the answer to the second question.

Source: Adapted from Schuman and Presser (1981:29).

---

topics: concern about crime and attitudes toward a new anti–drunk-driving law. A random half of the respondents heard questions about the drunk-driving law first; the other half heard about crime first. I examined the results to see whether there was any *context effect*—a difference by topic order. I found that respondents who were asked about the drunk-driving law first expressed less fear about crime than did those who were asked about crime first. Likewise, they were more supportive of the drunk-driving law than were those who first heard about crime. The first topic created a context within which respondents answered questions on the second topic. After they were asked about crime in general and thought about violent crime, drunk driving may have appeared to be a less important issue. By contrast, after they were asked about drunk driving and thought about drunk driving as a crime, they may have expressed less concern about crime in general.

Respondents answer all questions based on a context of preceding questions and the interview setting. A researcher needs to remember that the more ambiguous a question's meaning, the stronger the context effects, because respondents will draw on the context to interpret and understand the question. Previous questions on the same topic and heard just before a question can have a large context effect. For example, Sudman and associates (1996:90–91) contrasted three ways of asking how much a respondent followed politics. When they asked the question alone, about 21 percent of respondents said they followed politics "now and then" or "hardly at all." When they asked the question after asking what the respondent's elected representative recently did, the percentage who said they did not follow nearly doubled, going to 39 percent. The knowledge question about the representative made many respondents feel that they did not really know much. When a question about the amount of "public relations work" the elected representative provided to the area came between the two questions, 29 percent of respondents said they did not follow politics. This question gave respondents an excuse for not knowing the first question—they could blame their representative for their ignorance. The context of a question can make a difference and researchers need to be aware of it at all times.

Format and Layout. There are two format or layout issues: the overall physical layout of the questionnaire and the format of questions and responses.

Questionnaire Layout. Layout is important, whether a questionnaire is for an interviewer or for the respondent. Questionnaires should be clear, neat, and easy to follow. Give each question a number and put identifying information (e.g., name of organization) on questionnaires. Never cramp questions together or create a confusing appearance. A few cents saved in postage or printing will ultimately cost more in terms of lower validity due to a lower response rate or of confusion of interviewers and respondents. Make a *cover sheet* or face sheet for each interview, for administrative use. Put the time and date of interview, the interviewer, the respondent identification number, and the interviewer's comments and observations on it. A professional appearance with high-quality graphics, space between questions, and good layout improves accuracy and completeness and helps the questionnaire flow.

Give interviewers or respondents instructions on the questionnaire. Print instructions in a different style from the questions (e.g., in a different color or font or in all capitals) to distinguish them. This is so an interviewer can easily distinguish between questions for respondents and instructions intended for the interviewer alone.

Layout is crucial for mail questionnaires because there is no friendly interviewer to interact with the respondent. Instead, the questionnaire's appearance persuades the respondent. In mail surveys, include a polite, professional cover letter on letterhead stationery, identifying the researcher and offering a telephone number for questions. Details matter. Respondents will be turned off if they receive a bulky brown envelope with bulk postage addressed to Occupant or if the questionnaire does not fit into the return envelope. Always end with "Thank you for your participation." Interviewers and questionnaires should leave respondents with a positive feeling about the survey and a sense that their participation is appreciated.

Question design matters. One study of college students asked how many hours they studied per day. Some students saw five answer choices ranging from 0.5 hour to more than 2.5 hours; others saw five answer choices ranging from less than 2.5 hours to more than 4.5 hours. Of students who saw the first set, 77 percent said they studied under 2.5 hours versus 31 percent of those receiving the second set. When the mail questionnaire and telephone interview were compared, 58 percent of students hearing the first set said under 2.5 hours, but there was no change among those hearing the second set. More than differences in response categories were involved, because when students were asked about hours of television watching per day with similar response categories and then the alternative response categories made no difference. What can we learn from this? Respondents without clear answers tend to rely on questionnaire response categories for guidance and more anonymous answering formats tend to yield more honest responses (see Dillman 2000:32–39 for more details).

Question Format. Survey researchers decide on a format for questions and responses. Should respondents circle responses, check boxes, fill in dots, or put an × in a blank? The principle is to make responses unambiguous. Boxes or brackets to be checked and numbers to be circled are usually clearest. Also, listing responses down a page rather than across makes them easier to see (see Box 7.5). As mentioned before, use arrows and instructions for contingency questions. Visual aids are also helpful. For example, hand out thermometer-like drawings to respondents

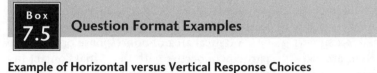

Question Format Examples

Example of Horizontal versus Vertical Response Choices

Do you think it is too easy or too difficult to get a divorce, or is it about right?

☐ Too Easy   ☐ Too Difficult   ☐ About Right

Do you think it is too easy or too difficult to get a divorce, or is it about right?

☐ Too Easy
☐ Too Difficult
☐ About Right

Example of a Matrix Question Format

	Strongly Agree	Agree	Disagree	Strongly Disagree	Don't Know
The teacher talks too fast.	☐	☐	☐	☐	☐
I learned a lot in this class.	☐	☐	☐	☐	☐
The tests are very easy.	☐	☐	☐	☐	☐
The teacher tells many jokes.	☐	☐	☐	☐	☐
The teacher is organized.	☐	☐	☐	☐	☐

Examples of Some Response Category Choices

Excellent, Good, Fair, Poor
Approve/Disapprove
Favor/Oppose
Strongly Agree, Agree, Somewhat Agree, Somewhat Disagree, Disagree, Strongly Disagree
Too Much, Too Little, About Right
Better, Worse, About the Same
Regularly, Often, Seldom, Never
Always, Most of Time, Some of Time, Rarely, Never
More Likely, Less Likely, No Difference
Very Interested, Interested, Not Interested

when asking about how warm or cool they feel toward someone. A *matrix question* (or grid question) is a compact way to present a series of questions using the same response categories. It saves space and makes it easier for the respondent or interviewer to note answers for the same response categories.

Nonresponse. The failure to get a valid response from every sampled respondent weakens a survey. Have you ever refused to answer a survey? In addition to research surveys, people are asked to respond to many requests from charities, marketing firms, candidate polls, and so forth. Charities and marketing firms get low response rates, whereas government organizations get much higher cooperation rates. Nonresponse can be a major problem for survey research because if a high proportion of the sampled respondents do not respond, researchers may not be able to generalize results, especially if those who do not respond differ from those who respond.

Public cooperation in survey research has declined over the past 20 to 30 years across many countries, with the Netherlands having the highest refusal rate, and with refusal rates as high as 30 percent in the United States.[12] There is both a growing group of "hard core" refusing people and a general decline in participation because many people feel there are too many surveys. Other reasons for refusal include a fear of crime and strangers, a more hectic life-style, a loss of privacy, and a rising distrust of authority or government. The misuse of the survey to sell products or persuade people, poorly designed questionnaires, and inadequate explanations of surveys to respondents also increase refusals for legitimate surveys.

Survey researchers can improve eligibility rates by careful respondent screening, better sample-frame definition, and multilingual interviewers. They can decrease refusals by sending letters in advance of an interview, offering to reschedule interviews, using small incentives (i.e., small gifts), adjusting interviewer behavior

and statements (i.e., making eye contact, expressing sincerity, explaining the sampling or survey, emphasizing importance of the interview, clarifying promises of confidentiality, etc.). Survey researchers can also use alternative interviewers (i.e., different demographic characteristics, age, race, gender, or ethnicity), use alternative interview methods (i.e., phone versus face to face), or accept alternative respondents in a household.

A critical area of nonresponse or refusal to participate occurs with the initial contact between an interviewer and a respondent. A face-to-face or telephone interview must overcome resistance and reassure respondents.

Research on the use of incentives found that prepaid incentives appear to increase respondent cooperation in all types of surveys. They do not appear to have negative effects on survey composition or future participation.

There is a huge literature on ways to increase response rates for mail questionnaires (see Box 7.6).[13] Heberlein and Baumgartner (1978, 1981) reported 71 factors affecting mail questionnaire response rates.

TYPES OF SURVEYS: ADVANTAGES AND DISADVANTAGES

Mail and Self-Administered Questionnaires

Advantages. Researchers can give questionnaires directly to respondents or mail them to respondents who read instructions and questions, then record their answers. This type of survey is by far the cheapest, and it can be conducted by a single researcher. A researcher can send questionnaires to a wide geographical area. The respondent can complete the questionnaire when it is convenient and can check personal records if necessary. Mail questionnaires offer anonymity and avoid interviewer bias. They can be effective, and response rates may be high for an educated target population that has a strong interest in the topic or the survey organization.

Box
7.6
Ten Ways to Increase Mail Questionnaire Response

1. Address the questionnaire to specific person, not "Occupant," and send it first class.

2. Include a carefully written, dated cover letter on letterhead stationery. In it, request respondent cooperation, guarantee confidentiality, explain the purpose of the survey, and give the researcher's name and phone number.

3. *Always* include a postage-paid, addressed return envelope.

4. The questionnaire should have a neat, attractive layout and reasonable page length.

5. The questionnaire should be professionally printed and easy to read, with clear instructions.

6. Send two follow-up reminder letters to those not responding. The first should arrive about one week after sending the questionnaire, the second a week later. Gently ask for cooperation again and offer to send another questionnaire.

7. Do not send questionnaires during major holiday periods.

8. Do not put questions on the back page. Instead, leave a blank space and ask the respondent for general comments.

9. Sponsors that are local and are seen as legitimate (e.g., government agencies, universities, large firms, etc.) get a better response.

10. Include a small monetary inducement ($1) if possible.

Disadvantages. Since people do not always complete and return questionnaires, the biggest problem with mail questionnaires is a low response rate. Most questionnaires are returned within two weeks, but others trickle in up to two months later. Researchers can raise response rates by sending nonrespondents reminder letters, but this adds to the time and cost of data collection.

A researcher cannot control the conditions under which a mail questionnaire is completed. A questionnaire completed during a drinking party by a dozen laughing people may be returned along with one filled out by an earnest respondent. Also, no one is present to clarify questions or to probe for more information when respondents give incomplete answers. Someone other than the sampled respondent (e.g., spouse, new resident, etc.) may open the mail and complete the questionnaire without the researcher's knowledge. Different respondents can complete the questionnaire weeks apart or answer questions in a different order than that intended by researchers. Incomplete questionnaires can also be a serious problem.

Researchers cannot visually observe the respondent's reactions to questions, physical characteristics, or the setting. For example, an impoverished 70-year-old White woman living alone on a farm could falsely state that she is a prosperous 40-year-old Asian male doctor living in a town with three children. Such extreme lies are rare, but serious errors can go undetected.

The mail questionnaire format limits the kinds of questions that a researcher can use. Questions requiring visual aids (e.g., look at this picture and tell me what you see), open-ended questions, many contingency questions, and complex questions do poorly in mail questionnaires. Likewise, mail questionnaires are ill suited for the illiterate or near-illiterate in English. Questionnaires mailed to illiterate respondents are not likely to be returned; if they are completed and returned, the questions were probably misunderstood, so the answers are meaningless (see Table 7.4).

Web Surveys

Access to the Internet and e-mail has become widespread since the late-1990s across most advanced nations. For example, 3 percent of the U.S. population had e-mail in 1994; only 10 years later about 75 percent of households had Internet connections.

TABLE 7.4   Types of Surveys and Their Features

Features	Type of Survey			
	Mail Questionnaire	*Web Survey*	*Telephone Interview*	*Face-to-Face Interview*
Administrative Issues				
Cost	Cheap	Cheapest	Moderate	Expensive
Speed	Slowest	Fastest	Fast	Slow to moderate
Length (number of questions)	Moderate	Moderate	Short	Longest
Response rate	Lowest	Moderate	Moderate	Highest
Research Control				
Probes possible	No	No	Yes	Yes
Specific respondent	No	No	Yes	Yes
Question sequence	No	Yes	Yes	Yes
Only one respondent	No	No	Yes	Yes
Visual observation	No	No	No	Yes
Success with Different Questions				
Visual aids	Limited	Yes	None	Yes
Open-ended questions	Limited	Limited	Limited	Yes
Contingency questions	Limited	Yes	Yes	Yes
Complex questions	Limited	Yes	Limited	Yes
Sensitive questions	Some	Yes	Limited	Limited
Sources of Bias				
Social desirability	Some	Some	Some	Most
Interviewer bias	None	None	Some	Most
Respondent's reading skill	Yes	Yes	No	No

Advantages. Web-based surveys over the Internet or by e-mail are very fast and inexpensive. They allow flexible design and can use visual images, or even audio or video in some Internet versions. Despite great flexibility, the basic principles for question writing and for paper questionnaire design generally apply.

Disadvantages. Web surveys have three areas of concern: coverage, privacy and verification, and design issues. The first concern involves sampling and unequal Internet access or use. Despite high coverage rates, older, less-educated, lower-income, and more rural people are less likely to have good Internet access. In addition, many people have multiple e-mail addresses, which limits using them for sampling purposes. Self-selection is a potential problem with web surveys. For example, a marketing department could get very distorted results of the population of new car buyers. Perhaps half of the new car buyers for a model are over age 55, but 75 percent of respondents to a web survey are under age 32 and only 8 percent are over age 55. Not only would the results be distorted by age but the relatively small percentage of over-55 respondents may not be representative of all over-55 potential new car buyers (e.g., they may be higher income or more educated).

A second concern is protecting respondent privacy and confidentiality. Researchers should encrypt collected data, only use secure websites and erase nonessential respondent identification or linking information on a daily or weekly basis. They should develop a system of respondent verification to ensure that only the sampled respondent participates and does so only once. This may involve a system such as giving each respondent a unique PIN number to access the questionnaire.

A third concern involves the complexity of questionnaire design. Researchers need to check and verify the compatibility of various web software and hardware combinations for respondents using different computers. Researchers are still learning what is most effective for web surveys. It is best to provide screen-by-screen questions and make an entire question visible on the screen at one time in a consistent format with drop-down boxes for answer choices. It is best to include a progress indicator (as motivation), such as a clock or waving hand. Visual appearance of a screen, such as the range of colors and fonts, should be kept simple for easy readability and consistency. Be sure to provide very clear instructions for all computer actions (e.g., use of drop-down screens) where they are needed and include "click here" instructions. Also, make it easy for respondents to move back and forth across questions. Researchers using web surverys need to avoid technical glitches at the implementation stage by repeated pretesting, having a dedicated server, and obtaining sufficient broadband to handle high demand.

Telephone Interviews

Advantages. The telephone interview is a popular survey method because about 95 percent of the population can be reached by telephone. An interviewer calls a respondent (usually at home), asks questions, and records answers. Researchers sample respondents from lists, telephone directories, or random digit dialing, and can quickly reach many people across long distances. A staff of interviewers can interview 1,500 respondents across a nation within a few days and, with several callbacks, response rates can reach 90 percent. Although this method is more expensive than a mail questionnaire, the telephone interview is a flexible method with most of the strengths of face-to-face interviews but for about half the cost. Interviewers control the sequence of questions and can use some probes. A specific respondent is chosen and is likely to answer all the questions alone. The researcher knows when the questions were answered and can use contingency questions effectively, especially with computer-assisted telephone interviewing (CATI) (to be discussed).

Disadvantages. Higher cost and limited interview length are among the disadvantages of telephone interviews. In addition, respondents without telephones are impossible to reach, and the call may come at an inconvenient time. The use of an interviewer reduces anonymity and introduces potential interviewer bias. Open-ended questions are difficult to use, and questions requiring visual aids are impossible. Interviewers can only note serious disruptions (e.g., background noise) and respondent tone of voice (e.g., anger or flippancy) or hesitancy.

Face-to-Face Interviews

Advantages. Face-to-face interviews have the highest response rates and permit the longest questionnaires. Interviewers also can observe the surroundings and can use nonverbal communication and visual aids. Well-trained interviewers can ask all types of questions, can ask complex questions, and can use extensive probes.

Disadvantages. High cost is the biggest disadvantage of face-to-face interviews. The training, travel, supervision, and personnel costs for interviews can be high. Interviewer bias is also greatest in face-to-face interviews. The appearance, tone of voice, question wording, and so forth of the interviewer may affect the respondent. In addition, interviewer supervision is less than for telephone interviews, which supervisors monitor by listening in.[14]

INTERVIEWING

The Role of the Interviewer

Interviews to gather information occur in many settings. Survey research interviewing is a specialized kind of interviewing. As with most interviewing, its goal is to obtain accurate information from another person.[15]

The survey interview is a social relationship. Like other social relationships, it involves social roles, norms, and expectations. The interview is a short-term, secondary social interaction between two strangers with the explicit purpose of one person's obtaining specific information from the other. The social roles are those of the interviewer and the interviewee or respondent. Information is obtained in a structured conversation in which the interviewer asks prearranged questions and records answers, and the respondent answers. It differs in several ways from ordinary conversation (see Table 7.5).

An important problem for interviewers is that many respondents are unfamiliar with the survey respondents' role. As a result, they substitute another role that may affect their responses. Some believe the interview is an intimate conversation or therapy session, some see it as a bureaucratic exercise in completing forms, some view it as a citizen referendum on policy choices, some view it as a testing situation, and some consider it as a form of deceit in which interviewers are trying to trick or entrap respondents. Even in a well-designed, professional survey, follow-up research found that only about half the respondents understand questions exactly as intended by researchers. Respondents reinterpreted questions to make them applicable to their ideosynctic, personal situations or to make them easy to answer.[16]

The role of interviewers is difficult. They obtain cooperation and build rapport, yet remain neutral and objective. They encroach on the respondents' time and privacy for information that may not directly benefit the respondents. They try to reduce embarrassment, fear, and suspicion so that respondents feel comfortable revealing information. They may explain the nature of survey research or give hints about social roles in an interview. Good interviewers monitor the pace and direction of the social interaction as well as the content of answers and the behavior of respondents.

Survey interviewers are nonjudgmental and do not reveal their opinions, verbally or nonverbally (e.g., by a look of shock). If a respondent asks for an interviewer's opinion, he or she po-

TABLE 7.5   Differences between Ordinary Conversation and a Structured Survey Interview

Ordinary Conversation	The Survey Interview
1. Questions and answers from each participant are relatively equally balanced.	1. Interviewer asks and respondent answers most of the time.
2. There is an open exchange of feelings and opinions.	2. Only the respondent reveals feelings and opinions.
3. Judgments are stated and attempts made to persuade the other of a particular points of view.	3. Interviewer is nonjudgmental and does not try to change respondent's opinions or beliefs.
4. A person can reveal deep inner feelings to gain sympathy or as a therapeutic release.	4. Interviewer tries to obtain direct answers to specific questions.
5. Ritual responses are common (e.g., "Uh huh," shaking head, "How are you?" "Fine").	5. Interviewer avoids making ritual responses that influence a respondent and also seeks genuine answers, not ritual responses.
6. The participants exchange information and correct the factual errors that they are aware of.	6. Respondent provides almost all information. Interviewer does not correct a respondent's factual errors.
7. Topics rise and fall and either person can introduce new topics. The focus can shift directions or digress to less relevant issues.	7. Interviewer controls the topic, direction, and pace. He or she keeps the respondent "on task," and irrelevant diversions are contained.
8. The emotional tone can shift from humor, to joy, to affection, to sadness, to anger, and so on.	8. Interviewer attempts to maintain a consistently warm but serious and objective tone throughout.
9. People can evade or ignore questions and give flippant or noncommittal answers.	9. Respondent should not evade questions and should give truthful, thoughtful answers.

Source: Adapted from Gorden (1980:19–25) and Sudman and Bradburn (1983:5–10).

litely redirects the respondent and indicates that such questions are inappropriate. For example, if a respondent asks, "What do you think?" the interviewer may answer, "Here, we are interested in what *you* think; what I think doesn't matter." Likewise, if the respondent gives a shocking answer (e.g., "I was arrested three times for beating my infant daughter and burning her with cigarettes"), the interviewer does not show shock, surprise, or disdain but treats the answer in a matter-of-fact manner. He or she helps respondents feel that they can give any truthful answer.

You might ask, "If the survey interviewer must be neutral and objective, why not use a robot or machine?" Machine interviewing has not been successful because it lacks the human warmth, sense of trust, and rapport that an interviewer creates. An interviewer helps define the situation and ensures that respondents have the information sought, understand what is expected, give relevant answers, are motivated to cooperate, and give serious answers.

Interviewers do more than interview respondents. Face-to-face interviewers spend only about 35 percent of their time interviewing. About 40 percent is spent in locating the correct respondent, 15 percent in traveling, and 10 percent in studying survey materials and dealing with administrative and recording details.[17]

Stages of an Interview

The interview proceeds through stages, beginning with an introduction and entry. The interviewer gets in the door, shows authorization, and reassures and secures cooperation from the respondent. He or she is prepared for reactions such as, "How did you pick me?" "What good will this do?" "I don't know about this," "What's this about, anyway?" The interviewer can explain why the specific respondent is interviewed and not a substitute.

The main part of the interview consists of asking questions and recording answers. The interviewer uses the exact wording on the questionnaire—no added or omitted words and no rephrasing. He or she asks all applicable questions in order, without returning to or skipping questions unless the directions specify this. He or she goes at a comfortable pace and gives nondirective feedback to maintain interest.

In addition to asking questions, the interviewer accurately records answers. This is easy for closed-ended questions, where interviewers just mark the correct box. For open-ended questions, the interviewer's job is more difficult. He or she listens carefully, must have legible writing, and must record what is said verbatim without correcting grammar or slang. More important, the interviewer never summarizes or paraphrases. This causes a loss of information or distorts answers. For example, the respondent says, "I'm really concerned about my daughter's heart problem. She's only 10 years old and already she has trouble climbing stairs. I don't know what she'll do when she gets older. Heart surgery is too risky for her and it costs so much. She'll have to learn to live with it." If the interviewer writes, "concerned about daughter's health," much is lost.

The interviewer knows how and when to use probes. A *probe* is a neutral request to clarify an ambiguous answer, to complete an incomplete answer, or to obtain a relevant response. Interviewers recognize an irrelevant or inaccurate answer and use probes as needed.[18] There are many types of probes. A three- to five-second pause is often effective. Nonverbal communication (e.g., tilt of head, raised eyebrows, or eye contact) also works well. The interviewer can repeat the question or repeat the reply and then pause. She or he can ask a neutral question, such as, "Any other reasons?" "Can you tell me more about that?" "How do you mean?" "Could you explain more for me?" (see Box 7.7).

The last stage is the exit, when the interviewer thanks the respondent and leaves. He or she then goes to a quiet, private place to edit the questionnaire and record other details such as the date, time, and place of the interview; a thumbnail sketch of the respondent and interview situation; the respondent's attitude (e.g., serious, angry, or laughing); and any unusual circumstances (e.g., "Telephone rang at question 27 and respondent talked for four minutes before the interview started again"). He or she notes anything disruptive that happened during the interview (e.g., "Teenage son entered room, sat at opposite end, turned on television with the volume loud, and watched a music video"). The interviewer also records personal feelings and anything that was suspected (e.g., "Respondent became nervous and fidgeted when questioned about his marriage").

Training Interviewers

A large-scale survey requires hiring multiple interviewers. Few people appreciate the difficulty of the interviewer's job. A professional-quality interview requires the careful selection of inter-

Box 7.7	Example of Probes and Recording Full Responses to Closed Questions

Interviewer Question: What is your occupation?

Respondent Answer: I work at General Motors.
  Probe: What is your job at General Motors? What type of work do you do there?

Interviewer Question: How long have you been unemployed?

Respondent Answer: A long time.
  Probe: Could you tell me more specifically when your current period of unemployment began?

Interviewer Question: Considering the country as a whole, do you think we will have good times during the next year, or bad times, or what?

Respondent Answer: Maybe good, maybe bad, it depends, who knows?
  Probe: What do you expect to happen?

Record Response to a Closed Question

Interviewer Question: On a scale of 1 to 7, how do you feel about capital punishment or the death penalty, where 1 is strongly in favor of the death penalty, and 7 is strongly opposed to it?
(Favor) 1 __   2 __   3 __   4 __   5 __   6 __   7 __   (Oppose)

Respondent Answer: About a 4. I think that all murderers, rapists, and violent criminals should get death, but I don't favor it for minor crimes like stealing a car.

---

viewers and extensive training. As with any employment situation, adequate pay and good supervision are important for consistent high-quality performance. Unfortunately, professional interviewing has not always paid well or provided regular employment. In the past, interviewers were largely drawn from a pool of middle-aged women willing to accept irregular part-time work.

Good interviewers are pleasant, honest, accurate, mature, responsible, moderately intelligent, stable, and motivated. They have a nonthreatening appearance, have experience with many different types of people, and possess poise and tact. Researchers may consider interviewers' physical appearance, age, race, sex, languages spoken, and even the sound of their voice.

Professional interviewers will receive a two-week training course. It includes lectures and reading, observation of expert interviewers, mock interviews in the office and in the field that are recorded and critiqued, many practice interviews, and role-playing. The interviewers learn about survey research and the role of the interviewer. They become familiar with the questionnaire and the purpose of questions, although not with the answers expected.

The importance of carefully selecting and training interviewers was evident during the 2004 U.S. presidential election. Exit polls are quick, very short surveys conducted outside a polling place for people immediately after they voted. On Election Day of 2004 exit polls showed candidate John Kerry well ahead, but after final votes were counted he lost to his opponent, George W. Bush. A major cause of the mistake was that the research organization, paid $10 million by six major news organizations to conduct the exit polls, had hired many young inexperienced interviewers and gave them only minimal training. Younger voters tended to support John Kerry, whereas older voters tended to support George Bush. The young inexperienced interviewers were less successful in gaining cooperation from older voters and felt more comfortable handing the questionnaire to someone of a similar age. As a result, exit poll participants did not reflect the composition of all voters and poll results showed greater support for Kerry than actually existed among all voters.[19]

Although interviewers largely work alone, researchers use an interviewer supervisor in large-scale surveys with several interviewers. Supervisors are familiar with the area, assist with problems, oversee the interviewers, and ensure that work is completed on time. For telephone interviewing, this includes helping with calls, checking when interviewers arrive and leave, and monitoring interview calls. In face-to-face interviews, supervisors check to find out whether the interview actually took place. This means calling back or sending a confirmation postcard to a sample of respondents. They can also check the response rate and incomplete questionnaires to see whether interviewers are obtaining cooperation, and they may reinterview a small subsample, analyze answers, or observe interviews to see whether interviewers are accurately asking questions and recording answers.

Interviewer Bias

Survey researchers proscribe interviewer behavior to reduce bias. This goes beyond reading each question exactly as worded. Ideally, the actions of a particular interviewer will not affect how a respondent answers, and responses will not vary from what they would be if asked by any other interviewer.

Survey researchers know that interviewer expectations can create significant bias. Interviewers who expect difficult interviews have them, and those who expect certain answers are more likely to get them (see Box 7.8). Proper interviewer behavior and exact question reading may be difficult, but the issue is larger.

The social setting in which the interview occurs can affect answers, including the presence of other people. For example, students answer differently depending on whether they are asked questions at home or at school. In general, survey researchers do not want others present because they may affect respondent answers. It may not always make a difference, however, especially if the others are small children.[20]

An interviewer's visible characteristics, including race and gender, often affect interviews and respondent answers, especially for questions about issues related to race or gender. For example, African American and Hispanic American respondents express different policy positions on race- or ethnic-related issues depending on the apparent race or ethnicity of the interviewer. This occurs even with telephone interviews when a respondent has clues about the interviewer's race or ethnicity. In general, interviewers of the same ethnic-racial group get more accurate answers.[21] Gender also affects interviews both in terms of obvious issues, such as sexual behavior, as well as support for gender-related collective action or gender equality.[22] Survey researchers need to note the race and gender of both interviewers and respondents.

Computer-Assisted Telephone Interviewing

Advances in computer technology and lower computer prices have enabled professional survey research organizations to install *computer-assisted telephone interviewing (CATI)* systems.[23] With CATI, the interviewer sits in front of a computer and makes calls. Wearing a headset

Box 7.8	Interviewer Characteristics Can Affect Responses

Example of Interviewer Expectation Effects

Asked by Female Interviewer Whose Own	Female Respondent Reports That Husband Buys Most Furniture
Husband buys most furniture	89%
Husband does not buy most furniture	15%

Example of Race or Ethnic Appearance Effects

Interviewer	Percentage Answering Yes to:	
	"Do you think there are too many Jews in government jobs?"	"Do you think that Jews have too much power?"
Looked Jewish with Jewish-sounding name	11.7	5.8
Looked Jewish only	15.4	15.6
Non-Jewish appearance	21.2	24.3
Non-Jewish appearance and non-Jewish-sounding name	19.5	21.4

Note: Racial stereotypes held by respondents can affect how they respond in interviews.
Source: Adapted from Hyman (1975:115, 163).

and microphone, the interviewer reads the questions from a computer screen for the specific respondent who is called, then enters the answer via the keyboard. Once he or she enters an answer, the computer shows the next question on the screen.

Computer-assisted telephone interviewing speeds interviewing and reduces interviewer errors. It also eliminates the separate step of entering information into a computer and speeds data processing. Of course, CATI requires an investment in computer equipment and some knowledge of computers. The CATI system is valuable for contingency questions because the computer can show the questions appropriate for a specific respondent; interviewers do not have to turn pages looking for the next question. In addition, the computer can check an answer immediately after the interviewer enters it. For example, if an interviewer enters an answer that is impossible or clearly an error (e.g., an *H* instead of an *M* for "Male"), the computer will request another answer. Innovations with computers and web surveys also help to gather data on sensitive issue (see Box 7.9).

Several companies have developed software programs for personal computers that help researchers develop questionnaires and analyze survey data. They provide guides for writing questions, recording responses, analyzing data,

Computer-Aided Surveys and Sensitive Topics

The questioning format influences how respondents answer questions about sensitive topics. Formats that permit the greater respondent anonymity, such as a self-administered questionnaire or the web survey, are more likely to elicit honest responses than one that requires interaction with another person, such as in a face-to-face interview or telephone interview. One of a series of computer-based technological innovations is called *computer-assisted self-administered interviews (CASAI)*. It appears to improve respondent comfort and honesty in answering questions on sensitive topics. In CASAI, respondents are "interviewed" with questions that are asked on a computer screen or heard over earphones. The respondents answer by moving a computer mouse or entering information using a computer keyboard. Even when a researcher is present in the same room, the respondent is semi-insulated from human contact and appears to feel comfortable answering questions about sensitive issues.

and producing reports. The programs may speed the more mechanical aspects of survey research—such as typing questionnaires, organizing layout, and recording responses—but they cannot substitute for a good understanding of the survey method or an appreciation of its limitations. The researcher must still clearly conceptualize variables, prepare well-worded questions, design the sequence and forms of questions and responses, and pilot-test questionnaires. Communicating unambiguously with respondents and eliciting credible responses remain the most important parts of survey research.

THE ETHICAL SURVEY

Like all social research, people can conduct surveys in ethical or unethical ways. A major ethical issue in survey research is the invasion of privacy. Survey researchers can intrude into a respondent's privacy by asking about intimate actions and personal beliefs. People have a right to privacy. Respondents decide when and to whom to reveal personal information. They are likely to provide such information when it is asked for in a comfortable context with mutual trust, when they believe serious answers are needed for legitimate research purposes, and when they believe answers will remain confidential. Researchers should treat all respondents with dignity and reduce anxiety or discomfort. They are also responsible for protecting the confidentiality of data.

A second issue involves voluntary participation by respondents. Respondents agree to answer questions and can refuse to participate at any time. They give "informed consent" to participate in research. Researchers depend on respondents' voluntary cooperation, so researchers need to ask well-developed questions in a sensitive way, treat respondents with respect, and be very sensitive to confidentiality.

A third ethical issue is the exploitation of surveys and pseudosurveys. Because of its popularity, some people use surveys to mislead others. A *pseudosurvey* is when someone who has little or no real interest in learning information from a respondent uses the survey format to try to persuade someone to do something. Charlatans use the guise of conducting a survey to invade privacy, gain entry into homes, or "suggle" (sell in the guise of a survey). I personally experienced a type of pseudosurvey known as a "suppression poll" in the 1994 U.S. election campaign. In this situation, an unknown survey organization telephoned potential voters and asked whether the voter supported a given candidate. If the voter supported the candidate, the interviewer next asked whether the respondent would still support the candidate if he or she knew that the candidate had an unfavorable characteristic (e.g., had been arrested for drunk driving, used illegal drugs, raised the wages of convicted criminals in prison, etc.). The goal of the interview was not to measure candidate support; rather, it was to identify a candidate's supporters then attempt to suppress voting. Although they are illegal, no one has been prosecuted for using this campaign tactic.

Another ethical issue is when people misuse survey results or use poorly designed or purposely rigged surveys. Why does this occur? People may demand answers from surveys that surveys cannot provide and not understand a survey's limitations. Those who design and prepare surveys may lack sufficient training to conduct a legitimate survey. Unfortunately, policy decisions are sometimes made based on careless or poorly designed surveys. They often result in waste or human hardship. This is why legitimate researchers conducting methodologically rigorous survey research are important.

The media report more surveys than other types of social research, yet sloppy reporting of survey results permits abuse.[24] Few people reading survey results may appreciate it, but researchers should include details about the survey (see Box 7.10) to reduce the misuse of survey research and increase questions about surveys that lack such information. Survey researchers urge the media to include such information, but it is rarely included. Over 88 percent of reports on surveys in the mass media fail to reveal the researcher who conducted the survey, and only 18 percent provide details on how the survey was conducted.[25] Currently, there are no quality-control standards to regulate the opinion polls or surveys reported in the U.S. media. Researchers have made unsuccessful attempts since World War II to require adequate samples, interviewer training and supervision, satisfactory questionnaire design, public availability of results, and controls on the integrity of survey organizations.[26] As a result, the mass media report both biased and misleading survey results and rigorous, professional survey results without making any distinction. It is not surprising that public confusion and a distrust of all surveys occur.

Box 7.10	Ten Items to Include When Reporting Survey Research

1. The sampling frame used (e.g., telephone directories)
2. The dates on which the survey was conducted
3. The population that the sample represents (e.g., U.S. adults, Australian college students, housewives in Singapore)
4. The size of the sample for which information was collected
5. The sampling method (e.g., random)
6. The exact wording of the questions asked
7. The method of the survey (e.g., face to face, telephone)
8. The organizations that sponsored the survey (paid for it and conducted it)
9. The response rate or percentage of those contacted who actually completed the questionnaire
10. Any missing information or "don't know" responses when results on specific questions are reported

CONCLUSION

In this chapter, you learned about survey research. You also learned some principles of writing good survey questions. There are many things to avoid and to include when writing questions. You learned about the advantages and disadvantages of three types of survey research: mail, telephone interviews, and face-to-face interviews. You saw that interviewing, especially face-to-face interviewing, can be difficult.

Although this chapter focused on survey research, researchers use questionnaires to measure variables in other types of quantitative research (e.g., experiments). The survey, often called the sample survey because random sampling is usually used with it, is a distinct technique. It is a process of asking many people the same questions and examining their answers.

Survey researchers try to minimize errors, but survey data often contain them. Errors in surveys can compound each other. For example, errors can arise in sampling frames, from nonresponse, from question wording or order, and from interviewer bias. Do not let the existence of errors discourage you from using the survey, however. Instead, learn to be very careful when designing survey research and cautious about generalizing from the results of surveys.

Key Terms

closed-ended question
computer-assisted telephone interviewing (CATI)
context effect
contingency question
cover sheet
double-barreled question
floaters
full-filter question
funnel sequence
interview schedule
matrix question
open-ended question
order effects
partially open question
prestige bias
probe
quasi-filter question
response set
social desirability bias
standard-format question
threatening questions
wording effects

Endnotes

1. Sudman and Bradburn (1983:39) suggested that even simple questions (e.g., "What brand of soft drink do you usually buy?") can cause problems.

Respondents who are highly loyal to one brand of traditional carbonated sodas can answer the question easily. Other respondents must implicitly address the following questions to answer the question as it was asked: (a) What time period is involved—the past month, the past year, the last 10 years? (b) What conditions count—at home, at restaurants, at sporting events? (c) Buying for oneself alone or for other family members? (d) What is a "soft drink"? Do lemonade, iced tea, mineral water, or fruit juices count? (e) Does "usually" mean a brand purchased as 51 percent or more of all soft drink purchases, or the brand purchased more frequently than any other? Respondents rarely stop and ask for clarification; they make assumptions about what the researcher means.

2. See Dykema and Schaeffer (2000) and Sudman and colleagues (1996:197–226).

3. See Ostrom and Gannon (1996).

4. See Bradburn (1983), Bradburn and Sudman (1980), and Sudman and Bradburn (1983) on threatening or sensitive questions. Backstrom and Hursh-Cesar (1981:219) and Warwick and Lininger (1975:150–151) provide useful suggestions as well.

5. On how "Who knows who lives here?" can be complicated, see Martin (1999) and Tourangeau et al. (1997).

6. For a discussion of the "don't know," "no opinion," and middle positions in response categories, see Backstrom and Hursh-Cesar (1981:148–149), Bishop (1987), Bradburn and Sudman (1988: 154), Brody (1986), Converse and Presser (1986:35–37), Duncan and Stenbeck (1988), and Sudman and Bradburn (1983:140–141).

7. The disagree/agree versus specific alternatives debate can be found in Bradburn and Sudman (1988:149–151), Converse and Presser (1986:38–39), and Schuman and Presser (1981:179–223).

8. The ranking versus ratings issue is discussed in Alwin and Krosnick (1985) and Krosnick and Alwin (1988). Also see Backstrom and Hursh-Cesar (1981:132–134) and Sudman and Bradburn (1983:156–165) for formats of asking rating and ranking questions.

9. See Foddy (1993) and Presser (1990).

10. Studies by Krosnick (1992) and Narayan and Krosnick (1996) show that education reduces response-order (primacy or recency) effects, but

Knäuper (1999) found that age is strongly associated with response-order effects.

11. This example comes from Strack (1992).
12. For a discussion, see Couper, Singer et al. (1998), de Heer (1999), Keeter et al. (2000), Sudman and Bradburn (1983:11), and "Surveys Proliferate, but Answers Dwindle," *New York Times,* October 5, 1990, p. 1. Smith (1995) and Sudman (1976:114–116) also discuss refusal rates.
13. Bailey (1987:153–168), Church (1993), Dillman (1978, 1983), Fox and colleagues (1988), Goyder (1982), Heberlein and Baumgartner (1978, 1981), Hubbard and Little (1988), Jones (1979), and Willimack and colleagues (1995) discuss increasing return rates in surveys
14. For a comparison among types of surveys, see Backstrom and Hursh-Cesar (1981:16–23), Bradburn and Sudman (1988:94–110), Dillman (1978:39–78), Fowler (1984:61–73), and Frey (1983:27–55).
15. For more on survey research interviewing, see Brenner and colleagues (1985), Cannell and Kahn (1968), Converse and Schuman (1974), Dijkstra and van der Zouwen (1982), Foddy (1993), Gorden (1980), Hyman (1975), and Moser and Kalton (1972:270–302).
16. See Turner and Martin (1984:262–269, 282).
17. From Moser and Kalton (1972:273).
18. The use of probes is discussed in Backstrom and Hursh-Cesar (1981:266–273), Gorden (1980:368–390), and Hyman (1975:236–241).
19. Report by Jacques Steinberg (2005). "Study Cites Human Failings in Election Day Poll System," *New York Times* (January 20, 2005).
20. See Bradburn and Sudman (1980), Pollner and Adams (1997), and Zane and Matsoukas (1979).
21. The race or ethnicity of interviewers is discussed in Anderson and colleagues (1988), Bradburn (1983), Cotter and colleagues (1982), Davis (1997), Finkel and colleagues (1991), Gorden (1980:168–172), Reese and colleagues (1986), Schaffer (1980), Schuman and Converse (1971), and Weeks and Moore (1981).
22. See Catania and associates (1996) and Kane and MacAulay (1993).
23. CATI is discussed in Bailey (1987:201–202), Bradburn and Sudman (1988:100–101), Frey (1983:24–25, 143–149), Groves and Kahn (1979:226), Groves and Mathiowetz (1984), and Karweit and Meyers (1983).
24. On reporting survey results in the media, see Channels (1993) and MacKeun (1984).
25. See Singer (1988).
26. From Turner and Martin (1984:62).

CHAPTER 8

Experimental Research

INTRODUCTION

Experimental research builds on the principles of a positivist approach more directly than do the other research techniques. Researchers in the natural sciences (e.g., chemistry and physics), related applied fields (e.g., agriculture, engineering, and medicine), and the social sciences conduct experiments. The logic that guides an experiment on plant growth in biology or testing a metal in engineering is applied in experiments on human social behavior. Although it is most widely used in psychology, the experiment is found in education, criminal justice, journalism, marketing, nursing, political science, social work, and sociology. This chapter focuses first on the experiment conducted in a laboratory under controlled conditions, then looks at experiments conducted in the field.

The experiment's basic logic extends commonsense thinking. Commonsense experiments are less careful or systematic than scientifically based experiments. In commonsense language, an *experiment* is when you modify something in a situation, then compare an outcome to what existed without the modification. For example, I try to start my car. To my surprise, it does not start. I "experiment" by cleaning off the battery connections, then try to start it again. I modified something (cleaned the connections) and compared the outcome (whether the car started) to the previous situation (it did not start). I began with an implicit "hypothesis"—a buildup of crud on the connections is the reason the car is not starting, and once the crud is cleaned off, the car will start. This illustrates three things researchers do in experiments: (1) begin with a hypothesis, (2) modify something in a situation, and (3) compare outcomes with and without the modification.

Compared to the other social research techniques, experimental research is the strongest for testing causal relationships because the three conditions for causality (temporal order, association, and no alternative explanations) are best met in experimental designs.

Research Questions Appropriate for an Experiment

The Issue of an Appropriate Technique. Some research questions are better addressed using certain techniques. New researchers often ask, Which technique (e.g., experiments and surveys) best fits which research question? There is no easy answer, because the match between a research question and technique is not fixed but depends on informed judgment. You can develop judgment from reading research reports, understanding the strengths and weaknesses of different techniques, assisting more experienced researchers with their research, and gaining practical experience.

Research Questions for Experimental Research. The experiment allows a researcher to focus sharply on causal relations, and it has practical advantages over other techniques, but it also has limitations. The research questions most appropriate for an experiment fit its strengths and limitations.

The questions appropriate for using an experimental logic confront ethical and practical limitations of intervening in human affairs for research purposes. It is immoral and impossible to manipulate many areas of human life for research purposes. The pure logic of an experiment has an experimenter intervene or induce a change in some focused part of social life, then examine the consequences that result from the change or intervention. This usually means that the experiment is limited to research questions in which a researcher is able to manipulate conditions. Experimental research cannot answer questions such as, Do people who complete a college education increase their annual income more than people who do not? Do children raised with younger siblings develop better leadership skills than children without siblings? Do people who belong to more organizations vote more often in elections? This is because an experimenter often cannot manipulate conditions or intervene. He or she cannot randomly assign thousands to attend college and prevent others from attending to discover who later earns more income. He or she cannot induce couples to have either many children or a single child so he or she can examine how leadership skills develop in children. He or she cannot compel people to join or quit organizations then see whether they vote. Experimenters are highly creative in simulating such interventions or conditions, but they cannot manipulate many of the variables of interest to fit the pure experimental logic.

The experiment is usually best for issues that have a narrow scope or scale. This strength allows experimenters to assemble and "run" many experiments with limited resources in a short period. Some carefully designed experiments require assembling only 50 or 60 volunteers and can be completed in one or two months. In general, the experiment is better suited for micro-level (e.g., individual or small-group phenomena) than for macro-level concerns or questions. Experiments can rarely address questions that require looking at conditions across an entire society or across decades. The experiment also limits one's ability to generalize to larger settings (see External Validity and Field Experiments later in this chapter).

Experiments encourage researchers to isolate and target the impact that arises from one or a few causal variables. This strength in demonstrating causal effects is a limitation in situations where a researcher tries to examine numerous variables simultaneously. The experiment is rarely appropriate for research questions or issues that require a researcher to examine the impact of dozens of diverse variables all together. Although the accumulated knowledge from many individual experiments, each focused on one or two variables, advances understanding, the approach of experimental research differs from doing research on a highly complex situation in which one examines how dozens of variables operate simultaneously.

Often, researchers study closely related topics using either an experimental or a nonexperi-

mental method. For example, a researcher may wish to study attitudes toward people in wheelchairs. An experimenter might ask people to respond (e.g., Would you hire this person? How comfortable would you be if this person asked you for a date?) to photos of some people in wheelchairs and some people not in wheelchairs. A survey researcher might ask people their opinions about people in wheelchairs. The field researcher might observe people's reactions to someone in a wheelchair, or the researcher himself or herself might be in wheelchair and carefully note the reactions of others.

RANDOM ASSIGNMENT

Social researchers frequently want to compare. For example, a researcher has two groups of 15 students and wants to compare the groups on the basis of a key difference between them (e.g., a course that one group completed). Or a researcher has five groups of customers and wants to compare the groups on the basis of one characteristic (e.g., geographic location). The cliché, "Compare apples to apples, don't compare apples to oranges," is not about fruit; it is about comparisons. It means that a valid comparison depends on comparing things that are fundamentally alike. Random assignment facilitates comparison in experiments by creating similar groups.

When making comparisons, researchers want to compare cases that do not differ with regard to variables that offer alternative explanations. For example, a researcher compares two groups of students to determine the impact of completing a course. In order to be compared, the two groups must be similar in most respects except for taking the course. If the group that completed the course is also older than the group that did not, for example, the researcher cannot determine whether completing the course or being older accounts for differences between the groups.

Why Randomly Assign?

Random assignment is a method for assigning cases (e.g., individuals, organizations, etc.) to groups for the purpose of making comparisons. It is a way to divide or sort a collection of cases into two or more groups in order to increase one's confidence that the groups do not differ in a systematic way. It is a mechanical method; the assignment is automatic, and the researcher cannot make assignments on the basis of personal preference or the features of specific cases.

Random assignment is random in a statistical or mathematical sense, not in an everyday sense. In everyday speech, *random* means unplanned, haphazard, or accidental, but it has a specialized meaning in mathematics. In probability theory, *random* describes a process in which each case has a known chance of being selected. Random selection lets a researcher calculate the odds that a specific case will be sorted into one group over another. Random means a case has an exactly equal chance of ending up in one or the other group. The great thing about a random process is that over many separate random occurrences, predictable things happen. Although the process itself is entirely due to chance and does not allow predicting a specific outcome at one specific time, it obeys mathematical laws that makes very accurate predictions possible when conducted over a large number of situations.

Random assignment or randomization is unbiased because a researcher's desire to confirm a hypothesis or a research subject's personal interests do not enter into the selection process. *Unbiased* does not mean that groups with identical characteristics are selected in each specific situation of random assignment. Instead, it says that the probability of selecting a case can be mathematically determined, and, in the long run, the groups will be identical.

Sampling and random assignment are processes of selecting cases for inclusion in a study. When a researcher randomly assigns, he or she sorts a collection of cases into two or more groups using a random process. In random sampling, he or she selects a smaller subset of cases from a larger pool of cases (see Figure 8.1). Ideally, a researcher will both randomly sample and randomly assign. He or she can first sample to obtain a smaller set of cases (e.g., 150 people out of 20,000) and then use random assignment to divide the sample into groups (e.g., divide the 150 people into three groups of 50). Unfortunately, few social science experimenters use random samples. Most begin with a convenience sample then randomly assign.

How to Randomly Assign

Random assignment is very simple in practice. A researcher begins with a collection of cases (individuals, organizations, or whatever the unit of analysis is), then divides it into two or more groups by a random process, such as asking people to count off, tossing a coin, or throwing dice. For example, a researcher wants to divide 32 people into two groups of 16. A random method is writing each person's name on a slip of paper, putting the slips in a hat, mixing the slips with eyes closed, then drawing the first 16 names for group 1 and the second 16 for group 2.

Matching versus Random Assignment

You might ask, If the purpose of random assignment is to get two (or more) equivalent groups, would it not be simpler to match the characteristics of cases in each group? Some researchers match cases in groups on certain characteristics, such as age and sex. Matching is an alternative to random assignment, but it is an infrequently used one.

Matching presents a problem: What are the relevant characteristics to match on, and can one locate exact matches? Individual cases differ in thousands of ways, and the researcher cannot know which might be relevant. For example, a researcher compares two groups of 15 students. There are 8 males in one group, which means there should be 8 males in the other group. Two males in the first group are only children; one is from a divorced family, one from an intact family. One is tall, slender, and Jewish; the other is short, heavy, and Methodist. In order to match groups, does the researcher have to find a tall Jewish male only child from a divorced home and a short Methodist male only child from an intact home? The tall, slender, Jewish male only child is 22 years old and is studying to become a physician. The short, heavy Methodist male is 20 years old and wants to be an accountant. Does the researcher also need to match the age and career aspirations of the two males? True matching soon becomes an impossible task.

EXPERIMENTAL DESIGN LOGIC

The Language of Experiments

Experimental research has its own language or set of terms and concepts. You already encountered the basic ideas: random assignment and independent and dependent variables. In experimental research, the cases or people used in research projects and on whom variables are measured are called the *subjects*.

Parts of the Experiment.   We can divide the experiment into seven parts. Not all experiments

FIGURE 8.1   **Random Assignment and Random Sampling**

Random Sampling

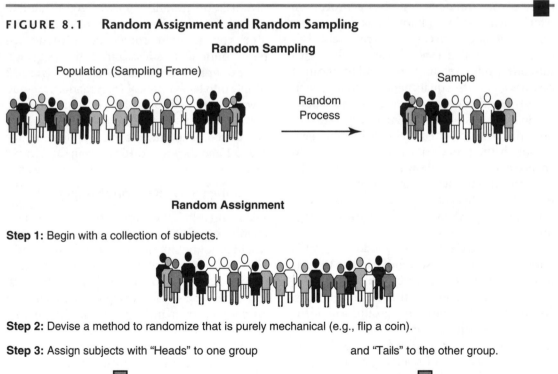

Population (Sampling Frame)

Random Process

Sample

Random Assignment

Step 1: Begin with a collection of subjects.

Step 2: Devise a method to randomize that is purely mechanical (e.g., flip a coin).

Step 3: Assign subjects with "Heads" to one group   and "Tails" to the other group.

Control Group

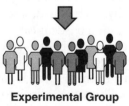

Experimental Group

have all these parts, and some have all seven parts plus others. The following seven, to be discussed here, make up a true experiment:

1. Treatment or independent variable
2. Dependent variable
3. Pretest
4. Posttest
5. Experimental group
6. Control group
7. Random assignment

In most experiments, a researcher creates a situation or enters into an ongoing situation, then modifies it. The *treatment* (or the stimulus or manipulation) is what the researcher modifies. The term comes from medicine, in which a physician administers a treatment to patients; the physician intervenes in a physical or psychological condition to change it. It is the independent variable or a combination of independent variables. In earlier examples of measurement, a researcher developed a measurement instrument or indicator (e.g., a survey question), then applied it to a person or case. In experiments, researchers "measure" independent variables by creating a condition or situation. For example, the independent variable is "degree of fear or anxiety"; the levels are high fear and low fear. Instead of asking subjects whether they are fearful, experimenters put subjects into either a high-fear or a low-fear situation. They measure the independent variable by manipulating conditions so that some subjects feel a lot of fear and others feel little.

Researchers go to great lengths to create treatments. Some are as minor as giving different groups of subjects different instructions. Others can be as complex as putting subjects into situations with elaborate equipment, staged physical settings, or contrived social situations to manipulate what the subjects see or feel. Researchers want the treatment to have an impact and produce specific reactions, feelings, or behaviors.

Dependent variables or outcomes in experimental research are the physical conditions, so-cial behaviors, attitudes, feelings, or beliefs of subjects that change in response to a treatment. Dependent variables can be measured by paper-and-pencil indicators, observation, interviews, or physiological responses (e.g., heartbeat or sweating palms).

Frequently, a researcher measures the dependent variable more than once during an experiment. The *pretest* is the measurement of the dependent variable prior to introduction of the treatment. The *posttest* is the measurement of the dependent variable after the treatment has been introduced into the experimental situation.

Experimental researchers often divide subjects into two or more groups for purposes of comparison. A simple experiment has two groups, only one of which receives the treatment. The *experimental group* is the group that receives the treatment or in which the treatment is present. The group that does not receive the treatment is called the *control group*. When the independent variable takes on many different values, more than one experimental group is used.

We can review the variables in the three experiments used as examples in previous chapters. In Chapter 2 you read about an experiment by Brase and Richmond (2004) about doctor–patient interactions and perceptions. After random assignment, subjects saw same- and opposite-gender models identified as being medical doctors but who wore either informal or formal/traditional attire (independent variable). The experimenters then measured the subjects' judgments about trust in the physican and the physician's abilities (dependent variable). In Goar and Sell's (2005) experiment about mixed race task groups described in Chapter 4, randomly assigned three-person groups were told they were either to a complete complex task requiring diverse skills or not (independent variable). The experimenters measured the time it took the group to complete a task and involvement by group members of different races (dependent variable). In the study on college women with tattoos discussed in Chapter 5 by

Hawkes, Senn, and Thorn (2004), randomly assigned subjects were asked to read one of five scenarios about a 22-year-old college student woman who had a tattoo (independent variable). The experimenters then measured the subjects' feelings about the woman and tattoo using a semantic differential, a Feminist scale, and a Women's Movement and Neosexisms scale (dependent variables).

Steps in Conducting an Experiment. Following the basic steps of the research process, experimenters decide on a topic, narrow it into a testable research problem or question, then develop a hypothesis with variables. Once a researcher has the hypothesis, the steps of experimental research are clear.

A crucial early step is to plan a specific experimental design (to be discussed). The researcher decides the number of groups to use, how and when to create treatment conditions, the number of times to measure the dependent variable, and what the groups of subjects will experience from beginning to end. He or she also develops measures of the dependent variable and pilot-tests the experiment (see Box 8.1).

The experiment itself begins after a researcher locates subjects and randomly assigns them to groups. Subjects are given precise, preplanned instructions. Next, the researcher measures the dependent variable in a pretest before the treatment. One group is then exposed to the treatment. Finally, the researcher measures the dependent variable in a posttest. He or she also interviews subjects about the experiment before they leave. The researcher records measures of the dependent variable and examines the results for each group to see whether the hypothesis receives support.

Control in Experiments. Control is crucial in experimental research. A researcher wants to control all aspects of the experimental situation to isolate the effects of the treatment and eliminate alternative explanations. Aspects of an experimental situation that are not controlled by

> **Box 8.1   Steps in Conducting an Experiment**
>
> 1. Begin with a straightforward hypothesis appropriate to the experimental research.
> 2. Decide on an experimental design that will test the hypothesis within practical limitations.
> 3. Decide how to introduce the treatment or create a situation that induces the independent variable.
> 4. Develop a valid and reliable measure of the dependent variable.
> 5. Set up an experimental setting and conduct a pilot test of the treatment and dependent variable measures.
> 6. Locate appropriate subjects or cases.
> 7. Randomly assign subjects to groups (if random assignment is used in the chosen research design) and give careful instructions.
> 8. Gather data for the pretest measure of the dependent variable for all groups (if a pretest is used in the chosen design).
> 9. Introduce the treatment to the experimental group only (or to relevant groups if there are multiple experimental groups) and monitor all groups.
> 10. Gather data for posttest measure of the dependent variable.
> 11. *Debrief* the subjects by informing them of the true purpose and reasons for the experiment. Ask subjects what they thought was occurring. Debriefing is crucial when subjects have been deceived about some aspect of the experiment.
> 12. Examine data collected and make comparisons between different groups. Where appropriate, use statistics and graphs to determine whether or not the hypothesis is supported.

the researcher are alternatives to the treatment for change in the dependent variable and undermine his or her attempt to establish causality definitively.

Experimental researchers use deception to control the experimental setting. *Deception* occurs when the researcher intentionally misleads subjects through written or verbal instructions, the actions of others, or aspects of the setting. It may involve the use of *confederates* or stooges—people who pretend to be other subjects or bystanders but who actually work for the researcher and deliberately mislead subjects. Through deception, the researcher tries to control what the subjects see and hear and what they believe is occurring. For example, a researcher's instructions falsely lead subjects to believe that they are participating in a study about group cooperation. In fact, the experiment is about male/female verbal interaction, and what subjects say is being secretly tape recorded. Deception lets the researcher control the subjects' definition of the situation. It prevents them from altering their cross-sex verbal behavior because they are unaware of the true research topic. By focusing their attention on a false topic, the researcher induces the unaware subjects to act "naturally." For realistic deception, researchers may invent false treatments and dependent variable measures to keep subjects unaware of the true ones. The use of deception in experiments raises ethical issues (to be discussed).

Types of Design

Researchers combine parts of an experiment (e.g., pretests, control groups, etc.) together into an *experimental design*. For example, some designs lack pretests, some do not have control groups, and others have many experimental groups. Certain widely used standard designs have names.

You should learn the standard designs for two reasons. First, in research reports, researchers give the name of a standard design instead of describing it. When reading reports, you will be able to understand the design of the experiment if you know the standard designs. Second, the standard designs illustrate common ways to combine design parts. You can use them

for experiments you conduct or create your own variations.

The designs are illustrated with a simple example. A researcher wants to learn whether wait staff (waiters and waitresses) receive more in tips if they first introduce themselves by first name and return to ask "Is everything fine?" 8 to 10 minutes after delivering the food. The dependent variable is the size of the tip received. The study occurs in two identical restaurants on different sides of a town that have had the same types of customers and average the same amount in tips.

Classical Experimental Design.   All designs are variations of the *classical experimental design,* the type of design discussed so far, which has random assignment, a pretest and a posttest, an experimental group, and a control group.

Example.   The experimenter gives 40 newly hired wait staff an identical two-hour training session and instructs them to follow a script in which they are not to introduce themselves by first name and not to return during the meal to check on the customers. They are next randomly divided into two equal groups of 20 and sent to the two restaurants to begin employment. The experimenter records the amount in tips for all subjects for one month (pretest score). Next, the experimenter "retrains" the 20 subjects at restaurant 1 (experimental group). The experimenter instructs them henceforth to introduce themselves to customers by first name and to check on the customers, asking, "Is everything fine?" 8 to 10 minutes after delivering the food (treatment). The group at restaurant 2 (control group) is "retained" to continue without an introduction or checking during the meal. Over the second month, the amount of tips for both groups is recorded (posttest score).

Preexperimental Designs.   Some designs lack random assignment and are compromises or shortcuts. These *preexperimental designs* are used in situations where it is difficult to use the classical design. They have weaknesses that make inferring a causal relationship more difficult.

One-Shot Case Study Design. Also called the one-group posttest-only design, the *one-shot case study design* has only one group, a treatment, and a posttest. Because there is only one group, there is no random assignment.

Example. The experimenter takes a group of 40 newly hired wait staff and gives all a two-hour training session in which they are instructed to introduce themselves to customers by first name and to check on the customers, asking, "Is everything fine?" 8 to 10 minutes after delivering the food (treatment). All subjects begin employment, and the experimenter records the amount in tips for all subjects for one month (posttest score).

One-Group Pretest-Posttest Design. This design has one group, a pretest, a treatment, and a posttest. It lacks a control group and random assignment.

Example. The experimenter takes a group of 40 newly hired wait staff and gives all a two-hour training session. They are instructed to follow a script in which they are not to introduce themselves by first name and not to return during the meal to check on the customers. All begin employment, and the experimenter records the amount in tips for all subjects for one month (pretest score). Next, the experimenter "retrains" all 40 subjects (experimental group). The experimenter instructs the subjects henceforth to introduce themselves to customers by first name and to check on the customers, asking, "Is everything fine?" 8 to 10 minutes after delivering the food (treatment). Over the second month, the amount of tips is recorded (posttest score).

This is an improvement over the one-shot case study because the researcher measures the dependent variable both before and after the treatment. But it lacks a control group. The researcher cannot know whether something other than the treatment occurred between the pretest and the posttest to cause the outcome.

Static Group Comparison. Also called the posttest-only nonequivalent group design, *static group comparison* has two groups, a posttest, and treatment. It lacks random assignment and a pretest. A weakness is that any posttest outcome difference between the groups could be due to group differences prior to the experiment instead of to the treatment.

Example. The experimenter gives 40 newly hired wait staff an identical two-hour training session and instructs them to follow a script in which they are not to introduce themselves by first name and not to return during the meal to check on the customers. They can choose one of the two restaurants to work at, so long as each restaurant ends up with 20 people. All begin employment. After one month, the experimenter "retrains" the 20 subjects at restaurant 1 (experimental group). The experimenter instructs them henceforth to introduce themselves to customers by first name and to check on the customers, asking, "Is everything fine?" 8 to 10 minutes after delivering the food (treatment). The group at restaurant 2 (control group) is "retained" to continue without an introduction or checking during the meal. Over the second month, the amount of tips for both groups is recorded (posttest score).

Quasi-Experimental and Special Designs. These designs, like the classical design, make identifying a causal relationship more certain than do preexperimental designs. *Quasi-experimental designs* help researchers test for causal relationships in a variety of situations where the classical design is difficult or inappropriate. They are called *quasi* because they are variations of the classical experimental design. Some have randomization but lack a pretest, some use more than two groups, and others substitute many observations of one group over time for a control group. In general, the researcher has less control over the independent variable than in the classical design (see Table 8.1).

TABLE 8.1   A Comparison of the Classical Experimental Design with Other Major Designs

Design	Random Assignment	Pretest	Posttest	Control Group	Experimental Group
Classical	Yes	Yes	Yes	Yes	Yes
One-Shot Case Study	No	No	Yes	No	Yes
One-Group Pretest Postest	No	Yes	Yes	No	Yes
Static Group Comparison	No	No	Yes	Yes	Yes
Two-Group Posttest Only	Yes	No	Yes	Yes	Yes
Time Series Designs	No	Yes	Yes	No	Yes

Two-Group Posttest-Only Design.   This is identical to the static group comparison, with one exception: The groups are randomly assigned. It has all the parts of the classical design except a pretest. The random assignment reduces the chance that the groups differed before the treatment, but without a pretest, a researcher cannot be as certain that the groups began the same on the dependent variable.

In a study using a two-group posttest-only design with random assignment, Rind and Strohmetz (1999) examined messages about a upcoming special written on the back of customers' checks. The subjects were 81 dining parties eating at an upscale restaurant in New Jersey. The treatment was whether a female server wrote a message about an upcoming restaurant special on the back of a check and the dependent variable was the size of tips. The server with two years' experience was given a randomly shuffled stack of cards, half of which said No Message and half of which said Message. Just before she gave a customer his or her check, she randomly pulled a card from her pocket. If it said Message, she wrote about an upcoming special on the back of the customer's check. If it said No Message, she wrote nothing. The experimenters recorded the amount of the tip and the number of people at the table. They instructed the server to act the same toward all customers. The results showed that higher tips came from customers who received the message about upcoming specials.

Interrupted Time Series.   In an *interrupted time series* design, a researcher uses one group and makes multiple pretest measures before and after the treatment. For example, after remaining level for many years, in 1995, cigarette taxes jumped 35 percent. Taxes remained relatively constant for the next 10 years. The hypothesis is that increases in taxes lower cigarette consumption. A researcher plots the rate of cigarette consumption for 1985 through 2005. The researcher notes that cigarette consumption was level during the 10 years prior to the new taxes, then dropped in 1995 and stayed about the same for the next 10 years.

Equivalent Time Series.   An *equivalent time series* is another one-group design that extends over a time period. Instead of one treatment, it has a pretest, then a treatment and posttest, then treatment and posttest, then treatment and posttest, and so on. For example, people who drive motorcycles were not required to wear helmets before 1985, when a law was passed requiring helmets. In 1991, the law was repealed because of pressure from motorcycle clubs. The helmet law was reinstated in 2003. The researcher's hypothesis is that wearing protective helmets lowers the number of head injury deaths in motorcycle accidents. The researcher plots head injury death rates in motorcycle accidents over time. The rate was very high prior to 1985, dropped sharply between 1985 and 1991, then returned to pre-1985 levels between 1991 and 2003, then dropped again from 2003 to the present.

Latin Square Designs.   Researchers interested in how several treatments given in different sequences or time orders affect a dependent variable can use a *Latin square design.* For example, a junior high school geography instructor has three units to teach students: map reading, using a compass, and the longitude/latitude (LL) system. The units can be taught in any order, but the teacher wants to know which order most helps students learn. In one class, students first learn to read maps, then how to use a compass, then the LL system. In another class, using a compass comes first, then map reading, then the LL system. In a third class, the instructor first teaches the LL system, then compass usage, and ends with map reading. The teacher gives tests after each unit, and students take a comprehensive exam at the end of the term. The students were randomly assigned to classes, so the instructor can see whether presenting units in one sequence or another resulted in improved learning.

Solomon Four-Group Design.   A researcher may believe that the pretest measure has an influence on the treatment or dependent variable. A pretest can sometimes sensitize subjects to the treatment or improve their performance on the posttest (see the discussion of testing effect to come). Richard L. Solomon developed the *Solomon four-group design* to address the issue of pretest effects. It combines the classical experimental design with the two-group posttest-only design and randomly assigns subjects to one of

four groups. For example, a mental health worker wants to determine whether a new training method improves clients' coping skills. The worker measures coping skills with a 20-minute test of reactions to stressful events. Because the clients might learn coping skills from taking the test itself, a Solomon four-group design is used. The mental health worker randomly divides clients into four groups. Two groups receive the pretest; one of them gets the new training method and the other gets the old method. Another two groups receive no pretest; one of them gets the new method and the other the old method. All four groups are given the same posttest and the posttest results are compared. If the two treatment (new method) groups have similar results, and the two control (old method) groups have similar results, then the mental health worker knows pretest learning is not a problem. If the two groups with a pretest (one treatment, one control) differ from the two groups without a pretest, then the worker concludes that the pretest itself may have an effect on the dependent variable.

Factorial Designs.   Sometimes, a research question suggests looking at the simultaneous effects of more than one independent variable. A *factorial design* uses two or more independent variables in combination. Every combination of the categories in variables (sometimes called *factors*) is examined. When each variable contains several categories, the number of combinations grows very quickly. The treatment or manipulation is not each independent variable; rather, it is each combination of the categories.

The treatments in a factorial design can have two kinds of effects on the dependent variable: main effects and interaction effects. Only *main effects* are present in one-factor or single-treatment designs. In a factorial design, specific combinations of independent variable categories can also have an effect. They are called *interaction effects* because the categories in a combination interact to produce an effect beyond that of each variable alone.

FIGURE 8.2   Blame, Resistance, and Schema: Interaction Effect

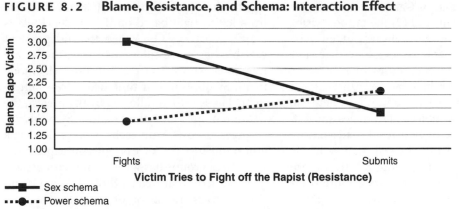

Interaction effects are illustrated in Figure 8.2, which uses data from a study by Ong and Ward (1999). As part of a study of 128 female undergraduates at the National University of Singapore, Ong and Ward measured which of two major ways subjects understood the crime of rape. Some of the women primarily understood it as sex and due to the male sex drive (sex schema); others understood it as primarily an act of male power and domination of a woman (power schema). The researchers asked the subjects to read a realistic scenario about the rape of a college student at their university. One randomly selected group of subjects read a scenario in which the victim tried to fight off the rapist. In the other set, she passively submitted. The researchers next asked the subjects to evaluate the degree to which the rape victim was at blame or responsible for the rape.

Results showed that the women who held the sex schema (and who also tended to embrace traditionalist gender role beliefs) more strongly blamed the victim when she resisted. Blame decreased if she submitted. The women who held a power schema (and who also tended to be nontraditionalists) were less likely to blame the victim if she fought. They blamed her more if she passively submitted. Thus, the subjects' responses to the victim's act of resisting the attack varied by, or interacted with, their understand-

ing of the crime of rape (i.e., the rape schema held by each subject). The researchers found that two rape schemas caused subjects to interpret victim resistance in opposite ways for the purpose of assigning responsibility for the crime.

Researchers discuss factorial design in a shorthand way. A "two by three factorial design" is written 2 × 3. It means that there are two treatments, with two categories in one and three categories in the other. A 2 × 3 × 3 design means that there are three independent variables, one with two categories and two with three categories each.

The previously discussed experiment by Hawkes, Seen, and Thorn (2004) on tattoos among college women used a 3 × 2 × 2 × 2 × 2 factorial design. The full study considered four independent variables, one with three categories, the rest having two categories, and it had three measures of the dependent variable. The dependent variable measures included a Semantic Differential measure (which contained three dimensions). In addition, experimenters had subjects complete a Neosexism measure (an 11-item, 5-point Likert Scale statements summed into an index) and a measure of Feminism and Women's Movement Support (a 10-item, 5-point Likert Scale summed into an index). The experimenters manipulated two independent variables in the descriptions of the tattoo read by subjects: (1) whether the woman had no tattoo, a tattoo smaller than a Canadian $1 coin, or larger than a $1 coin; and (2) the tattoo's visiblity as always hidden versus always hidden. Two independent variables were not manipulated but were preexisting characteristics of researcher subjects, (3) whether the subject him/herself had a tattoo or not, and (4) the subject's gender. The study included 268 subjects, 122 males and 146 females, of them 43 (or 16 percent) had a tattoo.

The study results showed that subjects viewed college women without a tattoo more positivity and female subjects were more positive toward a college woman having a tattoo than male subjects. There was also a significant effect for visibility, with more favorable attitudes for a nonvisible tattoo. Generally, subjects who had tattoos themselves were more favorable toward the woman having a tattoo. Size of tattoo had little effect. Men and women with a tattoo were more favorable, regardless of tattoo size, while those without a tattoo were negative. In addition, gender made no difference toward size of tattoo. The experiment had many specific findings for each combination of the five independent variables. One specific finding was that female subjects who had a tattoo themselves were least likely to react negatively to a larger tattoo. Results from the attitude measures suggest that "the tattooed woman may be seen by some as flaunting her freedom from gender norms or as threatening women's traditional place in society" (Hawkes, Seen, and Thorn 2004:603).

Design Notation

Experiments can be designed in many ways. *Design notation* is a shorthand system for symbolizing the parts of experimental design. Once you learn design notation, you will find it easier to think about and compare designs. For example, design notation expresses a complex, paragraph-long description of the parts of an experiment in five or six symbols arranged in two lines. It uses the following symbols: O = observation of dependent variable; X = treat-

ment, independent variable; R = random assignment. The Os are numbered with subscripts from left to right based on time order. Pretests are O_1, posttests O_2. When the independent variable has more than two levels, the Xs are numbered with subscripts to distinguish among them. Symbols are in time order from left to right. The R is first, followed by the pretest, the treatment, and then the posttest. Symbols are arranged in rows, with each row representing a group of subjects. For example, an experiment with three groups has an R (if random assignment is used), followed by three rows of Os and Xs. The rows are on top of each other because the pretests, treatment, and posttest occur in each group at about the same time. Table 8.2 gives the notation for many standard experimental designs.

INTERNAL AND EXTERNAL VALIDITY

The Logic of Internal Validity

Internal validity means the ability to eliminate alternative explanations of the dependent variable. Variables, other than the treatment, that affect the dependent variable are threats to internal validity. They threaten the researcher's ability to say that the treatment was the true causal factor producing change in the dependent variable. Thus, the logic of internal validity is to rule out variables other than the treatment by controlling experimental conditions and through experimental designs. Next, we examine major threats to internal validity.

Threats to Internal Validity

The following are nine common threats to internal validity.[1]

Selection Bias.   *Selection bias* is the threat that research participants will not form equivalent groups. It is a problem in designs without ran-

TABLE 8.2   Summary of Experimental Designs with Notation

Name of Design	Design Notation
Classical experimental design	R ⟨ O / O ⟩ X O / O
Preexperimental Designs	
One-shot case study	X O
One-group pretest-posttest	O X O
Static group comparison	X O / O
Quasi-Experimental Designs Two-group posttest only	R ⟨ X ⟩ O / O
Interrupted time series	O O O O X O O O
Equivalent time series	O X O X O X O X O
Latin square designs	R ⟨ O X_a O X_b O X_c O O X_b O X_a O X_c O O X_c O X_b O X_a O O X_a O X_c O X_b O O X_b O X_c O X_a O O X_c O X_a O X_b O ⟩

Solomon four-group design	R ⟨ O X O
	 O O
	      X O
	           O ⟩

Factorial designs	R ⟨ X_1 Z_1 O X_1 Z_2 O X_2 Z_1 O X_2 Z_2 O ⟩

dom assignment. It occurs when subjects in one experimental group have a characteristic that affects the dependent variable. For example, in an experiment on physical aggressiveness, the treatment group unintentionally contains subjects who are football, rugby, and hockey players, whereas the control group is made up of musicians, chess players, and painters. Another example is an experiment on the ability of people to dodge heavy traffic. All subjects assigned to one group come from rural areas, and all subjects in the other grew up in large cities. An examination of pretest scores helps a researcher detect this threat, because no group differences are expected.

History.   This is the threat that an event unrelated to the treatment will occur during the experiment and influence the dependent variable. *History effects* are more likely in experiments that continue over a long time period. For example, halfway through a two-week experiment to evaluate subjects' attitudes toward space travel, a spacecraft explodes on the launch pad, killing the astronauts. The history effect can occur in the cigarette tax example discussed earlier (see the discussion of interrupted time-series design). If a public antismoking campaign or reduced cigarette advertising also began in 1989, it would be hard to say that higher taxes caused less smoking.

Maturation.   This is the threat that some biological, psychological, or emotional process within the subjects and separate from the treatment will change over time. *Maturation* is more common in experiments over long time periods. For example, during an experiment on reasoning ability, subjects become bored and sleepy and, as a result, score lower. Another example is an experiment on the styles of children's play between grades 1 and 6. Play styles are affected by physical, emotional, and maturation changes that occur as the children grow older, instead of or in addition to the effects of a treatment. Designs with a pretest and control group help researchers determine whether maturation or history effects are present, because both experimental and control groups will show similar changes over time.

Testing.   Sometimes, the pretest measure itself affects an experiment. This *testing effect* threatens internal validity because more than the treatment alone affects the dependent variable. The Solomon four-group design helps a researcher detect testing effects. For example, a researcher gives students an examination on the first day of class. The course is the treatment. He or she tests learning by giving the same exam on the last day of class. If subjects remember the pretest questions and this affects what they learned (i.e., paid attention to) or how they answered questions on the posttest, a testing effect is present. If testing

effects occur, a researcher cannot say that the treatment alone has affected the dependent variable.

Instrumentation.   This threat is related to reliability. It occurs when the *instrument* or dependent variable measure changes during the experiment. For example, in a weight-loss experiment, the springs on the scale weaken during the experiment, giving lower readings in the posttest. Another example might have occurred in an experiment by Bond and Anderson (1987) on the reluctance to transmit bad news. The experimenters asked subjects to tell another person the results of an intelligence test and varied the test results to be either well above or well below average. The dependent variable was the length of time it took to tell the test taker the results. Some subjects were told that the session was being videotaped. During the experiment, the video equipment failed to work for one subject. If it had failed to work for more than one subject or had worked for only part of the session, the experiment would have had instrumentation problems. (By the way, subjects took longer to deliver bad news only if they thought they were doing so publicly—that is, being videotaped.)

Mortality.   *Mortality,* or attrition, arises when some subjects do not continue throughout the experiment. Although the word *mortality* means death, it does not necessarily mean that subjects have died. If a subset of subjects leaves partway through an experiment, a researcher cannot know whether the results would have been different had the subjects stayed. For example, a researcher begins a weight-loss program with 50 subjects. At the end of the program, 30 remain, each of whom lost 5 pounds with no side effects. The 20 who left could have differed from the 30 who stayed, changing the results. Maybe the program was effective for those who left, and they withdrew after losing 25 pounds. Or perhaps the program made subjects sick and forced them to quit. Researchers should notice and report the number of subjects in each group during pretests and posttests to detect this threat to internal validity.

Statistical Regression.   *Statistical regression* is not easy to grasp intuitively. It is a problem of extreme values or a tendency for random errors to move group results toward the average. It can occur in two ways.

One situation arises when subjects are unusual with regard to the dependent variable. Because they begin as unusual or extreme, subjects are unlikely to respond further in the same direction. For example, a researcher wants to see whether violent films make people act violently. He or she chooses a group of violent criminals from a high-security prison, gives them a pretest, shows violent films, then administers a posttest. To the researcher's shock, the prisoners are slightly less violent after the film, whereas a control group of prisoners who did not see the film are slightly more violent than before. Because the violent criminals began at an extreme, it is unlikely that a treatment could make them more violent; by random chance alone, they appear less extreme when measured a second time.[2]

A second situation involves a problem with the measurement instrument. If many research participants score very high (at the ceiling) or very low (at the floor) on a variable, random chance alone will produce a change between the pretest and the posttest. For example, a researcher gives 80 subjects a test, and 75 get perfect scores. He or she then gives a treatment to raise scores. Because so many subjects already had perfect scores, random errors will reduce the group average because those who got perfect scores can randomly move in only one direction—to get some answers wrong. An examination of scores on pretests will help researchers detect this threat to internal validity.

Diffusion of Treatment or Contamination. *Diffusion of treatment* is the threat that research participants in different groups will communicate with each other and learn about the other's treatment. Researchers avoid it by isolating groups or having subjects promise not to reveal anything to others who will become subjects. For example, subjects participate in a day-long experiment on a new way to memorize words. During a break, treatment-group subjects tell those in the control group about the new way to memorize, which control-group subjects then use. A researcher needs outside information, such as postexperiment interviews, with subjects to detect this threat.

Experimenter Expectancy.   Although it is not always considered a traditional internal validity problem, the experimenter's behavior, too, can threaten causal logic.[3] A researcher may threaten internal validity, not by purposefully unethical behavior but by indirectly communicating *experimenter expectancy* to subjects. Researchers may be highly committed to the hypothesis and indirectly communicate desired findings to the subjects. For example, a researcher studies the effects of memorization training on student learning ability, and also sees the grade transcripts of subjects. The researcher believes that students with higher grades tend to do better at the training and will learn more. Through eye contact, tone of voice, pauses, and other nonverbal communication, the researcher unconsciously trains the students with higher grades more intensely; the researcher's nonverbal behavior is the opposite for students with lower grades.

Here is a way to detect experimenter expectancy. A researcher hires assistants and teaches them experimental techniques. The assistants train subjects and test their learning ability. The researcher gives the assistants fake transcripts and records showing that subjects in one group are honor students and the others are failing, although in fact the subjects are identical. Experimenter expectancy is present if the fake honor students, as a group, do much better than the fake failing students.

The *double-blind experiment* is designed to control researcher expectancy. In it, people who have direct contact with subjects do not know the details of the hypothesis or the treatment. It is *double* blind because both the subjects and those in contact with them are blind to details of the experiment (see Figure 8.3). For example, a researcher wants to see if a new drug is effective. Using pills of three colors—green, yellow, and pink—the researcher puts the new drug in the yellow pill, puts an old drug in the pink one, and makes the green pill a *placebo*—a false treatment that appears to be real (e.g., a sugar pill without any physical effects). Assistants who give the pills and record the effects do not know which color

contains the new drug. Only another person who does not deal with subjects directly knows which colored pill contains the drug and it is he or she who examines the results.

External Validity and Field Experiments

Even if an experimenter eliminates all concerns about internal validity, external validity remains a potential problem. *External validity* is the ability to generalize experimental findings to events and settings outside the experiment itself. If a

FIGURE 8.3   Double-Blind Experiments: An Illustration of Single-Blind, or Ordinary, and Double-Blind Experiments

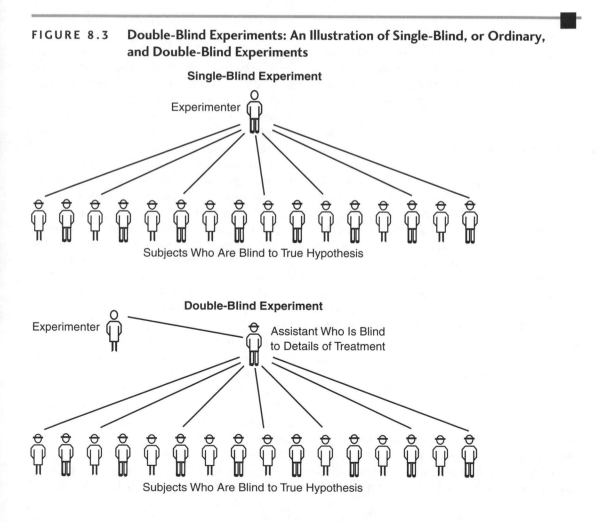

study lacks external validity, its findings hold true only in experiments, making them useless to both basic and applied science.

Reactivity.   Research participants might react differently in an experiment than they would in real life because they know they are in a study; this is called *reactivity*. The *Hawthorne effect* is a specific kind of reactivity.[4] The name comes from a series of experiments by Elton Mayo at the Hawthorne, Illinois, plant of Westinghouse Electric during the 1920s and 1930s. Researchers modified many aspects of working conditions (e.g., lighting, time for breaks, etc.) and measured productivity. They discovered that productivity rose after each modification, no matter what it was. This curious result occurred because the workers did not respond to the treatment but to the additional attention they received from being part of the experiment and knowing that they were being watched. Later research questioned whether this occurred, but the name is used for an effect from the attention of researchers. A related effect is the effect of something new, which may wear off over time.

Field Experiments.   So far, this chapter has focused on experiments conducted under the controlled conditions of a laboratory. Experiments are also conducted in real-life or field settings where a researcher has less control over the experimental conditions. The amount of control varies on a continuum. At one end is the highly controlled *laboratory experiment,* which takes place in a specialized setting or laboratory; at the opposite end is the *field experiment,* which takes place in the "field"—in natural settings such as a subway car, a liquor store, or a public sidewalk. Subjects in field experiments are usually unaware that they are involved in an experiment and react in a natural way. For example, researchers have had a confederate fake a heart attack on a subway car to see how the bystanders react.[5]

Dasgupta and Asgari (2004) tested the hypothesis that stereotypical beliefs weaken when a person encounters people who contradict the stereotype, especially if the others are respected. They used both a laboratory experiment (with a two-group, posttest-only design) and a field experiment. Past studies focused on out-group stereotypes, but the authors wanted to examine the hypothesis for an in-group, women. In the laboratory experiment, experimenters randomly assigned female subjects to view either (1) a set of photographs and biographies of 16 famous women leaders or (2) photos and descriptions of 16 flowers. The experimenters used deception and told subjects the study was about testing memory. The dependent variable was attitudes and beliefs about women and was measured with a Implicit Association Test (IAT). The results showed that subjects associated gendered first names (e.g., John vs. Emily) with leadership or follower traits (e.g., assertive and sympathetic). A high IAT score indicated that a subject viewed women more than men as having leadership more than supportive traits. The researchers also used a scale on beliefs about women. They found support for the hypothesis that exposure to famous women in leadership positions increased IAT scores, compared to exposure to neutral information about flowers. The field experiment had a pretest and a posttest but no random assignment. Subjects were females who attended two colleges in the same town. One was a coeducational college and the other had all female students. Subjects were recruited from first-year classes at the beginning of the academic year and completed the IAT measure, the beliefs about women scale, and a general campus questionnaire. The experimenters documented that the all-female college had more females in administrative and faculty leadership positions. Pretest IAT scores were very similar, with subjects from coeducational college having slightly lower scores. This helped the experimenters to check for possible selection bias. Subjects were contacted one year later and asked to complete the same measures as presented in the posttest. Experimenters watched very carefully for experimental mortality since some students stopped attending college or did not complete later surveys. The IAT scores for subjects at the coeducational college declined (i.e., they were less likely to see females as having leadership traits), whereas the IAT scores for subjects at the all-female college greatly increased. In addition, the experimenters found that the more female teachers a student had at either college, the higher the posttest IAT scores, and this was especially the case for math and sciences courses. Thus, exposure to women in leadership positions caused the IAT scores to increase, whereas the absence of such exposure, if anything, lowered the scores.

Von Larr and colleagues (2005) used a field experiment to test the well-known *contact hypothesis* that says intergroup contact reduces racial–ethnic prejudice as people replace their stereotypes with personal experience, although this happens so long as the contact involves people of equal status pursuing common goals in a cooperative setting and is approved by authorities. In addition, informal contact in which people get to know about out-group members as acquaintances also reduces out-group prejudice. The experiment took place at UCLA, where the student body is very racially and ethnically diverse. Unless they preselect a roommate, incoming students are randomly assigned roommates. About 20 percent of students choose a roommate and the rest are randomly assigned. The authors measured student background and attitudes among nearly 3,800 new incoming students using a panel design across five time periods—before college entry (summer 1996) and during the spring of each of the next four years (1997–2000) with surveys (20-minute telephone interviews). The dependent variable was the students' racial–ethnic attitudes and included questions about roommates, other friends, interracial dating, multiculturalism, symbolic racism, and feelings about various racial–ethnic groups. These were the experiment's pretest and multiple posttest measures. Experimenters watched very carefully for exper-

imental mortality, since some students stopped attending college, left college dormitories, or did not complete the later surveys. They tested the hypotheses that students who were randomly assigned to live with an out-group member (the independent variable) developed less prejudicial attitudes toward members of that out-group. They found that compared to pretest measures, prejudicial attitudes declined as predicted by the contact hypothesis with one exception. Apparently having an Asian American roommate worked in the opposite way and actually increased prejudice, especially among the White students.

Experimenter control relates to internal and external validity. Laboratory experiments tend to have greater internal validity but lower external validity; that is, they are logically tighter and better controlled, but less generalizable. Field experiments tend to have greater external validity but lower internal validity; that is, they are more generalizable but less controlled. Quasi-experimental designs are common in field experiments. Table 8.3 summarizes threats to internal and external validity.

TABLE 8.3   Major Internal and External Validity Concerns

Internal Validity	External Validity and Reactivity
Selection bias	Hawthorne effect
History effect	
Maturation	
Testing	
Instrumentation	
Experimental mortality	
Statistical regression	
Diffusion of treatment	
Experimenter expectancy	

PRACTICAL CONSIDERATIONS

Every research technique has informal tricks of the trade. These are pragmatic, commonsense ideas that account for the difference between the successful research projects of an experienced researcher and the difficulties a novice researcher faces. Three are discussed here.

Planning and Pilot-Tests

All social research requires planning, and most quantitative researchers use pilot-tests. During the planning phase of experimental research, a researcher thinks of alternative explanations or threats to internal validity and how to avoid them. The researcher also develops a neat and well-organized system for recording data. In addition, he or she devotes serious effort to pilot-testing any apparatus (e.g., computers, video cameras, tape recorders, etc.) that will be used in the treatment situation, and he or she must train and pilot-test confederates. After the pilot-tests, the researcher should interview the pilot subjects to uncover aspects of the experiment that need refinement.

Instructions to Subjects

Most experiments involve giving instructions to subjects to set the stage. A researcher should word instructions carefully and follow a prepared script so that all subjects hear the same thing. This ensures reliability. The instructions are also important in creating a realistic cover story when deception is used.

Postexperiment Interview

At the end of an experiment, the researcher should interview subjects, for three reasons. First, if deception was used, the researcher needs to debrief the research participants, telling them the true purpose of the experiment and answering questions. Second, he or she can learn what the subjects thought and how their definitions of the situation affected their behavior. Finally, he or she can explain the importance of not revealing the true nature of the experiment to other potential participants.

RESULTS OF EXPERIMENTAL RESEARCH: MAKING COMPARISONS

Comparison is the key to all research. By carefully examining the results of experimental research, a researcher can learn a great deal about threats to internal validity, and whether the treatment has an impact on the dependent variable. For example, in the Bond and Anderson (1987) experiment on delivering bad news, discussed earlier, it took an average of 89.6 and 73.1 seconds to deliver favorable versus 72.5 or 147.2 seconds to deliver unfavorable test scores in private or public settings, respectively. A comparison shows that delivering bad news in public takes the longest, whereas good news takes a bit longer in private.

A more complex illustration of such comparisons is shown in Figure 8.4 on the results of a series of five weight-loss experiments using the classical experimental design. In the example, the 30 research participants in the experimental group at Enrique's Slim Clinic lost an average of 50 pounds, whereas the 30 in the control group did not lose a single pound. Only one person dropped out during the experiment. Susan's Scientific Diet Plan had equally dramatic results, but 11 people in her experimental group dropped out. This suggests a problem with experimental mortality. People in the experimental group at Carl's Calorie Counters lost 8 pounds, compared to 2 pounds for the control group, but the control group and the experimental group began with an average of 31 pounds difference in weight. This suggests a problem with selection bias. Natalie's Nutrition Center had no experimental mortality or selection bias problems, but those in the experimental group lost no more weight than those in the control group. It ap-

FIGURE 8.4   Comparisons of Results, Classical Experimental Design, Weight-Loss Experiments

Enrique's Slim Clinic				Natalie's Nutrition Center		
	Pretest	Posttest			Pretest	Posttest
Experimental	190 (30)	140 (29)	Experimental		190 (30)	188 (29)
Control group	189 (30)	189 (30)	Control group		192 (29)	190 (28)

Susan's Scientific Diet Plan				Pauline's Pounds Off		
	Pretest	Posttest			Pretest	Posttest
Experimental	190 (30)	141 (19)	Experimental		190 (30)	158 (30)
Control group	189 (30)	189 (28)	Control group		191 (29)	159 (28)

Carl's Calorie Counters		
	Pretest	Posttest
Experimental	160 (30)	152 (29)
Control group	191 (29)	189 (29)

pears that the treatment was not effective. Pauline's Pounds Off also avoided selection bias and experimental mortality problems. People in her experimental group lost 32 pounds, but so did those in the control group. This suggests that the maturation, history, or diffusion of treatment effects may have occurred. Thus, the treatment at Enrique's Slim Clinic appears to be the most effective one. See Box 8.2 for a practical application of comparing experimental results.

Box
8.2   A "Natural" Field Experiment on Law Compliance in New Orleans

Occasionally, a "natural" experiment is possible due to public policy changes or a government intervention, and researchers are able to measure, participate, and learn from it and conduct a field experiment with high *external validity*. This occurred in New Orleans, Lousiana. Until the mid-1990s, laws on selling liquor to underage customers were barely enforced in New Orleans. If caught, the offending liquor retailer met privately with the liquor commission and paid a small fine. Enforcing liquor laws was low priority for state and local government, so only three enforcement officers monitored 5,000 alcohol outlets in the New Orleans area. When public officials planned to shift enforcement priorities, Scribner and Cohen (2001) examined its impact. They had several people who clearly looked under 18 years old attempt to purchase alcoholic beverages illegally (the law required being at least 21 years of age) at 143 randomly selected liquor outlets between November 1995 and January 1996 (Time 0). The percentage who could buy liquor illegally was the *pretest measure.* After assessing the rate of illegal sales, the *dependent variable,* the police issued citations to 51 of the sales outlets, the primary *independent variable*

BOX 8.2 Continued

or treatment. About the same time, government officials initiated a media campaign urging better law compliance. There were *two posttest measures*, first in March to April 1996 (Time 1) and again in November 1996 to January 1997 (Time 2), during which the experimenters checked the 143 outlets.

DEPENDENT VARIABLE: PERCENTAGE WHO OBEY THE LAW

	Pretest (Time 0)	Media Campaign	Posttest 1 (Time 1)	Posttest 2 (Time 2)	No. of Retail Liquor Outlets
Experimental (citation)	6.7%		51%	29%	45
Control (no citation)	13.3%		35%	17%	98
Total	11.1%		40%	21%	143

The results allow us to compare rates of illegal selling activity before and after citations plus media campaign (*pretest* and *posttest* measures) and to compare outlets that received citations (*experimental group*) with those that did not receive citations and only had media exposure (*control group*). We see that the citations and campaign did not stop the illegal activity, but it had some effect. The impact was greater on outlets that experienced direct punishment. In addition, by adding a later follow-up (Time 2), we see how the law-enforcement impact slowly decayed over time. As frequently happens in a natural experiment, internal validity is threatened: First, the pretest measure shows a difference in the two sets of outlets, with outlets that received the treatment showing higher rates of illegal behavior; this is potential *selection bias*. Second, the media campaign occurred for all outlets, so the treatment is really a citation plus the media campaign. The authors noted that they had intended to compare the New Orleans area with another area with neither the media nor

the citation campaign, but were unable to do so. Since outlets that did not receive the treatment (i.e., a citation for law violation) probably learned about it from others in the same business, a form of *diffusion of the treatment* could be operating. Third, the researchers report that they began with 155 outlets, but studied only 143 because 12 outlets went out of business during the study. The authors noted that none of the outlets that stopped selling alcohol closed due to new law enforcement, but if those outlets that received citations had more problems and were more likely to go out of business, it suggests *experimental mortality*. The experimenters did not mention any external events in New Orleans that happened during the time of the study (e.g., a publicized event such as underage drinker dying of alcohol poisoning from overdrinking). Researchers need to be aware of potential external events when a study continues for a long time and consider possible *history effects*.

A WORD ON ETHICS

Ethical considerations are a significant issue in experimental research because experimental research is intrusive (i.e., it interferes). Treatments may involve placing people in contrived social settings and manipulating their feelings or behaviors. Dependent variables may be what subjects say or do. The amount and type of intrusion is limited by ethical standards. Researchers must be very careful if they place research participants in physical danger or in embarrassing or anxiety-inducing situations. They must painstakingly monitor events and control what occurs.

Deception is common in social experiments, but it involves misleading or lying to subjects. Such dishonesty is not condoned unconditionally and is acceptable only as the means to achieve a goal that cannot be achieved otherwise. Even for a worthy goal, deception can be used only with restrictions. The amount and type of deception should not go beyond what is minimally necessary, and research participants should be debriefed.

CONCLUSION

In this chapter, you learned about random assignment and the methods of experimental research. Random assignment is an effective way to create two (or more) groups that can be treated as equivalent and hence compared. In general, experimental research provides precise and relatively unambiguous evidence for a causal relationship. It follows the positivist approach, produces quantitative results that can be analyzed with statistics, and is often used in evaluation research (see Box 8.2).

This chapter also examined the parts of an experiment and how they can be combined to produce different experimental designs. In addition to the classical experimental design, you learned about preexperimental and quasi-experimental designs. You also learned how to express them using design notation.

You learned that internal validity—the internal logical rigor of an experiment—is a key idea in experimental research. Threats to internal validity are possible alternative explanations to the treatment. You also learned about external validity and how field experiments maximize external validity.

The real strength of experimental research is its control and logical rigor in establishing evidence for causality. In general, experiments tend to be easier to replicate, less expensive, and less time consuming than the other techniques. Experimental research also has limitations. First, some questions cannot be addressed using experimental methods because control and experimental manipulation are impossible. Another limitation is that experiments usually test one or a few hypotheses at a time. This fragments knowledge and makes it necessary to synthesize results across many research reports. External validity is another potential problem because many experiments rely on small nonrandom samples of college students.[6]

You learned how a careful examination and comparison of results can alert you to potential problems in research design. Finally, you saw some practical and ethical considerations in experiments.

In the next chapters, you will examine other research techniques. The logic of the nonexperimental methods differs from that of the experiment. Experimenters focus narrowly on a few hypotheses. They usually have one or two independent variables, a single dependent variable, a few small groups of subjects, and an independent variable that the researcher induces. By contrast, other social researchers test many hypotheses at once. For example, survey researchers measure a large number of independent and dependent variables and use a larger number of randomly sampled subjects. Their independent variables are usually preexisting conditions in research participants.

Key Terms

classical experimental design
control group
debrief
deception
demand characteristics
design notation
diffusion of treatment
double-blind experiment

equivalent time series
experimental design
experimental group
factorial design
field experiment
Hawthorne effect
history effects
interaction effect
interrupted time series
laboratory experiment
Latin square design
maturation
mortality
one-shot case study
placebo
posttest
preexperimental designs
pretest
quasi-experimental designs
random assignment
reactivity
selection bias
Solomon four-group design

static group comparison
treatment

Endnotes

1. For additional discussions of threats to internal validity, see Cook and Campbell (1979:51–68), Kercher (1992), Smith and Glass (1987), Spector (1981:24–27), and Suls and Rosnow (1988).
2. This example is borrowed from Mitchell and Jolley (1988:97).
3. Experimenter expectancy is discussed in Aronson and Carlsmith (1968:66–70), Dooley (1984:151–153), and Mitchell and Jolley (1988:327–329).
4. The Hawthorne effect is described in Roethlisberger and Dickenson (1939), Franke and Kaul (1978), and Lang (1992). Also see the discussion in Cook and Campbell (1979:123–125) and Dooley (1984:155–156). Gillespie (1988, 1991) discussed the political context of the experiments.
5. See Piliavin and associates (1969).
6. See Graham (1992) and Sears (1986).

CHAPTER 9

Nonreactive Research and Secondary Analysis

INTRODUCTION

Experiments and survey research are both *reactive;* that is, the people being studied are aware of that fact. The techniques in this chapter address a limitation of reactive measures. You will learn about four research techniques that are *nonreactive;* that is, the people being studied are not aware that they are part of a research project. Nonreactive techniques are largely based on positivist principles but are also used by interpretive and critical researchers.

The first technique we will consider is less a distinct technique than a loose collection of inventive nonreactive measures. It is followed by content analysis, which builds on the fundamentals of quantitative research design and is a well-developed research technique. Existing statistics and secondary analysis, the last two techniques, refer to the collection of already existing information from government documents or previous surveys. Researchers examine the existing data in new ways to address new questions. Although the data may have been reactive when first collected, a researcher can address new questions without reactive effects.

NONREACTIVE MEASUREMENT

The Logic of Nonreactive Research

Nonreactive measurement begins when a researcher notices something that indicates a variable of interest. The critical thing about nonreactive or *unobtrusive measures* (i.e., measures that are not obtrusive or intrusive) is that the people being studied are not aware of it but leave evidence of their social behavior or actions "naturally." The observant researcher infers from the evidence to behavior or attitudes without disrupting the people being studied. Unnoticed observation is also a type of nonreactive measure. For example, McKelvie and Schamer (1988) unobtrusively observed whether drivers stopped at stop signs. They made observations during both daytime and nighttime. Observers noted whether the driver was male or female; whether the driver was alone or with passengers; whether other traffic was present; and whether the car came to a complete stop, a slow stop, or no stop. Later, we will contrast this type of observation to a slightly different type used in field research.

Varieties of Nonreactive or Unobtrusive Observation

Nonreactive measures are varied, and researchers have been creative in inventing indirect ways to measure social behavior (see Box 9.1). Because the measures have little in common except being nonreactive, they are best learned through examples. Some are *erosion measures,* where selective wear is used as a measure, and some are *accretion measures,* where the measures are deposits of something left behind.[1]

Researchers have examined family portraits in different historical eras to see how gender relations within the family are reflected in seating patterns. Urban anthropologists have examined the contents of garbage dumps to learn about life-styles from what is thrown away (e.g., liquor bottles indicate level of alcohol consumption). Based on garbage, people underreport their

---

Box 9.1 Finding Data on Tombstones

Foster and colleagues (1998) examined the tombstones in 10 cemeteries in an area of Illinois for the period from 1830 to 1989. They retrieved data on birth and death dates and gender from over 2,000 of the 2,028 burials. The researchers learned the area differed from some national trends. They found that conceptions had two peaks (spring and winter), females aged 10 to 64 had a higher death rate than males, and younger people died in late summer but older people in late winter.

liquor consumption by 40 to 60 percent (Rathje and Murphy, 1992:71). Researchers have studied the listening habits of drivers by checking what stations their radios are tuned to when cars are repaired. They have measured interest in different exhibits by noting worn tiles on the floor in different parts of a museum. They have studied differences in graffiti in male versus female high school restrooms to show gender differences in themes. Some have examined high school yearbooks to compare the high school activities of those who had psychological problems in latter life versus those who did not. (Also see Box 9.2.)

Recording and Documentation

Creating nonreactive measures follows the logic of quantitative measurement. A researcher first conceptualizes a construct, then links the construct to nonreactive empirical evidence, which is its measure. The operational definition of the variable includes how the researcher systematically notes and records observations.

Box 9.2	**Examples of Nonreactive Measures**

Physical Traces

Erosion: Wear suggests greater use.
Example: A researcher examines children's toys at a day care that were purchased at the same time. Worn-out toys suggest greater interest by the children.

Accretion: Accumulation of physical evidence suggests behavior.
Example: A researcher examines the brands of aluminum beverage cans in trash or recycling bins in male and female dormitories. This indicates the brands and types of beverages favored by each sex.

Archives

Running Records: Regularly produced public records may reveal much.
Example: A researcher examines marriage records for the bride and groom's ages. Regional differences suggest that the preference for males marrying younger females is greater in certain areas of the country.

Other Records: Irregular or private records can reveal a lot.

Example: A researcher finds the number of reams of paper purchased by a college dean's office for 10 years when student enrollment was stable. A sizable increase suggests that bureaucratic paperwork has increased.

Observation

External Appearance: How people appear may indicate social factors.
Example: A researcher watches students to see whether they are more likely to wear their school's colors and symbols after the school team won or lost.

Count Behaviors: Counting how many people do something can be informative.
Example: A researcher counts the number of men and women who come to a full stop and those who come to a rolling stop at a stop sign. This suggests gender difference in driving behavior.

Time Duration: How long people take to do things may indicate their attention.
Example: A researcher measures how long men and women pause in front of the painting of a nude man and in front of a painting of a nude woman. Time may indicate embarrassment or interest in same or cross-sex nudity by each sex.

Because nonreactive measures indicate a construct indirectly, the researcher needs to rule out reasons for the observation other than the construct of interest. For example, a researcher wants to measure customer walking traffic in a store. The researcher's measure is dirt and wear on floor tiles. He or she first clarifies what the customer traffic means (e.g., Is the floor a path to another department? Does it indicate a good location for a visual display?) Next, he or she systematically measures dirt or wear on the tiles, compares it to that in other locations, and records results on a regular basis (e.g., every month). Finally, the researcher rules out other reasons for the observations (e.g., the floor tile is of lower quality and wears faster, or the location is near an outside entrance).

CONTENT ANALYSIS

What Is Content Analysis?

Content analysis is a technique for gathering and analyzing the content of text. The *content* refers to words, meanings, pictures, symbols, ideas, themes, or any message that can be communicated. The *text* is anything written, visual, or spoken that serves as a medium for communication. It includes books, newspaper and magazine articles, advertisements, speeches, official documents, films and videotapes, musical lyrics, photographs, articles of clothing, and works of art.

The content analysis researcher uses objective and systematic counting and recording procedures to produce a quantitative description of the symbolic content in a text.[2] There are also qualitative or interpretive versions of content analysis, but in this chapter the emphasis is on quantitative data about a text's content.

Content analysis is nonreactive because the process of placing words, messages, or symbols in a text to communicate to a reader or receiver occurs without influence from the researcher who analyzes its content. For example, I, as author of this book, wrote words and drew diagrams to communicate research methods content to you, the student. The way the book was written and the way you read it are without any knowledge or intention of its ever being content analyzed.

Content analysis lets a researcher reveal the content (i.e., messages, meanings, etc.) in a source of communication (i.e., a book, article, movie, etc.). It lets him or her probe into and discover content in a different way from the ordinary way of reading a book or watching a television program.

With content analysis, a researcher can compare content across many texts and analyze it with quantitative techniques (e.g., charts and tables). In addition, he or she can reveal aspects of the text's content that are difficult to see. For example, you might watch television commercials and feel that non-Whites rarely appear in commercials for expensive consumer goods (e.g., luxury cars, furs, jewelry, perfume, etc.). Content analysis can document—in objective, quantitative terms—whether your vague feelings based on unsystematic observation are true. It yields repeatable, precise results about the text.

Content analysis involves random sampling, precise measurement, and operational definitions for abstract constructs. Coding turns aspects of content that represent variables into numbers. After a content analysis researcher gathers the data, he or she analyzes them with statistics in the same way that an experimenter or survey researcher would.

Topics Appropriate for Content Analysis

Researchers have used content analysis for many purposes: to study themes in popular songs and religious symbols in hymns, trends in the topics that newspapers cover and the ideological tone of newspaper editorials, sex-role stereotypes in textbooks or feature films, how often people of different races appear in television commercials and programs, answers to open-ended survey questions, enemy propaganda during wartime, the covers of popular magazines, personality characteristics from suicide notes, themes in advertising messages, gender differences in conversations, and so on.

Generalizations that researchers make on the basis of content analysis are limited to the cultural communication itself. Content analysis cannot determine the truthfulness of an assertion or evaluate the aesthetic qualities of literature. It reveals the content in text but cannot interpret the content's significance. Researchers should examine the text directly.

Content analysis is useful for three types of research problems. First, it is helpful for problems involving a large volume of text. A researcher can measure large amounts of text (e.g., years of newspaper articles) with sampling and multiple coders. Second, it is helpful when a topic must be studied "at a distance." For example, content analysis can be used to study historical documents, the writings of someone who has died, or broadcasts in a hostile foreign country. Finally, content analysis can reveal messages in a text that are difficult to see with casual observation. The creator of the text or those who read it may not be aware of all its themes, biases, or characteristics. For example, authors of preschool picture books may not consciously intend to portray children in traditional stereotyped sex roles, but a high degree of sex stereotyping has been revealed through content analysis.[3]

Measurement and Coding

General Issues. Careful measurement is crucial in content analysis because a researcher converts diffuse and murky symbolic communication into precise, objective, quantitative data. He or she carefully designs and documents procedures for coding to make replication possible. The researcher operationalizes constructs in content analysis with a coding system. A *coding system* is a set of instructions or rules on how to systematically observe and record content from text. A researcher tailors it to the specific type of text or communication medium being studied (e.g., television drama, novels, photos in magazine advertisements, etc.). The coding system also depends on the researcher's unit of analysis. For example, in the study by Lauzen and Dozier (2005) on gender stereotypes in the most popular U.S. films in 2002 (discussed in Chapter 4), the authors developed a coding system based on prior studies of prime-time television shows and film.

Units. The unit of analysis can vary a great deal in content analysis. It can be a word, a phrase, a theme, a plot, a newspaper article, a character, and so forth. In addition to units of analysis, researchers use other units in content analysis that may or may not be the same as units of analysis: recording units, context units, and enumeration units. There are few differences among them, and they are easily confused, but each has a distinct role. In simple projects, all three are the same.

What Is Measured? Measurement in content analysis uses *structured observation:* systematic, careful observation based on written rules. The rules explain how to categorize and classify observations. As with other measurement, categories should be mutually exclusive and exhaustive. Written rules make replication possible and improve reliability. Although researchers begin with preliminary coding rules, they often conduct a pilot study and refine coding on the basis of it.

Coding systems identify four characteristics of text content: frequency, direction, intensity, and space. A researcher measures from one to all four characteristics in a content analysis research project.

Frequency. *Frequency* simply means counting whether or not something occurs and, if it occurs, how often. For example, how many elderly people appear on a television program within a given week? What percentage of all characters are they, or in what percentage of programs do they appear?

Direction.   *Direction* is noting the direction of messages in the content along some continuum (e.g., positive or negative, supporting or opposed). For example, a researcher devises a list of ways an elderly television character can act. Some are positive (e.g., friendly, wise, considerate) and some are negative (e.g., nasty, dull, selfish).

Intensity.   *Intensity* is the strength or power of a message in a direction. For example, the characteristic of forgetfulness can be minor (e.g., not remembering to take your keys when leaving home, taking time to recall the name of someone you have not seen in years) or major (e.g., not remembering your name, not recognizing your children).

Space.   A researcher can record the size of a text message or the amount of space or volume allocated to it. *Space* in written text is measured by counting words, sentences, paragraphs, or space on a page (e.g., square inches). For video or audio text, space can be measured by the amount of time allocated. For example, a TV character may be present for a few seconds or continuously in every scene of a two-hour program.

Coding, Validity, and Reliability

Manifest Coding.   Coding the visible, surface content in a text is called *manifest coding*. For example, a researcher counts the number of times a phrase or word (e.g., *red*) appears in written text, or whether a specific action (e.g., a kiss) appears in a photograph or video scene. The coding system lists terms or actions that are then located in text. A researcher can use a computer program to search for words or phrases in text and have a computer do the counting work. To do this, he or she learns about the computer program, develops a comprehensive list of relevant words or phrases, and puts the text into a form that computers can read.[4]

Manifest coding is highly reliable because the phrase or word either is or is not present. Unfortunately, manifest coding does not take the connotations of words or phrases into account. The same word can take on different meanings depending on the context. The possibility that there are multiple meanings of a word limits the measurement validity of manifest coding.

For example, I read a book with a *red* cover that is a real *red* herring. Unfortunately, its publisher drowned in *red* ink because the editor could not deal with the *red* tape that occurs when a book is *red* hot. The book has a story about a *red* fire truck that stops at *red* lights only after the leaves turn *red*. There is also a group of *Reds* who carry *red* flags to the little *red* schoolhouse. They are opposed by *red*-blooded *red*necks who eat *red* meat and honor the *red,* white, and blue. The main character is a *red*-nosed matador who fights *red* foxes, not bulls, with his *red* cape. *Red*-lipped little *Red* Riding Hood is also in the book. She develops *red* eyes and becomes *red*-faced after eating a lot of *red* peppers in the *red* light district. She is given a *red* backside by her angry mother, a *red*head.

In the study of gender stereotypes in films in 2002, Lauzen and Dozier (2005) largely used manifest coding. Coders coded each character in a film as male or female, the estimated age of each character in one of 7 categories, the occupation of each character, and whether a character was formally appointed to provide guidance or direction in a group or informally emgered in such a function.

Latent Coding.   A researcher using *latent coding* (also called *semantic analysis*) looks for the underlying, implicit meaning in the content of a text. For example, a researcher reads an entire paragraph and decides whether it contains erotic themes or a romantic mood. The researcher's coding system has general rules to guide his or her interpretation of the text and for determining whether particular themes or moods are present.

Latent coding tends to be less reliable than manifest coding. It depends on a coder's knowledge of language and social meaning.[5] Training, practice, and written rules improve reliability, but still it is difficult to consistently identify themes, moods, and the like. Yet, the validity of latent coding can exceed that of manifest coding because people communicate meaning in many implicit ways that depend on context, not just in specific words.

A researcher can use both manifest and latent coding. If the two approaches agree, the final result is strengthened; if they disagree, the researcher may want to reexamine the operational and theoretical definitions.

Intercoder Reliability. Content analysis often involves coding information from a very large number of units. A research project might involve observing the content in dozens of books, hundreds of hours of television programming, or thousands of newspaper articles. In addition to coding the information personally, a researcher may hire assistants to help with the coding. He or she teaches coders the coding system and trains them to fill out a recording sheet. Coders should understand the variables, follow the coding system, and ask about ambiguities. A researcher records all decisions he or she makes about how to treat a new specific coding situation after coding begins so that he or she can be consistent.

A researcher who uses several coders must *always* check for consistency across coders. He or she does this by asking coders to code the same text independently and then checking for consistency across coders. The researcher measures *intercoder reliability* with a statistical coefficient that tells the degree of consistency among coders. The coefficient is *always* reported with the results of content analysis research. There are several intercoder reliability measures that range from 0 to 1, with 1.0 signifying perfect agreement among coders. An interreliability coeffi-

cent of .80 or better is generally required, although .70 may be acceptable for exploratory research. When the coding process stretches over a considerable time period (e.g., more than three months), the researcher also checks reliability by having each coder independently code samples of text that were previously coded. He or she then checks to see whether the coding is stable or changing. For example, six hours of television episodes are coded in April and coded again in July without the coders looking at their original coding decisions. Large deviations in coding necessitate retraining and coding the text a second time.

In the study of the 100 most popular U.S. films of 2002 by Lauzen and Dozier (2005), three graduate students worked as coders. During an initial training period they studied the coding system and variable definitions. Next, the coders practiced by coding independent of one another several films that were not in the study then comparing and discussing results. For coding of study films, 10 percent of all films were double coded to calculate intercoder reliability measures. Intercorder reliability measures were calculated for each variable. For the gender of the major character in the film it was .99, for occupation of the chacters it was .91, and for the age of characters it was .88.

Content Analysis with Visual Material. Using content analysis to study visual "text," such as photographs, paintings, statues, buildings, clothing, and videos and film, is difficult. It communicates messages or emotional content indirectly through images, symbols, and metaphors. Moreover, visual images often contain mixed messages at multiple levels of meaning.

To conduct content analysis on visual text, the researcher must "read" the meaning(s) within visual text. He or she must interpret signs and discover the meanings attached to symbolic images. Such "reading" is not mechanical (i.e., image *X* always means *G*); it depends heavily on the cultural context because the meaning of an image is culture bound. For example, a red light does not inevitably mean "stop"; it means "stop" only in cultures where people have given it that meaning. People construct cultural meanings that they attach to symbolic images, and the meanings can change over time. Some meanings are clearer and more firmly attached to symbols and images than others.

Most people share a common meaning for key symbols of the dominant culture, but some people may read a symbol differently. For example, one group of people may "read" a national flag to mean patriotism, duty to nation, and honor of tradition. For others, the same flag evokes fear, and they read it to indicate government oppression, abuse of power, and military aggression. A researcher pursuing the content analysis of images needs to be aware of divergent readings of symbols for people in different situations or who may have diverse beliefs and experiences.

Sociopolitical groups may invent or construct new symbols with attached meanings (e.g., a pink triangle came to mean gay pride). They may wrestle for control of the meaning of major existing symbols. For example, some people want to assign a Christian religious meaning to the Christmas tree; others want it to represent a celebration of tradition and family values without specific religious content; others see its origins as an anti-Christian pagan symbol; and still others want it to mean a festive holiday season for commercial reasons. Because images have symbolic content with complex, multilayer meaning, researchers often combine qualitative judgments about the images with quantitative data in content analysis.

For example, Chavez (2001) conducted a content analysis of the covers of major U.S. magazines that dealt with the issue of immigration into the United States. Looking at the covers of 10 magazines from the mid-1970s to the mid-1990s, he classified the covers as having one of three major messages: affirmative, alarmist, or neutral or balanced. Beyond his classification and identifying trends in messages, he noted how the mix of people (i.e., race, gender, age,

and dress) in the photographs and the recurrent use of major symbols, such as the Statute of Liberty or the U.S. flag, communicated messages.

Chavez argued that magazine covers are a site, or location, where cultural meaning is created. Visual images on magazine covers have multiple levels of meaning, and viewers construct specific meanings as they read the image and use their cultural knowledge. Collectively, the covers convey a worldview and express messages about a nation and its people. For example, a magazine cover that displayed the icon of the Statute of Liberty as strong and full of compassion (message: welcome immigrants) was altered to have strong Asian facial features (message: Asian immigrants distorted the national culture and altered the nation's racial make-up), or holding a large stop sign (message: go away immigrants). Chavez (2001: 44) observed that "images on magazines both refer to, and in the process, help to structure and construct contemporary 'American' identity." (See Box 9.3 for another content analysis example.)

How to Conduct Content Analysis Research

Question Formulation.   As in most research, content analysis researchers begin with a research question. When the question involves variables that are messages or symbols, content analysis may be appropriate. For example, I want to study how newspapers cover a political campaign. My construct "coverage" includes the amount of coverage, the prominence of the coverage, and whether the coverage favors one candidate over another. I could survey people about what they think of the newspaper coverage, but a better strategy is to examine the newspapers directly using content analysis.

Units of Analysis.   A researcher decides on the units of analysis (i.e., the amount of text that is assigned a code). For example, for a political campaign, each issue (or day) of a newspaper is the unit of analysis.

Box
9.3   Advertising and Race–Ethnicity in America

Two studies that examined race–ethnicity and advertising in the United States illustrate how content analysis is conducted. Mastro and Stern (2003) wanted to see whether television advertising represents major racial–ethnic groups proportionate to their presence in U.S. society. They examined a one-week random sample of prime-time television programming for six U.S. television networks (ABC, CBS, NBC, Fox, UPN, and WB) drawn from a three-week period in February 2001. Prime time was Monday through Saturday 8:00 P.M. to 11:00 P.M. EST and Sunday 7:00–11:00 P.M. Four undergraduate students were trained as coders. They used two units of analysis: a commercial (excluding local commercials, political advertisements, and trailers for upcoming programs) and the first three speaking characters in a commercial. Variables included product type based on a 30-product coding scheme, setting (e.g., work, outdoors), relation to product (e.g., endorse, use, neither or both), job authority, family status, social authority, sexual gazing, and affective state (e.g., cry, show anger, laugh). Other variables included respect shown for a character, character's age, and affability (friendly or hostile). The study coded 2,880 commercials with 2,315 speaking characters, among whom 2,290 had a race–ethnicity identified. Data analysis found that African American characters were most often shown advertising financial services (19 percent) or food (17 percent), Asians were associated with technology products (30 percent), and Latinos were shown selling soap (40 percent). In general, Whites were slightly overrepresented, Blacks equally represented, but Asians, Latinos, and Native Americans underrepresented. For example, Latinos are 12 percent of the population but had 1 percent of speaking parts, and were usually scantly clad young people with noticeable accents. The authors said that African Americans appear in commercials in a way that approximates their proportion in the United States, but other racial minorities are underrepresented or limited to specific products.

In another study, Mastro and Atkin (2002) examined whether alcohol advertising to promote brands and make drinking appear glamorous influenced high school students who are too young to drink legally. They looked at alcohol signs and billboards in a Mexican-American Chicago neighborhood. They first photographed all outdoor billboards and signs concerning alcohol in the neighborhood over a two-day period in March 1999. After a period of coder training, two female graduate students content-analyzed the photographs, coding the following variables: product type, product name, number of human models, and the race, age, gender of each model. More subjective-latent aspects of models coded included attractiveness, sexiness, stylishness, friendliness, and activity level. In addition, placement of products and colors in the billboard were coded. Coders also classified an overall theme of the billboard as romance, individuality, relaxation, sports, adventure, or tradition. Next, a questionnaire was developed for students at a high school in the neighborhood where 89 percent of the students were Mexican American. Students in grades 10, 11, and 12 were asked to volunteer to complete the survey across a three-day period and 123 completed it. Questionnaire items asked about attention, exposure, recall, and brand exposure to the outdoor signs and billboards as well as drinking intention, approval of underage drinking, and pro-drinking beliefs. Results showed that a student's recall of billboard images did not affect his or her drinking attitudes. However, brand exposure and accepting the themes in the billboards were associated with greater approval of underage drinking. The general impact on the students was present but not strong. The authors suggested that the weak impact was because there were few Mexican American models and the models were older. Also, survey measures of family beliefs suggested that the influence of the student's family and culture may have weakened the billboard's impact on pro-drinking attitudes.

Sampling. Researchers often use random sampling in content analysis. First, they define the population and the sampling element. For example, the population might be all words, all sentences, all paragraphs, or all articles in certain types of documents over a specified time period. Likewise, it could include each conversation, situation, scene, or episode of certain types of television programs over a specified time period. For example, I want to know how women and minorities are portrayed in U.S. weekly newsmagazines. My unit of analysis is the article. My population includes all articles published in *Time, Newsweek,* and *U.S. News and World Report* between 1985 and 2005. I first verify that the three magazines were published in those years and define precisely what is meant by an "article." For instance, do film reviews count as articles? Is there a minimum size (two sentences) for an article? Is a multipart article counted as one or two articles?

Second, I examine the three magazines and find that the average issue of each contains 45 articles and that the magazines are published 52 weeks per year. With a 20-year time frame, my population contains over 140,000 articles ($3 \times 45 \times 52 \times 20 = 140{,}400$). My sampling frame is a list of all the articles. Next, I decide on the sample size and design. After looking at my budget and time, I decide to limit the sample size to 1,400 articles. Thus, the sampling ratio is 1 percent. I also choose a sampling design. I avoid systematic sampling because magazine issues are published cyclically according to the calendar (e.g., an interval of every 52nd issue results in the same week each year). Because issues from each magazine are important, I use stratified sampling. I stratify by magazine, sampling $1{,}400/3 = 467$ articles from each. I want to ensure that articles represent each of the 20 years, so I also stratify by year. This results in about 23 articles per magazine per year.

Finally, I draw the random sample using a random-number table to select 23 numbers for the 23 sample articles for each magazine for each year. I develop a sampling frame worksheet to keep track of my sampling procedure. See Table 9.1 for a sampling frame worksheet in which 1,398 sample articles are randomly selected from 140,401 articles.

Variables and Constructing Coding Categories. In my example, I am interested in the construct of an African American or Hispanic American woman portrayed in a significant leadership role. I must define "significant leadership role" in operational terms and express it as written rules for classifying people named in an article. For example, if an article discusses the achievements of someone who is now dead, does the dead person have a significant role? What is a significant role—a local Girl Scout leader or a corporate president?

I must also determine the race and sex of people named in the articles. What if the race and sex are not evident in the text or accompanying photographs? How do I decide on the person's race and sex?

Because I am interested in positive leadership roles, my measure indicates whether the role was positive or negative. I can do this with either latent or manifest coding. With manifest coding, I create a list of adjectives and phrases. If someone in a sampled article is referred to with one of the adjectives, then the direction is decided. For example, the terms *brilliant* and *top performer* are positive, whereas *drug kingpin* and *uninspired* are negative. For latent coding, I create rules to guide judgments. For example, I classify stories about a diplomat resolving a difficult world crisis, a business executive unable to make a firm profitable, or a lawyer winning a case into positive or negative terms. (Relevant questions for coding each article are in Box 9.4.)

In addition to written rules for coding decisions, a content analysis researcher creates a *recording sheet* (also called a *coding form* or *tally sheet*) on which to record information (see Box 9.5). Each unit should have a separate recording sheet. The sheets do not have to be pieces of paper; they can be $3'' \times 5''$ or $4'' \times 6''$ file cards, or lines in a computer record or file. When a lot

TABLE 9.1   Excerpt from Sampling Frame Worksheet

Magazine	Issue	Article	Number	Article In Sample?*	Sampled Article ID
Time	January 1–7, 1985	pp. 2–3	000001	No	
Time	"	p. 4, bottom	000002	No	
Time	"	p. 4, top	000003	Yes—1	0001
•					
•					
•					
Time	March 1–7, 2005	pp. 2–5	002101	Yes—10	0454
Time	"	p. 6, right column	002102	No	
Time	"	p. 6, left column	002103	No	
Time	"	p. 7	002104	No	
•					
•					
•					
Time	December 24–31, 2005	pp. 4–5	002201	Yes—22	0467
Time	"	p. 5, bottom	002202	No	
Time	"	p. 5, top	002203	Yes—23	0468
Newsweek	January 1–7, 1985	pp. 1–2	010030	No	
Newsweek	"	p. 3	010031	Yes—1	0469
•					
•					
•					
U.S. News	December 25–31, 2005	p. 62	140401	Yes—23	1389

*"Yes" means the number was chosen from a random number table. The number after the dash is a count of the number of articles selected for a year.

Box 9.4   Example of Latent Coding Questions, Magazine Article Leadership Role Study

1. *Characteristics of the article.* What is the magazine? What is the date of the article? How large is the article? What was its topic area? Where did it appear in the issue? Were photographs used?

2. *People in the article.* How many people are named in the article? Of these, how many are significant in the article? What is the race and sex of each person named?

3. *Leadership roles.* For each significant person in the article, which ones have leadership roles? What is the field of leadership or profession of the person?

4. *Positive or negative roles.* For each leadership or professional role, rate how positively or negatively it is shown. For example, 5 = highly positive, 4 = positive, 3 = neutral, 2 = negative, 1 = highly negative, 0 = ambiguous.

Box 9.5	Example of Recording Sheet

Blank Example

Professor Neuman, Sociology Department   Coder:_____

Minority/Majority Group Representation in Newsmagazines Project

ARTICLE #_____   MAGAZINE:_____   DATE:_____   SIZE:_____ col. in.

Total number of people named _____   Number of Photos _____

No. people with significant roles: _____   Article Topic:_____

Person_____:	Race:_____	Gender:_____	Leader?:_____	Field?_____	Rating:_____
Person_____:	Race:_____	Gender:_____	Leader?:_____	Field?_____	Rating:_____
Person_____:	Race:_____	Gender:_____	Leader?:_____	Field?_____	Rating:_____
Person_____:	Race:_____	Gender:_____	Leader?:_____	Field?_____	Rating:_____
Person_____:	Race:_____	Gender:_____	Leader?:_____	Field?_____	Rating:_____
Person_____:	Race:_____	Gender:_____	Leader?:_____	Field?_____	Rating:_____
Person_____:	Race:_____	Gender:_____	Leader?:_____	Field?_____	Rating:_____
Person_____:	Race:_____	Gender:_____	Leader?:_____	Field?_____	Rating:_____

Example of Completed Recording Sheet for One Article

Professor Neuman, Sociology Department   Coder: Susan J.

Minority/Majority Group Representation in Newsmagazines Project

ARTICLE # 0454   MAGAZINE: Time   DATE: March 1–7, 2005   SIZE: 14 col. in.

Total number of people named 5   Number of Photos 0

No. people with significant roles: 4   Article Topic: Foreign Affairs

Person 1 :	Race: White	Gender: M	Leader?: Y	Field? Banking	Rating: 5
Person 2 :	Race: White	Gender: M	Leader?: N	Field? Government	Rating: NA
Person 3 :	Race: Black	Gender: F	Leader?: Y	Field? Civil Rights	Rating: 2
Person 4 :	Race: White	Gender: F	Leader?: Y	Field? Government	Rating: 0
Person _____:	Race: _____	Gender: _____	Leader?: _____	Field?_____	Rating: _____
Person _____:	Race: _____	Gender: _____	Leader?: _____	Field?_____	Rating: _____
Person _____:	Race: _____	Gender: _____	Leader?: _____	Field?_____	Rating: _____
Person _____:	Race: _____	Gender: _____	Leader?: _____	Field?_____	Rating: _____

of information is recorded for each recording unit, more than one sheet of paper can be used. When planning a project, researchers calculate the work required. For example, during my pilot-test, I find that it takes an average of 15 minutes to read and code an article. This does not include sampling or locating magazine articles. With approximately 1,400 articles, that is 350 hours of coding, not counting time to verify the accuracy of coding. Because 350 hours is about nine weeks of nonstop work at 40 hours a week, I should consider hiring assistants as coders.

Each recording sheet has a place to record the identification number of the unit and spaces for information about each variable. I also put identifying information about the research project on the sheet in case I misplace it or it looks similar to other sheets I have. Finally, if I use multiple coders, the sheet reminds the coder to check intercoder reliability and, if necessary, makes it possible to recode information for inaccurate coders. After completing all recording sheets and checking for accuracy, I can begin data analysis.

Inferences

The inferences a researcher can or cannot make on the basis of results is critical in content analysis. Content analysis describes what is in the text. It cannot reveal the intentions of those who created the text or the effects that messages in the text have on those who receive them. For example, content analysis shows that children's books contain sex stereotypes. That does not necessarily mean that children's beliefs or behaviors are influenced by the stereotypes; such an inference requires a separate research project on how children's perceptions develop.

EXISTING STATISTICS/ DOCUMENTS AND SECONDARY ANALYSIS

Appropriate Topics

Many types of information about the social world have been collected and are available to the researcher. Some information is in the form of statistical documents (books, reports, etc.) that contain numerical information. Other information is in the form of published compilations available in a library or on computerized records. In either case, the researcher can search through collections of information with a re-

search question and variables in mind, and then reassemble the information in new ways to address the research question.

It is difficult to specify topics that are appropriate for existing statistics research because they are so varied. Any topic on which information has been collected and is publicly available can be studied. In fact, existing statistics projects may not fit neatly into a deductive model of research design. Rather, researchers creatively reorganize the existing information into the variables for a research question after first finding what data are available.

Experiments are best for topics where the researcher controls a situation and manipulates an independent variable. Survey research is best for topics where the researcher asks questions and learns about reported attitudes or behavior. Content analysis is best for topics that involve the content of messages in cultural communication.

Existing statistics research is best for topics that involve information routinely collected by large bureaucratic organizations. Public or private organizations systematically gather many types of information. Such information is gathered for policy decisions or as a public service. It is rarely collected for purposes directly related to a specific research question. Thus, existing statistics research is appropriate when a researcher wants to test hypotheses involving variables that are also in official reports of social, economic, and political conditions. These include descriptions of organizations or the people in them. Often, such information is collected over long time periods. For example, existing statistics can be used by a researcher who wants to see whether unemployment and crime rates are associated in 150 cities across a 20-year period.

Downey (2005) conducted an existing statistics study on racial inequality (Black/White) and living near a toxic pollution site in Detroit. He used census data on the population/housing and manufacturing directories of manufacturing facilities. He also identified highly polluting industries and used the Environmental Protection Agency's inventory of toxic chemicals. His unit of analysis was the census tract. Downey tested competing models of environmental inequality: (1) racist siting policy: toxic sites were placed in Black residential areas, (2) economic inequality: low-income people who are disproportionately Black move into areas near toxic sites because they find low-cost housing there, and (3) residential segregation: Whites move into specific areas and keep out non-Whites. He found greatest support for the residential segregation model. Paradoxically, it meant that Blacks were less likely than Whites to live close to a toxic pollution site. This was because Whites had obtained housing near the factories where they worked and kept Blacks from moving in but those factories were the major sources of toxic pollution.

Social Indicators

During the 1960s, some social scientists, dissatisfied with the information available to decision makers, spawned the "social indicators' movement" to develop indicators of social well-being. Many hoped that information about social well-being could be combined with widely used indicators of economic performance (e.g., gross national product) to better inform government and other policymaking officials. Thus, researchers wanted to measure the quality of social life so that such information could influence public policy.[6]

Today, there are many books, articles, and reports on social indicators, and even a scholarly journal, *Social Indicators Research,* devoted to the creation and evaluation of social indicators. The U.S. Census Bureau produced a report, *Social Indicators,* and the United Nations has many measures of social well-being in different nations.

A *social indicator* is any measure of social well-being used in policy. There are many specific indicators that are operationalizations of well-being. For example, social indicators have been developed for the following areas: population, family, housing, social security and welfare,

health and nutrition, public safety, education and training, work, income, culture and leisure, social mobility, and public participation.

A more specific example of a social indicator is the FBI's uniform crime index. It indicates the amount of crime in U.S. society. Social indicators can measure negative aspects of social life, such as the infant mortality rate (the death rate of infants during the first year of life) or alcoholism, or they can indicate positive aspects, such as job satisfaction or the percentage of housing units with indoor plumbing. Social indicators often involve implicit value judgments (e.g., which crimes are serious or what constitutes a good quality of life).

Locating Data

Locating Existing Statistics.   The main sources of existing statistics are government or international agencies and private sources. An enormous volume and variety of information exists. If you plan to conduct existing statistics research, it is wise to discuss your interests with an information professional—in this case, a reference librarian, who can point you in the direction of possible sources.

Many existing documents are "free"—that is, publicly available at libraries—but the time and effort it takes to search for specific information can be substantial. Researchers who conduct existing statistics research spend many hours in libraries or on the Internet. After the information is located, it is recorded on cards, graphs, or recording sheets for later analysis. Often, it is already available in a format for computers to read. For example, instead of recording voting data from books, a researcher could use a social science data archive at the University of Michigan (to be discussed).

There are so many sources that only a small sample of what is available is discussed here. The single-most valuable source of statistical information about the United States is the *Statistical Abstract of the United States,* which has been published annually (with a few exceptions) since

1878. The *Statistical Abstract* is available in all public libraries and on the Internet and can be purchased from the U.S. Superintendent of Documents. It is a selected compilation of the many official reports and statistical tables produced by U.S. government agencies. It contains statistical information from hundreds of more detailed government reports. You may want to examine more specific government documents. (The detail of what is available in government documents is mind boggling. For example, you can learn that there were two African American females over the age of 75 in Tucumcari City, New Mexico, in 1980.)

The *Statistical Abstract* has over 1,400 charts, tables, and statistical lists from over 200 government and private agencies. It is hard to grasp all that it contains until you skim through the tables. A two-volume set summarizes similar information across many years; it is called *Historical Statistics of the U.S.: Colonial Times to 1970.*

Most governments publish similar statistical yearbooks. Australia's Bureau of Statistics produces *Yearbook Australia,* Statistics Canada produces *Canada Yearbook,* New Zealand's Department of Statistics publishes *New Zealand Official Yearbook,* and in the United Kingdom, the Central Statistics Office publishes *Annual Abstract of Statistics.*[7] Many nations publish books with historical statistics, as well.

Locating government statistical documents is an art in itself. Some publications exist solely to assist the researcher. For example, the *American Statistics Index: A Comprehensive Guide* and *Index to the Statistical Publications of the U.S. Government and Statistics Sources: A Subject Guide to Data on Industrial, Business, Social Education, Financial and Other Topics for the U.S. and Internationally* are two helpful guides for the United States.[8] The United Nations and international agencies such as the World Bank have their own publications with statistical information for various countries (e.g., literacy rates, percentage of the labor force working in agriculture, birth rates)—for example, the *Demographic Yearbook,* *UNESCO Statistical Yearbook,* and *United Nations Statistical Yearbook.*

In addition to government statistical documents, there are dozens of other publications. Many are produced for business purposes and can be obtained only for a high cost. They include information on consumer spending, the location of high-income neighborhoods, trends in the economy, and the like.[9]

Over a dozen publications list characteristics of businesses or their executives. These are found in larger libraries. Three such publications are as follows:

Dun and Bradstreet Principal Industrial Businesses is a guide to approximately 51,000 businesses in 135 countries with information on sales, number of employees, officers, and products.

Who Owns Whom comes in volumes for nations or regions (e.g., North America, the United Kingdom, Ireland, and Australia). It lists parent companies, subsidiaries, and associated companies.

Standard and Poor's Register of Corporations, Directors and Executives lists about 37,000 U.S. and Canadian companies. It has information on corporations, products, officers, industries, and sales figures.

Many biographical sources list famous people and provide background information on them. These are useful when a researcher wants to learn about the social background, career, or other characteristics of famous individuals. The publications are compiled by companies that send out questionnaires to people identified as "important" by some criteria. They are public sources of information, but they depend on the cooperation and accuracy of individuals who are selected.

Politics has its own specialized publications. There are two basic types. One has biographical information on contemporary politicians. The other type has information on voting, laws enacted, and the like. Here are three examples of political information publications for the United States:

Almanac of American Politics is a biannual publication that includes photographs and a short biography of U.S. government officials. Committee appointments, voting records, and similar information are provided for members of Congress and leaders in the executive branch.

America Votes: A Handbook of Contemporary American Election Statistics contains detailed voting information by county for most statewide and national offices. Primary election results are included down to the county level.

Vital Statistics on American Politics provides dozens of tables on political behavior, such as the campaign spending of every candidate for Congress, their primary and final votes, ideological ratings by various political organizations, and a summary of voter registration regulations by state.

Another source of public information consists of lists of organizations (e.g., business, educational, etc.) produced for general information purposes. A researcher can sometimes obtain membership lists of organizations. There are also publications of public speeches given by famous people.

Secondary Survey Data. Secondary analysis is a special case of existing statistics; it is the re-analysis of previously collected survey or other data that were originally gathered by others. As opposed to primary research (e.g., experiments, surveys, and content analysis), the focus is on analyzing rather than collecting data. Secondary analysis is increasingly used by researchers. It is relatively inexpensive; it permits comparisons across groups, nations, or time; it facilitates replication; and it permits asking about issues not thought of by the original researchers.

Large-scale data collection is expensive and difficult. The cost and time required for a major national survey that uses rigorous techniques are prohibitive for most researchers. Fortunately, the organization, preservation, and dissemination of major survey data sets have improved. Today, there are archives of past surveys that are open to researchers.

The Inter-University Consortium for Political and Social Research (ICPSR) at the University of Michigan is the world's major archive of social science data. Over 17,000 survey research and related sets of information are stored and made available to researchers at modest costs. Other centers hold survey data in the United States and other nations.[10]

A widely used source of survey data for the United States is the *General Social Survey (GSS)*, which has been conducted annually in most years by the National Opinion Research Center at the University of Chicago. In recent years, it has covered other nations as well. The data are made publicly available for secondary analysis at a low cost (see Box 9.6).

Limitations

Despite the growth and popularity of secondary data analysis and existing statistics research, there are limitations in their use. The use of such techniques is not trouble free just because a government agency or research organization gathered the data. One danger is that a researcher may use secondary data or existing statistics that are inappropriate for his or her research question. Before proceeding, a researcher needs to consider units in the data (e.g., types of people, organizations), the time and place of data collection, the sampling methods used, and the specific issues or topics covered in the data (see Box 9.7). For example, a researcher wanting to examine racial–ethnic tensions between Latinos and Anglos in the United States uses secondary data that includes only the Pacific Northwest and New England states should reconsider the question or the use of data.

Box 9.6 The General Social Survey

The General Social Survey (GSS) is the best-known set of survey data used by social researchers for secondary analysis. The mission of the GSS is "to make timely, high quality, scientifically relevant data available to the social science research community" (Davis and Smith, 1992:1). It is available in many computer-readable formats and is widely accessible for a low cost. Neither datasets nor codebooks are copyrighted. Users may copy or disseminate them without obtaining permission. You can find results using the GSS in over 2,000 research articles and books.

The National Opinion Research Center (NORC) has conducted the GSS almost every year since 1972. A typical year's survey contains a random sample of about 1,500 adult U.S. residents. A team of researchers selects some questions for inclusion, and individual researchers can recommend questions. They repeat some questions and topics each year, include some on a four- to six-year cycle, and add other topics in specific years. For example, in 1998, the special topic was job experiences and religion,

and in 2000, it was intergroup relations and multiculturalism.

Interviewers collect the data through face-to-face interviews. The NORC staff carefully selects interviewers and trains them in social science methodology and survey interviewing. About 120 to 140 interviewers work on the GSS each year. About 90 percent are women, and most are middle aged. The NORC recruits bilingual and minority interviewers. Interviewers with respondents are race-matched with respondents. Interviews are typically 90 minutes long and contain approximately 500 questions. The response rate has been 71 to 79 percent. The major reason for nonresponse is a refusal to participate.

The International Social Survey Program conducts similar surveys in other nations. Beginning with the German ALLBUS and British Social Attitudes Survey, participation has grown to include 33 nations. The goal is to conduct on a regular basis large-scale national general surveys in which some common questions are asked across cooperating nations.

A second danger is that the researcher does not understand the substantive topic. Because the data are easily accessible, researchers who know very little about a topic could make erroneous assumptions or false interpretations about results. Before using any data, a researcher needs to be well informed about the topic. For example, if a researcher uses data on high school graduation rates in Germany without understanding the Germany secondary education system with its distinct academic and vocational tracks, he or she may make serious errors in interpreting results.

A third danger is that a researcher may quote statistics in great detail to give an impression of scientific rigor. This can lead to the *fallacy of misplaced concreteness,* which occurs when someone gives a false impression of preci-

sion by quoting statistics in greater detail than warranted and "overloading" the details. For example, existing statistics report that the population of Australia is 19,169,083, but it is better to say that it is a little over 19 million. One might calculate the percentage of divorced people as 15.65495 in a secondary data analysis of the 2000 General Social Survey, but it is better to report that about 15.7 percent of people are divorced.[11]

Units of Analysis and Variable Attributes.   A common problem in existing statistics is finding the appropriate units of analysis. Many statistics are published for aggregates, not the individual. For example, a table in a government document has information (e.g., unemployment rate, crime rate, etc.) for a state, but the unit of analysis for the research question is the individual

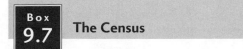

Box 9.7   The Census

Almost every country conducts a census, or a regular count of its population. For example, Australia has done so since 1881, Canada since 1871, and the United States since 1790. Most nations conduct a census every 5 or 10 years. In addition to the number of people, census officials collect information on topics such as housing conditions, ethnicity, religious affiliation, education, and so forth.

The census is a major source of high-quality existing statistical data, but it can be controversial. In Canada, an attempt to count the number of same-sex couples living together evoked public debate about whether the government should document the changes in society. In Great Britain, the Muslim minority welcomed questions about religion in the 2001 census because they felt that they had been officially ignored. In the United States, the measurement of race and ethnicity was hotly debated, so in the 2000 census, people could place themselves in multiple racial/ethnic categories.

The U.S. 2000 census also generated a serious public controversy because it missed thousands of people, most from low-income areas with concentrations of recent immigrants and racial minorities. Some double counting also occurred of people in high income areas where many owned second homes. A contentious debate arose among politicians to end miscounts by using scientific sampling and adjusting the census. The politicians proved to be less concerned about improving the scientific accuracy of the census than retaining traditional census methods that would benefit their own political fortunes or help their constituencies, because the government uses census data to draw voting districts and allocate public funds to areas.

obtain raw information on each respondent from archives.

A related problem involves the categories of variable attributes used in existing documents or survey questions. This is not a problem if the initial data were gathered in many highly refined categories. The problem arises when the original data were collected in broad categories or ones that do not match the needs of a researcher. For example, a researcher is interested in people of Asian heritage. If the racial and ethnic heritage categories in a document are "White," "Black," and "Other," the researcher has a problem. The "Other" category includes people of Asian and other heritages. Sometimes information was collected in refined categories but is published only in broad categories. It takes special effort to discover whether more refined information was collected or is publicly available.

Validity.   Validity problems occur when the researcher's theoretical definition does not match that of the government agency or organization that collected the information. Official policies and procedures specify definitions for official statistics. For example, a researcher defines a *work injury* as including minor cuts, bruises, and sprains that occur on the job, but the official definition in government reports only includes injuries that require a visit to a physician or hospital. Many work injuries, as defined by the researcher, would not be in official statistics. Another example occurs when a researcher defines people as *unemployed* if they would work if a good job were available, if they have to work part time when they want full-time work, and if they have given up looking for work. The official definition, however, includes only those who are now actively seeking work (full or part time) as unemployed. The official statistics exclude those who stopped looking, who work part time out of necessity, or who do not look because they believe no work is available. In both cases, the researcher's definition differs from that in official statistics (see Box 9.8).

(e.g., "Are unemployed people more likely to commit property crimes?"). The potential for committing the ecological fallacy is very real in this situation. It is less of a problem for secondary survey analysis because researchers can

Box 9.8	Official Unemployment Rates versus the Nonemployed

In most countries, the official unemployment rate measures only the unemployed (see below) as a percent of all working people. It would be 50 percent higher if two other categories of nonemployed people were added: involuntary part-time workers and discouraged workers (see below). In some countries (e.g., Sweden and United States), it would be nearly double if it included these people. This does not consider other nonworking people, transitional self-employed, or the underemployed (see below). What a country measures is a theoretical and conceptual definition issue: What construct should an unemployment rate measure and why measure it?

An economic policy or labor market perspective says the rate should measure those ready to enter the labor market immediately. It defines nonworking people as a supply of high-quality labor, an input for use in the economy available to employers. By contrast, a social policy or human resource perspective says the rate should measure those who are not currently working to their fullest potential. The rate should represent people who are not or cannot fully utilize their talents, skills, or time to the fullest. It defines nonworking people as a social problem of individuals unable to realize their capacity to be productive, contributing members of society.

Categories of Nonemployed/Fully Utilized

Unemployed people	People who meet three conditions: lack a paying job outside the home, are taking active measures to find work, can begin work immediately if it is offered.
Involuntary part-time workers	People with a job, but work irregularly or fewer hours than they are able and willing.
Discouraged workers	People able to work and who actively sought it for some time, but being unable to find it, have given up looking.
Other nonworking	Those not working because they are retired, on vacation, temporarily laid off, semidisabled, homemakers, full-time students, or in the process of moving.
Transitional self-employed	Self-employed who are not working full time because they are just starting a business or are going through bankruptcy.
Underemployed	Persons with a temporary full-time job for which they are seriously overqualified. They seek a permanent job in which they can fully apply their skills and experience.

Source: Adapted from *The Economist,* July 22, 1995, p. 74.

Another validity problem arises when official statistics are a surrogate or proxy for a construct in which a researcher is really interested. This is necessary because the researcher cannot collect original data. For example, the researcher wants to know how many people have been robbed, so he or she uses police statistics on rob-

bery arrests as a proxy. But the measure is not entirely valid because many robberies are not reported to the police, and reported robberies do not always result in an arrest.

A third validity problem arises because the researcher lacks control over how information is collected. All information, even that in official government reports, is originally gathered by people in bureaucracies as part of their jobs. A researcher depends on them for collecting, organizing, reporting, and publishing data accurately. Systematic errors in collecting the initial information (e.g., census people who avoid poor neighborhoods and make up information, or people who put a false age on a driver's license); errors in organizing and reporting information (e.g., a police department that is sloppy about filing crime reports and loses some); and errors in publishing information (e.g., a typographical error in a table) all reduce measurement validity.

This kind of problem happened in U.S. statistics on the number of people permanently laid off from their jobs. A university researcher reexamined the methods used to gather data by the U.S. Bureau of Labor Statistics and found an error. Data on permanent job losses come from a survey of 50,000 people, but the government agency failed to adjust for a much higher survey nonresponse rate. The corrected figures showed that instead of a 7 percent decline in the number of people laid off between 1993 and 1996, as had been first reported, there was no change.[12]

Reliability. Problems with reliability can plague existing statistics research. Reliability problems develop when official definitions or the method of collecting information changes over time. Official definitions of work injury, disability, unemployment, and the like change periodically. Even if a researcher learns of such changes, consistent measurement over time is impossible. For example, during the early 1980s, the method for calculating the U.S. unemployment rate changed. Previously, the unemployment rate was calculated as the number of unemployed persons divided by the number in the civilian work force. The new method divided the number of unemployed by the civilian work force plus the number of people in the military. Likewise, when police departments computerize their records, there is an apparent increase in crimes reported, not because crime increases but due to improved record keeping.

Reliability can be a serious problem in official government statistics. This goes beyond recognized problems, such as the police stopping poorly dressed people more than well-dressed people, hence poorly dressed, lower-income people appear more often in arrest statistics. For example, the U.S. Bureau of Labor Statistics found a 0.6 percent increase in the female unemployment rate after it used gender-neutral measurement procedures. Until the mid-1990s, interviewers asked women only whether they had been "keeping house or something else?" The women who answered "keeping house" were categorized as housewives, and not unemployed. Because the women were not asked, this occurred even if the women had been seeking work. Once women were asked the same question as men, "Were you working or something else?" more women said they were not working but doing "something else" such as looking for work. This shows the importance of methodological details in how government statistics get created.

Researchers often use official statistics for international comparisons but national governments collect data differently and the quality of data collection varies. For example, in 1994, the official unemployment rate reported for the United States was 7 percent, Japan's was 2.9 percent, and France's was 12 percent. If the nations defined and gathered data the same way, including discouraged workers and involuntary part-time workers rates, the rates would have been 9.3 percent for the United States, 9.6 percent for Japan, and 13.7 percent for France. To evaluate the quality of official government statistics, *The Economist* magazine asked a team of 20 leading statisticians to evaluate the statistics of 13 nations based on freedom from political interference, reliability, statistical methodology, and coverage of topics. The top five nations in order were Canada, Australia, Holland, France, and Sweden. The United States was tied for sixth with Britain and Germany. The United States spent more per person gathering its statistics than all nations except Australia and it released data the fastest. The quality of U.S. statistics suffered from being highly decentralized, having fewer statisticians employed than any nation, and politically motivated cutbacks on the range of data collected.[13]

Missing Data.   One problem that plagues researchers who use existing statistics and documents is that of missing data. Sometimes, the data were collected but have been lost. More frequently, the data were never collected. The decision to collect official information is made within government agencies. The decision to ask questions on a survey whose data are later made publicly available is made by a group of researchers. In both cases, those who decide what to collect may not collect what another researcher needs in order to address a research question. Government agencies start or stop collecting information for political, budgetary, or other reasons. For example, during the early 1980s, cost-cutting measures by the U.S. federal government stopped the collection of much information that social researchers had found

valuable. Missing information is especially a problem when researchers cover long time periods. For instance, a researcher interested in the number of work stoppages and strikes in the United States can obtain data from the 1890s to the present, except for a five-year period after 1911 when the federal government did not collect the data. (See Box 9.9 for an existing statistics example.)

ISSUES OF INFERENCE AND THEORY TESTING

Inferences from Nonreactive Data

A researcher's ability to infer causality or test a theory on the basis of nonreactive data is limited. It is difficult to use unobtrusive measures to establish temporal order and eliminate alternative explanations. In content analysis, a researcher cannot generalize from the content to its effects on those who read the text, but can only use the correlation logic of survey research

---

Box 9.9   Existing Statistics, Androgynous First Names, and Collective Behavior

An androgynous first name is one that can be for either a girl or boy without clearly marking the child's gender. Some argue that the feminist movement decreased gender marking in a child's name as part of its broader societal influence to reduce gender distinctions and inequality. Others observe that gender remains the single-most predominant feature of naming in most societies. Even when racial groups or social classes invent distinctive new first names, the gender distinctions are retained.

Lieberson and colleagues (2000) examined existing statistical data in the form of computerized records from the birth certificates of 11 million births of White children in the state of Illinois from 1916 to 1989. They found that androgynous first names are

rare (about 3 percent) and that there has been a very slight historical trend toward androgyny, but only in very recent years. In addition, parents give androgynous names to girls more than to boys, and gender segregation in naming is unstable (i.e., a name tends to lose its androgynous meaning over time). The authors noted that the way parents name children mimics a pattern of collective behavior found to operate in another research area: the racial segregation of neighborhoods. Change in residence is unequal among races with less movement by the dominant group; the less powerful group moves to occupy areas that the dominant group has abandoned; and integration is unstable, with new segregation reappearing after some time.

to show an association among variables. Unlike the ease of survey research, a researcher does not ask respondents direct questions to measure variables, but relies on the information available in the text.

Ethical Concerns

Ethical concerns are not at the forefront of most nonreactive research because the people being studied are not directly involved. The primary ethical concern is the privacy and confidentiality of using information gathered by someone else. Another ethical issue is that official statistics are social and political products. Implicit theories and value assumptions guide which information is collected and the categories used when gathering it. Measures or statistics that are defined as official and collected on a regular basis are objects of political conflict and guide the direction of policy. By defining one measure as official, public policy is shaped toward outcomes that would be different if an alternative, but equally valid, measure had been used. For example, the collection of information on many social conditions (e.g., the number of patients who died while in public mental hospitals) was stimulated by political activity during the Great Depression of the 1930s. Previously, the conditions were not defined as sufficiently important to warrant public attention. Likewise, information on the percentage of non-White students enrolled in U.S. schools at various ages is available only since 1953, and for specific non-White races only since the 1970s. Earlier, such information was not salient for public policy.

The collection of official statistics stimulates new attention to a problem, and public concern about a problem stimulates the collection of new official statistics. For example, drunk driving became a bigger issue once statistics were collected on the number of automobile accidents and on whether alcohol was a factor in an accident.

Political and social values influence decisions about which existing statistics to collect. Most official statistics are designed for top-down bureaucratic or administrative planning purposes. They may not conform to a researcher's purposes or the purposes of people opposed to bureaucratic decision makers. For example, a government agency measures the number of tons of steel produced, miles of highway paved, and average number of people in a household. Information on other conditions such as drinking-water quality, time needed to commute to work, stress related to a job, or number of children needing child care may not be collected because officials say it is unimportant. In many countries, the gross national product (GNP) is treated as a critical measure of societal progress. But GNP ignores noneconomic aspects of social life (e.g., time spent playing with one's children) and types of work (e.g., housework) that are not paid. The information available reflects the outcome of political debate and the values of officials who decide which statistics to collect.[14]

CONCLUSION

In this chapter, you have learned about several types of nonreactive research techniques. They are ways to measure or observe aspects of social life without affecting those who are being studied. They result in objective, numerical information that can be analyzed to address research questions. The techniques can be used in conjunction with other types of quantitative or qualitative social research to address a large number of questions.

As with any form of quantitative data, researchers need to be concerned with measurement issues. It is easy to take available information from a past survey or government document, but what it measures may not be the construct of interest to the researcher.

You should be aware of two potential problems in nonreactive research. First, the availability of existing information restricts the questions that a researcher can address. Second, the nonreactive variables often have weaker validity because they do not measure the construct of interest. Although existing statistics and secondary data analysis are low-cost research techniques, the researcher lacks control over, and substantial knowledge of, the data collection process. This introduces a potential source of errors about which researchers need to be especially vigilant and cautious.

In the next chapter, we move from designing research projects and collecting data to analyzing data. The analysis techniques apply to the quantitative data you learned about in the previous chapters. So far, you have seen how to move from a topic, to a research design and measures, to collecting data. Next, you will learn how to look at data and see what they can tell you about a hypothesis or research question.

Key Terms

accretion measures
coding
coding system
content analysis
erosion measures
fallacy of misplaced concreteness
General Social Survey (GSS)
latent coding
manifest coding
nonreactive
recording sheet
Statistical Abstract of the United States
structured observation
text
unobtrusive measures

Endnotes

1. See Webb and colleagues (1981:7–11).
2. For definitions of content analysis, see Holsti (1968:597), Krippendorff (1980:21–24), Markoff and associates (1974:5–6), Stone and Weber (1992), and Weber (1983, 1984, 1985:81, note 1).
3. Weitzman and colleagues (1972) is a classic in this type of research.

4. Stone and Weber (1992) and Weber (1984, 1985) summarized computerized content analysis techniques.
5. See Andren (1981:58–66) for a discussion of reliability. Coding categorization in content analysis is discussed in Holsti (1969:94–126).
6. A discussion of social indicators can be found in Carley (1981). Also see Bauer (1966), Duncan (1984:233–235), Juster and Land (1981), Land (1992), and Rossi and Gilmartin (1980).
7. Many non-English yearbooks are also produced; for example, *Statistiches Jahrbuch* for the Federal Republic of Germany, *Annuaire Statistique de la France* for France, *Year Book Australia* for Australia, and Denmark's *Statiskisk Ti Arsoversigt.* Japan produces an English version of its yearbook called the *Statistical Handbook of Japan.*
8. Guides exist for the publications of various governments—for example, the *Guide to British Government Publications, Australian Official Publications,* and *Irish Official Publications.* Similar publications exist for most nations.
9. See Churchill (1983:140–167) and Stewart (1984) for lists of business information sources.
10. Other major U.S. archives of survey data include the National Opinion Research Center, University of Chicago; the Survey Research Center, University of California–Berkeley; the Behavioral Sciences Laboratory, University of Cincinnati; Data and Program Library Service, University of Wisconsin–Madison; the Roper Center, University of Connecticut–Storrs; and the Institute for Research in Social Science, University of North Carolina–Chapel Hill. Also see Kiecolt and Nathan (1985) and Parcel (1992).
11. For a discussion of these issues, see Dale and colleagues (1988:27–31), Maier (1991), and Parcel (1992). Horn (1993:138) gives a good discussion with examples of the fallacy of misplaced concreteness.
12. See Stevenson (1996).
13. See *The Economist,* "The Good Statistics Guide" (September 11, 1993), "The Overlooked Housekeeper" (February 5, 1994), and "Fewer Damned Lies?" (March 30, 1996).
14. See Block and Burns (1986), Carr-Hill (1984), Hindess (1973), Horn (1993), Maier (1991), and Van den Berg and Van der Veer (1985).

Analysis of Quantitative Data

INTRODUCTION

If you read a research report or article based on quantitative data, you will probably find charts, graphs, and tables full of numbers. Do not be intimidated by them. A researcher provides the charts, graphs, and tables to give you, the reader, a condensed picture of the data. The charts and tables allow you to see the evidence collected. When you collect your own quantitative data, you will want to use similar techniques to help you see what is inside the data. You will need to organize and manipulate the data so they can reveal things of interest. In this chapter, you will learn the fundamentals of organizing and analyzing quantitative data. The analysis of quantitative data is a complex field of knowledge. This chapter covers only the basic statistical concepts and data-handling techniques necessary to understand social research.

Data collected using the techniques in the past chapters are in the form of numbers. The numbers represent values of variables, which measure characteristics of subjects, respondents, or other cases. The numbers are in a raw form, on questionnaires, note pads, recording sheets, or paper. Researchers reorganize them into a form suitable for computers, present charts or graphs to summarize their features, and interpret or give theoretical meaning to the results.

DEALING WITH DATA

Coding Data

Before a researcher examines quantitative data to test hypotheses, he or she needs to organize them in a different form. You encountered the idea of coding data in the last chapter. Here, data *coding* means systematically reorganizing raw numerical data into a format that is easy to analyze using computers. Researchers create and consistently apply rules for transferring information from one form to another.

Coding can be a simple clerical task when the data are recorded as numbers on well-organized recording sheets. However, it gets complex when the data are not well organized or not originally in the form of numbers. Researchers develop rules to assign certain numbers to variable attributes. For example, a researcher codes males as 1 and females as 2. Each category of a variable and missing information needs a code. A *codebook* is a document (i.e., one or more pages) describing the coding procedure and the location of data for variables in a format that computers can use.

When you code data, it is essential to create a well-organized, detailed codebook and make multiple copies of it. If you do not write down the details of the coding procedure, or if you misplace the codebook, you have lost the key to the data and may have to recode the data again.

Researchers begin to think about a coding procedure and codebook before they collect data. For example, a survey researcher precodes a questionnaire before collecting data. *Precoding* means placing the code categories (e.g., 1 for male, 2 for female) on the questionnaire.[1] Sometimes, to reduce dependence on a codebook, survey researchers also place the location in the computer format on the questionnaire.

If a researcher does not precode, the first step after collecting data is to create a codebook. He or she also gives each case an identification number to keep track of the cases. Next, the researcher transfers the information from each questionnaire into a format that computers can read.

Entering Data

Most computer programs designed for statistical analysis need the data in a grid format. In the grid, each row represents a respondent, subject, or case. A column or a set of columns represents specific variables. It is possible to go from a column and row location (e.g., row 7, column 5) back to the original source of data (e.g., a questionnaire item on marital status for respondent 8).

For example, a researcher codes survey data for three respondents in a format for computers like that presented in Figure 10.1. People cannot

FIGURE 10.1   Coded Data for Three Cases and Codebook

Exerpt from Survey Questionnaire

Respondent ID _____   Interviewer Name _____

Note the Respondent's Sex: ____ Male   ____ Female

1. The first question is about the president of the United States. Do you Strongly Agree, Agree, Disagree, Strongly Disagree, or Have No Opinion about the following statement:
   The President of the United States is doing a great job.

   ____ Strong Agree   ____ Agree   ____ Disagree   ____ Strong Disagree   ____ No Opinion

2. How old are you? _____

Excerpt of Coded Data

                              Column
0000000000111111111122222222223333333333444 ... etc. (tens)
12345678901234567890123456789012345678901 2 ... etc. (ones)
01 212736302 182738274 10239 18.82 3947461 ... etc.
02 213334821 124988154 21242 18.21 3984123 ... etc.
03 420123982 113727263 12345 17.36 1487645 ... etc.
etc.
Raw data for first three cases, columns 1 through 42.

Excerpt from Codebook

Column	Variable Name	Description
1–2	ID	Respondent identification number
3	BLANK	
4	Interviewer	Interviewer who collected the data: 1 = Susan 2 = Xia 3 = Juan 4 = Sophia 5 = Clarence
5	Sex	Interviewer report of respondent's sex 1 = Male, 2 = Female
6	PresJob	The president of the United States is doing a great job. 1 = Strongly Agree 2 = Agree 3 = No Opinion 4 = Disagree 5 = Strongly Disagree Blank = missing information

easily read it, and without the codebook, it is worthless. It condenses answers to 50 survey questions for three respondents into three lines or rows. The raw data for many research projects look like this, except that there may be over 1,000 rows, and the lines may be over 100 columns long. For example, a 15-minute telephone survey of 250 students produces a grid of data that is 250 rows by 240 columns.

The codebook in Figure 10.1 says that the first two numbers are identification numbers. Thus, the example data are for the first (01), second (02), and third (03) respondents. Notice that researchers use zeroes as place holders to reduce confusion between 1 and 01. The 1s are always in column 2; the 10s are in column 1. The codebook says that column 5 contains the variable "sex": Cases 1 and 2 are male and Case 3 is female. Column 4 tells us that Carlos interviewed Cases 1 and 2, and Sophia Case 3.

There are four ways to get raw quantitative data into a computer:

1. *Code sheet.* Gather the information, then transfer it from the original source onto a grid format (code sheet). Next, type what is on the code sheet into a computer, line by line.
2. *Direct-entry method, including CATI.* As information is being collected, sit at a computer keyboard while listening to/observing the information and enter the information, or have a respondent/subject enter the information himself or herself. The computer must be preprogrammed to accept the information.
3. *Optical scan.* Gather the information, then enter it onto optical scan sheets (or have a respondent/subject enter the information) by filling in the correct "dots." Next, use an optical scanner or reader to transfer the information into a computer.
4. *Bar code.* Gather the information and convert it into different widths of bars that are associated with specific numerical values,

then use a bar-code reader to transfer the information into a computer.

Cleaning Data

Accuracy is extremely important when coding data. Errors made when coding or entering data into a computer threaten the validity of measures and cause misleading results. A researcher who has a perfect sample, perfect measures, and no errors in gathering data, but who makes errors in the coding process or in entering data into a computer, can ruin a whole research project.

After very careful coding, the researcher verifies the accuracy of coding, or "cleans" the data. He or she may code a 10 to 15 percent random sample of the data a second time. If no coding errors appear, the researcher proceeds; if he or she finds errors, the researcher rechecks all coding.

When the data are in the computer, researchers verify coding in two ways. *Possible code cleaning* (or *wild code checking*) involves checking the categories of all variables for impossible codes. For example, respondent sex is coded 1 = Male, 2 = Female. Finding a 4 for a case in the field for the sex variable indicates a coding error. A second method, *contingency cleaning* (or *consistency checking*), involves cross-classifying two variables and looking for logically impossible combinations. For example, education is cross-classified by occupation. If a respondent is recorded as never having passed the eighth grade and also is recorded as being a legitimate medical doctor, the researcher checks for a coding error.

A researcher can modify data after they are in the computer. He or she may not use more refined categories than were used when collecting the original data, but may combine or group information. For example, the researcher may group ratio-level income data into five ordinal categories. Also, he or she can combine information from several indicators to create a new variable or add the responses to several questionnaire items into an index score.

RESULTS WITH ONE VARIABLE

Frequency Distributions

The word *statistics* can mean a set of collected numbers (e.g., numbers telling how many people live in a city) as well as a branch of applied mathematics used to manipulate and summarize the features of numbers. Social researchers use both types of statistics. Here, we focus on the second type—ways to manipulate and summarize numbers that represent data from a research project.

Descriptive statistics describe numerical data. They can be categorized by the number of variables involved: univariate, bivariate, or multivariate (for one, two, and three or more variables). *Univariate statistics* describe one variable (*uni-* refers to one; *-variate* refers to variable). The easiest way to describe the numerical data of one variable is with a *frequency distribution.* It can be used with nominal-, ordinal-, interval-, or ratio-level data and takes many forms. For example, I have data for 400 respondents. I can summarize the information on the gender of respondents at a glance with a raw count or a percentage frequency distribution (see Figure 10.2). I can present the same information in graphic form. Some common types of graphic representations are the *histogram, bar chart,* and *pie chart.* Bar charts or graphs are used for discrete variables. They can have a vertical or horizontal orientation with a small space between the bars. The terminology is not exact, but histograms are usually upright bar graphs for interval or ratio data.

For interval- or ratio-level data, a researcher often groups the information into categories. The grouped categories should be mutually exclusive. Interval- or ratio-level data are often plotted in a *frequency polygon.* In it the number of cases or frequency is along the vertical axis, and the values of the variable or scores are along the horizontal axis. A polygon appears when the dots are connected.

Measures of Central Tendency

Researchers often want to summarize the information about one variable into a single number. They use three measures of central tendency, or measures of the center of the frequency distribution: mean, median, and mode, which are often called *averages* (a less precise and less clear way of saying the same thing). Each measure of central tendency goes with data having a specific level of measurement (see Table 10.1).

The *mode* is the easiest to use and can be used with nominal, ordinal, interval, or ratio data. It is simply the most common or frequently occurring number. For example, the mode of the following list is 5: 6 5 7 10 9 5 3 5. A distribution can have more than one mode. For example, the mode of this list is both 5 and 7: 5 6 1 2 5 7 4 7. If the list gets long, it is easy to spot the mode in a frequency distribution—just look for the most frequent score. There will always be at least one case with a score that is equal to the mode.

The *median* is the middle point. It is also the 50th percentile, or the point at which half the cases are above it and half below it. It can be used with ordinal-, interval-, or ratio-level data (but not nominal level). You can "eyeball" the mode, but computing a median requires a little more work. The easiest way is first to organize the scores from highest to lowest, then count to the middle. If there is an odd number of scores, it is simple. Seven people are waiting for a bus; their ages are: 12 17 20 27 30 55 80. The median age is 27. Note that the median does not change easily. If the 55-year-old and the 80-year-old both got on one bus, and the remaining people were joined by two 31-year-olds, the median remains unchanged. If there is an even number of scores, things are a bit more complicated. For example, six people at a bus stop have the following ages: 17 20 26 30 50 70. The median is somewhere between 26 and 30. Compute the median by adding the two middle scores together and dividing by 2, or 26 + 30 = 56/2 = 28. The median

FIGURE 10.2   Examples of Univariate Statistics

Raw Count Frequency Distribution			Percentage Frequency Distribution	
Gender	*Frequency*		*Gender*	*Percentage*
Male	100		Male	25%
Female	300		Female	75%
Total	400		Total	100%

Bar Chart of Same Information

Males

Females

Example of Grouped Data Frequency Distribution

First Job Annual Income		*N*
Under $5,000		25
$5,000 to $9,999		50
$10,000 to $15,999		100
$16,000 to $19,999		150
$20,000 to $29,999		50
$30,000 and over		25
	Total	400

Example of Frequency Polygon

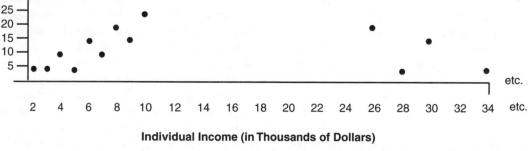

TABLE 10.1   Measures of Central Tendency and Levels of Measurement

Level of Measurement	Measure of Central Tendency		
	Mode	Median	Mean
Nominal	Yes		
Ordinal	Yes	Yes	
Interval	Yes	Yes	Yes
Ratio	Yes	Yes	Yes

age is 28, even though no person is 28 years old. Note that there is no mode in the list of six ages because each person has a different age.

The *mean,* also called the arithmetic average, is the most widely used measure of central tendency. It can be used *only* with interval- or ratio-level data.[2] Compute the mean by adding up all scores, then divide by the number of scores. For example, the mean age in the previous example is $17 + 20 + 26 + 30 + 50 + 70 = 213; 213/6 = 35.5$. No one in the list is 35.5 years old, and the mean does not equal the median.

The mean is strongly affected by changes in extreme values (very large or very small). For example, the 50- and 70-year-old left and were replaced with two 31-year-olds. The distribution now looks like this: 17 20 26 30 31 31. The median is unchanged: 28. The mean is $17 + 20 + 26 + 30 + 31 + 31 = 155; 155/6 = 25.8$. Thus, the mean dropped a great deal when a few extreme values were removed.

If the frequency distribution forms a "normal" or bell-shaped curve, the three measures of central tendency equal each other. If the distribution is a *skewed distribution* (i.e., more cases are in the upper or lower scores), then the three will not be equal. If most cases have lower scores with a few extreme high scores, the mean will be the highest, the median in the middle, and the

mode the lowest. If most cases have higher scores with a few extreme low scores, the mean will be the lowest, the median in the middle, and the mode the highest. In general, the median is best for skewed distributions, although the mean is used in most other statistics (see Figure 10.3).

Measures of Variation

Measures of central tendency are a one-number summary of a distribution; however, they give only its *center.* Another characteristic of a distribution is its spread, dispersion, or variability around the center. Two distributions can have identical measures of central tendency but differ in their spread about the center. For example, seven people are at a bus stop in front of a bar. Their ages are 25 26 27 30 33 34 35. Both the median and the mean are 30. At a bus stop in front of an ice cream store, seven people have the identical median and mean, but their ages are 5 10 20 30 40 50 55. The ages of the group in front of the ice cream store are spread more from the center, or the distribution has more variability.

Variability has important social implications. For example, in city X, the median and mean family income is $35,600 per year, and it has zero variation. *Zero variation* means that every family has an income of exactly $35,600. City Y has the same median and mean family income, but 95 percent of its families have incomes of $12,000 per year and 5 percent have incomes of $300,000 per year. City X has perfect income equality, whereas there is great inequality in city Y. A researcher who does not know the variability of income in the two cities misses very important information.

Researchers measure variation in three ways: range, percentile, and standard deviation. *Range* is the simplest. It consists of the largest and smallest scores. For example, the range for the bus stop in front of the bar is from 25 to 35, or $35 - 25 = 10$ years. If the 35-year-old got onto a bus and was replaced by a 60-year-old, the range would change to $60 - 25 = 45$ years. Range has limitations. For example, here are two

FIGURE 10.3   Measures of Central Tendency

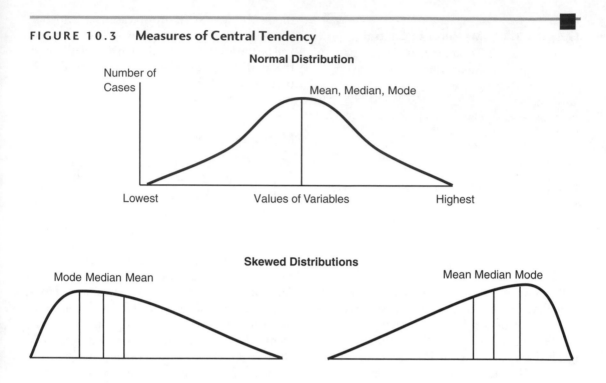

groups of six with a range of 35 years: 30 30 30 30 30 65 and 20 45 46 48 50 55.

Percentiles tell the score at a specific place within the distribution. One percentile you already learned is the median, the 50th percentile. Sometimes the 25th and 75th percentiles or the 10th and 90th percentiles are used to describe a distribution. For example, the 25th percentile is the score at which 25 percent of the distribution have either that score or a lower one. The computation of a percentile follows the same logic as the median. If I have 100 people and want to find the 25th percentile. I rank the scores and count up from the bottom until I reach number 25. If the total is not 100, I simply adjust the distribution to a percentage basis.

Standard deviation is the most difficult to compute measure of dispersion; it is also the most comprehensive and widely used. The range and percentile are for ordinal-, interval-, and ratio-level data, but the standard deviation requires an interval or ratio level of measurement.

It is based on the mean and gives an "average distance" between all scores and the mean. People rarely compute the standard deviation by hand for more than a handful of cases because computers and calculators can do it in seconds.

Look at the calculation of the standard deviation in Figure 10.4. If you add up the absolute difference between each score and the mean (i.e., subtract each score from the mean), you get zero. This is because the mean is equally distant from all scores. Also notice that the scores that differ the most from the mean have the largest effect on the sum of squares and on the standard deviation.

The standard deviation is used for comparison purposes. For example, the standard deviation for the schooling of parents of children in class A is 3.317 years; for class B, it is 0.812; and for class C, it is 6.239. The standard deviation tells a researcher that the parents of children in class B are very similar, whereas those for class C are very different. In fact, in class B, the school-

---

FIGURE 10.4   The Standard Deviation

Steps in Computing the Standard Deviation
1. Compute the mean.
2. Subtract the mean from each score.
3. Square the resulting difference for each score.
4. Total up the squared differences to get the sum of squares.
5. Divide the sum of squares by the number of cases to get the variance.
6. Take the square root of the variance, which is the standard deviation.

Example of Computing the Standard Deviation
[8 respondents, variable = years of schooling]

Score	Score – Mean	Squared (Score – Mean)
15	15 – 12.5 = 2.5	6.25
12	12 – 12.5 = –0.5	.25
12	12 – 12.5 = –0.5	.25
10	10 – 12.5 = –2.5	6.25
16	16 – 12.5 = 3.5	12.25
18	18 – 12.5 = 5.5	30.25
8	8 – 12.5 = 4.5	20.25
9	9 – 12.5 = –3.5	12.25

Mean = 15 + 12 + 12 + 10 + 16 + 18 + 8 + 9 = 100, 100/8 = 12.5
Sum of squares = 6.25 + .25 + .25 + 6.25 + 12.25 + 30.25 + 20.25 + 12.25 = 88
Variance = Sum of squares/Number of cases = 88/8 = 11
Standard deviation = Square root of variance = !11 = 3.317 years.
Here is the standard deviation in the form of a formula with symbols.

Symbols:
X = SCORE of case Σ = Sigma (Greek letter) for sum, add together
$\bar{X}$ = MEAN N = Number of cases

Formula:[a]

$$\text{Standard deviation} = \sqrt{\frac{\Sigma (X - \bar{X})^2}{N}}$$

---

[a] There is a slight difference in the formula depending on whether one is using data for the population or a sample to estimate the population parameter.

---

ing of an "average" parent is less than a year above or below than the mean for all parents, so the parents are very homogeneous. In class C, however, the "average" parent is more than six years above or below the mean, so the parents are very heterogeneous.

The standard deviation and the mean are used to create z-scores. *Z-scores* let a researcher compare two or more distributions or groups. The z-score, also called a *standardized score,* expresses points or scores on a frequency distribution in terms of a number of standard deviations from the mean. Scores are in terms of their relative position within a distribution, not as absolute values.

For example, Katy, a sales manager in firm A, earns $50,000 per year, whereas Mike in firm B earns $38,000 per year. Despite the absolute income differences between them, the managers are paid equally relative to others in the same firm. Katy is paid more than two-thirds of other employees in her firm, and Mike is also paid more than two-thirds of the employees in his firm.

Z-scores are easy to calculate from the mean and standard deviation (see Box 10.1). For example, an employer interviews students from

Kings College and Queens College. She learns that the colleges are similar and that both grade on a 4.0 scale. Yet, the mean grade-point average at Kings College is 2.62 with a standard deviation of .50, whereas the mean grade-point average at Queens College is 3.24 with a standard deviation of .40. The employer suspects that grades at Queens College are inflated. Suzette from Kings College has a grade-point average of 3.62, and Jorge from Queens College has a grade-point average of 3.64. Both students took the same courses. The employer wants to adjust the grades for the grading practices of the two colleges (i.e., create standardized scores). She calculates z-scores by subtracting each student's score from

---

Box 10.1   Calculating Z-Scores

Personally, I do not like the formula for z-scores, which is:

   Z-score = (Score − Mean)/Standard Deviation,

or in symbols:

$$z = \frac{X - \bar{X}}{\delta}$$

where: X = score, $\bar{X}$ = mean, δ = standard deviation

I usually rely on a simple conceptual diagram that does the same thing and that shows what z-scores really do. Consider data on the ages of schoolchildren with a mean of 7 years and a standard deviation of 2 years. How do I compute the z-score of 5-year-old Miguel, or what if I know that Yashohda's z-score is a +2 and I need to know her age in years? First, I draw a little chart from −3 to +3 with zero in the middle. I will put the mean value at zero, because a z-score of zero is the mean and z-scores measure distance above or below it. I stop at 3 because virtually all cases fall within 3 standard deviations of the mean in most situations. The chart looks like this:

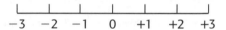

Now, I label the values of the mean and add or subtract standard deviations from it. One standard deviation above the mean (+1) when the mean is 7 and standard deviation is 2 years is just 7 + 2, or 9 years. For a −2 z-score, I put 3 years. This is because it is 2 standard deviations, of 2 years each (or 4 years), lower than the Mean of 7. My diagram now looks like this:

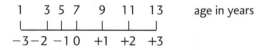

It is easy to see that Miguel, who is 5 years old, has a z-score of −1, whereas Yashohda's z-score of +2 corresponds to 11 years old. I can read from z-score to age, or age to z-score. For fractions, such as a z-score of −1.5, I just apply the same fraction to age to get 4 years. Likewise, an age of 12 is a z-score of +2.5.

the mean, then dividing by the standard deviation. For example, Suzette's z-score is 3.62 − 2.62 = 1.00/.50 = 2, whereas Jorge's z-score is 3.64 − 3.24. = .40/.40 = 1. Thus, the employer learns that Suzette is two standard deviations above the mean in her college, whereas Jorge is only one standard deviation above the mean for his college. Although Suzette's absolute grade-point average is lower than Jorge's, relative to the students in each of their colleges Suzette's grades are much higher than Jorge's.

RESULTS WITH TWO VARIABLES

A Bivariate Relationship

Univariate statistics describe a single variable in isolation. *Bivariate statistics* are much more valuable. They let a researcher consider two variables together and describe the relationship between variables. Even simple hypotheses require two variables. Bivariate statistical analysis shows a *relationship* between variables—that is, things that appear together.

Statistical relationships are based on two ideas: covariation and independence. *Covariation* means that things go together or are associated. To covary means to vary together; cases with certain values on one variable are likely to have certain values on the other one. For example, people with higher values on the income variable are likely to have higher values on the life expectancy variable. Likewise, those with lower incomes have lower life expectancy. This is usually stated in a shorthand way by saying that income and life expectancy are related to each other, or covary. We could also say that knowing one's income tells us one's probable life expectancy, or that life expectancy depends on income.

Independence is the opposite of covariation. It means there is no association or no relationship between variables. If two variables are independent, cases with certain values on one variable do not have any particular value on the other variable. For example, Rita wants to know whether number of siblings is related to life expectancy. If the variables are independent, then people with many brothers and sisters have the same life expectancy as those who are only children. In other words, knowing how many brothers or sisters someone has tells Rita nothing about the person's life expectancy.

Most researchers state hypotheses in terms of a causal relationship or expected covariation; if they use the null hypothesis, the hypothesis is that there is independence. It is used in formal hypothesis testing and is frequently found in inferential statistics (to be discussed).

Three techniques help researchers decide whether a relationship exists between two variables: (1) a scattergram, or a graph or plot of the relationship; (2) cross-tabulation, or a percentaged table; and (3) measures of association, or statistical measures that express the amount of covariation by a single number (e.g., correlation coefficient).

Seeing the Relationship: The Scattergram

What Is a Scattergram (or Scatterplot)? A *scattergram* is a graph on which a researcher plots each case or observation, where each axis represents the value of one variable. It is used for variables measured at the interval or ratio level, rarely for ordinal variables, and never if either variable is nominal. There is no fixed rule for which variable (independent or dependent) to place on the horizontal or vertical axis, but usually the independent variable (symbolized by the letter X) goes on the horizontal axis and the dependent variable (symbolized by Y) on the vertical axis. The lowest value for each should be the lower left corner and the highest value should be at the top or to the right.

How to Construct a Scattergram. Begin with the range of the two variables. Draw an axis with the values of each variable marked and write numbers on each axis (graph paper is helpful).

Next, label each axis with the variable name and put a title at the top.

You are now ready for the data. For each case, find the value of each variable and mark the graph at a place corresponding to the two values. For example, a researcher makes a scattergram of years of schooling by number of children. He or she looks at the first case to see years of schooling (e.g., 12) and at the number of children (e.g., 3). Then he or she goes to the place on the graph where 12 for the "schooling" variable and 3 for the "number of children" variable intersect and puts a dot for the case.

The scattergram in Figure 10.5 is a plot of data for 33 women. It shows a *negative relationship* between the years of education the woman completed and the number of children she gave birth to.

What Can You Learn from the Scattergram?
A researcher can see three aspects of a bivariate relationship in a scattergram: form, direction, and precision.

Form. Relationships can take three forms: independence, linear, and curvilinear. *Independence* or no relationship is the easiest to see. It looks like a random scatter with no pattern, or a straight line that is exactly parallel to the horizontal or vertical axis. A *linear relationship* means that a straight line can be visualized in the middle of a maze of cases running from one corner to another. A *curvilinear relationship* means that the center of a maze of cases would form a U curve, right side up or upside down, or an S curve.

Direction. Linear relationships can have a positive or negative direction. The plot of a *positive* relationship looks like a diagonal line from the lower left to the upper right. Higher values on X tend to go with higher values on Y, and vice versa. The income and life expectancy example described a positive linear relationship.

A *negative* relationship looks like a line from the upper left to the lower right. It means that higher values on one variable go with lower val-

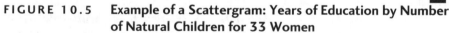

FIGURE 10.5   Example of a Scattergram: Years of Education by Number of Natural Children for 33 Women

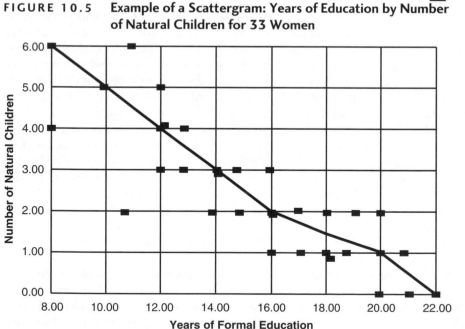

ues on the other. For example, people with more education are less likely to have been arrested. If we look at a scattergram of data on a group of males where years of schooling (X axis) are plotted by number of arrests (Y axis), we see that most cases (or men) with many arrests are in the lower right, because most of them completed few years of school. Most cases with few arrests are in the upper left because most have had more schooling. The imaginary line for the relationship can have a shallow or a steep slope. More advanced statistics provide precise numerical measures of the line's slope.

Precision.   Bivariate relationships differ in their degree of precision. *Precision* is the amount of spread in the points on the graph. A high level of precision occurs when the points hug the line that summarizes the relationship. A low level occurs when the points are widely spread around the line. Researchers can "eyeball" a highly precise relationship. They can also use advanced statistics to measure the precision of a relationship in a way that is analogous to the standard deviation for univariate statistics.

Bivariate Tables

What Is a Bivariate Table?   The bivariate contingency table is widely used. It presents the same information as a scattergram in a more condensed form. The data can be measured at any level of measurement, although interval and ratio data must be grouped if there are many different values. The table is based on *cross-tabulation;* that is, the cases are organized in the table on the basis of two variables at the same time.

A *contingency table* is formed by cross-tabulating two or more variables. It is contingent because the cases in each category of a variable get distributed into each category of a second (or additional) variable. The table distributes cases into the categories of multiple variables at the same time and shows how the cases, by category of one variable, are "contingent upon" the categories of other variables.

Figure 10.6 is a raw count or frequency table. Its cells contain a count of the cases. It is easy to make, but interpreting a raw count table is difficult because the rows or columns can have different totals, and what is of real interest is the relative size of cells compared to others.

Researchers convert raw count tables into percentaged tables to see bivariate relationships. There are three ways to percentage a table: by row, by column, and for the total. The first two are often used and show relationships.

Is it best to percentage by row or column? Either can be appropriate. Let us first review the mechanics of percentaging a table. When calculating column percentages, compute the percentage each cell is of the column total. This includes the total column or marginal for the column variable. For example, the first column total is 26 (there are 26 people under age 30), and the first cell of that column is 20 (there are 20 people under age 30 who agree). The percentage is 20/26 = 0.769 or 76.9 percent. Or, for the first number in the marginal, 37/101 = 0.366 = 36.6 percent (see Table 10.2). Except for rounding, the total should equal 100 percent.

Computing row percentages is similar. Compute the percentage of each cell as a percentage of the row total. For example, using the same cell with 20 in it, we now want to know what percentage it is of the row total of 37, or 20/37 = 0.541 = 54.1 percent. Percentaging by row or column gives different percentages for a cell unless the marginals are the same.

The row and column percentages let a researcher address different questions. The row percentage table answers the question. Among those who hold an attitude, what percentage come from each age group? It says of respondents who agree, 54.1 percent are in the under-30 age group. The column percentage table addresses the question: Among those in each age group, what percentage hold different attitudes? It says that among those who are under 30, 76.9 percent agree. From the row percentages, a researcher learns that a little over half of those who agree are under 30 years old, whereas from col-

FIGURE 10.6   Age Group by Attitude about Changing the Drinking Age, Raw Count Table

Raw Count Table (a)	Age Group (b)				
Attitude (b)	*Under 30*	*30–45*	*46–60*	*61 and Older*	**Total (c)**
Agree	20	10	4	3	37
No opinion	3 (d)	10	10	2	25
Disagree	3	5	21	10	39
Total (c)	26	25	35	15	101

Missing cases (f) = 8.   (e)

The Parts of a Table

(a) Give each table a *title*, which names variables and provides background information.

(b) Label the row and column variable and give a name to each of the variable categories.

(c) Include the totals of the columns and rows. These are called the *marginals*. They equal the univariate frequency distribution for the variable.

(d) Each number or place that corresponds to the intersection of a category for each variable is a *cell of a table.*

(e) The numbers with the labeled variable categories and the totals are called the *body of a table.*

(f) If there is missing information (cases in which a respondent refused to answer, ended interview, said "don't know," etc.), report the number of missing cases near the table to account for all original cases.

umn percentages, the researcher learns that among the under-30 people, over three-quarters agree. One way of percentaging tells about people who have specific attitudes; the other tells about people in specific age groups.

A researcher's hypothesis may imply looking at row percentages or the column percentages. When beginning, calculate percentages each way and practice interpreting, or figuring out, what each says. For example, my hypothesis is that age affects attitude, so column percentages are most helpful. However, if my interest was in describing the age make-up of groups of people with different attitudes, then row percentages are appropriate.

Unfortunately, there is no "industry standard" for putting independent and dependent variables in a percentage table as row or column, or for percentage by row and column. A majority of researchers place the independent variable as the column and percentage by column, but a large minority put the independent variable as the row and percentage by row.

Reading a Percentaged Table.   Once you understand how a table is made, reading it and figuring out what it says are much easier. To read a table, first look at the title, the variable labels, and any background information. Next, look at the direction in which percentages have been computed—in rows or columns. Notice that the percentaged tables in Table 10.2 have the same title. This is because the same variables are used. It would have helped to note how the data were percentaged in the title, but this is rarely done. Sometimes, researchers present abbreviated tables and omit the 100 percent total or the marginals, which adds to the confusion. It is best to include all the parts of a table and clear labels.

Researchers read percentaged tables to make comparisons. Comparisons are made in the opposite direction from that in which per-

centages are computed. A rule of thumb is to compare across rows if the table is percentaged down (i.e., by column) and to compare up and down in columns if the table is percentaged across (i.e., by row).

For example, in row-percentaged Table 10.2, compare columns or age groups. Most of those who agree are in the youngest group, with the proportion declining as age increases. Most no-opinion people are in the middle-age groups, whereas those who disagree are older, especially in the 46-to-60 group. When reading column-

TABLE 10.2 **Age Group by Attitude about Changing the Drinking Age, Percentaged Tables**

Column-Percentaged Table

Attitude	Under 30	30–45	46–60	61 and Older	Total
Agree	76.9%	40%	11.4%	20%	36.6%
No opinion	11.5	40	28.6	13.3	24.8
Disagree	11.5	20	60	66.7	38.6
Total	99.9	100	100	100	100
(N)	(26)*	(25)*	(35)*	(15)*	(101)*

Missing cases = 8

Row-Percentaged Table

Attitude	Under 30	30–45	46–60	61 and Older	Total	(N)
Agree	54.1%	27%	10.8%	8.1%	100%	(37)*
No opinion	12	40	40	8	100	(25)*
Disagree	7.7	12.8	53.8	25.6	99.9	(39)*
Total	25.7	24.8	34.7	14.9	100.1	(101)*

Missing cases = 8

*For percentaged tables, provide the number of cases or N on which percentages are computed in parentheses near the total of 100%. This makes it possible to go back and forth from a percentaged table to a raw count table and vice versa.

percentaged Table 10.2, compare across rows. For example, a majority of the youngest group agree, and they are the only group in which most people agree. Only 11.5 percent disagree, compared to a majority in the two oldest groups.

It takes practice to see a relationship in a percentaged table. If there is no relationship in a table, the cell percentages look approximately equal across rows or columns. A linear relationship looks like larger percentages in the diagonal cells. If there is a curvilinear relationship, the largest percentages form a pattern across cells. For example, the largest cells might be the upper right, the bottom middle, and the upper left. It is easiest to see a relationship in a moderate-sized table (9 to 16 cells) where most cells have some cases (at least five cases are recommended) and the relationship is strong and precise.

Principles of reading a scattergram can help you see a relationship in a percentaged table. Imagine a scattergram that has been divided into 12 equal-sized sections. The cases in each section correspond to the number of cases in the cells of a table that is superimposed onto the scattergram. The table is a condensed form of the scattergram. The bivariate relationship line in a scattergram corresponds to the diagonal cells in a percentaged table. Thus, a simple way to see strong relationships is to circle the largest percentage in each row (for row-percentaged tables) or column (for column-percentaged tables) and see if a line appears.

The circle-the-largest-cell rule works—with one important caveat. The categories in the percentages table *must* be ordinal or interval and in the same order as in a scattergram. In scattergrams the lowest variable categories begin at the bottom left. If the categories in a table are not ordered the same way, the rule does not work.

For example, Table 10.3a looks like a positive relationship and Table 10.3b like a negative relationship. Both use the same data and are percentaged by row. The actual relationship is negative. Look closely—Table 10.3b has age categories ordered as in a scattergram. When in doubt, return to the basic difference between

TABLE 10.3a   Age by Schooling

Age	Years of Schooling				Total
	0–11	12	13–14	16+	
Under 30	5%	25	30	40	100
30–45	15	25	40	20	100
46–60	35	45	12	8	100
61+	45	35	15	5	100

TABLE 10.3b   Age by Schooling

Age	Years of Schooling				Total
	0–11	12	13–14	16+	
61+	45%	35	15	5	100
46–60	35	45	12	8	100
30–45	15	25	40	20	100
Under 30	5	25	30	40	100

positive and negative relationships. A positive relationship means that as one variable increases, so does the other. A negative relationship means that as one variable increases, the other decreases.

Bivariate Tables without Percentages. Researchers condense information in another kind of bivariate table with a measure of central tendency (usually the mean) instead of percentages. It is used when one variable is nominal or ordinal and another is measured at the interval or ratio level. The mean (or a similar measure) of the interval or ratio variable is presented for each category of the nominal or ordinal variable. All cases are divided into the ordinal or nominal variable categories; then the mean is calculated for the cases in each variable category from the raw data.

Table 10.4 shows the mean age of people in each of the attitude categories. The results sug-

TABLE 10.4 Attitude about Changing the Drinking Age by Mean Age of Respondent

Drinking Age Attitude	Mean Age	(N)
Agree	26.2	(37)
No opinion	44.5	(25)
Disagree	61.9	(39)

Missing cases = 8

gest that the mean age of those who disagree is much higher than for those who agree or have no opinion.

Measures of Association

A *measure of association* is a single number that expresses the strength, and often the direction, of a relationship. It condenses information about a bivariate relationship into a single number.

There are many measures of association. The correct one depends on the level of measurement. Many measures are called by letters of the Greek alphabet. Lambda, gamma, tau, chi (squared), and rho are commonly used measures. The emphasis here is on interpreting the measures, not on their calculation. In order to understand each measure, you will need to complete a beginning statistics course.

If there is a strong association or relationship, then few errors are made predicting a second variable on the basis of knowledge of the first, or the proportion of errors reduced is large. A large number of correct guesses suggests that the measure of association is a nonzero number if an association exists between the variables. Table 10.5 describes five commonly used bivariate measures of association. Notice that most range from −1 to +1, with negative numbers in-

dicating a negative relationship and positive numbers a positive relationship. A measure of 1.0 means a 100 percent reduction in errors, or perfect prediction.

MORE THAN TWO VARIABLES

Statistical Control

Showing an association or relationship between two variables is not sufficient to say that an independent variable *causes* a dependent variable. In addition to temporal order and association, a researcher must eliminate alternative explanations—explanations that can make the hypothesized relationship spurious. Experimental researchers do this by choosing a research design that physically controls potential alternative explanations for results (i.e., that threaten internal validity).

In nonexperimental research, a researcher controls for alternative explanations with statistics. He or she measures possible alternative explanations with *control variables,* then examines the control variables with multivariate tables and statistics that help him or her decide whether a bivariate relationship is spurious. They also show the relative size of the effect of multiple independent variables on a dependent variable.

A researcher controls for alternative explanations in multivariate (more than two variables) analysis by introducing a third (or sometimes a fourth or fifth) variable. For example, a bivariate table shows that taller teenagers like sports more than shorter ones do. But the bivariate relationship between height and attitude toward sports may be spurious because teenage males are taller than females, and males tend to like sports more than females. To test whether the relationship is actually due to sex, a researcher must *control for* gender; in other words, effects of sex are statistically *removed.* Once this is done, a researcher can see whether the bivariate relationship between height and attitude toward sports remains.

TABLE 10.5   Five Measures of Association

Lambda is used for nominal-level data. It is based on a reduction in errors based on the mode and ranges between 0 (independence) and 1.0 (perfect prediction or the strongest possible relationship).

Gamma is used for ordinal-level data. It is based on comparing pairs of variable categories and seeing whether a case has the same rank on each. Gamma ranges from −1.0 to +1.0, with 0 meaning no association.

Tau is also used for ordinal-level data. It is based on a different approach than gamma and takes care of a few problems that can occur with gamma. Actually, there are several statistics named tau (it is a popular Greek letter), and the one here is Kendall's tau. Kendall's tau ranges from −1.0 to +1.0, with 0 meaning no association.

Rho is also called Pearson's product moment correlation coefficient (named after the famous statistician Karl Pearson and based on a product moment statistical procedure). It is the most commonly used measure of correlation, the correlation statistic people mean if they use the term *correlation* without identifying it further. It can be used only for data measured at the interval or ratio level. Rho is used for the mean and standard deviation of the variables and tells how far cases are from a relationship (or regression) line in a scatterplot. Rho ranges from −1.0 to +1.0, with 0 meaning no association. If the value of rho is squared, sometimes called *R*-squared, it has a unique proportion reduction in error meaning. *R*-squared tells how the percentage in one variable (e.g., the dependent) is accounted for, or explained by, the other variable (e.g., the independent). Rho measures linear relationships only. It cannot measure nonlinear or curvilnear relationships. For example, a rho of zero can indicate either no relationship or a curvilinear relationship.

Chi-squared has two different uses. It can be used as a measure of association in descriptive statistics like the others listed here, or in inferential statistics. Inferential statistics are briefly described next. As a measure of association, chi-squared can be used for nominal and ordinal data. It has an upper limit of infinity and a lower limit of zero, meaning no association.

Summary of Measures of Association

Measure	Greek Symbol	Type of Data	High Association	Independence
Lambda	λ	Nominal	1.0	0
Gamma	γ	Ordinal	+1.0, −1.0	0
Tau (Kendall's)	τ	Ordinal	+1.0, −1.0	0
Rho	ρ	Interval, ratio	+1.0, −1.0	0
Chi-square	χ^2	Nominal, ordinal	Infinity	0

A researcher controls for a third variable by seeing whether the bivariate relationship persists within categories of the control variable. For example, a researcher controls for sex, and the relationship between height and sports attitude persists. This means that tall males and tall females both like sports more than short males and short females do. In other words, the control variable has no effect. When this is so, the bivariate relationship is not spurious.

If the bivariate relationship weakens or disappears after the control variable is considered, it means that tall males are no more likely than short males to like sports, and tall females are no more likely to like sports than short females. It indicates that the initial bivariate relationship is spurious and suggests that the third variable, sex, and not height, is the true cause of differences in attitudes toward sports.

Statistical control is a key idea in advanced statistical techniques. A measure of association like the correlation coefficient only suggests a relationship. Until a researcher considers control variables, the bivariate relationship could be spurious. Researchers are cautious in interpreting bivariate relationships until they have considered control variables.

The Elaboration Model of Percentaged Tables

Constructing Trivariate Tables.   In order to meet all the conditions needed for causality, researchers want to "control for" or see whether an alternative explanation explains away a causal relationship. If an alternative explanation explains a relationship, then the bivariate relationship is spurious. Alternative explanations are operationalized as third variables, which are called *control variables* because they control for alternative explanation.

One way to take such third variables into consideration and see whether they influence the bivariate relationship is to statistically introduce control variables using trivariate or three-variable tables. Trivariate tables differ slightly from bivariate tables; they consist of multiple bivariate tables.

A trivariate table has a bivariate table of the independent and dependent variable for each category of the control variable. These new tables are called *partials*. The number of partials depends on the number of categories in the control variable. Partial tables look like bivariate tables, but they use a subset of the cases. Only cases with a specific value on the control variable are

in the partial. Thus, it is possible to break apart a bivariate table to form partials, or combine the partials to restore the initial bivariate table.

Trivariate tables have three limitations. First, they are difficult to interpret if a control variable has more than four categories. Second, control variables can be at any level of measurement, but interval or ratio control variables must be grouped (i.e., converted to an ordinal level), and how cases are grouped can affect the interpretation of effects. Finally, the total number of cases is a limiting factor because the cases are divided among cells in partials. The number of cells in the partials equals the number of cells in the bivariate relationship multiplied by the number of categories in the control variable. For example, a control variable has three categories, and a bivariate table has 12 cells, so the partials have $3 \times 12 = 36$ cells. An average of five cases per cell is recommended, so the researcher will need $5 \times 36 = 180$ cases at minimum.

For three variables, three bivariate tables are logically possible. In the example, the combinations are (1) gender by attitude, (2) age group by attitude, and (3) gender by age group. The partials are set up on the basis of the initial bivariate relationship. The independent variable in each is "age group" and the dependent variable is "attitude." "Gender" is the control variable. Thus, the trivariate table consists of a pair of partials, each showing the age/attitude relationship for a given gender.

A researcher's theory suggests the hypothesis in the initial bivariate relationship; it also tells him or her which variables provide alternative explanations (i.e., the control variables). Thus, the choice of the control variable is based on theory.

The *elaboration paradigm* is a system for reading percentaged trivariate tables.[3] It describes the pattern that emerges when a control variable is introduced. Five terms describe how the partial tables compare to the initial bivariate table, or how the original bivariate relationship changes after the control variable is considered. The examples of patterns presented here show strong cases. More advanced statistics are needed when the differences are not as obvious.

The *replication pattern* is the easiest to understand. It is when the partials replicate or reproduce the same relationship that existed in the bivariate table before considering the control variable. It means that the control variable has no effect.

The *specification pattern* is the next easiest pattern. It occurs when one partial replicates the initial bivariate relationship but other partials do not. For example, you find a strong (negative) bivariate relationship between automobile accidents and college grades. You control for gender and discover that the relationship holds only for males (i.e., the strong negative relationship was in the partial for males, but not for females). This is specification because a researcher can specify the category of the control variable in which the initial relationship persists.

The control variable has a large impact in both the interpretation and explanation patterns. In both, the bivariate table shows a relationship that disappears in the partials. In other words, the relationship appears to be independence in the partials. The two patterns cannot be distinguished by looking at the tables alone. The difference between them depends on the location of the control variable in the causal order of variables. Theoretically, a control variable can be in one of two places, either between the original independent and dependent variables (i.e., the control variable is intervening), or before the original independent variable.

The *interpretation pattern* describes the situation in which the control variable intervenes between the original independent and dependent variables. For example, you examine a relationship between religious upbringing and abortion attitude. Political ideology is a control variable. You reason that religious upbringing affects current political ideology and abortion attitude. You theorize that political ideology is logically prior to an attitude about a specific issue, like abortion. Thus, religious upbringing causes political ideology, which in turn has an impact on abortion attitude. The control variable is an intervening variable, which helps you interpret the meaning of the complete relationship.

The *explanation pattern* looks the same as interpretation. The difference is the temporal order of the control variable. In this pattern, a control variable comes before the independent variable in the initial bivariate relationship. For example, the original relationship is between religious upbringing and abortion attitude, but now gender is the control variable. Gender comes before religious upbringing because one's sex is fixed at birth. The explanation pattern changes how a researcher explains the results. It implies that the initial bivariate relationship is spurious.

The *suppressor variable pattern* occurs when the bivariate tables suggest independence but a relationship appears in one or both of the partials. For example, religious upbringing and abortion attitude are independent in a bivariate table. Once the control variable "region of the country" is introduced, religious upbringing is associated with abortion attitude in the partial tables. The control variable is a suppressor variable because it suppressed the true relationship. The true relationship appears in the partials. (See Table 10.6 for a summary of the elaboration paradigm.)

Multiple Regression Analysis

Multiple regression is a statistical technique whose calculation is beyond the level in this book. Although it is quickly computed by the appropriate statistics software, a background in statistics is needed to prevent making errors in its calculation and interpretation. It requires interval- or ratio-level data. It is discussed here for two reasons. First, it controls for many alternative explanations and variables simultaneously (it is rarely possible to use more than one control variable at a time using percentaged tables). Second, it is widely used in sociology, and you are likely to encounter it when reading research reports or articles.

TABLE 10.6   Summary of the Elaboration Paradigm

Pattern Name	Pattern Seen When Comparing Partials to the Original Bivariate Table
Replication	Same relationship in both partials as in bivariate table.
Specification	Bivariate relationship is only seen in one of the partial tables.
Interpretation	Bivariate relationship weakens greatly or disappears in the partial tables (control variable is intervening).
Explanation	Bivariate relationship weakens greatly or disappears in the partial tables (control variable is before independent variable).
Suppressor variable	No bivariate relationship; relationship appears in partial tables only.

EXAMPLES OF ELABORATION PATTERNS

Replication

Bivariate Table				**Partials**			
					Control = Low		Control = High
	Low	High			Low	High	Low	High
Low	85%	15%		Low	84%	16%	86%	14%
High	15%	85%		High	16%	84%	14%	86%

Interpretation or Explanation

Bivariate Table				**Partials**			
					Control = Low		Control = High
	Low	High			Low	High	Low	High
Low	85%	15%		Low	45%	55%	55%	45%
High	15%	85%		High	55%	45%	45%	55%

Specification

Bivariate Table				**Partials**			
					Control = Low		Control = High
	Low	High			Low	High	Low	High
Low	85%	85%		Low	95%	5%	50%	50%
High	15%	15%		High	5%	95%	50%	50%

Suppressor Variable

Bivariate Table				**Partials**			
					Control = Low		Control = High
	Low	High			Low	High	Low	High
Low	54%	46%		Low	84%	16%	14%	86%
High	46%	54%		High	16%	84%	86%	14%

Multiple regression results tell the reader two things. First, the results have a measure called *R*-squared (R^2), which tells how well a set of variables explains a dependent variable. *Explain* means reduced errors when predicting the dependent variable scores on the basis of information about the independent variables. A good model with several independent variables might account for, or explain, a large percentage of variation in a dependent variable. For example, an R^2 of .50 means that knowing the independent and control variables improves the accuracy of predicting the dependent variable by 50 percent, or half as many errors are made as would be made without knowing about the variables.

Second, the regression results measure the direction and size of the effect of each variable on a dependent variable. The effect is measured precisely and given a numerical value. For example, a researcher can see how five independent or control variables simultaneously affect a dependent variable, with all variables controlling for the effects of one another. This is especially valuable for testing theories that state that multiple independent variables cause one dependent variable.

The effect on the dependent variable is measured by a standardized regression coefficient or the Greek letter beta (β). It is similar to a correlation coefficient. In fact, the beta coefficient for two variables equals the *r* correlation coefficient.

Researchers use the beta regression coefficient to determine whether control variables have an effect. For example, the bivariate correlation between *X* and *Y* is .75. Next, the researcher statistically considers four control variables. If the beta remains at .75, then the four control variables have no effect. However, if the beta for *X* and *Y* gets smaller (e.g., drops to .20), it indicates that the control variables have an effect.

Consider an example of regression analysis with age, income, education, and region as independent variables. The dependent variable is a

TABLE 10.7   Example of Multiple Regression Results

Dependent Variable Is Political Ideology Index (High Score Means Very Liberal)

Independent Variable	Standardized Regression Coefficients
Region = South	−.19
Age	.01
Income	−.44
Years of education	.23
Religious attendance	−.39
$R^2 = .38$	

score on a political ideology index. The multiple regression results show that income and religious attendance have large effects, education and region minor effects, and age no effect. All the independent variables together have a 38 percent accuracy in predicting a person's political ideology (see Table 10.7). The example suggests that high income, frequent religious attendance, and a southern residence are positively associated with conservative opinions, whereas having more education is associated with liberal opinions. The impact of income is more than twice the size of the impact of living in a southern region. We have been examining descriptive statistics (see Table 10.8); next, we look at a different type: inferential statics.

INFERENTIAL STATISTICS

The Purpose of Inferential Statistics

Researchers often want to do more than describe; they want to test hypotheses, know whether sample results hold true in a popula-

TABLE 10.8   **Summary of Major Types of Descriptive Statistics**

Type of Technique	Statistical Technique	Purpose
Univariate	Frequency distribution, measure of central tendency, standard deviation, z-score	Describe one variable.
Bivariate	Correlation, percentage table, chi-square	Describe a relationship or the association between two variables.
Multivariate	Elaboration paradigm, multiple regression	Describe relationships among several variables, or see how several independent variables have an effect on a dependent variable.

tion, and decide whether differences in results (e.g., between the mean scores of two groups) are big enough to indicate that a relationship really exists. Inferential statistics use probability theory to test hypotheses formally, permit inferences from a sample to a population, and test whether descriptive results are likely to be due to random factors or to a real relationship.

This section explains the basic ideas of inferential statistics but does not deal with inferential statistics in any detail. This area is more complex than descriptive statistics and requires a background in statistics.

Inferential statistics rely on principles from probability sampling, where a researcher uses a random process (e.g., a random number table) to select cases from the entire population. Inferential statistics are a precise way to talk about how confident a researcher can be when inferring from the results in a sample to the population.

You have already encountered inferential statistics if you have read or heard about "statistical significance" or results "significant at the .05 level." Researchers use them to conduct various statistical tests (e.g., a *t*-test or an *F*-test). Statistical significance is also used in formal hypothesis testing, which is a precise way to decide whether to accept or to reject a null hypothesis.[4]

Statistical Significance

Statistical significance means that results are not likely to be due to chance factors. It indicates the probability of finding a relationship in the sample when there is none in the population. Because probability samples involve a random process, it is always possible that sample results will differ from a population parameter. A researcher wants to estimate the odds that sample results are due to a true population parameter or to chance factors of random sampling. Statistical significance uses probability theory and specific statistical tests to tell a researcher whether the results (e.g., an association, a difference between two means, a regression coefficient) are produced by random error in random sampling.

Statistical significance only tells what is likely. It cannot prove anything with absolute certainty. It states that particular outcomes are more or less probable. Statistical significance is *not* the same as practical, substantive, or theoretical significance. Results can be statistically significant but theoretically meaningless or trivial. For example, two variables can have a statistically significant association due to coincidence, with no logical connection between them (e.g., length of fingernails and ability to speak French).

Levels of Significance

Researchers usually express statistical significance in terms of levels (e.g., a test is statistically significant at a specific level) rather than giving the specific probability. The *level of statistical significance* (usually .05, .01, or .001) is a way of talking about the likelihood that results are due to chance factors—that is, that a relationship appears in the sample when there is none in the population. If a researcher says that results are significant at the .05 level, this means the following:

- Results like these are due to chance factors only 5 in 100 times.
- There is a 95 percent chance that the sample results are not due to chance factors alone, but reflect the population accurately.
- The odds of such results based on chance alone are .05, or 5 percent.
- One can be 95 percent confident that the results are due to a real relationship in the population, not chance factors.

These all say the same thing in different ways. This may sound like the discussion of sampling distributions and the central limit theorem in the chapter on sampling. It is not an accident. Both are based on probability theory, which researchers use to link sample data to a population. Probability theory lets us predict what happens in the long run over many events when a random process is used. In other words, it allows precise prediction over many situations in the long run, but not for a specific situation. Since we have one sample and we want to infer to the population, probability theory helps us estimate the odds that our particular sample represents the population. We cannot know for certain unless we have the whole population, but probability theory lets us state our confidence—how likely it is that the sample shows one thing while something else is true in the population. For example, a sample shows that college men

and women differ in how many hours they study. Is the result due to an unusual sample, and there is really no difference in the population, or does it reflect a true difference between the sexes in the population?

Type I and Type II Errors

The logic of statistical significance is based on stating whether chance factors produce results. You may ask, Why use the .05 level? It means a 5 percent chance that randomness could cause the results. Why not use a more certain standard—for example, a 1 in 1,000 probability of random chance? This gives a smaller chance that randomness versus a true relationship caused the results.

There are two answers. The simple answer is that the scientific community has informally agreed to use .05 as a rule of thumb for most purposes. Being 95 percent confident of results is the accepted standard for explaining the social world.

A second answer involves a tradeoff between making two types of logical errors. A *Type I error* occurs when the researcher says that a relationship exists when in fact none exists. It means falsely rejecting a null hypothesis. A *Type II error* occurs when a researcher says that a relationship does not exist, but in reality it does. It means falsely accepting a null hypothesis (see Table 10.9). Of course, researchers want to avoid both kinds of errors. They want to say that there is a relationship in the data only when it does exist and that there is no relationship only when there really is none, but they face a dilemma: As the odds of making one type of error decline, the odds of making the opposite error increase.

The idea of Type I and Type II errors may seem difficult at first, but the same logical dilemma appears in many other settings. For example, a judge can err by deciding that an accused person is guilty when in fact he or she is innocent. Or the judge can err by deciding that a person is innocent when in fact he or she is

TABLE 10.9   Type I and Type II Errors

	True Situation in the World	
What the Researcher Says	*No Relationship*	*Causal Relationship*
No relationship	No error	Type II error
Causal relationship	Type I error	No error

guilty. The judge does not want to make either error. A judge does not want to jail the innocent or to free the guilty. The judge must render a judgment based on limited information and balance the two types of errors. Likewise, a physician has to decide whether to prescribe a new medication for a patient. The physician can err by thinking that the medication will be effective and has no side effects when, in fact, it has a serious side effect, such as causing blindness. Or the physician can err by holding back an effective medication because of fear of serious side effects when in fact there are none. The physican does not want to make either error. By making the first error, the physican causes great harm to the patient and may even face a lawsuit. By making the second error, the physican does not help the patient get better. Again, a judgment must be made that balances two types of possible errors.

We can put the ideas of statistical significance and the two types of error together. An overly cautious researcher sets a high level of significance. For example, the researcher might use the .0001 level. He or she attributes the results to chance unless they are so rare that they would occur by chance only 1 in 10,000 times. Such a high standard means that the researcher is most likely to err by saying results are due to chance when in fact they are not. He or she may falsely accept the null hypothesis when there is a causal relationship (a Type II error). By contrast, a risk-taking researcher sets a low level of significance,

such as .10. His or her results indicate a relationship would occur by chance 1 in 10 times. He or she is likely to err by saying that a causal relationship exists, when in fact random factors (e.g., random sampling error) actually cause the results. The researcher is likely to falsely reject the null hypothesis (Type I error). In sum, the .05 level is a compromise between Type I and Type II errors.

The statistical techniques of inferential statistics are precise and rely on the relationship between sampling error, sample size, and central limit theorem. The power of inferential statistics is their ability to let a researcher state, with specific degrees of certainty, that specific sample results are likely to be true in a population. For example, a researcher conducts statistical tests and finds that a relationship is statistically significant at the .05 level. He or she can state that the sample results are probably not due to chance factors. Indeed, there is a 95 percent chance that a true relationship exists in the social world.

Tests for inferential statistics are limited. The data must come from a random sample, and tests only take into account sampling errors. Nonsampling errors (e.g., a poor sampling frame or a poorly designed measure) are not considered. Do not be fooled into thinking that such tests offer easy, final answers. Many computer programs quickly do the calculation for inferential and descriptive statistics (see Box 10.2).

Box
10.2   Statistical Programs on Computers

Almost every social researcher who needs to calculate many statistics does so with a computer program, often using a basic spreadsheet program, such as Excel. Unfortunately, spreadsheets are designed for accounting and bookkeeping functions. They include statistics, but are clumsy and limited for that purpose. There are many computer programs designed for calculating general statistics. The marketplace can be confusing to a beginner, for products evolve rapidly with changing computer technology.

In recent years, the software has become less demanding for a user. The most popular programs in the social sciences are Minitab, Microcase, and SPSS (Statistical Package for the Social Sciences). Others include SAS (Statistical Analysis System), STATISTICA by StratSoft, and Strata. Many began as simple, low-cost programs for research purposes.

The most widely used program for statistics in the social sciences in SPSS. Its advantages are that social researchers used it extensively for over three decades, it includes many ways to manipulate quantitative data, and it contains most statistical measures. A disadvantage is that it can take a long time to learn because of its many options and complex statistics. Also, it is expensive to purchase unless the user gets an inexpensive, "stripped down" student version included with a textbook or workbook.

As computer technology makes using a statistics program easier, the danger increases that some people will use the programs, but not understand statistics or what the programs are doing. They can easily violate basic assumptions required by a statistical procedure, use the statistics improperly, and produce results that are pure nonsense but that look very technically sophisticated.

CONCLUSION

You have learned about organizing quantitative data to prepare them for analysis and about analyzing them (organizing data into charts or tables, or summarizing them with statistical measures). Researchers use statistical analysis to test hypotheses and answer research questions. The chapter explained how data must first be coded and then analyzed using univariate or bivariate statistics. Bivariate relationships might be spurious, so control variables and multivariate analysis are often necessary. You also learned some basics about inferential statistics.

Beginning researchers sometimes feel their results should support a hypothesis. *There is nothing wrong with rejecting a hypothesis.* The goal of scientific research is to produce knowledge that truly reflects the social world, not to defend pet ideas or hypotheses. Hypotheses are theoretical guesses based on limited knowledge; they need to be tested. Excellent-quality research can find that a hypothesis is wrong, and poor-quality research can support a hypothesis. Good research depends on high-quality methodology, not on supporting a specific hypothesis.

Good research means guarding against possible errors or obstacles to true inferences from data to the social world. Errors can enter into the research process and affect results at many places: research design, measurement, data collection, coding, calculating statistics and constructing tables, or interpreting results. Even if a researcher can design, measure, collect, code, and calculate without error, another step in the research process remains. It is to interpret the tables, charts, and statistics, and to answer the question: What does it all mean? The only way to assign meaning to facts, charts, tables, or statistics is to use theory.

Data, tables, or computer output cannot answer research questions. The facts do not speak for themselves. As a researcher, you must return to your theory (i.e., concepts, relationships among concepts, assumptions, theoretical definitions) and give the results meaning. Do not lock yourself into the ideas with which you began. There is room for creativity, and new ideas are generated by trying to figure out what results really say. It is important to be careful in designing and conducting research so that you can look at the results as a reflection of something in the social world and not worry about whether they are due to an error or an artifact of the research process itself.

Before we leave quantitative research, there is one last issue. Journalists, politicians, and others increasingly use statistical results to make a point or bolster an argument. This has not produced greater accuracy and information in public debate. More often, it has increased confusion and made it more important to know what statistics can and cannot do. The cliché that you can prove anything with statistics is false; however, people can and do *misuse* statistics. Through ignorance or conscious deceit, some people use statistics to manipulate others. The way to protect yourself from being misled by statistics is not to ignore them or hide from the numbers. Rather, it is to understand the research process and statistics, think about what you hear, and ask questions.

We turn next to qualitative research. The logic and purpose of qualitative research differ from those of the quantitative, positivist approach of the past chapters. It is less concerned with numbers, hypotheses, and causality and more concerned with words, norms and values, and meaning.

Key Terms

bar chart
bivariate statistics
body of a table
cell of a table
code sheets
codebook
contingency cleaning
contingency table
control variable
covariation
cross-tabulation
curvilinear relationship
descriptive statistics
direct entry method
elaboration paradigm
explanation pattern
frequency distribution
frequency polygon
independence
interpretation pattern
level of statistical significance
linear relationship
marginals
mean
median
mode
normal distribution
partials
percentile
pie chart
possible code cleaning
range
replication pattern
scattergram
skewed distribution
specification pattern
standard deviation
statistical significance
suppressor variable pattern
Type I error
Type II error
univariate statistics
z-score

Endnotes

1. Note that coding sex as 1 = Male, 2 = Female, or as 0 = Male, 1 = Female, or reversing the sex for numbers is arbitrary. The only reason numbers are used instead of letters (e.g., *M* and *F*) is because many computer programs work best with all numbers. Sometimes coding data as a zero can

create confusion, so the number 1 is usually the lowest value.

2. There are other statistics to measure a special kind of mean for ordinal data and for other special situations, which are beyond the level of discussion in this book.

3. For a discussion of the elaboration paradigm and its history, see Babbie (1998:393–401) and Rosenberg (1968).

4. In formal hypothesis testing, researchers test the *null hypothesis*. They usually want to reject the null because rejection of the null indirectly supports the alternative hypothesis to the null, the one they deduced from theory as a tentative explanation.

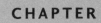

Field Research

INTRODUCTION

This chapter and the two that follow shift from the quantitative style of the past several chapters to the qualitative research style. The qualitative and the quantitative styles can differ a great deal. This chapter describes field research, also called *ethnography* or *participant-observation research*. It is a qualitative style in which a researcher directly observes and participates in small-scale social settings in the present time and in the researcher's home culture.

Many students are excited by field research because it involves hanging out with some exotic group of people. There are no cold mathematics or complicated statistics, and no abstract deductive hypotheses. Instead, there is direct, face-to-face social interaction with "real people" in a natural setting.

In field research, the individual researcher directly talks with and observes the people being studied. Through interaction over months or years, the researcher learns about them, their life histories, their hobbies and interests, and their habits, hopes, fears, and dreams. Meeting new people, developing friendships, and discovering new social worlds can be fun. It is also time consuming, emotionally draining, and sometimes physically dangerous.

Research Questions Appropriate for Field Research

Field research is appropriate when the research question involves learning about, understanding, or describing a group of interacting people. It is usually best when the question is: How do people do Y in the social world? or What is the social world of X like? It can be used when other methods (e.g., survey, experiments) are not practical, as in studying street gangs.

Field researchers study people in a location or setting. It has been used to study entire communities. Beginning field researchers should start with a relatively small group (30 or fewer) who interact with each other on a regular basis in a relatively fixed setting (e.g., a street corner, church, bar, beauty salon, baseball field, etc.).

In order to use consistent terminology, we can call the people who are studied in a field setting *members*. They are insiders or natives in the field and belong to a group, subculture, or social setting that the "outsider" field researcher wants to penetrate and learn about.

Field researchers have explored a wide variety of social settings, subcultures, and aspects of social life[1] (see Figure 11.1). Places my students have conducted successful short-term, small-scale field research studies include a beauty salon, day-care center, bakery, bingo parlor, bowling alley, church, coffee shop, laundromat, police dispatch office, nursing home, tattoo parlor, and weight room.

Ethnography and Ethnomethodology.   Two modern extensions of field research, ethnography and ethnomethodology, build on the social constructionist perspective. Each is redefining how field research is conducted. They are not yet the core of field research, so they are discussed only briefly here.

Ethnography comes from cultural anthropology.[2] *Ethno* means people or folk, and *graphy* refers to describing something. Thus *ethnography* means describing a culture and understanding another way of life from the native point of view. Ethnography assumes that people make inferences—that is, go beyond what is explicitly seen or said to what is meant or implied. People display their culture (what people think, ponder, or believe) through behavior (e.g., speech and actions) in specific social contexts. Displays of behavior do not give meaning; rather, meaning is inferred, or someone figures out meaning. Moving from what is heard or observed to what is actually meant is at the center of ethnography. For example, when a student is invited to a "kegger," the student infers that it is an informal party with other student-aged people at which beer will be served, based on his or her cultural knowledge. Cultural knowledge includes symbols, songs, sayings, facts, ways of behaving, and objects (e.g.,

FIGURE 11.1   Examples of Field Research Sites/Topics

Small-Scale Settings

Passengers in an airplane
Bars or taverns
Battered women's shelters
Camera clubs
Laundromats
Social movement organizations
Social welfare offices
Television stations
Waiting rooms

Community Settings

Retirement communities
Small towns
Urban ethnic communities
Working-class neighborhoods

Children's Activities

Children's playgrounds
Little League baseball
Youth in schools
Junior high girl groups

Occupations

Airline attendants
Artists
Cocktail waitresses
Dog catchers

Door-to-door salespersons
Factory workers
Gamblers
Medical students
Female strippers
Police officers
Restaurant chefs
Social workers
Taxi drivers

Deviance and Criminal Activity

Body/genital piercing and branding
Cults
Drug dealers and addicts
Hippies
Nude beaches
Occult groups
Prostitutes
Street gangs, motorcycle gangs
Street people, homeless shelters

Medical Settings and Medical Events

Death
Emergency rooms
Intensive care units
Pregnancy and abortion
Support groups for Alzheimer's caregivers

telephones, newspapers, etc.). We learn the culture by watching television, listening to parents, observing others, and the like.

Cultural knowledge includes both explicit knowledge, what we know and talk about, and tacit knowledge, what we rarely acknowledge. For example, *explicit knowledge* includes the social event (e.g., a "kegger"). Most people can easily describe what happens at one. *Tacit knowledge* includes the unspoken cultural norm for the proper distance to stand from others. People are generally unaware that they use this norm. They feel unease or discomfort when the norm is violated, but it is difficult to pinpoint the source of discomfort. Ethnographers describe the explicit and tacit cultural knowledge that members use. Their detailed descriptions and careful analysis take what is described apart and put it back together.

Ethnomethodology is a distinct approach developed in the 1960s, with its own unique terminology. It combines theory, philosophy, and method. Some do not consider it a part of sociology.

A simple definition of *ethnomethodology* is the study of commonsense knowledge. Ethnomethodologists study common sense by observing its creation and use in ongoing social interaction in natural settings. Ethnomethodology is a radical or extreme form of field research, based on phenomenological philosophy and a social constructionist approach. It involves the specialized, highly detailed analysis of micro-situations (e.g., transcripts of short conversations or videotapes of social interactions). Compared to other field research, it is more concerned about method and argues that research findings result as much from the method used as from the social life studied.

Ethnomethodology assumes that social meaning is fragile and fluid, not fixed, stable, or solid. Meaning is constantly being created and re-created in an ongoing process. For this reason, ethnomethodologists analyze language, including pauses and the context of speech. They assume that people "accomplish" commonsense understanding by using tacit social-cultural rules, and social interaction is a process of reality construction. People interpret everyday events by using cultural knowledge and clues from the social context. Ethnomethodologists examine how ordinary people in everyday settings apply tacit rules to make sense of social life (e.g., to know whether or not someone is joking).

Ethnomethodologists examine ordinary social interaction in great detail to identify the rules for constructing social reality and common sense, how these rules are applied, and how new rules are created. For example, they argue that standardized tests or survey interviews measure a person's ability to pick up implicit clues and apply common sense more than measuring objective facts.

THE LOGIC OF FIELD RESEARCH

What Is Field Research?

It is difficult to pin down a specific definition of *field research* because it is more of an orientation toward research than a fixed set of techniques to apply.[3] A field researcher uses various methods to obtain information. A *field researcher* is a resourceful, talented individual who has ingenuity and an ability to think on her or his feet while in the field.

Field research is based on naturalism, which is also used to study other phenomena (e.g., oceans, animals, plants, etc.). *Naturalism* involves observing ordinary events in natural settings, not in contrived, invented, or researcher-created settings. Research occurs in the field and outside the safe settings of an office, laboratory, or classroom.

A field researcher's goal is to examine social meanings and grasp multiple perspectives in natural social settings. He or she wants to get inside the meaning system of members and then return to an outside or research viewpoint. To do this, the researcher switches perspectives and looks at the setting from multiple points of view simultaneously.

Field research is usually conducted by a single individual, although small teams have been effective (see Box 11.1). The researcher is directly involved in and part of the social world studied, so his or her personal characteristics are relevant in research. The researcher's direct involvement in the field often has an emotional impact. Field research can be fun and exciting, but it can also disrupt one's personal life, physical security, or mental well-being. More than other types of social research, it reshapes friendships, family life, self-identity, and personal values.

Steps in a Field Research Project

Naturalism and direct involvement mean that field research is less structured than quantitative research. This makes it essential for a researcher to be well organized and prepared for the field. It also means that the steps of a project are not entirely predetermined but serve as an approximate guide or road map (see Box 11.2).

Box 11.1   **What Do Field Researchers Do?**

A field researcher does the following:

1. Observes ordinary events and everyday activities as they happen in natural settings, in addition to any unusual occurrences

2. Becomes directly involved with the people being studied and personally experiences the process of daily social life in the field setting

3. Acquires an insider's point of view while maintaining the analytic perspective or distance of an outsider

4. Uses a variety of techniques and social skills in a flexible manner as the situation demands

5. Produces data in the form of extensive written notes, as well as diagrams, maps, or pictures to provide very detailed descriptions

6. Sees events holistically (e.g., as a whole unit, not in pieces) and individually in their social context

7. Understands and develops empathy for members in a field setting, and does not just record "cold" objective facts

8. Notices both explicit (recognized, conscious, spoken) and tacit (less recognized, implicit, unspoken) aspects of culture

9. Observes ongoing social processes without upsetting, disrupting, or imposing an outside point of view

10. Copes with high levels of personal stress, uncertainty, ethical dilemmas, and ambiguity

Box 11.2   **Steps in Field Research**

1. Prepare oneself, read the literature, and defocus.

2. Select a field site and gain access to it.

3. Enter the field and establish social relations with members.

4. Adopt a social role, learn the ropes, and get along with members.

5. Watch, listen, and collect quality data.

6. Begin to analyze data and to generate and evaluate working hypotheses.

7. Focus on specific aspects of the setting and use theoretical sampling.

8. Conduct field interviews with member informants.

9. Disengage and physically leave the setting.

10. Complete the analyses and write the research report.

Note: There is no fixed percentage of time needed for each step. For a rough approximation, Junker (1960:12) suggested that, once in the field, the researcher should expect to spend approximately one-sixth of his or her time observing, one-third recording data, one-third of the time analyzing data, and one-sixth reporting results. Also see Denzin (1989:176) for eight steps of field research.

Flexibility. Field researchers rarely follow fixed steps. In fact, flexibility is a key advantage of field research, which lets a researcher shift direction and follow leads. Good field researchers recognize and seize opportunities, "play it by ear," and rapidly adjust to fluid social situations.

A field researcher does not begin with a set of methods to apply or explicit hypotheses to test. Rather, he or she chooses techniques on the basis of their value for providing information. In the beginning, the researcher expects little control over data and little focus. Once socialized to the setting, however, he or she focuses the inquiry and asserts control over the data.

Getting Organized in the Beginning. Human and personal factors can play a role in any research project, but they are crucial in field research. Field projects often begin with chance occurrences or a personal interest. Field researchers can begin with their own experiences, such as working at a job, having a hobby, or being a patient or an activist.

Field researchers use the skills of careful looking and listening, short-term memory, and regular writing. Before entering the field, a new researcher practices observing the ordinary details of situations and writing them down. Attention to details and short-term memory can improve with practice. Likewise, keeping a daily diary or personal journal is good practice for writing field notes.

As with all social research, reading the scholarly literature helps the researcher learn concepts, potential pitfalls, data collection methods, and techniques for resolving conflicts. In addition, a field researcher finds diaries, novels, journalistic accounts, and autobiographies useful for gaining familiarity and preparing emotionally for the field.

Field research begins with a general topic, not specific hypotheses. A researcher does not get locked into any initial misconceptions. He or she needs to be well informed but open to discovering new ideas. Finding the right questions to ask about the field takes time.

A researcher first empties his or her mind of preconceptions. The researcher should move outside his or her comfortable social niche to experience as much as possible in the field without betraying a primary commitment to being a researcher.

Another preparation for field research is self-knowledge. A field researcher needs to know himself or herself and reflect on personal experiences. He or she can expect anxiety, self-doubt, frustration, and uncertainty in the field. Especially in the beginning, the researcher may feel that he or she is collecting the wrong data and may suffer emotional turmoil, isolation, and confusion. He or she often feels doubly marginal: an outsider in the field setting and also distant from friends, family, and other researchers.[4] The relevance of a researcher's emotional make-up, personal biography, and cultural experiences makes it important to be aware of his or her personal commitments and inner conflicts (see Box 11.3). Fieldwork can have a strong impact on a researcher's identity and outlook. Researchers may be personally transformed by the field experience. Some adopt new values, interests, and moral commitments, or change their religion or political ideology.[5]

CHOOSING A SITE AND GAINING ACCESS

Although a field research project does not proceed by fixed steps, some common concerns arise in the early stages. These include selecting a site and gaining access to the site, entering the field, learning the ropes, and developing rapport with members in the field.

Selecting a Site and Entering

Where to Observe. Field researchers talk about doing research on a setting, or *field site,* but this term is misleading. A site is the context in which events or activities occur, a socially defined territory with shifting boundaries. A social group may interact across several physical sites. For example, a college football team may interact on the playing field, in the locker room, in a dormitory, at a training camp, or at a local hangout. The team's field site includes all five locations.

The field site and research question are bound together, but choosing a site is not the same as focusing on a case for study. A *case* is a social relationship or activity; it can extend beyond the boundaries of the site and have links to other social settings. A researcher selects a site, then identifies cases to examine within it—for example, how football team members relate to authority figures.

Selecting a field site is an important decision, and researchers take notes on the site selection processes. Three factors are relevant when choosing a field research site: richness of data, unfamiliarity, and suitability.[6] Some sites are more likely than others to provide rich data. Sites that present a web of social relations, a variety of activities, and diverse events over time provide richer, more interesting data. Beginning

| Box 11.3 | **Field Research at a Country and Western Bar** |

Eliasoph (1998) conducted field research on several groups in a California community to understand how Americans avoid political expression. One was a social club. Eliasoph describes herself as an "urban, bicoastal, bespectacled, Jewish, Ph.D. candidate from a long line of communists, atheists, liberals, book-readers, ideologues, and arguers" (p. 270). The social club's world was very foreign to her. The social club, the Buffalos, centered on country and western music at a bar, the Silverado Club. She describes it:

The Silverado huddled on a vast, rutted parking lot on what was once wetlands and now was a truck stop, a mile and a half from Amargo's [town name] nuclear battleship station. Occasional gulleys of salt water cattails poked through the wide flat miles of paved malls and gas stations. Giant four-wheeled-drive vehicles filled the parking lot, making my miniature Honda look like a toy. . . . Inside the windowless Silverado, initial blinding darkness gave way to a huge Confederate flag pinned up behind the bandstand, the standard collection of neon beer signs and beer mirrors, men in cowboys hats, cowboys

shirts and jeans, women in curly perms and tiered flounces of lace or denim skirts, or jeans, and belts with their names embroidered in glitter on the back. (1998:92)

Eliasoph introduced herself as a student. During her two years of research, she endured smoke-filled rooms as well as expensive beer and bottled-water prices; attended a wedding and many dance lessons; and participated in countless conversations and heard many abusive sexist/racist jokes. She listened, asked questions, observed, and took notes in the bathroom. When she returned home after hours with club members, it was to a university crowd who had little understanding of the world she was studying. For them, witty conversation was central and being bored was to be avoided. The club members used more nonverbal than verbal communication and being bored, or sitting and doing nothing, was just fine. The research forced Eliasoph to reexamine her own views and tastes, which she had taken for granted.

field researchers should choose an unfamiliar setting. It is easier to see cultural events and social relations in a new site. When "casing" possible field sites, one must consider such practical issues as the researcher's time and skills, serious conflicts among people in the site, the researcher's personal characteristics and feelings, and access to parts of a site.

A researcher's ascriptive characteristics (e.g., age, gender, race) can limit access. Physical access to a site can be an issue. Sites are on a continuum, with open and public areas (e.g., public restaurants, airport waiting areas, etc.) at one end and closed and private settings (e.g., private firms, clubs, activities in a person's home, etc.) at the other. A researcher may find that he or she is not welcome or not allowed on the site, or there are legal and political barriers to access. Laws

and regulations in institutions (e.g., public schools, hospitals, prisons, etc.) restrict access. In addition, institutional review boards may limit field research on ethical grounds.

Level of Involvement. Field roles can be arranged on a continuum by the degree of detachment or involvement a researcher has with members. At one extreme is a detached outsider; at the other extreme is an intimately involved insider.

The field researcher's level of involvement depends on negotiations with members, specifics of the field setting, the researcher's personal comfort, and the particular role adopted in the field. Many move from outsider to insider levels with more time in the field. Each level has its advantages and disadvantages.

Different field researchers advocate different levels of involvement.

Roles at the outsider end of the continuum reduce the time needed for acceptance, make overrapport less an issue, and can sometimes help members open up. They facilitate detachment and protect the researcher's self-identity. A researcher feels marginal. Although there is less risk of "going native," he or she is also less likely to know an insider's experience and misinterpretation is more likely. To really understand social meaning for those being studied, the field researcher must participate in the setting, as others do.

By contrast, roles at the insider end of the continuum facilitate empathy and sharing of a member's experience. The goal of fully experiencing the intimate social world of a member is achieved. Nevertheless, a lack of distance from, too much sympathy for, or overinvolvement with members is likely. A researcher's reports may be questioned, data gathering is difficult, there can be a dramatic impact on the researcher's self, and the distance needed for analysis may be hard to attain.

Gatekeepers.   A gatekeeper is someone with the formal or informal authority to control access to a site.[7] It can be the thug on the corner, an administrator of a hospital, or the owner of a business. Informal public areas (e.g., sidewalks, public waiting rooms, etc.) rarely have gatekeepers; formal organizations have authorities from whom permission must be obtained.

Field researchers expect to negotiate with gatekeepers and bargain for access. The gatekeepers may not appreciate the need for conceptual distance or ethical balance. The researcher must set nonnegotiable limits to protect research integrity. If there are many restrictions initially, a researcher can often reopen negotiations later, and gatekeepers may forget their initial demands as trust develops. It is ethically and politically astute to call on gatekeepers. Researchers do not expect them to listen to research concerns or care about the findings, except insofar as these findings might provide evidence for someone to criticize them.

Dealing with gatekeepers is a recurrent issue as a researcher enters new levels or areas. In addition, a gatekeeper can shape the direction of research. In some sites, gatekeeper approval creates a stigma that inhibits the cooperation of members. For example, prisoners may not be cooperative if they know that the prison warden gave approval to the researcher.

Strategy for Entering

Entering a field site requires having a flexible strategy or plan of action, negotiating access and relations with members, and deciding how much to disclose about the research to field members or gatekeepers.

Planning.   Entering and gaining access to a field site is a process that depends on commonsense judgment and social skills. Field sites usually have different levels or areas, and entry is an issue for each. Entry is more analogous to peeling the layers of an onion than to opening a door. Moreover, bargains and promises of entry may not remain stable over time. A researcher needs fallback plans or may have to return later for renegotiation. Because the specific focus of research may not emerge until later in the research process or may change, it is best to avoid being locked into specifics by gatekeepers.

Negotiation.   Social relations are negotiated and formed throughout the process of fieldwork.[8] Negotiation occurs with each new member until a stable relationship develops to gain access, develop trust, obtain information, and reduce hostile reactions. The researcher expects to negotiate and explain what he or she is doing over and over in the field (see Normalizing Social Research later in the chapter).

Deviant groups and elites often require special negotiations for gaining access. To gain access to deviant subcultures, field researchers have used contacts from the researcher's private life, gone to social welfare or law-enforcement agencies where the deviants are processed, advertised for volunteers, offered a service (e.g., counseling) in exchange for access, or gone to a location where deviants hang out and joined a group.

Disclosure. A researcher must decide how much to reveal about himself or herself and the research project. Disclosing one's personal life, hobbies, interests, and background can build trust and close relationships, but the researcher will also lose privacy, and he or she needs to ensure that the focus remains on events in the field.

A researcher also decides how much to disclose about the research project. Disclosure ranges on a continuum from fully covert research, in which no one in the field is aware that research is taking place, to the opposite end, where everyone knows the specifics of the research project. The degree and timing of disclosure depends on a researcher's judgment and particulars in the setting. Disclosure may unfold over time as the researcher feels more secure.

Researchers disclose the project to gatekeepers and others unless there is a good reason for not doing so, such as the presence of gatekeepers who would seriously limit or inhibit research for illegitimate reasons (e.g., to hide graft or corruption). Even in these cases, a researcher may disclose his or her identity as a researcher, but may pose as one who seems submissive, harmless, and interested in nonthreatening issues.

Learning the Ropes

After a field site is selected and access obtained, researchers must learn the ropes, develop rapport with members, adopt a role in the setting, and maintain social relations. Before confronting such issues, the researcher should ask: How will I present myself? What does it mean for me to be a "measurement instrument"? How can I assume an "attitude of strangeness"?

Presentation of Self. People explicitly and implicitly present themselves to others. We display who we are—the type of person we are or would like to be—through our physical appearance, what we say, and how we act. The presentation of self sends a symbolic message. It may be, "I'm a serious, hard-working student," "I'm a warm and caring person," "I'm a cool jock," or "I'm a rebel and party animal." Many selves are possible, and presentations of selves can differ depending on the occasion.

A field researcher is conscious of the presentation of self in the field. For example, how should he or she dress in the field? The best guide is to respect both oneself and those being studied. Do not overdress so as to offend or stand out, but copying the dress of those being studied is not always necessary. A professor who studies street people does not have to dress or act like one; dressing and acting informally is sufficient. Likewise, more formal dress and professional demeanor are required when studying corporate executives or top officials.

A researcher must be aware that self-presentation will influence field relations to some degree. It is difficult to present a highly deceptive front or to present oneself in a way that deviates sharply from the person one is ordinarily.

Researcher as Instrument. The researcher is the instrument for measuring field data. This has two implications. First, it puts pressure on the researcher to be alert and sensitive to what happens in the field and to be disciplined about recording data. Second, it has personal consequences. Fieldwork involves social relationships and personal feelings. Field researchers are flexible about what to include as data and admit their own subjective insights and feelings. Personal, subjective experiences are part of field data. They are valuable both in themselves and for interpreting events in the field. Instead of trying to be objective and eliminate personal reactions, field researchers treat their feelings toward field events as data.

Field research can heighten a researcher's awareness of personal feelings. For example, a researcher may not be fully aware of personal feelings about nudity until he or she is in a nudist colony, or about personal possessions until he or she is in a setting where others "borrow" many items. The researcher's own surprise, indignation, or questioning then may become an opportunity for reflection and insight.

An Attitude of Strangeness.   It is hard to recognize what we are very close to. The everyday world we inhabit is filled with thousands of details. If we paid attention to everything all the time, we would suffer from severe information overload. We manage by ignoring much of what is around us and by engaging in habitual thinking. Unfortunately, we fail to see the familiar as distinctive, and assume that others experience reality just as we do. We tend to treat our own way of living as natural or normal.

Field research in familiar surroundings is difficult because of a tendency to be blinded by the familiar. By studying other cultures, researchers encounter dramatically different assumptions about what is important and how things are done. This confrontation of cultures, or culture shock, has two benefits: It makes it easier to see cultural elements and it facilitates self-discovery. Researchers adopt the attitude of strangeness to gain these benefits. The *attitude of strangeness* means questioning and noticing ordinary details or looking at the ordinary through the eyes of a stranger. Strangeness helps a researcher overcome the boredom of observing ordinary details. It helps him or her see the ordinary in a new way, one that reveals aspects of the setting of which members are not consciously aware. A field researcher adopts both a stranger's and an insider's point of view.

People rarely recognize customs they take for granted. For example, when someone gives us a gift, we say thank you and praise the gift. By contrast, gift-giving customs in many cultures include complaining that the gift is inadequate. The attitude of strangeness helps make the tacit culture visible—for example, that gift givers expect to hear "Thank you" and "The gift is nice," and become upset otherwise.

Strangeness also encourages a researcher to reconsider his or her own social world. Immersion in a different setting breaks old habits of thought and action. He or she finds reflection and introspection easier and more intense when encountering the unfamiliar, whether it is a different culture or a familiar culture seen through a stranger's eyes.

Building Rapport

A field researcher builds rapport by getting along with members in the field. He or she forges a friendly relationship, shares the same language, and laughs and cries with members. This is a step toward obtaining an understanding of members and moving beyond understanding to empathy—that is, seeing and feeling events from another's perspective.

It is not always easy to build rapport. The social world is not all in harmony, with warm, friendly people. A setting may contain fear, tension, and conflict. Members may be unpleasant, untrustworthy, or untruthful; they may do things that disturb or disgust a researcher. An experienced researcher is prepared for a range of events and relationships. He or she may find, however, that it is impossible to penetrate a setting or get really close to members. Settings where cooperation, sympathy, and collaboration are impossible require different techniques.[9]

Charm and Trust.   A field researcher needs social skills and personal charm to build rapport. Trust, friendly feelings, and being well liked facilitate communication and help him or her to understand the inner feelings of others. There is no magical way to do this. Showing a genuine concern for and interest in others, being honest, and sharing feelings are good strategies, but they are not foolproof. It depends on the specific setting and members.

Many factors affect trust and rapport—how a researcher presents himself or herself; the role he or she chooses for the field; and the events that encourage, limit, or make it impossible to achieve trust. Trust is not gained once and for all. It is a developmental process built up over time through many social nuances (e.g., sharing of personal experiences, story telling, gestures, hints, facial expressions). It is constantly re-created and seems easier to lose once it has been built up than to gain in the first place.

Establishing trust is important, but it does not ensure that all information will be revealed. It may be limited to specific areas. For example, trust can be built up regarding financial matters but not to disclose intimate dating behavior. Trust may have to be created anew in each area of inquiry; it requires constant reaffirmation.

Understanding. Rapport helps field researchers understand members, but understanding is a precondition for greater depth, not an end in itself. It slowly develops in the field as the researcher overcomes an initial bewilderment with a new or unusual language and system of social meaning. Once he or she attains an understanding of the member's point of view, the next step is to learn how to think and act within a member's perspective. This is *empathy,* or adopting another's perspective. Empathy does not necessarily mean sympathy, agreement, or approval; it means feeling things as another does. Rapport helps create understanding and ultimately empathy, and the development of empathy facilitates greater rapport.

RELATIONS IN THE FIELD

You play many social roles in daily life—daughter/son, student, customer, sports fan—and maintain social relations with others. You choose some roles and others are structured for you. Few have a choice but to play the role of son or daughter. Some roles are formal (e.g., bank teller, police chief, etc.), others are informal (flirt, elder statesperson, buddy, etc.). You can switch roles, play multiple roles, and play a role in a particular way. Field researchers play roles in

the field. In addition, they learn the ropes and maintain relations with members.

Roles in the Field

Preexisting versus Created Roles. At times, a researcher adopts an existing role. Some existing roles provide access to all areas of the site, the ability to observe and interact with all members, the freedom to move around, and a way to balance the requirements of researcher and member. At other times, a researcher creates a new role or modifies an existing one. Duneier (1999), in his four-year study of New York City street vendors, assumed the role of browser, customer, and even magazine vendor.

Limits on the Role Chosen. The field roles open to a researcher are affected by ascriptive factors and physical appearance. He or she can change some aspects of appearance, such as dress or hairstyle, but not ascriptive features such as age, race, gender, and attractiveness. Nevertheless, such factors can be important in gaining access and can restrict the available roles. For example, Gurney (1985) reported that being a female in a male-dominated setting required extra negotiations and "hassles." Nevertheless, her gender provided insights and created situations that would have been absent with a male researcher.

Since many roles are sex-typed, gender is an important consideration. Female researchers often have more difficulty when the setting is perceived as dangerous or seamy and where males are in control (e.g., police work, fire fighting, etc.). They may be shunned or pushed into limiting gender stereotypes (e.g., "sweet kid," "mascot," "loud mouth," etc.).

New researchers face embarrassment, experience discomfort, and are overwhelmed by the details in the field. For example, in her study of U.S. relocation camps for Japanese Americans during World War II, respected field researcher Rosalie Wax (1971) reported that she endured the discomfort of 120-degree Fahrenheit temperatures, filthy and dilapidated living conditions, dysentery, and mosquitoes. She felt isolated, she cried a lot, and she gained 30 pounds from compulsive eating. After months in the field, she thought she was a total failure; she was distrusted by members and got into fights with the camp administration.

Maintaining a "marginal" status is stressful; it is difficult to be an outsider who is not fully involved, especially when studying settings full of intense feelings (e.g., political campaigns, religious conversions, etc.). The loneliness and isolation of fieldwork may combine with the desire to develop rapport and empathy to cause overinvolvement. A researcher may "go native" and drop the professional researcher's role to become a full member of the group being studied. Or the researcher may feel guilt about learning intimate details as members drop their guard, and may come to overidentify with members.

Normalizing Social Research. A field researcher not only observes and investigates members in the field but is observed and investigated by members as well. In overt field research, members are usually initially uncomfortable with the presence of a researcher. Most are unfamiliar with field research and fail to distinguish between sociologists, psychologists, counselors, and social workers. They may see the researcher as an outside critic or spy, or as a savior or all-knowing expert.

An overt field researcher must *normalize social research*—that is, help members redefine social research from something unknown and threatening to something normal and predictable. He or she can help members manage research by presenting his or her own biography, explaining field research a little at a time, appearing nonthreatening, or accepting minor deviance in the setting (e.g., minor violations of official rules).

Maintaining Relations

Social Relations. With time, a field researcher develops and modifies social relationships.

Members who are cool at first may warm up later. Or they may put on a front of initial friendliness, and their fears and suspicions surface only later. A researcher is in a delicate position. Early in a project, when not yet fully aware of everything about a field site, the researcher does not form close relationships because circumstances may change. Yet, if he or she does develop close friends, they can become allies who will defend the researcher's presence and help him or her gain access.

A field researcher monitors how his or her actions or appearance affects members. For example, a physically attractive researcher who interacts with members of the opposite sex may encounter crushes, flirting, and jealousy. He or she develops an awareness of these field relations and learns to manage them.

In addition to developing social relationships, a field researcher must be able to break or withdraw from relationships as well. Ties with one member may have to be broken in order to forge ties with others or to explore other aspects of the setting. As with the end of any friendly relationship, the emotional pain of social withdrawal can affect both the researcher and the member. The researcher must balance social sensitivity and the research goals.

Small Favors. Exchange relationships develop in the field, in which small tokens or favors, including deference and respect, are exchanged. A researcher may gain acceptance by helping out in small ways. Exchange helps when access to sensitive issues is limited. A researcher may offer small favors but not burden members by asking for return favors. As the researcher and members share experiences and see each other again, members recall the favors and reciprocate by allowing access. For example, Duneier (1999) used the small favor of watching the tables of street vendors when they had to leave for a short time, such as to use the bathroom.

Conflicts in the Field. Fights, conflict, and disagreements can erupt in the field, or a researcher may study groups with opposing positions. In such situations, the researcher will feel pressure to take sides and will be tested to see if he or she can be trusted. In such occasions, a researcher usually stays on the neutral sidelines and walks a tightrope between opposing sides. This is because once he or she becomes aligned with one side, the researcher will cut off access to the other side. In addition, he or she will see the situation from only one point of view.

Appearing Interested. Field researchers maintain an *appearance of interest* in the field. An experienced researcher appears to be interested in and involved with field events by statements and behaviors (e.g., facial expression, going for coffee, organizing a party, etc.) even if he or she is not truly interested. This is because field relations may be disrupted if the researcher appears to be bored or distracted. Putting up such a temporary front of involvement is a common small deception in daily life and is part of being polite.

Of course, selective inattention (i.e., not staring or appearing not to notice) is also part of acting polite. If a person makes a social mistake (e.g., accidentally uses an incorrect word, passes gas, etc.), the polite thing to do is to ignore it. Selective inattention is used in fieldwork, as well. It gives an alert researcher an opportunity to learn by casually eavesdropping on conversations or observing events not meant to be public.

OBSERVING AND COLLECTING DATA

This section looks at how to get good qualitative field data. Field data are what the researcher experiences and remembers, and what are recorded in field notes and become available for systematic analysis.

Watching and Listening

Observing. In the field, researchers pay attention, watch, and listen carefully. They use all the senses, noticing what is seen, heard, smelled, tasted, or touched. The researcher becomes an instrument that absorbs all sources of information.

A field researcher carefully scrutinizes the physical setting to capture its atmosphere. He or she asks: What is the color of the floor, walls, ceiling? How large is the room? Where are the windows and doors? How is the furniture arranged, and what is its condition (e.g., new or old and worn, dirty or clean)? What type of lighting is there? Are there signs, paintings, plants? What are the sounds or smells?

Why bother with such details? You may have noticed that stores and restaurants often plan lighting, colors, and piped-in music to create a certain atmosphere. Maybe you know that used-car sales people spray a new-car scent into cars or that shops in shopping malls intentionally send out the odor of freshly made cookies. These subtle, unconscious signals influence human behavior.

Observing in field research is often detailed, tedious work. Instead of the quick flash, motivation arises out of a deep curiosity about the details. Good field researchers are intrigued about details that reveal "what's going on here" through careful listening and watching. Field researchers believe that the core of social life is communicated through the mundane, trival, everyday minutia. This is what people often overlook, but field researchers need to learn how to notice.

In addition to physical surroundings, a field researcher observes people and their actions, noting each person's observable physical characteristics: age, sex, race, and stature. People socially interact differently depending on whether another person is 18, 40, or 70 years old; male or female; White or non-White; short and frail or tall, heavyset, and muscular. When noting such characteristics, the researcher is included. For example, an attitude of strangeness heightens sensitivity to a group's racial composition. A researcher who ignores the racial composition of a group of Whites in a multiracial society because he or she too is White is being racially insensitive.

The researcher records such details because something of significance *might* be revealed. It is better to err by including everything than to ignore potentially significant details. For example, "The tall, White muscular 19-year-old male sprinted into the brightly lit room just as the short, overweight Black woman in her sixties eased into a battered chair" says much more than "One person entered, another sat down."

A field researcher notes aspects of physical appearance such as neatness, dress, and hairstyle because they express messages that can affect social interactions. People spend a great deal of time and money selecting clothes, styling and combing hair, grooming with make-up, shaving, ironing clothes, and using deodorant or perfumes. These are part of their presentation of self. Even people who do not groom, shave, or wear deodorant present themselves and send a symbolic message by their appearance. No one dresses or looks "normal." Such a statement suggests that a researcher is not seeing the social world through the eyes of a stranger or is insensitive to social signals.

Behavior is also significant. A field researcher notices where people sit or stand, the pace at which they walk, and their nonverbal communication. People express social information, feelings, and attitudes through nonverbal communication, including gestures, facial expressions, and how one stands or sits (standing stiffly, sitting in a slouched position, etc.). People express relationships by how they position themselves in a group and through eye contact. A researcher may read the social communication of people by noting that they are standing close together, looking relaxed, and making eye contact.

A field researcher also notices the context in which events occur: Who was present? Who just arrived or left the scene? Was the room hot and stuffy? Such details may help the researcher assign meaning and understand why an event occurred. If they are not noticed, the details are lost, as is a full understanding of the event.

Serendipity is important in field research. Many times, a field researcher does not know the relevance of what he or she is observing until later. This has two implications. First is the importance of keen observation and excellent notes at all times, even when "nothing seems to be happening." Second is the importance of looking back over time and learning to appreciate wait time. Most field researchers say that they spend a lot of time "waiting." Novice field researchers get frustrated with the amount of time they seem to "waste," either waiting for other people or waiting for events to occur.

A field researcher needs must be attuned to the rhythms of the setting, operate on other people's schedules, and observe how events occur within their own flow of time. Wait time is not always wasted time. Wait time is time for reflection, for observing details, for developing social relations, for building rapport, and for becoming a familiar sight to people in the field setting. Wait time also displays that a researcher is committed and serious; perseverance is a significant trait field researchers need to cultivate. The researcher may be impatient to get in, get the research over, and get on with his or her "real life" but for the people in the field site, this *is* real life. The researcher should subordinate his or her personal wants to the demands of the field site.

Listening.   A field researcher listens carefully to phrases, accents, and incorrect grammar, listening both to *what* is said and *how* it is said or what was implied. For example, people often use phrases such as "you know" or "of course" or "et cetera." A field researcher knows the meaning behind such phrases. He or she can try to hear everything, but listening is difficult when many conversations occur at once or when eavesdropping. Luckily, significant events and themes usually recur.

Taking Notes

Most field research data are in the form of field notes. Full field notes can contain maps, diagrams, photographs, interviews, tape recordings, videotapes, memos, artifacts or objects from the field, notes jotted in the field, and detailed notes written away from the field. A field researcher expects to fill many notebooks, or the equivalent in computer memory. He or she may spend more time writing notes than being in the field. Some researchers produce 40 single-spaced pages of notes for three hours of observation. With practice, even a new field researcher can produce several pages of notes for each hour in the field.

Writing notes is often boring, tedious work that requires self-discipline. The notes contain extensive descriptive detail drawn from memory. A researcher makes it a daily habit or compulsion to write notes immediately after leaving the field. The notes must be neat and organized because the researcher will return to them over and over again. Once written, the notes are private and valuable. A researcher treats them with care and protects confidentiality. Field notes may be of interest to hostile parties, blackmailers, or legal officials, so some researchers write field notes in code.

A researcher's state of mind, level of attention, and conditions in the field affect note taking. He or she will usually begin with relatively short one- to three-hour periods in the field before writing notes.

Types of Field Notes. Field researchers take notes in many ways.[10] The recommendations here (also see Box 11.4) are suggestions. Full field notes have several types or levels. Five levels will be described. It is usually best to keep all the notes for an observation period together and to distinguish types of notes by separate pages. Some researchers include inferences with direct observations if they are set off by a visible device such as brackets or colored ink. The quantity of notes varies across types. For example, six hours in the field might result in 1 page of jotted notes, 40 pages of direct observation, 5 pages of researcher inference, and 2 pages total for methodological, theoretical, and personal notes.

Jotted Notes. It is nearly impossible to take good notes in the field. Even a known observer

in a public setting looks strange when furiously writing. More important, when looking down and writing, the researcher cannot see and hear what is happening. The attention given to note writing is taken from field observation where it belongs. The specific setting determines whether any notes in the field can be taken. The researcher may be able to write, and members may expect it, or he or she may have to be secretive (e.g., go to the restroom).

Jotted notes are written in the field. They are short, temporary memory triggers such as words, phrases, or drawings taken inconspicuously, often scribbled on any convenient item (e.g., napkin, matchbook). They are incorporated into direct observation notes but are never substituted for them.

Direct Observation Notes. The basic source of field data are notes a researcher writes immediately after leaving the field, which he or she can add to later. The notes should be ordered chronologically with the date, time, and place on each entry. They serve as a detailed description of what the researcher heard and saw in concrete, specific terms. To the extent possible, they are an exact recording of the particular words, phrases, or actions.

A researcher's memory improves with practice. A new researcher can soon remember exact phrases from the field. Verbatim statements should be written with double quote marks to distinguish them from paraphrases. Dialogue accessories (nonverbal communication, props, tone, speed, volume, gestures) should be recorded as well. A researcher records what was actually said and does not clean it up; notes include ungrammatical speech, slang, and misstatements (e.g., write, "Uh, I'm goin' home, Sal," not "I am going home, Sally").

A researcher puts concrete details in notes, not summaries. For example, instead of, "We talked about sports," he or she writes, "Anthony argued with Sam and Jason. He said that the Cubs would win next week because they traded for a new shortstop, Chiappetta. He also said

Box 11.4   Recommendations for Taking Field Notes

1. Record notes as soon as possible after each period in the field, and do not talk with others until observations are recorded.

2. Begin the record of each field visit with a new page, with the date and time noted.

3. Use jotted notes only as a temporary memory aid, with key words or terms, or the first and last things said.

4. Use wide margins to make it easy to add to notes at any time. Go back and add to the notes if you remember something later.

5. Plan to type notes and keep each level of notes separate so it will be easy to go back to them later.

6. Record events in the order in which they occurred, and note how long they last (e.g., a 15-minute wait, a one-hour ride).

7. Make notes as concrete, complete, and comprehensible as possible.

8. Use frequent paragraphs and quotation marks. Exact recall of phrases is best, with double quotes; use single quotes for paraphrasing.

9. Record small talk or routines that do not appear to be significant at the time; they may become important later.

10. "Let your feelings flow" and write quickly without worrying about spelling or "wild ideas." Assume that no one else will see the notes, but use pseudonyms.

11. Never substitute tape recordings completely for field notes.

12. Include diagrams or maps of the setting, and outline your own movements and those of others during the period of observation.

13. Include the researcher's own words and behavior in the notes. Also record emotional feelings and private thoughts in a separate section.

14. Avoid evaluative summarizing words. Instead of "The sink looked disgusting," say, "The sink was rust-stained and looked as if it had not been cleaned in a long time. Pieces of food and dirty dishes looked as if they had been piled in it for several days."

15. Reread notes periodically and record ideas generated by the rereading.

16. Always make one or more backup copies, keep them in a locked location, and store the copies in different places in case of fire.

---

that the team was better than the Mets, who he thought had inferior infielders. He cited last week's game where the Cubs won against Boston by 8 to 3." A researcher notes who was present, what happened, where it occurred, when, and under what circumstances. New researchers may not take notes because "nothing important happened." An experienced researcher knows that events when "nothing happened" can reveal a lot. For example, members may express feelings and organize experience into folk categories even in trivial conversations.

Researcher Inference Notes. A field researcher listens to members in order to "climb into their skin" or "walk in their shoes." This involves a three-step process. The researcher listens without applying analytical categories; he or she compares what is heard to what was heard at other times and to what others say; then the researcher applies his or her own interpretation to infer or figure out what it means. In ordinary interaction, we do all three steps simultaneously and jump quickly to our own inferences. A field researcher learns to look and listen without inferring or imposing an interpretation. His or her observations without inferences go into *direct observation notes.*

A researcher records inferences in a separate section that is keyed to direct observations. People never see social relationships, emotions, or meaning. They see specific physical actions and hear words, then use background cultural knowledge, clues from the context, and what is done or said to assign social meaning. For example, one does not see *love* or *anger;* one sees and hears specific actions (red face, loud voice, wild gestures, obscenities) and draw inferences from them (the person is angry).

People constantly infer social meaning on the basis of what they see and hear, but not always correctly. For example, my niece visited me and accompanied me to a store to buy a kite. The clerk at the cash register smiled and asked her whether she and her "Daddy" (looking at me) were going to fly the kite that day. The clerk observed our interaction, then inferred a father/daughter, not an uncle/niece relationship. She saw and heard a male adult and a female child, but she inferred the social meaning incorrectly.

A researcher keeps inferred meaning separate from direct observation because the meaning of actions is not always self-evident. Sometimes, people try to deceive others. For example, an unrelated couple register at a motel as Mr. and Mrs. Smith. More frequently, social behavior is ambiguous or multiple meanings are possible. For example, I see a White male and female, both in their late twenties, get out of a car and enter a restaurant together. They sit at a table, order a meal, and talk with serious expressions in hushed tones, sometimes leaning forward to hear each other. As they get up to leave, the woman, who has a sad facial expression and appears ready to cry, is briefly hugged by the male. They then leave together. Did I witness a couple breaking up, two friends discussing a third, two people trying to decide what to do because they have discovered that their spouses are

having an affair with each other, or a brother and sister whose father just died?

Analytic Notes. Researchers make many decisions about how to proceed while in the field. Some acts are planned (e.g., to conduct an interview, to observe a particular activity, etc.) and others seem to occur almost out of thin air. Field researchers keep methodological ideas in analytic notes to record their plans, tactics, ethical and procedural decisions, and self-critiques of tactics.

Theory emerges in field research during data collection and is clarified when a researcher reviews field notes. Analytic notes have a running account of a researcher's attempts to give meaning to field events. He or she thinks out loud in the notes by suggesting links between ideas, creating hypotheses, proposing conjectures, and developing new concepts.

Analytic memos are part of the theoretical notes. They are systematic digressions into theory, where a researcher elaborates on ideas in depth, expands on ideas while still in the field, and modifies or develops more complex theory by rereading and thinking about the memos.

Personal Notes. As discussed earlier, personal feelings and emotional reactions become part of the data and color what a researcher sees or hears in the field. A researcher keeps a section of notes that is like a personal diary. He or she records personal life events and feelings in it ("I'm tense today. I wonder if it's because of the fight I had yesterday with Chris," "I've got a headache on this gloomy, overcast day").

Personal notes serve three functions: They provide an outlet for a researcher and a way to cope with stress; they are a source of data about personal reactions; and they give him or her a way to evaluate direct observation or inference notes when the notes are later reread. For example, if the researcher was in a good mood during observations, it might color what he or she observed (see Figure 11.2).

FIGURE 11.2   Types of Field Notes

Direct Observation	Inference	Analytic	Personal Journal
Sunday, October 4. Kay's Kafe 3:00 pm. Large White male in mid-40s, overweight, enters. He wears worn brown suit. He is alone; sits at booth #2. Kay comes by, asks, "What'll it be?" Man says, "Coffee, black for now." She leaves and he lights cigarette and reads menu. 3:15 pm. Kay turns on radio.	Kay seems friendly today, humming. She becomes solemn and watchful. I think she puts on the radio when nervous.	Women are afraid of men who come in alone since the robbery.	It is raining. I am feeling comfortable with Kay but am bored today.

Maps and Diagrams. Field researchers often make maps and draw diagrams or pictures of the features of a field site. This serves two purposes: It helps a researcher organize events in the field and it helps convey a field site to others. For example, a researcher observing a bar with 15 stools may draw and number 15 circles to simplify recording (e.g., "Yosuke came in and sat on stool 12; Phoebe was already on stool 10"). Field researchers find three types of maps helpful: spatial, social, and temporal. The first helps orient the data; the latter two are preliminary forms of data analysis. A *spatial map* locates people, equipment, and the like in terms of geographical physical space to show where activities occur (Figure 11.3A). A *social map* shows the number or variety of people and the arrangements among them of power, influence, friendship, division of labor, and so on (Figure 11.3B). A *temporal map* shows the ebb and flow of people, goods, services, and communications, or schedules (Figure 11.3C).

Machine Recordings to Supplement Memory. Tape recorders and videotapes can be helpful supplements in field research. They never substitute for field notes or a researcher's presence in the field. They cannot be introduced into all field sites, and can be used only after a researcher develops rapport. Recorders and videotapes provide a close approximation to what occurred and a permanent record that others can review. They serve as "jotted notes" to help a researcher recall events and observe what is easy to miss. Nevertheless, these items can create disruption and an increased awareness of surveillance. Researchers who rely on them must address associated problems (e.g., ensure that batteries are fresh and there are enough blank tapes). Also, relistening to or viewing tapes can be time consuming. For example, it may take over 100 hours to listen to 50 hours recorded in the field. Transcriptions of tape are expensive and not always accurate; they do not always convey subtle contextual meanings or mumbled words. Duneier (1999) had a tape recorder on all the time in his study of New York City street vendors. He made others aware of the machine and took reponsibility for what behaviors he focused on, and he left the machine visible. The taping may have created some distortion but it also provided a record of everyday routines. He also had a collaborator who took a large collection of photographs of his field site and informants, which helped him to see things differently.

FIGURE 11.3   Types of Maps Used in Field Research

A Spatial Map

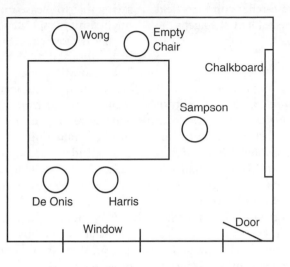

B Social Map

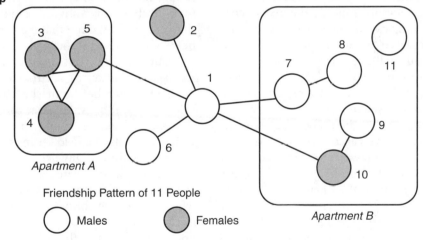

Friendship Pattern of 11 People

○ Males   ● Females

C Temporal Map

Day of Week, Buzz's Bar

	Mon	Tue	Wed	Thr	Fri	Sat
Open 10:00	Old Drunks	Old Drunks	Old Drunks	Old Drunks	Skip Work or Leave Early	Going to Fish
5:00	Football Watchers	Neighbors and Bridge Players	Softball Team (All-Male Night)	Young Crowd	Loud Music, Mixed Crowd	Loners and No Dates
Close 1:00						

Interview Notes.   If a researcher conducts field interviews (to be discussed), he or she keeps the interview notes separate.

Data Quality

Reliability in Field Research.   The reliability of field data addresses the question: Are researcher observations about a member or field event internally and externally consistent? *Internal consistency* refers to whether the data are plausible given all that is known about a person or event, eliminating common forms of human deception. In other words, do the pieces fit together into a coherent picture? For example, are a member's actions consistent over time and in different social contexts? *External consistency* is achieved by verifying or cross-checking observations with other, divergent sources of data. In other words, does it all fit into the overall context? For example, can others verify what a researcher observed about a person? Does other evidence confirm the researcher's observations?

Reliability in field research also includes what is not said or done, but is expected. Such omissions can be significant but are difficult to detect. For example, when observing a cashier end her shift, a researcher notices that the money in the cash drawer is not counted. He or she may notice the omission only if other cashiers always count the money at the end of the shift.

Reliability in field research depends on a researcher's insight, awareness, suspicions, and questions. He or she looks at members and events from different angles (legal, economic, political, personal) and mentally asks questions: Where does the money come from for that? What do those people do all day?

Field researchers depend on what members tell them. This makes the credibility of members and their statements part of reliability. To check member credibility, a researcher asks: Does the person have a reason to lie? Is she in a position to know that? What are the person's values and how might that shape what she says? Is he just

saying that to please me? Is there anything that might limit his spontaneity?

Field researchers take subjectivity and context into account as they evaluate credibility. They know that a person's statements or actions are affected by subjective perceptions. Statements are made from a particular point of view and colored by an individual's experiences. Instead of evaluating each statement to see if it is true, a field researcher finds statements useful in themselves. Even inaccurate statements and actions can be revealing from a researcher's perspective.

As mentioned before, actions and statements are shaped by the context in which they appear. What is said in one setting may differ in other contexts. For example, when asked "Do you dance?" a member may say no in a public setting full of excellent dancers, but yes in a semiprivate setting with few good dancers and different music. It is not that the member is lying but that the answer is shaped by the context.

Duneier (1999) has warned us to avoid the *ethnographic fallacy*. It occurs when a field researcher takes what he or she observes at face value, does not question what people in a field site say, and focuses solely on the immediate concrete details of a field setting while ignoring larger social forces. Duneier noted that he tried to avoid the fallacy by being aware of larger social context and forces. Thus, he studied people who took responsibilty for their own failures (such as dropping out of school in the ninth grade) and blamed themselves. Duneier was fully aware from many other studies of the larger forces (e.g., family situation, violence, poor quality school, racial prejudice, joblessness) that often contributed to their experience of failure.[11]

Validity in Field Research.   Validity in field research is the confidence placed in a researcher's analysis and data as accurately representing the social world in the field. Replicability is not a criterion because field research is virtually impossible to replicate. Essential aspects of the field change: The social events and context change, the members are different, the individual researcher differs, and so on. There are four kinds of validity or tests of research accuracy: ecological validity, natural history, member validation, and competent insider performance.

- *Ecological validity.* Validity is achieved by describing the studied social world in a manner that matches what it would be without a research presence. Ecological validity suggests that events and interactions would occur the same without a researcher there and without being part of a research study.
- *Natural history.* Validity is achieved by offering a highly detailed description of how the research was conducted. Natural history offers readers a close-up view of a researcher's actions, assumptions, and procedures for evaluation.
- *Member validation.* Validity is achieved by asking members of a field site to review and verify the accuracy of the description of their intimate social world. Possible limitations of member validation are that different members may have conflicting perspectives, members may object to an unfavorable portrayal their social world, or members may not recognize parts of a description that go beyond their own narrow perspective.[12]
- *Competent insider performance.* Validity is achieved by a researcher interacting identically to or "passing" as an insider or member of the field site. This form of validity is reached when a researcher truly understands insider assumptions, knows and acts based on tacit local social rules or knowledge, and can tell and get insider jokes.

Focusing and Sampling

Focusing. The field researcher first gets a general picture, then focuses on a few specific problems or issues (see Figure 11.4). A researcher decides on specific research questions and devel-

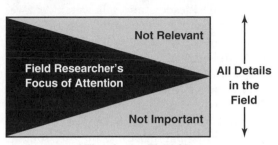

FIGURE 11.4 Focusing in Field Research

→ Amount of Time in the Field Site →

ops hypotheses only after being in the field and experiencing it firsthand. At first, everything seems relevant; later, however, selective attention focuses on specific questions and themes.

Sampling. Field researchers often use nonprobability samples, such as snowball sampling. Many times the field research is sampling different types of units. A field researcher may take a smaller, selective set of observations from all possible observations, or sample times, situations, types of events, locations, types of people, or contexts of interest. For example, a researcher samples time by observing a setting at different times. He or she observes at all times of the day, on every day of the week, and in all seasons to get a full sense of how the field site stays the same or changes. It is often best to overlap when sampling (e.g., to have sampling times from 7:00 A.M. to 9:00 A.M., from 8:00 A.M. to 10:00 A.M., from 9:00 A.M. to 11:00 A.M., etc.).

A researcher often samples locations because one location may give depth, but a narrow perspective. Sitting or standing in different locations helps the researcher get a sense of the whole site. For example, the peer-to-peer behavior of school teachers usually occurs in a faculty lounge, but it also occurs at a local bar when teachers gather or in a classroom temporarily used for a teacher meeting. In addition, researchers trace the paths of members to various field locations.

Field researchers sample people by focusing their attention on different kinds of people (old-timers and newcomers, old and young, males and females, leaders and followers). As a researcher identifies types of people, or people with opposing outlooks, he or she tries to interact with and learn about all types. A field researcher also samples various kinds of events, such as routine, special, and unanticipated. Routine events (e.g., opening up a store for business) happen every day and should not be considered unimportant simply because they are routine. Special events (e.g., annual office party) are announced and planned in advance. They focus member attention and reveal aspects of social life not otherwise visible. Unanticipated events are those that just happen to occur while a researcher is present (e.g., unsupervised workers when the manager gets sick and cannot oversee workers at a store for a day). In this case, the researcher sees something unusual, unplanned, or rare by chance.

THE FIELD RESEARCH INTERVIEW

So far, you have learned how field researchers observe and take notes. They also interview members, but field interviews differ from survey research interviews. This section introduces the field interview.

The Field Interview

Field researchers use unstructured, nondirective, in-depth interviews, which differ from formal survey research interviews in many ways (see Table 11.1). The field interview involves asking questions, listening, expressing interest, and recording what was said. It is a joint production of a researcher and a member. Members are active participants whose insights, feelings, and cooperation are essential parts of a discussion process that reveals subjective meanings.

Field research interviews go by many names: unstructured, depth, ethnographic, open-ended, informal, and long. Generally, they involve one or more people being present, occur in the field, and are informal and nondirective (i.e., the respondent may take the interview in various directions).

A field interview involves a mutual sharing of experiences. A researcher might share his or her background to build trust and encourage the informant to open up, but does not force answers or use leading questions. She or he encourages and guides a process of mutual discovery.

In field interviews, members express themselves in the forms in which they normally speak, think, and organize reality. A researcher retains members' jokes and narrative stories in their natural form and does not repackage them into a standardized format. The focus is on the members' perspectives and experiences. In order to stay close to a member's experience, the researcher asks questions in terms of concrete examples or situations—for example, "Could you tell me things that led up to your quitting in June?" instead of "Why did you quit your job?"

Field interviews can occur in a series over time. A researcher begins by building rapport and steering conversation away from evaluative or highly sensitive topics. He or she avoids probing inner feelings until intimacy is established, and even then, the researcher expects apprehension. After several meetings, he or she may be able to probe more deeply into sensitive issues and seek clarification of less sensitive issues. In later interviews, he or she may return to topics and check past answers by restating them in a nonjudgmental tone and asking for verification—for example, "The last time we talked, you said that you started taking things from the store after they reduced your pay. Is that right?"

The field interview is closer to a friendly conversation than the stimulus/response model found in a survey research interview. You are familiar with a friendly conversation. It has its own informal rules and the following elements: (1) a greeting ("Hi, it's good to see you again"); (2) the absence of an explicit goal or purpose (we don't say, "Let's now discuss what we did last weekend"); (3) avoidance of repetition (we don't say, "Could you clarify what you said about"); (4) question asking ("Did you see the race yesterday?"); (5) expressions of interest ("Really? I wish I could have been there!"); (6) expressions of ignorance ("No, I missed it. What happened?"); (7) turn taking, so the encounter is balanced (one person does not always ask questions and the other only answer); (8) abbreviations ("I missed the Derby, but I'm going to the Indy," not "I missed the Kentucky Derby horse race but I will go to the Indianapolis 500 auto-

motive race"); (9) a pause or brief silence when neither person talks is acceptable; (10) a closing (we don't say, "Let's end this conversation"; instead, we give a verbal indicator before physically leaving: "I've got to get back to work now—see ya tomorrow").

The field interview differs from a friendly conversation. It has an explicit purpose—to learn about the informant and setting. A researcher includes explanations or requests that diverge from friendly conversations. For example, he or she may say, "I'd like to ask you about . . ." or "Could you look at this and see if I've

TABLE 11.1   Survey Interviews versus Field Research Interviews

Typical Survey Interview	Typical Field Interview
1. It has a clear beginning and end.	1. The beginning and end are not clear. The interview can be picked up later.
2. The same standard questions are asked of all respondents in the same sequence.	2. The questions and the order in which they are asked are tailored to specific people and situations.
3. The interviewer appears neutral at all times.	3. The interviewer shows interest in responses, encourages elaboration.
4. The interviewer asks questions, and the respondent answers.	4. It is like a friendly conversational exchange, but with more interviewer questions.
5. It is almost always with one respondent alone.	5. It can occur in group setting or with others in area, but varies.
6. It has a professional tone and businesslike focus; diversions are ignored.	6. It is interspersed with jokes, asides, stories, diversions, and anecdotes, which are recorded.
7. Closed-ended questions are common, with rare probes.	7. Open-ended questions are common, and probes are frequent.
8. The interviewer alone controls the pace and direction of interview.	8. The interviewer and member jointly control the pace and direction of the interview.
9. The social context in which the interview occurs is ignored and assumed to make little difference.	9. The social context of the interview is noted and seen as important for interpreting the meaning of responses.
10. The interviewer attempts to mold the framework communication pattern into a standard.	10. The interviewer adjusts to the member's norms and language usage.

Source: Adapted from Briggs (1986), Denzin (1989), Douglas (1985), Misher (1986), Spradley (1979a).

written it down right?" The field interview is less balanced. A higher proportion of questions come from the researcher, who expresses more ignorance and interest. Also, it includes repetition, and a researcher asks the member to elaborate on unclear abbreviations.

Kissane (2003) used depth interviews in her field study of low-income women in Philadelphia (discussed in Chapter 6). Interviews lasted from 30 minutes to three hours. Kissane noted that she asked the women what services they used, and then named specific agencies. Often a woman would then say she was aware of the named agency. She asked the women to describe their experiences with various agencies, when they had used them or if they would use services of various agencies, and what other social services they used. Open-ended interviewing allowed her to see the women's decision-making process.

Types of Questions in Field Interviews

Many field researchers ask three types of questions in a field interview: descriptive, structural, and contrast questions. All are asked concurrently, but each type is more frequent at a different stage in the research process (see Figure 11.5). During the early stage, a researcher primarily asks descriptive questions, then gradually

adds structural questions until, in the middle stage after analysis has begun, they make up a majority of the questions. Contrast questions begin to appear in the middle of a field research study and increase until, by the end, they are asked more than any other type.[13]

A *descriptive question* is used to explore the setting and learn about members. Descriptive questions can be about time and space—for example, "Where is the bathroom?" "When does the delivery truck arrive?" "What happened Monday night?" They can also be about people and activities: "Who is sitting by the window?" "What is your uncle like?" "What happens during the initiation ceremony?" They can be about objects: "When do you use a saber saw?" "Which tools do you carry with you on an emergency water leak job?" Questions asking for examples are descriptive questions—for example, "Could you give me an example of a great date?" "What were your experiences as a postal clerk?" Descriptive questions may ask about hypothetical situations: "If a student opened her book during the exam, how would you deal with it?" They also ask members about the argot of the setting: "What do you call a deputy sheriff?" (The answer is a "county Mountie.")

A researcher introduces a *structural question* after spending time in the field and starting to analyze data. It begins after a researcher organizes specific field events, situations, and conversations into conceptual categories. For example, a researcher's observations of a highway truck-stop restaurant revealed that the employees informally classify customers who patronize the truck stop. In a preliminary analysis, he or she creates a conceptual category of kinds of customers and has members verify the categories with structural questions. A common way to pose a structural question is to ask the members whether a category includes elements in addition to those already identified—for example, "Are there any types of customers other than regulars, greasers, pit stoppers, and long haulers?" In addition, a researcher asks for confirmation: "Is a greaser a type of customer that

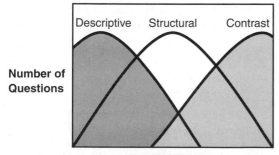

FIGURE 11.5   Types of Questions in Field Research Interviews

Descriptive   Structural   Contrast

Number of Questions

Time in the Field

you serve?" "Would a pit stopper ever eat a three-course dinner?"

The *contrast question* builds on the analysis already verified by structural questions. Contrast questions focus on similarities or differences between elements in categories or between categories. The researcher asks members to verify the similarities and differences: "You seem to have a number of different kinds of customers come in here. I've heard you call some customers 'regulars' and others 'pit stoppers.' How are a regular and a pit stopper alike?" or "Is the difference between a long hauler and a greaser that the greaser doesn't tip?" or "Two types of customers just stop to use the restroom—entire families and a lone male. Do you call both pit stoppers?"

Informants

An informant or key actor in field research is a member with whom a field researcher develops a relationship and who tells about, or informs on, the field.[14] Who makes a good informant? The ideal informant has four characteristics:

1. The informant is totally familiar with the culture and is in position to witness significant events. He or she lives and breathes the culture and engages in routines in the setting without thinking about them.
2. The individual is currently involved in the field. Ex-members who have reflected on the field may provide useful insights, but the longer they have been away from direct involvement, the more likely it is that they have reconstructed their recollections.
3. The person can spend time with the researcher. Interviewing may take many hours, and some members are simply not available for extensive interviewing.
4. Nonanalytic individuals make better informants. A nonanalytic informant is familiar with and uses native folk theory or pragmatic common sense. This is in contrast to the analytic member, who preanalyzes the

setting, using categories from the media or education.

A field researcher may interview several types of informants. Contrasting types of informants who provide useful perspectives include rookies and old-timers, people in the center of events and those on the fringes of activity, people who recently changed status (e.g., through promotion) and those who are static, frustrated or needy people and happy or secure people, the leader in charge and the subordinate who follows. A field researcher expects mixed messages when he or she interviews a range of informants.

Interview Context

Field researchers recognize that a conversation in a private office may not occur in a crowded lunchroom. Often, interviews take place in the member's home environment so that he or she is comfortable. This is not always best. If a member is preoccupied or there is no privacy, a researcher will move to another setting (e.g., restaurant or university office).

The interview's meaning is shaped by its Gestalt or whole interaction of a researcher and a member in a specific context. For example, a researcher notes nonverbal forms of communication that add meaning, such as a shrug, a gesture, and so on.

LEAVING THE FIELD

Work in the field can last for a few weeks to a dozen years. In either case, at some point work in the field ends. Some researchers (e.g., Schatzman and Strauss, 1973) suggest that the end comes naturally when theory building ceases or reaches a closure; others feel that fieldwork could go on without end and that a firm decision to cut off relations is needed.

Experienced field researchers anticipate a process of disengaging and exiting the field. Depending on the intensity of involvement and the length of time in the field, the process can be disruptive or emotionally painful for both the researcher and the members. A researcher may experience the emotional pain of breaking intimate friendships when leaving the field. He or she may feel guilty and depressed immediately before and after leaving. He or she may find it difficult to let go because of personal and emotional entanglements. If the involvement in the field was intense and long, and the field site differed from his or her native culture, the researcher may need months of adjustment before feeling at home with his or her original cultural surroundings.

Once a researcher decides to leave—because the project reaches a natural end and little new is being learned, or because external factors force it to end (e.g., end of a job, gatekeepers order the researcher out, etc.)—he or she chooses a method of exiting. The researcher can leave by a quick exit (simply not return one day) or slowly withdraw, reducing his or her involvement over weeks. He or she also needs to decide how to tell members and how much advance warning to give.

The exit process depends on the specific field setting and the relationships developed. In general, a researcher lets members know a short period ahead of time. He or she fulfills any bargains or commitments that were made and leaves with a clean slate. Sometimes, a ritual or ceremony, such as a going-away party or shaking hands with everyone, helps signal the break for members. Maintaining friendships with members is also possible and is preferred by feminist researchers.

A field researcher is aware that leaving affects members. Some members may feel hurt or rejected because a close social relationship is ending. They may react by trying to pull a researcher back into the field and make him or her more of a member, or they may become angry and resentful. They may grow cool and distant because of an awareness that the researcher is really an outsider. In any case, fieldwork is not fin-

ished until the process of disengagement and exiting is complete.

FOCUS GROUPS

The *focus group* is a special qualitative research technique in which people are informally "interviewed" in a group-discussion setting.[15] Focus group research has grown over the past 20 years. The procedure is that a researcher gathers together 6 to 12 people in a room with a moderator to discuss a few issues. Most focus groups last about 90 minutes. The moderator is trained to be nondirective and to facilitate free, open discussion by all group members (i.e., not let one person dominate the discussion). Group members should be homogenous, but not include close friends or relatives. In a typical study, a researcher uses four to six separate groups. Focus group topics might include public attitudes (e.g., race relations, workplace equality), personal behaviors (e.g., dealing with AIDS), a new product (e.g., breakfast cereal), a political candidate, or a number of other topics. Researchers often combine focus groups with quantitative research, and the procedure has its own specific strengths and weaknesses (see Box 11.5).

Several years ago, I conducted an applied study on why parents and students chose to attend a private high school. In addition to collecting quantitative survey data, I formed six focus groups, each with 8 to 10 students from the high school. A trained college-student moderator asked questions, elicited comments from group members, and prevented one person from dominating discussions. The six groups were co-ed and contained members of either one grade level or two adjacent grades (e.g., freshmen and sophomores). Students discussed their reasons for attending the high school and whether specific factors were important. I tape-recorded the discussions, which lasted about 45 minutes, then analyzed the tapes to understand what the students saw as important to their decisions. In ad-

Box 11.5	Advantages and Limitations of Focus Groups

Advantages

- The natural setting allows people to express opinions/ideas freely.
- Open expression among members of marginalized social groups is encouraged.
- People tend to feel empowered, especially in action-oriented research projects.
- Survey researchers are provided a window into how people talk about survey topics.
- The interpretation of quantitative survey results is facilitated.
- Participants may query one another and explain their answers to each other.

Limitations

- A "polarization effect" exists (attitudes become more extreme after group discussion).
- Only one or a few topics can be discussed in a focus group session.
- A moderator may unknowingly limit open, free expression of group members.
- Focus group participants produce fewer ideas than in individual interviews.
- Focus group studies rarely report all the details of study design/procedure.
- Researchers cannot reconcile the differences that arise between individual-only and focus group-context responses.

dition, the data helped when interpreting the survey data.

ETHICAL DILEMMAS OF FIELD RESEARCH

The direct personal involvement of a field researcher in the social lives of other people raises many ethical dilemmas. The dilemmas arise when a researcher is alone in the field and has little time to make a moral decision. Although he or she may be aware of general ethical issues before entering the field, they arise unexpectedly in the course of observing and interacting in the field. We will look at four ethical issues in field research: deception, confidentiality, involvement with deviants, and publishing reports.[16]

Deception

Deception arises in several ways in field research: The research may be covert; it may assume a false role, name, or identity; or it may mislead members in some way. The most hotly debated of the ethical issues arising from deception is that of covert versus overt field research. Some support it and see it as necessary for entering into and gaining a full knowledge of many areas of social life. Others oppose it and argue that it undermines a trust between researchers and society. Although its moral status is questionable, there are some field sites or activities that can only be studied covertly. Covert research is never preferable and never easier than overt research because of the difficulties of maintaining a front and the constant fear of getting caught.

Confidentiality

A researcher learns intimate knowledge that is given in confidence. He or she has a moral obligation to uphold the confidentiality of data. This includes keeping information confidential from others in the field and disguising members' names in field notes. Sometimes a field researcher cannot directly quote a person. One strategy is instead of reporting the source as an informant, the researcher can find documentary evidence that says the same thing and use the document (e.g., an old memo, a newspaper article, etc.) as if it were the source of the information.

Involvement with Deviants

Researchers who conduct field research on deviants who engage in illegal behavior face additional dilemmas. They know of and may sometimes be involved in illegal activity. This *guilty knowledge* is of interest not only to law-enforcement officials but also to other deviants.[17] The researcher faces a dilemma of building trust and rapport with the deviants, yet not becoming so involved as to violate his or her basic personal moral standards. Usually, the researcher makes an explicit arrangement with the deviant members.

Publishing Field Reports

The intimate knowledge that a researcher obtains and reports creates a dilemma between the right of privacy and the right to know. A researcher does not publicize member secrets, violate privacy, or harm reputations. Yet, if he or she cannot publish anything that might offend or harm someone, part of what the researcher learned will remain hidden, and it may be difficult for others to believe the report if a researcher omits critical details. Some researchers ask members to look at a report to verify its accuracy and to approve of their portrayal in print. For marginal groups (e.g., addicts, prostitutes, crack users), this may not be possible, but researchers must respect member privacy. On the other hand, censorship or self-censorship can be a danger. A compromise position is for a researcher to publish truthful but unflattering material after consideration and only if it is essential to the researcher's arguments.

CONCLUSION

In this chapter, you learned about field research and the field research process (choosing a site and gaining access, relations in the field, observing and collecting data, and the field interview). Field researchers begin data analysis and theorizing during the data collection phase.

You can now appreciate implications of saying that in field research, the researcher is directly involved with those being studied and is immersed in a natural setting. Doing field research usually has a greater impact on the researcher's emotions, personal life, and sense of self than doing other types of research. Field research is difficult to conduct, but it is a way to study parts of the social world that otherwise could not be studied.

Good field research requires a combination of skills. In addition to a strong sense of self, the best field researchers possess an incredible ability to listen and absorb details, tremendous patience, sensitivity and empathy for others, superb social skills, a talent to think very quickly "on one's feet," the ability see subtle interconnections among people and/or events, and a superior ability to express oneself in writing.

Field research is strongest when a researcher studies a small group of people interacting in the present. It is valuable for micro-level or small-group face-to-face interaction. It is less effective when the concern is macro-level processes and social structures. It is nearly useless for events that occurred in the distant past or processes that stretch across decades. Historical-comparative research, discussed in the next chapter, is better suited to investigating these types of concerns.

Key Terms

analytic memos
appearance of interest
attitude of strangeness
contrast question
descriptive question
direct observation notes
ecological validity
ethnography
ethnographic fallacy
ethnomethodology
external consistency
field site

focus group
go native
guilty knowledge
internal consistency
jotted notes
member validation
naturalism
normalize social research
structural question

Endnotes

1. For studies of these sites or topics, see Neuman (2000, 2003). On studies of children or schools, see Corsaro (1994), Corsaro and Molinari (2000), Eder (1995), Eder and Kinney (1995), Kelle (2000), and Merten (1999). On studies of homeless people, see Lankenau (1999), and on studies of female strippers, see Wood (2000).

2. Ethnography is described in Agar (1986), Franke (1983), Hammersley and Atkinson (1983), Sanday (1983), and Spradley (1979a:3–12, 1979b:3–16).

3. For a general discussion of field research and naturalism, see Adler and Adler (1994), Georges and Jones (1980), Holy (1984), and Pearsall (1970). For discussions of contrasting types of field research, see Clammer (1984), Gonor (1977), Holstein and Gubrium (1994), Morse (1994), Schwandt (1994), and Strauss and Corbin (1994).

4. See Lofland (1976:13–23) and Shaffir and colleagues (1980:18–20) on feeling marginal.

5. See Adler and Adler (1987:67–78).

6. See Hammersley and Atkinson (1983:42–45) and Lofland and Lofland (1995:16–30).

7. For more on gatekeepers and access, see Beck (1970:11–29), Bogdan and Taylor (1975:30–32), and Wax (1971:367).

8. Negotiation in the field is discussed in Gans (1982), Johnson (1975:58–59, 76–77), and Schatzman and Strauss (1973:22–23).

9. See Douglas (1976), Emerson (1981:367–368), and Johnson (1975:124–129) on the question of whether the researcher should always be patient, polite, and considerate.

10. For more on ways to record and organize field data, see Bogdan and Taylor (1975:60–73), Hammersley and Atkinson (1983:144–173), and Kirk and Miller (1986: 49–59).

11. See Duneier (1999:342–343) for detailed discussion.

12. For more on validity in field research, see Briggs (1986:24), Bogdan and Taylor (1975), Douglas (1976), Emerson (1981:361–363), and Sanjek (1990).

13. The types of questions are adapted from Spradley (1979a, 1979b).

14. Field research informants are discussed in Dean and associates (1969), Kemp and Ellen (1984), Schatzman and Strauss (1973), Spradley (1979a:46–54), and Whyte (1982).

15. For a discussion of focus groups, see Bischoping and Dykema (1999), Churchill (1983:179–184), Krueger (1988), Labaw (1980:54–58), and Morgan (1996).

16. See Lofland and Lofland (1995:26, 63, 75, 168–177), Miles and Huberman (1994:288–297), and Punch (1986).

17. Fetterman (1989) discusses the idea of guilty knowledge.

CHAPTER 12

Historical-Comparative Research

INTRODUCTION

Some students find historical-comparative research difficult and uninteresting because they do not know much about various countries or history, which is often necessary to appreciate this type of research and studies that use it. They may feel that historical-comparative studies are beyond their immediate daily experiences and not relevant. Yet, explaining and understanding major events in the world around them—an attack by terrorists, a nation going to war, the source of racism, large-scale immigration, violence based on religious hatred, urban decay—depend on historical-comparative research.

The classic social thinkers in the nineteenth century, such as Emile Durkheim, Karl Marx, and Max Weber, who founded the social sciences, used a historical and comparative method. This method is used extensively in a few areas of sociology (e.g., social change, political sociology, social movements, and social stratification) and has been applied in many others, as well (e.g., religion, criminology, sex roles, race relations, and family). Although much social research focuses on current social life in one country, historical and/or comparative studies have become more common in recent years.

Historical-comparative social research is a collection of techniques and approaches. Some blend into traditional history, others extend quantitative social research. The focus of this chapter is on the distinct type of social research that puts historical time and/or cross-cultural variation at the center of research—that is, the type of research that treats what is studied as part of the flow of history and situated in a cultural context.

Research Questions Appropriate for Historical-Comparative Research

Historical-comparative research is a powerful method for addressing big questions: How did major societal change take place? What fundamental features are common to most societies?

Why did current social arrangements take a certain form in some societies but not in others? For example, historical-comparative researchers have addressed the questions of what caused societal revolutions in China, France, and Russia (Skocpol, 1979); how major social institutions, such as medicine, have developed and changed over two centuries (Starr, 1982); how basic social relationships, such as feelings about the value of children, change (Zelizer, 1985); how recent changes in major cities, such as New York, London, and Tokyo, reveal the rise of a new global urban system (Sassen, 2001), and, as the study discussed in Chapter 2 by Marx (1998) asked, why Brazil, South Africa, and the United States developed different racial relations.[1]

Historical-comparative research is suited for examining the combinations of social factors that produce a specific outcome (e.g., civil war). It is also appropriate for comparing entire social systems to see what is common across societies and what is unique. An H-C researcher may apply a theory to specific cases to illustrate its usefulness. He or she brings out or reveals the connections between divergent social factors or groups. And, he or she compares the same social processes and concepts in different cultural or historical contexts. For example, Switzerland and United States have been compared in terms of the use of direct democracy and women's right to vote. Similar forms of lcoal government allowed direct democracy to spread in parts of both countries (Kriesi and Wisler, 1999). Although some U.S. states granted women to right to vote in the 1800s, the Swiss women did not get the right to vote until 1990 because, unlike the U.S. movement, the Swiss suffrage movement believed in consensus politics and local autonomy and relied on government parties for direction (Banaszak, 1996).

Researchers also use the H-C method to reinterpret data or challenge old explanations. By asking different questions, finding new evidence, or assembling evidence in a different way, the H-C rescarcher raises questions about old explanations and finds support for new ones by interpreting the data in its cultural-historical context.

Historical-comparative research can strengthen conceptualization and theory building. By looking at historical events or diverse cultural contexts, a researcher can generate new concepts and broaden his or her perspectives. Concepts are less likely to be restricted to a single historical time or to a single culture; they can be grounded in the experiences of people living in specific cultural and historical contexts.[2]

A difficulty in reading H-C studies is that one needs a knowledge of the past or other cultures to fully understand them. Readers who are familiar with only their own cultures or contemporary times may find it difficult to understand the H-C studies or classical theorists. For example, it is difficult to understand Karl Marx's *The Communist Manifesto* without a knowledge of the conditions of feudal Europe and the world in which Marx was writing. In that time and place, serfs lived under severe oppression. Feudal society included caste-based dress codes in cities and a system of peonage that forced serfs to give a large percent of their product to landlords. The one and only Church had extensive landholdings, and tight familial ties existed among the aristocracy, landlords, and Church. Modern readers might ask, Why did the serfs not flee if conditions were so bad? The answer requires an understanding of the conditions at the time. The serfs had little chance to survive in European forests living on roots, berries, and hunting. Also, no one would aid a fleeing serf refugee because the traditional societies did not embrace strangers, but feared them.

THE LOGIC OF HISTORICAL-COMPARATIVE RESEARCH

The terms used for H-C research can be confusing. Researchers may mean different things when they say *historical, comparative,* and *historical-comparative.* The key question is: Is there a distinct historical-comparative method and logic?

The Logic of Historical-Comparative Research and Quantitative Research

Quantitative versus Historical-Comparative Research. One source of the confusion is that both positivist quantitatively oriented and interpretive (or critical) qualitatively oriented researchers study historical or comparative issues. Positivist researchers reject the idea that there is a distinct H-C method. They measure variables, test hypotheses, analyze quantitative data, and replicate research to discover generalizable laws that hold across time and societies. They see no fundamental difference between quantitative social research and historical-comparative research.

Most social research examines social life in the present in a single nation—that of the researcher. Historical-comparative research can be organized along three dimensions: Is the focus on what occurs in one nation, a small set of nations, or many nations? Is the focus on a single time period in the past, across many years, or a recent time period? Is the analysis based primarily on quantitative or qualitative data?

The Logic of Historical-Comparative Research and Interpretive Research

A distinct, qualitative historical-comparative type of social research differs from the positivist approach and from an extreme interpretive approach. Historical-comparative researchers who use case studies and qualitative data may depart from positivist principles. Their research is an intensive examination of a limited number of cases in which social meaning and context are critical. Case studies, even on one nation, can be very important. Case studies can elaborate historical processes and specify concrete historical details (see Box 12.1).

Scholars who adopt the positivist approach to social science criticize the historical-compar-

Box 12.1   Women of the Klan

In *Women of the Klan,* Kathleen Blee (1991) noted that, prior to her research, no one had studied the estimated 500,000 women in the largest racist, right-wing movement in the United States. She suggested that this may have been due to an assumption that women were apolitical and passive. Her six years of research into the unknown members of a secret society over 60 years ago shows the ingenuity needed in historical-sociological research.

Blee focused on the state of Indiana, where as many as 32 percent of White Protestant women were members of the Ku Klux Klan at its peak in the 1920s. In addition to reviewing published studies on the Klan, her documentary investigation included newspapers, pamphlets, and unpublished reports. She conducted library research on primary and secondary materials at over half a dozen college, government, and historical libraries. The historical photographs, sketches, and maps in the book give readers a feel for the topic.

Finding information was difficult. Blee did not have access to membership lists. She identified Klan women by piecing together a few surviving rosters, locating newspaper obituaries that identified women as Klan members, scrutinizing public notices or anti-Klan documents for the names of Klan women, and interviewing surviving women of the Klan.

To locate survivors 60 years after the Klan was active, Blee had to be persistent and ingenious. She mailed a notice about her research to every local newspaper, church bulletin, advertising supplement, historical society, and public library in Indiana. She obtained 3 written recollections, 3 unrecorded interviews, and 15 recorded interviews. Most of her informants were over age 80. They recalled the Klan as an important part of their lives. Blee verified parts of their memories through newspaper and other documentary evidence.

Membership in the Klan remains controversial. In the interviews, Blee did not reveal her opinions about the Klan. Although she was tested, Blee remained neutral and did not denounce the Klan. She stated, "My own background in Indiana (where I lived from primary school through college) and white skin led informants to assume—lacking spoken evidence to the contrary—that I shared their worldview" (p. 5). She did not find Klan women brutal, ignorant, and full of hatred. Blee got an unexpected response to a question on why the women had joined the Klan. Most were puzzled by the question. To them it needed no explanation—it was just "a way of growing up" and "to get together and enjoy."

---

ative approach for using a small number of cases. They believe that historical-comparative research is inadequate because it rarely produces probabilistic causal generalizations that they take as indicating a "true" (i.e., positivist) science.

Like interpretive field researchers, H-C researchers focus on culture, try to see through the eyes of those being studied, reconstruct the lives of the people studied, and examine particular individuals or groups. An extremist interpretive position says that an empathic understanding of the people being studied is the sole goal of social research. It takes a strict, idiographic, descriptive

approach and rejects causal statements, systematic concepts, or abstract theoretical models. In the extremist interpretive approach, each social setting is unique and comparisons are impossible.

A Distinct Historical-Comparative Approach

The distinct historical-comparative research method avoids the excesses of the positivist and extreme interpretive approaches. It combines a sensitivity to specific historical or cultural contexts with theoretical generalization. The logic and goals of H-C research are closer to those of field research than to positivist approaches. The following discussion describes similarities between H-C research and field research, and six more unique features of historical-comparative research (see Table 12.1).

Similarities to Field Research.   First, both H-C research and field research recognize that the researcher's point of view is an unavoidable part of research. Both involve interpretation, which introduces the interpreter's location in time, place, and worldview. Historical-comparative research does not try to produce a single, unequivocal set of objective facts. Rather, it is a confrontation of old with new or of different worldviews. It recognizes that a researcher's reading of historical or comparative evidence is influenced by an awareness of the past and by living in the present.

TABLE 12.1   Summary of a Comparison of Approaches to Research: The Qualitative versus Quantitative Distinction

Topic	Both Field and H-C	Quantitative
Researcher's perspective	Include as an intergral part of the research process	Remove from research process
Approach to data	Immersed in many details to acquire understanding	Precisely operationalize variables
Theory and data	Grounded theory, dialogue between data and concepts	Deductive theory compared with empirical data
Present findings	Translate a meaning system	Test hypotheses
Action/structure	People construct meaning but within structures	Social forces shape behavior
Laws/generalization	Limited generalizations that depend on context	Discover universal, context-free laws

Features of Distinct H-C Research Approach

Topic	Historical Comparative Researcher's Approach
Evidence	Reconstructs from fragments and incomplete evidence
Distortion	Guards against using own awareness of factors outside the social or historical context
Human role	Includes the consciousness of people in a context and uses their motives as causal factors
Causes	Sees cause as contingent on conditions, beneath the surface, and due to a combination of elements
Micro/macro	Compares whole cases and links the micro to macro levels or layers of social reality
Cross-contexts	Moves between concrete specifics in a context and across contexts for more abstract comparisons

Second, both field and H-C research examine a great diversity of data. In both, the researcher becomes immersed in data to gain an empathic understanding of events and people. Both capture subjective feelings and note how everyday, ordinary activities signify important social meaning.

The researcher inquires, selects, and focuses on specific aspects of social life from the vast array of events, actions, symbols, and words. An H-C researcher organizes data and focuses attention on the basis of evolving concepts. He or she examines rituals and symbols that dramatize culture (e.g., parades, clothing, placement of objects, etc.) and investigates the motives, reasons, and justifications for behaviors.

Third, both field and H-C researchers use *grounded theory*. Theory usually emerges during the process of data collection.

Next, in both field and H-C research the researcher's meaning system frequently differs from that of the people he or she studies, but he or she tries to penetrate and understand their point of view. Once the life, language, and perspective of the people being studied have been mastered, the researcher "translates" it for others who read his or her report.

Fifth, both field and H-C researchers focus on process and sequence. They see the passage of time and process as essential to how people construct social reality. This is related to how both are sensitive to an ever-present tension between agency—the active moving fluid side of people changing social reality—and structure—the fixed regularities and patterns that shape social life. For both types of research social reality simultaneously is what people create and something that imposes restrictions on human choice.[3]

Sixth, generalization and theory are limited in field and H-C research. Historical and cross-cultural knowledge is incomplete and provisional, based on selective facts and limited questions. Neither deduces propositions or tests hypotheses in order to uncover fixed laws. Likewise, replication is unrealistic because each researcher has a unique perspective and assembles a unique body of evidence. Instead, researchers offer plausible accounts and limited generalizations.

Unique Features of Historical-Comparative Research. Despite its many similarities to field research, some important differences distinguish H-C research. Research on the past and on an alien culture share much in common, and what they share distinguishes them from other approaches.

First, H-C research usually relies on limited and indirect evidence. Direct observation or involvement by a researcher is often impossible. An H-C researcher reconstructs what occurred from the evidence, but cannot have absolute confidence in the reconstruction. Historical evidence depends on the survival of data from the past, usually in the form of documents (e.g., letters and newspapers). The researcher is limited to what has not been destroyed and what leaves a trace, record, or other evidence behind.

Historical-comparative researchers must also interpret the evidence. Different people looking at the same evidence often ascribe different meanings to it, so a researcher must reflect on evidence. An understanding of it based on a first glance is rarely possible. To do this, a researcher becomes immersed in and absorbs details about a context. For example, a researcher examining the family in the past or a distant country needs to be aware of the full social context (e.g., the nature of work, forms of communication, transportation technology, etc.). He or she looks at maps and gets a feel for the laws in effect, the condition of medical care, and common social practices. For example, the meaning of "a visit by a family member" is affected by conditions such as roads of dirt and mud, the inability to call ahead of time, and the lives of people who work on a farm with animals that need constant watching.

A reconstruction of the past or another culture is easily distorted. Compared to the people being studied, a researcher is usually more aware of events occurring prior to the time studied, events occurring in places other than the location studied, and events that occurred after the period studied. This awareness gives the researcher a greater sense of coherence than was experienced by those living in the past or in an isolated social setting that he or she guards against in a reconstruction.

Historical-comparative researchers recognize the capacity of people to learn, make decisions, and act on what they learn to modify the course of events. For example, if a group of people are aware of or gain consciousness of their own past history and avoid the mistakes of the past, they may act consciously to alter the course of events. Of course, people will not necessarily learn or act on what they have learned, and if they do act they will not necessarily be successful. Nevertheless, people's capacity to learn introduces indeterminacy into historical-comparative explanations.

An H-C researcher wants to find out whether people viewed various courses of action as plausible. Thus, the worldview and knowledge of the people under study shaped what they saw as possible or impossible ways to achieve goals. The researcher asks whether people were conscious of certain things. For example, if an army knew an enemy attack was coming and so decided to cross a river in the middle of the night, the action "crossing the river" would have a different meaning than in the situation where the army did not know the enemy was approaching.

A historical-comparative researcher integrates the micro (small-scale, face-to-face interaction) and macro (large-scale social structures) levels. The H-C researcher describes both levels or layers of reality and links them to each other. For example, an H-C researcher examines the details of individual biographies by reading diaries or letters to get a feel for the individuals: the food they ate, their recreational pursuits, their clothing, their sicknesses, their relations with friends, and so on. He or she links this micro-level view to macro-level processes: increased immigration, mechanization of produc-

tion, proletarianization, tightened labor markets, and the like.

Historical-comparative researchers shift between details of specific context and making a general comparison. A researcher examines specific contexts, notes similarities and differences, then generalizes. Comparative researchers compare across cultural-geographic units (e.g., urban areas, nations, societies, etc.).[4] Historical researchers investigate past contexts, usually in one culture (e.g., periods, epochs, ages, eras, etc.), for sequence and comparison. Of course, a researcher can combine both to investigate multiple cultural contexts in one or more historical contexts. Yet, each period or society has its unique causal processes, meaning systems, and social relations, which may lack equivalent elements across the units. This produces a creative tension between the concrete specifics in a context and the abstract ideas a researcher uses to make links across contexts.

The use of transcultural concepts in comparative analysis is analogous to the use of transhistorical ones in historical research.[5] In comparative research, a researcher translates the specifics of a context into a common, theoretical language. In historical research, theoretical concepts are applied across time.

STEPS IN A HISTORICAL-COMPARATIVE RESEARCH PROJECT

In this section, we turn to the process of doing H-C research. Conducting historical-comparative research does not involve a rigid set of steps and, with only a few exceptions, it does not use complex or specialized techniques.

Conceptualizing the Object of Inquiry

An H-C researcher begins by becoming familiar with the setting and conceptualizing what is being studied. He or she may start with a loose model or a set of preliminary concepts and apply them to a specific setting. The provisional concepts contain implicit assumptions or organizing categories to "package" observations and guide a search through evidence.

If a researcher is not already familiar with the historical era or comparative settings, he or she conducts an orientation reading (reading several general works). This will help the researcher grasp the specific setting, assemble organizing concepts, subdivide the main issue, and develop lists of questions to ask. It is impossible to begin serious research without a framework of assumptions, concepts, and theory. Concepts and evidence interact to stimulate research. For example, Skocpol (1979) began her study of revolution with puzzles in macro-sociological theory and the histories of specific revolutions. The lack of fit between histories of revolutions and existing theories stimulated her research.

Locating Evidence

Next, a researcher locates and gathers evidence through extensive bibliographic work. A researcher uses many indexes, catalogs, and reference works that list what libraries contain. For comparative research, this means focusing on specific nations or units and on particular kinds of evidence within each. The researcher frequently spends many weeks searching for sources in libraries, travels to several different specialized research libraries, and reads dozens (if not hundreds) of books and articles. Comparative research often involves learning one or more foreign languages.

As the researcher masters the literature and takes numerous detailed notes, he or she completes many specific tasks: creating a bibliography list (on cards or computer) with complete citations, taking notes that are neither too skimpy nor too extensive (i.e., more than one sentence but less than dozens of pages of quotes), leaving margins on note cards for adding themes later on, taking all notes in the same format (e.g., on cards, paper, etc.), and developing a file on themes or working hypotheses.

A researcher adjusts initial concepts, questions, or focus on the basis of what he or she discovers in the evidence and considers a range of research reports at different levels of analysis (e.g., general context and detailed narratives on specific topics).

Evaluating Quality of Evidence

The H-C researcher gathers evidence with two questions in mind: How relevant is the evidence to emerging research questions and evolving concepts? How accurate and strong is the evidence?

As the focus of research shifts, evidence that was not relevant can become relevant. Likewise, some evidence may stimulate new avenues of inquiry and a search for additional confirming evidence. An H-C researcher reads evidence for three things: the implicit conceptual frameworks, particular details, and empirical generalizations. He or she evaluates alternative interpretations of evidence and looks for "silences," or cases where the evidence fails to address an event, topic, or issue. For example, when examining a group of leading male merchants in the 1890s, a researcher finds that the evidence and documents about them ignore their wives and many servants.

Organizing Evidence

As a researcher gathers evidence and locates new sources, he or she begins to organize the data. Obviously, it is unwise to take notes madly and let them pile up haphazardly. A researcher begins a preliminary analysis by noting low-level generalizations or themes. Next, a researcher organizes evidence, using theoretical insights to stimulate new ways to organize data and for new questions to ask of evidence.

The interaction of data and theory means that a researcher goes beyond a surface examination of the evidence to develop new concepts by critically evaluating the evidence based on theory. For example, a researcher reads a mass of evidence about a protest movement. The preliminary analysis organizes the evidence into a theme: People who are active in protest interact with each other and develop shared cultural meanings. He or she examines theories of culture and movements, then formulates a new concept: "oppositional movement subculture." The researcher then uses this concept to reexamine the evidence.

Synthesizing

The next step is is to synthesize evidence. Once most of the evidence is in, the researcher refines concepts, creates new ones, and moves toward a general explanatory model. Concrete events in the evidence give meaning to new concepts. The researcher looks for patterns across time or units, and draws out similarities and differences with analogies. He or she organizes divergent events into sequences and groups them together to create a larger picture. Plausible explanations are then developed that subsume both concepts and evidence into a coherent whole. The researcher then reads and rereads notes and sorts and resorts them into piles or files on the basis of organizing schemes. He or she looks for links or connections while looking at the evidence in different ways.

Synthesis links specific evidence with an abstract model of underlying relations or causal mechanisms. Researchers may use metaphors. For example, mass frustration leading to a revolution is "like an emotional roller coaster drop" in which things seem to be getting better, and then there is a sudden letdown after expectations have risen very fast. The models are sensitizing devices.

Writing a Report

Assembling evidence, arguments, and conclusions into a report is always a crucial step, but more than in quantitative approaches, the careful crafting of evidence and explanation makes or breaks H-C research. A researcher distills

mountains of evidence into exposition and prepares extensive footnotes. She or he must also weave together the evidence and arguments to communicate a coherent, convincing picture or "tell a story" to readers.

DATA AND EVIDENCE IN HISTORICAL CONTEXT

Types of Historical Evidence

First, some terms need clarification. *History* means the events of the past (e.g., it is *history* that the French withdrew troops from Vietnam), a record of the past (e.g., a *history* of French involvement in Vietnam), and a discipline that studies the past (e.g., a department of *history*). *Historiography* is the method of doing historical research or of gathering and analyzing historical evidence. Historical sociology is a part of historical-comparative research.

Researchers draw on four types of historical evidence or data: primary sources, secondary sources, running records, and recollections.[6] Traditional historians rely heavily on primary sources. H-C researchers often use secondary sources or the different data types in combination.

Primary Sources.   The letters, diaries, newspapers, movies, novels, articles of clothing, photographs, and so forth of those who lived in the past and have survived to the present are *primary sources.* They are found in archives (a place where documents are stored), in private collections, in family closets, and in museums (see Box 12.2). Today's documents and objects (our letters, television programs, commercials, clothing, automobiles) will be primary sources for future historians. An example of a classic primary source is a bundle of yellowed letters written by a husband away at war to his wife and found in an attic by a researcher.

Published and unpublished written documents are the most important type of primary

Box 12.2 Using Archival Data

The archive is the main source for primary historical materials. Archives are accumulations of documentary materials (papers, photos, letters, etc.) in private collections, museums, libraries, or formal archives.

Location and Access

Finding whether a collection exists on a topic, organization, or individual can be a long, frustrating task of many letters, phone calls, and referrals. If the material on a person or topic does exist, it may be scattered in multiple locations. Gaining access may depend on an appeal to a family member's kindness for private collections or traveling to distant libraries and verifying one's reason for examining many dusty boxes of old letters. Also, the researcher may discover limited hours (e.g., an archive is open only four days a week from 10 A.M. to 5 P.M., but the researcher needs to inspect the material for 40 hours).

Sorting and Organization

Archive material may be unsorted or organized in a variety of ways. The organization may reflect criteria that are unrelated to the researcher's interests. For example, letters and papers may be in chronological order, but the researcher is interested only in letters to four professional colleagues over three decades, not daily bills, family correspondence, and so on.

Technology and Control

Archival materials may be in their original form, on microforms, or, more rarely, in an electronic form. Researchers may be allowed only to take notes, not make copies, or they may be allowed only to see select parts of the whole collection. Researchers become frustrated with the limitations of having to read dusty papers in one specific room and being allowed only to take notes by pencil for the few hours a day the archive is open to the public.

Tracking and Tracing

One of the most difficult tasks in archival research is tracing common events or persons through the materials. Even if all material is in one location, the same event or relationship may appear in several places in many forms. Researchers sort through mounds of paper to find bits of evidence here and there.

Drudgery, Luck, and Serendipity

Archival research is often painstaking slow. Spending many hours pouring over partially legible documents can be very tedious. Also, researchers will often discover holes in collections, gaps in a series of papers, or destroyed documents. Yet, careful reading and inspection of previously untouched material can yield startling new connections or ideas. The researcher may discover unexpected evidence that opens new lines of inquiry (see Elder et al., 1993, and Hill, 1993).

---

source. Researchers find them in their original form or preserved in microfiche or on film. They are often the only surviving record of the words, thoughts, and feelings of people in the past. Written documents are helpful for studying societies and historical periods with writing and literate people. A frequent criticism of written sources is that they were largely written by elites or those in official organizations; thus, the views of the illiterate, the poor, or those outside official social institutions may be overlooked. For example, it was illegal for slaves in the United States to read or write, and thus written sources on the experience of slavery have been indirect or difficult to find.

The written word on paper was the main medium of communication prior to the widespread use of telecommunications, computers, and video technology to record events and ideas. In fact, the spread of forms of communication that do not leave a permanent physical record (e.g., telephone conversations, computer records, and television or radio broadcasts), and which have largely replaced letters, written ledgers, and newspapers, may make the work of future historians more difficult.

Secondary Sources. Primary sources have realism and authenticity, but the practical limitation of time can restrict research on many primary sources to a narrow time frame or location. To get a broader picture, many H-C researchers use *secondary sources,* the writings of specialist historians who have spent years studying primary sources.

Running Records. *Running records* consist of files or existing statistical documents maintained by organizations. An example of a running record is a file in a country church that contains a record of every marriage and every death from 1910 to the present.

Recollections. The words or writings of individuals about their past lives or experiences based on memory are *recollections.* These can be in the form of memoirs, autobiographies, or interviews. Because memory is imperfect, recollections are often distorted in ways that primary sources are not. For example, Blee (1991) interviewed a woman in her late eighties about being in the Ku Klux Klan (see Box 12.1).

In gathering *oral history,* a type of recollection, a researcher conducts unstructured interviews with people about their lives or events in the past. This approach is especially valuable for nonelite groups or the illiterate. The oral history technique began in the 1930s and now has a professional association and scholarly journal devoted to it.

Research with Secondary Sources

Uses and Limitations. Social researchers often use secondary sources, the books and articles written by historians, as evidence of past conditions.[7] Secondary sources have limitations and need to be used with caution.

Limitations of secondary historical evidence include problems of inaccurate historical accounts and a lack of studies in areas of interest. Such sources cannot be used to test hypotheses. Post facto (after-the-fact) explanations cannot meet positivist criteria of falsifiability, because few statistical controls can be used and replication is impossible. Yet, historical research by others plays an important role in developing general explanations, among its other uses. For example, such research substantiates the emergence and evolution of tendencies over time.

Potential Problems. The many volumes of secondary sources present a maze of details and interpretations for an H-C researcher. He or she must transform the mass of descriptive studies into an intelligible picture that is consistent with the richness of the evidence. It also must bridge the many specific time periods or locales. The researcher faces potential problems with secondary sources.

One problem is that historians rarely present theory-free, objective "facts." They implicitly frame raw data, categorize information, and shape evidence using concepts. The historian's concepts are a mixture drawn from journalism, the language of historical actors, ideologies, philosophy, everyday language in the present, and social science. Most are vague, applied inconsistently, and not mutually exclusive nor exhaustive. For example, a historian describes a group of people in a nineteenth-century town as upper class, but never defines the term and fails to link it to any theory of social classes. The historian's implicit theories constrain the evidence and the social researcher may be looking for evidence for explanations that are contrary to ones implicitly being used by historians in secondary sources.

Historians also select some information from all possible evidence. Yet, the H-C researcher does not know how this was done. Without knowing the selection process, a historical-comparative researcher must rely on the historian's judgments, which can contain biases.[8] For example, a historian reads 10,000 pages of newspapers, letters, and diaries, then boils down this information into summaries and selected quotes in a 100-page book. An H-C researcher does not know whether information that the historian left out is relevant for his or her purposes.

The typical historian's research practice also introduces an individualist bias. A heavy reliance on primary sources and surviving artifacts combines with an atheoretical orientation to produce a narrow focus on the actions of specific people. This particularistic, micro-level view directs attention away from integrating themes or patterns. This emphasis on the documented activities of specific individuals is a type of theoretical orientation.[9]

Another problem is in the organization of the evidence. Tradional historians organize evidence as a *narrative history*. This compounds problems of undefined concepts and the selection of evidence. In the historical narrative, material is chronologically organized around a single coherent "story." Each part of the story is connected to each other part by its place in the time order of events. Together, all the parts form a unity or whole. Conjuncture and contingency are key elements of the narrative form—that is, if X (or X plus Z) occurred, then Y would occur, and if X (or X plus Z) had not occurred, something else would have followed. The contingency creates a logical interdependency between earlier and later events.

A difficulty of the narrative is that the primary organizing tool—time order or position in a sequence of events—does not denote theoretical or historical causality. In other words, the narrative meets only one of the three criteria for establishing causality—that of temporal order. Moreover, narrative writing frequently obscures causal processes. This occurs when a historian includes events in the narrative to enrich the background or context, to add color, but that have no causal significance. Likewise, he or she presents events with a delayed causal impact, or events that are temporarily "on hold" with a causal impact occuring at some unspecified later time.

Also, narratives rarely explicitly indicate how combination or interaction effects operate, or the relative size of different factors. For example, the historian discusses three conditions as causing an event. Yet, rarely do readers know which is most important or whether all three conditions must operate together to have a causal impact, but no two conditions alone, or no single condition alone, creates the same impact.[10]

The narrative organization creates difficulties for the researcher using secondary sources and creates conflicting findings. The H-C researcher must read though weak concepts, unknown selection criteria, and unclear casual logic. Theory may reside beneath the narrative but it remain implicit and hidden.

Two last problems are that a historian is influenced by when he or she is writing and historiographic schools. Various schools of historiography (e.g., diplomatic, demographic, ecological, psychological, Marxist, intellectual, etc.) have their own rules for seeking evidence and asking questions, and they give priority to certain types of explanatory factors. Likewise, a historian writing today will examine primary materials differently from how those writing in the past, such as 1920s, did.

Research with Primary Sources

The historian is the major issue when using secondary sources. When using primary sources, the biggest concern is that only a fraction of everything written or used in the past has survived into the present. Moreover, what survived is a nonrandom sample of what once existed.

Historical-comparative researchers attempt to read primary sources with the eyes and assumptions of a contemporary who lived in the past. This means "bracketing," or holding back knowledge of subsequent events and modern values. For example, when reading a source produced by a slave holder, moralizing against slavery or faulting the author for not seeing its evil is not worthwhile. The H-C researcher holds back moral judgments and becomes a moral relativist while reading primary sources.

Another problem is that locating primary documents is a time-consuming task. A researcher must search through specialized indexes and travel to archives or specialized libraries. Primary sources are often located in a dusty, out-of-the-way room full of stacked cardboard boxes containing masses of fading documents. These may be incomplete, unorganized, and in various stages of decay. Once the documents or other primary sources are located, the researcher evaluates them by subjecting them to external and internal criticism (see Figure 12.1).

External criticism means evaluating the authenticity of a document itself to be certain that it is not a fake or a forgery. Criticism involves asking: Was the document created when it is claimed to have been, in the place where it was supposed to be, and by the person who claims to be its author? Why was the document produced to begin with, and how did it survive?

Once the document passes as being authentic, a researcher uses *internal criticism,* an examination of the document's contents to establish credibility. A researcher evaluates whether what is recorded was based on what the author directly witnessed or is secondhand information. This requires examining both the literal meaning of what is recorded and the subtle connotations or intentions. The researcher notes other events, sources, or people mentioned in the document and asks whether they can be verified. He or she examines implicit assumptions or value positions, and the relevant conditions under which the document was produced is noted (e.g., during wartime or under a totalitarian regime). The researcher also considers language usage at the time and the context of statements within the document to distill a meaning.

In an H-C study of Chinese migrant networks in Peru, Chicago, and Hawaii early in the twentieth century, McKeown (2001) used both primary and secondary historical sources and running records. He considered events over nearly a century of history and in three nations, and everything from major international events and national laws to individual family biographies. He relied on secondary sources for major national or international events. Although his study was primarily historical and qualitative, he also examined quantitative data from running records and provided graphs, charts, and tables of statistics. His evidence also included geographic maps and photographs, quotes from 100-year-old telegrams, official government documents, original newspaper reports, and selections from personal letters in three languages. By comparing Chinese migrants over a long historical period and in divergent social-cultural settings, he could trace the formation and operation of transnational communities and social

FIGURE 12.1   Internal and External Criticism

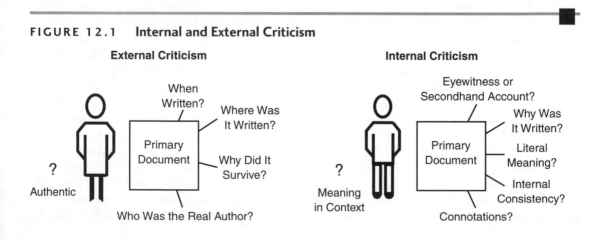

identities. He learned that networks with links back to villages in China and crossing several national borders helped to sustain a vibrant, interacting community. The network was held together by social relations from the village of origin, clan, family, business transactions, and shared language and customs. One of McKeown's major arguments is that a perspective based solely on nations can limit a researcher's ability to see a social community that is transnational and the hybrid of multiple cultures. Many aspects of the transnational community developed in reaction to specific interactions that occurred locally.

COMPARATIVE RESEARCH

Types of Comparative Research

A Comparative Method. Comparative research is more of a perspective or orientation than a separate research technique. In this section, we consider its strengths.

Problems in other types of research are magnified in a comparative study.[11] Holt and Turner (1970:6) said, "In principle, there is no difference between comparative cross-cultural research and research conducted in a single society. The differences lie, rather, in the magnitude of certain types of problems." A comparative perspective exposes weaknesses in research design and helps a researcher improve the quality of research. The focus of comparative research is on similarities and differences between units.

Comparative research helps a researcher identify aspects of social life that are general across units (e.g., cultures), as opposed to being limited to one unit alone. All researchers want to generalize to some degree. Positivist researchers are interested in discovering general laws or patterns of social behavior that hold across societies. But most positivist research is not comparative.

The comparative orientation improves measurement and conceptualization. Concepts developed by researchers who conduct research across several social units or settings are less likely to apply only to a specific culture or setting. It is difficult for a researcher to detect hidden biases, assumptions, and values until he or she applies a concept in different cultures or settings. Different social settings provide a wider range of events or behavior, and the range in one culture is usually narrower than for human behavior in general. Thus, research in a single culture or setting focuses on a restricted range of possible social activity. For example, two researchers, Hsi-Ping and Abdul, examine the relationship between the age at which a child is weaned and the onset of emotional problems. Hsi-Ping looks only at U.S. data, which show a range from 5 to 15 months at weaning, and indicate that emotional problems increase steadily as age of weaning increases. She concludes that late weaning causes emotional problems. Abdul looks at data from 10 cultures and discovers a range from 5 to 36 months at weaning. He finds that the rate of emotional problems rises with age of weaning until 18 months; it then peaks and falls to a lower level. Abdul arrives at more accurate conclusions: Emotional problems are likely for weaning between the ages of 6 and 24 months, but weaning either earlier or later reduces the chances of emotional problems. Hsi-Ping reached false conclusions about the relationship because of the narrow range of weaning age in the United States.

The way comparative research raises new questions and stimulates theory building is a major strength. For example, Lamont (2000) compared samples of blue-collar and lower–white-collar workers in France and the United States for their justifications and forms of argument used to explain racial differences. She drew random samples from telephone directories of Whites and Blacks in the suburbs of Paris and New York City and interviewed respondents for two hours. Lamont found that the arguments of racists and antiracists alike differed widely between France and the United States. People use arguments and rationales closely tied to the dominant cultural themes of their society. For example, in the United States, there is a long history of using biological inferiority to explain racial differences. This declined greatly but it still exists, yet such a rationale is absent in France. In the United States, the market has near-sacred status and both racist and antiracists frequently used the market and personal economic success in their arguments, but the market factor was absent in France because it is not viewed as a fair and efficient mechanism for allocating resources. The French use cultural arguments, egalitarianism, and the universality of all humans much more than Americans. In fact, the idea of a fundamental equality among all human beings was nearly absent among the justifications given in the United States. Such a discrepancy stimulates researchers to seek explanations for the relationship and to develop new research questions.

Comparative research also has limitations. It is more difficult, more costly, and more time consuming than research that is not comparative. The types of data that can be collected and problems with equivalence (to be discussed) are also frequent problems.

Another limitation is the number of cases. Comparative researchers can rarely use random sampling. Sufficient information is not available for all of the approximately 150 nations in the world. It is unavailable for a nonrandom subset (poor countries, nondemocratic countries, etc.). In addition, can a researcher treat all nations as equal units when some have over a billion people and others only 100,000? The small number of cases creates a tendency for researchers to particularize and see each case as unique, limiting generalization. For example, a researcher examines five cases (e.g., countries), but the units differ from each other in 20 ways. It is difficult to test theory or determine relationships when there are more different characteristics than units.

A third limitation is that comparative researchers can apply, not test, theory, and can make only limited generalizations. Despite the ability to use and consider cases as wholes in

H-C research, rigorous theory testing or experimental research is rarely possible. For example, a researcher interested in the effects of economic recessions cannot cause one group of countries to have a recession while others do not. Instead, the researcher waits until a recession occurs and then looks at other characteristics of the country or unit.

The Units Being Compared

Culture versus Nation.   For convenience, comparative researchers often use the nation-state as their unit of analysis. The nation-state is the major unit used in thinking about the divisions of people across the globe today. Although it is a dominant unit in current times, it is neither an inevitable nor a permanent one; in fact, it has been around for only about 300 years.

The nation-state is a socially and politically defined unit. In it, one government has sovereignty (i.e., military control and political authority) over populated territory. Economic relations (e.g., currency, trade, etc.), transportation routes, and communication systems are integrated within territorial boundaries. The people of the territory usually share a common language and customs, and there is usually a common educational system, legal system, and set of political symbols (e.g., flag, national anthem, etc.). The government claims to represent the interests of all people in the territory under its control.

The nation-state is not the only unit for comparative research. It is frequently a surrogate for culture, which is more difficult to define as a concrete, observable unit. *Culture* refers to a common identity among people based on shared social relations, beliefs, and technology. Cultural differences in language, customs, traditions, and norms often follow national lines. In fact, sharing a common culture is a major factor causing the formation of distinct nation-states.

The boundaries of a nation-state may not match those of a culture. In some situations, a single culture is divided into several nations; in other cases, a nation-state contains more than one culture. Over the past centuries, boundaries between cultures and distinct vibrant cultures have been destroyed, rearranged, or diffused as territory around the world was carved into colonies or nation-states by wars and conquest. For instance, European empires imposed arbitrary boundaries over several cultural groups in nations that were once colonies. Likewise, new immigrants or ethnic minorities are not always assimilated into the dominant culture in a nation. For example, one region of a nation may have people with a distinct ethnic backgrounds, languages, customs, religions, social institutions, and identities (e.g., the province of Quebec in Canada). Such intranational cultures can create regional conflict, since ethnic and cultural identities are the basis for nationalism.

The nation-state is not always the best unit for comparative research. A researcher should ask: What is the relevant comparative unit for my research question—the nation, the culture, a small region, or a subculture? For example, a research question is: Are income level and divorce related (i.e., are higher-income people less likely to divorce?)? A group of people with a distinct culture, language, and religion live in one region of a nation. Among them, income and divorce are not related; elsewhere in the nation, however, where a different culture prevails, income and divorce are related. If a researcher uses the nation-state as his or her unit, the findings could be ambiguous and the explanation weak. Instead of assuming that each nation-state has a common culture, a researcher may find that a unit smaller than the nation-state is more appropriate.

Galton's Problem. The issue of the units of comparison is related to a problem named after Sir Francis Galton (1822–1911). When researchers compare units or their characteristics, they want the units to be distinct and separate from each other. If the units are not different but are actually the subparts of a larger unit, then researchers will find spurious relationships. For example, the units are the states and provinces in

Canada, France, and the United States; a researcher discovers a strong association between speaking English and having the dollar as currency, or speaking French and using the franc as currency. Obviously, the association exists because the units of analysis (i.e., states or provinces) are subparts of larger units (i.e., nations). The features of the units are due to their being parts of larger units and not to any relationship among the features. Social geographers also encounter this because many social and cultural features diffuse across geographic space.

Galton's problem is an important issue in comparative research because cultures rarely have clear, fixed boundaries. It is hard to say where one culture ends and another begins, whether one culture is distinct from another, or whether the features of one culture have diffused to another over time. Galton's problem occurs when the relationship between two variables in two different units is actually due to a common origin, and they are not truly distinct units (see Figure 12.2).

Galton's problem originated with regard to comparisons across cultures, but it applies to historical comparisons also. It arises when a researcher asks whether units are really the same or different in different historical periods. For example, is the Cuba of 1875 the same country as the Cuba of 2005? Do 130 years since the end of Spanish colonialism, the rise of U.S. influence, independence, dictatorship, and a communist revolution fundamentally change the unit?

Data in Cross-Cultural Research

Comparative Field Research. Comparative researchers use field research and participant observation in cultures other than their own. Anthropologists are specially trained and prepared for this type of research. The exchange of methods between anthropological and field research suggests that there are small differences between field research in one's own society and in another culture. Field research in a different culture is usually more difficult and places more requirements on the researcher.

FIGURE 1 2 . 2   Galton's Problem

Galton's problem occurs when a researcher observes the same social relationship (represented by X) in different settings or societies (represented as A, B, and C) and falsely concludes that the social relationship arose independently in these different places. The researcher may believe he or she has discovered a relationship in three separate cases. But the actual reason for the occurrence of the social relation may be a shared or common origin that has diffused from one setting to others. This is a problem because the researcher who finds a relationship (e.g., a marriage pattern) in distinct settings or units of analysis (e.g., societies) may believe it arose independently in different units. This belief suggests that the relationship is a human universal. The researcher may be unaware that in fact it exists because people have shared the relationship across units.

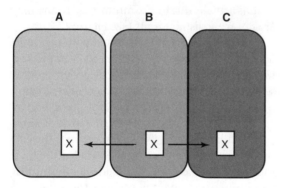

Existing Sources of Qualitative Data.   Comparative researchers can use secondary sources. For example, a researcher who conducts a comparative study of the Brazilian, Canadian, and Japanese educational systems can read studies by researchers from many countries, including Brazil, Canada, and Japan, which describe the education systems in the three nations.

There may have been 5,000 different cultures throughout human history; about 1,000 of

them have been studied by social researchers. A valuable source of ethnographic data on different cultures is the *Human Relations Area Files (HRAF)* and the related *Ethnographic Atlas*.[12] The HRAF is a collection of field research reports that bring together information from ethnographic studies on various cultures, most of which are primitive or small tribal groupings. Extensive information on nearly 300 cultures has been organized by social characteristics or practices (e.g., infant feeding, suicide, childbirth, etc.). A study on a particular culture is divided up, and its information on a characteristic is grouped with that from other studies. This makes it easy to compare many cultures on the same characteristic. For example, a researcher interested in inheritance can learn that of 159 different cultures in which it has been studied, 119 have a patrilineal form (father to son), 27 matrilineal (mother to daughter), and 13 mixed inheritance.

Researchers can use the HRAF to study relationships among several characteristics of different cultures. For example, to find out whether sexual assault against women, or rape, is associated with patriarchy (i.e., the holding of power and authority by males), a researcher can examine the presence of sexual assault and the strength of patriarchy in many cultures.

Using the HRAF does have limitations, however. First, the quality of the original research reports depends on the initial researcher's length of time in the field, familiarity with the language, and prior experience, as well as on the explicitness of the research report. Also, the range of behavior observed by the initial researcher and the depth of inquiry can vary. In addition, the categorization of characteristics in the HRAF can be crude. Another limitation involves the cultures that have been studied. Western researchers have made contact with and conducted field research on a limited number of cultures prior to these cultures' contact with the outside world. The cultures studied are not a representative sample of all the human cultures that existed. In addition, Galton's problem (discussed earlier) can be an issue.

Cross-National Survey Research. Survey research was discussed in a previous chapter. This section examines issues that arise when a researcher uses the survey technique in other cultures. The limitations of a cross-cultural survey are not different in principle from those of a survey within one culture. Nevertheless, they are usually much greater in magnitude and severity.

Survey research in a different culture requires that the researcher possess an in-depth knowledge of its norms, practices, and customs. Without such an in-depth knowledge, it is easy to make serious errors in procedure and interpretation. Knowing another language is not enough. A researcher needs to be multicultural and thoroughly know the culture in addition to being familiar with the survey method. Substantial advance knowledge about the other culture is needed prior to entering it or planning the survey. Close cooperation with the native people of the other culture is also essential.

A researcher's choice of the cultures or nations to include in a cross-cultural survey should be made on both substantive (e.g., theoretical, research question) and practical grounds. Each step of survey research (question wording, data collection, sampling, interviewing, etc.) must be tailored to the culture in which it is conducted. One critical issue is how the people from the other culture experience the survey. In some cultures, the survey and interviewing itself may be a strange, frightening experience, analogous to a police interrogation.

Sampling for a survey is also affected by the cultural context. Comparative survey researchers must consider whether accurate sampling frames are available, the quality of mail or telephone service, and transportation to remote rural areas. They need to be aware of such factors as how often people move, the types of dwellings in which people live, the number of people in a dwelling, the telephone coverage, or typical rates of refusal. Researchers must tailor the sampling unit to the culture and consider how basic units, such as the family, are defined in that culture. Special samples or methods for locating people for a sample may be required.

Questionnaire writing problems in the researcher's own culture are greatly magnified when studying a different culture. A researcher needs to be especially sensitive to question wording, questionnaire length, introductions, and topics included. He or she must be aware of local norms and of the topics that can and cannot be addressed by survey research. For example, open questions about political issues, alcohol use, religion, or sexuality may be taboo. In addition to these cultural issues, translation and language equivalency often pose serious problems (see Equivalence in Historical-Comparative Research). Techniques such as back translation (to be discussed) and the use of bilingual people are helpful, but often it is impossible to ask the exact same question in a different language.

Interviewing requires special attention in cross-cultural situations. Selection and training of interviewers depends on the education, norms, and etiquette of the other culture. The interview situation raises issues such as norms of privacy, ways to gain trust, beliefs about confidentiality, and differences in dialect. For example, in some cultures, an interviewer must spend a day in informal discussion before achieving the rapport needed for a short formal interview.

Existing Sources of Quantitative Data. Quantitative data for many variables are available for different nations. In addition, large collections of quantitative data have been assembled. They gather information on many variables from other sources (e.g., newspaper articles, official government statistics, United Nations reports).

There are significant limitations on existing cross-national data, many of which are shared by other existing statistics. The theoretical definition of variables and the reliability of data collection can vary dramatically across nations.

Missing information is a frequent limitation. Intentional misinformation in the official data from some governments can be a problem. Another limitation involves the nations on which data are collected. For example, during a 35-year period, new nations come into existence and others change their names or change their borders.

The existing data are available in major national data archives in a form that computers can read, and researchers can conduct secondary analysis on international existing statistics data. For example, Sutton (2004) conducted a quantitative, statistical study on 15 nations between 1960 and 1990. Researchers have long observed that imprisonment rates do not closely follow changes in crime rates. Sutton tested the Rusche and Kirchheimer thesis. It says that unemployment rates cause a rise in imprisonment rates because imprisonment is a government attempt to control a surplus of unemployed working-class males in the population who could become unruly and dangerous to the social order. Basically, it predicts that prisons will be filled when many workers are out of work and will empty out when the economy is booming. Sutton gathered data from government statistical yearbooks of the 15 countries, from publications by international organizations such as the World Health Organization and the International Labor Organization, and from prior social science studies that identified features of several nations, such as their unionization pattern, political party structure, and so forth. Sutton found only limited support for the original thesis, but he documented a strong effect from several other factors. He argued that the effect of unemployment on imprisonment was probably spurious (see the discussion of a spurious relationship in Chapters 2, 4, and 10 of this book). Sutton found that specific features of the nation's political organization and labor market structure appeared to cause both specific unemployment patterns and different imprisonment policies. In short, when low-income people and workers were politically weak compared to wealthy people and corporation owners, both unemployment and imprisonment rates rise compared to times when low-income people and workers have greater political power and influence.

EQUIVALENCE IN HISTORICAL-COMPARATIVE RESEARCH

The Importance of Equivalence

Equivalence is a critical issue in all research. It is the issue of making comparisons across divergent contexts, or whether a researcher, living in a specific time period and culture, correctly reads, understands, or conceptualizes data about people from a different historical era or culture. Without equivalence, a researcher cannot use the same concepts or measures in different cultures or historical periods, and this makes comparison difficult, if not impossible. It is similar to the problems that arise with measurement validity in quantitative research.

Types of Equivalence

The equivalence issue has implications for H-C research. A researcher might misunderstand or misinterpret events in a different era or culture. Assuming that the interpretation is correct, a researcher may find it difficult to conceptualize and organize the events to make comparisons across times or places. If he or she fully grasps another culture, a researcher may still find it difficult to communicate with others from his or her own time and culture. The equivalence issue can be divided into four subtypes: lexicon equivalence, contextual equivalence, conceptual equivalence, and measurement equivalence.

Lexicon Equivalence. *Lexicon equivalence* is the correct translation of words and phrases, or finding a word that means the same thing as another word. This is clearest between two languages. For example, in many languages and cultures there are different forms of address and pronouns for intimates (e.g., close friends and family members) and subordinates (e.g., younger persons and lower-status people) from those used in unknown or public settings or for persons of higher social status. There are no directly equal linguistic forms of speech in English, although the idea of close personal versus public relations exists in English-speaking cultures. In such languages, switching pronouns when saying, "How are you today?" might indicate a change in status or in the social relationship. One would have to indicate it in another, perhaps nonverbal, way if speaking in English. In cultures where age is an important status (e.g., Japan), many status-based words exist that are absent in English. One cannot say, for example, "my brother" without indicating whether one is speaking of an older or younger brother, and separate words are used for "my younger brother" or "my older brother."

Comparative researchers often use a technique called *back translation* to achieve lexicon equivalence. In back translation, a phrase or question is translated from one language to another and then back again. For example, a phrase in English is translated into Korean and then independently translated from Korean back into English. A researcher then compares the first and second English versions. For example, in a study to compare knowledge of international issues by U.S. and Japanese college students, the researchers developed a questionnaire in English. They next had a team of Japanese college faculty translate the questionnaire into Japanese. Some changes were made in the questionnaire. When they used back translation, they discovered "30 translating errors, including some major ones" (Cogan et al., 1988: 285).

Back translation does not help when words for a concept do not exist in a different language (e.g., there is no word for *trust* in Hindi, for *loyalty* in Turkish, for *privacy* in Chinese, or for *good quarrel* in Thai). Thus, translation may require complex explanations, or a researcher may not be able to use certain concepts.

Lexicon equivalence can be significant in historical research because the meaning of words changes over time, even in the same language. The greater the distance in time, the greater the chance that an expression will have a different meaning or connotation. For example, today the word *weed* refers to unwanted plants or to marijuana, but in Shakespeare's era, the word meant clothing (see Box 12.3).

Contextual Equivalence. *Contextual equivalence* is the correct application of terms or concepts in different social or historical contexts. It is an attempt to achieve equivalence within specific contexts. For example, in cultures with different dominant religions, a religious leader (e.g., priest, minister, or rabbi) can have different roles, training, and authority. In some contexts, priests are full-time male professionals who are wealthy, highly esteemed, well-educated community leaders and also wield political power. In other contexts, a priest is anyone who rises above others in a congregation on a temporary basis but is without power or standing in

---

Box 12.3 Cross-Cultural Answers to Survey Questions

The meaning of a statement or answer to a question often depends on the customs of a culture, the social situation, and the manner in which the answer is spoken. The manner of answering can reverse the different meanings of the same answer based on the manner in which the answer was spoken.

Manner in Which Answer Spoken	Answer to Question	
	Yes	*No*
Polite	No	Yes
Emphatic	Yes	No

Source: Adapted from Hymes (1970:329).

the community. Priests in such a context may be less well educated, have low incomes, and be viewed as foolish but harmless people. A researcher who asks about "priests" without noticing the context could make serious errors in interpretations.

Context also applies across historical eras. For example, *attending college* has a different meaning today than in a historical context in which only the richest 1 percent of the population attended college, most colleges had fewer than 500 students, all were private all-male institutions that did not require a high school diploma for entry, and a college curriculum consisted of classical languages and moral training. Attending college 100 years ago was not the same as it is today; the historical context has altered the meaning of attending college.

Conceptual Equivalence.   The ability to use the same concept across divergent cultures or historical eras is *conceptual equivalence.* Researchers live within specific cultures and historical eras. Their concepts are based on their experiences and knowledge from their own culture and era. Researchers may try to stretch their concepts by learning about other cultures or eras, but their views of other cultures or eras are colored by their current life situations. This creates a persistent tension and raises the question: Can a researcher create concepts that are simultaneously true reflections of life experiences in different cultures or eras and that also make sense to him or her?

The issue of a researcher's concept is a special case of a larger issue, because concepts can be incompatible across different time periods or cultures. Is it possible to create concepts that are true, accurate, and valid representations of social life in two or more cultural or historical settings that are very different? For example, the word *class* exists in many societies, but the system of classes (i.e., the role of income, wealth, job, education, status, relation to means of production), the number of classes, the connota-

tions of being in a particular class, and class categories or boundaries differ across societies, making the study of social class across societies difficult.

At times, the same or a very similar concept exists across cultures but in different forms or degrees of strength. For example, in many Asian societies, there is a marked difference between the outward, public presentation and definition of self and the private, personal presentation and the definition of self. What one reveals and shows externally is often culturally detached from true, internal feelings. Some languages mark this linguistically, as well. The idea of a distinct self for public, nonfamily, or nonprivate situations exists in Western cultures, as well, but it is much weaker and less socially significant. In addition, many Western cultures assume that the inner self is "real" and should be revealed, an assumption that is not always shared cross-culturally.

At other times, there is no direct cultural equivalent. For example, there is no direct Western conceptual equivalent for the Japanese *ie.* It is translated as family system, but this idea was created by outsiders to explain Japanese behavior. The *ie* includes a continuing line of familial descent going back generations and continuing into the future. Its meaning is closer to a European lineage "house" among the feudal nobility than the modern household or even an extended family. It includes ancestors, going back many generations, and future descendants, with branches created by noninheriting male offspring (or adopted sons). It can also include a religious identity and property-holding dimensions (as land or a business passed down for generations). It can include feelings of obligation to one's ancestors and feelings to uphold any commitments they may have made. The *ie* is also embedded in a web of hierarchical relationships with other *ie* and suggests social position or status in a community.

Conceptual equivalence also applies to the study of different historical eras. For example, measuring income is very different in a historical era with a largely noncash society in which most people grow their own food, make their own furniture and clothing, or barter goods. Where money is rarely used, it makes no sense to measure income by number of dollars earned. Counting hogs, acres of land, pairs of shoes, servants, horse carriages, and the like may be more appropriate.

Measurement Equivalence. *Measurement equivalence* means measuring the same concept in different settings. If a researcher develops a concept appropriate to different contexts, the question remains: Are different measures necessary in different contexts for the same concept? The measurement equivalence issue suggests that an H-C researcher must examine many sources of partial evidence in order to measure or identify a theoretical construct. When evidence exists in fragmentary forms, he or she must examine extensive quantities of indirect evidence in order to identify constructs.

ETHICS

Historical-comparative research shares the ethical concerns found in other nonreactive research techniques. The use of primary historical sources occasionally raises special ethical issues. First, it is difficult to replicate research based on primary material. The researcher's selection criteria for use of evidence and external criticism of documents places a burden on the integrity of the individual researcher.

Second, the right to protect one's privacy may interfere with the right to gather evidence. A person's descendants may want to destroy or hide private papers or evidence of scandalous behavior. Even major political figures (e.g., presidents) want to hide embarrassing official documents. Comparative researchers must be sensitive to cultural and political issues of cross-cultural interaction. They need to learn what is considered

offensive within a culture. Sensitivity means showing respect for the traditions, customs, and meaning of privacy in a host country. For example, it may be taboo for a man to interview a married woman without her husband present.

In general, a researcher who visits another culture wants to establish good relations with the host country's government. He or she will not take data out of the country without giving something (e.g., results) in return. The military or political interests of the researcher's home nation or the researcher's personal values may conflict with official policy in the host nation. A researcher may be suspected of being a spy or may be under pressure from his or her home country to gather covert information.

Sometimes, the researcher's presence or findings may cause diplomatic problems. For example, a researcher who examines health care practices in a country, then declares that official government policy is to ignore treating a serious illness can expect serious controversy. Likewise, a researcher who is sympathetic to the cause of groups who oppose the government may be threatened with imprisonment or asked to leave the country. Social researchers who conduct research in any country should be aware of such issues and the potential consequences of their actions.

CONCLUSION

In this chapter, you have learned methodological principles for an inquiry into historical and comparative materials. The H-C approach is appropriate when asking big questions about macro-level change, or for understanding social processes that operate across time or are universal across several societies. Historical-comparative research can be carried out in several ways, but a distinct qualitative H-C approach is similar to that of field research in important respects.

Historical-comparative research involves a different orientation toward research more than it means applying specialized techniques. Some specialized techniques are used, such as the external criticism of primary documents, but the most vital feature is how a researcher approaches a question, probes data, and moves toward explanations.

Historical-comparative research is more difficult to conduct than research that is neither historical nor comparative, but the difficulties are present to a lesser degree in other types of social research. For example, issues of equivalence exist to some degree in all social research. In H-C research, however, the problems cannot be treated as secondary concerns. They are at the forefront of how research is conducted and determine whether a research question can be answered.

Key Terms

back translation
conceptual equivalence
contextual equivalence
external criticism
Galton's problem
Human Relations Area Files (HRAF)
internal criticism
lexicon equivalence
measurement equivalence
oral history
primary sources
recollections
running records
secondary sources

Endnotes

1. See Mahoney (1999) for major works of historical-comparative research.
2. See Calhoun (1996), McDaniel (1978), Przeworski and Teune (1970), and Stinchcombe (1978) for additional discussion.
3. For additional discussion, see Sewell (1987).
4. See Naroll (1968) for a discussion of difficulties in creating distinctions. Also see Whiting (1968).
5. Transhistorical concepts are discussed by others, such as Bendix (1963), Przeworski and Teune (1970), and Smelser (1976).
6. See Lowenthal (1985:187).
7. Bendix (1978:16) distinguished between the *judgments* of historians and the *selections* of sociologists.
8. Bonnell (1980:161), Finley (1977:132), and Goldthorpe (1977:189–190) discussed how historians use concepts. Selection in this context is discussed by Abrams (1982:194) and Ben-Yehuda (1983).
9. For introductions to how historians see their method, see Barzun and Graff (1970), Braudel (1980), Cantor and Schneider (1967), Novick (1988), or Shafer (1980).
10. The narrative is discussed in Abbott (1992), Gallie (1963), Gotham and Staples (1996), Griffin (1993), McLennan (1981:76–87), Runciman (1980), and Stone (1987:74–96).
11. For more on the strengths and limitations of comparative research, see Anderson (1973), Holt and Turner (1970), Kohn (1987), Ragin (1987), Smelser (1976), Vallier (1971a, 1971b), Walton (1973), and Whiting (1968).
12. For more on the *Human Relations Area File* and the *Ethnographic Atlas,* see Murdock (1967, 1971) and Whiting (1968).

Analysis of Qualitative Data

INTRODUCTION

Qualitative data come in the form of photos, written words, phrases, or symbols describing or representing people, actions, and events in social life. Qualitative researchers rarely use statistical analysis. This does not mean that qualitative data analysis is based on vague impressions. It can be systematic and logically rigorous, although in a different way from quantitative or statistical analysis. Over time qualitative data analysis has become more explicit, although no single qualitative data analysis approach is widely accepted.

This chapter is divided into four parts. First, the similarities and differences between qualitative and quantitative data analysis are discussed. Next is a look at how researchers use coding and concept/theory building in the process of analyzing qualitative data. Third is a review of some of the major analytic strategies researchers deploy and ways they think about linking qualitative data with theory. Last is a brief review of other techniques researchers use to manage and examine patterns in the qualitative data they have collected.

COMPARING METHODS OF DATA ANALYSIS

Similarities

Both styles of research involve researchers inferring from the empirical details of social life. To *infer* means to pass a judgment, to use reasoning, and to reach a conclusion based on evidence. In both forms of data analysis, the researcher carefully examines empirical information to reach a conclusion. The conclusion is reached by reasoning, simplifying the complexity in the data, and abstracting from the data, but this varies by the style of research. Both forms of data analysis anchor statements about the social world and are faithful to the data.

Qualitative as well as quantitative analysis involves a public method or process. Researchers systematically record or gather data and in so doing make accessible to others what they did. Both types of researchers collect large amounts of data, describe the data, and document how they collected and examined it. The degree to which the method is standardized and visible may vary, but all researchers reveal their study design in some way.

All data analysis is based on comparison. Social researchers compare features of the evidence they have gathered internally or with related evidence. Researchers identify multiple processes, causes, properties, or mechanisms within the evidence. They then look for patterns—similarities and differences, aspects that are alike and unlike. Both qualitative and quantitative researchers strive to avoid errors, false conclusions, and misleading inferences. Researchers are also alert for possible fallacies or illusions. They sort through various explanations, discussions, and descriptions, and evaluate merits of rivals, seeking the more authentic, valid, true, or worthy among them.

Differences

Qualitative data analysis differs from quantitative analysis in four ways. First, quantitative researchers choose from a specialized, standardized set of data analysis techniques. Hypothesis testing and statistical methods vary little across different social research projects. Quantitative analysis is highly developed and builds on applied mathematics. By contrast, qualitative data analysis is less standardized. The wide variety in qualitative research is matched by the many approaches to data analysis.

A second difference is that quantitative researchers do not begin data analysis until they have collected all of the data and condensed them into numbers. They then manipulate the numbers in order to see patterns or relationships. Qualitative researchers can look for patterns or relationships, but they begin analysis early in a research project, while they are still collecting data. The results of early data analysis guide subsequent data collection. Thus, analysis is less a distinct final stage of research than a dimension of research that stretches across all stages.

Another difference is the relationship between data and social theory. Quantitative researchers manipulate numbers that represent empirical facts to test theoretical hypotheses. By contrast, qualitative researchers create new concepts and theory by blending together empirical evidence and abstract concepts. Instead of testing a hypothesis, a qualitative analyst may illustrate or color in evidence showing that a theory, generalization, or interpretation is plausible.

The fourth difference is the degree of abstraction or distance from the details of social life. In all data analysis, a researcher places raw data into categories that he or she manipulates in order to identify patterns. Quantitative researchers assume that social life can be represented by using numbers. When they manipulate the numbers according to the laws of statistics, the numbers reveal features of social life. Qualitative analysis does not draw on a large, well-established body of formal knowledge from mathematics and statistics. The data are in the form of words, which are relatively imprecise, diffuse, and context-based, and can have more than one meaning.

Explanations and Qualitative Data

Qualitative explanations take many forms. A qualitative researcher does not have to choose between a rigid idiographic/nomothetic dichotomy—that is, between describing specifics and verifying universal laws. Instead, a researcher develops explanations or generalizations that are close to concrete data and contexts but are more than simple descriptions. He or she usually uses a lower-level, less abstract theory, which is grounded in concrete details. He or she may

build new theory to create a realistic picture of social life and stimulate understanding more than to test a causal hypothesis. Explanations tend to be rich in detail, sensitive to context, and capable of showing the complex processes or sequences of social life. The explanations may be causal, but this is not always the case. The researcher's goal is to organize specific details into a coherent picture, model, or set of interlocked concepts.

A qualitative researcher divides explanations into two categories: highly unlikely and plausible. The researcher is satisfied by building a case or supplying supportive evidence. He or she may eliminate some theoretical explanations from consideration while increasing the plausibility of others because only a few explanations will be consistent with a pattern in the data. Qualitative analysis can eliminate an explanation by showing that a wide array of evidence contradicts it. The data might support more than one explanation, but *all* explanations will not be consistent with it. In addition to eliminating less plausible explanations, qualitative data analysis helps to verify a sequence of events or the steps of a process. This temporal ordering is the basis of finding associations among variables, and it is useful in supporting causal arguments.

CODING AND CONCEPT FORMATION

Qualitative researchers often use general ideas, themes, or concepts as analytic tools for making generalizations. Qualitative analysis often uses nonvariable concepts or simple nominal-level variables.

Conceptualization

Quantitative researchers conceptualize and refine variables in a process that comes before data collection or analysis. By contrast, qualitative researchers form new concepts or refine concepts that are grounded in the data. Concept formation is integral to data analysis and begins during data collection. Conceptualization is how a qualitative researcher organizes and makes sense of the data.

A qualitative researcher organizes data into categories on the basis of themes, concepts, or similar features. He or she develops new concepts, formulates conceptual definitions, and examines the relationships among concepts. Eventually, he or she links concepts to each other in terms of a sequence, as oppositional sets (X is the opposite of Y) or as sets of similar categories that he or she interweaves into theoretical statements. Qualitative researchers conceptualize or form concepts as they read through and ask critical questions of data (e.g., field notes, historical documents, secondary sources, etc.). The questions can come from the abstract vocabulary of a discipline such as sociology—for example: Is this a case of class conflict? Was role conflict present in that situation? Is this a social movement? Questions can also be logical—for example: What was the sequence of events? How does the way it happened here compare to over there? Are these the same or different, general or specific cases? Researchers often conceptualize as they code qualitative data.

In qualitative data analysis, ideas and evidence are mutually interdependent. This applies particularly to case study analysis. Cases are not given preestablished empirical units or theoretical categories apart from data; they are defined by data and theory. By analyzing a situation, the researcher organizes data and applies ideas simultaneously to create or specify a case. Making or creating a case, called *casing*, brings the data and theory together. Determining what to treat as a case resolves a tension or strain between what the researcher observes and his or her ideas about it.

Coding Qualitative Data

A quantitative researcher codes after all the data have been collected. He or she arranges measures of variables, which are in the form of numbers, into a machine-readable form for statistical analysis.

Coding data has a different meaning in qualitative research. A researcher codes by organizing the raw data into conceptual categories and creates themes or concepts. Instead of a simple clerical task, coding is an integral part of data analysis guided by the research question. Coding encourages higher-level thinking about the data and moves a researcher toward theorical generalizations.

Coding is two simultaneous activities: mechanical data reduction and analytic data categorization. Coding data is the hard work of reducing mountains of raw data into manageable piles. In addition to making a large mass of data manageable, it is how a researcher imposes order on the data. Coding also allows a researcher to quickly retrieve relevant parts of the data. Between the moments of thrill and inspiration, coding qualitative data, or filework, can be wearisome and tedious.

Open Coding.   *Open coding* is performed during a first pass through recently collected data. The researcher locates themes and assigns initial codes or labels in a first attempt to condense the mass of data into categories. He or she slowly reads field notes, historical sources, or other data, looking for critical terms, key events, or themes, which are then noted. Next, he or she writes a preliminary concept or label at the edge of a note card or computer record and highlights it with brightly colored ink or in some similar way. The researcher is open to creating new themes and to changing these initial codes in subsequent analysis. A theoretical framework helps if it is used in a flexible manner.

Open coding brings themes to the surface from deep inside the data. The themes are at a low level of abstraction and come from the researcher's initial research question, concepts in the literature, terms used by members in the social setting, or new thoughts stimulated by immersion in the data.

An example of this is found in LeMasters's (1975) field research study of a working-class tavern when he found that marriage came up in many conversations. If he open coded field notes, he might have coded a block of field notes with the theme *marriage*. Following is an example of hypothetical field notes that can be open coded with the theme *marriage:*

> I wore a tie to the bar on Thursday because I had been at a late meeting. Sam noticed it immediately and said. "Damn it, Doc. I wore one of them things once—when I got married—and look what happened to me! By God, the undertaker will have to put the next one on." I ordered a beer, then asked him, "Why did you get married?" He replied, "What the hell you goin' to do? You just can't go on shacking up with girls all your life—I did plenty of that when I was single" with a smile and wink. He paused to order another beer and light a cigarette, then continued, "A man, sooner or later, likes to have a home of his own, and some kids, and to have that, you have to get married. There's no way out of it—they got you hooked." I said, "Helen [his wife] seems like a nice person." He returned, "Oh, hell, she's not a bad kid, but she's a god-damn woman and they get under my skin. They piss me off. If you go to a party, just when you start having fun, the wife says 'let's go home.' " (Adapted from LeMasters, 1975:36–37)

Historical-comparative researchers also use open coding. For example, a researcher studying the Knights of Labor, an American nineteenth-century movement for economic and political reform, reads a secondary source about the activities of a local branch of the movement in a specific town. When reading and taking notes, the researcher notices that the Prohibition party was important in local elections and that temperance was debated by members of the local branch. The researcher's primary interest is in the internal structure, ideology, and growth of the Knights movement. Temperance is a new and unexpected category. The researcher codes the notes with the label "temperance" and includes it as a possible theme.

Qualitative researchers vary in the units they code. Some code every line or every few words; others code paragraphs and argue that much of the data are not coded and are dross or left over. The degree of detail in coding depends on the research question, the "richness" of the data, and the researcher's purposes.

Open-ended coding extends to analytic notes or memos that a researcher writes to himself or herself while collecting data. Researchers should write memos on their codes (see the later discussion in Analytic Memo Writing).

Axial Coding.   This is a "second pass" through the data. During open coding, a researcher focuses on the actual data and assigns code labels for themes. There is no concern about making connections among themes or elaborating the concepts that the themes represent. By contrast, in *axial coding,* the researcher begins with an organized set of initial codes or preliminary concepts. In this second pass, he or she focuses on the initial coded themes more than on the data. Additional codes or new ideas may emerge during this pass, and the researcher notes them; but his or her primary task is to review and examine initial codes. He or she moves toward organizing ideas or themes and identifies the axis of key concepts in analysis.

During axial coding, a researcher asks about causes and consequences, conditions and interactions, strategies and processes, and looks for categories or concepts that cluster together. He or she asks questions such as: Can I divide existing concepts into subdimensions or subcategories? Can I combine several closely related concepts into one more general one? Can I organize categories into a sequence (i.e., A, then B, then C), or by their physical location (i.e., where they occur), or their relationship to a major topic of interest? For example, a field researcher studying working-class life divides the general issue of marriage into subparts (e.g., engagement, weddings). He or she marks all notes involving parts of marriage and then relates marriage to themes of sexuality, division of labor in household tasks, views on children, and so on. When the theme reappears in different places, the researcher makes comparisons so he or she can see new themes (e.g., men and women have different attitudes toward marriage).

In the example of historical research on the Knights of Labor, a researcher looks for themes related to temperance. He or she looks for discussions of saloons, drinking or drunkenness, and relations between the movement and political parties that support or oppose temperance. Themes that cluster around temperance could also include drinking as a form of recreation, drinking as part of ethnic culture, and differences between men and women regarding drinking.

Axial coding not only stimulates thinking about linkages between concepts or themes but it also raises new questions. It can suggest dropping some themes or examining others in more depth. In addition, it reinforces the connections between evidence and concepts. As a researcher consolidates codes and locates evidences, he or she finds evidence in many places for core themes and builds a dense web of support in the qualitative data for them. This is analogous to the idea of multiple indicators described with regard to reliability and measuring variables. The connection between a theme and data is strengthened by multiple instances of empirical evidence.

Selective Coding.   By the time a researcher is ready for this last pass through the data, he or she has identified the major themes of the research project. *Selective coding* involves scanning data and previous codes. Researchers look selectively for cases that illustrate themes and make comparisons and contrasts after most or all data collection is complete. They begin after they have well-developed concepts and have started to organize their overall analysis around several

core generalizations or ideas. For example, a researcher studying working-class life in a tavern decides to make gender relations a major theme. In selective coding, the researcher goes through his or her field notes, looking for differences in how men and women talk about dating, engagements, weddings, divorce, extramarital affairs, or husband/wife relations. He or she then compares male and female attitudes on each part of the theme of marriage.

Likewise, the researcher studying the Knights of Labor decides to make the movement's failure to form alliances with other political groups a major theme. The researcher goes through his or her notes looking for compromise and conflict between the Knights and other political parties, including temperance groups and the Prohibition party. The array of concepts and themes that are related to temperance in axial coding helps him or her discover how the temperance issue facilitated or inhibited alliances.

During selective coding, major themes or concepts ultimately guide the researcher's search. He or she reorganizes specific themes identified in earlier coding and elaborates more than one major theme. For example, in the working-class tavern study, the researcher examines opinions on marriage to understand both the theme of gender relations and the theme of different stages of the life cycle. He or she does this because marriage can be looked at both ways. Likewise, in the Knights of Labor study, the researcher can use temperance to understand the major theme of failed alliances and also to understand another theme, sources of division within the movement that were based on ethnic or religious differences among members (see Figure 13.1).

Analytic Memo Writing

Qualitative researchers are compulsive note-takers. Their data are recorded in notes, they write comments on their research strategy in notes, and so on. They keep their notes organized in

FIGURE 13.1   The Coding Process for Qualitative Data Analysis

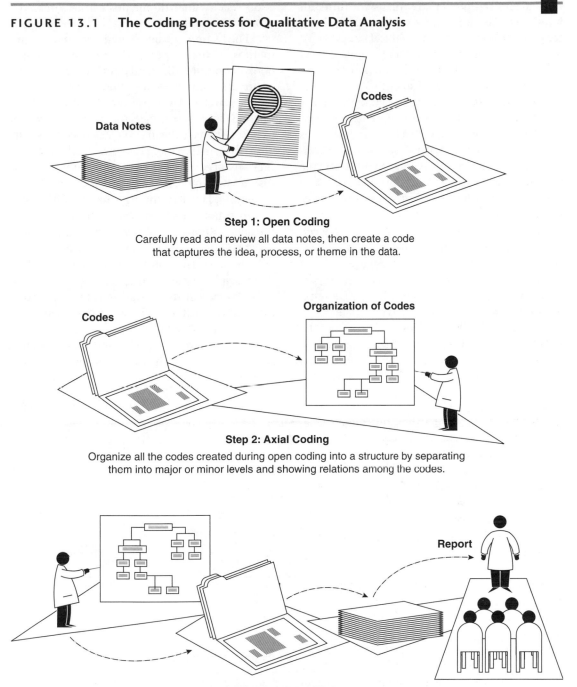

Step 1: Open Coding

Carefully read and review all data notes, then create a code
that captures the idea, process, or theme in the data.

Step 2: Axial Coding

Organize all the codes created during open coding into a structure by separating
them into major or minor levels and showing relations among the codes.

Step 3: Selective Coding

Take the organized codes from the axial coding process and review the codes in the original
data notes to select the best illustrations for entering them into a final report.

files, and often have many files with different kinds of notes: a file on methodological issues (e.g., locations of sources or ethical issues), a file of maps or diagrams, a file on possible overall outlines of a final report or chapter, a file on specific people or events, and so on.

The *analytic memo* is a special type of note. It is a memo or discussion of thoughts and ideas about the coding process that a researcher writes to himself or herself. Each coded theme or concept forms the basis of a separate memo, and the memo contains a discussion of the concept or theme. The rough theoretical notes form the beginning of analytic memos.

The analytic memo forges a link between the concrete data or raw evidence and more abstract, theoretical thinking (see Figure 13.2). It contains a researcher's reflections on and thinking about the data and coding. The researcher adds to the memo and uses it as he or she passes through the data with each type of coding. The memos form the basis for analyzing data in the research report. In fact, rewritten sections from

good-quality analytic memos can become sections of the final report.

The technology involved in writing analytic memos is simple: pen and paper, a few notebooks, computer files, and photocopies of notes. There are many ways to write analytic memos; each researcher develops his or her own style or method. Some researchers make multiple copies of notes, then cut them and place selections into an analytic memo file. This works well if the data files are large and the analytic memos are kept distinct within the file (e.g., on different-colored paper or placed at the beginning). Other researchers link the analytic memo file locations to the data notes where a theme appears. Then it is easy to move between the analytic memo and the data. Because data notes contain links or marked themes, it is easy to locate specific sections in the data. An intermediate strategy is to keep a running list of locations where a major theme appears in the raw data.

As a researcher reviews and modifies analytic memos, he or she discusses ideas with col-

FIGURE 13.2   Analytic Memos and Other Files

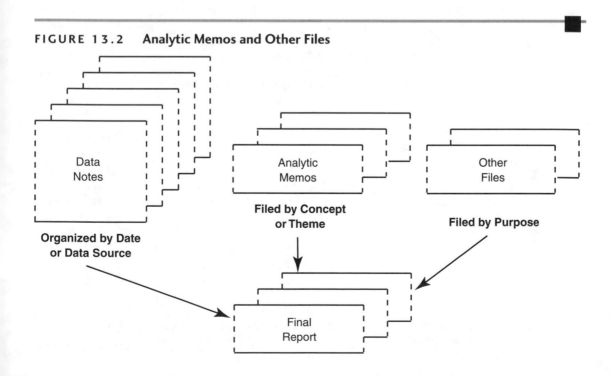

leagues, and returns to the literature with a focus on new issues. Analytic memos may help to generate potential hypotheses, which can be added and dropped as needed, and to develop new themes or coding systems.

ANALYTIC STRATEGIES FOR QUALITATIVE DATA

Techniques of coding and memo writing are approaches to the analysis of qualitative data. Most qualitative researchers use these techniques to some degree, often combined with a more specific strategy for the analysis of qualitative data. In this section you will learn about four strategies researchers use to analyze qualitative data: the narrative, ideal types, successive approximation, and the illustrative method.

Compared to the analysis of quantitative data, strategies for qualitative data are more diverse, less standardized, and less explicitly outlined by researchers. Only in the past decade have researchers started to explain and outline exactly how they analyze qualitative data.

In general, *data analysis* means a search for patterns in data—recurrent behaviors, objects, or a body of knowledge. Once a pattern is identified, it is interpreted in terms of a social theory or the setting in which it occurred. The qualitative researcher moves from the description of a historical event or social setting to a more general interpretation of its meaning.

The Narrative

You encountered the narrative in the last chapter on historical-comparative research. In field research, it is also called a *natural history* or *realist tale approach*. The narrative is a largely atheoretical description. The researcher–author "disappears" from the analysis and presents the concrete details in chronological order as if they were the product of a unique and "naturally unfolding" sequence of events. He or she simply "tells a story" of what occurred.

Some argue that the narrative approach is a presentation of data without analysis. There can be analysis in a narrative, but it is "light" and subtle. In the narrative method, a researcher assembles the data into a descriptive picture or account of what occurred, but he or she largely leaves the data to "speak for themselves." He or she interjects little in the form of new systematic concepts, external theories, or abstract models. The explanation resides not in abstract concepts and theories, but in a combination of specific, concrete details. The researcher presents or reveals the social reality as members in a field setting experience it, or the worldview of specific historical actors at a particular point in time. By using little commentary, a researcher tries to convey an authentic feel for life's complexity as experienced by particular people in specific circumstances, and does not derive abstract principles or identify generalizable analytic patterns.

In the narrative, data are "analyzed" or "explained" in the terminology and concepts of the people being studied. The analysis appears in how a researcher organizes the data for presentation and tells the story. It appears in a greater attention to particular people, events, or facts, and it relies on literary devices—the creative selection of particular words to tell a story, describe a setting, show character development, and present dramatic emphasis, intrigue, or suspense.

Researchers debate the usefulness of the narrative strategy. On the one hand, it provides rich concrete detail and clearly demonstrates the temporal ordering of processes or specific events. It captures a high degree of complexity and conveys a nuanced understanding of how particular events or factors mutually affect each other. The narrative allows the researcher to assemble very specific concrete details (i.e., the names, actions, and words of specific people and the detailed descriptions of particular events at specific times) that may be idiosyncratic but that contribute to a complete explanation. On the other hand, many researchers criticize the narrative approach for being too complex, particular, and idiosyncratic. It does not provide generalizations. The narrative may present an overwhelming array of particular details, but not provide a general explanation that researchers can apply to other people, situations, or time periods (see Box 13.1).

Ideal Types

Max Weber's *ideal type* is used by many qualitative researchers. Ideal types are models or mental abstractions of social relations or processes. They are pure standards against which the data

or "reality" can be compared. An ideal type is a device used for comparison, because no reality ever fits an ideal type. For example, a researcher develops a mental model of the ideal democracy or an ideal college beer party. These abstractions, with lists of characteristics, do not describe any specific democracy or beer party; nevertheless, they are useful when applied to many specific cases to see how well each case measures up to the ideal. This stage can be used with the illustrative method described earlier.

Weber's method of ideal types also complements John Stuart Mill's method of agreement.

Box 13.1   The Narrative

Many qualitative researchers, especially feminist researchers, use the narrative because they believe it best enables them to retain a richness and authenticity from their original data sources (i.e., individual personal stories or events in ethnographies, or specific historical events). In simple terms, the narrative is story telling. In it, an author presents two or more events in temporal and causal sequences. Some narratives are complex, with elements such as (1) a summary statement of the entire story; (2) an orientation that identifies specific times, places, persons, and situations; (3) complicating actions or twists in the plot of "what happened"; (4) an evaluation or emotional assessment of the narrative's meaning or signifigance; (5) a resolution or what occured after a dramatic high point that resolves a suspenseful climatic event; and (6) a coda or signal that the narrative is ending.

People frequently tell one another stories in daily life. They usually structure or organize their narratives into one of several recognized patterns, often recounting it with visual clues, gestures, or voice intonations for dramatic emphasis. The structure may include plot lines, core metaphors, and rhetorical devices that draw on familiar cultural and personal models to effectively communicate meanings to others.

The narrative is found in literature, artistic expressions, types of therapy, judicial inquiries, social or political histories, biography and autobiography, medical case histories, and journalistic accounts. As a way to organize, analyze, and present qualitative social science data, the narrative shares many features with other academic and cultural communication forms, but it differs from the positivist model for organizing and reporting on data. The positivist model emphasizes using impersonal, abstract, "neutral" language and a standardized analytic approach.

Many qualitative researchers argue that researchers who adopt the positivist model are simply using an alternative form of narrative, one with specialized conventions. These conventions encourage formal analytic models and abstract theories, but such models or theories are not necessarily superior to a story-telling narrative. Positivist data analysis and reporting conventions have two negative effects. First, they make it easier for researchers to lose sight of the concrete actual events and personal experiences that comprise social science data. Second, they make it more difficult for researchers to express ideas and build social theories in a format that most people find to be familiar and comfortable.

With the method of agreement, a researcher's attention is focused on what is common across cases, and he or she looks for common causes in cases with a common outcome. By itself, the method of agreement implies a comparison against actual cases. This comparison of cases could also be made against an idealized model. A researcher could develop an ideal type of a social process or relationship, then compare specific cases to it.

Qualitative researchers have used ideal types in two ways: to contrast the impact of contexts and as analogy.

Contrast Contexts. Researchers who adopt a strongly interpretive approach may use ideal types to interpret data in a way that is sensitive to the context and cultural meanings of members. They do not test hypotheses or create a generalizable theory, but use the ideal type to bring out the specifics of each case and to emphasize the impact of the unique context.

Researchers making contrasts between contexts often choose cases with dramatic contrasts or distinctive features. For example, in *Work and Authority in Industry,* Reinhard Bendix (1956) compared management relations in very different contexts: Czarist Russia and industrializing England.

When comparing contexts, researchers do not use the ideal type to illustrate a theory in different cases or to discover regularities. Instead, they accentuate the specific and the unique. Other methods of analysis focus on the general and ignore peculiarities. By contrast, a researcher who uses ideal types can show how unique features shape the operation of general processes.

Analogies. Ideal types are used as analogies to organize qualitative data. An *analogy* is a statement that two objects, processes, or events are similar to each other. Researchers use analogies to communicate ideas and to facilitate logical comparisons. Analogies transmit information about patterns in data by referring to something that is already known or an experience familiar to the reader. They can describe relationships buried deep within many details and are a shorthand method for seeing patterns in a maze of specific events. They also make it easier to compare social processes across different cases or settings. For example, a researcher says that a room went silent after person X spoke: "A chill like a cold gust of air" spread through the room. This does not mean that the room temperature dropped or that a breeze was felt, but it succinctly expresses a rapid change in emotional tone. Likewise, a researcher reports that gender relations in society Y were such that women were "viewed like property and treated like slaves." This does not mean that the legal and social relations between genders were identical to those of slave owner and slave. It implies that an ideal type of a slave-and-master relationship would show major similarities to the evidence on relations between men and women if applied to society Y.

The use of analogies to analyze qualitative data serves as a heuristic device (i.e., a device that helps one learn or see). It can represent something that is unknown and is especially valuable when researchers attempt to make sense of or explain data by referring to a deep structure or an underlying mechanism. Ideal types do not provide a definitive test of an explanation. Rather, they guide the conceptual reconstruction of the mass of details into a systematic format.

Successive Approximation

Successive approximation involves repeated iterations or cycling through steps, moving toward a final analysis. Over time, or after several iterations, a researcher moves from vague ideas and concrete details in the data toward a comprehensive analysis with generalizations. This is similar to the three kinds of coding discussed earlier.

A researcher begins with research questions and a framework of assumptions and concepts. He or she then probes into the data, asking questions of the evidence to see how well the concepts fit the evidence and reveal features of the data. He or she also creates new concepts by abstracting from the evidence and adjusts concepts to fit the evidence better. The researcher then collects additional evidence to address unresolved issues that appeared in the first stage, and repeats the process. At each stage, the evidence and the theory shape each other. This is called *successive approximation* because the modified concepts and the model approximate the full evidence and are modified over and over to become successively more accurate.

Each pass through the evidence is provisional or incomplete. The concepts are abstract, but they are rooted in the concrete evidence and reflect the context. As the analysis moves toward generalizations that are subject to conditions and contingencies, the researcher refines generalizations and linkages to reflect the evidence better. For example, a historical-comparative researcher believes that historical reality is not even or linear; rather, it has discontinuous stages or steps. He or she may divide 100 years of history into periods by breaking continuous time into discrete units or periods and define the periods theoretically. Theory helps the researcher identify what is significant and what is common within periods or between different periods.

The researcher cannot determine the number and size of periods and the breaks between them until after the evidence has been examined. He or she may begin with a general idea of how many periods to create and what distinguishes them but will adjust the number and size of the periods and the location of the breaks after reviewing the evidence. The researcher then reexamines the evidence with added data, readjusts the periodization, and so forth. After several cycles, he or she approximates a set of periods in 100 years on the basis of successively theorizing and looking at evidence.

The Illustrative Method

Another method of analysis uses empirical evidence to illustrate or anchor a theory. With the *illustrative method,* a researcher applies theory to a concrete historical situation or social setting, or organizes data on the basis of prior theory. Preexisting theory provides the *empty boxes.* The researcher sees whether evidence can be gathered to fill them. The evidence in the boxes confirms or rejects the theory, which he or she treats as a useful device for interpreting the social world. The theory can be in the form of a general model, an analogy, or a sequence of steps.

There are two variations of the illustrative method. One is to show that the theoretical model illuminates or clarifies a specific case or single situation. A second is the parallel demonstration of a model in which a researcher juxtaposes multiple cases (i.e., units or time periods) to show that the theory can be applied in multiple cases. In other cases, the researcher illustrates theory with specific material from multiple cases. An example of parallel demonstration is found in Paige's (1975) study of rural class conflict. Paige first developed an elaborate model of conditions that cause class conflict, and then provided evidence to illustrate it from Peru, Angola, and Vietnam. This demonstrated the applicability of the model in several cases. (See Box 13.2 for a summary of types.)

Box 13.2 **A Summary of Four Strategies for Qualitative Data Analysis**

1. *The narrative.* Tell a detailed story about a particular slice of social life.
2. *Ideal types.* Compare qualitative data with a pure model of social life.
3. *Successive approximation.* Repeatedly move back and forth between data and theory, until the gap between them shrinks or disappears.
4. *The illustrative method.* Fill the "empty boxes" of theory with qualitative data.

OTHER TECHNIQUES

Qualitative researchers use many analysis techniques. Here is a brief look at other techniques to illustrate the variety.

Network Analysis

The idea of social networks was discussed with network theory and with snowball sampling. Qualitative researchers often "map" the connections among a set of people, organizations, events, or places. Using sociograms and similar mapping techniques, they can discover, analyze, and display sets of relations. For example, in a company, Harry gives Sue orders, Sue and Sam consult and help one another. Sam gets materials from Sandra. Sandra socializes with Mary. Researchers find that networks help them see and understand the structure of complex social relations.

Time Allocation Analysis

Time is an important resource. Researchers examine the way people or organizations spend or invest time to reveal implicit rules of conduct or priorities. Researchers document the duration or amount of time devoted to various activities. Qualitative researchers examine the duration or amount of time devoted to activities. An analysis of how people, groups, or organizations allocate the valuable resources they control (such as time, space, money, prestige) can reveal a lot about their real, as contrasted with officially professed, priorities. Often, people are unaware of or do not explicitly acknowledge the importance of an activity on which they spent time. For example, a researcher notices that certain people are required to wait before seeing a person, whereas others do not wait. The researcher may analyze the amount of time, who waits, what they do while waiting, and whether they feel waiting is just. Or the researcher documents that people say that a certain celebration in a corporation is not important. Yet, everyone attends and spends two hours at the event. The collective allocation of two hours during a busy week for the celebration signals its latent or implicit importance in the culture of the corporation.

Flowchart and Time Sequence

In addition to the amount of time devoted to various activities, researchers analyze the order of events or decisions. Historical researchers have traditionally focused on documenting the sequence of events, but comparative and field researchers also look at flow or sequence. In addition to when events occur, researchers use the idea of a decision tree or flowchart to outline the order of decisions, to understand how one event or decision is related to others. For example, an activity as simple as making a cake can be outlined (see Figure 13.3). The idea of mapping out steps, decisions, or events and looking at their interrelationship has been applied to many settings.

Multiple Sorting Procedure

Multiple sorting is a technique similar to domain analysis that a researcher can use in field research or oral history. Its purpose is to discover how people categorize their experiences or classify items into systems of "similar" and "different." The multiple sorting procedure has been adopted by cognitive anthropologists and psychologists. It can be used to collect, verify, or analyze data. Here is how it works. The researcher gives those being studied a list of terms, photos, places, names of people, and so on, and asks them to organize the lists into categories or piles. The subjects or members use categories of their own devising. Once sorted, the researcher asks about the criteria used. The subjects are then given the items again and asked to sort them in other ways. There is a similarity to Thurstone scaling in that people sort items, but here, the number of piles and type of items differ. More significantly, the purpose of the sorting is not to create a uniform scale but to discover the variety

FIGURE 13.3   Partial Flowchart of Cake Making

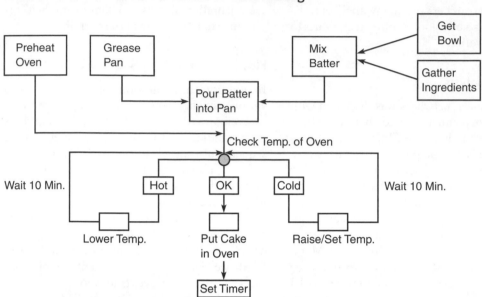

of ways people understand the world. For example (Canter et al., 1985:90), a gambler sorts a list of eight gambling establishments five times. Each sort has three to four categories. One of the sorts organized them based on "class of casino" (high to low). Other sorts were based on "frills," "size of stake," "make me money," and "personal preference." By examining the sorts, the researcher sees how others organize their worlds.

Diagrams

Qualitative researchers have moved toward presenting their data analysis in the form of diagrams and charts. Diagrams and charts help them organize ideas and systematically investigate relations in the data, as well as communicate results to readers. Researchers use spatial or temporal maps, typologies, or sociograms.

Quantitative researchers have developed many graphs, tables, charts, and pictorial devices to present information. Miles and Huberman (1994) argued that data display is a critical part

of qualitative analysis. In addition to taxonomies, maps, and lists, they suggested the use of flowcharts, organizational charts, causal diagrams, and various lists and grids to illustrate analysis (see Figure 13.4).

SOFTWARE FOR QUALITATIVE DATA

Quantitative researchers have used computers for nearly 40 years to generate tables, graphs, and charts to analyze and present numerical data. By contrast, qualitative researchers moved to computers and diagrams only in the past decade. A researcher who enters notes in a word-processing program may quickly search for words and phrases that can be adapted to coding data and linking codes to analytic memos. Word processing can also help a researcher revise and move codes and parts of field notes.

New computer programs are continuously being developed or modified, and most come

FIGURE 13.4 **Examples of the Use of Diagrams in Qualitative Analysis**

	EXAMPLE 1			
Person	Worked Before College	Part-Time Job in College	Pregnant Now	Had Own Car
John	Yes	Yes	N/A	No
Mary	Yes	DK	No	Yes
Martin	No	Yes	N/A	Yes
Yoshi	Yes	No	Yes	Yes

DK = don't know, N/A = not applicable

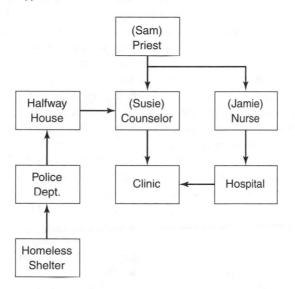

with highly detailed and program-specific user manuals. The review here does not go into detail about specific software. It covers only the major approaches to qualitative data analysis at this time.

Some programs perform searches of text documents. What they do is similar to the searching function available in most word-processing software. The specialized text retrieval programs are faster and have the capability of finding close matches, slight misspellings, similar-sounding words, and synonyms. For example, when a researcher looks for the keyword *boat*, the program might also tell whether any of the following appeared: *ship, battleship, frigate,*

rowboat, schooner, vessel, yacht, steamer, ocean liner, tug, canoe, skiff, cutter, aircraft carrier, dinghy, scow, galley, ark, cruiser, destroyer, flagship, and *submarine.* In addition, some programs permit the combination of words or phrases using logical terms *(and, or, not)* in what are called *Boolean searches.* For example, a researcher may search long documents for when the keywords *college student* and *drinking* and *smoking* occur within four sentences of one another, but only when the word *fraternity* is not present in the block of text. This Boolean search uses *and* to seek the intersection of *college student* with either of two behaviors that are connected by the logical term *or*, whereas the logical search word *not* excludes situations in which the term *fraternity* appears.

Most programs show the keyword or phrase and the surrounding text. The programs may also permit a researcher to write separate memos or add short notes to the text. Some programs count the keywords found and give their location. Most programs create a very specific index for the text, based only on the terms of interest to the researcher.

Textbase managers are similar to text retrieval programs. The key difference is their ability to organize or sort information about search results. They allow researchers to sort notes by a key idea or to add factual information. For example, when the data are detailed notes on interviews, a researcher can add information about the date and length of the interview, gender of interviewee, location of interview, and so on. The researcher can then sort and organize each interview or part of the interview notes using a combination of key words and added information.

In addition, some programs have *Hypertext* capability. Hypertext is a way of linking terms to other information. It works such that clicking the mouse on one term causes a new screen (one that has related information) to appear. The researcher can identify keywords or topics and link them together in the text. For example, a field researcher wants to examine the person Susan and the topic of hair (including haircuts, hairstyles, hair coloring, and hats or hair covering). The researcher can use Hypertext to connect all places Susan's name appears to discussions of hair. By the mouse clicking on Susan's name, one block of text quickly jumps to another in the notes to see all places where Susan and the hair topic appear together.

Code-and-retrieve programs allow a researcher to attach codes to lines, sentences, paragraphs, or blocks of text. The programs may permit multiple codes for the same data. In addition to attaching codes, most programs also allow the researcher to organize the codes. For example, a program can help a researcher make outlines or "trees" of connections (e.g., trunks, branches, and twigs) among the codes, and among the data to which the codes refer. The qualitative data are rearranged in the program based on the researcher's codes and the relations among codes that a researcher specifies.

CONCLUSION

In this chapter, you have learned how researchers analyze qualitative data. In many respects, qualitative data are more difficult to deal with than data in the form of numbers. Numbers have mathematical properties that let a researcher use statistical procedures. Qualitative analysis requires more effort by an individual researcher to read and reread data notes, reflect on what is read, and make comparisons based on logic and judgment.

Most forms of qualitative data analysis involve coding and writing analytic memos. Both are labor-intensive efforts by the researcher to read over data carefully and think about them seriously. In addition, you learned about methods that researchers have used for the analysis of qualitative data. They are a sample of the many methods of qualitative data analysis. You also learned about the importance of thinking about negative evidence and events that are not present in the data.

This chapter ends the section of the book on research design, data collection, and data analysis. Social research also involves preparing reports on a research project, which is addressed in the next chapter.

Key Terms

axial coding
empty boxes
illustrative method
narrative history
open coding
selective coding
successive approximation

Writing the Research Report

INTRODUCTION

The previous chapters have looked at how to design studies, gather data, and analyze the data. Yet, a research project is not complete until the researcher shares the results with others. Communicating results and how a study was conducted with others is a critical last step in the research process. It is usually in the form of a written report. Chapter 1 discussed how the scientific community emphasizes that researchers make public how they conducted their research and their findings. In this chapter, you will learn about writing a report on one's research.

THE RESEARCH REPORT

Why Write a Report?

After a researcher completes a project or a significant phase of a large project, it is time to communicate the findings to others through a research report. You can learn a lot about writing a research report by reading many reports and taking a course in scientific and technical writing.

A *research report* is a written document (or oral presentation based on a written document) that communicates the methods and findings of a research project to others. It is more than a summary of findings; it is a record of the research process. A researcher cannot wait until the research is done to think about the report; he or she must think ahead to the report and keep careful records while conducting research. In addition to findings, the report includes the reasons for initiating the project, a description of the project's steps, a presentation of data, and a discussion of how the data relate to the research question or topic.

The report tells others what you, the researcher, did and what you discovered. In other words, the research report is a way of disseminating knowledge. As you saw in Chapter 1, the research report plays a significant role in binding together the scientific community. Other reasons for writing a report are to fulfill a class or job assignment, to meet an obligation to an organization that paid for the research, to persuade a professional group about specific aspects of a problem, or to tell the general public about findings. Communicating with the general public is rarely the primary method for communication of scientific results; it is usually a second stage of dissemination.

The Writing Process

Your Audience.   Professional writers say: Always know for whom you are writing. This is because communication is more effective when it is tailored to a specific audience. You should write a research report differently depending on whether the primary audience is an instructor, students, professional social scientists, practitioners, or the general public. It goes without saying that the writing should be clear, accurate, and organized.

Instructors assign a report for different reasons and may place requirements on how it is written. In general, instructors want to see writing and an organization that reflect clear, logical thinking. Student reports should demonstrate a solid grasp of substantive and methodological concepts. A good way to do this is to use technical terms explicitly *when appropriate;* they should not be used excessively or incorrectly.

When writing for students, it is best to define technical terms and label each part of the report. The discussion should proceed in a logical, step-by-step manner with many specific examples. Use straight-forward language to explain how and why you conducted the various steps of the research project. One strategy is to begin with the research question, then structure the report as an answer.

Scholars do not need definitions of technical terms or explanations of why standard procedures (e.g., random sampling) were used. They are interested in how the research is linked to abstract theory or previous findings in the literature. They want a condensed, detailed description of research design. They pay close attention to how variables are measured and the methods of data collection. Scholars like a compact, tightly written, but extensive section on data analysis, with a meticulous discussion of results.

Practitioners prefer a short summary of how the study was conducted and results presented in a few simple charts and graphs. They like to see an outline of alternative paths of action implied by results with the practical outcomes of pursuing each path. Practitioners must be cautioned not to overgeneralize from the results of one study. It is best to place the details of research design and results in an appendix.

When writing for the general public, use simple language, provide concrete examples, and focus on the practical implications of findings for social problems. Do not include details of research design or of results, and be careful not to make unsupported claims when writing for the public. Informing the public is an important service, which can help nonspecialists make better judgments about public issues.

Style and Tone.   Research reports are written in a narrow range of styles and have a distinct tone. Their purpose is to communicate clearly the research method and findings.

Style refers to the types of words chosen by the writer and the length and form of sentences or paragraphs used. *Tone* is the writer's attitude or relation toward the subject matter. For example, an informal, conversational style (e.g., colloquial words, idioms, clichés, and incomplete sentences) with a personal tone (e.g., these are my feelings) is appropriate for writing a letter to a close friend, but not for research reports. Research reports have a formal and succinct (saying a lot in few words) style. The tone expresses distance from the subject matter; it is professional and serious. Field researchers sometimes use an informal style and a personal tone, but this is the exception. Avoid moralizing and flowery language. The goal is to inform, not to advocate a position or to entertain.

A research report should be objective, accurate, and clear. Check and recheck details (e.g., page references in citations) and fully disclose how you conducted the research project. If readers detect carelessness in writing, they may question the research itself. The details of a research project can be complex, and such complexity means that confusion is always a danger. It makes clear writing essential. Clear writing can be achieved by thinking and rethinking the research problem and design, explicitly defining terms, writing with short declarative sentences, and limiting conclusions to what is supported by the evidence.

Organizing Thoughts.   Writing does not happen magically or simply flow out of a person when he or she puts pen to paper (or fingers to keyboard) although many people have such an illusion. Rather, it is hard work, involving a sequence of steps and separate activities that result in a final product. Writing a research report is not radically different from other types of writing. Although some steps differ and the level of complexity may be greater, most of what a good writer does when writing a long letter, a poem, a set of instructions, or a short story applies to writing a research report.

First, a writer needs something about which to write. The "something" in the research report includes the topic, research question, design and measures, data collection techniques, results, and implications. With so many parts to write about, organization is essential. The most basic tool for organizing writing is the outline. Outlines help a writer ensure that all ideas are included and that the relationship between them is clear. Outlines are made up of topics (words or phrases) or sentences. Most of us are familiar with the basic form of an outline (see Figure 14.1).

Outlines can help the writer, but they can also become a barrier if they are used improperly. An outline is simply a tool to help the writer organize ideas. It helps (1) put ideas in a sequence (e.g., what will be said first, second, and

FIGURE 14.1   Form of Outline

I. First major topic	One of the most important
A. Subtopic of topic I	Second level of importance
1. Subtopic of A	Third level of importance
a. Subtopic of 1	Fourth level of importance
b. Subtopic of 1	''
(1) Subtopic of b	Fifth level of importance
(2) Subtopic of b	''
(a) Subtopic of (2)	Sixth level of importance
(b) Subtopic of (2)	''
i. Subtopic of (b)	Seventh level of importance
ii. Subtopic of (b)	''
2. Subtopic of A	Third level of importance
B. Subtopic of topic I	Second level of importance
II. Second major topic	One of the most important

third); (2) group related ideas together (e.g., these are similar to each other but they differ from those); and (3) separate the more general, or higher-level, ideas from more specific ideas, and the specific ideas from very specific details.

Some students feel that they need a complete outline before writing, and that once an outline is prepared, deviations from it are impossible. Few writers begin with a complete outline. The initial outline is sketchy because until you write everything down, it is impossible to put all ideas in a sequence, group them together, or separate the general from the specific. For most writers, new ideas develop or become clearer in the process of writing itself.

A beginning outline may differ from the final outline by more than degree of completeness. The process of writing may not only reveal or clarify ideas for the writer but it will also stimulate new ideas, new connections between ideas, a different sequence, or new relations between the general and the specific. In addition, the process of writing may stimulate reanalysis or a reexamination of the literature or findings. This does not mean beginning all over again. Rather, it means keeping an open mind to new insights and being candid about the research project.

Back to the Library.   Few researchers finish their literature review before completing a research project. The researcher should be familiar with the literature before beginning a project, but will need to return to the literature after completing data collection and analysis, for several reasons. First, time has passed between the beginning and the end of a research project, and new studies may have been published. Second, after completing a research project, a researcher will know better what is or is not central to the study and may have new questions in mind when rereading studies in the literature. Finally, when writing the report, researchers may find that notes are not complete enough or a detail is missing in the citation of a reference source (see Box 14.1). The visit to the library after data collection is less extensive and more selective or focused than that conducted at the beginning of research.

When writing a research report, researchers frequently discard some of the notes and sources that were gathered prior to completing the research project. This does not mean that the initial library work and literature review were a waste of time and effort. Researchers expect that some of the notes (e.g., 25 percent) taken before

Box 14.1 Formats for Reference Lists, Using American Sociological Association Style

Books

First-Edition Books

Eliasoph, Nina. 1998. *Avoiding Politics: How Americans Produce Apathy in Everyday Life.* New York: Cambridge University Press.

Glynn, Carroll J., Susan Herbst, Garrett J. O'Keefe and Robert Y. Shapiro. 1999. *Public Opinion.* Boulder, CO: Westview Press.

Later Editions of Books

Portes, Alejandro and Ruben G. Rumbaut. 1996. *Immigrant America: A Portrait, 2d ed.* Berkeley: University of California Press.

[Abbreviations are 2d ed., 3d ed., Rev. ed., 2 vols.]

One Volume of Multivolume Book

Marx, Karl. [1887] 1967. *Capital: Critique of Political Economy, Volume 1, The Process of Capitalist Production.* Translated by Frederick Engles. Reprint. New York: International Publishers.

Translated Books

Durkheim, Emile. 1933. *The Division of Labor in Society.* Translated by George Simpson. New York: Free Press.

Weber, Max. 1958. *The Protestant Ethic and the Spirit of Capitalism.* Translated by Talcott Parsons. New York: Charles Scribner's Sons.

Edited Books

Danziger, Sheldon and Peter Gottschalk, eds. 1993. *Uneven Tides: Rising Inequality in America.* New York: Russell Sage Foundation.

Republished Books

Mason, Edward S. [1957] 1964. *Economic Concentration and the Monopoly Problem.* Reprint. New York: Atheneum.

Articles from Books or Scholarly Journals

Wright, Erik Olin. 1997. "Rethinking, Once Again, the Concept of Class Structure." Pp. 41–72 in *Reworking Class,* edited by J. Hall. Ithaca: Cornell University Press.

Van Tubergen, Frank. 2005. "Self Employment of Immigrants: A Cross-National Study of 17 Western Societies." *Social Forces* 84:709–32.

[*Note*: Omit issue number except when each issue is renumbered beginning with page 1. Then give volume(issue):pages—for example, 84(2):709–33.]

Articles from Magazines and Newspapers

Janofsky, Michael. "Shortage of Housing for Poor Grows in the U.S." *New York Times* (April 29, 1998), p. A14.

Nichols, John. 1998. "How Al Gore Has It Wired" *Nation 267* (July 20, 1998): 11–16.

[It is not always necessary to include page numbers for newspapers].

Book Reviews

Academic Journals

Bergen, Raquel Kennedy. 1998. Review of *A Woman Scorned: Acquaintance Rape on Trial,* by Peggy Reeves Sanday. *Contemporary Sociology* 27:98–99.

Popular Magazines

Wolfe, Alan. 2001. Review of *Heaven Below: Early Pentacostals and American Culture,* by Grant Wacker. *New Republic,* 225 (September 10):59–62.

Government Documents

U.S. Bureau of Census. 2006. *Statistical Abstract of the United States, 125th ed.* Washington DC: U.S. Government Printing Office.

Doctoral Dissertations and Theses

King, Andrew J. 1976. "Law and Land Use in Chicago: A Pre-History of Modern Zoning." Ph.D. dissertation, Department of Sociology, University of Wisconsin, Madison, WI.

Unpublished Papers, Policy Reports and Presented Papers

Haines, Herbert H. 1980. "Ideological Distribution and Racial Flank Effects in Social Movements" Pre-

BOX 14.1   Continued

sented at the annual meeting of the American Sociological Association, August, New York City.

Internet Sources

[*Note:* The date retrieved is the date that the reader located and read the work on the Internet.]

Announcement or Personal Home Page
American Sociological Association 1999. *Journals and Newsletters.* Retrieved January 16, 1999. http://www.asanet.org/Pubs/publicat.html

On-Line Journal Article
Sosteric, Mike, Mike Gismondi and Gina Ratkovic. 1998. "The University, Accountability, and Market Discipline in the Late 1990s." *Electronic Journal of Sociology* April 1988, Vol. 3. Retrieved January 16, 1999. http://www.sociology.org/content/vol003.003/sosteric.html

Newspaper Article
Lee, Don. 1999. "State's Job Growth Hits Unexpected Cold Spell." *Los Angeles Times* (January 16). Retrieved January 16, 1999. http://www.latimes.com/HOME/BUSINESS/topstory.html

Journal Abstract or Book Review
Stanbridge, Karen. 2005. Review of *The New Transnational Activism* by Sidney Tarrow. *Canadian Journal of Sociology Online.* Retrieved January 12, 2006. http://www.cjsonline.ca/reviews/transnatl.html.

---

completing the project will become irrelevant as the project gains focus. They do not include notes or references in a report that are no longer relevant, for they distract from the flow of ideas and reduce clarity.

Returning to the library to verify and expand references focuses ideas. It also helps avoid plagiarism. *Plagiarism* is a serious form of cheating, and many universities expel students caught engaging in it. If a professional ever plagiarizes in a scholarly journal, it is treated as a very serious offense. Take careful notes and identify the exact source of phrases or ideas to avoid unintentional plagiarism. Cite the sources of both directly quoted words and paraphrased ideas. For direct quotes, include the location of the quote with page numbers in the citation.

Using another's written words and failing to give credit is wrong, but paraphrasing is less clear. *Paraphrasing* is not using another's exact words; it is restating another's ideas in your own words, condensing at the same time. Researchers regularly paraphrase, and good paraphrasing requires a solid understanding of what is being paraphrased. It means more than replacing another's words with synonyms; paraphrasing is borrowing an idea, boiling it down to its essence, and giving credit to the source.

Steps in Writing

Writing is a process. The way to learn to write is by writing. It takes time and effort, and it improves with practice. There is no single correct way to write, but some methods are associated with good writing. The process has three steps:

1. *Prewriting.* Prepare to write by arranging notes on the literature, making lists of ideas, outlining, completing bibliographic citations, and organizing comments on data analysis.
2. *Composing.* Get your ideas onto paper as a first draft by freewriting, drawing up the bibliography and footnotes, preparing data for presentation, and forming an introduction and conclusion.

3. *Rewriting*. Evaluate and polish the report by improving coherence, proofreading for mechanical errors, checking citations, and reviewing voice and usage.

Many people find that getting started is difficult. Beginning writers often jump to the second step and end there, which results in poor-quality writing. *Prewriting* means that a writer begins with a file folder full of notes, outlines, and lists. You must think about the form of the report and audience. Thinking time is important. It often occurs in spurts over a period of time before the bulk of composing begins.

Some people become afflicted with a strange ailment called *writer's block* when they sit down to compose writing. It is a temporary inability to write when the mind goes blank, the fingers freeze, and panic sets in. Writers from beginners through experts occasionally experience it. If you experience it, calm down and work on overcoming it.

Numerous writers begin to compose by freewriting—that is, they sit down and write down everything they can as quickly as it enters the mind. Freewriting establishes a link between a rapid flow of ideas in the mind and writing. When you freewrite, you do not stop to reread what you wrote, you do not ponder the best word, you do not worry about correct grammar, spelling, or punctuation. You just put ideas on paper as quickly as possible to get and keep the creative juices or ideas flowing. You can later clean up what you wrote.

Writing and thinking are so intertwined that it is impossible to know where one ends and the other begins. This means that if you plan to sit and stare at the wall, the computer output, the sky, or whatever until all thoughts become totally clear before beginning, you may not get anything written. Writing itself can ignite the thinking process.

Rewriting. Perhaps one in a million writers is a creative genius who can produce a first draft that communicates with astounding accuracy and clarity. For the rest of us mortals, writing means that rewriting—and rewriting again—is necessary. For example, Ernest Hemingway is reported to have rewritten the end of *Farewell to Arms* 39 times. It is not unusual for a professional researcher to rewrite a report a dozen times. Do not become discouraged. If anything, rewriting reduces the pressure; it means you can start writing soon and get out a rough draft that you can polish later. Plan to rewrite a draft at least three or four times. A draft is a complete report, from beginning to end, not a few rough notes or an outline.

Rewriting helps a writer express himself or herself with a greater clarity, smoothness, precision, and economy of words. When rewriting, the focus is on clear communication, not pompous or complicated language. Rewriting means slowly reading what you have written and, if necessary, reading out loud to see if it sounds right. It is a good idea to share your writing with others. Professional writers often have others read and criticize their writing. New writers soon learn that friendly, constructive criticism is very valuable. Sharing your writing with others may be difficult at first because it means exposing your written thoughts and encouraging criticism. Yet, the purpose of the criticism is to clarify writing, and the critic is doing you a favor.

Rewriting involves two processes: revising and editing. *Revising* is inserting new ideas, adding supporting evidence, deleting or changing ideas, moving sentences around to clarify meaning, or strengthening transitions and links between ideas. *Editing* means cleaning up and tightening the more mechanical aspects of writing, such as spelling, grammar, usage, verb tense, sentence length, and paragraph organization. When you rewrite, go over a draft and revise it brutally to improve it. This is easier if some time passes between a draft and rewriting. Phrases that seemed satisfactory in a draft may look fuzzy or poorly connected after a week or two (see Box 14.2).

Even if you have not acquired typing skills, it is a good idea to type and print out at least one

Box 14.2   Suggestions for Rewriting

1. *Mechanics.* Check grammar, spelling, punctuation, verb agreement, verb tense, and verb/subject separation with each rewrite. Remember that each time new text is added, new errors can creep in. Mistakes are not only distracting but they also weaken the confidence readers place in the ideas you express.

2. *Usage.* Reexamine terms, especially key terms, when rewriting to see whether you are using the exact word that expresses your intended meaning. Do not use technical terms or long words unnecessarily. Use the plain word that best expresses meaning. Get a thesaurus and use it. A *thesaurus* is an essential reference tool, like a dictionary, that contains words of similar meaning and can help you locate the exact word for a meaning you want to express. Precise thinking and expression requires precise language. Do not say *average* if you use the *mean*. Do not say *mankind* or *policeman* when you intend *people* or *police officer*. Do not use *principal* for *principle*.

3. *Voice.* Writers of research reports often make the mistake of using the passive instead of the active voice. It may appear more authoritative, but passive voice obscures the actor or subject of action. For example, the passive, *The relationship between grade in school and more definite career plans was confirmed by the data* is better stated as the active, *The data confirm the relationship between grade in school and more definite career plans.* The passive, *Respondent attitude toward abortion was recorded by an interviewer* reads easier in the active voice: *An interviewer recorded respondent attitude toward abortion.* Also avoid unnecessary qualifying language, such as *seems to* or *appears to.*

4. *Coherence.* Sequence, steps, and transitions should be logically tight. Try reading the entire report one paragraph at a time. Does the paragraph contain a unified idea? A topic sentence?

Is there a transition between paragraphs within the report?

5. *Repetition.* Remove repeated ideas, wordiness, and unnecessary phrases. Ideas are best stated once, forcefully, instead of repeatedly in an unclear way. When revising, eliminate deadwood (words that add nothing) and circumlocution (the use of several words when one more precise word will do). Directness is preferable to wordiness. The wordy phrase, *To summarize the above, it is our conclusion in light of the data that X has a positive effect of considerable magnitude on the occurrence of Y, notwithstanding the fact that Y occurs only on rare occasions,* is better stated, *In sum, we conclude that X has a large positive effect on Y, but Y occurs infrequently.*

6. *Structure.* Research reports should have a transparent organization. Move sections around as necessary to fit the organization better, and use headings and subheadings. A reader should be able to follow the logical structure of a report.

7. *Abstraction.* A good research report mixes abstract ideas and concrete examples. A long string of abstractions without the specifics is difficult to read. Likewise, a mass of specific concrete details without periodic generalization also loses readers.

8. *Metaphors.* Many writers use metaphors to express ideas. Phrases like *the cutting edge, the bottom line,* and *penetrating to the heart* are used to express ideas by borrowing images from other contexts. Metaphors can be an effective method of communication, but they need to be used sparingly and with care. A few well-chosen, consistently used, fresh metaphors can communicate ideas quickly and effectively; however, the excessive use of metaphors, especially overused metaphors (e.g., the *bottom line*), is a sloppy, unimaginative method of expression.

draft before the final draft. This is because it is easier to see errors and organization problems in a clean, typed draft. Feel free to cut and paste, cross out words, or move phrases on the printed copy.

Good keyboarding skills and the ability to use a word processor are extremely valuable when writing reports and other documents. Serious professionals find that the time they invest into building keyboard skills and learning to use a word processor pays huge dividends later. Word processors not only make editing much easier but they also check spelling and offer synonyms. In addition, there are programs that check grammar. You cannot rely on the computer program to do all the work, but it makes writing easier. The speed and ease that a word processor offers is so dramatic that few people who become skilled at using one ever go back to writing by hand or typing.

One last suggestion: Rewrite the introduction and title after completing a draft so that they accurately reflect what is said. Titles should be short and descriptive. They should communicate the topic and the major variables to readers. They can describe the type of research (e.g., "An experiment on . . .") but should not have unnecessary words or phrases (e.g., "An investigation into the . . .").

The Quantitative Research Report

The principles of good writing apply to all reports, but the parts of a report differ depending on whether the research is quantitative or qualitative. Before writing any report, read reports on the same kind of research for models.

We begin with the quantitative research report. The sections of the report roughly follow the sequence of steps of a research project.

Abstract or Executive Summary. Quantitative research reports usually begin with a short summary or abstract. The size of an abstract varies; it can be as few as 50 words (this paragraph has 90 words) or as long as a full page. Most scholarly

journal articles have abstracts that are printed on the first page of the article. The abstract has information on the topic, the research problem, the basic findings, and any unusual research design or data collection features.

Reports of applied research that are written for practitioners have a longer summary called the *executive summary.* It contains more detail than an article abstract and includes the implications of research and major recommendations made in the report. Although it is longer than an abstract, an executive summary rarely exceeds four or five pages.

Abstracts and executive summaries serve several functions: For the less interested reader, they tell what is in a report; for readers looking for specific information, they help the reader determine whether the full report contains important information. Readers use the abstract or summary to screen information and decide whether the entire report should be read. It gives serious readers who intend to read the full report a quick mental picture of the report, which makes reading the report easier and faster.

Presenting the Problem. The first section of the report defines the research problem. It can be placed in one or more sections with titles such as "Introduction," "Problem Definition," "Literature Review," "Hypotheses," or "Background Assumptions." Although the subheadings vary, the contents include a statement of the research problem and a rationale for what is being examined. Here, researchers explain the significance of and provide a background to the research question. They explain the significance of the research by showing how different solutions to the problem lead to different applications or theoretical conclusions. Introductory sections frequently include a context literature review and link the problem to theory. Introductory sections also define key concepts and present conceptual hypotheses.

Describing the Methods. The next section of the report describes how the researcher designed the study and collected the data. It goes by several names (e.g., "Methods," "Research Design," or "Data") and may be subdivided into other parts (e.g., "Measures," "Sampling," or "Manipulations"). It is the most important section for evaluating the methodology of the project. The section answers several questions for the reader:

1. What type of study (e.g., experiment, survey) was conducted?
2. Exactly how were data collected (e.g., study design, type of survey, time and location of data collection, experimental design used)?
3. How were variables measured? Are the measures reliable and valid?
4. What is the sample? How many subjects or respondents are involved in the study? How were they selected?
5. How were ethical issues and specific concerns of the design dealt with?

Results and Tables.   After describing how data were collected, methods of sampling, and measurement, you then present the data. This section presents—it does not discuss, analyze, or interpret—the data. Researchers sometimes combine the "Results" section with the next section, called "Discussion" or "Findings."

Researchers make choices in how to present the data. When analyzing the data, they look at dozens of univariate, bivariate, and multivariate tables and statistics to get a feel for the data. This does not mean that every statistic or table is in a final report. Rather, the researcher selects the minimum number of charts or tables that fully inform the reader and rarely present the raw data itself. Data analysis techniques should summarize the data and test hypotheses (e.g., frequency distributions, tables with means and standard deviations, correlations, and other statistics).

A researcher wants to give a complete picture of the data without overwhelming the reader—not provide data in excessive detail nor present irrelevant data. Readers can make their own interpretations. Detailed summary statistics belong in appendixes.

Discussion.   In the discussion section, researchers give the reader a concise, unambiguous interpretation of its meaning. The discussion is not a selective emphasis or partisan interpretation; rather, it is a candid discussion of what is in the "Results" section. The "Discussion" section is separated from the results so that a reader can examine the data and arrive at different interpretations.

Beginning researchers often find it difficult to organize the "Discussion" section. One approach is to organize the discussion according to hypotheses, discussing how the data relate to each hypothesis. In addition, researchers should discuss unanticipated findings, possible alternative explanations of results, and weaknesses or limitations.

Drawing Conclusions.   Researchers restate the research question and summarize findings in the conclusion. Its purpose is to summarize the report, and it is sometimes titled "Summary."

The only sections after the conclusion are the references and appendixes. The "References" section contains only sources that were referred to in the text or notes of the report. Appendixes, if used, usually contain additional information on methods of data collection (e.g., questionnaire wording) or results (e.g., descriptive statistics). The footnotes or endnotes in quantitative research reports expand or elaborate on information in the text. Researchers use them sparingly to provide secondary information that clarifies the text but might distract from the flow of the reading.

The Qualitative Research Report

Compared to quantitative research, it is more difficult to write a report on qualitative social research. It has fewer rules and less structure. Nevertheless, the purpose is the same: to clearly communicate the research process and the data collected through the process.

Quantitative reports present hypotheses and evidence in a logically tight and condensed style. By contrast, qualitative reports tend to be longer, and book-length reports are common. The greater length is for five reasons:

1. The data in a qualitative report are more difficult to condense. Data are in the form of words, pictures, or sentences and include many quotes and examples.

2. Qualitative researchers try to create a subjective sense of empathy and understanding among readers in addition to presenting factual evidence and analytic interpretations. Detailed descriptions of specific settings and situations help readers better understand or get a feel for settings. Researchers attempt to transport the reader into the subjective world view and meaning system of a social setting.

3. Qualitative researchers use less standardized techniques of gathering data, creating analytic categories, and organizing evidence. The techniques applied may be particular to individual researchers or unique settings. Thus, researchers explain what they did and why, because it has not been done before.

4. Exploring new settings or constructing new theory is a common goal in qualitative research. The development of new concepts and the examination of relationships among them adds to the length of reports. Theory flows out of evidence, and detailed descriptions demonstrate how the researcher created interpretations.

5. Qualitative researchers may use more varied and literary writing styles, which increases length. They have greater freedom to employ literary devices to tell a story or recount a tale.

Field Research.   Field research reports rarely follow a fixed format with standard sections, and theoretical generalizations and data are not separated into distinct sections. Generalizations are intertwined with the evidence, which takes the form of detailed description with frequent quotes.

Researchers balance the presentation of data and analysis to avoid an excessive separation of data from analysis, called the *error of segregation.* This occurs when researchers separate data from analysis so much that readers cannot see the connection.[1]

The tone of field research reports is less objective and formal, and more personal. Field research reports may be written in the first person (i.e., using the pronoun *I*) because the researcher was directly involved in the setting, interacted with the people studied, and was the measurement "instrument." The decisions or indecisions, feelings, reactions, and personal experiences of the researcher are parts of the field research process.

Field research reports often face more skepticism than quantitative reports do. This makes it essential to assess an audience's demands for evidence and to establish credibility. The key is to provide readers with enough evidence so that they believe the recounted events and accept the interpretations as plausible. A degree of selective observation is accepted in field research, so the critical issue is whether other observers could reach the same conclusion if they examined the same data.

Field researchers face a data reduction dilemma when presenting evidence. Most data are in the form of an enormous volume of field notes, but a researcher cannot directly share all the observations or recorded conversations with the readers. For example, in their study of medical students, *Boys in White,* Becker and colleagues (1961) had about 5,000 pages of single-spaced field notes. Field researchers include only about 5 percent of their field notes in a report as quotes. The remaining 95 percent is not wasted; there is just no room for it. Thus, writers select quotes and indirectly convey the rest of the data to readers.

There is no fixed organization for a field research report, although a literature review often appears near the beginning. There are many acceptable organizational forms. Lofland (1976) suggests the following:

1. Introduction
   a. Most general aspects of situation
   b. Main contours of the general situation
   c. How materials were collected
   d. Details about the setting
   e. How the report is organized
2. The situation
   a. Analytic categories
   b. Contrast between situation and other situations
   c. Development of situation over time
3. Strategies
4. Summary and implications

Devices for organizing evidence and analysis also vary a great deal. For example, writers can organize the report in terms of a *natural history,* an unfolding of events as you discovered them, or as a *chronology,* following the developmental cycle or career of an aspect of the setting or people in it. Another possibility is to organize the report as a *zoom lens,* beginning broadly and then focusing increasingly narrowly on a specific topic. Statements can move from universal statements about all cultures, to general statements about a specific cultures, to statements about a specific cultural scene, to specific statements about an aspect of culture, to specific statements about specific incidents.

Field researchers also organize reports by themes. A writer chooses between using abstract analytic themes and using themes from the categories used by the people who were studied. The latter gives readers a vivid description of the setting and displays knowledge of the language, concepts, categories, and beliefs of those being written about.[2]

Field researchers discuss the methods used in the report, but its location and form vary. One technique is to interweave a description of the setting, the means of gaining access, the role of the researcher, and the subject–researcher relationship into the discussion of evidence and analysis. This is intensified if the writer adopts what Van Maanen (1988:73) called a "confessional" style of writing.

A chronological, zoom lens, or theme-based organization allows placing the data collection method near the beginning or the end. In book-length reports, methodological issues are usually discussed in a separate appendix.

Field research reports can contain transcriptions of tape recordings, maps, photographs, or charts illustrating analytic categories. They supplement the discussion and are placed near the discussion they complement. Qualitative field research can use creative formats that differ from the usual written text with examples from field notes. Harper's (1982) book contains many photographs with text. The photographs give a visual inventory of the settings described in the text and present the meanings of settings in the terms of those being studied. For example, field research articles have appeared in the form of all photographs, a script for a play, or a documentary film.[3]

Direct, personal involvement in the intimate details of a social setting heightens ethical concerns. Researchers write in a manner that protects the privacy of those being studied and helps prevent the publication of a report from harming those who were studied. They usually change the names of members and exact locations in field reports. Personal involvement in field research leads researchers to include a short autobiography. For example, in the appendix to *Street Corner Society,* the author, William Foote Whyte (1955), gave a detailed account of the occupations of his father and grandfather, his hobbies and interests, the jobs he held, how he ended up going to graduate school, and how his research was affected by his getting married.

Historical-Comparative Research.   There is no single way to write a report on historical-comparative research. Most frequently, researchers "tell a story" or describe details in general analytic categories. The writing usually goes beyond description and includes limited generalizations and abstract concepts.

Historical-comparative researchers rarely describe their methods in great detail. Explicit sections of the report or an appendix that describes the methods used are unusual. Occasionally, a book-length report contains a bibliographic essay that discusses major sources used. More often, numerous detailed footnotes or endnotes describe the sources and evidence. For example, a 20-page report on quantitative or field research typically has 5 to 10 notes, whereas an H-C research report of equal length may have 40 to 60 notes.

Historical-comparative reports can contain photographs, maps, diagrams, charts, or tables of statistics throughout the report and in the section that discusses evidence that relates to them. The charts, tables, and so forth supplement a discussion or give the reader a better feel for the places and people being described. They are used in conjunction with frequent quotes as one among several types of evidence. Historical-comparative reports rarely summarize data to test specific hypotheses as quantitative research does. Instead, the writer builds a web of meaning or descriptive detail and organizes the evidence itself to convey interpretations and generalizations.

There are two basic modes of organizing H-C research reports: by topic and chronologically. Most writers mix the two types. For example, information is organized chronologically within topics, or organized by topic within chronological periods. Occasionally other forms of organization are used—by place, by individual person, or by major events. If the report is truly comparative, the writer has additional options, such as making comparisons within topics. Box 14.3 provides a sample of some techniques used by historical-comparative researchers to organize evidence and analysis.

Some H-C researchers mimic the quantitative research report and use quantitative research techniques. They extend quantitative research rather than adopt a distinct historical-comparative research method. Their reports follow the model of a quantitative research report.

You learned about the narrative strategy of qualitative data analysis in Chapter 13. Researchers who use this strategy often adopt a narrative style of report writing. Researchers who use the narrative style organize their data chronologically and try to "tell a story" around specific individuals and events.

The Research Proposal

What Is the Proposal?   A research *proposal* is a document that presents a plan for a project to reviewers for evaluation. It can be a supervised project submitted to instructors as part of an educational degree (e.g., a master's thesis or a Ph.D. dissertation) or it can be a research project proposed to a funding agency. Its purpose is to convince reviewers that you, the researcher, are capable of successfully conducting the proposed research project. Reviewers have more confidence that a planned project will be successfully completed if the proposal is well written and organized, and if you demonstrate careful planning.

The proposal is similar to a research report, but it is written before the research project begins. A proposal describes the research problem and its importance, and gives a detailed account of the methods that will be used and why they are appropriate.

The proposal for quantitative research has most of the parts of a research report: a title, an abstract, a problem statement, a literature review, a methods or design section, and a bibliography. It lacks results, discussion, and conclusion sections. The proposal has a plan for data collection and analysis (e.g., types of statistics). It frequently includes a schedule of the steps to be undertaken and an estimate of the time required for each step.

Proposals for qualitative research are more difficult to write because the research process itself is less structured and preplanned. The re-

Box 14.3

Ten Features to Consider When Writing a Report on Historical-Comparative Research

1. *Sequence.* Historical-comparative researchers are sensitive to the temporal order of events and place a series of events in order to describe a process. For example, a researcher studying the passage of a law or the evolution of a social norm may break the process into a set of sequential steps.

2. *Comparison.* Comparing similarities and differences lies at the heart of comparative-historical research. Make comparisons explicit and identify both similarities and differences. For example, a researcher comparing the family in two historical periods or countries begins by listing shared and nonshared traits of the family in each setting.

3. *Contingency.* Researchers often discover that one event, action, or situation depends on or is conditioned by others. Outlining the linkages of how one event was contingent on others is critical. For example, a researcher examining the rise of local newspapers notes that it depended on the spread of literacy.

4. *Origins and consequences.* Historical-comparative researchers trace the origins of an event, action, organization, or social relationship back in time, or follow its consequences into subsequent time periods. For example, a researcher explaining the end of slavery traces its origins to many movements, speeches, laws, and actions in the preceding fifty years.

5. *Sensitivity to incompatible meaning.* Meanings change over time and vary across cultures. Historical-comparative researchers ask themselves whether a word or social category had the same meaning in the past as in the present or whether a word in one culture has a direct translation in another culture. For example, a college degree had a different meaning in a historical era when it was extremely expensive and less than 1 percent of the 18- to 22-year-old population received a degree compared to the late twentieth century, when college became relatively accessible.

6. *Limited generalization.* Overgeneralization is always a potential problem in historical-comparative research. Few researchers seek rigid, fixed laws in historical, comparative explanation. They qualify statements or avoid strict determination. For example, instead of a blanket statement that the destruction of the native cultures in areas settled by European Whites was the inevitable consequence of advanced technological culture, a researcher may list the specific factors that combined to explain the destruction in particular social-historical settings.

7. *Association.* The concept of association is used in all forms of social research. As in other areas, historical-comparative researchers identify factors that appear together in time and place. For example, a researcher examining a city's nineteenth-century crime rate asks whether years of greater migration into the city are associated with higher crime rates and whether those arrested tended to be recent immigrants.

8. *Part and whole.* It is important to place events in their context. Writers of historical-comparative research sketch linkages between parts of a process, organization, or event and the larger context in which it is found. For example, a researcher studying a particular political ritual in an eighteenth-century setting describes how the ritual fit within the eighteenth-century political system.

9. *Analogy.* Analogies can be useful. The overuse of analogy or the use of an inappropriate analogy is dangerous. For example, a researcher examines feelings about divorce in country X and describes them as "like feelings about death" in country Y. This analogy requires a description of "feelings about death" in country Y.

Box 14.3 *Continued*

10. *Synthesis.* Historical-comparative researchers often synthesize many specific events and details into a comprehensive whole. Synthesis results from weaving together many smaller generalizations and interpretations into coherent main themes. For example, a researcher studying the French Revolution synthesizes specific generalizations about changes in social structure, international pressures, agricultural dislocation, shifting popular beliefs and problems with government finances into a compact, coherent explanation. Researchers using the narrative form summarize the argument in an introduction or conclusion. It is a motif or theme embedded within the description. Thus, theoretical generalizations are intertwined with the evidence and appear to flow inductively out of the detailed evidence.

---

searcher prepares a problem statement, literature review, and bibliography. He or she demonstrates an ability to complete a proposed qualitative project in two ways. First, the proposal is well written, with an extensive discussion of the literature, significance of the problem, and sources. This shows reviewers familiarity with qualitative research and the appropriateness of the method for studying the problem. Second, the proposal describes a qualitative pilot study. This demonstrates motivation, familiarity with research techniques, and ability to complete a report about unstructured research.

Proposals to Fund Research. The purpose of a research grant is to provide the resources needed to help complete a worthy project. Researchers whose primary goal is to use funding for personal benefit or prestige, to escape from other activities, or to build an "empire" are less successful. The strategies of proposal writing and getting grants has become an industry called *grantsmanship.*

There are many sources of funding for research proposals. Colleges, private foundations, and government agencies have programs to award grants to researchers. Funds may be used to purchase equipment, to pay your salary or that of others, for research supplies, for travel to collect data, or for help with the publication of results. The degree of competition for a grant varies a great deal, depending on the source. Some sources fund more than 3 out of 4 proposals they receive, others fund fewer than 1 in 20.

The researcher needs to investigate funding sources and ask questions: What types of projects are funded—applied versus basic research, specific topics, or specific research techniques? What are the deadlines? What kind (e.g., length, degree of detail, etc.) of proposal is necessary? How large are most grants? What aspects (e.g., equipment, personnel, travel, etc.) of a project are or are not funded? There are many sources of information on funding sources. Librarians or officials who are responsible for research grants at a college are good resource people. For example, private foundations are listed in an annual publication, *The Foundation Directory. The Guide to Federal Funding for Social Scientists* lists sources in the U.S. government. In the United States, there are many newsletters on funding sources and two national computerized databases, which subscribers can search for funding sources. Some agencies periodically issue *requests for proposals (RFPs)* that ask for proposals to conduct research on a specific issue. Researchers need to learn about funding sources because it is essential to send the proposal to an appropriate source in order to be successful.

Researchers should show a track record of past success in the proposal, especially if they are going to be in charge of the project. The researcher in charge of a research project is the *principal investigator (PI)* or project director. Proposals usually include a curriculum vitae or academic resumé, letters of support from other researchers, and a record of past research. Reviewers feel safer investing funds in a project headed by someone who already has research experience than in a novice. One can build a track record with small research projects or by assisting an experienced researcher before seeking funding as a principal investigator.

The reviewers who evaluate a proposal judge whether the proposal project is appropriate to the funding source's goals. Most funding sources have guidelines stating the kinds of projects they fund. For example, programs that fund basic research have the advancement of knowledge as a goal. Programs that fund applied research often have improvements in the delivery of services as a goal. Instructions specify page length, number of copies, deadlines, and the like. Follow all instructions exactly.

Proposals should be neat and professional looking. The instructions usually ask for a detailed plan for the use of time, services, and personnel. These should be clearly stated and realistic for the project. Excessively high or low estimates, unnecessary add-ons, or omitted essentials will lower how reviewers evaluate a proposal. Creating a budget for a proposed project is complicated and usually requires technical assistance. For example, pay rates, fringe benefit rates, and so on that must be charged may not be easy to obtain. It is best to consult a grants officer at a college or an experienced proposal writer. In addition, endorsements or clearances of regulations are often necessary (e.g., IRB approval). Proposals should also include specific plans for disseminating results (e.g., publications, presentations before professional groups, etc.) and a plan for evaluating whether the project met its objectives.

The proposal is a kind of contract between researcher and the funding source. Funding agencies often require a final report, including details on how funds were spent, the findings, and an evaluation of whether the project met its objectives. Failure to spend funds properly, complete the project described in the proposal, or file a final report may result in a researcher being barred from receiving future funding or facing legal action. A serious misuse of funds may result in the banning of others at the same institution from receiving future funding.

The process of reviewing proposals after they are submitted to a funding source takes anywhere from a few weeks to almost a year, depending on the funding source. In most cases, reviewers rank a large group of proposals, and only highly ranked proposals receive funding. A proposal often undergoes a peer review in which the reviewers know the proposer from the vitae in the proposal, but the proposer does not know the reviewers. Sometimes a proposal is reviewed by nonspecialists or nonresearchers. Instructions on preparing a proposal indicate whether to write for specialists in a field or for an educated general audience.

If a proposal is funded, celebrate, but only for a short time. If the proposal is rejected, which is more likely, do not despair. Most proposals are rejected the first or second time they are submitted. Many funding sources provide written reviewer evaluations of the proposal. Always request them if they are provided. Sometimes, a courteous talk on the telephone with a person at the funding source will reveal the reasons for rejection. Strengthen and resubmit a proposal on the basis of the reviewer's comments. Most funding sources accept repeated resubmissions of revised proposals, and proposals that have been revised may be stronger in subsequent competitions.

If a proposal has been submitted to an appropriate funding source and all instructions are followed, reviewers are more likely to rate it high when:

- It addresses an important research question. It builds on prior knowledge and represents a substantial advance of knowledge for basic research. It documents a major social problem and holds promise for solutions for applied research.

- It follows all instructions, is well written, and is easy to follow, with clearly stated objectives.
- It completely describes research procedures that include high standards of research methodology, and it applies research techniques that are appropriate to the research question.
- It includes specific plans for disseminating the results and evaluating whether the project has met its objectives.
- The project is well designed and shows serious planning. It has realistic budgets and schedules.
- The researcher has the necessary experience or background to complete the project successfully.

CONCLUSION

Clearly communicating results is a vital part of the larger scientific enterprise, as are the ethics and politics of social research.

I want to end this chapter by urging you, as a consumer of social research or a new social researcher, to be self-aware. Be aware of the place of the researcher in society and of the societal context of social research itself. Social researchers, and sociologists in particular, bring a unique perspective to the larger society.

Key Terms

editing
error of segregation
executive summary
grantsmanship
paraphrasing
plagiarism
prewriting
principal investigator
request for proposals (RFPs)
revising
rewriting
zoom lens

Endnotes

1. The error of segregation is discussed in Lofland and Lofland (1984:146).
2. See Van Maanen (1988:13).
3. See Becker and associates (1989), Dabbs (1982), and Jackson (1978).

Following the definition, the number in parentheses indicates the chapter in which the term first appears in the text and is in the Key Terms section. Italicized terms refer to terms defined elsewhere in this glossary.

Abstract A term with two meanings in literature reviews: a short summary of a scholarly journal article that usually appears at its beginning, and a reference tool for locating scholarly journal articles. (4)

Accretion measures *Nonreactive measures* of the residue of the activity of people or what they leave behind. (9)

Action research study A type of *applied social research* in which a researcher treats knowledge as a form of power and abolishes the division between creating knowledge and using knowledge to engage in political action. (1)

Alternative hypothesis A *hypothesis* paired with a *null hypothesis* stating that the *independent variable* has an effect on a *dependent variable.* (4)

Analytic memo The written notes a qualitative researcher takes during data collection and afterwards to develop concepts, themes, or preliminary generalizations. (11)

Anonymity Research participants remain anonymous or nameless. (3)

Appearance of interest A technique in field research in which researchers maintain relations in a *field site* by pretending to be interested and excited by the activities of those studied, even though they are actually uninterested or very bored. (11)

Applied research Research that attempts to solve a concrete problem or address a specific policy question and that has a direct, practical application. (1)

Association A co-occurrence of two events, factors, characteristics, or activities, such that when one happens, the other is likely to occur as well. Many statistics measure this. (2)

Assumption Parts of social theories that are not tested, but act as starting points or basic beliefs about the world. They are necessary to make other theoretical statements and to build social theory. (2)

Attitude of strangeness A technique in *field research* in which researchers study a *field site* by mentally adjusting to "see" it for the first time or as an outsider. (11)

Attributes The categories or levels of a *variable.* (4)

Axial coding A second coding of *qualitative data* after *open coding.* The researcher organizes the codes, develops links among them, and discovers key analytic categories. (13)

Back translation A technique in comparative research for checking *lexicon equivalence.* A researcher translates spoken or written text from an original language into a second language, then translates the same text in the second language back into the original language, then compares the two original language texts. (12)

Bar chart A display of *quantitative data* for one variable in the form of rectangles where longer rectangles indicate more cases in a variable category. Usually, it is used with discrete data and there is a small space between rectangles. They can have a horizontal or vertical orientation. Also called bar graphs. (10)

Basic social research   Research designed to advance fundamental knowledge about the social world. (1)

Bivariate statistics   Statistical measures that involve two variables only. (10)

Blame analysis   A counterfeit argument presented as if it were a theoretical explanation that substitutes attributing blame for a *causal explanation* and implies an intention or negligence, or responsibility for an event or situation. (2)

Body of a table   The center part of a *contingency table*. It contains all the cells, but not the totals or labels. (10)

Bogardus social distance scale   A *scale* that measures the distance between two or more social groups by having members of one group express the point at which they feel comfortable with various types of social interaction or closeness with members of the other group(s). (5)

Case study   Research, usually qualitative, on one or a small number of cases in which a researcher carefully examines a large number of details about each case. (1)

Causal explanation   A statement in social theory about why events occur that is expressed in terms of causes and effects. They correspond to associations in the empirical world. (2)

Cell of a table   A part of the *body of a table*. In a *contingency table*, it shows the distribution of cases into categories of variables as a specific number or percentage. (10)

Central limit theorem   A lawlike mathematical relationship that states: Whenever many *random samples* are drawn from a *population* and plotted, a *normal distribution* is formed, and the center of such a distribution for a variable is equal to its *population parameter*. (6)

Citation   Details of a scholarly journal article's location that helps people find it quickly. (4)

Classical experimental design   An *experimental design* that has *random assignment,* a *control group,* an *experimental group,* and *pretests* and *posttests* for each group. (8)

Classification   Complex, multidimensional concepts that have subtypes. They are parts of social theories between one simple concept and a full theoretical explanation. (2)

Closed-ended questions   A type of *survey research* question in which respondents must choose from a fixed set of answers. (7)

Cluster sampling   A type of *random sample* that uses multiple stages and is often used to cover wide geographic areas in which aggregated units are randomly selected then *samples* are drawn from the sampled aggregated units, or clusters. (6)

Code sheets   Paper with a printed grid on which a researcher records information so that it can be easily entered into a computer. It is an alternative to *direct-entry method* and using optical-scan sheets. (10)

Codebook   A document that describes the procedure for coding variables and their location in a format for computers. (10)

Coding   The process of converting raw information or data into another form for analysis. In *content analysis,* it is a means for determining how to convert symbolic meanings in *text* into another form, usually numbers (see *Coding system*); in *quantitative data* analysis, it is a means for assigning numbers; and in *qualitative data* analysis, it is a series of steps for reading raw notes and assigning codes or conceptual terms (see *Axial coding, Open coding, Selective coding*). (9)

Coding system   A set of instructions or rules used in *content analysis* to explain how to systematically convert the symbolic content from *text* into *quantitative data.* (9)

Cohort study   A type of *longitudinal research* in which a researcher focuses on a category of people who share a similar life experience in a specified time period. (1)

Computer-assisted telephone interviewing (CATI)   *Survey research* in which the interviewer sits before a computer screen and keyboard and uses the computer to read questions that are asked in a telephone interview, then enters answers directly into the computer. (7)

Concept cluster   A collection of interrelated ideas that share common *assumptions,* belong to the same larger social theory, and refer to one another. (2)

Conceptual definition   A careful, systematic definition of a construct that is explicitly written to clarify one's thinking. It is often linked to other concepts or theoretical statements. (5)

Conceptual equivalence   In *historical-comparative research,* the issue of whether the same ideas or concepts occur or can be used to represent phenomena across divergent cultural or historical settings. (12)

Conceptual hypothesis   A type of *hypothesis* in which the researcher expresses variables in abstract, conceptual terms and expresses the relationship among variables in a theoretical way. (5)

Conceptualization   The process of developing clear, rigorous, systematic *conceptual definitions* for abstract ideas/concepts. (5)

Concurrent validity   *Measurement validity* that relies on a preexisting and already accepted measure to verify the indicator of a construct. (5)

Confidence interval   A range of values, usually a little higher and lower than a specific value found in a *sample,* within which a researcher has a specified and high degree of confidence that the *population parameter* lies. (6)

Confidentiality   Information with participant names attached, but the researcher holds it in confidence or keeps it secret from the public. (3)

Content analysis   Research in which one examines patterns of symbolic meaning within written text, audio, visual, or other communication medium. (9)

Content validity   *Measurement validity* that requires that a measure represent all the aspects of the conceptual definition of a construct. (5)

Context effect   An effect in *survey research* when an overall tone or set topics heard by a respondent

affects how he or she interprets the meaning of subsequent questions. (7)

Contextual equivalence   The issue in *historical-comparative research* of whether social roles, norms, or situations across different cultures or historical periods are equivalent or can be compared. (12)

Contingency cleaning   Cleaning data using a computer in which the researcher looks at the combination of categories for two variables for logically impossible cases. (10)

Contingency question   A type of *survey research* question in which the respondent next goes to one or another later question based on his or her answer. (7)

Contingency table   A table that shows the *cross-tabulation* of two or more variables. It usually shows *bivariate quantitative data* for variables in the form of percentages across rows or down columns for the categories of one variable. (10)

Continuous variable   Variables measured on a continuum in which an infinite number of finer gradations between variable *attributes* are possible. (5)

Contrast question   A type of interview question asked late in *field research* in which the researcher verifies the correctness of distinctions found among categories in the meaning system of people being studied. (11)

Control group   The group that does not get the *treatment* in *experimental research.* (8)

Control variable   A "third" variable that shows whether a *bivariate relationship* holds up to alternative explanations. It can occur before or between other variables. (10)

Covariation   The idea that two variables vary together, such that knowing the values in one variable provides information about values found in another variable. (10)

Cover sheet   One or more pages at the beginning of a *questionnaire* with information about an interview or respondent. (7)

Criterion validity   *Measurement validity* that relies on some independent, outside verification. (5)

Crossover design A design to reduce creating inequality; it is when a study group that gets no treatment in the first phase of the experiment becomes the group with the treatment in the second phase, and vice versa. (3)

Cross-sectional research Research in which a researcher examines a single point in time or takes a one-time snapshot approach. (1)

Cross-tabulation Placing data for two variables in a *contingency table* to show the number or percentage of cases at the intersection of categories of the two variables. (10)

Curvilinear relationship A relationship between two variables such that as the values of one variable increase, the values of the second show a changing pattern (e.g., first decrease then increase then decrease). It is not a *linear relationship*. (10)

Data The *empirical evidence* or information that a person gathers carefully according to established rules or procedures; it can be qualitative or quantitative. (1)

Debrief When a researcher gives a true explanation of the experiment to subjects after using *deception*. (8)

Deception When an experimenter lies to subjects about the true nature of an experiment or creates a false impression through his or her actions or the setting. (8)

Deductive approach An approach to inquiry or social theory in which one begins with abstract ideas and principles then works toward concrete, *empirical evidence* to test the ideas. (2)

Demand characteristics A type of *reactivity* in which the subjects in *experimental research* pick up clues about the *hypothesis* and alter their behavior accordingly. (8)

Dependent variable The effect variable that is last and results from the causal variable(s) in a *causal explanation*. Also the variable that is measured in the *pretest* and *posttest* and that is the result of the *treatment* in *experimental research*. (4)

Descriptive question A type of question asked early in *field research*. The researcher seeks basic information (e.g., who, what, when, where) about the *field site*. (11)

Descriptive research Research in which one "paints a picture" with words or numbers, presents a profile, outlines stages, or classifies types. (1)

Descriptive statistics A general type of simple statistics used by researchers to describe basic patterns in the data. (10)

Design notation The name of a symbol system used to discuss the parts of an experiment and to make diagrams of them. (8)

Deviant case sampling A type of *nonrandom sample*, especially used by qualitative researchers, in which a researcher selects unusual or nonconforming cases purposely as a way to provide greater insight into social processes or a setting. (6)

Diffusion of treatment A threat to *internal validity* that occurs when the *treatment* "spills over" from the *experimental group*, and *control group* subjects modify their behavior because they learn of the *treatment*. (8)

Direct-entry method A method of entering data into a computer by typing data without code or optical scan sheets. (10)

Direct observation notes Notes taken in *field research* that attempt to include all details and specifics of what the researcher heard or saw in a *field site*. They are written in a way that permits multiple interpretations later. (11)

Discrete variables Variables in which the *attributes* can be measured only with a limited number of distinct, separate categories. (5)

Double-barreled question A problem in *survey research* question wording that occurs when two ideas are combined into one question, and it is unclear whether the answer is for the combination of both or one or the other question. (7)

Double-blind experiment A type of *experimental research* in which neither the subjects nor the person who directly deals with the subjects for the experimenter knows the specifics of the experiment. (8)

Ecological fallacy   Something that appears to be a *causal explanation* but is not. It occurs because of a confusion about *units of analysis*. A researcher has *empirical evidence* about an *association* for large-scale units or huge aggregates, but *overgeneralizes* to make theoretical statements about an *association* among small-scale units or individuals. (4)

Ecological validity   A way to demonstrate the authenticity and trustworthiness of a *field research* study by showing that the researcher's descriptions of the field site matches those of the members from the site and that the researcher was not a major disturbance. (11)

Editing   A step in the writing process that is part of *rewriting*, in which a writer cleans up and tightens the language and checks grammar, verb agreement, usage, sentence length, and paragraph organization to improve communication. (14)

Elaboration paradigm   A system for describing patterns evident among tables when a *bivariate contingency table* is compared with *partials* after the *control variable* has been added. (10)

Empirical evidence   The observations that people experience through their senses—touch, sight, hearing, smell, and taste; these can be direct or indirect. (1)

Empirical generalization   A quasi-theoretical statement that summarizes findings or regularities in *empirical evidence*. It uses few if any abstract concepts and only makes a statement about a recurring pattern that researchers observe. (2)

Empirical hypothesis   A type of *hypothesis* in which the researcher expresses variables in specific terms and expresses the *association* among the measured indicators of observable, *empirical evidence*. (5)

Empty boxes   A name for conceptual categories in an explanation that a researcher uses as part of the *illustrative method* of *qualitative data* analysis. (13)

Equivalent time-series design   An *experimental design* in which there are several repeated *pretests, posttests,* and *treatments* for one group often over a period of time. (8)

Erosion measures   *Nonreactive measures* of the wear or deterioration on surfaces due to the activity of people. (9)

Error of segregation   A mistake that can occur when writing qualitative research in which a writer separates concrete *empirical* details from abstract ideas too much. (14)

Ethnographic fallacy   When a field researcher takes what is observed at face value, fails to question what members of a *field site* say, and only focuses on the immediate concrete details of a setting while ignoring larger social forces. (11)

Ethnography   An approach to *field research* that emphasizes providing a very detailed description of a different culture from the viewpoint of an insider in that culture in order to permit a greater understanding of it. (11)

Ethnomethodology   An approach to social science that combines philosophy, social theory, and method to study. (11)

Evaluation research study   A type of *applied research* in which one tries to determine how well a program or policy is working or reaching its goals and objectives. (1)

Executive summary   A summary of a research project's findings placed at the beginning of a report for an applied, nonspecialist audience. Usually a little longer than an *abstract*. (14)

Exhaustive attributes   The principle that response categories in a *scale* or other measure should provide a category for all possible responses (i.e., every possible response fits into some category). (5)

Existing statistics research   Research in which one examines numerical information from government documents or official reports to address new research questions. (1)

Experimental design   Arranging the parts of an experiment and putting them together. (8)

Experimental group The group that receives the *treatment* in *experimental research.* (8)

Experimental research Research in which one intervenes or does something to one group of people but not to another, then compares results for the two groups. (1)

Explanation pattern A pattern in the *elaboration paradigm* in which the *bivariate contingency table* shows a relationship, but the *partials* show no relationship and the *control variable* occurs prior to the *independent variable.* (10)

Explanatory research Research that focuses on why events occur or tries to test and build social theory. (1)

Exploratory research Research into an area that has not been studied and in which a researcher wants to develop initial ideas and a more focused research question. (1)

External consistency A way to achieve *reliability* of data in *field research* in which the researcher cross-checks and verifies *qualitative data* using multiple sources of information. (11)

External criticism In historical research, a way to check the authenticity of *primary sources* by accurately locating the place and time of its creation (e.g., it is not a forgery). (12)

External validity The ability to generalize from *experimental research* to settings or people that differ from the specific conditions of the study. (5)

Face validity A type of *measurement validity* in which an indicator "makes sense" as a measure of a construct in the judgment of others, especially those in the scientific community. (5)

Factorial design A type of *experimental design* that considers the impact of several *independent variables* simultaneously. (8)

Fallacy of misplaced concreteness When a person uses too many digits in a quantitative measure in an attempt to create the impression that the data are accurate or the researcher is highly capable. (9)

Field experiment *Experimental research* that takes place in a natural setting. (8)

Field research A type of qualitative research in which a researcher directly observes the people being studied in a natural setting for an extended period. Often, the researcher combines intense observing with participation in the people's social activities. (1)

Field site The one or more natural locations where a researcher conducts *field research.* (11)

First-order interpretation In qualitative research, what the people who are being studied actually feel and think. (4)

Floaters Respondents who lack a belief or opinion, but who give an answer anyway if asked in a *survey research* question. Often, their answers are inconsistent. (7)

Focus groups A type of group interview in which an interviewer asks questions to the group, and answers are given in an open discussion among the group members. (11)

Frequency distribution A table that shows the distribution of cases into the categories of one variable (i.e., the number or percent of cases in each category). (10)

Frequency polygon A graph of connected points showing the distribution of how many cases fall into each category of a variable. (10)

Full-filter question A type of *survey research* question in which respondents are first asked whether they have an opinion or know about a topic, then only the respondents with an opinion or knowledge are asked a specific question on the topic. (7)

Functional theory A type of social theory based on biological analogies, in which the social world or its parts are seen as systems, with its parts serving the needs of the system. (2)

Funnel sequence A way to order *survey research* questions in a questionnaire from general ones to specific. (7)

Galton's problem In comparative research, the problem of finding correlations or *associations* among variables or characteristics in multiple cases or units, when the characteristics are actually diffused from a single unit or have a common origin. Thus, a researcher cannot really treat the multiple units (e.g., countries, cultures, etc.) as being wholly separate. (12)

General Social Survey (GSS)   A survey of a *random sample* of about 1,500 U.S. adults that has been conducted in most years between 1972 and the present and is available for many researchers to analyze. (9)

Go native   What happens when a researcher in *field research* gets overly involved and loses all distance or objectivity and becomes like the people being studied. (11)

Grantsmanship   The strategies and skills of locating appropriate funding sources and preparing high-quality proposals for research funding. (14)

Grounded theory   Social theory that is rooted in observations of specific, concrete details. (2)

Guilty knowledge   When a researcher in *field research* learns of illegal, unethical, or immoral actions by the people in the *field site* that is not widely known. (11)

Guttman scaling   A *scale* that researchers use after data are collected to reveal whether a hierarchical pattern exists among responses, such that people who give responses at a "higher level" also tend to give "lower-level" ones. (5)

Halo effect   An error often made when people use personal experience as an alternative to science for acquiring knowledge. It is when a person overgeneralizes from what he or she accepts as being highly positive or prestigious and lets its strong reputation or prestige "rub off" onto other areas. (1)

Haphazard sampling   A type of *nonrandom sample* in which the researcher selects anyone he or she happens to come across. (6)

Hawthorne effect   An effect of *reactivity* named after a famous case in which subjects reacted to the fact that they were in an experiment more than they reacted to the *treatment*. (8)

Hidden populations   People who engage in clandestine, deviant, or concealed activities and who are difficult to locate and study. (6)

Historical-comparative research   Research in which one examines different cultures or periods to better understand the social world. (1)

History effects   A threat to *internal validity* due to something that occurs and affects the *dependent variable* during an experiment, but which is unplanned and outside the control of the experimenter. (8)

Human Relations Area Files (HRAF)   An extensive catalog and comprehensive collection of *ethnographies* on many cultures (mostly preliterate) that permits a researcher to compare across cultural units. (12)

Hypothesis   The statement from a *causal explanation* or a *proposition* that has at least one *independent* and one *dependent variable*, but it has yet to be empirically tested. (4)

Ideal type   A pure model about an idea, process, or event. One develops it to think about it more clearly and systematically. It is used both as a method of *qualitative data* analysis and in *social theory* building. (2)

Idiographic   An approach that focuses on creating detailed descriptions of specific events in particular time periods and settings. It rarely goes beyond *empirical generalizations* to abstract social theory or *causal laws*. (2)

Illustrative method   A method of *qualitative data* analysis in which a researcher takes the concepts of a *social theory* or explanation and treats them as *empty boxes* to be filled with *empirical* examples and descriptions. (13)

Independence   The absence of a *statistical relationship* between two variables (i.e., when knowing the values on one variable provides no information about the values that will be found on another variable). There is no *association* between them. (10)

Independent variable   The first variable that causes or produces the effect in a *causal explanation*. (4)

Index   The summing or combining of many separate measures of a construct or variable. (5)

Inductive approach An approach to inquiry or social theory in which one begins with concrete empirical details, then works toward abstract ideas or general principles. (2)

Inferential statistics A branch of applied mathematics or statistics based on a *random sample*. It lets a researcher make precise statements about the level of confidence he or she has in the results of a *sample* being equal to the *population parameter*. (6)

Informed consent An agreement by participants stating they are willing to be in a study after they learn something about what the research procedure will involve. (3)

Institutional Review Board A committee of researchers and community members that oversees, monitors, and reviews the impact of research procedures on human participants and applies ethical guidelines by reviewing research procedures at a preliminary stage when first proposed. (3)

Interaction effect The effect of two *independent variables* that operate simultaneously together. The effect of the variables together is greater than what would occur from a simple addition of the effects from each. The variables operate together on one another to create an extra "boost." (8)

Internal consistency A way to achieve *reliability* of data in *field research* in which a researcher examines the data for plausibility and sees whether they form a coherent picture, given all that is known about a person or event, trying to avoid common forms of deception. (11)

Internal criticism How historical researchers establish the authenticity and credibility of *primary sources* and determine its accuracy as an account of what occurred. (12)

Internal validity The ability of experimenters to strengthen a *causal explanation*'s logical rigor by eliminating potential alternative explanations for an *association* between the *treatment* and the *dependent variable* through an *experimental design*. (5)

Interpretation pattern A pattern in the *elaboration paradigm* in which the *bivariate contingency table* shows a relationship, but the *partials* show no relationship and the *control variable* is intervening in the *causal explanation*. (10)

Interrupted time series An *experimental design* in which the *dependent variable* is measured periodically across many time points, and the *treatment* occurs in the midst of such measures, often only once. (8)

Interval level of measurement A *level of measurement* that identifies differences among variable *attributes*, ranks, and categories, and that measures distance between categories, but there is no true zero. (5)

Intervening variable A variable that is between the initial causal variable and the final effect variable in a *causal explanation*. (4)

Interview schedule The name of a *survey research questionnaire* when a telephone or face-to-face interview is used. (7)

Jotted notes In *field research*, what a researcher inconspicuously writes while in the *field site* on whatever is convenient in order to "jog the memory" later. (11)

Laboratory experiment *Experimental research* that takes place in an artificial setting over which the experimenter has great control. (8)

Latent coding A type of *content analysis* coding in which a researcher identifies subjective meaning such as general themes or motifs in a communication medium. (9)

Latin square design An *experimental design* used to examine whether the order or sequence in which subjects receive multiple versions of the *treatment* has an effect. (8)

Level of analysis A way to talk about the scope of a *social theory, causal explanation, proposition, hypothesis,* or theoretical statement. The range of phenomena it covers, or to which it applies, goes from social psychological (*micro level*) to organizational (*meso level*) to large-scale social structure (*macro level*). (4)

Level of measurement A system that organizes the information in the measurement of variables into four general levels, from *nominal level* to *ratio level.* (5)

Level of statistical significance A set of numbers researchers use as a simple way to measure the degree to which a *statistical relationship* results from random factors rather than the existence of a true relationship among variables. (10)

Lexicon equivalence Finding equivalent words or phrases to express the identical meaning in different languages or in the translation from one language to another (see *Back translation*). (12)

Likert scale A *scale* often used in *survey research* in which people express attitudes or other responses in terms of several *ordinal-level* categories (e.g., agree, disagree) that are ranked along a continuum. (5)

Linear relationship An *association* between two variables that is positive or negative across the attributes or levels of the variables. When plotted in a *scattergram,* the basic pattern of the *association* forms a straight line, not a curve or other pattern. (10)

Linear research path Research that proceeds in a clear, logical, step-by-step straight line. It is more characteristic of a quantitative than a qualitative approach to social research. (4)

Literature review A systematic examination of previously published studies on a research question, issue, or method that a researcher undertakes and integrates together to prepare for conducting a study or to bring together and summarize the "state of the field." (4)

Longitudinal research Research in which the researcher examines the features of people or other units at multiple points in time. (1)

Macro-level theory Social theories and explanations about more abstract, large-scale, and broad-scope aspects of social reality, such as social change in major institutions (e.g., the family, education, etc.) in a whole nation across several decades. (2)

Manifest coding A type of *content analysis* coding in which a researcher first develops a list of spe-

cific words, phrases, or symbols, then finds them in a communication medium. (9)

Marginals The totals in a *contingency table,* outside the *body of a table.* (10)

Matrix question A type of *survey research* question in which a set of questions is listed in a compact form together, all questions sharing the same set of answer categories. (7)

Maturation A threat to *internal validity* in *experimental research* due to natural processes of growth, boredom, and so on, that occur to subjects during the experiment and affect the *dependent variable.* (8)

Mean A measure of central tendency for one variable that indicates the arithmetic average (i.e., the sum of all scores divided by the total number of scores). (10)

Measurement equivalence In *historical-comparative research,* creating or locating measures that will accurately represent the same construct or variable in divergent cultural or historical settings. (12)

Measurement validity How well an *empirical* indicator and the *conceptual definition* of the construct that the indicator is supposed to measure "fit" together. (5)

Median A measure of central tendency for one variable indicating the point or score at which half the cases are higher and half are lower. (10)

Member validation A way to demonstrate the authenticity and trustworthiness of a *field research* study by having the people who were studied (i.e., members) read and confirm as being true that which the *researcher* has reported. (11)

Meso-level theory Social theories and explanations about the middle level of social reality between a broad and narrow scope, such as the development and operation of social organizations, communities, or social movements over a five-year period. (2)

Micro-level theory Social theories and explanations about the concrete, small-scale, and narrow level of reality, such as face-to-face interaction in small groups during a two-month period. (2)

Mode   A measure of central tendency for one variable that indicates the most frequent or common score. (10)

Mortality   Threats to *internal validity* due to subjects failing to participate through the entire experiment. (8)

Multiple indicators   Many procedures or instruments that indicate, or provide evidence of, the presence or level of a variable using *empirical evidence.* Researchers use the combination of several together to measure a variable. (5)

Mutually exclusive attributes   The principle that response categories in a *scale* or other measure should be organized so that a person's responses fit into only one category (i.e., categories should not overlap). (5)

Narrative history   A type of writing about a historical setting in which the writer attempts to "tell a story" by following chronological order, describing particular people and events, and focusing on many colorful details. (13)

Naturalism   The principle that researchers should examine events as they occur in natural, everyday ongoing social settings. (11)

Negative relationship   An *association* between two variables such that as values on one variable increase, values on the other variable fall or decrease. (2)

Nominal-level measurement   The lowest, least precise *level of measurement* for which there is only a difference in type among the categories of a variable. (5)

Nomothetic   An approach based on laws or one that operates according to a system of laws. (2)

Nonlinear research path   Research that proceeds in a circular, back-and-forth manner. It is more characteristic of a qualitative than a quantitative style to social research. (4)

Nonrandom sample   A type of sample in which the sampling elements are selected using something other than a mathematically random process. (6)

Nonreactive   Measures in which people being studied are unaware that they are in a study. (9)

Normal distribution   A "bell-shaped" frequency polygon for a distribution of cases, with a peak in the center and identical curving slopes on either side of the center. It is the distribution of many naturally occurring phenomena and is a basis of much statistical theory. (10)

Normalize social research   Techniques in *field research* used by researchers to make the people being studied feel more comfortable with the research process and to help them accept the researcher's presence. (11)

Null hypothesis   A *hypothesis* that says there is no relationship or *association* between two variables, or no effect. (4)

One-shot case study   An *experimental design* with only an *experimental group* and a *posttest,* no *pretest.* (8)

Open coding   A first coding of *qualitative data* in which a researcher examines the data to condense them into preliminary analytic categories or codes for analyzing the data. (13)

Open-ended question   A type of *survey research* question in which respondents are free to offer any answer they wish to the question. (7)

Operational definition   The definition of a variable in terms of the specific activities to measure or indicate it with *empirical evidence.* (5)

Operationalization   The process of moving from the *conceptual definition* of a construct to a set of specific activities or measures that allow a researcher to observe it *empirically* (i.e., its *operational definition*). (5)

Oral history   A type of *recollection* in which a researcher interviews a person about the events, beliefs, or feelings in the past that were directly experienced. (12)

Order effects   An effect in *survey research* in which respondents hear some specific questions before others, and the earlier questions affect their answers to later questions. (7)

Ordinal-level measurement   A *level of measurement* that identifies a difference among categorics of a variable and allows the categories to be rank ordered. (5)

Overgeneralization An error that people often make when using personal experience as an alternative to science for acquiring knowledge. It occurs when some evidence supports a belief, but a person falsely assumes that it applies to many other situations, too. (1)

Panel study A powerful type of *longitudinal research* in which a researcher observes exactly the same people, group, or organization across multiple time points. (1)

Paradigm A general organizing framework for *social theory* and *empirical* research. It includes basic *assumptions,* major questions to be answered, models of good research practice and theory, and methods for finding the answers to questions. (2)

Parameter A characteristic of the entire *population* that is estimated from a *sample.* (6)

Paraphrasing When a writer restates or rewords the ideas of another person, giving proper credit to the original source. (14)

Partially open question A type of *survey research* question in which respondents are given a fixed set of answers to choose from, but in addition, an "other" category is offered so that they can specify a different answer. (7)

Partials In *contingency tables* for three variables, tables that show the *association* between the *independent* and *dependent variables* for each category of a *control variable.* (10)

Percentile A measure of dispersion for one variable that indicates the percentage of cases at or below a score or point. (10)

Pie chart A display of numerical information on one variable that divides a circle into fractions by lines representing the proportion of cases in the variable's *attributes.* (10)

Placebo A false *treatment* or one that has no effect in an experiment. It is sometimes called a "sugar pill" that a *subject* mistakes for a true *treatment.* (8)

Plagiarism A type of unethical behavior in which one uses the writings or ideas of another without giving proper credit. It is "stealing ideas." (3, 14)

Population The name for the large general group of many cases from which a researcher draws a *sample* and which is usually stated in theoretical terms. (6)

Positive relationship An *association* between two variables such that as values on one increase, values on the other also increase. (2)

Possible code cleaning Cleaning data using a computer in which the researcher looks for responses or answer categories that cannot have cases. (10)

Posttest The measurement of the *dependent variable* in *experimental research* after the *treatment.* (8)

Praxis An idea in critical social science that social theory and everyday practice interact or work together, mutually affecting one another. This interaction can promote social change. (2)

Prediction A statement about something that is likely to occur in the future. (2)

Predictive validity *Measurement validity* that relies on the occurrence of a future event or behavior that is logically consistent to verify the indicator of a construct. (5)

Preexperimental designs *Experimental designs* that lack *random assignment* or use shortcuts and are much weaker than the *classical experimental design.* They may be substituted in situations where an experimenter cannot use all the features of a *classical experimental design,* but have weaker *internal validity.* (8)

Premature closure An error that is often made when using personal experience as an alternative to science for acquiring knowledge. It occurs when a person feels he or she has the answers and does not need to listen, seek information, or raise questions any longer. (1)

Prestige bias A problem in *survey research* question writing that occurs when a highly respected group or individual is linked to one of the answers. (7)

Pretest The measurement of the *dependent variable* of an experiment prior to the *treatment*. (8)

Prewriting A very early step in the writing process, when one writes without worrying about word choice, spelling, or grammar, but tries to let "ideas flow" as quickly as possible to connect thinking processes with writing. (14)

Primary sources *Qualitative data* or *quantitative data* used in historical research. It is evidence about past social life or events that was created and used by the persons who actually lived in the historical period. (12)

Principal investigator (PI) The person who is primarily in charge of research on a project that is sponsored or funded by an organization. (14)

Principle of voluntary consent An ethical principle of social research that people should never participate in research unless they first explicitly agree to do so. (3)

Probability proportionate to size (PPS) An adjustment made in *cluster sampling* when each cluster does not have the same number of *sampling elements*. (6)

Probe A follow-up question or action in *survey research* used by an interviewer to have a respondent clarify or elaborate on an incomplete or inappropriate answer. (7)

Proposition A basic statement in social theory that two ideas or variables are related to one another. It can be true or false (e.g., most sex offenders were themselves sexually abused when growing up), conditional (e.g., if a foreign enemy threatens, then the people of a nation will feel much stronger social solidarity), and/or causal (e.g., poverty causes crime). (2)

Public sociology Social science that seeks to enrich public debates over moral and political issues by infusing them with social theory and research and tries to generate a conversation between researchers and public. Often uses *action research* and a *critical social science* approach with its main audience being non-experts and practitioners. (3)

Purposive sampling A type of *nonrandom sample* in which the researcher uses a wide range of methods to locate all possible cases of a highly specific and difficult-to-reach *population*. (6)

Qualitative data Information in the form of words, pictures, sounds, visual images, or objects. (1)

Quantitative data Information in the form of numbers. (1)

Quasi-experimental designs *Experimental designs* that are stronger than *preexperimental designs*. They are variations on the *classical experimental design* that an experimenter uses in special situations or when an experimenter has limited control over the *independent variable*. (8)

Quasi-filter questions A type of *survey research* question including the answer choice "no opinion" or "don't know." (7)

Quota sampling A type of *nonrandom sample* in which the researcher first identifies general categories into which cases or people will be selected, then he or she selects a predetermined number of cases in each category. (6)

Random assignment Dividing subjects into groups at the beginning of *experimental research* using a random process, so the experimenter can treat the groups as equivalent. (8)

Random digit dialing (RDD) A method of randomly selecting cases for telephone interviews that uses all possible telephone numbers as a *sampling frame*. (6)

Random number table A list of numbers that has no pattern in them and that is used to create a random process for selecting cases and other randomization purposes. (6)

Random sample A type of *sample* in which the researcher uses a *random number table* or similar mathematical random process so that each *sampling element* in the *population* will have an equal probability of being selected. (6)

Range A measure of dispersion for one variable indicating the highest and lowest scores. (10)

Ratio-level measurement The highest, most precise *level of measurement* for which variable *attributes* can be rank ordered, the distance between the *attributes* precisely measured, and an absolute zero exists. (5)

Reactivity   The general threat to *external validity* that arises because subjects are aware that they are in an experiment and being studied. (8)

Recollections   The words or writings of people about their life experiences after some time has passed. The writings are based on a memory of the past, but may be stimulated by a review of past objects, photos, personal notes, or belongings. (12)

Recording sheet   Pages on which a researcher writes down what is coded in *content analysis*. (9)

Reductionism   Something that appears to be a *causal explanation*, but is not, because of a confusion about *units of analysis*. A researcher has *empirical evidence* for an association at the level of individual behavior or very small-scale units, but *overgeneralizes* to make theoretical statements about very large-scale units. (4)

Reliability   The dependability or consistency of the measure of a variable. (5)

Replication   The principle that researchers must be able to repeat scientific findings in multiple studies to have a high level of confidence that the findings are true. (2)

Replication pattern   A pattern in the *elaboration paradigm* in which the *partials* show the same relationship as in a *bivariate contingency table* of the *independent* and *dependent variable* alone. (10)

Request for proposal (RFP)   An announcement by a funding organization that it is willing to fund research and it is soliciting written plans of research projects. (14)

Research fraud   A type of unethical behavior in which a researcher fakes or invents data that he or she did not really collect, or fails to honestly and fully report how he or she conducted a study. (3)

Response set   An effect in *survey research* when respondents tend to agree with every question in a series rather than thinking through their answer to each question. (7)

Revising   A step in the writing process that is part of *rewriting* in which a writer adds ideas or evidence, and deletes, rearranges, or changes ideas to improve clarity and better communicate meaning. (14)

Rewriting   A step in the writing process in which the writer goes over a previous draft to improve communication of ideas and clarity of expression. (14)

Running records   A special type of *existing statistics research* used in historical research because the files, records, or documents are maintained in a relatively consistent manner over a period of time. (12)

Sample   A smaller set of cases a researcher selects from a larger pool and generalizes to the *population*. (6)

Sampling distribution   A distribution created by drawing many *random samples* from the same *population*. (6)

Sampling element   The name for a case or single unit to be selected. (6)

Sampling error   How much a *sample* deviates from being representative of the *population*. (6)

Sampling frame   A list of cases in a *population*, or the best approximation of it. (6)

Sampling interval   The inverse of the *sampling ratio*, which is used in *systematic sampling* to select cases. (6)

Sampling ratio   The number of cases in the *sample* divided by the number of cases in the *population* or the *sampling frame*, or the proportion of the *population* in the *sample*. (6)

Scale   A type of *quantitative data* measure often used in *survey research* that captures the intensity, direction, level, or potency of a variable construct along a continuum. Most are at the *ordinal level* of measurement. (5)

Scattergram   A diagram to display the *statistical relationship* between two variables based on plotting each case's values for both of the variables. (10)

Scientific community A collection of people who share a system of rules and attitudes that sustain the process of producing scientific knowledge. (1)

Scientific method The process of creating new knowledge using the ideas, techniques, and rules of the *scientific community*. (1)

Scientific misconduct When someone engages in *research fraud, plagiarism,* or other unethical conduct that significantly deviates from the accepted practice for conducting and reporting research within the *scientific community*. (3)

Secondary sources *Qualitative data* and *quantitative data* used in historical research. Information about events or settings are documented or written later by historians or others who did not directly participate in the events or setting. (12)

Second-order interpretation In qualitative research, what a researcher believes the people being studied feel and think. (4)

Selection bias A threat to *internal validity* when groups in an experiment are not equivalent at the beginning of the experiment. (8)

Selective coding A last pass at coding *qualitative data* in which a researcher examines previous codes to identify and select illustrative data that will support the conceptual coding categories that he or she developed. (13)

Selective observation The tendency to take notice of certain people or events based on past experience or attitudes. (1)

Semantic differential A *scale* in which people are presented with a topic or object and a list of many polar opposite adjectives or adverbs. They are to indicate their feelings by marking one of several spaces between two adjectives or adverbs. (5)

Sequential sampling A type of *nonrandom sample* in which a researcher tries to find as many relevant cases as possible, until time, financial resources, or his or her energy are exhausted, or until there is no new information or diversity from the cases. (6)

Simple random sampling A type of *random sample* in which a researcher creates a *sampling frame* and uses a pure random process to select cases. Each *sampling element* in the *population* will have an equal probability of being selected. (6)

Skewed distribution A distribution of cases among the categories of a variable that is not *normal* (i.e., not a "bell shape"). Instead of an equal number of cases on both ends, more are at one of the extremes. (10)

Snowball sampling A type of *nonrandom sample* in which the researcher begins with one case, then, based on information about interrelationships from that case, identifies other cases, and then repeats the process again and again. (6)

Social desirability bias A bias in *survey research* in which respondents give a "normative" response or a socially acceptable answer rather than give a truthful answer. (7)

Social impact assessment study A type of *applied social research* in which a researcher estimates the likely consequences or outcome of a planned intervention or intentional change to occur in the future. (1)

Social research A process in which a researcher combines a set of principles, outlooks, and ideas with a collection of specific practices, techniques, and strategies to produce knowledge. (1)

Sociogram A diagram or "map" that shows the network of social relationships, influence patterns, or communication paths among a group of people or units. (6)

Solomon four-group design An *experimental design* in which *subjects* are randomly assigned to two *control groups* and two *experimental groups*. Only one *experimental group* and one *control group* receive a *pretest*. All four groups receive a posttest. (8)

Special populations People who lack the necessary cognitive competency to give real informed consent or people in a weak position who might comprise their freedom to refuse to participate in a study. (3)

Specification pattern   A pattern in the *elaboration paradigm* in which the *bivariate contingency table* shows a relationship. One of the *partial tables* shows the relationship, but other tables do not. (10)

Spuriousness   A statement that appears to be a *causal explanation,* but is not because of a hidden, unmeasured, or initially unseen variable. The unseen variable comes earlier in the temporal order, and it has a causal impact on what was initially posited to be the *independent variable* as well as the *dependent variable.* (4)

Standard deviation   A measure of dispersion for one variable that indicates an average distance between the scores and the *mean.* (10)

Standard-format question   A type of *survey research* question in which the answer categories fail to include "no opinion" or "don't know." (7)

Standardization   The procedure to statistically adjust measures to permit making an honest comparison by giving a common basis to measures of different units. (5)

Static group comparison   An *experimental design* with two groups, no *random assignment,* and only a *posttest.* (8)

Statistic   A numerical estimate of a *population parameter* computed from a *sample.* (6)

Statistical Abstract of the United States   A U.S. government publication that appears annually and contains an extensive compilation of statistical tables and information. (9)

Statistical significance   A way to discuss the likelihood that a finding or *statistical relationship* in a *sample* is due to the random factors rather than due to the existence of an actual relationship in the entire *population.* (10)

Stratified sampling   A type of *random sample* in which the researcher first identifies a set of *mutually exclusive* and *exhaustive* categories, then uses a random selection method to select cases for each category. (6)

Structural question   A type of question in *field research* interviews in which the researcher attempts to verify the correctness of placing terms or events into the categories of the meaning system used by people being studied. (11)

Structured observation   A method of watching what is happening in a social setting that is highly organized and that follows systematic rules for observation and documentation. (9)

Subjects   The name for people who are studied and participate in *experimental research.* (8)

Successive approximation   A method of *qualitative data* analysis in which the researcher repeatedly moves back and forth between the *empirical data* and the abstract concepts, theories, or models. (13)

Suppressor variable pattern   A pattern in the *elaboration paradigm* in which no relationship appears in a *bivariate contingency table,* but the *partials* show a relationship between the variables. (10)

Survey research   Quantitative social research in which one systematically asks many people the same questions, then records and analyzes their answers. (1)

Systematic sampling   A type of *random sample* in which a researcher selects every *k*th (e.g., 12th) case in the *sampling frame* using a *sampling interval.* (6)

Target population   The name for the large general group of many cases from which a *sample* is drawn and which is specified in very concrete terms. (6)

Text   A general name for symbolic meaning within a communication medium measured in *content analysis.* (9)

Third-order interpretation   In qualitative research, what a researcher tells the reader of a research report that the people he or she studied felt and thought. (4)

Threatening questions   A type of *survey research* question in which respondents are likely to cover up or lie about their true behavior or beliefs because they fear a loss of self-image or that they may appear to be undesirable or deviant. (7)

Time-series study   Any research that takes place over time, in which different people or cases may be looked at in each time point. (1)

Treatment   What the *independent variable* in *experimental research* is called. (8)

Type I error   The logical error of falsely rejecting the *null hypothesis.* (10)

Type II error   The logical error of falsely accepting the *null hypothesis.* (10)

Unidimensionality   The principle that when using *multiple indicators* to measure a construct, all the indicators should consistently fit together and indicate a single construct. (5)

Unit of analysis   The kind of empirical case or unit that a researcher observes, measures, and analyzes in a study. (4)

Univariate statistics   Statistical measures that deal with one variable only. (10)

Universe   The broad class of units that are covered in a *hypothesis.* All the units to which the findings of a specific study might be generalized. (4)

Unobtrusive measures   Another name for *nonreactive measures.* It emphasizes that the people being studied are not aware of it because the measures do not intrude. (9)

Validity   A term meaning truth that can be applied to the logical tightness of *experimental design,* the ability to generalize findings outside a study, the quality of measurement, and the proper use of procedures. (5)

Variable   A concept or its *empirical* measure that can take on multiple values. (4)

Verstehen   A German word that translates as understanding; specifically, it means an empathic understanding of another's worldview. (2)

Whistle-blower   A person who sees ethical wrongdoing, tries to correct it internally but then informs an external audience, agency, or the media. (3)

Wording effects   An effect that occurs when a specific term or word used in a *survey research* question affects how respondents answer the question. (7)

Zoom lens   An organizational form often used by field researchers when writing reports that begin broadly then become narrow, focused, and specific. (14)

Z-score   A way to locate a score in a distribution of scores by determining the number of *standard deviations* it is above or below the *mean* or arithmetic average. (10)

Abbott, Andrew. (1992). From causes to events. *Sociological Methods and Research,* 20:428–455.

Abrams, Philip. (1982). *Historical sociology.* Ithaca, NY: Cornell University Press.

Adams, Peter. (2004). "Gambling Impact Assessment" Centre for Gambling Studies, University of Auckland. www.waitakere.govt.nz/AbtCnl/pp/pdf/partoneintro.pdf, downloaded 08/15/05.

Adler, Patricia A., and Peter Adler. (1987). *Membership roles in field research.* Beverly Hills, CA: Sage.

Adler, Patricia A., and Peter Adler. (1993). Ethical issues in self-censorship. In *Research on sensitive topics,* edited by C. Renzetti and R. Lee, pp. 249–266. Thousand Oaks, CA: Sage.

Adler, Patricia A., and Peter Adler. (1994). Observational techniques. In *Handbook of qualitative research,* edited by N. Denzin and Y. Lincoln, pp. 377–392. Thousand Oaks, CA: Sage.

Agar, Michael. (1986). *Speaking of ethnography.* Beverly Hills, CA: Sage.

Alwin, Duane F., and Jon A. Krosnick. (1985). The measurement of values in surveys. *Public Opinion Quarterly,* 49:535–552.

American Sociological Association. (1997). *American Sociological Association style guide,* 2nd ed. Washington, DC: American Sociological Association.

Anderson, Barbara A., Brian D. Silver, and Paul R. Abramson. (1988). The effects of the race of interviewer on race-related attitudes of black respondents in SRC/CPS national election studies. *Public Opinion Quarterly,* 52:289–324.

Anderson, R. Bruce W. (1973). On the comparability of meaningful stimuli in cross-cultural research. In *Comparative research methods,* edited by D. Warwick and S. Osherson, pp. 149–186. Englewood Cliffs, NJ: Prentice-Hall.

Andolina, Molly W., and Jeremy Mayer. (2003). Demographic shifts and racial attitudes. *The Social Science Journal,* 40:19–31.

Andren, Gunnar. (1981). Reliability and content analysis. In *Advances in content analysis,* edited by K. Rosengren, pp. 43–67. Beverly Hills, CA: Sage.

Aronson, Elliot, and J. Merrill Carlsmith. (1968). Experimentation in social psychology. In *The handbook of social psychology, Vol. 2: Research methods,* edited by G. Lindzey and E. Aronson, pp. 1–78. Reading, MA: Addison-Wesley.

Babbie, Earl. (1989). *The practice of social research,* 5th ed. Belmont, CA: Wadsworth. (6th ed., 1992; 8th ed., 1998; 9th ed., 2001; 10th ed., 2004.)

Backstrom, Charles H., and Gerald Hursh-Cesar. (1981). *Survey research,* 2nd ed. New York: Wiley.

Bailey, Kenneth D. (1987). *Methods of social research,* 3rd ed. New York: Free Press.

Banaszak, Lee Ann. (1996). *Why movements succeed or fail.* Princeton NJ: Princeton University Press.

Barzun, Jacques, and Henry F. Graff. (1970). *The modern researcher,* rev. ed. New York: Harcourt, Brace and World.

Bauer, Raymond, ed. (1966). *Social indicators.* Cambridge, MA: MIT Press.

Beck, Bernard. (1970). Cooking welfare stew. In *Pathways to data,* edited by R. W. Habenstein, pp. 7–29. Chicago: Aldine.

Beck, Richard A. (1995). Publishing evaluation research. *Contemporary Sociology,* 24:9–12.

Becker, Howard S., Blanche Geer, Everett C. Hughes, and Anselm Strauss. (1961). *Boys in white: Student culture in medical school.* Chicago: University of Chicago Press.

Becker, Howard S., Michal M. McCall, and Lori V. Morris. (1989). Theatres and communities. *Social Problems,* 36:93–116.

Ben-Yehuda, Nachman. (1983). History, selection and randomness—Towards an analysis of social historical explanations. *Quality and Quantity,* 17:347–367.

Bendix, Reinhard. (1956). *Work and authority in industry.* New York: Wiley.

Bendix, Reinhard. (1963). Concepts and generalizations in comparative sociological studies. *American Sociological Review*, 28:91–116.

Bendix, Reinhard. (1978). *Kings or people: Power and the mandate to rule.* Berkeley: University of California Press.

Best, Joel. (2001). *Damned lies and statistics: Untangling numbers from the media, politicians, and activists.* Berkeley: University of California Press.

Bischoping, Katherine, and Jennifer Dykema. (1999). Toward a social psychological programme for improving focus group methods of developing questionnaires. *Journal of Official Statistics*, 15:495–516.

Bishop, George F. (1987). Experiments with the middle response alternative in survey questions. *Public Opinion Quarterly*, 51:220–232.

Blee, Kathleen M. (1991). *Women of the Klan: Racism and gender in the 1920s.* Berkeley: University of California Press.

Block, Fred, and Gene A. Burns. (1986). Productivity as a social problem: The uses and misuses of social indicators. *American Sociological Review*, 51:767–780.

Blum, Debra E. (1989). Dean charged with plagiarizing a dissertation for his book on Muzak. *Chronicle of Higher Education*, 35, A17.

Bogdan, Robert, and Steven J. Taylor. (1975). *Introduction to qualitative research methods: A phenomenological approach to the social sciences.* New York: Wiley.

Bond, Charles F., Jr., and Evan L. Anderson. (1987). The reluctance to transmit bad news: Private discomfort or public display? *Journal of Experimental Social Psychology*, 23:176–187.

Bonnell, Victoria E. (1980). The uses of theory, concepts and comparison in historical sociology. *Comparative Studies in Society and History*, 22:156–173.

Bradburn, Norman M. (1983). Response effects. In *Handbook of survey research*, edited by P. Rossi, J. Wright, and A. Anderson, pp. 289–328. Orlando, FL: Academic.

Bradburn, Norman M., and Seymour Sudman. (1980). *Improving interview method and questionnaire design.* San Francisco: Jossey-Bass.

Bradburn, Norman M., and Seymour Sudman. (1988). *Polls and surveys.* San Francisco: Jossey-Bass.

Brase, Gary L. and Jullian Richmond. (2004). The white-coat effect. *Journal of Applied Social Psychology* 34:2469–2483.

Braudel, Fernand. (1980). *On history*, trans. Sarah Matthews. Chicago: University of Chicago Press.

Brenner, Michael, Jennifer Brown, and David Canter, eds. (1985). *The research interview: Uses and approaches.* Orlando, FL: Academic Press.

Briggs, Charles L. (1986). *Learning how to ask.* New York: Cambridge University Press.

Broad, W. J., and N. Wade. (1982). *Betrayers of the truth.* New York: Simon and Schuster.

Broadhead, Robert, and Ray Rist. (1976). Gatekeepers and the social control of social research. *Social Problems*, 23:325–336.

Brody, Charles J. (1986). Things are rarely black or white. *American Journal of Sociology*, 92:657–677.

Burawoy, Michael. (2004). Public sociologies. *Social Forces*, 82:1603–1618.

Burawoy, Michael. (2005). For public sociology. *American Sociological Review* 70:4–28.

Calhoun, Craig. (1996). The rise and domestication of historical sociology. In *The historical turn in the human sciences*, edited by T. J. McDonald, pp. 305–337. Ann Arbor: University of Michigan Press.

Cannell, Charles F., and Robert L. Kahn. (1968). Interviewing. In *Handbook of social psychology*, 2nd ed., Vol. 2, edited by G. Lindzey and E. Aronson, pp. 526–595. Reading, MA: Addison-Wesley.

Canter, David, Jennifer Brown, and Linda Goat. (1985). Multiple sorting procedure for studying conceptual systems. In *The research interview: Uses and approaches*, edited by M. Brenner, J. Brown, and D. Canter, pp. 79–114. New York: Academic Press.

Cantor, Norman F., and Richard I. Schneider. (1967). *How to study history.* New York: Thomas Y. Crowell.

Carley, Michael. (1981). *Social measurement and social indicators.* London: George Allen and Unwin.

Carr-Hill, Roy A. (1984). The political choice of social indicators. *Quality and Quantity*, 18:173–191.

Catania, Joseph, D. Dinson, J. Canahola, L. Pollack, W. Hauck, and T. Coates. (1996). Effects of interviewer gender, interviewer choice and item wording on responses to questions concerning sexual behavior. *Public Opinion Quarterly*, 60:345–375.

Chafetz, Janet Saltzman. (1978). *A primer on the construction and testing of theories in sociology.* Itasca, IL: Peacock.

Channels, Noreen L. (1993). Anticipating media coverage. In *Research on sensitive topics,* edited by C. Renzetti and R. Lee, pp. 267–280. Thousand Oaks, CA: Sage.

Chavez, Leo R. (2001). *Covering immigration.* Berkeley: University of California Press.

Cherlin, Andrew J., Linda Burton, Tera Hurt, and Diane Purvin. (2004). The influence of physical and sexual abuse on marriage and cohabitation. *American Sociological Review* 69:768–789.

Chicago manual of style for authors, editors and copywriters, 13th ed., revised and expanded. (1982). Chicago: University of Chicago Press.

Church, Allan H. (1993). Estimating the effect of incentives on mail survey response rates: A meta analysis. *Public Opinion Quarterly,* 57:62–80.

Churchill, Gilbert A., Jr. (1983). *Marketing research,* 3rd ed. New York: Dryden.

Clammer, John. (1984). Approaches to ethnographic research. In *Ethnographic research: A guide to general conduct,* edited by R. F. Ellen, pp. 63–85. Orlando: Academic Press.

Cogan, Johan, Judith Torney-Purta, and Douglas Anderson. (1988). Knowledge and attitudes toward global issues: Students in Japan and the United States. *Comparative Education Review,* 32: 283–297.

Cole, Stephen, and Linda Perlman Gordon. (1995). *Making sciencey.* Cambridge MA: Harvard University Press.

Converse, Jean M., and Stanley Presser. (1986). *Survey questions.* Beverly Hills, CA: Sage.

Converse, Jean M., and Howard Schuman. (1974). *Conversations at random.* New York: Wiley.

Cook, Thomas D., and Donald T. Campbell. (1979). *Quasi-experimentation.* Chicago: Rand McNally.

Corsaro, William. (1994). Discussion, debate, and friendship processes. *Sociology of Education,* 67:1–26.

Corsaro, William, and Luisa Molinari. (2000). Priming events and Italian children's transition from preschool to elementary school: Representations and action. *Social Psychology Quarterly,* 63:16–33.

Cotter, Patrick R., Jeffrey Cohen, and Philip B. Coulter. (1982). Race of interview effects in telephone interviews. *Public Opinion Quarterly,* 46:278–286.

Couper, Mick P., Eleanor Singer, et al. (1998). Participation in the 1990 decennial census. *American Politics Quarterly,* 26:59–81.

Craib, Ian. (1984). *Modern social theory: From Parsons to Habermas.* New York: St. Martin's Press.

Crane, Diana. (1972). *Invisible colleges.* Chicago: University of Chicago Press.

Crozat, Matthew. (1998). Are the times a-changin'? Assessing the acceptance of protest in Western democracies. In *The movement society,* edited by D. Meyer and S. Tarrow, pp. 59–81. Totowa, NJ: Rowman and Littlefield.

Dabbs, James M., Jr. (1982). Making things visible. In *Varieties of qualitative research,* edited by J. Van Maanen, J. Dabbs, Jr., and R. R. Faulkner, pp. 31–64. Beverly Hills, CA: Sage.

Dale, Angela, S. Arber, and Michael Procter. (1988). *Doing secondary analysis.* Boston: Unwin Hyman.

D'Antonio, William. (August 1989). Executive Office Report: Sociology on the move. *ASA Footnotes,* 17, p. 2.

Dasgupta, Nilanjana, and Shaki Asgari. (2004). Seeing is believing. *Journal of Experimental Social Psychology* 40:642–658.

Davis, Darren W. (1997). The direction of race of interviewer effects among African-Americans: Donning the black mask. *American Journal of Political Science,* 41:309–322.

Davis, James A., and Tom W. Smith. (1992). *The NORC General Social Survey: A user's guide.* Newbury Park, CA: Sage.

Dawes, R. M., and T. W. Smith. (1985). Attitude and opinion measurement. In *Handbook of social psychology,* 3rd ed., Vol. 1, edited by G. Lindzey and E. Aronson, pp. 509–566. New York: Random House.

Dean, John P., Robert L. Eichhorn, and Lois R. Dean. (1969). Fruitful informants for intensive interviewing. In *Issues in participant observation,* edited by G. McCall and J. L. Simmons, pp. 142–144. Reading, MA: Addison-Wesley.

De Heer, Wim. (1999). International response trends: Results from an international survey. *Journal of Official Statistics,* 15:129–142.

Denzin, Norman K. (1989). *The research act,* 3rd ed. Englewood Cliffs, NJ: Prentice-Hall.

deVaus, D. A. (1986). *Surveys in social research.* Boston: George Allen and Unwin.

Diener, Edward, and Rick Crandall. (1978). *Ethics in social and behavioral research.* Chicago: University of Chicago Press.

Dijkstra, Wil, and Johannes van der Zouwen, eds. (1982). *Response behavior in the survey interview.* New York: Academic Press.

Dillman, Don A. (1978). *Mail and telephone surveys: The total design method.* New York: Wiley.

Dillman, Don A. (1983). Mail and other self-administered questionnaires. In *Handbook of survey research,* edited by P. Rossi, J. Wright, and A. Anderson, pp. 359–377. Orlando, FL: Academic Press.

Dillman, Don A. (1991). The design and administration of mail surveys. *Annual Review of Sociology,* 17:225–249.

Dillman, Don A. (2000). *Mail and Internet surveys,* 2nd ed. New York: Wiley.

Dooley, David. (1984). *Social research methods.* Englewood Cliffs, NJ: Prentice-Hall.

Douglas, Jack D. (1976). *Investigative social research.* Beverly Hills, CA: Sage.

Douglas, Jack D. (1985). *Creative interviewing.* Beverly Hills, CA: Sage.

Downey, Liam. (2005). The unintended significance of race. *Social Forces,* 83:971–1008.

Draus, Paul J., Harvey Siegal, Robert Carlson, Russell Falck, and Jichuan Wang. (2005). Cracking in the heartland. *Sociological Quarterly* 46:165–189.

Duncan, Otis Dudley. (1984). *Notes on social measurement.* New York: Russell Sage Foundation.

Duncan, Otis Dudley, and Magnus Stenbeck. (1988). No opinion or not sure? *Public Opinion Quarterly,* 52:513–525.

Duneier, Mitchell. (1999). *Sidewalk.* New York: Farrar, Straus and Giroux.

Durkheim, Emile. (1938). *Rules of the sociological method,* trans. Sarah Solovay and John Mueller, edited by G. Catlin. Chicago: University of Chicago Press.

Durkheim, Emile. (1951). *Suicide.* (Translated from original 1897 work by John A. Spalding and George Simpson). New York: Free Press.

Dykema, Jennifer, and Nora Cate Schaeffer. (2000). Events, instruments, and reporting errors. *American Sociological Review,* 65:619–629.

Edelman, Lauren, Sally R. Fuller, and Iona Mara-Drita. (2001). Diversity rhetoric and the managerialization of law. *American Journal of Sociology,* 106:1589–1641.

Eder, Donna. (1995). *School talk.* New Brunswick, NJ: Rutgers University Press.

Eder, Donna, and David Kinney. (1995). The effect of middle school extracurricular activities on adolescents' popularity and peer status. *Youth and Society,* 26:298–325.

Elder, Glen H., Jr., Eliza Pavalko, and Elizabeth Clipp. (1993). *Working with archival data.* Thousand Oaks, CA: Sage.

Elder, Joseph W. (1973). Problems of crosscultural methodology. In *Comparative social research,* edited by M. Armer and A. D. Grimshaw, pp. 119–144. New York: Wiley.

Eliasoph, Nina. (1998). *Avoiding politics.* New York: Cambridge University Press.

Emerson, Robert M. (1981). Observational field work. *Annual Review of Sociology,* 7:351–378.

Felson, Richard. (1991). Blame analysis. *American Sociologist,* 22:5–24.

Felson, Richard, and Stephen Felson. (1993). Predicaments of men and women. *Society,* 30:16–20.

Fernandez, Roberto M. (2001). Skill-biased technological change and wage inequality. *American Journal of Sociology,* 107:273–321.

Fetterman, David M. (1989). *Ethnography: Step by step.* Newbury Park, CA: Sage.

Finkel, Steven E., Thomas M. Guterbock, and Marian J. Borg. (1991). Race-of-interviewer effects in a pre-election poll: Viriginia 1989. *Public Opinion Quarterly,* 55:313–330.

Finley, M. I. (Summer 1977). Progress in historiography. *Daedalus,* pp. 125–142.

Foddy, William. (1993). *Constructing questions for interviews and questionnaires.* New York: Cambridge University Press.

Foster, Gary S., Richard L. Hummel, and Donald J. Adamchak. (1998). Patterns of conception, natality and mortality from midwestern cemeteries. *Sociological Quarterly,* 39:473–490.

Fowler, Floyd J., Jr. (1984). *Survey research methods.* Beverly Hills, CA: Sage.

Fowler, Floyd J., Jr. (1992). How unclear terms can affect survey data. *Public Opinion Quarterly,* 56:218–231.

Fox, Richard, Melvin R. Crask, and Jonghoon Kim. (1988). Mail survey response rate. *Public Opinion Quarterly,* 52:467–491.

Franke, Charles O. (1983). Ethnography. In *Contemporary field research,* edited by R. M. Emerson, pp. 60–67. Boston: Little, Brown.

Franke, Richard H., and James D. Kaul. (1978). The Hawthorne experiments. *American Sociological Review,* 43:623–643.

Freeman, Howard, and Peter H. Rossi. (1984). Furthering the applied side of sociology. *American Sociological Review,* 49:571–580.

Frey, James H. (1983). *Survey research by telephone.* Beverly Hills, CA: Sage.

Gallie, W. B. (1963). The historical understanding. *History and Theory,* 3:149–202.

Gamson, William A. (1992). *Talking politics.* Cambridge: Cambridge University Press.

Gans, Herbert J. (1982). The participant observer as a human being: Observations on the personal aspects of fieldwork. In *Field research,* edited by R. G. Burgess, pp. 53–61. Boston: George Allen and Unwin.

Garza, Cecilia, and Michael Landeck. (2004). College freshmen at risk. *Social Science Quarterly,* 85:1390–1400.

George, Alexander, and Andrew Bennett. (2005). *Case studies and theory development in the social sciences.* Cambridge, MA: MIT Press.

Georges, Robert A., and Michael O. Jones. (1980). *People studying people.* Berkeley: University of California Press.

Gibelman, Margaret. (2001). Learning from the mistakes of others. *Journal of Social Work Education,* 37: 241–255.

Gillespie, Richard. (1988). The Hawthorne experiments and the politics of experimentation. In *The rise of experimentation in American psychology,* edited by J. Morawski, pp. 114–137. New Haven, CT: Yale University Press.

Gillespie, Richard. (1991). *Manufacturing knowledge.* New York: Cambridge University Press.

Goar, Carla, and Jane Sell. (2005). Using Task Definition to Modify Racial Inequality within Task Groups. *Sociological Quarterly,* 46:525–543.

Goldner, Jesse A. (1998). The unending saga of legal controls over scientific misconduct. *American Journal of Law & Medicine,* 24:293–344.

Goldthorpe, John. (1977). The relevance of history to sociology. In *Sociological research methods,* edited by M. Bulmer, pp. 178–191. London: Macmillan.

Gonor, George. (1977). "Situation" versus "frame": The "interactionist" and the "structuralist" analysis of everyday life. *American Sociological Review,* 42:854–867.

Gorden, Raymond. (1980). *Interviewing: Strategy, techniques and tactics,* 3rd ed. Homewood, IL: Dorsey Press.

Gorden, Raymond. (1992). *Basic interviewing skills.* Itasca, IL: Peacock.

Gordon, Phyllis, D. Feldman, J. Tantillo, and K. Perrone. (2004). Attitudes regarding interpersonal relationships with persons with mental illness and mental retardation. *Journal of Rehabilitation,* 70:50–56.

Gotham, Kevin Fox, and William G. Staples. (1996). Narrative analysis and the new historical sociology. *Sociological Quarterly,* 37:481–502.

Goyder, John C. (1982). Factors affecting response rates to mailed questionnaires. *American Sociological Review,* 47:550–554.

Graham, Sandra. (1992). Most of the subjects were white and middle class. *American Psychologist,* 47:629–639.

Griffin, Larry J. (1992). Comparative-historical analysis. In *Encyclopedia of sociology,* Vol. 1, edited by E. and M. Borgatta, pp. 263–271. New York: Macmillan.

Griffin, Larry J. (1993). Narrative, event structure analysis and causal interpretation in historical sociology. *American Journal of Sociology,* 98:1094–1133.

Groves, Robert M., and Robert L. Kahn. (1979). *Surveys by telephone.* New York: Academic Press.

Groves, Robert M., and Nancy Mathiowetz. (1984). Computer assisted telephone interviewing: Effects on interviewers and respondents. *Public Opinion Quarterly,* 48:356–369.

Gurney, Joan Neff. (1985). Not one of the guys: The female researcher in a male dominated setting. *Qualitative Sociology,* 8:42–62.

Hage, Jerald. (1972). *Techniques and problems of theory construction in sociology.* New York: Wiley.

Hagstrom, Warren. (1965). *The scientific community.* New York: Basic Books.

Hammersley, Martyn, and Paul Atkinson. (1983). *Ethnography: Principles in practice.* London: Tavistock.

Harper, Douglas. (1982). *Good company.* Chicago: University of Chicago Press.

Harris, Sheldon H. (2002). *Factories of death.* New York: Taylor & Francis.

Hawkes, Daina, Charlene Senn, and Chantal Thorn. (2004). Factors that influence attitudes toward women with tattoos. *Sex Roles,* 50:593–604.

Hearnshaw, L. S. (1979). *Cyril Burt: Psychologist.* London: Holder and Stoughten.

Heberlein, Thomas A., and Robert Baumgartner. (1978). Factors affecting response rates to mailed questionnaires. *American Sociological Review,* 43:447–462.

Heberlein, Thomas A., and Robert Baumgartner. (1981). Is a questionnaire necessary in a second mailing? *Public Opinion Quarterly,* 45:102–107.

Herring, Lee, and Johanna Ebner. (May/June 2005). Sociologists' impact interpretation of federal welfare legislation. *American Sociological Association Footnotes,* 33, p. 3.

Hill, Michael R. (1993). *Archival strategies and techniques.* Thousand Oaks, CA: Sage.

Hindess, Barry. (1973). *The use of official statistics in sociology: A critique of positivism and ethnomethodology.* New York: Macmillan.

Hippler, Hans J., and Norbert Schwartz. (1986). Not forbidding isn't allowing. *Public Opinion Quarterly,* 50:87–96.

Hirschman, Albert O. (1970). *Exit, voice, and loyalty: Response to decline in firms, organizations and states.* Cambridge, MA: Harvard University Press.

Holden, Constance. (2000). Psychologist made up sex bias results. *Science,* 294:2457.

Holstein, James A., and Jaber F. Gubrium. (1994). Phenomenology, ethnomethodology and interpretative practice. In *Handbook of qualitative research,* edited by N. Denzin and Y. Lincoln, pp. 262–272. Thousand Oaks, CA: Sage.

Holsti, Ole R. (1968). Content analysis. In *Handbook of social psychology,* 2nd ed., Vol. 2, edited by G. Lindzey and E. Aronson, pp. 596–692. Reading, MA: Addison-Wesley.

Holsti, Ole R. (1969). *Content analysis for the social sciences and humanities.* Reading, MA: Addison-Wesley.

Holt, Robert T., and John E. Turner. (1970). The methodology of comparative research. In *The methodology of comparative research,* edited by R. Holt and J. Turner, pp. 1–20. New York: Free Press.

Holy, Ladislav. (1984). Theory, methodology and the research process. In *Ethnographic research: A guide to general conduct,* edited by R. F. Ellen, pp. 13–34. Orlando: Academic Press.

Horn, Robert V. (1993). *Statistical indicators for the economic and social sciences.* Cambridge: Cambridge University Press.

Hubbard, Raymond, and Eldon Little. (1988). Promised contributions to charity and mail survey responses: Replication with extension. *Public Opinion Quarterly,* 52:223–230.

Humphreys, Laud. (1975). *Tearoom Trade: Impersonal sex in public places.* Chicago: Aldine.

Hyman, Herbert H. (1975). *Interviewing in social research.* Chicago: University of Chicago Press.

Hyman, Herbert H. (1991). *Taking society's measure: A personal history of survey research.* New York: Russell Sage.

Hymes, Dell. (1970). Linguistic aspects of comparative political research. In *The methodology of comparative research,* edited by R. Holt and J. Turner, pp. 295–341. New York: Free Press.

Jackson, Bruce. (1978). Killing time: Life in the Arkansas penitentiary. *Qualitative Sociology,* 1:21–32.

Jackson, Bruce. (1987). *Fieldwork.* Urbana: University of Illinois Press.

Johnson, John M. (1975). *Doing field research.* New York: Free Press.

Jones, J. H. (1981). *Bad blood: The Tuskegee syphilis experiment.* New York: Free Press.

Jones, Wesley H. (1979). Generalizing mail survey inducement methods: Populations' interactions with anonymity and sponsorship. *Public Opinion Quarterly,* 43:102–111.

Junker, Buford H. (1960). *Field work.* Chicago: University of Chicago Press.

Juster, F. Thomas, and Kenneth C. Land, eds. (1981). *Social accounting systems: Essays on the state of the art.* New York: Academic Press.

Kalmijn, Matthijus. (1991). Shifting boundaries: Trends in religious and educational homogamy. *American Sociological Review,* 56:786–801.

Kane, Emily W., and Laura J. MacAulay. (1993). Interview gender and gender attitudes. *Public Opinion Quarterly,* 57:1–28.

Kaplan, Abraham. (1964). *The conduct of inquiry: Methodology for behavioral science.* New York: Harper & Row.

Karweit, Nancy, and Edmund D. Meyers, Jr. (1983). Computers in survey research. In *Handbook of survey research,* edited by P. Rossi, J. Wright, and A. Anderson, pp. 379–414. Orlando, FL: Academic Press.

Katzer, Jeffrey, Kenneth H. Cook, and Wayne W. Crouch. (1982). *Evaluating information: A guide for users of social science research,* 2nd ed. Reading, MA: Addison-Wesley.

Katzer, Jeffrey, Kenneth H. Cook, and Wayne W. Crouch. (1991). *Evaluating information: A guide for users of social science research,* 3rd ed. New York: McGraw-Hill.

Keeter, Scott, et al. (2000). Consequences of reducing non-response in a national telephone survey. *Public Opinion Quarterly,* 64:125–148.

Kelle, Helga. (2000). Gender and territoriality in games played by nine to twelve-year-old schoolchildren. *Journal of Contemporary Ethnography,* 29:164–197.

Kelman, Herbert. (1982). Ethical issues in different social science methods. In *Ethical issues in social science research,* edited by T. Beauchamp, R. Faden, R. J. Wallace, and L. Walters, pp. 40–99. Baltimore: Johns Hopkins University Press.

Kemp, Jeremy, and R. F. Ellen. (1984). Informants. In *Ethnographic research: A guide to general conduct,* edited by R. F. Ellen, pp. 224–236. Orlando: Academic Press.

Kercher, Kyle. (1992). Quasi-experimental research designs. In *Encyclopedia of sociology,* Vol. 3, edited by E. and M. Borgatta, pp. 1595–1613. New York: Macmillan.

Kidder, Louise H., and Charles M. Judd. (1986). *Research methods in social relations,* 5th ed. New York: Holt, Rinehart and Winston.

Kiecolt, K. Jill, and Laura E. Nathan. (1985). *Secondary analysis of survey data.* Beverly Hills, CA: Sage.

Kirk, Jerome, and Marc L. Miller. (1986). *Reliability and validity in qualitative research.* Beverly Hills, CA: Sage.

Kissane, Rebecca Joyce. (2003). What's need go to do with it? *Journal of Sociology and Social Welfare,* 30:137–148.

Kleg, Milton, and Kaoru Yamamoto. (1998). As the world turns. *Social Science Journal,* 35:183–190.

Knäuper, Bärbel. (1999). The impact of age and education on response order effects in attitude measurement. *Public Opinion Quarterly,* 63:347–370.

Kohn, Melvin L. (1987). Cross-national research as an analytic strategy. *American Sociological Review,* 52:713–731.

Koretz, Daniel. (Summer 1988). Arriving in Lake Wobegon. *American Educator,* 12:8–15.

Kriesi, Hanspeter, and Dominique Wisler. (1999). The impact of social movements on political institutions. In *How social movements matter,* edited by M. Giugni, D. McAdam, and Tilly, pp. 42–65. Minneapolis: University of Minnesota Press.

Krippendorff, Klaus. (1980). *Content analysis: An introduction to its methodology.* Beverly Hills, CA: Sage.

Krosnick, Jon. (1992). The impact of cognitive sophistication and attitude importance on response-order and question-order effects. In *Context effects,* edited by N. Schwarz and Sudman, pp. 203–218. New York: Springer-Verlag.

Krosnick, Jon, and Duane Alwin. (1988). A test of the form-resistant correlation hypothesis: Ratings, rankings, and the measurement of values. *Public Opinion Quarterly,* 52:526–538.

Krueger, Richard A. (1988). *Focus groups: A practical guide for applied research.* Beverly Hills, CA: Sage.

Kusserow, Richard P. (March 1989). *Misconduct in scientific research.* Report of the Inspector General of the U.S. Department of Health and Human Services. Washington, DC: Department of Health and Human Services.

Labaw, Patricia J. (1980). *Advanced questionnaire design.* Cambridge, MA: Abt Books.

Lamont, Michèle. (2000). The rhetorics of racism and anti-racism in France and the United States. In *Rethinking comparative cultural sociology,* edited by M. Lamont and L. Thèvenot, pp. 25–55. New York: Cambridge University Press.

Land, Kenneth. (1992). Social indicators. *Encyclopedia of sociology,* Vol. 4, edited by E. and M. Borgatta, pp. 1844–1850. New York: Macmillan.

Lang, Eric. (1992). Hawthorne effect. *Encyclopedia of sociology,* Vol. 2, edited by E. and M. Borgatta, pp. 793–794. New York: Macmillan.

Lankenau, Stephen E. (1999). Stronger than dirt. *Journal of Contemporary Ethnography,* 28:288–318.

Lauzen, Martha M., and David M. Dozier. (2005). Maintaining the double standard: Portrayals of age and gender in popular films. *Sex Roles,* 52:437–446.

LeMasters, E. E. (1975). *Blue collar aristocrats.* Madison: University of Wisconsin Press.

Lieberson, Stanley, Susan Dumais, and Shyon Baumann. (2000). The instability of androgynous names. *American Journal of Sociology,* 105:1249–1287.

Lifton, Robert J. (1986). *Nazi doctors.* New York: Basic Books.

Lofland, John. (1976). *Doing social life.* New York: Wiley.

Lofland, John, and Lyn H. Lofland. (1984). *Analyzing social settings,* 2nd ed. Belmont, CA: Wadsworth.

Lofland, John, and Lyn H. Lofland. (1995). *Analyzing social settings,* 3rd ed. Belmont, CA: Wadsworth.

Logan, John. (1991). Blaming the suburbs? *Social Science Quarterly,* 72:476–503.

Lowenthal, David. (1985). *The past is a foreign country.* New York: Cambridge University Press.

Lu, Shun, and Gary Alan Fine. (1995). The presentation of ethnic authenticity. *Sociological Quarterly,* 36:535–553.

MacKeun, Michael B. (1984). Reality, the press and citizens' political agendas. In *Surveying subjective phenomena,* Vol. 2, edited by C. Turner and E. Martin, pp. 443–473. New York: Russell Sage Foundation.

Mahoney, James. (1999). Nominal, ordinal, and narrative appraisal in macrocausal analysis. *American Journal of Sociology,* 104:1154–1196.

Maier, Mark H. (1991). *The data game.* Armonk, NY: M. E. Sharpe.

Markoff, John, Gilbert Shapiro, and Sasha R. Weitman. (1974). Toward the integration of content analysis and general methodology. In *Sociological methodology, 1974,* edited by D. Heise, pp. 1–58. San Francisco: Jossey-Bass.

Martin, Elizabeth. (1999). Who knows who lives here? *Public Opinion Quarterly,* 63:200–236.

Marx, Anthony W. (1998). *Making race and nation.* New York: Cambridge University Press.

Mastro, Dana E., and Charles Atkin. (2002). Exposure to alcohol billboards and beliefs and attitudes toward drinking among Mexican American high school students. *Howard Journal of Communications,* 13:129–151.

Mastro, Dana E., and Susannah Stern. (2003). Representations of race in television commercials. *Journal of Broadcasting and Electronic Media,* 47:638–647.

McCall, George. (1969). Quality control in participant observation. In *Issues in participant observation,* edited by G. McCall and J. L. Simmons, pp. 128–141. Reading, MA: Addison-Wesley.

McDaniel, Timothy. (1978). Meaning and comparative concepts. *Theory and Society,* 6:93–118.

McKelvie, Stuart J., and Linda A. Schamer. (1988). Effects of night, passengers and sex on driver behavior at stop signs. *Journal of Social Psychology,* 128:658–690.

McKeown, Adam. (2001). *Chinese migrants' networks and cultural change.* Chicago: University of Chicago Press.

McLennan, Gregor. (1981). *Marxism and the methodologies of history.* London: Verso.

Merten, Don E. (1999). Enculturation into secrecy among junior high school girls. *Journal of Contemporary Ethnography,* 28:107–138.

Merton, Robert K. (1957). *Social theory and social structure.* New York: Free Press.

Merton, Robert K. (1967). *On theoretical sociology.* New York: Free Press.

Merton, Robert K. (1970). *Science, technology and society in seventeenth century England.* New York: Harper & Row.

Merton, Robert K. (1973). *The sociology of science.* Chicago: University of Chicago Press.

Miles, Matthew B., and A. Michael Huberman. (1994). *Qualitative data analysis,* 2nd ed. Thousand Oaks, CA: Sage.

Milgram, Stanley. (1963). Behavioral study of obedience. *Journal of Abnormal and Social Psychology,* 6:371–378.

Milgram, Stanley. (1965). Some conditions of obedience and disobedience to authority. *Human Relations,* 18:57–76.

Milgram, Stanley. (1974). *Obedience to authority.* New York: Harper & Row.

Mishler, Elliot G. (1986). *Research interviewing.* Cambridge, MA: Harvard University Press.

Mitchell, Alison. (May 17, 1997). Survivors of Tuskegee study get apology from Clinton. *New York Times.*

Mitchell, Mark, and Janina Jolley. (1988). *Research design explained.* New York: Holt, Rinehart and Winston.

Molotch, Harvey, William Freudenburg, and Krista Paulsen. (2000). History repeats itself, but how? City character, urban tradition, and the accomplishment of place. *American Sociological Review,* 65:791–823.

Monaghan, Peter. (April 7, 1993a). Facing jail, a sociologist raises question about a scholar's right to protect sources. *Chronicle of Higher Education,* p. A10.

Monaghan, Peter. (May 26, 1993b). Sociologist is jailed for refusing to testify about research subject. *Chronicle of Higher Education,* p. A10.

Monaghan, Peter. (September 1, 1993c). Sociologist jailed because he "wouldn't snitch" ponders the way research ought to be done. *Chronicle of Higher Education*, pp. A8–A9.

Morgan, David L. (1996). Focus groups. *Annual Review of Sociology*, 22: 129–152.

Morse, Janice M. (1994). Designing funded qualitative research. In *Handbook of qualitative research*, edited by N. Denzin and Y. Lincoln, pp. 220–235. Thousand Oaks, CA: Sage.

Moser, C. A., and G. Kalton. (1972). *Survey methods in social investigation.* New York: Basic Books.

Mulkay, Michael. (1979). *Science and the sociology of knowledge.* London: George Allen and Unwin.

Mulkay, M. J. (1991). *Sociology of science.* Philadelphia: Open University Press.

Mullins, Nicholas C. (1971). *The art of theory: Construction and use.* New York: Harper & Row.

Murdock, George P. (1967). Ethnographic atlas. *Ethnology*, 6:109–236.

Murdock, George P. (1971). *Outline of cultural materials*, 4th ed. New Haven, CT: Human Relations Area Files.

Musick, Marc A., John Wilson, and William Bynum. (2000). Race and formal volunteering. *Social Forces*, 78:1539–1571.

Narayan, Sowmya, and John A. Krosnick. (1996). Education moderates some response effects in attitude measurement. *Public Opinion Quarterly*, 60:58–88.

Naroll, Raoul. (1968). Some thoughts on comparative method in cultural anthropology. In *Methodology in social research*, edited by H. Blalock and A. Blalock, pp. 236–277. New York: McGraw-Hill.

National Science Board. (2002). *Science and engineering indicators—2002.* Arlington, VA: National Science Foundation (NSB-02–1).

Neuman, W. Lawrence. (1992). Gender, race and age differences in student definitions of sexual harassment. *Wisconsin Sociologist*, 29:63–75.

Neuman, W. Lawrence. (2000). *Social research methods*, 4th ed. Boston: Allyn and Bacon.

Neuman, W. Lawrence. (2003). *Social research methods*, 5th ed. Boston: Allyn and Bacon.

Novick, Peter. (1988). *That noble dream.* New York: Cambridge University Press.

Oesterle, Sabrina, Monica Kirkpatrick Johnson, and Jeylan T. Mortimer. (2004). Volunteerism during the transition to adulthood. *Social Forces*, 82:1123–1149.

Ong, Andy S. J., and Colleen A. Ward. (1999). The effects of sex and power schemas, attitudes toward women, and victim resistance on rape attributions. *Journal of Applied Social Psychology*, 29:362–376.

Ostrom, Thomas M., and Katherine M. Gannon. (1996). Exemplar generation. In *Answering questions*, edited by N. Schwarz and S. Sudman, pp. 293–318. San Francisco: Jossey-Bass.

Pager, Devah, and Lincoln Quillian. (2005). Walking the talk? *American Sociological Review*, 70:355–380.

Paige, Jeffrey M. (1975). *Agrarian revolution.* New York: Free Press.

Parcel, Toby L. (1992). Secondary data analysis and data archives. *Encyclopedia of sociology*, Vol. 4, edited by E. and M. Borgatta, pp. 1720–1728. New York: Macmillan.

Patton, Michael Quinn. (2001). *Qualitative research and evaluation methods*, 3rd ed. Thousand Oaks, CA: Sage.

Pearsall, Marion. (1970). Participant observation as role and method in behavioral research. In *Qualitative methodology*, edited by W. J. Filstead, pp. 340–352. Chicago: Markham.

Phillips, Bernard. (1985). *Sociological research methods: An introduction.* Homewood, IL: Dorsey.

Piliavin, Irving M., J. Rodin, and Jane A. Piliavin. (1969). Good samaritanism: An underground phenomenon? *Journal of Personality and Social Psychology*, 13:289–299.

Pollner, Melvin, and Richard Adams. (1997). The effect of spouse presence on appraisals of emotional support and household strain. *Public Opinion Quarterly*, 61:615–626.

Presser, Stanley. (1990). Measurement issues in the study of social change. *Social Forces* 68:856–868.

Przeworski, Adam, and Henry Teune. (1970). *The logic of comparative inquiry.* New York: Wiley.

Punch, Maurice. (1986). *The politics and ethics of fieldwork.* Beverly Hills, CA: Sage.

Ragin, Charles C. (1987). *The comparative method.* Berkeley: University of California Press.

Ragin, Charles C. (1992). Introduction: Cases of "what is a case?" In *What is a case*, edited by C. Ragin and H. Becker, pp. 1–18. New York: Cambridge University Press.

Rampton, Sheldon, and John Stauber. (2001). *Trust us, we're experts.* New York: Putnam.

Rathje, William, and Cullen Murphy. (1992). *Rubbish: The archaeology of garbage.* New York: Vintage.

Reese, Stephen, W. Danielson, P. Shoemaker, T. Chang, and H. Hsu. (1986). Ethnicity of interview effects among Mexican Americans and Anglos. *Public Opinion Quarterly,* 50:563–572.

Reynolds, Paul Davidson. (1971). *A primer in theory construction.* Indianapolis: Bobbs-Merrill.

Reynolds, Paul Davidson. (1979). *Ethical dilemmas and social science research.* San Francisco: Jossey-Bass.

Reynolds, Paul Davidson. (1982). *Ethics and social science research.* Englewood Cliffs, NJ: Prentice-Hall.

Rind, Bruce, and David Strohmetz. (1999). Effect on restaurant tipping of a helpful message written on the back of customers' checks. *Journal of Applied Social Psychology,* 29:139–144.

Roethlisberger, F. J., and W. J. Dickenson. (1939). *Management and the worker.* Cambridge, MA: Harvard University Press.

Roscigno, Vincent J., and William Danaher. (2001). Media and mobilization: The case of Radio and Southern Textile Worker Insurgency, 1929–1934. *American Sociological Review,* 66:21–48.

Rosenberg, Morris. (1968). *The logic of survey analysis.* New York: Basic Books.

Rossi, Robert J., and Kevin J. Gilmartin. (1980). *The handbook of social indicators.* New York: Garland STPM Press.

Rueschemeyer, Dietrich, Evelyne Huber Stephens, and John D. Stephens. (1992). *Capitalist development and democracy.* Chicago: University of Chicago Press.

Runciman, W. G. (1980). Comparative sociology or narrative history. *European Journal of Sociology,* 21:162–178.

Sanday, Peggy Reeves. (1983). The ethnographic paradigm(s). In *Qualitative methodology,* edited by J. Van Maanen, pp. 19–36. Beverly Hills, CA: Sage.

Sanders, Jimy, Victor Nee, and Scott Sernau. (2002). Asian immigrants' reliance on social ties in a multiethnic labor market. *Social Forces,* 81:281–314.

Sanjek, Roger. (1978). A network method and its uses in urban anthropology. *Human Organization,* 37:257–268.

Sanjek, Roger. (1990). On ethnographic validity. In *Field notes,* edited by R. Sanjek, pp. 385–418. Ithaca, NY: Cornell University Press.

Sassen, Saskia. (2001). *The global city.* New York: Princeton University Press.

Schacter, Daniel L. (2001). *The seven deadly sins of memory.* Boston: Houghton Mifflin.

Schaffer, Nora Cate. (1980). Evaluating race-of-interviewer effects in a national survey. *Sociological Methods and Research,* 8:400–419.

Schatzman, Leonard, and Anselm L. Strauss. (1973). *Field research.* Englewood Cliffs, NJ: Prentice-Hall.

Schuman, Howard, and Jean M. Converse. (1971). Effects of black and white interviewers on black response in 1968. *Public Opinion Quarterly,* 65:44–68.

Schuman, Howard, and Stanley Presser. (1981). *Questions and answers in attitude surveys: Experiments on question form, wording and content.* New York: Academic Press.

Schwandt, Thomas A. (1994). Constructivist, interpretivist approaches to human inquiry. In *Handbook of qualitative research,* edited by N. Denzin and Y. Lincoln, pp. 118–137. Thousand Oaks, CA: Sage.

Scribner, Richard, and Deborah Cohen. (2001). The effect of enforcement on merchant compliance with the minimum legal drinking age law. *Journal of Drug Issues,* 31:857–867.

Sears, David O. (1986). College sophomores in the laboratory. *Journal of Personality and Social Psychology,* 51: 515–530.

Sewell, William H., Jr. (1987). Theory of action, dialectic, and history. *American Journal of Sociology,* 93:166–171.

Shafer, Robert Jones. (1980). *A guide to historical method,* 3rd ed. Homewood, IL: Dorsey.

Shaffir, William B., Robert A. Stebbins, and Allan Turowetz. (1980). Introduction. In *Fieldwork experience,* edited by W. B. Shaffir, R. Stebbins, and A. Turowetz, pp. 3–22. New York: St. Martin's Press.

Singer, Eleanor. (1988). Surveys in the mass media. In *Surveying social life: Papers in honor of Herbert H. Hyman,* edited by H. O'Gorman, pp. 413–436. Middletown, CT: Wesleyan University Press.

Singleton, Royce, Jr., B. Straits, Margaret Straits, and Ronald McAllister. (1988). *Approaches to social research.* New York: Oxford University Press.

Skidmore, William. (1979). *Theoretical thinking in sociology,* 2nd ed. New York: Cambridge University Press.

Skocpol, Theda. (1979). *States and social revolutions.* New York: Cambridge University Press.

Smelser, Neil J. (1976). *Comparative methods in the social sciences.* Englewood Cliffs, NJ: Prentice-Hall.

Smith, Mary Lee, and Gene V. Glass. (1987). *Research and evaluation in education and the social sciences.* Englewood Cliffs, NJ: Prentice-Hall.

Smith, Tom W. (1987). That which we call welfare by any other name would smell sweeter. *Public Opinion Quarterly,* 51:75–83.

Smith, Tom W. (1995). Trends in non-response rates. *International Journal of Public Opinion Research,* 7:156–171.

Snow, David, and Leon Anderson. (1991). Researching the homeless. In *A case for the case study,* edited by Joe R. Feagan, Anthony M. Orum, and Gideon Sjoberg, pp. 148–173. Chapel Hill: University of North Carolina Press.

Snow, David, and Leon Anderson. (1992). *Down on their luck.* Berkeley: University of California Press.

Snow, David, Sarah A. Soule, and Daniel M. Cress. (2005). Identifying the precipitants of homeless process across 17 U.S. cities, 1980–1990. *Social Forces,* 83:1183–1210.

Spector, Paul E. (1981). *Research designs.* Beverly Hills, CA: Sage.

Spradley, James P. (1979a). *The ethnographic interview.* New York: Holt, Rinehart and Winston.

Spradley, James P. (1979b). *Participant observation.* New York: Holt, Rinehart and Winston.

Stack, Steven, Ira Wasserman, and Roger Kern. (2004). Adult social bonds and use of Internet pornography. *Social Science Quarterly,* 85:75–88.

Starr, Paul. (1982). *The social transformation of American medicine.* New York: Basic Books.

Stevenson, Richard W. (October 16, 1996). U.S. to revise its estimate of layoffs. *New York Times.*

Stewart, David W. (1984). *Secondary research: Information sources and methods.* Beverly Hills, CA: Sage.

Stinchcombe, Arthur L. (1968). *Constructing social theories.* New York: Harcourt, Brace and World.

Stinchcombe, Arthur L. (1973). Theoretical domains and measurement, Part 1. *Acta Sociologica,* 16:3–12.

Stinchcombe, Arthur L. (1978). *Theoretical methods in social history.* New York: Academic Press.

Stone, Lawrence. (1987). *The past and present revisited.* Boston: Routledge and Kegan Paul.

Stone, Philip J., and Robert P. Weber. (1992). Content analysis. In *Encyclopedia of sociology,* Vol. 1, edited by E. and M. Borgatta, pp. 290–295. New York: Macmillan.

Strack, Fritz. (1992). "Order effects" in survey research. In *Context effects in social and psychological re-*search, edited by N. Schwarz and S. Sudman, pp. 23–24. New York: Springer-Verlag.

Strauss, Anselm. (1987). *Qualitative analysis for social scientists.* New York: Cambridge University Press.

Strauss, Anselm, and Juliet Corbin. (1990). *Basics of qualitative research.* Newbury Park, CA: Sage.

Strauss, Anselm, and Juliet Corbin. (1994). Grounding theory methodology. In *Handbook of qualitative research,* edited by N. Denzin and Y. Lincoln, pp. 273–285. Thousand Oaks, CA: Sage.

Sudman, Seymour. (1976). Sample surveys. *Annual Review of Sociology,* 2:107–120.

Sudman, Seymour. (1983). Applied sampling. In *Handbook of survey research,* edited by P. Rossi, J. Wright, and A. Anderson, pp. 145–194. Orlando, FL: Academic Press.

Sudman, Seymour, and Norman M. Bradburn. (1983). *Asking questions.* San Francisco: Jossey-Bass.

Sudman, Seymour, Norman M. Bradburn, and Norbert Schwarz. (1996). *Thinking about answers.* San Francisco: Jossey-Bass.

Suls, Jerry M., and Ralph L. Rosnow. (1988). Concerns about artifacts in psychological experiments. In *The rise of experimentation in American psychology,* edited by J. Morawski, pp. 153–187. New Haven, CT: Yale University Press.

Sutton, John R. (2004). The political economy of imprisonment in affluent western democrcies, 1960–1990. *American Sociological Review,* 69:170–189.

Taylor, Charles. (1979). Interpretation and the sciences of man. In *Interpretative social science: A reader,* edited by P. Rabinow and W. Sullivan, pp. 25–72. Berkeley: University of California Press.

Taylor, Steven. (1987). Observing abuse. *Qualitative Sociology,* 10:288–302.

Tourangeau, Roger, et al. (1997). Who lives here? *Journal of Official Statistics,* 13:1–18.

Turner, Charles, and Elizabeth Martin, eds. (1984). *Surveying subjective phenomena,* Vol. 1. New York: Russell Sage Foundation.

Turner, Stephen P. (1980). *Sociological explanation as translation.* New York: Cambridge University Press.

Tyldum, Guri, and Anette Brunovskis. (2005). Describing the unobserved. *International Migration,* 43:17–34.

Vallier, Ivan, ed. (1971a). *Comparative methods in sociology.* Berkeley: University of California Press.

Vallier, Ivan. (1971b). Empirical comparisons of social structure. In *Comparative methods in sociology,* edited by I. Vallier, pp. 203–263. Berkeley: University of California Press.

Van den Berg, Harry, and Cees Van der Veer. (1985). Measuring ideological frames of references. *Quality and Quantity,* 19:105–118.

Van Laar, Colette, Shana Levin, Stacey Sinclair, and Jim Sidanius. (2005). The effect of university roommate contact on ethnic attitudes and behavior. *Journal of Experimental Social Psychology,* 41:329–345.

Van Maanen, John. (1982). Fieldwork on the beat. In *Varieties of qualitative research,* edited by J. Van Maanen, J. Dabbs, Jr., and R. Faulkner, pp. 103–151. Beverly Hills, CA: Sage.

Van Maanen, John. (1988). *Tales of the field.* Chicago: University of Chicago Press.

Van Poppel, Frans, and L. Day. (1996). A test of Durkheim's theory of suicide—Without committing the "ecological fallacy." *American Sociological Review,* 61:500–507.

Vaquera, Elizabeth, and Grace Kao. (2005). Private and public displays of affection among interracial and intra-racial adolescent couples. *Social Science Quarterly,* 86:484–508.

Vidich, Arthur Joseph, and Joseph Bensman. (1968). *Small town in mass society,* rev. ed. Princeton, NJ: Princeton University Press.

Wade, Nicholas. (1976). IQ and heredity. *Science,* 194: 916–919.

Walton, John. (1973). Standardized case comparison. In *Comparative social research,* edited by M. Armer and A. Grimshaw, pp. 173–191. New York: Wiley.

Warwick, Donald P. (1982). Types of harm in social science research. In *Ethical issues in social science research,* edited by T. Beauchamp, R. Faden, R. J. Wallace, and L. Walters, pp. 101–123. Baltimore: Johns Hopkins University Press.

Warwick, Donald P., and Charles A. Lininger. (1975). *The sample survey.* New York: McGraw-Hill.

Wax, Rosalie H. (1971). *Doing fieldwork: Warnings and advice.* Chicago: University of Chicago Press.

Wax, Rosalie H. (1979). Gender and age in fieldwork and fieldwork education. *Social Problems,* 26:509–522.

Webb, Eugene J., Donald T. Campbell, Richard D. Schwartz, Lee Sechrest, and Janet Belew Grove.

(1981). *Nonreactive measures in the social sciences,* 2nd ed. Boston: Houghton Mifflin.

Weber, Robert P. (1983). Measurement models for content analysis. *Quality and Quantity,* 17:127–149.

Weber, Robert P. (1984). Computer assisted content analysis: A short primer. *Qualitative Sociology,* 7:126–149.

Weber, Robert P. (1985). *Basic content analysis.* Beverly Hills, CA: Sage.

Weeks, M. F., and R. P. Moore. (1981). Ethnicity of interviewer effects on ethnic respondents. *Public Opinion Quarterly,* 45:245–249.

Weinstein, Deena. (1979). Fraud in science. *Social Science Quarterly,* 59:639–652.

Weiss, Carol H. (1997). *Evaluation.* Englewood Cliffs, NJ: Prentice Hall.

Weiss, Janet A., and Judith E. Gruber. (1987). The managed irrelevance of educational statistics. In *The politics of numbers,* edited by W. Alonso and P. Starr, pp. 363–391. New York: Russell Sage Foundation.

Weitzer, Ronald, and Steven Tuch. (2004). Race and perceptions of police misconduct. *Social Problems,* 51:305–325.

Weitzer, Ronald, and Steven Tuch. (2005). Racially biased policing. *Social Forces,* 83:1009–1030.

Weitzman, Lenore, D. Eifler, E. Hokada, and C. Ross. (1972). Sex role socialization in picture books for preschool children. *American Journal of Sociology,* 77:1125–1150.

Whiting, John W. M. (1968). Methods and problems in cross-cultural research. In *The handbook of social psychology,* 2nd ed., edited by G. Lindzey and E. Aronson, pp. 693–728. Reading, MA: Addison-Wesley.

Whyte, William Foote. (1955). *Street corner society: The social structure of an Italian slum,* 2nd ed. Chicago: University of Chicago Press.

Whyte, William Foote. (1982). Interviewing in field research. In *Field research,* edited by R. G. Burgess, pp. 111–122. Boston: George Allen and Unwin.

Whyte, William Foote. (1984). *Learning from the field.* Beverly Hills: Sage.

Williams, Peter, and David Wallace. (1989). *Unit 731: Japan's secret biological warfare in World War II.* New York: Free Press.

Willimack, Diane K., Howard Schuman, Beth-Ellen Pennell, and James M. Lepkowski. (1995). Effects of prepaid non-monetary incentives on response rates and response quality in face-to-face survey. *Public Opinion Quarterly,* 59:78–92.

Wood, Elizabeth Anne. (2000). Working in the fantasy factory. *Journal of Contemporary Ethnography,* 29:5–32.

Zane, Anne, and Euthemia Matsoukas. (1979). Different settings, different results? A comparison of school and home responses. *Public Opinion Quarterly,* 43:550–557.

Zelizer, Viviana A. (1985). *Pricing the priceless child.* New York: Basic Books.

Ziman, John. (August 19, 1999). Social rules of the game in doing science. *Nature,* 400:721.

Zimbardo, Philip G. (1972). Pathology of imprisonment. *Society,* 9:4–6.

Zimbardo, Philip G. (1973). On the ethics of intervention in human psychological research. *Cognition,* 2:243–256.

Zimbardo, Philip G., et al. (April 8, 1973). The mind is a formidable jailer. *New York Times Magazine,* 122:38–60.

Zimbardo, Philip G., et al. (1974). The psychology of imprisonment: Privation, power and pathology. In *Doing unto others,* edited by Z. Rubin. Englewood Cliffs, NJ: Prentice-Hall.

Scholarly Journals in the Social Sciences in English

GENERAL SOCIAL SCIENCE

American Behavioral Scientist
Annals of the American Academy of Political and Social Science
Evaluation Practice (American Evaluation Association)
Evaluation Review
Human Relations
Public Opinion Quarterly (American Association for Public Opinion)
Rationality and Society
Social Science Journal (Western Social Science Association)
Social Science Quarterly (Southwestern Social Science Association)
Theory and Society

ANTHROPOLOGY

American Anthropologist (American Anthropological Association)
American Ethnologist (American Ethnological Society)
Critique of Anthropology
Ethnology
Human Organization (Society for Applied Anthropology)
Mankind Quarterly (Institute for the Study of Man)

CRIMINOLOGY/SOCIOLOGY OF LAW

Contemporary Crisis
Crime and Delinquency (National Council on Crime and Delinquency)
Crime, Law and Social Change
Criminal Justice and Behavior (American Association of Correctional Psychologists)
Criminology (American Society of Criminology)
Journal of Criminal Law and Criminology
Journal of Research in Crime and Delinquency (National Council on Crime and Delinquency)
Journal of Quantitative Criminology
Law and Social Inquiry (American Bar Association)
Law and Society Review (Law and Society Association)
Social Justice: A Journal of Crime, Conflict and World Order

RACE/ETHNIC RELATIONS

Ethnic Forum
Ethnic Groups
Ethnic and Racial Studies
Hispanic Journal of Behavioral Sciences
Journal of American Ethnic History
Journal of Black Studies
Negro Educational Review
Phylon: The Atlanta University Review of Race and Culture
Race and Class (Institute of Race Relations)
Review of Black Political Economy (National Economic Association)

COMPARATIVE-HISTORICAL RESEARCH

Comparative Political Studies
Comparative Studies in Society and History
Cross-Cultural Research
Development and Change
Economic Development and Cultural Change
International Journal of Comparative Sociology
International Journal of Contemporary Sociology
International Migration Review
Journal of Cross-Cultural Psychology
Review (Fernand Braudel Center)
Social Science History

POLITICAL SCIENCE/POLITICAL SOCIOLOGY

American Journal of Political Science (Midwest Political Science Association)
American Political Science Review (American Political Science Review)
American Politics Quarterly
British Journal of Political Science
Canadian Journal of Political Science (Canadian Political Science Association; also in French)
Journal of Conflict Resolution
Journal of Political and Military Sociology
Journal of Politics (Southern Political Science Association)
Political Methodology
Political Science Quarterly (Academy of Political Science)
Politics and Society